Rites of Ordination
and Commitment in the Churches
of the Nordic Countries

Rites of Ordination and Commitment in the Churches of the Nordic Countries

THEOLOGY AND TERMINOLOGY

EDITOR:

Hans Raun Iversen

MUSEUM TUSCULANUM PRESS
UNIVERSITY OF COPENHAGEN
2006

Rites of Ordination and Commitment in the Churches of the Nordic Countries.
Theology and Terminology
© 2006, Museum Tusculanum Press and the authors
Edited by Hans Raun Iversen
Editorial assistant: Liselotte Malmgart
Editorial committee:
Gunnel Borgegaard,
Sven-Erik Brodd,
Risto Cantell,
Else-Britt Nilsen
and Einar Sigurbjörnsson
Secretary to the editorial committee: Ghita Olsen
Consultant: James F. Puglisi
English and theological language revision: Christine Hall
Cover design: Pernille Sys Hansen
Composition and printing: BookPartnerMedia A/S, Copenhagen
ISBN 87 635 0265 8

Front cover illustration: Toni Kaarttinen, Salvation Army (small picture in the centre).
Pastor's Ordination in Trinity Church, Copenhagen 1944, Bishop's Office (picture in the background).

Published with financial support from:
NOS-H, Joint Committee of the Nordic Research Councils
for the Humanities

Keywords:
ecumenical research, liturgy, Nordic countries, Nordic churches, ordination,
theology, bishop, priest, deacon, sacraments, consecration, religious life.

Museum Tusculanum Press
Njalsgade 94
DK-2300 København S
www.mtp.dk

Contents

CONTENTS

CONTENTS

Acknowledgments

Financial support for this volume has been provided by the Ansgar School of Theology and Mission, Stavanger, Norway, Baptist Union of Denmark, Church of Finland, Church of Sweden, Ekumeniskt Institut för Norden, Sigtuna, Dominican Sisters of Notre Dame de Grâce (Chatillon), Joint Committee for Nordic Research Councils for the Humanities (NOS-H, now NOS-HS), the Office of the Bishop of Iceland, Segelbergska Stiftelsen, Stockholm, University of Copenhagen and University of Greenland.

In addition to the contributions by the individual authors this publication has been made possible by the work of Gunnel Borgegaard, Sven-Erik Brodd, Risto Cantell, Else-Britt Nilsen, OP and Einar Sigurbjörnsson (editorial committee), Ghita Olsen (secretary to the editorial committee), James F. Puglisi, SA (consultant), Christine Hall (language revision), Liselotte Malmgart (editorial assistant) and Hans Raun Iversen (general editor).

Preface

The question of ordained ministry seems to be the most difficult and unsolvable problem between the different churches today. Where there is not sufficient agreement or consensus about it, possibilities of celebrating the Lord's Supper (the Holy Eucharist) together lie far beyond the horizon. The churches have not yet said all there is to say about ministry and ordination to the special ministry of the Church, hence this book, in which there are many surprises to be discovered on ministry and ordination in the Nordic countries.

It is not by chance that the churches have begun more discussions – within each church but also increasingly between the churches – on the question of ministry. The context in which the churches are living presents them with new questions and challenges about their service to the world. What is needed is a new and fresh look at these questions, especially at the way the churches fulfil the very service to the world that Christ himself commanded. The proclamation of the gospel is at stake since it is at the heart of the ministry entrusted first to the whole Church through baptism and, in a special way, to those who have been called and ordained for the equipping of the saints (cf. Eph. 4.11).

A unique situation exists in the Nordic countries: in all these countries there is a Lutheran majority living in ecumenical cooperation with other churches and ecclesial communities. In differing ways the Lutheran Churches have preserved a medieval tradition in their church life and structure. The ordained ministry is an integral part of this situation. In spite of this fact, differences have developed over the years in the actual practice of ordained ministry in each of these countries (Denmark, Finland, Iceland, Norway and Sweden). With this variation new terms have entered the vocabulary of each of the churches and it may even be said that different ways of understanding the meaning of ordination have begun to appear. For a number of years the discussion within the Nordic Lutheran Churches has been raising questions in this area. Moreover, the ecumenical context that has arisen in the Nordic countries has also precipitated a deeper questioning around the issues of ministry and ordination.

This book attempts to shed light on what the churches have discovered they hold in common and on areas where they recognise that there are divergences between them, both in relation to ordination and ministry and, in particular, to the theology and terminology of ordination.

The research process itself provides an example of how churches might be able to work through issues that seem to be difficult and divisive for them. The focus on liturgy could well be of use to the churches which are struggling with questions about liturgy as a place where the faith of the Church is proclaimed and confessed. Furthermore, all churches are facing the challenge of how to live out the reality of ministry in the world today. It is hoped that those who have the responsibility of leadership within their church will be interested in the implications that a serious reflection on the question of ordination and ordination rites might have for questions about how the Church should minister in the world today.

Although this book does not solve all the problems related to ordination and ministry, it does offer helpful insights to the churches, as they seek the visible unity of the Church of Jesus Christ.

Risto Cantell
James F. Puglisi, SA.

PART I

Introduction

Purpose, Background and Methodological Issues

Hans Raun Iversen

The Threefold Purpose of this Book

This book attempts first to introduce the profiles of the churches in the Nordic countries of Europe to a Nordic as well as a wider international readership, by picturing their stories and situations and by undertaking in-depth analyses of a central part of their faith and order, namely their rites of ordination and commitment.

Secondly, it aims to pioneer ecumenical study of the ministry of the Church by researching the theological self-understanding of the Nordic Churches as mirrored in their immensely diverse but nevertheless converging rites of ordination. It is the considered view of the editors that comparative studies of rites used in our churches may be one of today's most important ecumenical tasks.

Thirdly, this book identifies important theological issues related to the process by which churches come together in a better mutual understanding of ordained ministry. In doing this, the book also poses basic liturgical and ecumenical questions for the churches' work with rites of ordination and commitment.

Background and History

In 1997, following the debate on The Porvoo Common Statement, the Nordic Ecumenical Council decided to initiate a study of the *Theology and Terminology in Rites of Ordination in the Churches in the Nordic Countries*.[1] A Working Group was formed with Gunnel Borgegård, Director of the Nordic

---

1. The English version of The Porvoo Common Statement, which is a result of conversations concluded between the British and Irish Anglican Churches and the Nordic and

Ecumenical Council, Uppsala; Professor Sven-Erik Brodd, Uppsala; Dr. Risto Cantell, Director of the Church Department for International Relations, Helsinki, and Professor Ola Tjørhom, Stavanger.

This group arranged a consultation from 16th to 21st April 1998, in Farfa Sabina near Rome, with 17 participants from Nordic Churches and Schools of Theology. The Farfa consultation resulted in a common paper on the project and its methodology, related to preliminary presentations by three members of the Working Group.[2] Participants at the Farfa Consultation visited Dr. James F. Puglisi, Director of the *Centro Pro Unione* in Rome, and since then Dr. Puglisi has worked as a consultant to the project, participating in its conferences and Steering and Editorial Committee meetings. His *magnum opus* on ordination was adopted as a common reference work for the participants in their research.[3] In Farfa, Associate Professor Hans Raun Iversen, Copenhagen, took over as practical leader of the proposed project and applied for Project Preparation funds from NOS-H,[4] in January 1999, as it was decided that the work should be carried out as an academic research project, connected to the Faculties of Theology in the Nordic Universities.

From 15th to 16th February 1999, the new Steering Committee, Gunnel Borgegård, Uppsala; Professor Sven-Erik Brodd, Uppsala; Professor Einar Sigurbjörnsson, Reykjavik; Dr. Else-Britt Nilsen, Oslo; Dr. Yngvil Martola, Åbo; and Hans Raun Iversen, Copenhagen, met in Copenhagen to prepare the first

---

Baltic Lutheran Churches in 1992, is edited in *Together in Mission and Ministry: The Porvoo Common Statement with Essays on Church and Ministry in Northern Europe (London: Church House Publishing,* 1993). By 1996 the Evangelical-Lutheran Churches in the five Nordic countries had signed the Porvoo Common Statement, except for the Danish Evangelical-Lutheran Church (cf. the reports and reflections in Tjørhom 2002). Following up the Porvoo process, the Nordic Ecumenical Council has also been involved in special studies on the ministry of deacons in the Porvoo Churches, cf. Borgegård and Hall, 1999; Borgegård, Fanuelsen and Hall, 2000.

2. Preliminary papers: Sven-Erik Brodd, 'Theology and Terminology of Ordination: a Research Project on the Authorisation of Rites and Procedures in the Nordic Churches'; Risto Cantell, 'Preliminary Notes on how to analyse and compare Rites for Ordination, Blessing and Installation as Dogmatic Texts', and Ola Tjørhom, 'Differences between Ordination Liturgies and their Interpretation: Text and Context'. The meeting produced the common paper, 'Project and Methodology: The Theology and Terminology of Ordination –Preliminary Remarks and Observations on Framework, Method and Contents for a Proposed Nordic Research Project: Farfa 16-20 April, 1998'.

3. Puglisi, 1996, 1998, and 2001. For theological studies of liturgy Irwin 1994 was recommended.

4. NOS-H is a Nordic research fund set up by the Nordic National Research Councils for Humanities and Theology.

working conference, which was held at Dianalund, Filadelfia, Denmark, from 29th October to 1st November 1999, with 20 participants, of whom 13 had also been at the consultation in Farfa. As a result of this conference a project application, visualising the present book, was drawn up and sent to NOS-H in January 2000.[5] In June 2001, after an eighteen-month delay, research funds were awarded by NOS-H.

A second Steering Committee meeting was held in Uppsala from 25th to 26th September 2001 to agree the criteria for the case-studies proposed in Filadelfia. Synopses from the authors were collected and dealt with at a third Steering Committee meeting in Copenhagen from 25th to 26th January 2002. Thus prepared, the second Working Conference was held in Granavold near Oslo, from 26th to 29th April 2002, with 30 participants (13 of whom had been at Filadelfia). First drafts for the articles found in this book were presented and discussed intensively there. After the conference the fourth Steering Committee meeting drafted instructions for the second edition of the papers to be included in the book, for which the Steering Committee took over responsibility as Editorial Committee. In the meantime Dr. Yngvil Martola was replaced by Dr. Risto Cantell.

The first Editorial Committee meeting was held in Assisi, Italy, from 9th to 12th January 2003 to discuss the articles and the framework of this book. After a last revision of the articles the Editorial Committee had its final meeting from 24th to 27th October 2003 in Venice, paying special attention to the concluding Common Statement on the Meaning of Ordination (Part IV), for which the Editorial Committee takes collective responsibility.

It has been a challenge to get 23 busy colleagues to follow the working process and revise their own contributions over such a long period of research. It has, however, been important that nine participants contributed greatly to the continuity of the project by attending the consultation in Farfa as well as the Working Conferences in Filadelfia and Granavold: from Finland, Yngvil Martola and Risto Cantell; from Sweden, Gunnel Borgegård and Sven-Erik Brodd; from Norway, Else-Britt Nilsen and Bjørn Øyvind Fjeld; from Denmark, Bent Hylleberg and Hans Raun Iversen, and from Iceland, Einar Sigurbjørnsson. To this must be added the faithful co-operation, from the Farfa Consultation onwards, of the project consultant, Dr. James F. Puglisi.

Deliberately the project conferences have been open to participants from

---

5. Iversen, Hans Raun, 'Project Description: Theology and Terminology of Ordination, a Research Project on Rites for the Authorization of Ministry in the Nordic Churches', January 2000 and 2001.

the various Nordic churches, quite a number of whom have at the same time been dealing with ordination to ministry through involvement in liturgical and theological committees in their churches. Furthermore the ecumenical councils in the Nordic countries have arranged local study days on rites of ordination and commitment, where the national participants in the project have had the opportunity to discuss their research with participants from the local churches.[6]

The work on the editing of this book has been greatly supported by the service of the Revd Ghita Olsen, who has acted as secretary to the Steering and Editorial Committees, and Dr. Liselotte Malmgart, who has undertaken the final editorial work on the book. The language of the various contributions has been revised by Revd Deacon Christine Hall, Chichester, England. For this work and to all participants in the project during its six years of work and especially to the contributors to this book the editorial committee is most thankful. A final word of appreciation goes to NOS-H: this research, for which our universities could not find sufficient resources, has only been made possible by the funds awarded by them.

Scope and Methodology

The central focus of the research is the exploration of differences and convergences to be found in concepts of ordained ministries in the churches of the Nordic countries, in as far as they can be diagnosed from analysing these churches' rites of ordination. We have taken this line of research because the ordination rites very often seem to be the most communicatively significant as well as theologically condensed expressions of what churches think about their ordained ministries. We focus on the rites of ordination as text and performance. Keeping primarily to the rites as our common primary sources we also attempt to include the whole process of admission to ordained ministry as it sheds light on the theology of ordained ministry in our churches. In this way we picture the ecclesiology and especially the ecclesial reality of our churches.

Traditional ecumenical and dogmatic studies of ordained ministry may be labelled deductive when they find their material and come to their conclusions by focusing on the more or less historically fixed creeds and documents of the churches. Conversely, studies of the social roles of ordained ministers, as un-

---

6. Three contributions from the study day on ordination rites held at the University of Copenhagen, Denmark, were published in *Kritisk Forum for Praktisk Teologi* 93, September 2003.

dertaken, for example, by sociologists of religion, are empirical and inductive, since they collect as primary sources actions, experiences and expectations surrounding ordained ministers in their relations to parishes and churches. Studying present rites of ordination as text and performance, we study the religious practice of our churches. Methodologically our research is firstly inductive in as far as the 'texts' to be studied are initially established from actual practice in the churches (cf. what follows below on levels of analysis). After that procedure the research continues in a mainly deductive way, attempting to clarify the theology at work in the rites of ordination and commitment. We study ordination rites as expressions of the actual faith as well as of the working order of the churches. It might well be easier to conduct studies of the ministry of our churches purely dogmatically or sociologically. We do, however, think that, for our purpose as outlined above, it is more timely and fruitful to focus on the ordination practices of the churches and to face the hermeneutical and methodological challenges involved.

Hermeneutics

Rites – not least ordination rites – bring together past and present. They are rooted in old traditions, more or less adapted to the present situation, and at the same time claiming to articulate what the churches need to articulate today. This is true in a double sense of ordination: first, ordination texts do belong to tradition and have to be dealt with, analysed and understood according to the hermeneutical principles generally relevant when dealing with historical texts and traditions. Secondly – and even more significantly – in ordination a church places the person to be ordained within a tradition of ministry, which the newly ordained minister is now to guard, practise and transfer to new generations in that church. Therefore ordination rites are also to be understood in the context within which they are intended to communicate.

> Understanding is to be thought of less as a subjective act than as participating in an event of tradition, a process of transmission in which past and present are constantly mediated (Gadamer 1993:290).

This classic formulation of what understanding is about is relevant for the participant in ordination rites as well as for the student of such rites. In his *magnum opus* on hermeneutics Hans-Georg Gadamer emphasises that a for-understanding is always in play, whenever we try to understand a text or a tradition – and for that matter any message coming to us from outside (Gadamer 1993, 294, 55). Thus understanding is always a process, which takes the form of a hermeneutical circle, where we have to understand against the background of what we have already understood (Gadamer 1993, 292). To complicate matters it has to be remembered that the tradition itself, for example the rite of ordination, is also contributing to the for-understanding, because some people in the congregation may have experienced it before and others have their preconceived expectations from various other sources. For good or for ill the rite is always at work, as it has its *Wirkungsgeschichte* in the minds of most of us, before we participate in it – or study it.

The for-understanding by which we read or listen to a text or a rite is embedded in a specific 'horizon' which sets the limit for our understanding even though our horizons are capable of being opened and broadened. This is in fact what happens in true understanding, which takes place as a fusion of our horizon with the horizon of the new text or message (Gadamer 1993, 302-6). To understand in a proper historical way requires us to understand the question to which the text that we are dealing with was originally the answer (Gadamer 1993, 376). However, when we deal with legal and theological texts they are not only meant to be understood historically. They must be understood in terms of their message today, that is they must be applied in our current situation, if they are to be understood according to their intention (Gadamer 1993, 308).

However historically determined rites of ordination may be, they intend to speak more of present and future commitment than of historically past traditions and practices. They intend to transmit by actualising – and certainly not to betray by repeating in a mere historical sense – the theological content they received once upon a time.[7] To transmit the content and intention of a tradition, as it is intended in ordination, things may have to be said and performed in new ways in a new situation, in order to be faithful to the tradition in question. Using James F. Puglisi's examples and terminology, we may ask:

> Do our present-day institutions transmit the responsibility-in-solidarity of all Christians as well as did those of the early Church? Might a more active role in the choice of their ministers demonstrate that the Spirit is active in all the members of the Body of Christ? ... Do our theories of subjective vocation express the objective character and ecclesial nature of vocation to the ordained ministry, as we have seen in traditional practices? (Puglisi 2001:282).

---

7. Cf. Puglisi 2001, 279-83 dealing with 1 Cor. 11.23-26.

In studying our present ordination rites we must first let the rites speak for themselves by listening to them with the ears with which we may assume that Christians participating in them listen. This is in itself a great challenge as we study rites and traditions far beyond those of our own churches.[8] But we also need to understand the rites in the wider ecclesiastical and historical contexts to which they belong and in relation to the background against which they will be interpreted by church leaders in the individual churches. This requires us to understand the intention of the ordination rites against the background of the historical questions to which they provide the answers as well as the meaning of the answers that they communicate today.

Levels of Analysis

To a varying degree the different case-studies presented in Part II of this book cover various levels – or rather different combinations of levels – of analysis of ordination rites, as they can be described in the following four points:

1. The written rites must first be studied as *theological texts* to determine their basic characteristics and purposes, structures, specific terms, concepts and symbols that carry the meaning of the text and its theological content. In this way more or less closely related texts may be studied *comparatively* with the help of synoptic schemes of their various elements.[9] In reading ordination rites as texts it is also important to make the churches aware of what is actually being said in the texts that they use and which the churches have formally authorised in one way or another as their understanding of ministry and ordination. Even though the churches vary in their understanding of liturgy as an expression of faith and creeds (their understanding of *lex orandi lex credendi*), what the ordination texts literally say has to be taken seriously at the outset.

2. It is also important to study *the rites as they are actually celebrated and*

---

8. At the outset we had the idea that the authors of this book should not study only or primarily their own traditions. For practical reasons in the end most of the studies were undertaken by scholars who were personally related to at least some of the churches whose rites they have studied.

9. The synoptic schemes set up and used in these studies may be downloaded free from the editor's website, www.teol.ku.dk/ast/ansatte/Hans%20Raun%20Iversen-ordination. htm. Unfortunately, it was not possible to include the schemes here. It is however highly recommended that readers of this book read it in conjunction with the relevant synoptic schemes. The synoptic schemes are also recommended for teaching purposes and for enhancing creativity when working with rites of ordination and commitment.

performed. In many rites, those of the more established churches, for example, we find a number of rubrics on the celebration of the rite in brackets or in the margins, giving practical directions for its performance. In other cases it is necessary to observe the actual rite in practice to be sure who is participating and doing what, whether the rite includes vesting in special robes, symbols and so on. To understand what the churches are actually communicating to the members of their congregations and their wider surroundings this research method is indispensable.

3. Very often rites are only to be understood against the background of *the confessional standpoints and legally formulated regulations on ordination and ministry* that are supposed to be known at least to the central participants in the act of ordination. For a full understanding of their ordination rites, therefore, the faith and order of the churches may have to be taken into consideration.

4. Finally, it is often important to take account of *the historical background of ordination rites*. Ritual texts and practices are often directly dependent on previous texts from within the same churches or they may depend on inspiration from other churches and denominations, including ecumenical dialogues. These too may be influenced by specific social or ecclesiastical situations or processes during the history of the churches in which they originate. Such historical backgrounds must be taken into account for a fuller understanding of the texts, although the congregations and even the ministers officiating at the liturgies are often not aware of the historical determinatives behind their ritual texts.

Categories of Rites

Almost 200 rites have been studied at various degrees of depth during the research on the case studies in Part II of this book. Depending on how the calculation is made, a total of between 400 and 500 rites for different sorts of 'ordination' in the Nordic churches has been collected during the study process. The rites of most churches occur in many historical editions or different revised forms. A number of rites are to some extent common to different minority churches, which have put their own mark on them only to a limited degree. Many of the rites are translations of texts from mother churches or denominational headquarters and thus only slightly adapted to their specific Nordic context. It is therefore impossible to give an exact number for rites of ordination in the Nordic countries. Practically we have had to group the rites according to their functions and characteristics, distinguishing between:

1. *Rites for different types of ministries:* priestly, diaconal, catechetical, missionary, oversight or other. As shown below under Terminology, there is a great variation in the way churches label their various ministries. In some churches the agenda for ordination to different ministries are very similar or at least parallel, in others they differ significantly, depending on the kind of ministry which the candidate is entering by ordination. Among others Tjørhom (Part III.1) suggests that we should only and always use the label 'ordination' with reference to deacons, priests and bishops, whereas 'ordination' to all other forms of ministry should be called by other terms, such as 'installation', 'blessing', 'consecration' or 'intercessory prayers'. However, the material from the Nordic Churches cannot be organised according to such a simple pattern, as the variations are more complicated – and perhaps even more fruitful.

2. *Rites of ordination,* which admit candidates to ordained ministry and which may normally only take place once during the lifetime of a minister, and *rites of installation,* which will be repeated when a minister takes up a new responsibility in a new post. In some cases, for example, the admission of an ordained pastor to the function of a bishop, it is difficult to be sure whether the rite used is to be considered a rite of ordination or installation. Over against the rites for ordaining/installing are *rites of commitment,* for example to religious life, where the perspective of the rite will normally be for the lifetime of the candidate, but where the rite does not lead to ordained ministry or an office in the church.[10]

3. *Rites authorised by a church and unauthorised (or 'private') rites,* which different groups in the churches have used and/or are using to admit specific sorts of ministers to service. Examples of unauthorised rites are the rites that admit deacons and deaconesses to their service, which have been unauthorised for decades in some of the Evangelical-Lutheran Churches in the Nordic Countries.[11] The same is often the case

---

10. Cf. Nilssen on rites for perpetual commitment to religious life in the Nordic countries (Part II.4). Other rites, particularly older rites for the inauguration of deaconesses and missionaries may also have more the character of rites of commitment than of ordination.

11. Cf. Malmgart and Inghammar on the development of the 'ordination' of deaconesses and deacons in Denmark and Sweden (Part II.3) and Olsen on rites for the sending out of missionaries (Part II.5).

with rites for the sending out of missionaries. A particular example here is the group of *oral, i.e. not-written rites*, which are used for ordination especially in Pentecostal churches. They are not especially private as they are used publicly in the midst of the congregation, but they have no authorised form except for forms inherent in the oral tradition. Such rites can only be studied by recording and observing them during field work. Unfortunately we have not been able to include a study of totally non-written rites in this book.

Terminology

In the translation of the *Porvoo Common Statement* into the languages in the various Nordic countries it was once more observed that terminological questions are crucial and sometimes even detrimental to a common understanding of the theology of ordained ministry. We have made the very same observation during this project. Thus we have had to deal with terminological questions – especially at the following three basic levels:

1. Which term do different churches use for different sorts of acts of 'ordination' to different forms of ministry? And what is the difference between the various terms used in different connections, such as *'ordination', 'vielse', 'indvielse', 'vigning', 'vigsling', 'vigsla'* and *'vihkimys'*, to mention terms from the Nordic Lutheran Churches, which may be used interchangeably, though that is definitely not always the case? Already at this basic point confusion is imminent.[9]

2. What do the churches call the functions and positions of various ministries? Are they 'offices' *('ordines', 'embeder/embeter')* or 'services'/ 'ministries' *('diakonia', 'tjenester')* or something else? How far do the different titles carry different concepts of ordained ministry, as is indicated in the Church of Sweden which has replaced the use of *'ämbete'* (office) with *'vigningstjänst'* ('ordained ministry') in its Church ordinance?

3. What do the churches call particular forms of ministries? Are they 'bishops', 'pastors', 'deacons', 'catechists', 'missionaries', to mention only the English equivalents of the most commonly used Nordic terms? Or are they called by other titles, and if so, how far is this only

---

9. Cf. e.g. Einar Sigurbjörnsson on the translation of Roman Catholic rites into the Nordic languages (Part II.1). See further Brodd's analysis of a Swedish Free Chruch Handbook (Part II.4).

a question of terminology or how far do we have to see quite a different content in the ministries, when the terminology changes, for instance from '*prest*' to '*forstander*' or from '*biskop*' to '*tilsynsmann*' or '*generalsekretær*'?[13]

Some churches seem very concerned to have a precise – even dogmatically correct – terminology in their rites, though they do not always succeed in preserving it, when the rites are translated into different languages and related to different historical experiences with the different terms.[14] Others may be more liberal in constructing their rites – and thus later on end up asking dogmatic questions about the meaning of different terms, as is presently the case within the Church of Norway.[15] Others again may be very relaxed and pragmatic about the terminological questions, using the mainstream terminology of the place in order to communicate to the surroundings in the most efficient way. This is very much the case with the Salvation Army, when it calls its installations 'ordinations' and its officers 'pastors', as seems to fit the context, even though the Army is only in the process of turning to the theological self-understanding equivalent to the theology behind this terminology as it is being used in other local churches.[16]

It is obviously important to digest the terminology of the churches whose ordination rites we are dealing with. It is, however, equally important to analyse the different rites, with the help of the clarified terminology in the individual contributions to the analysis (as found in Part II). In an attempt to be faithful to the primary inductive approach of this research we have not tried to make all writers use a common terminology. On the contrary we have advised each author to clarify and use the terminology through which it is possible to work out the most consistent analysis of the rites chosen for analysis. There is always a sort of dialectic between the terminology and the theology of ordination. However, no conclusion about theology can be obtained from studying terminology alone, nor can the theology of a particular ordination rite be changed merely by changing its terminology. Terminology and theology have to be dealt with separately and at the same time as factors in dynamic relationship with one another.[17]

---

13. Cf. Fjeld's Appendix 3 (Part II.4).
14. Cf. Einar Sigurbjörnsson (Part II.1).
15. Cf. Fjeld on the Lutheran Churches in Norway (Part II.4).
16. Cf. Lydholm on ordination in the Salvation Army (Part II.5).
17. Cf. Tjørhom (Part III.1).

All attempts to systematize the different terms in use according to a common structure or comparative table have proved impossible or rather unfruitful, more confusing than enlightening. Two churches of the same denomination may use the same terms in different ways. It may also be so with churches related to one another and living within the same local culture using one and the same language. Even within the individual churches the use of terminology may be inconsistent as is the case in the Evangelical-Lutheran Church of Denmark where, since 1685, ordination has always been called '*vielse*' in the titles of ordination liturgies, even though the Danish word in theological, legal and everyday language is '*ordination*'. This is the case even in some of the rubrics in the rite itself.

It follows from what has been said so far that we have not been able to construct a theological or even a linguistic table of the terminology used in ordination rites in the Nordic countries. We have, however, developed a *Glossary of Nordic Terms* in which Else-Britt Nilsen has drawn up a list of the different Nordic terms which appear in this book.[18] We hope it will be helpful to readers as well as for future research in this area.

Texts and Contexts

In the above discussion on the principles of hermeneutics and methodology it was stressed that liturgical texts are developed, gain their meanings, are understood and thus to a certain extent determined within a variety of different contexts. We shall point to some of the most important of these:

1. First there is *the historical and cultural context.* Different liturgies are created and/or inculturated in all sorts of cultures all over the world. Christianity can in fact be seen as a movement of translation, as Christianity is always being passed on – and thus inculturated – by being translated (cf. Sanneh 1989). This is true of the Reformation Churches as it is very much of Christian mission today, and according to the theology of Vatican II, the inculturation of ordination rites implies not only new local terminologies but also new concepts of ministry and ordination. Whether these are faithful to the old ones or not; whether they are even better than the old ones, or more in accordance with the Gospel, will always be a matter for debate. The necessity for Christian

---

18. Historical surveys of basic terminology used when dealing with ordained ministries from the Early Church, at the Reformation and today can be found in Puglisi 1996, 212-15 and Puglisi 1998, 172-74.

theology and practice to be inculturated follows from the fundamentally incarnational character of Christianity. Inculturation is a requirement of the basic calling of the Church to follow Christ. The Church, however, is not Christ. Therefore it may fail or it may succeed when incarnating its theology and practice into a new culture. Incarnation and inculturation is, however, always a necessary form of life for a Christian Church.[19]

2. *The political context* is part of the historical and cultural contexts in which ordination rites are inculturated. Christianity is not meant to be without political consequences. Nor have political rulers ever left it alone: quite the opposite, they have always attempted in different ways to make the Church support or legitimise their politics. The relationships between Church and politics are thus manifold. A strong church like the Roman Catholic Church of medieval times may be placed over against the political rulers in conflict and/or cooperation. A traditional Lutheran State Church gets its protection from the King, who, for his part, uses the church in an attempt to control the people ideologically. A Free Church may work so hard to be free from the state that it tends to be more identified by its opposition to the state than by its faith in the Gospel. Thus the traces of current political circumstances are always found in the churches, most often also in the rites for the ordination of their priestly and spiritual leaders, in whom politicians may take a special interest.[20] In the modern setting of the Nordic countries, democracy is the dominant system of governance even within the churches. This raises the question of ordained ministers being reduced to democratically appointed civil servants or employees of the churches. How does that influence ordination rites? And if it does not, can the

---

19. Examples of the inculturation of ordination rites (and the theology and life of our churches in general) are found below in Lydholm's contribution on the Salvation Army in the different Nordic countries as well as in Olsen's study of rites for the ordination/blessing of missionaries. Illustrations are also found in the studies by Langgaard, Hansen and Einar Sigurbjörnsson & Kristján Valur Ingolfson on Greenland, the Faeroe Islands and Iceland.

20. Examples of political influence in ordination rites are very obvious in Langgaard's, Hansen's and Einar Sigurbjörnsson & Kristján Valur Ingolfson's studies of the rites of the former Danish 'colonies', Greenland, the Faeroe Islands and Iceland.

rites still be trustworthy expressions of ordained ministry, for which there are democratic election processes?[21]

3. A specific context of its own with both cultural and political connotations is *the gender context*, which has played a significant and explicit role during the last 50 years. During this time, most of the churches in the Nordic countries have debated, wrestled with the idea of women ministers and eventually introduced them.[22] On the one hand the question of gender in ordination rites goes with the question of the introduction of women ministers: on the other hand it goes beyond this question to involve the whole range of gender questions in Christian theology. Ultimately, it very much reflects the general status of gender issues in the societies in which the churches live.[23] As indicated by Ninna Beckmann (Part III.2), gender issues have been explicitly dealt with in only a very few places in the case studies in this book.

4. Finally, of all the contexts of ordination rites, the most immediate and thus important is always *the congregation present at the ordination*. This raises the question of the communicative ability of the rites. To what extent and in what way are they understood by the congregation present at ordinations in our churches? This of course depends on the language as well as the performance of the rites and not least on the way in which the congregation is included or excluded.[24]

The Theological Significance of Liturgy

Ordination rites are not only written and more or less historically determined and theologically reflective texts meant for celebration today. They are liturgies. What does that imply? This obviously depends on our concept(s) of

---

21. The challenge to the episcopate of the Church in a democratic society has been dealt with in *The Office of the Bishop* 1993, 123-130.
22. Cf. Beckmann (Part III.2).
23. Cf. Inghammar on the ordination of deaconesses and deacons (Part II.3).
24. The communication question is explicitly dealt with in Iversen's analysis of the rites of ordination of the Evangelical-Lutheran Church of Denmark and more generally by Einar Sigurbjörnsson in his analysis of a collection of the great Nordic hymns for ordination, the singing of which is a highly participatory and probably also very communicative part of ordination in the Evangelical-Lutheran Churches in the Nordic countries. (See Part II.6 for both articles.)

liturgy as the language of believers in their communication with God and their symbolic work for the world.[25]

Social anthropologists have developed multidimensional and very often conflicting theories about what is going on in rites and liturgies and to what effect. Social anthropological studies and theories could probably further the understanding of rites of ordination and commitment. However, the churches in various branches of the Christian Church have their own – significantly different – concepts of liturgy. Briefly speaking, in the Orthodox Churches *all that is important for theology is liturgy*.[26] The Roman Catholic Church would not go quite so far, but does stress the importance of having *a theology of liturgy*.[27] In his development of a Catholic understanding of the relationship between text and context in liturgical life Kevin W. Irwin stresses that liturgy is anamnetic-christological, recalling the redemptive deeds of Christ, epicletic-pneumatological, praying for and depending on the work of the Holy Spirit today, and ecclesiological-soteriological as a corporate act of prayer of the Church, through which salvation is mediated (Irwin 1994, 46-50). Protestant Churches, however, often seem to perform their liturgies as just another way of teaching the right theology in a certain situation by means of what the *Confessio Augustana,* for example, calls 'ceremonies'.

Liturgical studies often work with the thesis that the liturgies confess and express the basic creeds and theology of the churches – referring to the notion of *lex orandi, lex credendi*, which can be traced back to the early Church (cf. De Clerck 1994). This fifth century term is used today, for example, to describe the theological identity of the Anglican Church. The present studies are in line with this notion: ordination rites are used as a basic *locus theologicus*, that is, as the place to find the decisive theological material for research on ordained ministries in the Nordic Churches. In this process, it is important to respect the special character of rites: they are not to be dealt with as traditional dogmatic text, but as text enacted within a certain context in the Church. As noted above, the primary contexts of rites are not the historical, confessional or legal traditions of the churches, but the very congregational life in which they are enacted and which is being recreated by the liturgy celebrated in the midst of the congregation.

Among Protestant theologians it is, however, also common to point to the

---

25. Cf. the Greek term *'laos ergon'* (the work by or for the people) as the etymological basis for the English word 'liturgy'.
26. Cf. White (Part III.1).
27. Cf. De Clerck (Part III.2).

liturgy of the Church as *theologia prima*, in relation to which academic theology and the teachings of the Church are only *theologia secunda*, reflecting what is basically found – and brought into our world – by means of the liturgical life of the Church, which may also include its spiritual, diaconal and social life in a broader sense. *Theologia prima* is not only talking about God as *theologia secunda* is: it is talking with God. The primary advantage of liturgy compared with confessional teachings and academic theology is obviously that it is enacted and alive in a living dialogue with God. The importance of liturgy as living and life-giving in the Church is stressed, for example, by the Danish Lutheran theologian Regin Prenter:

> If liturgy is separated from theology, i.e. if it is no longer in its essence 'theology' or true witness to the revelation of God, it then becomes an end in itself, a 'good work', performed with the intention of pleasing God... If, on the other hand, theology is separated from liturgy, i.e. if it is no longer seen as a part of the liturgy of the Church, part of the living sacrifice of our bodies in the living service of God and our fellow men, it, too, becomes an end in itself, a human wisdom competing with and even rejecting the revelation of God.... These two dangers arising out of the neglect of the essential unity of liturgy and theology are, I think, imminent in our present situation in the Lutheran Church...If intellectualistic theology prevails in the Church it may transform that Church into a philosophical society or a Gnostic sect. If, on the other hand, ritualistic liturgy prevails, it may change the Christian faith into a mystery religion... If the Gospel is not proclaimed in the name of the Triune God as the living, prophetic and apostolic voice maintaining the personal relationship between God and people, a relationship, which we, using biblical terms, call a covenant, then there can be no true liturgy...Only when the preaching of the gospel is followed by the administration of the Holy Communion is it clearly manifested that the sacrifice of Jesus Christ in history is not simply an important fact of the past, the moral and religious evaluation of which is left to us, but, rather, that this sacrifice is God's ultimate dealing with his people and is valid for all places and all ages... The theology of the Church is liturgical, a part of the liturgy in the wider sense. Theology has no purpose in itself. It serves God and Neighbour. It is part of the sacrifice of our bodies to which we are called as the people of God... Theology is real only in so far as it is liturgy... (Prenter 1959).

An understanding of liturgy – including ordination rites – in line with Regin Prenter's standpoint is a common point of departure for the studies in this book. Even though some of the churches whose rites are examined do not officially value liturgy in this way, practically they seem to emphasise the importance of liturgy anyway, when they celebrate ordination. When we see ordination rites as liturgy it gives ordination some sort of sacramental character: something new is happening, something is given by God, when the person being ordained participates in the liturgy. It is possible to have *knowledge of liturgy*, but there is also a *knowledge in liturgy*, which people may have their share of, when participating in it. This notion of liturgy is well summarised in a quotation from *Paivi Jussila* (Part III.2):

> In academic theology, knowledge of God is normally limited to 'knowledge about'... Liturgy instead, does not seek theoretical or partial knowledge of God. It seeks God not as a piece of knowledge, but as a being. It aims at a unifying experience of communion. Knowledge without love leaves a human being in the state of terrifying loneliness and boredom...whereas liturgy is filled with praise and doxology.

The Structure of this Book

For the sake of non-Nordic readers of this work, the introduction is completed here by two short contributions which attempt to depict the various churches and their special historically determined context in the Nordic countries.

Part II below contains 19 different case studies of rites of ordination and commitment in the Nordic Churches. It begins with Roman Catholic and Orthodox rites and goes, via Lutheran rites for the ordination of bishops and pastors and a special section on rites of admission to diaconal ministry, to a section exploring the significance and meaning of rites of ordination and commitment in various denominational contexts. One section deals with the process of institutionalization and contextualization of the rites in various ecclesial contexts and Part II concludes with two articles attempting to see the rites through the experience of the congregation present.

Part III adds six articles on important ecumenical and liturgical contexts and perspectives related to the case studies in Part II. Finally, the conclusions in Part IV provide, after the general editor's comments and observations, a Common Statement on the Meaning of Ordination, for which the whole group of editors, who have worked together during the five years of the project, is collectively responsible.

The leadership of this Nordic project on the Theology and Terminology of Ordination Rites in the Churches of the Nordic Countries worked hard to invite scholars from all the churches in the Nordic area to participate and contribute equally in the study process that led up to this book, hoping thereby to cover the rites from the various churches on an equal basis. Now that we have come to the end it is obvious that more contributions might have given a fuller picture. We would like to have had more on the ordination rites in the western (Swedish and Finnish) tradition of the Nordic Lutheran Churches as well as a stronger representation from Pentecostal Churches and established churches, such as the Methodist and Anglican Churches, which are also present in the Nordic countries. More theoretical perspectives from social anthropology would also need to be integrated into future studies. Once more we remind colleagues and other readers that apart from this book we hope to have facilitated future research by making our synoptic tables of rites available on the internet (www.teol.ku.dk/ast/ansatte/Hans%20Raun%20Iversen-ordination.htm).

References

Borgegård, Gunnel and Hall, Christine (eds). 1999. *The Ministry of the Deacon, vol. 1. Anglican-Lutheran Perspectives.* Uppsala: Nordic Ecumenical Council.

Borgegård, Gunnel, Fanuelsen, Olav and Hall, Christine (eds). 2000. *The Ministry of the Deacon, vol. 2. Ecclesiological Explorations.* Uppsala: Nordic Ecumenical Council.

De Clerck, Paul. 1994. 'Lex orandi, lex credendi': the Original Sense and the historical Avatars of an Equivocal Adage, in *Studia Liturgica*, 24:2, 178-200.

Gadamer, Hans-Georg. *Truth and Method.* 2nd rev. ed. London: Sheed & Ward.

Irwin, Kevin W. 1994. *Context and Text: Method in Liturgical Theology.* Collegeville, Minn: The Liturgical Press.

Prenter, Regin. 1959. 'Liturgy and Theology', in *Liturgy, Theology, Music in the Lutheran Church.* Minneapolis, 33-42. Reprinted in Regin Prenter 1987. *Theologie und Gottesdienst: Gesammelte Aufsätze.* Århus: Forlaget Aros & Göttingen: Vandenhoch & Ruprecht, 131-159.

Puglisi, James F. 1996, 1998, and 2001. *The Process of Admission to Ordained Ministry*, Vols. I-III. Collegeville, Minn: The Liturgical Press.

Sanneh, Lamin. 1989. *Translating the Message: The Missionary Impact on Culture.* Maryknoll, N.Y.: Orbis Books.

The Office of the Bishop: Report of the official Working Group for Dialogue between the Church of Sweden and the Roman Catholic Diocese of Stockholm. 1993. Geneva: Lutheran World Federation.

Together in Mission and Ministry: The Porvoo Common Statement with Essays on Church and Ministry in Northern Europe. 1993. London: Church House Publishing.

Tjørhom, Ola (ed.). 2002. *Apostolicity and Unity: Essays on the Porvoo Common Statement.* Geneva: WCC Publications.

The Political, Ecclesial, and Religious Profile of the Nordic Countries

Hans Raun Iversen

It is both easy and difficult to describe the five Nordic countries in an international context. In terms of population, they are relatively small. At the same time they are quite homogeneous, though significantly different in their political, ecclesial and religious profiles.

In this short article we shall first depict the general political, ecclesial and religious profile of the five Nordic countries in its uniqueness and say what may be said about them all in common, before pointing to the most important differences between them. When similarities have been pointed out, we must immediately modify them by spelling out the important ways in which the situation is also diverse in the churches in the Nordic countries:

1. The Nordic countries are culturally homogeneous, highly developed welfare states, with high taxation, stable democracy and strong Social Democratic Parties, which have been in power for major parts of the time since World War II

1a. All the Nordic countries have significant indigenous minority groups in their population. Finland, Sweden and Norway include the Sami people (50-70,000) in their northern areas. Denmark includes Greenland (57,000) and the Faeroe Islands (48,000). As these minority groups only amount to a small percentage of the total population they are often neglected politically as well as religiously. In this book two articles deal with the specific situations in the Faeroe Islands and Greenland.

1b. Apart from gradual but fairly continuous immigration throughout most of their history, all the Nordic countries have had significant recent immigration, firstly by the guest workers of the 1960s and their families and, during recent decades, mainly by refugees. In Sweden and Denmark about 10% of the inhabitants today are of non-local ethnic origin, 3-4 % have a Muslim background, whereas the percentages are lower in Norway and especially in Iceland and Finland – primarily because of differences in their geographical position. Finland has also been more isolated because of the Finish language, which is totally different from the languages of the four other Nordic Countries, whose languages are similar.

1c. Furthermore the political culture varies in the five Nordic countries. Two of the countries, Sweden and Denmark, have been independent states for many centuries, for some periods acting as major, multi-ethnic states with involvements in international warfare and with various sorts of 'colonies'. The three other countries gained their full national independence more recently: Finland from Russia in 1917, Norway from Sweden in 1905 and Iceland from Denmark in 1944.

1d. To this are added differences in modern political experience due not least to different geographical positions. Until 1990 Finland was forced to act carefully in relation to its big eastern neighbour, the Soviet Union. Finland and 'neutral' Sweden nearby have never been members of NATO as the three western Nordic countries have. Today Finland is a full member of the European Union, even more committed than Sweden and Denmark, where the relationship to the rest of Europe is a debated and partly pragmatic matter. Norway, Iceland, the Faeroe Islands and Greenland are still formally outside the European Union.

2. Since the sixteenth century there have been – and to some extent there still are – strong relationships between the more or less monopolistic Lutheran national Churches in the Nordic countries, of which more than 80% of the population are still members, and the state.

2a. Since the Reformation there have been major differences between the western (Swedish) and eastern (Danish) ecclesial traditions in the national Lutheran Churches. The Reformation was radical, at least at the top level, in Denmark, where the church was more or less expropriated by the state in terms not only of property, but also of infrastructure, leadership and vision. In Sweden the Reformation was more moderate and gradual, and the church kept its identity and in major parts of its history also some independent, internal governance in relation to the state and even a direct influence on the state via the places that the clergy had in Parliament until 1861. This is reflected in the two different ordinals: in Denmark, partly including Norway and Iceland, and in Sweden, partly including Finland.[1]

2b. The religious and cultural revival movements in the nineteenth century also marked the national churches in different ways: in Sweden 6% of the population was organised into free churches, more or less inspired by the revival, outside the national church. In Norway and Iceland the comparable figure is 4 % and in Denmark and Finland, where the revivals were kept inside the national church, only 1 %. In Finland the Orthodox Church, with 1 % of the population as its members, has the same formal relationship with the state as the Lutheran Church. In recent years, immigration has changed this picture somewhat, as it has led to growth in the Roman Catholic Church, formerly only significant in Sweden, and to some extent also in the Pentecostal Churches.

2c. In all national Lutheran Churches internal church governance, bishops meetings, synods, diocesan councils and parish boards, have gradually been introduced and developed during the last century or two. In Denmark this is so far only the case at the congregational level. Against this background the churches have various degrees of independence today in their relations with the state: the Church of Sweden has had formal independence since 2000, in Norway a process towards independence has been started, in Finland and Iceland independence is strong in internal matters. In Denmark there is no formal independence, but a spreading out of influence between various church and state agencies.

2d. The legal position of free churches and other religious bodies outside the national churches also varies in the Nordic countries. In Sweden all religions are now treated equally in principle. The same is, to a great extent, the case in Norway, Iceland and Finland, though the national churches have special relations with the state. In Denmark the legal position of Christian denominations and other religions outside the national church is weaker and less clear.

3. The Nordic countries are highly secularised – with the world record in low rates of religious attendance, a low level of conformity among church members to the official teaching of the churches and a relatively low level of expectation of the churches by their members.

3a. The low rate of church attendance (2-4 % on a weekly basis), combined with the high rate of nominal church membership in the national Lutheran

---

1. Cf. Knuutila (Part II.2).

Churches (80-85 %) reflects, among other things, a situation in which almost five hundred years of relatively rigid, compulsory state church religion has prevented the majority of the people in the Nordic countries from ever having any sense of practical responsibility for the organisation of their own religion. This general tendency is, however, counteracted by a considerable number of church organisations, local as well as national, originally rooted in the revival movements, which are quite actively supported by volunteer members of the national church and the free churches.

3b. The passive attitude of most church members is also counter-balanced by a high degree of personal, existential, ethical and partly religious concern among individuals in general. The point is, however, that Nordic people do not look to their churches for answers to existential and ethical questions. In that respect they only have a limited sense of the classical meaning of 'Church'. There is on the other hand, strong evidence that the churches are still playing an important role as the implicit legitimating body of the Christian culture of their members. In most cases the members do not even think of creating alternatives to the established churches, to which they faithfully turn, when they are in need of baptism, confirmation, weddings or funerals.

3c. Among the Nordic countries the most affirmative attitude to the Church and classical Christian faith is found in Finland. Denmark seems to be leading in terms of low level of church attendance, followed by Sweden and Norway, where the revival movement and free churches have been and still are comparatively strong and thus also raise the average attendance. The lowest degree of conformity with the Christian teaching of the churches is usually found in Sweden, which is therefore often labelled the most secularized country in the world. On the other hand Christianity is even more invisible in public life in Denmark than in Sweden.

3d. 'I am Christian – in my own way' is the most popular religious statement in the Nordic countries. The supposedly very personal ways of being Christian in Nordic countries do, however, fit in to a common pattern of quite strong belief in the goodness of God, whoever that is, in the importance of good morals and in some sort of personal eternal life, though with only a weak relationship to the content of the Apostles' Creed, for example. In this first part of the twenty-first century globalisation, multiculturalism and the visible local presence of non-Christian religions tend to make the people of the Nordic countries more open and partly also more affirmative of Christianity without turning to regular church attendance or conformity with the official teaching of the churches.

References

Balling, J.L. and Lindhardt, P.G. 1967. *Den nordiske kirkes historie.* Copenhagen: Nyt Nordisk Forlag.

Church and State in Scandinavia. 1990. In *Studia Theologica, Scandinavian Journal of Theology*, Vol. 44: 1.

Den store danske encyklopædi. 2000-2001. Danmarks Nationalleksikon. Copenhagen: Gyldendalske Boghandel.

Gustafsson, Göran and Pettersson, Thorleif. 2000. *Folkkyrkor och religiös pluralism –den nordiska religiösa modellen.* Stockholm: Verbum.

Martin, David. 1978. *A General Theory of Secularization.* Oxford: Basil Blackwell.

Dahlgaard, Frank (ed.). *Nordic Statistical Yearbook.* Copenhagen: Nordic Council of Ministers.

Schjørring, Jens Holger (ed.). 2001. *Nordiske folkekirker i opbrud. National identitet og international nyorientering efter 1945.* Aarhus: Aarhus Universitetsforlag.

The Nordic Churches: A Brief Statistical Profile

Liselotte Malmgart

In the Nordic countries the majority of the population belong to the Lutheran Protestant Churches, but a wide range of other Christian churches and denominations also exist.

It is difficult to collect exactly comparable statistics from all the countries, and the situation is constantly changing. However, the estimates below give an impression of the situation of the Christian churches in the Nordic countries at the beginning of the twenty-first century.

Denmark

Approximately 84% of the 5.3 million Danes are members of the Evangelical-Lutheran Church of Denmark. The Roman Catholic Church is the second largest church in the country with around 35,000 members, but this is less than 1% of the population. Another 1% belongs to a number of smaller free churches, the largest being the Baptist Church and the Pentecostal congregations, each with a membership between 5,200 and 5,300.

Iceland

Iceland has a population of approximately 288,500 people and 86 % belong to the Evangelical-Lutheran Church of Iceland. Almost 5% are members of a number of smaller free Christian churches, the largest one being the Evangelical-Lutheran Free Church of Reykjavik (2%). Roughly 2% are Roman Catholics and only 2.4% of the population are registered as not belonging to any religious organisations.

Finland

Approximately 84.1% of the 5.2 million Finns belong to the Evangelical-Lutheran Church of Finland. The membership of the Orthodox Church is approximately 60,000 (1.1% of the population). Another 1.1% belong to other registered religious organisations, a statistic in which all faiths are included. In addition, about 1% of the population are members of Pentecostal congregations (until recently not registered as religious organisations).

Norway

Of 4.5 million Norwegians 85.7% belong to the Church of Norway and another 6.3% (including both Christians and non-Christians) belong to other registered communities of faith. Nearly 1% of the population belong to the Roman Catholic Church and about 1% to the Pentecostal congregations. The membership numbers for some of the free Christian churches can be found in Bjørn-Øyvind Fjeld's articles (Part II.4).

Sweden

Sweden has a population of 9 million, of which 79.6% are members of the Church of Sweden. The Protestant Free Churches are estimated to have a following of 2.4%, the largest being the Mission Covenant Church of Sweden ministering to 1.5% of the population. In addition to this, nearly 1.4% of the population are involved in the Pentecostal congregations.

Almost 1.6% belong to the Roman Catholic Church and close to 1% to one of fifteen orthodox and oriental 'immigrant' churches, the largest being the Syrian Orthodox Church with 29,000 members.

Sources

www.evl.fi; virtualfinland.fi; www.hagstofa.is; www.ssb.no; www.dst.dk; www.svenskakyrkan.se; www.sweden.se; www.sst.a.se
Nordic Statistical Yearbook 2003

PART II
Case Studies

1. Early Traditions of Ordination in the Nordic Context

The Roman Catholic and the Orthodox Churches are minority churches in the Nordic countries. Even so they play important roles in Nordic church life, the Orthodox Church foremost in Finland. Ordination in the Nordic countries thus has links to the early traditions that lie behind present-day Roman Catholic and Orthodox rites of ordination.

Einar Sigurbjörnsson examines the theology and terminology of Roman Catholic rites for the ordination of bishops, priests and deacons, as they have been translated – historically and recently – into the various languages of the five Nordic countries. Interestingly the translations of the authorised rites into the different, but (with the exception of Finnish) rather similar Nordic languages, have not been co-ordinated. They thus provide a good case study of the difficulties encountered, when translating a developed theology of ordination from its distinct language of origin (in this case, Latin) to other languages with their different linguistic roots and, in the case of Nordic languages, inherited *Wirkungsgeschichte* from former translations (Roman Catholic during the Middle Ages and Lutheran since the time of the Reformation). A mutual coordination of these translations and a deliberate consideration of connections and disconnections in relation to the language of the dominant Lutheran Churches in the Nordic countries would be desirable.

Metropolitan Johannes of Nicaea gives an account of the rites for the sacramental ordination of deacons, priests and bishops in the Orthodox Church of Finland. He emphasises that ordination is a participation in the *mysterion* of salvation. Ordination is thus a mystery which God performs through the Holy Spirit with the bishop as his tool. The essential prayers are said in a low voice or 'secretly', as the tradition puts it. Signifying their special position as personally entrusted representatives of one bishop, deacons and priests are always ordained one at a time – and by one bishop only. Conversely, at least two other bishops must assist the ordaining bishop at a bishop's ordination, as the bishops there present must represent Orthodox bishops in general. Further background information on the Orthodox understanding of liturgy and ordination is provided in *Grant White*'s article on Orthodox stances in recent ecumenical dialogues on the theology of ordained ministry (Part III.1).

Theology and Terminology in Roman Catholic Rites of Ordination in the Nordic Countries

Einar Sigurbjörnsson

The Reformation was established in the Nordic countries in the 1530s. From the sixteenth to the nineteenth centuries the only religion allowed was that of the Lutheran Church, and other Christian communities including the 'popish church' were banned. In the nineteenth century, the age of freedom, democracy came to the fore and constitutions granted freedom of religion to the people, although the Lutheran Church continued to be the established church of all the Nordic countries. Gradually other churches began working in these countries, among them the Roman Catholic Church which is now, at the beginning of the twenty-first century, a considerable force in the religious lives of the Nordic countries.

Although the liturgy of the Mass and other services were celebrated in Latin, the Mass and the daily office were translated and published for the benefit of the laity but not for general use.[1] The Second Vatican Council (1962-1965) effected a significant change when it recommended in its Constitution on the Liturgy (*Constitutio de Sacra Liturgia: Sacrosanctum Concilium*) that the liturgy of the Mass as well as other services should be celebrated in the vernacular (*Sacrosanctum Concilium* e. g. nos. 36 and 54, 828, 831). Following the recommendations of Vatican II the Roman Catholic Church, including the local churches in the Nordic countries, began the work of translating the liturgy of

---

1. In Iceland the Mass, both the ordinary and the propers, was translated and published in Latin and Icelandic in 1959: *Rómversk-kapólsk messubók fyrir sunnudaga og aðalhátíðisdaga kirkjuársins* I-III, 1959.

the Mass and other liturgies.[2] The translation work included the ordination rites.

The theology of worship formulated by Vatican II had its roots in the liturgical movement (J. A. Jungmann 1967). Instead of regarding liturgy as the activity of priests, liturgy is interpreted as the work of the whole community, the work of the royal and priestly People of God.[3] This understanding of liturgy was echoed in the ecclesiology of the Council as formulated in the Dogmatic Constitution on the Church (*Constitutio Dogmatica de Ecclesia: Lumen Gentium).* There the concept of the 'People of God' (*'populus Dei')* is the main concept related to the Church. This had far reaching consequences for the understanding of liturgy, including the understanding of the sacrament of order. Instead of defining ministry from a cultic point of view, the Council emphasized the pastoral duties of the ministry of the Church with its apex in episcopacy.[4]

The Medieval Doctrine of the Sacrament of Order

The sacrament of order was defined during the Middle Ages. It was defined at that time from the point of view of priesthood (*'sacerdotium').* There were seven orders: four minor orders, those of doorkeeper, reader, exorcist and acolyte, and three major orders, those of sub-deacon, deacon and priest. Thus the summit of the sacrament resided in ordination to the presbyterate. In their ordination, priests had the power to consecrate the body and blood of Christ conferred on them, and this was the aim of the sacrament (Thomas Aquinas V: 165). Priests or, rather, presbyters (*'presbyteri')* and bishops were equals as far as priesthood (*'sacerdotium')* was concerned and thus had equal powers over the sacramental body of Christ: their powers were unequal as far as power over the mystical body of Christ was concerned.[5]

This understanding of the sacrament of order was confirmed at the Council

2. In Iceland the ordinary of the Mass was published as early as 1969: *Rómversk kaþólsk messubók. Fastir liðir messunnar,* 1969.
3. *Constitutio de Sacra Liturgia* nos. 7 and 14 in Tanner 1990, II: 822, 824. See also the chapter on the renewal of the liturgy in Tanner, 1990, II: 825-830, e.g. no. 26: 'Liturgical events are not private actions but celebrations of the Church which is "the sacrament of unity", the holy people drawn into an ordered whole under the bishops'. Tanner, 1990, II: 826.
4. See Einar Sigurbjörnsson (1974). On the Roman Catholic understanding of ministry prior to Vatican II, see Persson (1961).
5. Thomas Aquinas, *Summa Theologiae* 2-2 q. 184 6 ad 1, in the edition of *Biblioteca de autores Cristianos* III: 1072; 3 q. 67 2 ad 2 and q. 82 1 ad 4, in the edition of *Biblioteca*

of Trent (Tanner 1990, II: 742-744; Denzinger and Schönmetzer 1967, no. 1763-1778). In its Decree on the Sacrament of Order the Council of Trent states in the first chapter that sacrifice and priesthood (*'sacrificium et sacerdotium'*) are intimately connected and that the Lord has instituted in the Church a visible sacrifice of the Eucharist (*'sanctum eucharistiae sacrificium visibile'*) which necessitates a visible and external priesthood (*'visibile et externum sacerdotium'*). The power of the priesthood to consecrate, offer and administer Christ's body and blood hence was given by the Lord to the apostles and their successors. In chapter two other ministries of minor and major orders are mentioned and are defined as assisting the priests (*'sacerdotes'*) through their ministries. In canon 6 the hierarchy of bishops, presbyters and deacons is said to be of divine origin.

Whilst the lesser orders from deacons down to doorkeepers are said to be ministers to the priests and, in chapter 4 of the Decree, bishops are said to belong to the hierarchical order as 'rulers of the Church of God', the Decree uses the terms priest and priesthood (*'sacerdos'* and *'sacerdotium'*) of both presbyters and bishops. The episcopal ministry is not defined. It is only stated that bishops are superior to presbyters and that their particular ministry is to confer the sacrament of confirmation, to ordain ministers and perform other duties which the lesser orders have no power to perform. Thus ministry and ordination were primarily regarded from a cultic point of view.

The Teaching of Vatican II

The sacrament of order received a new definition at the Second Vatican Council (Einar Sigurbjörnsson 1974). In the teaching of Vatican II the ministry of bishops was elevated to be regarded as the primary and chief ministry in the Church. Episcopal ordination was said to be the fullness of the sacrament of order. Contrary to the former emphasis which had concentrated on ordination as conferring the power of sanctification, ordination came to be seen as conveying the offices of sanctifying, teaching and governing (*Lumen Gentium* nn. 21 and 26, 865, 870). Presbyters were said to be ordained to participate in the ministry of bishops and to serve by their mandate, but nevertheless as true priests (*'sacerdotes'*) (*Lumen Gentium* n. 28, 873). Deacons were said not to be ordained to priesthood (*'sacerdotium'*) but to ministry (*'ministerium'*) and were

---

de autores Cristianos IV:530, 694. See also Einar Sigurbjörnsson 1974, 20-22. For me as a Lutheran it is interesting to see that Aquinas defines the word *'episcopus'* (bishop) as 'superintendent': *'Nam episcopi dicuntur ex eo quod superintendunt, sicut Augustinus dicit XIX De Civ. Dei.'* (*Summa Theologiae* 2-2 q. 184 6 ad 1.

seen as the servants of the bishop (*Lumen Gentium* n. 29, 874). With this reversal, Vatican II abandoned the specific western medieval understanding of ministry which emphasized the cultic role of the priest and returned to the early Church's understanding of the threefold ministry of the Church. This is also connected with the understanding of the Church as the People of God, which puts more emphasis on the pastoral function of the ordained ministry.[6]

The concept of the People of God is developed in the second chapter of the Vatican II Constitution on the Church. There it is emphasized that through baptism all members of God's people participate in the priesthood ('*sacerdotium*') of Christ (*Lumen Gentium* n. 10, 856-857). This is called the common priesthood of the faithful ('*sacerdotium commune fidelium*'). Besides this common priesthood there is a ministerial or hierarchical priesthood ('*sacerdotium ministeriale seu hierarchicum*') which 'in essence and not simply in degree' ('*essentia et non gradu tantum*') differs from the common priesthood of the faithful. The ministerial priest 'through the sacred power that he enjoys' is to form and govern the priestly people of God especially in the eucharistic sacrifice, which he offers to God in the name of the whole people. By virtue of their royal priesthood the faithful 'join in the offering of the Eucharist and they exercise their priesthood in receiving the sacraments, in prayer and thanksgiving, through the witness of a holy life, by self-denial and by active charity' (Tanner 1990, II: 857). Thus the concept of priesthood ('*sacerdotium*') is no longer simply a cultic concept but one which refers to the whole life of the People of God.

The main teaching of the third chapter which deals with the hierarchical constitution of the Church is that the ministerial priesthood, together with all prerogatives of the ministry or hierarchy, rests in the episcopate. At the beginning of chapter 3 it is emphasized that Christ instituted ministries in the Church to guide or lead his people. The ministers have sacred power ('*potestas sacra*') and chief among the ministers are the bishops who are the successors of the apostles in unity or communion with the Bishop of Rome, the successor of Peter. The bishops form a college ('*collegium episcoporum*', also called '*ordo episcoporum*', order of bishops) which is a continuation of the college of the apostles. It is Christ himself, as High Priest ('*Summus Pontifex*'), who is present through the bishops and acts in them and distributes his gifts. Presbyters are defined as helpers of the bishops. Hence it is the bishops who receive, at their ordination, the fullness of the sacrament of order. The fullness of ministry is conferred on them through the act of ordination: not only the office ('*munus*'

---

6. J. Puglisi 2001, 19-21, 41-42, cf. above on the liturgical theology of Vatican II.

instead of '*potestas*') of sanctifying, but also that of teaching and leading. According to the Constitution on the Church the institution of ministry is not connected to the institution of the Eucharist but to the giving of the Holy Spirit to the Apostles at Pentecost, and this gift they handed over to their helpers by the imposition of hands. Thus ministry is pneumatologically anchored and there is a close interaction between the sending ('*missio*') of Christ and the Church (Tanner 1990, II: 865).

Thus episcopal ordination grants participation in the threefold ministry of Christ, that of priest ('*sacerdos*'), teacher (or prophet) and pastor (or ruler or king). At the same time episcopal ordination is entry into the college of bishops, which can only act in communion with the Pope (art. 22, Tanner 1990, II: 865-867). And since the bishop is endowed with the fullness of the sacrament of order ('*plenitudine sacramenti Ordinis insignitus*'), he is 'the steward of the grace of the supreme priesthood' ('*oeconomus gratiae supremi sacerdotii*'), a quotation from a Byzantine rite of ordination (Tanner 1990, II: 870). This is evident above all in the Eucharist 'which he offers, or which he ensures is offered' ('*quam ipse offert vel offerri curat*') (Tanner 1990, II). The Church is present in each local church, and there it is the bishop who serves in sanctifying, teaching and leading, through his helpers the presbyters and deacons: 'In this way the divinely instituted ecclesiastical ministry is exercised in different orders by those who from ancient times are called bishops, priests and deacons' (*Lumen Gentium* n. 10, 856-857).

Of these ministries, the priests ('*presbyteri*') are most closely connected to the bishop by reason of priestly dignity ('*sacerdotali honore coniuncti*'). Priests do not possess the highest honour of the pontificate, and in the exercise of their power 'depend on the bishops' ('*Presbyteri, quamvis pontificatus apicem non habeant et in exercenda sua potestate ab Episcopis pendeant*'). Yet, they are united with them 'in priestly honour' ('*sacerdotali honore*') which they receive in ordination so that they are 'true priests of the new testament' ('*veri sacerdotes novi testamenti*'). Presbyters are co-operators and helpers of the order of bishops and form with the bishops one '*presbyterium*'. In their ministry they render the bishop in some way visible or represent the bishop (*Lumen Gentium* n. 28, 872-874).

Deacons receive less attention than bishops and presbyters. They are dealt with in article 29, and the tenor of the article is to establish a permanent diaconate instead of regarding the diaconate as only a degree in the hierarchy. Deacons are said to be inferior to bishops and presbyters. They are said to receive the laying-on of hands 'not for the priesthood ('*sacerdotium*') but for the ministry (*'ministerium'*)'.[7] Thus deacons stand between the laity and the hierarchy. They are ordained and as such are members of the hierarchy but do not participate in the ministerial or hierarchical priesthood but only in the common priesthood of the faithful.

The new Pontificale

In the aftermath of Vatican II the ordination rites together with other rites and liturgies of the Roman Catholic Church were revised in order to reflect this new understanding of ministry. This also applied to the rites of ordination (*Sacrosanctum Concilium* n. 76, 834). The first edition of the ordination rites appeared in 1968 under the title: *de Ordinatione Diaconi, Presbyteri et Episcopi* (*Pontificale* 1968). A new revised edition appeared in 1990 under the title: *de Ordinatione Episcopi, Presbyterorum et Diaconorum*.[8] Thus the structure was changed in order to reflect more the teaching of Vatican II:

> The structure of this book is changed in such a way that it begins with the Bishop, who has the fullness of the Sacrament of Holy Orders, in order to convey more clearly that priests are the Bishop's co-workers and that deacons are ordained for his service.[9]

There is not much difference between the two editions except in the prayer of ordination in the ordination of priests. The *anamnesis* part of the prayer was expanded to include more elements from salvation history.[10]

In both editions of the post-conciliar *Pontificale*, *'ordinatio'* is the common word for the ordination of bishops, priests and deacons but the older Post-Tridentine *Pontificale* distinguished between the *'ordinatio'* of deacons and priests (as well as the lower orders of the hierarchy) and *'consecratio'* of bishops. The officiating minister or 'ordainer' is in all rites a bishop. In the rite for the ordination of bishops he is called *'episcopus ordinans (principalis)'* and he is to

---

7. Tanner 1990 II: 874. The Latin reads: *'In gradu inferiori Hierarchiae sistunt Diaconi, quibus "non ad sacerdotium, sed ad ministerium"* (*Constitutiones Ecclesiae Ægyptiacæ*, III, 2), *manus imponuntur. Gratia etenim sacramentali roborati, in diaconia liturgiæ, verbi et caritatis Populo Dei, in communione cum Episcopo eiusque presbyterio, inserviunt'*.
8. *Pontificale* 1990. English translation: *The Roman Pontifical* 2000.
9. *The Roman Pontifical* 2000, 5. The Latin reads thus: *'Dispositio libri immutata est, ita ut initium sumendo ab Episcopo, qui plenitudinem sacri Ordinis habet, melius intellegatur quomodo presbyteri eius sint cooperatores et diaconi ad eius ministerium ordinentur'*. *Pontificale Romanum* 1990, III.
10. On the comparison between the two editions see Puglisi 2001, 34-41.

be assisted by at least two other bishops. In the other rites he is called *'Episcopus'*. At the ordination of priests, he is assisted by priests who also participate in the laying-on of hands during the prayer of ordination. At the ordination of deacons, the bishop is assisted by deacons except in the laying-on of hands which the bishop does alone.

There is an interesting change of terminology. In the 1968 *Pontificale*, the 'ordainer' at an episcopal ordination was called *'consecrator (principalis)'* corresponding to the older use of the Tridentine *Pontificale* where he was also called *'consecrator'*.[11]

The Translation of the Ordination Rites into the Nordic languages

The Nordic Editions of the Pontificale

The ordination rites have been translated into the Nordic languages, Danish, Swedish, Norwegian, Icelandic and Finnish. The Danish translation was published in 1994 and is a complete translation of the new *Pontificale* (*Det romerske pontifikale* 1994). It includes Paul VI's introduction to the *Pontificale* of 1968 and all the general rubrics. The Swedish translation is from 1991 and was published as a manuscript (*'provmanuskript'*, *Ordning* 1991). It contains only the rites themselves and the corresponding rubrics. The Norwegian translation appeared in a prayer book (*Bønnebok* 1990). It is a translation of the 1968 *Pontificale* and is not for the use of those officiating at the liturgy but for the laity, in order to inform them of the meaning of ordination and enable them to participate in the liturgy of ordination with understanding. The Icelandic translation is for the ordination of priests and was made on the occasion of the ordination of an Icelandic priest in the Roman Catholic Church of Iceland in 1996 (*Prestvígsla* 1996). The Finnish translations of the ordination rite for deacons, priests and bishops were also made for special occasions.[12]

---

11. In the case of other ordinations, the officiating minister or ordaining minister was called *'pontifex'* in the Tridentine *Pontificale*.
12. Tuomo T. Vimparin, *'Diakoniksi Vihkiminen'* (15.8.1998); Tuomo T. Vimparin, *'Papiksi Vihkiminen'* (P. Henrikin Katedraali, Helsinki 22.5.1999); Isä Józef Wróbelin SCJ, *'Piispaksi Vihkiminen'* (Johanneksen Kirkossa: Helsinki 27.1.2001). I thank Maria Junttila for providing this material.

On Terminology

The Roman Catholic churches of all the Nordic countries have based the terminology of their translations on the liturgical tradition of their respective countries. These traditions can be traced to the establishment of Christianity in the Nordic countries a thousand years ago. At the Reformation, the Lutheran Churches in the Nordic countries all maintained continuity with the medieval Church, as far as terminology was concerned, both with regard to liturgies and ministries. The main service was, for instance, called '*messa/messe/ mässa*', that is, Mass, and the ministers continued to be called priests and bishops. Although the Church Order of 1537 for Denmark, Norway and Iceland, uses '*minister*'('*þénari*') for 'priest' ('*prestur*') and '*superintendentes*' for 'bishops', the words 'priest' (the Latin original uses '*presbyter*') and 'bishop' ('*episcopus*') also appear and continued to be the terminology of the people in all these countries and soon also in official legal and liturgical texts.[13] Therefore, the terminology used in connection with worship and ministry is based on a very longstanding tradition.

When Christianity was established in the Nordic countries, the word '*prestur*' ('*präst*', '*præst*', '*prest*' – that is, 'priest') was used as a translation of two Latin words, '*sacerdos*' and '*presbyter*'. This seems to be the case with all Germanic languages, cf. German '*Priester*' and English '*priest*'. Etymologically, '*prestur*' is derived from the Latin '*presbyter*' which for that matter is only a latinization of the Greek '*presbyteros*', 'elder'. '*Presbyter*' referred to the seventh order in the hierarchy in which the person received '*sacerdotium*' or priesthood which sometimes was referred to as '*prestdómur*', sometimes as '*prestsembætti*'. In some Icelandic medieval sources the word '*kennimaður*' is used as a translation of '*sacerdos*' and '*kennimannsskapur*' for '*sacerdotium*'.[14] In medieval translations of the Bible, '*kennimaður*' was used for '*sacerdos*', for example, in Ps 110 (109), and this was also the case with the first Lutheran translations of the Bible into Icelandic.[15]

---

13. In the index of the first Icelandic translation of the 1537 Church Order, the chapter '*Ritus instituendi ministros*' is translated '*Hvernin að vígja á kennimenn*'. The second translation reads '*prestavígslu*'. *Diplomatarium islandicum* X, 127, 263. '*Kennimenn*' is also used in translation of '*conciniatores*'. See *Diplomatarium islandicum* X, 135, 269, the second translation reads '*predikararnir*', op. cit., 187.
14. '*Kennimaður*' means literally teacher or learned man and, hence, '*kennimaður*' is also used for learned men, the teachers of the church.
15. I had the opportunity to look up words relating to 'ordination', 'priesthood' and similar in the *Ordbog over det norrøne prosasprog* of the University of Copenhagen and thank the people there for their assistance, especially Mrs. Þorbjörg Helgadóttir.

The fact that the one word 'prestur/præst/präst' has been used as the translation of two Latin words, viz. *'presbyter'* and *'sacerdos'*, in the Nordic languages has caused some ambiguity both in translations of the Bible as well as in liturgical usage until today. The ambiguity appears in the translations of the Roman Catholic ordination rites where 'præst/präst/prest' are used both as a translation of *'sacerdos'* and *'presbyter'*. By reading the translations alone it is not clear whether 'præst/präst/prest' refers to *'presbyter'* or *'sacerdos'* or if 'præstembede/prästämbete' refers to *'presbyteratus'* or *'sacerdotium'*. The Danish translation sometimes translates *'sacerdotium'* as *'præstedømme'* but it is not entirely consistent.

For the word 'ordination' the Nordic translations use words which are derived from the old Nordic and Icelandic word *'vígsla'* (*'vielse'* in Danish and Norwegian, *'vigning'* in Swedish and *'Vihkiminien'* in Finnish). For 'ordination' the word used was *'vígsla'*, the corresponding verb being *'vígja'*. *'Vígsla'* was used as the translation not only of *'ordinatio'* but also of *'benedictio'*, *'consecratio'* and *'dedicatio'*. The coronation of kings was also referred to as *'vígsla'*, based on the medieval translation of 1 Sam. 16.13 on the anointing (*'vígsla'*) of David by Samuel. In medieval Icelandic texts such as the Sagas, *'vígsla'* is used as a translation of the Latin words *'ordinatio'*, *'consecratio'* and *'benedictio'*. This is due to the fact that for a long time these words were used without any clear difference between them in Latin Christianity (Puglisi 1996, I: 212-215; Kleinheyer 1984, 23). When canon law and theology began to differentiate between the ordination of priests and the consecration of bishops, this differentiation did not reach the Nordic countries and the words *'vígsla/ vielse/vigning'* have been used until now with both meanings. The word *'blessun'* (from the English 'blessing') is also known in medieval Icelandic sources and came to be used of benedictions in the liturgy, where the other Nordic speaking nations use *'velsignelse'*. The Danish word 'indvie/indvielse', which appeared in the 1685 Rite for the ordination/consecration of bishops (cf. Iversen, Part II.6), seems to be a translation of *'consecratio'* and appears in the Danish rite for the ordination of deacons (cf. also Iversen). It is interesting that the heading of the chapter on ordination in the Norwegian Prayer Book has the heading *'Ordinasjonen'*. In the preamble it talks about *'ordinasjonens sakrament'*. When it comes to describing the act, the chapter uses *'vielse'* and the verb *'vie'* (*Bønnebok* 1990, 650ff). The term 'ordination' does not appear in the Swedish and Danish translations or in the Finnish.

The Scandinavian Rites

A. Ordination of Bishops

In the Danish translation, '*episcopus ordinans*' is called '*hovedordinator*' but in the Swedish, Norwegian and Finnish translations he is called '*huvud/hoved-konsekrator/päävihkijär*' as was the case in the 1968 *Pontificale*. In the homily which is delivered at the ordination, the ministry to which the candidate is to be ordained is explained.[16] At the ordination of a bishop, the homily begins with the sending of the apostles by the Son and grounds the episcopal ministry in the fact that the apostles instituted helpers in order that Christ's commission might be carried out and by the laying-on of hands conferred on them '*Ordinis sacramentum plenitudo*'. All translations translate '*ordo*' as 'embede/ ämbete': '*som meddeler embedet i dets fylde*' (Danish) and '*som meddeler embedets sakrament i dets fylde*'/'*som skänker ämbetets sakrament i sin fullhet*' (Norwegian/ Swedish). It is interesting that the Danish translation reads 'the fullness of ministry' and does not mention sacrament. The ambiguity of the words '*presbyter*' and '*sacerdos*' appears when the homily talks of the relationship between the bishops and the presbyters. The Latin reads: '*In episcopo a presbyteris suis circumdato adest in medio vestri ipse Dominus noster Iesus Christus, Pontifex factus in æternum*'. The Danish translation reads: '*I biskoppen, omgivet af sine præster, er vor Herre Jesus Kristus selv til stede i jeres midte, for evigt indsat som Ypperstepræst*'. Similarly the Norwegian translation: '*I biskopen og det presteskap som omgir ham, er vår Herre Jesus Kristus selv tilstede i vår midte som den evige Yppersteprest*'. The Swedish translation uses the word '*presbyterium*' and reads: '*I biskopen och hans presbyterium som omger honom, är vår Herre Jesus Kristus själv närvarande i vår mitt som den evige Översteprästen*'.

In one of the vows the Swedish translation is interesting. The Latin reads: '*Vis plebem Dei sanctam, cum comministris tuis presbyteris et diaconis, ut pius pater, fovere et in viam salutis dirigere?*' While the Danish and Norwegian translations are literal and refer to presbyters and deacons as the bishop's '*medarbejdere*' (Danish) and '*medtjenere*' (Norwegian), the Swedish refers to them as participating in the ministry of the bishop: '*... tillsammans med prästerna och diakonerna, som har del i ditt ämbete ...*'. The Finnish translation has the same sense as the Swedish: '*...yhdessä palveluvirkaasi jakavien pappien ja diakonien kanssa...*'.

The last vow reads in Latin: '*Vis Deum omnipotentem pro populo sancto indesinenter orare et sine reprehensione summi sacerdotii munus explere?*'. Summi

---

16. In our collected material, we have none of these homilies in Finnish.

sacerdotii munus is translated as *'din ypperstepræstelige gerning'* in Danish and *'ditt översteprästerliga uppdrag'/'ditt yppersteprestelige opdrag'*, in Swedish, Norwegian and Finnish.

Prex Ordinationis is translated into Danish as *'vielsesbøn'* and into Finnish as *'vihkimisrukous'*. The Swedish version has *'konsekrationsbön'* (*'prex consecrationis'* which was used in the older edition of 1968). The Norwegians use *'vigselsbønn'*.

The beginning of the ordination prayer is an *anamnesis* and thanksgiving to God that, from the time of Abraham he has not left the Church or God's righteous people without *'principes et sacerdotes'*, leaders and priests. The *epiclesis* with the laying-on of hands which constitutes the ordination itself reads as follows in Latin:

> Et nunc effunde super hunc electum eam virtutem, quæ a te est, Spiritum principalem, quem dedisti dilecto Filio tuo Iesu Christo, quem ipse donavit sanctis Apostolis, qui constituerunt Ecclesiam per singula loca ut sanctuarium tuum, in gloriam et laudem indeficientem nominis tui.

'Spiritus principalis' points to *'principes'* in the first part of the prayer. The prayer asks for the spirit of leading or governing the Church.[17] Therefore, the Norwegians and Swedes translate *'spiritus principalis'* as *'lederskapets ånd/ande'*. The Finns stress the power of the Spirit, *'vahva Henki'* (the powerful Spirit). The Danes simply say *'den Helligånd'*, which does not wholly correspond to the meaning of the text.

In the subsequent passage the Latin text reads: 'Da ... huic servo tuo quem elegisti ad Episcopatum, ut pascat gregem sanctum tuum, et summum sacerdotium tibi exhibeat ... da ut virtute Spiritus summi sacerdotii habeat potestatem dimittendi peccata ...'. Here the Danish translation reads 'lad ham som du har udvalgt til biskop ... udøve sin tjeneste som ypperstepræst for dig ...' and '... lad ham ved kraften fra din Helligånd få ypperstepræstedømmets myndighed ...'. The Norwegian version is: '... la denne din tjener som du har utvalgt til biskop, være en yppersteprest ... i dine øyne'. 'Summi sacerdotii potestas' is translated as 'det yppersteprestelige embede'. The Swedish translation reads: '... låt denna din tjänare ...vara ... en överstepräst ... Skänk honom genom Anden, som är kraften i det översteprästerliga ämbetet ...'. Here the Danes render 'sacerdotium' as 'præstedømme'.

---

17. The English translation has 'governing spirit', *The Roman Pontifical*, 2000, 27.

B. Ordination of Priests

In the ordination of presbyters or priests, persons are made presbyters and receive the gift of *'sacerdotium'*. In rubric 112 it is explained: *'Per impositionem manuum Episcopi et Precem Ordinationis candidatis donum Spiritus Sancti pro munere presbyterorum confertur'*. Here *munus presbyterorum* – presbyteral office – is translated *'præsteembede/prästämbete'*. In the ordination of presbyters the ambiguity of having one word render two words in Latin is more apparent than in the rite for episcopal ordination. The general rubric quotes the Vatican II Decree on the Life and Ministry of Priests (*Presbyterorum Ordinis*) art. 2 and similarly *Lumen Gentium* art. 28 where it is emphasized that presbyters are co-operators with the bishops and share in their *'sacerdotium'* and *'missio'* and form one *'presbyterium'* with their bishop. The Danes translate *'sacerdotium'* here as *'præstedømme'* but the Swedes use *'prästerliga ämbete'* so that the adjective *'prästerlig'* here seems to refer to *'sacerdotium'*. *'Presbyterium'* is used in the Swedish translation but the Danish has *'præstekollegium'*, college of priests or presbyters. The rubrics are not translated into Norwegian or into Finnish.

After the initial ceremony of the election of the candidates, the bishop says: *'Auxiliante Domino Deo, et Salvatore nostro Iesu Christo, eligimus hos fratres nostros in Ordinem presbyterii'*. The Danes translate this as *'udtager vi denne vor broder til præst'* and the Norwegians as *'velger denne vor bror til prest'* and the Swedes as *'utser vi dessa våra bröder till prästerlig tjänst'*. Here *'præsteembede/ prästämbäte'* would seem to be more appropriate or more in line with rubric 112 than the words used. This seems to be the case in the Finnish translation: *'valitsemme veljemme Toumon papin virkaan'*. If the Swedes wished to render *'sacerdotium'* by using the adjective *'prästerlig'*, it is strange to use *'prästerlig tjänst'* here instead of *'prästämbete'*. In Icelandic the bishop says *'kjósum vér þennan bróður vorn til prestsvígslu'* – 'to ordination as priest' – but in the initial sentence *'ordo presbyterii'* is translated as *'gegna prestsverkum'*.

The homily begins by referring to the People of God as *'regale sacerdotium'* and yet *'ipse magnus Sacerdos noster, Iesus Christus, discipulos quosdam elegit, qui in Ecclesia sacerdotali officio publice pro hominibus ipsius nomine fungerentur'*. It says further, in line with *Lumen Gentium* art. 29, that ordinands *'ad sacerdotium in Ordine presbyterorum sunt ordinandi, ut Christo Magistro, Sacerdoti et Pastori inserviant ... Christo summo et æterno Sacerdoti configurandi, sacerdotio Episcoporum coniungendi, in veros Novi Testamenti sacerdotes consecrabuntur ad Evangelium prædicandum, populum Dei pascendum cultumque divinum in dominico præsertim sacrificio celebrandum'*.

The Danes translate *'ad sacerdotium in Ordine presbyterorum'* as *'vies til præst'* and *'sacerdotale officium'* as *'præstedømme'*. *'Sacerdotio Episcoporum coniungendi, in veros Novi Testamenti sacerdotes consecrabuntur'* is translated as *'ved at forenes med biskoppernes præstedømme indvies til sand præst i Den nye Pagt ...'* The Norwegians translate very similarly but speak of *'prestembede'* instead of *'præstedømme'*. The Swedes translate *'prästerlig tjänst'* and say that the presbyters participate in *'biskoparnas prästerliga ämbete genom vigningen till det Nya Testamentets sanna prästerliga tjänst ...'.*

When the ordaining bishop addresses the candidates themselves, he refers to them as *'Vos ... ad Ordinem presbyterii provehendi'.* This the Danes and the Norwegians translate as *'optages/opptas i præstestanden'* and the Swedes: *'Ni skall nu ta emot prästvigningens sakrament'* – 'receive the sacrament of order'. The same is the case when the vows are made and the bishop addresses the candidates *'priusquam ad Ordinem presbyterii accedatis'* for which the Danes say *'før du træder ind i præsternes stand'*, but the Swedes *'innan ni mottar vigningen till präster'* and the Norwegians *'før du kan vies til prest'.* In Finnish: *'ennen kuin sinut vihitään papiksi'.* At the end of the homily the bishop admonishes the candidates *'Munus ergo Christi Sacerdotis ... Munere denique Christi Capitis et Pastoris pro vestra parte fungentes ... Episcopi iuncti et suditi ...'.* The Danes translate *'munus Christi Sacerdotis'* as *'Kristi præstedømme'* and *'munus Christi'* as *'Kristi embede ...'.* The Norwegians translate these as *'Kristi prestegjerning'* and *'tjeneste for Kristus'* and the Swedes as *'Kristi prästämbete'* and *'Kristi uppdrag'.*[18]

In the vows the Latin text reads *'Ordo presbyterii'* and *'munus sacerdotii in gradu presbyterorum and Episcoporum Ordinis cooperatores'.* The Danes use *'præsternes stand'* and *'præsteembedet'* and *'biskoppernes trofaste medarbejdere'.* The Norwegians use *'vies til prest'* and *'trofast samarbeid med dine foresatte i bispeembedet'.* The Swedes speak about *'motta vigningen till präster'* and *'fullgöra den prästerliga tjänsten ... som biskopens ... medarbetare'.* The Icelandic has *'vígjast prestur og gegna prestsembætti'.*

The call to prayer speaks of *'presbyterii munus'*, which the Danes call *'præstens tjeneste'* and the Norwegians *'prestekallet'* but the Swedes *'prästerlig tjänst'* and the Icelanders *'prestsembætti'* like the Finns' *'papin virkaan'.*

In the prayer concluding the litany of saints the bishop prays *'gratiae sacerdotalis effunde virtutem'*, which is translated into Danish as *'præstedømmets nådekraft'* and into Norwegian as *'prestedømmets nåde'*, close to the Finnish *'pappeuden armo'.* The Swedes translate this with the words *'sakramentets kraft'* and in Icelandic this becomes *'með náð prestsdómsins'.*

The ordination prayer is called *'vielsesbøn'* (Danish), *'vigselsbøn'* (Norwe-

---

18. The homily has not been translated into Icelandic.

gian)[19] and *'vigningsbön'* (Swedish), *'vihkimisrukous'* (Finnish) and *'vígslubæn'* (Icelandic). In the *anamnesis*, ministry is related to the priestly people of God: *'Adesto, Domine ... qui ad efformandum populum sacerdotalem ministros Christi Filii tui, virtute Spiritus Sancti, in eodem diversis ordinibus disponis'.* The Danish translation is quite literal: *'... for at skabe dig et folk af præster, giver du det ved Helligåndens kraft tjenere for din Søn Jesus Kristus, enhver med sin gerning'.* The Swedish translation interprets this sentence to signify the general ministry of the whole priestly People of God: *'Du har gjort oss till ett folk av kungar och präster, där var och en efter sin gåva skall tjäna din Son, vår Herre Jesus Kristus, i den helige Andes kraft'.* The Finnish translation reads: *'Rakentaaksesi papillista kansaasi sinä annat kansasi avuksi Kristuksen palvelijoita hoitamaan sitä Pyhän Hengen voimalla palveluviran eri asteissa'.* In Icelandic, *'populus sacerdotalis'* is translated as *'prestasamfélag'.*

The *epiclesis* which constitutes the form of the sacrament says:

> Da, quæsumus, omnipotens Pater, in hos famulos tuos presbyterii digni-
> tatem; innova in visceribus eorum Spiritum sanctitatis; acceptum a te,
> Deus, secundi meriti munus obtineant, censuramque morum exemplo suæ
> conversationis insinuent.

The prayer says nothing about *'sacerdotium'.* The reference is to the *'presbyterium'* as a body into which the ordinand is received by his ordination. It is strange here that the Danes translate *'presbyterii dignitas'* as *'præstedømmets værdighed'* as they generally use *'præstedømme'* for *'sacerdotium'.* 'Præsteembede' would seem more appropriate here, which is also the case in the Swedish and Norwegian translations. The Swedes simply say *'prästämbetet',* but the Norwegians speak of *'prestembedets verdighe'* like the Finnish *'pappeuden arvo'.* The Icelanders have *'prestslegrar tignar'.*

C. Ordination of Deacons

The Ordination of deacons emphasizes that deacons are ministers or servants of the bishop and his presbyters, exercising duties which the bishop or a competent minister assigns to them. After the election of the candidate the bishop declares his willingness to admit the candidate to *Ordo diaconii.* The Danish and Norwegian translations say simply in the election *'udtager/velger vi*

---

19. The Norwegian translation is from the 1968 *Pontificale*, where the prayer of ordination is shorter than in the 1990 *Pontificale*, cf. *supra*.

denne vor broder til diakon'. The Swedish translation refers here to *'ordo dia-conorum'* as *'diakonatet': 'Väljer vi dessa våra bröder till diakonatet'.*

'Ordo diaconorum' is also mentioned in the homily. Here both the Swedish and the Norwegian translations say that the person is to be ordained deacon: *'vigas till diakoner'/'vies til diakon'.* The homily is not translated into Danish but in a rubric the bishop is referred to the model homily in the *Pontificale.* In the vows *'ordo diaconorum'* is also mentioned. This is translated as *'diakonernes stand'* in Danish, *'diakonin virkaan'* in Finnish, but the Swedish and Norwegian translations speak of *'vigning/vielse til diakon'.* In the vow the Latin uses *'consecrari'* which the Danes translate as *'indvies'* but the Swedes and Norwegians have *'vigas/vies'.*

Prex ordinationis is called *'vielsesbøn'* in Danish, *'vigselsbøn'* in Norwegian, *'vihkimisrukous'* in Finnish and *'vigningsbön'* in Swedish. In the anamnesis, the variety of ministries in the church of both the Old and the New Testament is mentioned, referring both to the Levites of the Old Testament and the seven helpers of the Apostles in Acts 6. In the introduction to the *epiclesis* the bishop prays for grace for those he is to ordain as deacons. Here the verb used is *'dedicare'.* All the translations except the Finnish render this as *'vie/viga'.* In Finnish it is *'aseta'.*

The *epiclesis* which constitutes the act is for the sevenfold gift of the Holy Spirit to strengthen the deacons in their service:

> Emitte in eos, Domine, quæsumus, Spiritum Sanctum, quo in opus min-isterii fideliter exsequendi munere septiformis tuæ gratiæ roborentur.

'Opus ministerii' is translated as *'tjeneste'* (Danish and Norwegian), *'tjänst'* (Swedish) and *'palvelutehtäväänsä'* (Finnish).

Conclusion

All the five translations are very good both theologically and terminologically. They are obviously based on the tradition of translation in the Nordic countries which can be traced very far back in history. This is also very important ecumenically. All the Nordic Churches could benefit from working together on terminology. This concerns, perhaps, especially the Lutheran and the Roman Catholic Churches which tend to use the same terminology for their ministries and ordinations. Of the four translations the Danish seems to be the most thorough or advanced. This is especially evident in the rite for the ordination of presbyters where the translation seeks to underline the difference between *'presbyter'* and *'sacerdos'* by using *'præsternes stand'*, *'præsteembede'* for *'presbyterium'*, *'presbyterii munus'* and *'ordo presbyterorum'*, and *'præstedømme'* for *'sacerdotium'* even if it is not quite consistent (cf. the *epiclesis* in the ordination of presbyters). All churches in the Nordic countries must work further on terminological issues. The word *'præstedømme'* (Danish/Norwegian), *'prestsdómur'* (Icelandic) and *'prästerskap'* (Swedish) could be used as a translation of *'sacerdotium'* but *'præstembede/ prästämbete/ prestsembætti'* for *'munus presbyterii'* and similar. There is obvious difficulty in finding a new word for *'sacerdos'* or *'presbyter'* because a mixture of the two can be traced back through many centuries. In the episcopal ordination, concepts such as *'ordo episcoporum'* and *'collegium episcoporum'* must be looked into as well as *'summum sacerdotium'* and similar expressions. In relation to deacons, clarification is needed on the concept of *'ministerium'*. The Swedes use the word *'diakonat'* for *'ordo diaconorum'* which is a good solution and could perhaps be used further, perhaps also for the *'opus ministerii'* of the *epiclesis* in the prayer of ordination.

References

Bønnebok for den katolske kirke (Oslo: St. Olav Forlag, 1990), 650-672.

Constitutio de Sacra Liturgia: Sacrosanctum Concilium (1963), in Tanner 1990, II: 820-843.

Constitutio Dogmatica de Ecclesia: Lumen Gentium (1964), in Tanner, 1990, II: 849-900.

Denzinger, H., and Schönmetzer, A.(eds), *Enchiridion Symbolorum, Definitionum et Declarationum de Rebus Fidei et Morum* (Freiburg: Herder, 1967).

Det romerske pontifikale. Fornyet udgave efter beslutning af II økumeniske Vatikankoncil udgived med pave Paul VIs bemyndigelse, godkendt af pave Johannes Paul II: bispe-, præste- og diakonvielse (København: Ansgarstiftelsens forlag, 1994).

Diplomatarium islandicum - Íslenskt fornbréfasafn X. 1911-1921 (Reykjavík: Hið íslenzka bókmenntafélag).

Einar Sigurbjörnsson, *Ministry within the People of God: The Development of the Doctrines on the Church and on the Ministry in the Second Vatican Council's DE ECCLESIA* (Lund: CWK Gleerup1974).

Jungmann, J. A., Constitution on the Sacred Liturgy, *Commentary on the Documents of Vatican II.* (Freiburg: Herder and Herder, 1967), I: 1-88.

Kleinheyer, B., Gottesdienst der Kirche. *Handbuch der Liturgiewissenschaft Teil 8: Sarkamentliche Feiern,* Vol. II. (Regensburg: Verlag Friedrich Pustet, 1984).

Ordning för biskopsvigning. Ordning för prästvigning. Ordning för diakonvign-

ing. Provmanuskript. augusti 1991. (Stockholm: Stockholms katolska stift. Katolska liturgiska nämnden).

Persson, P.E. *Kyrkans ämbete som Kristus-representation: En kritisk analys av nyare ämbetsteologi* (Lund: Gleerups, 1961).

Pontificale Romanum ex Decreto Sacrosancti Oecumenici Concilii Vaticani II Instauratum Auctoritate Pauli Pp. VI promulgatum: De Ordinatione Diaconi, Presbyteri et Episcopi,. (Vatican City: Typis polyglottis Vaticanis. Editio typica, 1968).

Pontificale Romanum ex Decreto Sacrosancti Oecumenici Concilii Vaticani II Renovatum Auctoritate Pauli Pp. VI editum Ioannis Pauli Pp. II cura recognitum: De Ordinatione Episcopi, Presbyterorum et Diaconorum (Vatican City: Typis polyglottis Vaticanis. Editio Typica Altera, 1990).

Prestvígsla. Með handayfirlagningu og bæn kirkjunnar vígir herra Jóhannes Gijsen Reykjavíkur biskup Atla Gunnar Jónsson til prests (Reykjavík, 7th September 1996. Dómkirkja Krists konungs Landakoti).

Puglisi, J.F., *The Process of Admission to Ordained Ministry. Vol. I: A Comparative Study. Epistemoligcal Principles and Roman Catholic Rites* (Collegeville, Minn: The Liturgical Press, 1996.); -, *The Process of Admission to Ordained Ministry Vol III: Contemporary Rites and General Conclusions* (Collegeville, Minn: The Liturgical Press, 2001).

Rómversk kaþólsk messubók. Fastir liðir messunnar (Reykjavík: Kaþólska kirkjan á Íslandi, 1969).

Rómversk-kaþólsk messubók fyrir sunnudaga og aðalhátíðisdaga kirkjuársins I-III (Reykjavík: Kaþólska kirkjan á Íslandi, 1959).

The Roman Pontifical Reformed by Decree of the Second Vatican Ecumenical Council Published by Authority of Pope Paul VI, Revised at the Direction of Pope John Paul II: Rites of Ordination of a Bishop, of Priests and of Deacons (Washington DC: International Commission on English in the Liturgy: Joint Commission of Catholic Bishops' Conferences. Second Typical Edition, 2000).

Tanner, N.P. (ed.), *Decrees of the Ecumenical Councils. Vol. II: Trent to Vatican II.* (London/Washington DC: Sheed & Ward/Georgetown University Press, 1990).

Thomas Aquinas. *Summa theologiae. Supplementum,* q. 37, a. 2, in the edition of *Biblioteca de autores Cristianos* (Madrid: 1965).

Sacramental Ordination in the Orthodox Church of Finland

Metropolitan Johannes of Nicaea

The Orthodox understanding of priesthood is the theme of another chapter in this book. Thus my own task is mainly to deal with the tradition of ordination in the Orthodox Church of Finland. In spite of this, I would like to offer some basic views on the doctrinal attitude of the Orthodox Church on this matter, as a kind of background to the Holy Mystery of ordination. In principle and quite particularly, also from the ecumenical point of view, it is essential that priesthood and ordination into it should be one of the Mysteries or Sacraments of the Church, instituted by Christ through the calling of the apostles, and not just a solemn human ceremony. In other words, priesthood in all times goes back, through the apostolic succession, to the aforementioned calling of the apostles. Although we shall deal with the matter more in detail later on, it seems proper to underline immediately in this connection that priesthood consists of three degrees of ordained men, that is, deacons, priests and bishops, and belongs fully and in a special way only to bishops, who ordain the members of the two lower degrees and act in that way as a tool of the Holy Spirit, who in reality is the acting factor. In this sense we can say that Christ himself is the real priest, shepherd and teacher of the Church. He is and remains the true Head of the Church. As to the relation between the bishop and the two lower degrees of priesthood, the priest and the deacon can be seen as entrusted representatives of the bishop. Through ordination and with the blessing of the bishop, they are empowered and authorized to perform some of the functions of the full priesthood, which belongs to the bishop on the basis of the apostolic succession.

The sacramental priesthood constitutes a guarantee of the continuous presence of Christ in the Church. The Church has been established by God in Christ, and she is united by Orthodox faith, divine law, priesthood and the mysteries. Thus the apostolic succession is based on two elements: an unbroken succession of ordination and the maintenance of genuine apostolic teaching.

The Ordination of Deacons

The diaconate constitutes the first degree of priesthood in the sacramental sense of the term. Before this degree, there exist two so-called minor degrees, which are not part of the sacramental priesthood but are necessary preliminary or preparatory steps for it. Readers or cantors and hypo-deacons or sub-deacons represent this group, whose members are blessed or set apart by the bishop outside the sanctuary, not within it as is the case for sacramental ordinations.

Sacramental ordinations all take place in the framework of the Divine Liturgy, but at different moments. Toward the end of the Liturgy, when the Holy Gifts, the eucharistic elements, have already been consecrated and the bishop has exclaimed, 'And may the mercy of our great God and Saviour Jesus Christ be with you all', there comes the moment for the ordination of the deacon. The bishop is seated in the sanctuary, either on the right side close to the *iconostasis* (*templon*, icon-screen) or in front of the holy table (altar) toward the left side of it. (There are also other practices.) The statement of the deacon's confessor concerning the canonical requirements for the ordination is read and the ordinand is led to the sanctuary by two deacons, who exclaim in turns, 'Command'. Inside the sanctuary the ordinand bows three times before the altar. One of the deacons says, 'Command, Most Reverend Master', and the ordinand bows before the bishop, who signs him with the sign of the Cross. The way of addressing the bishop varies in different languages and local churches. Additionally, the expression used in this connection may also be understood as meaning 'Everything is ready!'. Then the deacons lead the ordinand around the altar singing with those present in the sanctuary, 'O holy martyrs, who fought the good fight and have received your crowns, entreat the Lord that our souls may be saved'. The ordinand kisses the four corners of the altar while going around it. Then the same words are sung by the choir outside the sanctuary. After the first round the ordinand again bows down before the altar, then before the bishop and kisses his hand and his *epigonation* (a square-shaped garment worn at the bishop's side). Then follows the second round, during which those in the sanctuary sing, 'Glory to Thee, O Christ-God, the apostles' boast, the martyrs' joy, whose preaching was the consubstantial Trinity'.

Then the choir's turn comes again and they sing the above mentioned hymn. During this round, the ordinand again kisses the four corners of the altar. After the round, he again bows down before the altar, kisses it and the *omophorion* (a long scarf, the special sign of episcopacy) and the hand of the bishop. After that follows the third round in the same way as the two previous rounds. This time the following hymn is sung, 'Rejoice, O Isaiah! A Virgin is with child and shall bear a Son, Emmanuel, both God and man; and Orient is His name, whom magnifying we call the Virgin blessed'. Again follows the choir's turn. The ordinand acts as after the previous rounds, bows down before the altar and the bishop and kisses his hand.

After the three rounds comes the moment of the ordination proper. The bishop stands in front of the altar. The ordinand goes to the right side of the bishop and bows down saying in a low voice, 'O God, have mercy upon me, a sinner'. Then he bends his right knee, lays his palms upon the altar and places his forehead between his hands. After that the bishop lays the end of his *epitrachilion* (stole) upon his head and blesses him three times on his head. When the leading deacon has said 'Let us attend', the bishop says aloud the following prayer, 'The divine grace, which always heals that which is infirm and completes that which is wanting, ordains (the name of the ordinand) the devout sub-deacon a deacon. Wherefore, let us pray for him, that the grace of the all-holy Spirit may come upon him'. Here a few remarks regarding the central verb have to be made. In the Greek original usage we have a word, the basic meaning of which is 'to put at disposal'. It expresses in a simple and clear way the essence of the matter. Somebody is made a deacon; he is made to be at hand to serve as a deacon. In the usage of the Church, the verb then quite clearly received the meaning of ordaining. In certain translations this understanding has been expressly stated. Especially in the Slavonic tradition there is an addition in connection with the verb in question which reads, 'through the laying-on of hands'. This addition does not occur in the original tradition. Here we have to observe that the ordaining bishop does not refer to his own person. He is simply a tool, however necessary, and the acting factor is the grace of God. Then those in the sanctuary sing three times: 'Lord, have mercy'. The choir sings the same, often in Greek with the words, '*Kyrie eleison*'.

When the leading deacon has said, 'Let us pray to the Lord', the bishop reads the following prayer:

O Lord our God, who by Thy foreknowledge send down the fullness of the Holy Spirit upon those who are ordained by Thine inscrutable power to be Thy servants and to administer Thy spotless mysteries, preserve, O Sovereign Master, also this man, whom Thou hast been pleased to ordain through me to the service of the diaconate, in all soberness of life, holding the mystery of the faith in a pure conscience. Vouchsafe unto him the grace, which Thou didst grant unto Stephen, the first martyr, whom Thou didst also call to be the first in the work of Thy ministry, and make him worthy to administer after Thy pleasure in the degree which it has seemed good to Thee to confer upon him. For they who minister well, prepare for themselves a good degree. And manifest him as wholly Thy servant. For Thine is the kingdom and the power and the glory, of the Father and of the Son and of the Holy Spirit, now and ever and unto the ages of ages. Amen.

This prayer is said in a low voice, 'secretly', as the traditional expression has it, while the choir is singing continuously. It can also be mentioned, that the word 'man' does not occur in the original Greek as already the masculine pronoun expresses the same thing. While the bishop says this prayer, the leading deacon – or according to another tradition, the leading priest – reads in a low voice a series of petitions in the sanctuary. A petition for the ordaining bishop and for the candidate is included.

While the petitions in question are read, the bishop, keeping his hand on the ordinand, says the following prayer secretly:

O God our Saviour, who by Thine incorruptible voice appointed unto Thine apostles the law of the diaconate and manifested the first martyr, Stephen, as serving it and proclaimed him the first, who should exercise the office of a deacon, as it is written in Thy holy gospel: Whosoever desires to be the first among you, let him be your servant. O Master of all men, fill also this Thy servant, whom Thou hast graciously permitted to enter into the ministry of a deacon, with all faith and love and power and holiness through the inspiration of Thy holy and life-giving Spirit, for not through the laying-on of my hands, but through the presence of Thy rich bounties, is grace bestowed upon Thy worthy ones, that he, being devoid of all sin, may stand blameless before Thee on the terrible day of Thy promise.

Then the bishop raises the new deacon and looses his *orarion* (stole), which is bound cross-wise. Taking the *orarion* the bishop lays it on the left shoulder of the deacon, saying in a loud voice: *'Axios'* (worthy). Those inside the sanctuary sing three times *'Axios'* and the choir repeats the same. Then the bishop takes the deacon to the Holy Gate, says again *'Axios'* and greets the deacon with the words, 'Christ is in the midst of us'. The newly ordained deacon then starts taking part in the Liturgy. According to the Russian tradition he remains in the sanctuary and fans the Holy Gifts with a sacramental fan. There are certain other external differences between the older Greek tradition and the Russian tradition, but as they are without essential meaning, there is no special reason to describe them here.

It should be noted that only one man is ordained in one Liturgy, although there may be several candidates at the same time in the case of minor orders below the sacramentally ordained clergy. This and the fact that it is one bishop who ordains one deacon, creates a special relationship between the two and indicates that the deacon, whom the bishop has ordained, is the entrusted representative of his bishop, as we have mentioned earlier.

The Ordination of Priests

Many of the elements to which we have referred when dealing with the ordination of deacons also occur in the rite for the ordination of priests and there is no need to repeat them here. We shall mainly pay attention to those things which are characteristic of the ordination of priests.

First, some general remarks: the deacon who is to be ordained priest participates as a deacon in the Liturgy until the Cherubic Hymn. After this hymn he stands outside the Holy Gate and two deacons then lead him to the gate, where he is received by two priests. The bowing down, the circling of the altar and the singing are exactly as for him who is to be made a deacon. When the ordinand after the third round has bowed down before the bishop, the bishop leads him to the right corner of the altar and blesses him three times on the head. The ordinand kneels, now on both knees, and as in the case of ordination to the diaconate, the bishop lays the end of his *epitrachilion* on the head of the candidate and after having again blessed him reads in a loud voice the same prayer which is used at the ordaining of a deacon, except that instead of 'devout sub-deacon', he says 'devout deacon'. After this the bishop again blesses the candidate three times and says the following prayer:

> O God, who hast no beginning and no ending, who art older than any created thing, who crownest with the name of presbyter those whom Thou deemest worthy to serve the word of Thy truth in the divine ministry of this degree, deign, O Thou the Lord of all men, to preserve in pureness of life and in unswerving faith this man, upon whom Thou hast graciously been pleased to lay hands through me. Be favourably pleased to grant unto him the great grace of Thy Holy Spirit and make him wholly Thy servant, in all things acceptable unto Thee and worthily exercising the great honours of the priesthood, which Thou hast conferred upon him by Thy prescient power. For Thine is the majesty and Thine are the kingdom and

the power and the glory, of the Father and of the Son and of the Holy Spirit, now and ever and unto the ages of ages.

The candidate is then again blessed three times by the bishop, who says secretly:

O God, great in might and inscrutable in wisdom and marvellous in counsel above the sons of men, fill Thou, O Lord, with the gift of Thy Holy Spirit this man whom it has pleased Thee to ordain to the degree of priest, that he may be worthy to stand in innocence before Thine altar, to proclaim the Gospel of Thy Kingdom, to minister the Word of Thy truth, to offer unto Thee gifts and spiritual sacrifices, to renew Thy people through the laver of regeneration. That when he shall go to meet Thee at the second coming of our great God and Saviour Jesus Christ, Thine Only-begotten Son, he may receive the reward of a good steward in the degree committed unto him, through the plenitude of Thy goodness. Amen.

When the bishop has read the above-mentioned prayer, he raises the newly ordained and puts his *orarion* around his neck to hang down in front of him. (According to another custom, a priest's *epitrachilion* is brought to the bishop for the same purpose.) Then the bishop exclaims loudly '*Axios*'. The same is then sung by those in the sanctuary and after that by the choir. In a similar way the *zone* (cincture) and the *phelonion* (chasuble) are given to the new priest. Then the bishop takes him to the Holy Gate and exclaims again '*Axios*' before the faithful present in the church. The choir (with the people) sings the same. The bishop says, 'Christ is in the midst of us', and the new priest replies, 'He is and shall be', while kissing the shoulders and the hand of the bishop. After this the new priest takes his place among the other priests in the sanctuary.

Later on, when the holy gifts have been consecrated, the bishop gives the Holy Lamb (the consecrated bread) to the newly ordained priest on a *diskos* (paten) and says, 'Take this deposit and preserve it to the coming of our Lord Jesus Christ, who shall demand it from thee'. While taking it he kisses the hand of the bishop and says, 'Lord have mercy', placing the *diskos* on the holy table. Before the partaking of the holy gifts, when the bishop says, 'Holy things to the holy', the priest returns the *diskos* with the Holy Lamb to the bishop. On this occasion the new priest receives the Holy Communion before the other priests, against the normal rules of seniority. After the Liturgy the newly ordained priest receives his ordination certificate, signed by the bishop on the altar (according to the practice of Constantinople). In connection with the ordination, the new priest also receives a pectoral cross, according to the

Russian tradition also followed by the Orthodox Church of Finland. The use of this cross was introduced by order of the Russian Empress Catharine the Great at the end of the eighteenth century. In the old Orthodox Churches a so-called jewelled cross is sometimes granted by the bishop as a mark of distinction. When an unmarried priest is elevated to the rank of archimandrite, this always also implies the right to the jewelled cross.

The special prayers in connection with the ordinations of deacons and priests, described earlier in our text here, can also be taken as an expression of the duties and tasks of those who are ordained. Therefore, we here only refer to their contents. Particularly regarding the priests, the prayers deal with their functions in some detail.

As concerns the relationship of deacons and priests with their bishop, there are in the various local churches sometimes particular rules about this, but the basic principle is clearly expressed already in the Apostolic Canons, where it is stated in canon XXXIX (or XL according to another numbering), 'Let not the presbyters or deacons do anything without the sanction of the bishop; for he it is who is entrusted with the people of the Lord and of whom will be required the account of their souls'. The tradition that the deacon and the priest are ordained by one bishop is correspondingly based on the second canon in the same collection, where we read, 'Let a presbyter, deacon and the rest of the clergy be ordained by one bishop'. Here the rest of the clergy refers to the minor orders, which we have mentioned earlier.

The Ordination (Consecration) of Bishops

Here it should be mentioned that in the original Greek tradition the term *cheirotonia* is used of ordination for all the three degrees, although we have a different practice in English. (In the case of minor orders, the term is *cheirothesia*.) Here we follow the Greek practice. The rite itself is fairly extensive and the limited space allotted to us makes it necessary to choose among the material at our disposal, without, however, omitting anything essential.

When there is a new bishop-elect, his ordination also takes place within the Divine Liturgy. Before the ordination proper there is in some churches a separate rite for the so-called canonical nomination; in some other churches certain of the elements in it are included in the rite proper. There exist also certain other differences regarding the order of the ceremony. We follow here, in the main, the tradition of the Ecumenical Throne, with some exceptions.

The rite is conducted, in addition to the presiding bishop, by at least two other bishops. (Even several other hierarchs may participate. Under very special circumstances it is allowed that only two bishops take part.) This synod or college of bishops represents in principle the Orthodox episcopacy in general and manifests the fact that nobody can be made an Orthodox bishop by a single bishop only, but the apostolic office is conferred upon the ordinand by the whole Church.

The process of ordination begins with a ceremony immediately before the Divine Liturgy. The participating bishops sit on their thrones (chairs) in the nave, where the candidate is also led. (According to another, mainly Russian, tradition, they stand on a platform in the middle of the church.) There are various theologically insignificant differences between certain local traditions regarding the structure of the rite and also in some expressions used, but the essence of the rite remains everywhere the same.

The leading deacon proclaims in a loud voice, 'The beloved of God, elect and confirmed archimandrite (priest) NN, is led forth for ordination to the bishopric of the God-saved city NN'.

The presiding bishop then says to the candidate, 'Wherefore have you come and what do you ask of us?', and the bishop-elect replies, 'The ordination of the archipastoral grace, together with the priests of the most holy bishopric of NN'. (According to another tradition, he answers, 'The laying-on of hands, unto the grace of the episcopal office'.) After this the presiding bishop says, 'And how do you believe?', and the candidate reads the Nicene Creed. Then the presiding bishop says to him, 'Tell us more extensively how you believe concerning the properties of the three persons of the ineffable Godhead, and concerning the incarnation of the person of the Son and Word of God'. The candidate then gives a detailed answer to the question.

The presiding bishop still puts a further question and says, 'Declare to us also what you think about the canons of the holy apostles and the holy fathers and the traditions and regulations of the Church'. In his answer the candidate promises to observe the canons of the apostles, of the Seven Ecumenical Councils, and the traditions of the Church. He also assures his obedience to the head and the synod of his Church. Furthermore, he promises not to exercise any priestly or episcopal functions in another diocese without the permission of the bishop of the said diocese. The statements made by the candidate are given also in writing to the presiding bishop.

Finally, the presiding bishop, blessing the candidate, says, 'The grace of the Holy Spirit, through my humility, exalts thee, most beloved of God archimandrite (priest) NN to be the bishop-elect of the God-saved city NN'.

After this the liturgy begins. After the Cherubic Hymn the candidate is led to the Holy Gate, where he is received by the bishops in the sanctuary. He kneels down on both knees in the midst of the bishops, who take the Holy Gospel, open it and lay it upon his head, holding it there. The presiding bishop then says in a loud voice, 'By the election and approbation of the most

God-loving bishops and of all the consecrated council (synod), the divine grace, which always heals that which is infirm and completes that which is wanting, ordains the most God-loving archimandrite (priest) NN, duly elected bishop of the God-saved city NN. Wherefore, let us pray for him, that the grace of the all-holy Spirit may come upon him'. The presiding bishop makes three crosses above the head of him who is being consecrated and continues with this prayer:

> O Master, Lord our God, who through Thine all-laudable apostle Paul hast established for us an ordinance of degrees and ranks, unto the service and divine celebration of Thine august and all-spotless mysteries upon Thy holy altar; first apostles, secondly prophets, thirdly teachers, O Lord of all, who also hast graciously enabled this elected man to come under the yoke of the Gospel and the dignity of a bishop through this hand of mine and of the fellow-servants here present, strengthen Thou him by the inspiration and power and grace of Thy Holy Spirit, as Thou didst strengthen Thy holy apostles and prophets, as Thou didst anoint kings, as Thou didst ordain bishops, and make his bishopric to be blameless and adorning him with all dignity, present him holy, that he may be worthy to ask those things which are for the salvation of the people and that Thou mayest listen to him. For blessed is Thy name and glorified Thy Kingdom, of the Father and of the Son and of the Holy Spirit, now and ever and unto the ages of ages.

Then one of the other bishops says a series of petitions in a low voice, including a prayer for the new bishop.

The presiding bishop then continues with the following prayer:

> O Lord our God, who forasmuch as it is impossible for the nature of man to endure the essence of the Godhead, in Thy providence hast instituted for us teachers, suffering like us, to maintain Thine altar, that they may offer unto Thee sacrifice and oblation for all Thy people; O Lord, make also this man, who has been proclaimed a steward of the episcopal grace, to be like Thee, the true shepherd, who laid down Thy life for Thy sheep; to be a leader of the blind, a light to those who are in darkness, a reprover of the unwise, a teacher of the young, a lamp to the world: that having perfected the souls entrusted unto him in this present life, he may stand unashamed before Thy throne and receive the great reward which Thou hast prepared for those who have contended valiantly for the preaching of Thy Gospel. For Thine it is to show mercy and to save us, O God, and unto Thee we

ascribe glory, to the Father and to the Son and to the Holy Spirit, now and ever and unto the ages of ages. Amen.

After the 'Amen', the bishops put the book of the Gospel upon the altar and the new bishop is invested with his episcopal robes. The presiding bishop proclaims the traditional '*Axios*', which is repeated by the choir. After the end of the Liturgy the pastoral staff is given to the newly ordained bishop by the presiding bishop with these words, 'Receive the pastoral staff, that Thou mayest feed the flock of Christ entrusted unto thee, and be a staff and support unto those who are obedient. Lead the disobedient and the wayward unto correction, gentleness and obedience, and they shall continue in due submission'.

Also here there are certain differences in wording in the various local traditions, as has been mentioned before in connection with the prayers of the ordination rites. The character of the episcopal office is described in the above texts, in everything essential from the point of view of ecclesiology, although we have largely omitted the references to external ceremonies and symbolic details.

References

APXIEPATIKON. 1985. Edition of the Apostolic Diakonia. Ordination of deacons, priests and bishops, 80-95. Athens.

Catechism of the Christian Faith, 'The Living God'. 1980. Translated from French by Olga Dunlop, II: 300-311. New York.

Father Ambrosius and Markku Haapio (eds.). 1979. *Ortodoksinen Kirkko Suomessa,* 19-24. Lieto.

Hapgood, Isabel Florence (ed.). 1965. *Service Book of the Holy Orthodox-Catholic Apostolic Church,* 4th ed., 311-331. New York.

Larentzakis, Grigorios. 2000. *Die Ortodoxe Kirche,* 70-78. Wien.

Kazhdan, Alexander P. (ed.). 1991. *Oxford Dictionary of Byzantium.* I: 291-92, 417, 592; III: 1718. New York.

Panotes, Aristeides. 1962-68. *ΘΡΗΣΚΕΥΤΙΚΗ ΚΑΙ ΗΘΙΚΗ ΕΓΚΥΚΛΟΠΑΙΔΕΙΑ.* tomes I-XII. (deacons IV: 1156-1167; priests X: 581-583; bishops V: 782-783 and generally XII: 114-117). Athens.

Rinne, Johannes. 1971. *ΕΝΟΤΗΣ ΚΑΙ ΟΜΟΙΜΟΡΦΙΑ ΕΝ ΤΗ ΕΚΚΛΗΣΙΑ ΚΑΤΑ ΤΟ ΠΝΕΥΜΑ ΤΩΝ ΟΙΚΟΥΜΕΝΙΚΩΝ ΣΥΝΟΔΩΝ.* 1971. 67-69, 111-113. Thessaloniki.

2. Historically determined Lutheran Traditions of Ordination in the Nordic Countries

The significantly different ways of understanding ordained ministries in the otherwise closely interrelated Evangelical-Lutheran Churches in the five Nordic countries, all of them so-called folk churches, can be traced back to different developments during the time of the Reformation. Historically determined rites may be changed, but even so the traces of their predecessors are found in the new rites –positively, in that they keep to the tradition, or negatively, in that they react against it, perhaps to some degree even turning it upside down.

Jyrki Knuutila outlines the development of the two Lutheran traditions of rites for the ordination of pastors and bishops in the Nordic countries: the Swedish/Finnish tradition over against the Danish/Norwegian/Icelandic tradition.

Einar Sigurbjörnsson and Kristján Valur Ingólfsson examine the development of rites for the ordination of priests and bishops in the Evangelical-Lutheran Church of Iceland. Until the introduction of Home Rule in Iceland in 1904, Icelandic ordination rites were translations of the authorized rites of the governing power, Denmark. The first Icelandic rites, 1910 and 1934, were marked by nationalistic, purist tendencies and promoted theological liberalism in rebellion against (colonial Danish Lutheran) confessional Christianity. By1981 the Lutheran Church in Iceland had already introduced new rites in line with the ecumenical tendencies later on expressed in the Lima and Porvoo documents, even though former patterns are still traceable in these rites.

Jakub Reinert Hansen has examined the rites for the ordination of pastors in the Evangelical-Lutheran Church in the Faeroe Islands. Ordinations have only been carried out in the Faeroe Islands since 1967, after a vice-bishop was appointed in 1963 and a diocesan bishop in 1990. Each of the two bishops created their own rites, the 1967 rite being a free translation of the Danish unauthorized proposal of 1965, and the 1993 rite being a similarly free translation of the Danish 1898 rite. The question arises as to how it can be left to the bishop in charge to make his distinctively personal edition of a rite of the Danish Church personally selected by him.

Karen Langgård traces the development of Lutheran rites for the ordination of pastors and bishops in the Greenlandic language. Given Greenland's status as a Danish colony until 1953, with Christian mission being a more or less integrated part of colonial politics and administration, Greenlanders were only ordained in a few cases, where their pastoral service was badly needed, and ordination was clearly a conferral of Danish authority. Dealing in detail with the wording of the twentieth century ordination rites written in Greenlandic, Langgård demonstrates how these translations, related to biblical and hymn translations of their times, gradually abandon the most authoritarian images of the Christian God and the ordained minister in his service, which were introduced during colonial times.

The Ordination of Bishops and Pastors in the Rites of the Evangelical-Lutheran Churches in the five Nordic Countries

Jyrki Knuutila

This article examines how bishops and pastors are currently ordained in the Evangelical-Lutheran Churches in the five Nordic countries: Denmark, Norway, Iceland, Sweden and Finland. Rites for such ordinations exist in the Service Books of all five of these Nordic national churches. The material below focuses therefore on a total of ten rites dating from the latter part of the twentieth century. The structure and content of these rites is analysed and compared, in order to determine the extent to which they converge or diverge from each other; to ascertain what influence they have had over each other, and to identify any differences in content and terminology between the rites used for ordaining pastors and those used for ordaining bishops. This last task has been undertaken with a view to determining in what sense the ministries of bishop and pastor are regarded and understood as distinctive within the different churches.

The article also aims to explain the factors or elements which have influenced the development and content of these Nordic ordination rites. All the Nordic Evangelical-Lutheran Churches have had the status of established, national or state churches, and heads of state have nominated bishops and sometimes priests. This has bound bishops and some priests to governments, though they have not had the status of government officers in the strict sense of the term. This situation requires Nordic rites to be examined in their general historical context as well as from the more specific perspective of their church history. The rites are also examined here against the background of theological and ecumenical trends that have influenced the development of ecclesiology and of the Church's ministry during the twentieth century.

Ordination Rites in the Nordic Countries until the End of the Twentieth Century

The Nordic Rites are presented briefly and in catalogue form from medieval times to the end of the twentieth century as a historical background to the rites currently in use. For historical reasons the Danish, Norwegian and Icelandic Rites are presented together, as are the Swedish and Finnish Rites, for the same reasons.

Pre-Reformation Rites

In Scandinavia there is only one pre-Reformation source of episcopal ceremonial, the fifteenth century manuscript of the *Pontificale Roskildense*. The manuscript of the *Pontificale Lundense* also dates from the fifteenth century and includes additionally a rite for the ordination of priests (Strömberg 1955, 153-171, 244-260, 279-300).[1] Fragments of other Pontificals in several Nordic libraries are not sufficient to show how bishops and priests were ordained in the church provinces of Nidaros and Uppsala and their suffragan dioceses. All that can be said, according to Hilding Johansson, the Swedish scholar of liturgical history, is that those ceremonies too may well have been carried out in a way similar to the Lund usage (Johansson 1956, 205; Parvio 1970, 40).

Post-Reformation Rites

Bishops and pastors began to be ordained in accordance with evangelical order at the end of the 1530s in *Denmark*, which then included Norway and Iceland. The 1537 Danish Church Ordinance (*Kirkeordinansen,* hereafter KO*)* had rites for this purpose in Latin: a Church Ordinance also with ordination rites was published in Danish in 1539. The ordination rites in KO 1537/1539 were based on Danish medieval usage and on Martin Luther's rite for the ordination of pastors (von Sicard 1972, 293-294; Venge 1980, 298-299; Puglisi 1998, 31). The 1537 rite for the ordination of bishops was the oldest known from any Evangelical-Lutheran Church. This rite, and the rite for the ordination of pastors, was included with slight amendments in the 1685 Church Rites (hereafter CR 1685) and in the 1688 Altar Book *(Alterbog,* hereafter AB 1688), which was a reprint of it. The same rites were included in the 1898 Danish Church Rites (*Ritebog for den danske folkekirke,* hereafter RB 1898), approved in 1895.

---

1. These rites were in use in the church province of Lund and were influenced by the French-German *Pontificale* tradition and by the 1485 *Pontificale Romanum* (Strömberg 1955, 36-37, 48-49, 51-54, 58-72, 83-92).

There were several reprints of RB 1898 during the twentieth century in Denmark (see Pedersen 1948, 343; Villadsen 1994, 307). It is thus possible to speak of a Danish tradition of ordination rites from the Reformation to the first half of the twentieth century.[2] The 1898 rites for the ordination of bishops and pastors were used until 1987, when a new Service Book (*Gudstjenesteordning for Den Danske Folkekirke Ritebog*, hereafter GOD) was authorised. Its ordination rites were ostensibly the older Danish rites, with only minor amendments in structure and content (Eckerdal 1989, 57 and Iversen, Part II, 6).

Norway was part of Denmark until 1814, and Norwegian bishops and pastors were ordained in accordance with the rites in Danish KO 1537/1539, CR 1685 (1985) and AB 1688, which were used in Norway until the Norwegian Church's own ordinal was published in the 1889 *Alterbok* (hereafter AB 1889). There were no differences worth mentioning between Danish AB 1688 and Norwegian AB 1889. In practice, therefore, bishops and pastors in Norway were ordained in accordance with the rites in Danish AB 1688 until the beginning of the twentieth century. Despite the personal union between Norway and Sweden from 1814 to 1905, the Swedish practice of ordaining bishops and pastors did not influence Norwegian usage (Molland 1954, 349; Borregaard 1970, 122-124; Oftestad, Rasmussen and Schumacher 1991, 221). The work of liturgical renewal carried out in Norway during the nineteenth century came to an end with the publication of the 1920 *Alterbok* (hereafter AB 1920) but did not cause any significant changes in the ordination rites compared with those that had been in use since 1689. Several reprints of *AB 1920* were subsequently published (Flatø 1982, 78-82, 170-173; Fæhn 1984, 249-266). Thus effectively the Danish ordination rites were in use in Norway until well into the twentieth century. Ordination rites were included in the next Church of Norway Service Book (*Gudstjenestebok for den Norske Kirke*, hereafter GBN 1986-1991) which was drawn up as a result of the work of a Liturgical Commission between 1986 and 1991.[3] Some changes in structure and contents were this time made in the ordination rites as compared with older Norwegian rites.

Iceland was part of Denmark until 1944, and Danish-Norwegian ordination rites authorised between 1537 and 1898 were used there until the beginning of the twentieth century. The rite for the ordination of bishops in Danish

---

2. The structure of ordination rites according to the Danish tradition from the Reformation up to the first half of the twentieth century is given in the appendix (106-107 below).
3. Cf. Fjeld's first article (Part 2.4).

AB 1898 was used when a bishop was ordained in Reykjavik in 1908. However, this rite and the rite for the ordination of pastors were translated into Icelandic. The Icelandic Church's own Service Books, the *Helgisiðabók* of 1910 and the *Handbók* of 1934 (hereafter *HBI 1910* and *HBI 1934)* also contain both ordination rites. These were the rites of Danish AB 1898, with only minor amendments in structure and content. Changes in structure and content were also minor between HBI 1934 and the 1981 Liturgical Handbook of the Icelandic Church (*Handbók íslensku kirkjunnar*, hereafter HBI 1981*).*[4] Thus in practice, the Danish ordination tradition was also used in Iceland almost until the end of the twentieth century.

According to many scholars, bishops and pastors began to be ordained in the 1550s in *Sweden* which then included Finland. Unfinished rites drawn up for this purpose by Laurentius Petri, Archbishop of Uppsala, were first used. These rites appear complete and annotated in 1561, in his proposal for a Church Ordinance and were printed in the 1571 Swedish Church Ordinance (hereafter KO 1571).[5] However, scholars are not able on available evidence to explain how a deacon was ordained in accordance with evangelical order (Parvio 1970, 36-44; 1976, 55-54, 61-62; Andrén 1999, 69-72; Brodd 1999, 276-278).

The 1571 ordination rites were published with minor amendments in the 1686 Swedish Church Act (Kyrkio-Lag och Ordning, hereafter KL 1686). They were not printed in the Swedish Service Book *(Handbok)* until 1811. No significant changes were made in 1811 by comparison with corresponding

---

4. cf. Einar Sigurbjörnsson and Kristján Valur Ingolfsson (Part II.2).
5. The ordination rites in the 1571 Church Order were based on both the Swedish medieval tradition and on German models, in particular Martin Luther's rite for the ordination of pastors. The influence of Swedish medieval ordination rites for priests and bishops is evident in the ordination rites in *KO 1571*. A chalice and a Bible were given to pastors to symbolise their authority to teach and to dispense the sacraments. Furthermore, both rites were supposed to be performed in connection with Holy Communion. Laurentius Petri had based his ordination rites on the German rite for the ordination of pastors in the 1552 Mecklenburg Church Order. This rite, for its part, had been compiled based on Martin Luther's ordinal of 1535 (Färnström 1935, 237-240; 1956, 165-168; von Sicard 1972, 293-294; Yelverton 1958, 88; Parvio 1976, 56, 62; Puglisi 1996, 54). There were some similarities between the ordination rites in KO 1571 and the corresponding rites in Danish *KO 1537/1539*. The laying-on of hands was the only symbolic gesture in *KO 1571*. Bishops were no longer anointed. The King of Sweden Gustavus Vasa had been anointed at his coronation but bishops were no longer anointed at ordination during his reign (1523-1560) (Brodd 1999, 275). Both Rites in *KO 1571* have also been published in French (Dewailly 1985, 297-321).

ordination rites in *KL 1686*. Changes by comparison with previous rites were also minor in the ordination rites in the Swedish Service Books (*Kyrkohand-bok*) of 1868, 1894, 1917 and 1942 (hereafter HBS 1868 etc.).[6] It is thus possible to speak of a Swedish tradition of ordination rites from the Reformation to the latter part of the twentieth century. Some changes in structure and content were made in the ordination rites in the 1987 Swedish Service Book (*Kyrkohandboken,* hereafter HBS 1987 (1988)) compared with the older Swedish ordination tradition (Lempiäinen 1985, 225-30, 233-35).

Finland was a part of Sweden until the beginning of the nineteenth century, and bishops and pastors were ordained there in accordance with the rites found in *KO 1571* and *KL 1686*. The latter was translated into Finnish in 1688. The ordination rites in Swedish HBS 1811 were published in Finnish in 1817 though by then Finland was no longer part of Sweden. The first Finnish rites for the ordination of bishops and pastors were included in the 1886 Finnish Service Book (*Kirkkokäsikirja,* hereafter KK 1886), and, with only minor amendments, in subsequent Service Books in 1913, 1963 and 1984 (hereafter KK 1913 etc.). There were only minor structural differences between the nineteenth and twentieth century Finnish ordination rites and between the equivalent Swedish rites of the same period (Lempiäinen 1985, 225). Thus in practice, the Swedish ordination tradition was also used in Finland until the end of the twentieth century.

The Reform of the Nordic Rites in the late Twentieth Century

As mentioned above, all Nordic rites for the ordination of bishops and pastors were revised at the same time in the latter part of the twentieth century. Revised rites were authorised in Iceland in 1980, in Finland in 1984, in Sweden in 1987, in Norway in 1991 and in Denmark in 1987.

Although the newer ordination rites were based on older tradition, they were all reformed for several reasons,[7] in the first place as part of the liturgical renewal in the Nordic region at the end of the twentieth century, which was

---

6. HBS 1868 was a reprint of HBS 1811 with minor amendments, whilst HBS 1894, 1917 and 1942 had separate versions of the Swedish ordinal. The ordination rites used in manuscript in Sweden during the eighteenth century are not dealt with in this article. On those rites, see e.g. Kjöllerström 1971, 252-263, 271-277. The structure of ordination rites according to the Swedish tradition from the Reformation to the latter part of the twentieth century is given in the appendix (106-107 below).

7. This concurrent revision of ordination rites across the Nordic region was not a new

inspired by Roman Catholic and Protestant examples. One of the most important points of origin for the liturgical renewal of the Nordic rites was the Second Vatican Council (1962-1965). Liturgical research undertaken in connection with this work of reform contributed to the revision of the rites (VC II 1996, 20-24; Lempiäinen 1985, 225; Oftestad, Rasmussen and Schumacher 1991, 292-295). Secondly, the Nordic reform was stimulated by the Ecumenical Movement and the research on the theology and functions of the Church's ordained ministry which that movement inspired. In this respect, the influence of statements on ministry in two important ecumenical documents, *Baptism, Eucharist and Ministry* (BEM 1982) and *The Porvoo Common Statement* (1993), should be mentioned. The third reason for the reform of the rites was the influence of social change and the changing relationship between the state and the church and its effect on the link between the appointment of bishops and some priests and the governments in power.[8]

The Structure of Nordic Rites for the Ordination of Bishops and Pastors at the End of the Twentieth Century

The structure of the modern Nordic ordination rites is compared in figure 1, but not in chronological order. Only the elements mentioned as such within the rites themselves are included in the table, put side by side to facilitate comparison of their structural similarity and differences.

---

phenomenon. As mentioned before, the first ordination rites came into existence between the 1530s and 1550s in Denmark and Sweden. The oath of allegiance was added to these rites in the seventeenth century in both countries and was omitted from all other Nordic ordination rites, except for the Finnish rites, at the end of the nineteenth century. The most recent process of revision, again undertaken concurrently, indicates that the Nordic countries belong together culturally.

8. The Swedish Church became independent of the state in 2000; the church-state relationship is currently being debated in Denmark, Iceland and Norway. The ties between church and state have been looser in Finland than in the other Nordic countries since the nineteenth century, because Finland was a Grand Duchy of the Russian Empire from 1809. The Emperor of Russia, who professed the Orthodox faith, became at that time the highest ruler of the Lutheran Church in Finland in place of the King of Sweden. Thus, the Lutheran Church in Finland had to redefine its relationship with the government. This was completed in 1869 when the Church Act for the Evangelical-Lutheran Church of Finland was approved, giving a looser definition of the juridical status of the Finnish Lutheran Church than was the case of the churches in the other Nordic countries.

Figure 1

Content of Nordic Rites for the Ordination of Bishops and Pastors in the 1980s and 1990s

Point	Content	Denmark Bi	Pa	Norway Bi	Pa	Iceland Bi	Pa	Sweden Bi	Pa	Finland Bi	Pa
	Introduction										
1a.	Prelude with entrance procession	x	x	x	x	x	x				
1b.	Entrance prayer and procession							x	x	x	x
1c.	Entrance prayer and hymn	x	x	x^1	x^1	x^1	x^1				
2.	Entrance word			x	x			x	x	x	x
3.	Confession, *Kyrie, Gloria Patri*			x	x			x^2	x^2		
4.	Greetings	x	x								
5.	Collect	x	x	x	x	x	x				
6.	First Scripture reading	x	x			x					
7.	(Apostles') Creed	x	x								
8.	Hymn and short sermon	x^3	x	x^3	x	x	x^3				
	The ordination										
9a.	Presentation and prayer	x	x	x	x	x^4	x				
9b.	Hymn	x	x			x^5	x^5				
9c.	Presentation and reading of letter of power of attorney							x	x^6		
10.	Short sermon and prayer									x	x
11.	Hymn and prayer	x^7	x^7	x^8		x^{7a}	x^{7a}				
12.	Short sermon	x	x	x^9	x^9	x	x				
13.	Presentation and reading of letter of power of attorney									x	x^{6a}
14.	Scripture reading	x	x	x^{8a}	x	x^{10}	x^{10}	x	x	x	x
15.	(Apostles') Creed					x^{10}	x^{10}			x	x^{11}
16.	Brief sermon							x	x		
17.	Exhortation	x	x	x	x	x	x	x	x		
18.	Promises	x	x	x	x	x	x	x	x	x	x

No.	Item										
19a.	Hand shaking	x	x	x	x	x[12]	x[12]				
19b.	Solemn declaration							x	x		
19c.	Oath									x	x
20.	Creed (Nicene)							x	x		
21.	Prayer for the church and hymn							x	x		
22a.	Prayer, laying-on of hands and Lord's Prayer	x	x			x[13]	x[13]				
22b.	Prayer of blessing, laying-on of hands, vesting with episcopal or clerical vestments, Lord's Prayer or (Nicene) Creed and proclamation as bishop or pastor			x[14]	x[14]						
22c.	Prayer of blessing, laying-on of hands, vesting in episcopal or clerical vestments, handing over of letter of power of attorney or letter of ministerial authorisation, and confirmation of ordination							x[15]	x[15]		
22d.	Conferral of ministry and wish for divine help to fulfil promises, vesting in episcopal or clerical vestments, laying-on of hands, blessing and Lord's Prayer									x[16]	x[16]
23.	Hymn	x	x	x[17]	x	x	x				
24.	Invitation to congregation			x							
	Conclusion										
25.	Holy Mass	x[18]	x	x[18]	x[18]	x[18]	x	x[19]	x[19]	x[20]	x[20]
26.	Prayer of praise (*Benedicamus*) or hymn							x	x		
27.	Consecration and sending out for office			x[21]				x	x	x	x
28.	Hymn or postlude with procession	x	x	x[22]	x	x[22]	x[22]	x	x	x	x

Key to figure 1:
Bi Rites for the Ordination of Bishops
Pa Rites for the Ordination of Pastors
x Appears in the ordination rites.

x[1]   There is no prayer here.

x[2]   There is no *Kyrie* and *Gloria* here. Instead, confession, prayer for forgiveness and a thanks-giving prayer for the forgiveness of sins are mentioned as part of the ordination rite.

x[3]   There is no short sermon here.

x[4]   Here a report written by the ordinand on his/her life and the divine dispensation in his/her life is read.

x[5]   Here, in addition to the hymn, *Veni Sancte Spiritus* is sung as a responsory.

x[6]   The letter of power of attorney is read only in the rite for the ordination of a bishop.

x[6a] In fact, the presentation in the rite for the ordination of a bishop is carried out by the reading of the letter of power of attorney. No other words are used.

x[7]   The Danish version of the hymn *Veni Sancte Spiritus* precedes that prayer. The *Veni Sancte Spiritus* and the prayer may alternatively be in Latin.

x[7a] The Latin version of *Veni Sancte Spiritus* precedes the prayer, which is also in Latin.

x[8]   In fact, there is no prayer here. Instead a hymn or the first verse of the Norwegian version of *Veni Sancte Spiritus is sung.*

x[8a] *Veni Sancte Spiritus* is sung in the vernacular between the Scripture readings and at the end of them.

x[9]   A short sermon is delivered after the Scripture reading.

x[10] The Creed precedes the Scripture reading. Here the Apostles' Creed is read.

x[11] The Nicene Creed is read in the rite for the ordination of pastors.

x[12] Episcopal and clerical vestments are put on here.

x[13] Here the laying-on of hands, prayer of blessing and Lord's Prayer take place. The 'Amen' completes this part of the ordination rites.

x[14] The Lord's Prayer is read only in the rite for the ordination of pastors. The Creed is read only in the rite for the ordination of bishops.

x[15] The *Veni Sancte Spiritus* is sung in the vernacular while episcopal and clerical vestments are put on.

x[16] Ministry is assigned by proclamation. The letter of power of attorney is given here. The *Veni Sancte Spiritus* is sung in the vernacular while episcopal vestments are put on. It is also the practice to use it while pastors' vestments are put on, though this hymn in the ver-nacular is not mentioned in the rite for the ordination of pastors.

x[17] Hymn and sermon are mentioned here. The Holy Mass is celebrated after the sermon.

x[18] The new bishop is required to preach.

x[19] The offertory, preface, *Sanctus*, eucharistic prayer, Lord's Prayer, fraction, the Peace, *Agnus Dei*, distribution of Communion and prayer of thanksgiving are included in the ordination rites.

x[20] According to the rubrics given at the beginning of the rites, the ordination of bishops and pastors is to take place before the Eucharist. Thus, the Holy Mass is celebrated after ordination in both cases.

x[21] The responsory prayer is sung here.

x[22]   There is no separate mention of a hymn or postlude in this rite for the ordination of
bishops. However, these are the final parts of the Mass after a bishop's ordination.

Figure 1 indicates that 28 different elements or parts were used in the Nordic
ordination rites in the 1980s and 1990s.[9] These may be divided into three
sections: the introduction (points 1-8); the ordination (points 9-24) and the
conclusion (points 25-28). Most of the elements exist in more than one rite,
though some occur only in one (points 4, 7, 9c-10, 13, 19b-21, 22b-22d, 24,
26). It thus becomes clear that none of the Nordic rites is fully identical with
any of the others. However, all five rites have the same basic structure and
contain items from the introduction, the ordination and the conclusion. The
section on ordination is the largest and also the main section in all the Nordic
rites.[10] For the most part, the introductory and concluding sections contain
some parts of the Eucharist.

In addition, some similarities may be noticed. The ordination takes place in
connection with the Eucharist in all the Nordic rites.[11] This was the case from

---

9. There are 19 elements in the Danish and Norwegian, 18 in the Icelandic, 16 in the
   Swedish and 12 in the Finnish rites. Six of these occur only in the Swedish rites (See
   points 9c, 19b, 20-21, 22c, 26), four only in the Finnish rites (points 10, 13, 19c,
   22d), two only in the Norwegian (points 22b, 24) and one only in the Danish rites
   (point 7).

10. 53% (10 out of 19 elements) of the Danish and Norwegian rites are in the ordination
    section. The corresponding percentages for the other rites are: Icelandic rites 65% (11
    out of 17); Swedish rites 56% (9 out of 16) and Finnish rites 64% (7 out of 11).

11. However, the relationship between the Eucharist and the ordination proper varies: in
    Finland, the ordination is recognised as an element in its own right; it is not an actual
    part of the Eucharist (Perustelut 2001, 29). In Denmark and Iceland it is connected
    to the Eucharist a little more closely than in Finland, as evidenced by those parts of the
    Danish and Icelandic ordination rite, which are specifically parts of the eucharistic rite
    and are generated by the act of ordination: the Collect, the first Scripture reading and
    Apostles' Creed (points 5-7). In Norway and Sweden the ordination proper is per-
    ceived more clearly as part of the Eucharist than in Denmark and Iceland, as shown
    where parts of the eucharistic rite are included in the Norwegian rites (points 3, 5), i.e.
    the confession, the *Kyrie* and *Gloria* and the Collect, which is normally the Collect of
    the day, though another collect may be chosen (e.g. the Collect for the first Sunday
    after Easter). The Scripture readings most used (Is. 6.1–8; Rom. 12. 4–11; Eph.
    4.11–16; Matt. 9.35–38) are those that are linked with the doctrine of the Church's
    ministry, and its essential nature and obligations (GBN 1991-1996, 162). Of all the
    Nordic rites, the Swedish rites are most clearly seen and understood as parts of the
    Eucharist. The other rites may be celebrated in connection with it or they may be used
    separately and independently. The elements in the Swedish rites that illustrate this are
    the confession and the liturgical orders for Holy Communion (points 3, 25). The

the sixteenth to the twentieth centuries. The connection between the eucharistic rite and the ordination proper is natural because the duties of the Church's ordained ministers, as given in the act of ordination, are to preach the Word of God and dispense the sacraments.

Thus there are some common elements in all the Nordic rites: the Scripture readings, the promises, the Eucharist and a hymn or *postlude* with procession (points 14, 18, 25, 28). Furthermore, there are elements with the same contents located in different contexts in the rites: a procession (points 1a-1b); the presentation (points 9a, 9c, 13); a short sermon (points 10, 12, 16); the imposition of hands or laying-on of hands (points 22a-22d), and the Apostles' Creed (points 7, 15) or Nicene Creed (points 20, 22b). Prayers and hymns (points 1b, 1c, 5, 8, 9b, 10-11, 21, 22a-23, 26, 28) are included in all the Nordic rites. However, there is one common element, the exhortation, which is included in all except the Finnish rite (point 17).

The similarities mentioned in the Nordic rites originate in the traditional practice of ordination and in the theology of ordination. For example, Scripture readings, promises and the laying-on of hands (points 14, 18, 22a-22d) have been included in Nordic ordination rites since the medieval period (Strömberg 1955). The elements mentioned were also included in the sixteenth and seventeenth century ordination rites. However, in the latter case, the promises emphasised Reformation doctrine. The presentation (points 9a, 9c, 13) was added in rites influenced by Reformation thinking,[12] and the apostolic succession and blessing of the Church were conveyed symbolically by the laying-on of hands in accordance with the Reformation doctrine (Rietschel (and Graff) 1951, 853-854; Lempiäinen 1985, 223-224; Puglisi 1998, 4-23). The imposition of hands is mentioned in the documents of the Second Vatican

---

status of the ordination rites as part of the eucharistic rite has been further strengthened in Swedish liturgical renewal, which is ongoing (Kyrkohandboksgruppens förslag 2000, 270). At the turn of the twenty-first century, the aim of Finnish liturgical renewal is to link ordination to the Eucharist as a whole (Perustelut 2001, 29).

12. According to Reformation doctrine a person was to be called to office in due order by a congregation and charged with the main duties of office, i.e., to preach the Gospel and to dispense the sacraments. He was to have an inner calling to the ministry of the Church. The inner calling and the call of the congregation were confirmed publicly in the ordination of pastors. There were also other fundamental elements of ordination: the ordinand had to declare his support for Lutheran belief; the duties of ministry were to be read from the Bible and the duties of office stated (Lohse 1970, 51-57; Parvio 1970, 35-36; von Sicard 1972, 293-294; Parvio 1976, 54-55, 61-62; Brodd 1999, 272-275, 277-278).

Council as a very important element in the rite for the ordination of bishops (VC II. 1996:1: III: 76). The Porvoo Common Statement takes the same view (e.g., Porvoo 1993: IV, C 47). At the same time, Lutheran doctrine has always pointed out that everyting should be based on the Word of God. Therefore, Scripture reading has also been seen as a very important element in ordination. For all these reasons, it is not surprising that the elements mentioned were included in Nordic rites in the 1980s and 1990s.

Figure 1 also indicates differences in the Nordic rites. Common structural parts exist only in some of the Nordic ordination rites. There are 17 common elements in the Danish and Icelandic rites (points 1a, 1c, 5, 6, 8-9ab, 11-12, 14, 17-19a, 22a, 23) and 14 in the Danish, Norwegian and Icelandic Rites (points 1a, 1c, 5, 8-9a, 11-12, 14, 17-19a, 23). Six common parts exist in the Swedish and Finnish rites (points 1b, 2, 9c, 13, 19b-19c, 27). As for points 9c and 13 there is a question as to whether these elements are the same or not: they do not exist in exactly the same context in the Swedish and Finnish Rites. The same question arises at 19b and19c, though these parts are here differently named, 'solemn declaration' (in the Swedish Rite) and 'oath' (in the Finnish Rite). There is also one common part in the Norwegian and Swedish rites (point 3) and two in the Norwegian, Swedish and Finnish rites (points 2, 27), and one common element exists between the Icelandic and Finnish rites (point 15).

An overall picture of structural similarity emerges in the Nordic rites when the number of all common parts is calculated and displayed as a percentage of all 28 elements. The Danish and Icelandic rites have most common parts (60% of all elements). There are 50% common elements in the Danish, Norwegian and Icelandic rites, 21% in the Swedish and Finnish rites, 3% in the Swedish and Norwegian rites and 7% in the Norwegian, Swedish and Finnish rites. Except for the five common elements found in all the Nordic rites (points 14, 17-18, 25, 28, though Finnish rites have no point 17), the Swedish rites do not have any other common parts with Danish and Icelandic rites. The same is true of the Finnish and Danish rites. However, 3% of all elements are common to Icelandic and Finnish rites.

On the basis of this information, it is possible to determine the common parts that form a structural similarity especially between the Danish and Icelandic rites, but also between them and the Norwegian rites. This is clearly the case because Iceland was part of Denmark until 1944 and Norway was part of Denmark until 1814. Also, Danish rites were used in Iceland until the beginning of the twentieth century, with only minor changes in detail caused by Icelandic circumstances. Likewise, Norwegian rites in the nineteenth and twentieth centuries were not structurally different from the corresponding

Danish rites. The only differences between them were minor amendments in detail. It is thus possible to speak of a Danish group of ordination rites at the end of the twentieth century.[13]

It is understandable that there are common elements between the Swedish and Finnish rites because Finland was part of Sweden until 1809 and this is apparent in the structural similarity in Swedish and Finnish rites in the nineteenth and twentieth centuries. However, a structural similarity formed by common elements exists neither in Swedish, Danish and Icelandic rites nor in Danish and Finnish rites despite the number of parts common to all Nordic rites. Furthermore, one common element (the Apostles' Creed) in Icelandic and Finnish rites is not a sign of structural similarity formed by common elements between those two rites. The same fact will be noted in Norwegian, Swedish and Finnish rites which have two common elements (an entrance word and consecration and sending out for ministry) and in Norwegian and Swedish rites which have one common part (confession, *Kyrie* and *Gloria Patri*). There is thus also a Swedish group or family of ordination rites in Scandinavia at the end of the twentieth century.[14]

There are notable differences in structural form and content between the Danish and Swedish sixteenth to twentieth century ordination traditions (See the appendix, points 2a, 4-5, 8-12, 14, 17a,19-20, 22). Figure 1 and the appendix indicate that the Norwegian rites in GBN 1986-1991 differ from the Danish ordination tradition. For example, the first Scripture reading is lacking only in *GBN 1986-1991* (point 6 in figure 1, point 4 in the appendix, column 1). Furthermore, vesting in episcopal or clerical vestments, the calling to a congregation and the consecration and sending out for ministry are included only in *GBN 1986-1991*. Seen from this viewpoint, it is possible to conclude

---

13. There are however differences in the Danish group of ordination rites. Greetings (point 4) exist only in Danish rites, and only Norwegian rites have an entrance word, confession, *Kyrie* and *Gloria Patri*, calling, consecration and sending out for ministry (points 2-3, 24, 27). The first Scripture reading (point 6) is lacking in the Norwegian rites. Also some elements occur in different contexts in the Norwegian and Icelandic rites (Creed, points 15, 22b) from their context in the corresponding Danish rites.

14. There are also differences in the Swedish group of ordination rites. The confession, *Kyrie* and *Gloria Patri*, exhortation, hymn and prayer for the Church and the prayer of praise (*Benedicamus*) or hymn (points 3, 17, 21, 26) exist only in the Swedish rites. Moreover, the presentation, the reading of the letter of power of attorney and the short sermon (points 9c, 10, 13, 16) have a different context in the Swedish rites from their context in the Finnish rites.

that the Danish and Icelandic rites are more conservative than the corresponding Norwegian rites.

The Finnish rites in *KK 1984* remain more true to the Swedish ordination tradition than the Swedish rites in *HBS 1987*. This can be seen for example in the fact that Scripture reading precedes the Creed. Also, the short sermon is delivered before the presentation in the Swedish tradition and in the Finnish *KK 1984* (See figure 1, points 10, 13, and the appendix, points 6, 7b, column 2). Furthermore, the Prayer for the Church is included only in *HBS 1987*.[15] From this point of view, the Finnish rites are more conservative than the corresponding Swedish rites.

The Understanding of the Bishop's and Pastor's Ministry in the Nordic Rites

The different sections in all the Nordic rites have similar vernacular titles.[16] The vernacular concept for ordination *'vielse' / 'vigsling' / 'vígsla' / 'vigning' / 'vihkiminen'* is derived from the verb *'viga'* ('to ordain' in Danish, Norwegian, Icelandic, and Swedish) and *'vihkiä'* ('to ordain' in Finnish). Since medieval times, the meaning of this vernacular verb has been seen and understood in Nordic theological languages to mean 'bless' or 'consecrate' and 'sanctify' (Knuutila 1990, 52; Puglisi 1998, 14).[17] In accordance with this meaning, both a bishop and a pastor are 'blessed' or 'consecrated' for their ministries. They are also 'sanctified', i.e., set apart from the rest of the community for the ministry of the Church. In other words, a bishop is 'ordained', i.e., not only 'consecrated' or 'installed', according to all the Nordic rites in the 1980s and 1990s.

Figure 1 indicates that the same elements exist in all the Nordic rites for the

---

15. In the Swedish intercessory prayer for the Church (point 21), a blessing is asked for the Church and its ministers in order to spread the gospel and to bring 'justice and peace to the world'. This example shows that the theological emphasis that was dominant at the end of the twentieth century has been incorporated into the Swedish ordination rites.

16. The ordination of bishops / pastors is called in Danish *'Bispevielse' / 'Præstevielse'*, in Norwegian *'Vigsling til Biskop' / 'Vigsling til Prestetjenest'*; in Icelandic *'Biskupsvígsla' / 'Prestvígsla'*; in Swedish *'Biskopsvigning' / 'Prästvigning'*, and in Finnish *'Piispan vihkiminen virkaan' / 'Papiksi vihkiminen'*.

17. James F. Puglisi has dealt with the etymology of the German verb, *'weihen'*. This verb is a German synonym for *'ordinere' / 'vigsle' / 'vígja' / 'viga' / 'vihkiä'* in Danish, Norwegian, Icelandic, Swedish and Finnish respectively.

ordination of bishops and pastors (See points 1a-28).[18] Thus, bishops and pastors are ordained in the same way. This fact can be seen to be derived from the same vernacular concept, '*vielse*'/ '*vigsling*'/ '*vgsla*'/ '*vgning*'/'*vikhiminen*', in the titles of the Nordic rites.

It could be asked what the relationship is between the ministries of bishops and pastors. To answer this question the Lutheran doctrine of episcopacy must be studied from two points of view: the teachings of Martin Luther and the liturgical practice of ordaining bishops in the Evangelical-Lutheran Churches in the five Nordic countries from the Reformation until now.

It is difficult to reach a clear understanding of Martin Luther's view of the ministries of bishops and pastors on the basis of his writings. According to several scholars, Luther regarded the episcopacy as the part of ministry that is the office of preaching.[19] However, the ministry of bishops was considered to have different duties from that of pastors: these were to ensure the correct teaching and preaching of the Word of God, to visit the parishes, to ordain new pastors and to watch over their conduct. Furthermore, although a bishop or superintendent should already be an ordained pastor, he should also have an episcopal ordination[20] because the duties of a bishop's ministry require a separate ordination. As far as we know, Martin Luther did not draw up a liturgical rite for the ordination of bishops. However, his rite for the ordination of pastors is known to have been adapted for the ordination of bishops or

---

18. There are only two exceptions, in the Norwegian rites for the ordination of bishops and pastors: a hymn and prayer (point 11) and consecration and sending out for ministry (point 27) are included in the rite for the ordination of pastors but not in that of bishops.

19. Episcopacy was not a ministry ('*ordo*') of its own in the Middle Ages. For this reason, the consecration of bishops was based on the ordination of priests. The elected and nominated bishop was consecrated or blessed for his office by the anointing of his hands and the laying-on of hands. By consecration, a bishop was differentiated from a priest. The episcopal power or sacerdotal, kingly and teaching authority ('*potestas ordinis, iurisdictionis, magisterii*') and the apostolic succession have furthermore been identified. For that purpose the bishop was also given the insignia of episcopal rank (Crichton 1972, 288-289). In late medieval times, an ordained bishop and priest were considered to fulfil the duties of sacrificial priesthood ('*sacerdotium*') and the deacon the duties of ministry ('*ministerium*') (Brodd 1999, 271-272).

20. Martin Luther used several verbs meaning to ordain bishops: '*weihen*' ('to consecrate'), '*ordinieren*' ('to ordain') and '*einführen*' or '*einsetzen*' ('to install'). Puglisi has dealt with the difference between the concepts of 'ordination' and 'installation' (Puglisi 1998, 14, 26-27; Smith 2000).

superintendents,[21] thus emphasising the ordination of pastors as a precondition for that of bishops. One of the essential contents of Luther's rite for the ordination of pastors was to emphasise the preconditions of ministry: the call of a congregation and the inner call, or vocation. According to Luther, those should be confirmed publicly by the presentation and promises in the ordination rite. Another essential content was that of giving an ordained person the right publicly to preach the gospel and to dispense the sacraments and forgive sins. The rite contained readings from the Bible declaring the duties and rights of a pastor as well as prayers of blessing. The blessing was given by the laying-on of hands (Rietschel (and Graff) 1951, 853-854; Lohse 1970, 51-57; Parvio 1970, 35-36; 1976, 54-55,61-62; von Sicard 1972, 293-294; Puglisi 1998, 14-23, 26-27; Brodd 1999, 272-278; Smith 2000, 45-86).

The Evangelical-Lutheran Churches in the five Nordic countries have had their own rites for ordaining bishops from the Reformation until now. These rites began in the same way as the rites for the ordination of pastors.[22] A different concept for the ordination of bishops than for that of pastors has been used in the Swedish rites since the nineteenth century and in Finnish rites at the end of the nineteenth century and the beginning of the twentieth century.[23] Their use for the ordination of bishops cannot, however, be em-

---

21. Martin Luther published the rite for the ordination of pastors in 1535 to 1539. It was copied in different versions in several German Church Orders in the sixteenth century (Smith 2000, 46, 147-200).

22. The concepts 'vielse' / 'vigsling' / 'vígsla' / 'vigning' / 'vihkiminen' ('ordination') have been used in most of the rites (Puglisi 1998, 58-61). In the Swedish KO 1571, the vernacular verb, 'ordinera' ('to ordain') was included in the title of both rites.

23. In the nineteenth century Swedish Ordinals, the rite for the ordination of pastors was called 'vigning' ('ordination') and that of bishops 'installation' ('installation'). In Finnish ordinals at the end of the nineteenth and the beginning of the twentieth century, equivalent Finnish words were 'vihkiminen' in the rite for the ordination of pastors, and 'installaatio' in that of bishops (e.g. HBS 1894: 210, 220; KK 1886: 141, 151; KK 1913 (1941): 186, 194). Earlier the rites for the ordination of bishops and pastors had different names only in the Danish medieval and Reformation ordinals. In the Danish medieval Pontificale Roskildense (Strömberg 1955: 153, 244, 297, 299), the rite of ordination for priests was entitled 'Ordo, qualiter sacri ordines fieri debeant' ('Rite for creating sacred orders'). The concept of 'consecration' (in Latin, 'consecratio') was used in the title of the rite for the consecration of bishops. In KO 1537/1539 the rite for the ordination of bishops was called the same in Latin: 'Caerimoniis ordinabitur publice Superindentendens' and in Danish 'Med disse Ceremonier skal een Superattendent wiies' ('Ceremonies for the Ordination of Superintendent'). Titles for the rite for the ordination of pastors have been the same in Latin 'Ritus instituendi ministros' and in Danish 'Huorledis Kirckens tienere skulle tilskickis' ('Rite for the Installation of Ministers').

phasised too much because the distinction between the different concepts of ordination are, according to Puglisi, very minor (Puglisi 1998, 26-27). Rites for the ordination of pastors and bishops have had the same structural content. However, there have been some differences in detail (see the appendix and figure 1 at 7a-7b, 14a-14b, 17a-17b). Some elements (e.g., the exhortation in the Danish tradition and the promises in the Swedish tradition (See the appendix, points 15, 16a) differ in content, because of the different duties of each ministry. Thus, the rite for the ordination of bishops may be seen as based on that of pastors. The important elements in the ordination rite: the presentation, promises, Scripture readings, prayers and the laying-on of hands were part of both the Danish and Swedish traditions (See the appendix, points 3, 8, 13, 16a, 18). Thus, preconditions and the duties and rights of both ministries are stated in the rites.

Through similar titles, the structural content and important common elements in the Nordic rites for the ordination of bishops and pastors, the Lutheran doctrine of the ministry of bishops as part of that of pastors may be found in continuing existence.[24] From the ecumenical point of view, this is to be expected, as the Ecumenical Movement at the end of the twentieth century emphasised one apostolic ministry, that of the threefold ministry of bishops, priests and deacons (e.g., BEM 1991: M. 13; Porvoo 1993: B 41). Every ministry has, however, preconditions, duties and rights. We can now examine those preconditions as given in the rites.

Preconditions for the Ordination and Ministry of Bishops and Pastors
In the presentation (figure 1, points 9a, 9c, 13; HBI 1980 (1981): 184, 195-196; KK 1984 (1985): 108, 122; GBN 1986-1991 (1996): 163, 205; GOD 1987 (2001): 134, 161), preconditions for both ministries are found. First, the requirement of a call from the Church is stated very clearly in all the rites for the ordination of bishops in the Danish group of rites and also in the Swedish rite for the ordination of pastors. The reading of the letter of power of attorney symbolises this call in the rites for the ordination of bishops in the Swedish group.[25] Secondly, the call is stated very clearly in the rites for the ordination of pastors in the Danish group, where pastors are said 'to be or-

---

24. It is also noteworthy that the rite for the ordination of a bishop is referred to in the Porvoo Common Statement (1993) as 'ordination' or 'consecration', whereas in the documents of the Second Vatican Council the same rite is called the 'consecration' of a bishop in accordance with the Catholic tradition (VC II. 1996, 1: III: 76; Porvoo 1993: C 47-48).
25. In Sweden and Finland, a letter of power of attorney is read. This letter was signed by

dained in the apostolic way by prayer and the laying-on of hands'. This statement affirms that the concept 'Church' refers to the wider Church, that is, the Church of Christ, not just the Nordic churches. Thirdly, the personal nature of the call is emphasised by mentioning the ordinand by name in all presentations in the Nordic rites. The names of all the congregations which will be receiving new pastors are also read.[26] In conclusion, the call as featured in the presentation is in accordance with the Lutheran doctrine of preconditions for ordination and ministry.

The presentations have different wording and contents in the ordination rites for bishops and pastors. These differences point to one ministry which has both bishop's and pastor's functions. This is clear first in the Swedish rites, in which different preconditions are laid down for the ordination of bishops and for that of pastors. Bishops to be ordained must be elected and nominated and pastors must be called, approved and accepted. In addition, bishops to be ordained are described as 'elected'[27] only in the Danish rites for the ordination of bishops. This expression points to the episcopate as a ministry of the Church, despite the fact that new bishops were actually *nominated* by the head of state. Secondly, prayers are connected with the presentations in the rites of the Danish group (figure 1, point 9a; HBI 1980 (1981): 184-185, 196; GBN 1986-1991 (1996): 163-164, 206; GOD 1987 (2001): 134-135, 161-162). The different duties of bishops and pastors are mentioned in these prayers. For example in the Danish prayer, the bishop to be ordained is called a 'steward of the congregation' and a pastor to be ordained is called a 'preacher'.[28] In the Finnish rites, prayers are said in connection with a short sermon before the presentation (figure 1, point 10; KK 1984 (1985): 107-108, 121). A blessing is asked for bishops and pastors, that bishops may shepherd their flock and

---

the head of state, the King of Sweden or the President of Finland, until the end of the twentieth century, but is now signed by representatives of the Church, because bishops are no longer nominated by the head of state.

26. To be exact, the reading of names of congregations is not mentioned directly in the presentation in the Swedish rite for the ordination of pastors.

27. The election of a bishop was referred to earlier in the medieval rite for the ordination of a bishop in the *Pontificale Lundense*.

28. The prayers read in connection with the presentation have different wording in the Danish, Norwegian and Icelandic rites. In the Danish rites, there are three alternative prayers which have the same wording in the ordination rites for both bishops and pastors. However, all the prayers in question have the same substance: to ask a blessing for the ordinands and also for ordination. There are no such prayers in the Swedish group of rites.

pastors may preach God's word and teach.[29] In the ecumenical documents, the same duties of episcopal ministry are mentioned also as duties of the ministry of oversight (*episkopé*) (BEM 1991: M. 29; Porvoo 1993: B 41-45).

The duties mentioned for the ministry of bishops and pastors are derived from the Scripture readings in the Nordic rites (figure 1, point 14).[30] In some readings, reasons for the leadership of the congregation can also be found.[31] Some readings are included in the rites for the ordination of both bishops and pastors.[32] This is in accordance with current ecumenical understanding in which the duties of a bishop's ministry have been established as: preaching the Word, presiding at the sacraments, and administering discipline (e.g., BEM 1991: M. 29; Porvoo 1993: B 43). This fact emphasises that the ministries of bishops and pastors are included in the same apostolic ministry.

For preconditions and duties of ministries, the exhortation and promises (figure 1, points 17-18; N. B. Finnish rites do not have an exhortation) are also worth a closer look. They have slightly different wording in all the Nordic rites (HBI 1980 (1981): 187-188, 198-199; KK 1984 (1985): 110-111, 124-125; HBS 1987 (1988): 8-10, 21-23; GBN 1986-1991 (1996): 168-169, 210;

---

29. There are two alternative prayers in the Finnish rites for the ordination of pastors. In the second alternative, an idiomatic expression '*to differentiate the holy office*' (in Finnish '*pyhään virkaan erottaminen*') is used. This expression is a verbal relic from centuries when priesthood was thought to be a sacrament. There is no corresponding expression in the other Nordic rites. However, the expression '*the holy office*' has been used as an example at the conferral of the bishop's or pastor's ministry in the Norwegian rites (ABN 1920 (1945): 169, 184).

30. There are 44 lessons included in the Nordic rites. Several of them exist in more than one rite (e.g., Matt. 28.16-20; John 15.1-5; John 15.12-16; Acts 20.28-32; 1 Cor. 4.1-5; 2 Cor. 5.14b-20; Titus 1.5-9, and 1 Pet. 5.2-4). Lessons are normally chosen from the four Gospels, Paul's letter to the Corinthians, Ephesians, Philippians, Timothy and Titus and from the first letter of Peter. Lessons chosen from the Old Testament are only included in the Swedish rites. The same lessons have been included in the Nordic rites from the sixteenth to the twentieth centuries (e.g., KO 1537/1539: 64, 113-114, 142-143, 190-191, 241; KO 1571 (1971): 144-146, 170-171; KR 1685: 121, 123, 128; HBS 1894: 211-2214, 223-226; ABN 1920 (1945): 164-168, 178-182). The doctrine of the Church as the Church of Christ, of the minister as a servant of Christ, of justification and the duties of ministry and of sending out bishops and pastors for their ministries can be seen and understood to have its basis in those readings (e.g., Matt. 10.24-27; 28.16-20; John 15.1-5;12-16; 20;21-23; 1 Cor. 4.1-5; 2 Cor. 3.4-8; 5.14-21; Eph. 4.7-13; and Phil. 2.5-11.

31. For example: Phil. 2.5-11; 2 Tim 4.1-5; Titus 1.5-9; and 1 Pet. 5.2-4.

32. Matt. 28.16-20; John 15.1-9, in the Danish and Icelandic rites, and Matt. 28.18-20 in the Norwegian and Finnish rites.

GOD 1987 (2001): 144-145, 173). According to the exhortations in the Danish group of rites, bishops are to hold to the Confession and Doctrine of the Church and to be an example for people in their diocese. Pastors are to preach the gospel, dispense sacraments and be an example for people in the congregation. In the corresponding exhortations in the Swedish rites, two examples are given of the duties of a bishop and pastor: visitation for bishops and pastoral care for pastors. The same duties of a bishop's ministry are also mentioned as duties of *episkopé*, in ecumenical documents (BEM 1991: M. 29; Porvoo 1993: B 41-45).

In the promises in the Danish group of rites, ordinands are questioned briefly about their willingness to undertake the ministry of a bishop or pastor and to carry out their duties as mentioned in the exhortations.[33] Corresponding elements in the rites of the Swedish group have the same content relating to undertaking the ministry of the Church and carrying out its duties. However, the questions have a longer format.[34] There are four questions in the Swedish rites and three in the Finnish rites, and questions are asked about the ordinands' willingness to undertake the ministry of the Church, to uphold the doctrine of the Church, to carry out the duties of bishops' and pastors' ministries and to be an example in their diocese or congregation. There is also a fourth question in the Swedish rites in which the ordinands' intention to live among people bearing witness to God's love is ascertained.

These are the essential preconditions indicated in the promises. Through the ordaining minister's questions, the call of the Church is invited and the willingness of ordinands to accept the duties of office is examined. As the answers are given to the bishop, ordained persons are accepted into their ministries by the bishop on behalf of Church. This means that new bishops and pastors are chosen by the Church. On the other hand, the inner call or vocation of ordinands is part of the answers they make to the bishops. Thus all the preconditions for ministry are met in the promises. The inner call is mentioned very clearly only in the Icelandic rite for the ordination of a bishop. Here a report on the ordinand's life and of divine action in it, written by the candidate to be ordained bishop, is commanded to be read. A bishop is said to be called to the episcopal ministry *by the grace of God*. The call of the Church appears in the Danish and Icelandic rites for the ordination of pastors, in

---

33. Ordinands were also questioned in the same way in the early Danish ordination tradition (See the appendix, column 1, point 16a).
34. The promises also had the form of three questions in the early Swedish ordination tradition (See the appendix, column 2, point 16a).

which the question is asked by a bishop *by virtue of his episcopal ministry* (in the Danish Rite) or *on behalf of the Holy Church* (in the Icelandic rite). In addition, the call of the Church can be seen indirectly and understood to be invited when ordinands are mentioned by name. This procedure has been followed in the Danish rite for the ordination of pastors and in both Norwegian rites.

In the Danish group of rites, there is handshaking between the ordaining minister and the ordinands after the promises (figure 1, point 19a; HBI 1980 (1981): 188 199; GBN 1986-1991 (1996): 169, 210-211; GOD 1987 (2001): 145, 173).[35] This confirms the contract, which is made through the questions and affirmative answers between the ordaining minister and the ordinands (Iversen 2004: 10).[36] The same aim is achieved in the solemn declaration in the Swedish rites and in the oath in the Finnish rites (figure 1, point 19b-19c; KK 1984 (1985): 111, 125; HBS 1987 (1988): 10, 23).[37] The ordinands are mentioned by name and affirm or vow to keep the promises. In the Finnish rites, the first and last paragraphs of the oath[38] were reputedly read by the ordinands at the clerk's dictation. This format emphasises the supervising and

---

35. In the Middle Ages, a handshake was the sign of confirmation of a contract. It was added in the Danish rites in *KR 1685* partly because of the resurgence of feudalism during the time of absolute monarchy (from 1660) and partly because of Anglican influence. The aim of the handshake was to emphasise the allegiance of a pastor to the bishop and, through that episcopal ministry, also to the Church. Handshaking is also an expression of the Church's call.

36. Unlike Luther's rite, *KO 1537/1539* included a promise or a solemn affirmation or vow to the king. This was to be sworn before ordination in the church. The solemn affirmation was replaced by an oath in *CR 1685* (1985). In practice, the oath was sworn before the act of ordination in the church. In the nineteenth century, it could also take place after the act of ordination in the sacristy. The oath to the king was left out in *RB 1898*.

37. There was no such oath in the Swedish *KO 1571*. The form and content of the oath were developed during the seventeenth century as in Denmark because allegiance to the government was required of bishops and pastors. It was at that time that a new Church Act was prepared following a long process. A bishop and a pastor were to swear the oath of allegiance to the king, as well as hold to the Word of God and the Confession of the Church (e.g., HBS 1884: 210). The next step in this development was to add the reading of the letter of power of attorney and the conferral of ministry in the rite for the ordination of bishops in *HBS 1811*. However, the oath of allegiance was left out in *HBS 1894* as in Denmark, Norway and Iceland. In Finnish rites, the oath was included in *KK 1984*. The oath was understood generally as problematic in Finland also. Therefore, it could be sworn, for example, in the sacristy after the act of ordination (Lempiäinen 1985: 228-229, 233-234).

38. The oath was not included in the proposal for the new Finnish ordination rites in 2001 (Kirkollisten toimitusten kirja II 2001: 267, 281).

confirming role of a bishop, which is in accordance with the current ecumenical understanding of *episkopé* (e. g. BEM 1991: M. 29; Porvoo 1993: B 43).

In all the Nordic rites, prayer, the laying-on of hands and the Lord's Prayer (See figure 1, points 22a-22d: N. B. Prayer is not included in the Swedish rites) are officiated after confirmation of the contract between the ordaining minister and the ordinands. Other parts are included in the Norwegian, Swedish and Finnish rites (HBI 1980 (1981): 189, 199-200; KK 1984 (1985): 111-113, 125-126; HBS 1987 (1988): 13-14, 25-26; GBN 1986-1991 (1996): 169-170, 210-211; GOD 1987 (2001): 145-147, 174-175). These are the proclamation of the bishop and pastor in the Norwegian rites,[39] the handing over of the letter of power of attorney and confirmation of ordination in the Swedish and Finnish rites[40] and the vesting in episcopal and clerical vestments[41] in the Norwegian, Swedish and Finnish rites. In the Swedish and Finnish rites, *Veni, Sancte Spiritus*[42] is also sung in the vernacular while the vesting is taking place (figure 1, points 22b-22d).

---

39. The Nicene Creed is also read at this point in the Norwegian rites.

40. The letters of power of attorney for ministry have normally been signed by bishops. In addition, historically, there have been parishes in Sweden and Finland in which pastors have been elected by a king.

41. The medieval practice of vesting bishops and pastors in their episcopal and clerical vestments was reintroduced in the nineteenth and twentieth centuries in the Swedish and Finnish Rites (Lempiäinen 1985, 229, 234). In the Norwegian rites, bishops and pastors were not vested in their episcopal and liturgical vestments until *GBN 1986-1991*.

42. The *Veni Sancte Spiritus* in the vernacular is not mentioned in the Finnish rite for the ordination of pastors, but the practice is to use it while the pastors' vestments are being put on. It is sung in the rites of the Danish group between the presentation, hymn, short sermon and Scripture reading (Table, points 9a, 14. NB the Norwegian rites have no hymn or short sermon at that point). The *Veni Sancte Spiritus* has the nature of a blessing because it asks for the help of the Holy Spirit for the ordinands, as does the prayer that follows it. This hymn has been included in the Danish tradition since medieval times (Strömberg 1955, 168; KO 1537/39 (1989): 133, 141, 190, 239; KR 1685 (1985): 121, 128). Following this tradition the hymn may also be sung in Latin in the Danish and Icelandic rites. *Veni Sancte Spiritus* in a bishop's ordination is to be sung in vernacular form, according to Norwegian *AB 1889*. However, it could alternatively be sung in Latin (ABN 1920 (1945): 177-178; Flatø 1982, 78-79, 173). It is a very important element in the rites of the Danish group. It has not had the same significance in the rites of the Swedish group, where its use, in the vernacular, was not included until the beginning of the nineteenth century (See the appendix column 2). In the Swedish tradition, the hymn also has the nature of a blessing. This fact can be noted because the Holy Spirit is asked to bless the ordinands in the hymn and the prayer read after it.

Although Danish, Norwegian, Icelandic, Swedish and Finnish rites do not have all the previously mentioned elements, they form a whole that confers the bishop's or pastor's ministry. The theological content of this whole is first to confirm that ordained persons have been accepted by the Church and will now be sent out to their ministries.[43] Secondly, ordained bishops and pastors will be given all the rights and power of bishops' and pastors' ministries, i.e. the right to dispense the sacraments, teach and preach the Word of God, forgive sins and visit parishes, ordain new pastors and watch over their conduct. This is the rationale of the proclamation or handing over of the letter of power of attorney. The sending out for ministry is also symbolised by the imposition of hands and vesting in episcopal or clerical vestments. The apostolic succession and blessing of the Church is conveyed symbolically in accordance with the tradition of the Church.[44] Ordinands are also bound by the apostolic basis of the Church's ministry. This is currently seen and understood to be very important ecumenically. The ministry of bishops is said to have historical continuity and to serve the apostolicity, catholicity and unity of the Church's teaching, worship and sacramental life (e.g., BEM 1982: M. 13, 29 Porvoo 1993: A 39-40, C 47-49, D 50-51). The episcopal and clerical vestments are insignia of the rank, duties and rights of both ministries. Thirdly, in the reading of the prayer, the Lord's Prayer and the singing of *Veni Sancte Spiritus* in the vernacular, blessing and divine help are asked for the ordained to enable them to carry out their ministry and fulfil the promises they have made.

Conclusion

This article has presented research on the subject of the ordination of bishops and pastors in the five Nordic national churches at the turn of the twenty-first century.

Because the ordination of a bishop was a pre-Reformation ceremony, it was

---

43. This is particularly obvious in the Norwegian rite for the ordination of pastors and the Swedish and Finnish rites (Table, point 27). The Aaronic blessing is read in connection with the sending out. The meaning of this element is that the Church will not leave bishops or pastors without support. This is stated particularly in the Norwegian rite for the ordination of pastors, in which parishioners are asked to receive a new pastor and to support him or her by praying for them (Table, point 24).

44. Theologically, the concept of 'church' is seen and understood in the Nordic rites as an institution because ordinands are blessed by the ordaining minister, other bishops, pastors and lay people. The Lord's Prayer in the Danish, Norwegian, Icelandic and Finnish rites also points to the Church as the Church of Christ. A sign of this ministry is given to ordinands and they are blessed.

first officiated in accordance with the *Pontificale*, i.e., the book of episcopal services. In the Nordic countries, bishops and pastors continued to be ordained probably by using the rite from a medieval *Pontificale* until the first Reformation rites for their ordination were brought into use between the 1530s and 1550s. The use of these rites and the development of later rites to form two groups of rites used respectively in Denmark, Norway and Iceland and in Sweden and Finland, is given in detail above. All the ordination rites for the ministry of bishops and pastors currently in use in the Nordic national churches were authorised in the 1980s and 1990s as part of the revision of Danish, Norwegian, Icelandic, Swedish and Finnish ordinals.

All Nordic ordination rites used from the sixteenth century to the twentieth century have the same structural content. The rites contain hymns, prayers, Scripture readings, and short sermons, and also the ordination proper (presentation, exhortation, promises and conferral of ministry). Over and above the similarities in the five Nordic rites for the ordination of bishops and pastors there are also differences. As noted above, the rites divide into two groups: based: the Danish ordination tradition and the Swedish tradition, with Norwegian and Icelandic rites included in the Danish group and Finnish rites in the Swedish. Those two traditions can be explained by the history of the five Nordic countries. However, there are some differences within the Danish and Swedish traditions: Danish and Icelandic rites are more conservative than Norwegian rites; likewise Finnish rites by comparison with Swedish rites.

In the five late twentieth century Nordic rites for the ordination of bishops and pastors, the most important verbal differences are in the presentations, exhortations and promises. In the Danish tradition, the presentation and exhortation are more extensive in form and content than their counterparts in the Swedish tradition, in which the presentation is replaced by the reading of the letter of power of attorney and the promises are more extensive in form and content. After the promises, the handshaking takes place between the ordaining minister and the ordinands in the Danish tradition, while the solemn declaration or oath is made or sworn by the ordinands to the ordaining minister in the Swedish rite, differences that have a historical basis.

Each of the five Nordic churches has its own rites for ordaining bishops and they have the same constitutive elements as those for the ordination of pastors. Rites for the ordination of pastors and bishops have also had same structural content. These facts point to a doctrine of the same ministry, but with different duties. Thus, the rite for the ordination of bishops has been seen and understood to be based on that of a pastor's ordination. This is in accordance with Lutheran doctrine on the bishop's ministry as part of that of the pastor and with twentieth century ecumenical understanding. Both ministries have, however, their own preconditions, duties and rights.

In the presentations, the call of the Church is stated as a precondition for both ministries in accordance with Lutheran doctrine. The reading of the letter of power of attorney symbolises this call in the Swedish group of rites for the ordination of bishops. The body that calls, the Church of Christ, is identified very clearly in the Danish group's rites for the ordination of pastors. In the presentations in all the Nordic rites, the call is also introduced in the person of the ordinands. Different preconditions for the ministry of bishop and of pastor are clearly stated in the Swedish rites. Bishops should be elected and nominated and pastors should be called, approved and accepted.

The duties of both ministries are mentioned in the prayers read in connection with the presentations in the Danish group of rites; prayers are read in connection with the short sermon before the presentation in the Finnish rites and in the exhortations of both the Danish and the Swedish groups. Bishops are to uphold the Confession and Doctrine of the Church and be an example for the people in their diocese; they should visit parishes, ordain new pastors and watch over their conduct. Pastors should preach the gospel, dispense sacraments and be an example for people in their congregation and deliver pastoral care. Twentieth century ecumenical documents mention the same duties for the bishop's ministry, also mentioned as duties of the ministry of oversight, or *episkopé*.

In the promises in the Danish and Swedish groups of rites, ordinands are questioned about their willingness to undertake the ministry of the Church, to uphold the doctrine of the Church, to carry out the duties of bishops' and pastors' ministries and to be an example in the diocese or congregation. As their responses are required by the bishop, the ordained are clearly accepted into their ministries by the bishop on behalf of the Church. In other words, new bishops and pastors are chosen by the Church. However, the inner call or vocation of ordinands is declared in the answers to the bishop's questions. Thus all preconditions for accepting ministries are met in the promises. The inner call is mentioned very clearly only in the Icelandic Rite for the ordination of bishops. A contract results from the questions and affirmative answers between the ordaining minister and the ordinands. This contract is confirmed with handshaking in the Danish tradition and a solemn declaration or oath in the Swedish tradition. Thus, the supervising and confirming role of a bishop is emphasised. This is in accordance with the twentieth century understanding of *episkopé*.

Although the conferral of the bishop's and pastor's ministry takes different forms in different Nordic rites, they have the same theological content. The acceptance of ordained bishops and pastors is confirmed by sending them out to their ministries. Furthermore, ordained bishops and pastors are given all the rights and powers of their ministries: the right to dispense sacraments, teach and preach the Word of God, forgive sins and visit parishes, and to ordain new pastors and watch over their conduct. For this reason, the proclamation or handing over of the letter of power of attorney takes place in Norwegian, Swedish and Finnish rites. The sending out for ministry is symbolised by the imposition of hands and vesting in episcopal or clerical vestments. The apostolic succession and blessing of the Church are conveyed symbolically in accordance with the tradition of the Church and ordinands are bound by the apostolic basis of the Church's ministry which is very important in twentieth century ecumenism.

References

ABN. 1920. 1945. *Alterbok for den norske kirke.* 3. opl. Oslo: Forlagt av selskapet til kristlige andagtsbøkers utgivelse.

Andrén, Åke. 1999. *Sveriges kyrkohistoria 3.* Reformationstid. Trelleborg: Verbum.

Borregaard, S. 1970:116-124. The Post-Reformation Developments of Episcopacy in Denmark, Norway, and Iceland. In *Episcopacy in the Lutheran Church? Studies in the Development and Definition of the Office of Church Leadership.* Philadelphia: Fortress Press.

Brodd, Sven-Erik. 1999: 271-276 Kyrkans ämbete under reformationstiden. In *Sveriges kyrkohistoria 3.* Reformationstid. Trelleborg: Vebum.

CR 1685. 1985. Danmarks Og Norges Kirke-Rite. Haderslev: Genudgivet af udvalget for konvent for kirke og theologi 1985

Crichton, J. D. 1972: 288-289. Ordination, Medieval and Roman Catholic. In *A Dictionary of Liturgy & Worship.* Ed. J. G. Davies. Norwich: SCM Press.

Dewailly, L.-M. 1985. Laurentius Petri et la Kyrkoordning de 1571. In *Istina* 30,3. Paris.

Eckerdal, Lars, 1989:13-64. Indvielse til tjeneste i det kirkelige embede and Den danske folkekirkes indvielsesliturgiske tradition i et luthersk liturgisk fællesskab. In *Under bøn og håndspålæggelse. Indvielse af missionærer, diakoner og præster.* Copenhagen: Anis

Baptism, Eucharist and Ministry (BEM). 1982. Faith and Order Paper 111. Geneva: World Council of Churches.

Flatø, Lars. 1982. *Den store liturgirevisjonen i vår kirke 1886-1926. En kirkehistorisk undersøkelse.* Oslo: Land og kirke. Gyldendal norsk forlag.

Fæhn, Helge, 1984: 249-266. Liturgiene ved preste- og bispevielse i Norge. Fra reformasjonen till Alterboken 1920. In *Norsk Teologisk Tidsskrift 85 (1984)*. Oslo.

Färnström, Emil. 1935. *Om källorna till 1571 års kyrkoordning*. Lund Dissertation: Uppsala.

Färnström, Emil. 1956. *Laurentius Petris handskrivna kyrkordning av år 1561*. Samlingar och studier till svenksa kyrknas historia 34. Lund.

GBN 1986-1991. 1996. *Gudstjenestebok for den norske kirke. II*. Kirkelige handlingar. Oslo. Verbum.

GOD 1987. 2001. *Gudstenesteordning for Den Danske Folkekirke Ritebog from 1987*. Copenhagen: Det Kgl. Vajsenhus' Forlag.

HBF 1963. 1972. *Kyrkohandbok för den Evangelisk-lutherska Kyrkan i Finland III*. Kyrkliga förrättningar. Vasa.

HBF 1984. 1985. *Kyrkohandbok för den Evangelisk-lutherska Kyrkan i Finland III*. Vasa.

HBI 1980. 1981. *Handbók. Íslensku kirkjunnar*. Reykjavik.

HBS 1894. 1894. *Handbok för svenska kyrkan*. Stadfäst af Konungen år 1894. Lund.

HBS 1942. 1942. *Den svenska kyrkohandboken*. Stadfäst av Konungen år 1942. Uppsala.

HBS 1987. 1988. *Den svenska kyrkohandboken. II*. Vignings-, Sändnings-, Mottagnings- och Invigningshandlingar. Stockholm: Verbum.

Johansson, Hilding. 1956: 203-205. [En Recension av] Den pontifikala liturgin i Lund och Roskilde under medeltiden. In *Kyrkohistorisk årsskrift 1956*.

Kjöllerström, Sven. 1971: 201-277. Laurentius Petris Kyrkoordning 1571-1971. Tillkomst och användning. In *Den svenska kyrkoordningen jämte studier kring tillkomst, innehåll och användning*. Ed. Sven Kjöllerström. Lund: Håkan Ohlsson Förlag.

Kirkollisten toimitusten kirja II, 2001. *Suomen evankelis-luterilaisen kirkon kirkkokäsikirja III.Kirkollisten toimitusten kirja II. Vihkimiset, virkaan asettamiset ja tehtävään siunaamiset*. Suomen evankelis-luterilaisen kirkon kirkolliskokouksen vuonna 1988 asettaman käsikirjakomitena ehdotus. Jyväskylä

KKE 1859. *Kirkko-Käsikirja, jossa säätään, miten Jumalapalvelus ... Esitys*. Turku.

KK 1817. 1829. *Käsi-Kirja, jossa säätään, kuinga Jumalan-palvelus ...* Stockholm 1817.

KK 1886. 1888. *Kirkko-Käsikirja, jossa säädetään, miten Jumalanpalvelus ... 1886*. Ohjepainos. Helsinki.

KK 1913. 1941. *Suomen evankelis-luterilaisen kirkon kirkkokäsikirja*. Porvoo.

KK 1963. 1964. *Kirkollisten toimitusten kirja. XIX yleisen kirkolliskokouksen mukaisesti toimitetu ohjepainos. Pieksämäki:Suomen kirkon sisälähetysseura.*

Knuutila, Jyrki. 1990. *Avioliitto oikeudellisena ja kirkollisena instituutiona Suomessa vuoteen 1629.* Suomen kirkkohistoriallisen seuran toimituksia 151. Jyväskylä.

KL 1686. 1687. Kyrkio-Lag och Ordning. Stockholm.

KO 1537/1539. 1989. *Kirkeordinansen. Det danske Udkast til Kirkeordinansen (1537). Ordinatio Ecclesiastica Regnorum Daniæ e Norwegiæ et Ducatum Sleswecensis Holtsatiæ. (1537). Den danske Kirkeordinans (1539).* Tekstudgave med indledning og noter ved Martin Schwarz Lausten. Odense: Akademisk Forlag.

KO 1571. 1971. *Den svenska kyrkoordningen jämte studier kring tillkomst, innehåll och användning.* Ed. Sven Kjöllerström. Lund: Håkan Ohlssons Förlag.

KR 1685. 1985. *Danmarks Og Norgis Kirke-Rite.* Genudgivet af udvalged for konvent for kirkr og theologi 1985. Haderslev.

Kyrkohandboksgruppens förslag. 2000. *Kyrkohandboksgruppens förslag till Kyrkohandbok för Svenska kyrkan. Gudstjänstordning.* Svenska kyrkansa utredningar 2000:1. Stockholm.

Lempiäinen, Pentti. 1985. *Pyhät toimitukset.* 2. uud. p. Rauma. Kirjapaja.

Lindhard, P. G. 1977. De danske ordinations Riter. In *Kirkehistoriske samlinger 1977.*

Molland, E. 1954: 349. Alterbok. In *Aschehougs konversasjons leksikon I.* 4. Oslo: Forlagt av H. Aschehoug et co (W. Nygaard).

Oftestad, Bernt T. & Rasmussen, Tarald & Schumacher, Jan. 1991: 221-295. *Norsk kirkehistorie.* Oslo: Universitetsforlaget.

Parvio, Martti. 1970: 33-63. Piispanvirka Suomessa reformaation murroksessa. In *Finska kyrkohistoriska samfundets årsskrift 58-59 (1968-1969).* (English version: Parvio, Martti 1970: 125-137. The Post-Reformation Developments of Episcopacy in Sweden, Finland, and the Baltic States. In *Episcopacy in the Lutheran Church? Studies in the Development and Definition of the Office of Church Leadership.* Philadelphia: Fortress Press.

Parvio, Martti. 1976:51-65. Kirkon virka Suomessa reformaation murroskautena. In *XX varsinaisen kirkolliskokouksen asettaman virkakomitean loppumietintö. Liite B.* Suomen evankelis-luterilaisen kirkon kirkolliskokous. Kevätistunto 1976. Pieksämäki.

Pedersen, Jørgen. 1948: 342-343. Alterbog. In *Raunkjærs konversations leksikon. I.* Copenhagen: Det danske forlag.

Pernler, Sven-Erik. 1999. *Sveriges kyrkohistoria 2.* Hög- och senmedeltid. Trelleborg: Vebum.

Perustelut. 2001. *Perustelut. Kirkolliskokouksen vuonna 1988 asettaman käsikir-jakomitean ehdotus Kirkollisten toimitusten kirjaksi.* Suomen evankelis-lute-rilaisen kirkon keskushallinto. Sarja A 2001:2. Helsinki.

Puglisi, James F. 1998. *The Process of Admission to ordained Ministry. A Com-parative Study, vol. II: The First Lutheran, Reformed, Anglican and Wesleyan Rites.* (Collegeville, Minn.: Liturgical Press).

RBD 1991. 2001. *Gudstjenesteordning for Den Danske Folkekirke. Ritebog.* Copenhagen: Det Kgl. Vajsenhus' Forlag.

Rietschel, Gorg (& Graff, Paul). 1951. *Lehrbuch der Liturgik. I. Die Lehre vom Gemeindegottesdiest.* 2. neuarbeite Auflage von Paul Graff. Göttingen: Van-denhoeck & Ruprecht.

von Sicard, E. J. R. H. S. 1972: 293-294. Ordination, Lutheran. In *A Dic-tionary of Liturgy & Worship.* Ed. J. G. Davies. Norwich: SCM Press.

Smith, Ralph F. 2000. *Luther, Ministry and Ordination Rites in the Early Ref-ormation Church.* Renaissance and Baroque Studies and Texts 15. New York: Peter Lang.

Strömberg, Bengt. 1955. *Den pontifikala liturgin i Lund och Roskilde under medeltiden.* Studia theologica Lundensia. Skrifter utgivna av teologiska fakulteten i Lund. Lund: C W K Gleerup.

Together in Ministry and Mission. 1993. The Porvoo Common Statement with Essays on Church and Ministry in Northern Europe. London: Church House Publishing.

VC II. 1996. *Vatican Council II. Volume I. The Conciliar and Postconciliar Documents.* New Revised Edition. The Vatican Collection. Northport, New York & Dublin, Ireland: Costello Publishing Company, Inc. & Do-minican Publications.

Venge, Mikael. 1980. Tiden fra 1523 til 1559. In *Danmarks historie 2:1. Tiden 1340-1648. Første halvbind: 1340-1559.* Tønder: Gyldendal.

Villadsen, Holger. 1994: 307. Alterbog. In *Den Store Danske Encyklopædi I.* Haslev: Danmarks nationalleksikon.

Yelverton, Eric E. 1958. *An Archbishop of the Reformation. Laurentius Petri Nericius, Archbishop of Uppsala 1531-1573. A Study of His Liturgical Projects.* London: Epworth Press.

Appendix

Ordination Rites in the Danish and Swedish traditions from the Reformation to the mid-20th Century

Point	The Danish Tradition (Reformation to mid-20th Century[1]	The Swedish tradition (Reformation to mid-20th Century[2]
1.	Hymn	Hymn
2a.	Greeting (between liturgical leader and congregation)	
2b.		Entrance[3]
3.	Prayer	Prayer
4.	Scripture reading from an Epistle	
5.	Hymn	
6.	Short sermon	Short sermon
7a.		Reading of King's letter of power of attorney (for a bishop's ordination)
7b.	Presentation (announcement of the name of the candidate for ordination)	Presentation
8.	Call for prayer and a prayer	
9.	Lord's Prayer	
10a.	*Veni Sancte Spiritus*	
10b.	Hymn	
11.	Scripture reading from the Psalter	
12.	Prayer	
13.	Scripture reading	Scripture reading
14a.		Creed (bishop's ordination)
14b.		Creed (pastor's ordination)
15.	Exhortation on the ministry of a bishop/ pastor	Exhortation
16a.	Promises (candidates respond: 'Yes') – in accordance with the exhortation	Promises (candidates respond – 'Yes'
16b.	Handshake with the bishop and those assisting him	Oath

17a.		Conferral of bishop's office and handing over of King's letter of power of attorney
17b.	Conferral of the ministry of the Church	Conferral of ministry and bishop's letter of power of attorney
18.	Ordination prayer (concluding with the Lord's Prayer) during the laying-on of hands	Hymn (*Veni Sancte Spiritus* in the vernacular)[4], Lord's Prayer and a prayer during the laying-on of hands
19.		Sending out (for a pastor)
20.		Aaronic blessing
21.	Hymn	Hymn
22.	Sermon	
23.	Holy Communion	Holy Communion

1. 7b, 10a, 12-13, 15-16a 18, 21, 23 were included in *KO 1537/1539*. 4, 9, 11, 16b, 17b, 22 were added in *CR 1685*. 1-2a, 3, 5-6, 10b came into use in *RB 1898*. 9 and 21 are to be found only in *CR 1685*. (KO 1537/39 (1989): 112-114, 141-144, 188-191, 239-243; CR 1985 (1985): 119130; Lindhard 1977: 7-50; Eckerdal 1989: 20-21; Puglisi 1996: 32-38).

2. 6-7, 7b, 13, 7a, 14a, 15, 17b, 18 and 19 were included in the ordination rites in *KO 1571*. 16b was added in *KL 1686*. 1-2b, 7a, 14b, 17a and 20 were appended in *HBS 1811*. Many of them were already in use in the 18th and 19th Centuries. In KO 1571 and KL 1686, the short sermon and litany were preceded by a prayer. The Creed (point 14a) was read at the ordination of bishops in *KO 1571* and *KL 1686* after the promises. (KO 1571 (1971), 142-149, 169-173; KL 1686 (1986), XXI § 1-3, XXII § 1-2; HBS 1894: 210-219, 221-231; HBS 1942.333-359, Kjöllerström 1971: 252-263, 271-277. See also Puglisi 1996: 61–62).

3. A prayer was included at the entrance in the ordination rite for bishops in HBS 1894 and in both ordination rites in HBS 1942.

4. The *Veni, Sancte Spiritus* sung in the vernacular was included in the Swedish tradition from HBS 1811. However, a corresponding hymn in the vernacular (*'Nw bidie wij then helge And'*) is sung after the ordination proper, as an Introit hymn for the Holy Communion in KO 1571 and KL 1686.

Rites for the Ordination of Priests and Bishops in the Evangelical-Lutheran Church of Iceland

Einar Sigurbjörnsson and Kristján Valur Ingólfsson

When a new Service Book for the Evangelical-Lutheran Church of Iceland was published in 1910, it contained rites for the ordination of priests and bishops (*Helgisiðabók* 1910). This was the first time that rites for ordination had been published in an authorized Service Book. Until then the ordination rites were only in manuscripts used by the bishops themselves. From the introduction of the Church Order of Christian III in 1541, the rite for the ordination of priests followed that of the Church Order. The Danish-Norwegian Rite of 1685, although not formally ratified in Iceland, was soon, however, translated into Icelandic and the rite for the ordination of priests was used in Iceland. With two exceptions, Icelandic bishops were ordained in Copenhagen from 1540-1889, yet the rites for the ordination of bishops in the Church Order and in the 1685 Rite were translated into Icelandic. Until the publication of the Liturgical Handbook of the Icelandic Church in 1981, the ordination rites were only for priests and bishops (*Handbók* 1981). The 1981 Handbook added a rite for the ordination of deacons (*Handbók* 1981, 183-206).[1]

The Lutheran Reformation

At the time of the Reformation Iceland was part of the Danish-Norwegian Kingdom. Hence it was the Danish Church Order of 1537 that was inaugu-

---

1. On the diaconate in Iceland, see Olsen (Part II.3).

rated in Iceland.[2] During the Middle Ages, Iceland was divided into two dioceses, Skálholt, which comprised three-quarters of the country, and Hólar, which comprised one quarter. This division remained until 1801 when the See of Hólar was abolished by royal decree and the country made into one diocese with the See in the recently founded town of Reykjavík, to which the Skálholt See was moved by royal decree in 1785. The first Lutheran Bishop in Iceland, Gissur Einarsson (d. 1546) was appointed Bishop of Skálholt in 1540. He translated the Church Order from Latin into Icelandic and introduced it to the Icelandic Parliament, the *Althing*, in 1541. The *Althing* ratified it for the Skálholt diocese but Hólar diocese did not accept the Reformation for another ten years.

The first translation of the Church Order was not a complete one: it omitted some parts which were regarded as unnecessary for the Icelandic situation. It included the rite for the ordination of priests but not that for the ordination of bishops. Later in the sixteenth century, a complete translation was made containing also the rite for the ordination of bishops.[3] In the Church Order of 1537 there was a chapter on Norway, in which it was promised that a special Church Order would be made for Norway.[4] This happened in 1607. The Norwegian Church Order was ratified by Christian IV on 2nd July 1607 and introduced into Iceland by a royal decree of 29th November 1622 (*Kirkeordinansen av 1607, 1985; Kirkeordinants for Norge 1853, 150-170*). It was published in Iceland in 1635 (*Ein Kyrkiu* 1635; Manuscript JS 165. fol). This new order did not alter the liturgical guidelines or the ordination rites.

Gissur Einarsson's translation of the Church Order together with the translation of the New Testament in 1540 by Oddur Gottskálksson are very important both for the liturgical history of the Icelandic Church and for the cultural and literary history of the people. They enabled Icelanders to develop worship in their native language, develop hymnody and retain the continuity with the literary heritage of the Middle Ages in the Sagas and epic poems as well as biblical, hymnic and liturgical matters (Magnús Már Lárusson 1949,

2. *Kirkjuordinanzía Kristjáns konungs hins III.* Gissur Einarsson's translation is found in *Diplomatarium islandicum* X: 117-167. (*Diplomatarium islandicum* hereafter abbreviated as DI). See Lausten 1989.
3. DI X: 167-255; the Latin original in DI X: 257-328. Gissur Einarsson's translation contained Bugenhagen's chapters on canons and monasteries which were omitted in the later translation as the monasteries had then been abolished.
4. DI X: 243-244, 300; this chapter was omitted by Gissur Einarsson. See also Lausten 1989,137 (Latin text) and 233-234 (Danish text and editor's note).

1957; Steingrímur J. Þorsteinsson 1950; Guðrún Kvaran 1990; Stefán Karlsson 1985, 1990; Svavar Sigmundsson 1990; Þórir Óskarsson 1990).

In their work on the translation of liturgical texts the Icelandic Reformers made use of this heritage and used the terminology that had been used in medieval translations. Research on the earliest Reformation liturgies has shown that the Icelanders were very independent of the Danes in liturgical matters and in many ways developed their own liturgies (Einar Sigurbjörnsson 1979a, 1987; Arngrímur Jónsson 1993).

Until the nineteenth century, there were three liturgical books in Iceland (Páll Eggert Ólason 1924; Einar Sigurbjörnsson 1979b, 1996, 165-175):

The Service Book (*Graduale-Messusöngsbók* (Gradual)) contained the rites for the liturgy on Sundays and feast days together with hymns for the liturgy on each holy day (first published 1594).

The Priests' Manual (*Handbók fyrir presta á Íslandi*, (Manuale)) contained the lessons for each Sunday and holy day and the rite for baptism and so on – corresponding to the Danish *Alterbog* (published several times from the end of the sixteenth century).

The Hymnal (*Sálmabók*) which was used for devotions in the home and for private devotions (first edition 1589).

In 1801 the Gradual and the Hymnal were combined into one, as had been the case in Denmark for a long time, but the Priests' Manual continued to be published. In the twentieth century the Manual and the Service Book or order for worship were combined into one book which went through three editions in 1910, 1934 and 1981. The first two editions were published under the title *Helgisiðabók* (Liturgical Book) and the latest edition under the title *Handbók* (Handbook).

The Church Order

The ordination liturgies in the Church Order are faithful translations of the Latin original[5]. In Gissur Einarsson's translation, the chapter on the ordination of priests has the heading: '*Hvernig kirkjuþjenararnir skulu til skikkast, því að prestvíglsan er ekki annað heldur en kirkjunnar skikkan að kalla nokkurn til*

---

5. Cf. Iversen (Part II.6.)

orðsins þjónustu og helgana'.[6] This heading is a verbatim translation of the Latin title.[7] In the Preface where the contents of the Order are described, the chapter on ordination, which in Latin has the heading *'Ritus instituendi ministros'*, is called in Icelandic: *'Hvernig að vígja á kennimenn'* (DI X: 127). *'Kennimenn'* (plural of *'kennimaður'*, literally 'teacher', 'preacher') was in medieval litera- ture often used as a translation of *'sacerdos'* ('priest') both in biblical material, homilies and the Sagas. In the more recent translation this topic is called *'Um prestavígslu'*.[8] Also in the more recent translation the chapter on ordination has the heading: *'Um kirkjunnar þjenara, hvernig þeir skulu útveljast og vígjast'.*[9] Here the content of the chapter is put into the heading and the theological explanation of what ordination is forms the first sentence of the chapter: *'Fyrir því að prestavígslan er ekkert annað en ein skikkan í kristilegri kirkju með hverri að nokkrar persónur kallast til að þjóna Guðs orði og sakramentunum ...'.*[10]

The word used for ordination is the Old Icelandic and Nordic word *'vígsla'* with the verb *'vígja'.* In the Medieval Sagas and stories of bishops and in the translations of the legends of the saints these words are used about the ordi- nation of clergy and also the consecration of churches, blessings of houses and other objects. The Saga of the saintly Bishop Guðmundur Arason of Hólar (d. 1236) is interesting in this respect (Guðni Jónsson 1948, 177-410, e.g. 251- 252). Guðmundur blessed wells and springs all over the country and the verb used is *'vígja'.* In the more recent translation of the Church Order the verb *'ordinerast'* is used once.[11] This is in the introduction to the service of ordi- nation when it says that the person is to be ordained before the altar. Then the words *'ordinerast og skikkast'* ('to be ordained and appointed' or 'sent') are used.

In the rite for the ordination of priests, both translations render *'presbyter'* as *'prestur'* ('priest') and *'minister'* as *'þjenari'* ('minister', 'servant'). *'Þjenari'*,

---

6. 'How the ministers of the church shall be appointed because ordination of priests is nothing other than the custom of the church to call someone to the service of the word and sacraments', DI X: 143 (orthography modernized); the chapter on ordination is in DI X: 143-148. It is interesting that Gissur Einarsson translates 'sacrament' with the word *'helgan'* which literally means 'sanctification'.
7. *'Ritus instituendi ministros. Est autem ordinatio nihil aliud quam ritus ecclesiasticus vo- candi aliquem in ministerium Verbi & Sacramentorum, ...'* DI X: 275.
8. DI X: 177; cf. the Latin text, 263.
9. 'On the ministers of the Church, how they are to be elected and ordained.' DI X: 199 (orthography modernized); the chapter on ordination is in DI X: 199-205.
10. 'Since the ordination of priests is nothing other than a custom in the Christian Church by which some persons are called to serve the Word of God and the Sacraments . . .'
11. Cf. Einar Sigurbjörnsson (Part II.1).

however, soon disappeared and in the Gradual published in 1594, the word *'prestur'* is always used. Gissur follows the Latin original faithfully and uses 'superintendent' or *'superattendent'* where it appears in the original and 'bishop' where it says *'episcopus'* in the original. The more recent translation of the rite does the same, except in the rite for the ordination of priests, where the word 'bishop' is always used even where the original says superintendent.

As mentioned above, Gissur Einarsson did not translate the rite for the ordination of bishops. This appears first in the more recent translation (DI X: 249-254.). The heading of the chapter is: *'Með þessum eftirfylgjandi seremoníum skal einn superattendens vígjast á einhverjum sunnudegi eður á nokkurn annan helgan dag'.*[12] In the text itself the word 'bishop' is used and not 'superintendent' even if that is the word in the original. When the rite says that the passage from the chapter on the salaries of bishops is to be read explaining their duties, the beginning of that reading is interesting. The Latin original reads: *'Quia vero superattendentes, qui veri sunt ecclesiarum episcopi vel archepiscopi ...'.* (DI X: 292.). The translation reads: *'En með því að biskuparnir (sem vera skulu þeir réttu superattendentes, umsjónarmenn og erkibiskupar) ...'.*[13]

Although the rite for the ordination of bishops in the Church Order was translated, Icelandic bishops were ordained in Copenhagen after having been elected by the Icelandic *Althing* or Parliament. After the introduction of hereditary monarchy in 1661, where the king was to be the sole ruler of the realm, the *Althing* lost some of its prestige and it became more common that interested men applied for the bishoprics. One such person, Jón Vigfússon (1643-1690, bishop from 1684), a former judge who had lost his office but regained the king's favour, came in the summer of 1674 to the Bishop of Skálholt, Brynjólfur Sveinsson (1605-1675, bishop from 1639), with two letters from the king. One was a letter of appointment as Bishop of Hólar at the next vacancy. The other was a letter to Brynjólfur Sveinsson ordering him to ordain Jón Vigfússon. Brynjólfur Sveinsson, a staunch upholder of the rights of Iceland and the freedom of the church, evidently sensed a dangerous development here but did not disobey the king and ordained Jón Vigfússon as

---

12. 'By these ceremonies shall a superintendent be ordained on some Sunday or another holy day.' The Latin reads: *'Hisce cerimoniis ordinabitur publice Superintendens, dominica die aut festo'.* DI X: 303.
13. 'But since the bishops (who are to be the right superintendents, overseers and archbishops) ...' DI X: 230.

bishop on 23rd August 1674. However, his real feeling was probably shown in the selection of text for his sermon, (John 10.1):[14]

> Truly, truly, I say unto you, he who does not enter the sheepfold by the door but climbs in by another way, that man is a thief and a robber (Jón Halldórsson I 1903-1910, 291; Þórhallur Guttormsson 1973, 110).

The 1685 Rite

The Danish-Norwegian Church Rite of 1685[15] was never formally authorized in Iceland but it did have a great deal of influence on liturgical development in the eighteenth century (Jón Pjetursson 1890, 73; Einar Arnórsson 1912, 9; Björn Magnússon 1954; Einar Sigurbjörnsson 1996, 38). The Rite was soon translated and the rite for the ordination of priests was used in Iceland. The Latin oath was signed by all ordained priests.[16] Although the rite for the ordination of bishops was also translated, no bishop was ordained in Iceland except in 1797 when the last bishop appointed to the See of Skálholt, in accordance with a royal decree, was ordained in Hólar by the bishop there (Lovsamling 1855, 652-653; Einar Sigurbjörnsson 2000b). At the beginning of the eighteenth century the Icelandic bishops were appointed to draw up liturgical rites for Iceland and did so, but these were never formally ratified for Iceland (Manuscripts Lbs 5 fol; Lbs 410 4to). These proposed rites did not include ordination rites.

The Icelandic translation of the 1685 Danish Rite is very faithful to the original. The first sentence in the rite for the ordination of bishops reads: *'Biskuparnir skulu* innvígjast *til síns embættis ...'*, which is a literal translation of the Danish *'indvies'* ('to be consecrated'). In the rubrics the Latin words *'ordinator'* and *'ordinandus'* are not translated. The same is the case with the ordination of priests. The first sentence reads: *'Prestarnir* ordinerast *það snarasta ske kann ...'.* In the rubrics the words *'ordination'*, *'ordinandus'* and *'ordinator'* are not translated. This rite was used for ordinations in Iceland until the publication of the Service Book in 1910. Although the rite suggests that priests are to be ordained on a Wednesday or a Friday the custom in

---

14. Biblical quotations are from the *Revised Standard Version of the Bible* (New York, 1952).
15. Cf. Iversen (Part II.6).
16. Translations of the 1685 Rite containing the rite for the ordination of priests are found in Manuscripts Lbs 381.8vo and JS 13. 4to. The Manuscripts Lbs 496.4to and Lbs 401.4to are the same translations but also contain the rite for the ordination of bishops; I use here Lbs 496 4to.

Iceland was that priests were always ordained on a Sunday (Danmarks 1985, 127; Lbs 496 4to).

The ordination rites in both the Church Order and the 1685 Rite describe how ministers of the Church are made. There is a clear distinction between benefice and ministry. The benefice is presented by the secular authority but the ministry is conferred upon the person by the Church itself. The priests are to be ministers of the gospel in the local church; the bishops are made ministers of oversight ('episkopé') in the Church. Thus their ministry expresses the unity of the Church in the region or the catholicity of the Church.

The Nineteenth Century

The nineteenth century was the age of nationalism. In Iceland national awakening was very strongly connected with the demand for independence from Denmark. One form of Icelandic nationalism was linguistic purism, with the demand to purify the language of Danish words and expressions. Although the Icelandic language had changed very little as far as grammar and vocabulary is concerned, several expressions had been influenced by Danish and German. This was evident in the Bible, in hymns, and in the rites of the church. As nationalism increased towards the turn of the century, voices critical of religion in general and Christianity in particular became louder. Christianity was not only criticized for being outdated as a primitive world view, but also for being a foreign element. The Lutheran Church was especially criticized for having been forced upon the nation by a foreign king. The Bishop of Iceland who was appointed by the king to sit in the *Althing* was often criticized for being the king's representative and for acting contrary to national interest as far as demands for independence were concerned.

In 1866 Bishop Pétur Pétursson asked the Ministry for Church Affairs in Copenhagen for permission to revise the old Priests' Manual, a revision he said was necessary because of the new 1866 translation of the Bible and also for linguistic reasons (*Íslands biskupsdæmis* 1866-67, 89). The revised manual was published in 1869 (second edition 1879): *Handbók fyrir presta á Íslandi. Endurskoðuð*.

However, Pétur Pétursson's revision is more radical than the letter suggests and is in fact a new manual. What was new was mostly based on Bishop Mynster's proposal for a new Rite for Denmark in 1839: *Udkast til en Alterbog og et Kirke-Ritual for Danmark* (Einar Sigurbjörnsson 2000a; Jón Helgason

1922, 191-92*)*. This manual did not contain ordination rites but it did contain a rite for the dedication of churches based on Mynster's proposal.[17]

In 1874, on the occasion of the 1000th anniversary of the settlement of Iceland, King Christian IX of Denmark gave the Icelanders a constitution on matters pertaining to Iceland.[18] Among these special matters were ecclesiastical affairs and, according to § 45 of the Constitution, 'the Evangelical- Lutheran Church is the national Church of Iceland'.[19] The newly appointed legislature of Iceland very soon began revising laws pertaining to the Church (Magnús Jónsson 1952; Einar Sigurbjörnsson 1996, 39-41). Reform of the hymnal and of the liturgy was also regarded as urgent not least for purist and literary reasons (Einar Sigurbjörnsson 2000b, 2000c). A new hymnal was published in 1886, and in 1892 a committee was established to revise the liturgy and rites of the church. This committee published its suggestions or proposal for a new Service Book in 1897 which, however, did not contain ordination rites (Frumvarp 1897). The Service Book based on these proposals was first published in 1910 and authorized by the king on 22nd June.[20] In addition to the liturgy, collects, lessons and rites performed by priests, it also contained ordination rites for both priests and bishops, the first ordination rites published in Iceland (*Helgisiðabók* 1910, 106-112, 113-121).

Two years before the publication of the Service Book, the ordination of a bishop took place in Reykjavík Cathedral when Þórhallur Bjarnarson was ordained on 4th October 1908, the third episcopal ordination to take place in Iceland. On his appointment as bishop, Þórhallur Bjarnarson (1855-1916) insisted on being ordained in Iceland since his predecessor, Hallgrímur Sveinsson (1841-1909) was still alive and able to perform the ceremony. When Hallgrímur was appointed bishop in 1889 he went for his ordination to

---

17. *Handbók fyrir presta á Íslandi* (1969), 158-159. It is probable that Pétur Pétursson translated the rite for the ordination of priests, cf. below on the Service Book of 1910. Yet, I have not been able to find any manuscript of the Priests' Manual of 1869 among Pétur Pétursson's manuscripts in the Archives of the University-National Library of Iceland.

18. 'Stjórnarskrá um hin sérstaklegu málefni Íslands' (*Tíðindi* 1870-75, 3: 698-711). Iceland got home rule in 1904, independence in personal union with Denmark in 1918 and became a republic in 1944.

19. *Tíðindi* 1870-75, 3: 708. This paragraph is now no. 62 in the Constitution of the Republic of Iceland, *Lagasafn. Íslensk lög 1. október 1999*, 3.

20. Letter from the government to the Bishop of Iceland informing him of the king's permission to use the Service Book. *Stjórnartíðindi fyrir Ísland árið 1910 – Regjeringstidende for Island 1910*. Reykjavík. Nr. 89/1910, p. 164.

Copenhagen as had been the rule ever since the Reformation although his predecessor, Pétur Pétursson, was also still alive and would have been able to ordain his successor. Yet, nobody officially mentioned that he be ordained in Iceland. In 1908, the situation was different. Nationalism was at its highest. In the summer of 1908 a very decisive vote about the relationship with Denmark had taken place which the party that wanted independence had won by a large majority. If at this critical moment the newly elected bishop had gone to Denmark for his ordination, this would have caused further criticism of the church for being the representative of the foreign power in the country. In 1909 a law was passed stating that two suffragan bishops should be appointed, one for each of the two old dioceses, who would be able to ordain the Bishop of Iceland.[21]

In an article about the ordination of 1908 in the journal *Nýtt Kirkjublað* there is a good description of the service. There it says that the rite was a translation from the Danish Service Book but that the hymns sung were new. These new hymns are a cantata written by the poet priest and later suffragan bishop Valdimar Briem (1848-1930) and the music composed by the composer and organist Sigfús Einarsson (1877-1939) (*Nýtt kirkjublað* 1908, 235-240). When the Service Book was published two years later, the rite for the ordination of bishops was the same as had been used for the ordination of Þórhallur Bjarnarson two years previously, with only slight changes.

The 1910 Service Book: The Ordination of Priests

If the rite for the ordination of bishops is a translation of the latest Danish rite, the rite for the ordination of priests depends a great deal on the rite in the Mynster proposal of 1839 and at the same times retains some features of the 1685 Rite. In all probability, Bishop Pétur Pétursson had translated the rite with his work on the above mentioned 1869 Manual.

According to the Service Book the ordination of priests is to take place on a Sunday. It is interesting that it says in the introductory rubric that the ordinands are to assemble in the sacristy half an hour before the service begins for a confession of sins: at that time confession before Holy Communion was no longer obligatory but optional (*Helgisiðabók* 1910, 106, 90). The ordinands, the assistants (who were two or four priests) and the bishop are robed

---

21. At first the suffragan bishops continued to serve as priests in their parishes although they had been ordained bishops. Since 1990 the suffragan bishops have had a permanent ministry and occupy the old episcopal sees of Hólar and Skálholt.

in albs.[22] There is no mention of a cope but it is probably presupposed that the bishop would wear one as that had always been the case.

The service is to begin in a traditional manner with salutation and collect but, instead of the collect of the day, there is a special collect at the beginning which is a translation of the collect in Mynster's proposal of 1839:

> All loving God, the Father of our Lord Jesus Christ, let the ministers of the word propagate the salutary doctrine of your only Son from one generation to another. Give to the priests of the congregation the spirit of your wisdom, the spirit of strength and humility, so that they may in faithfulness guard the flock which Jesus Christ has bought with his own blood. Grant them your grace that they in all diligence guard themselves, so that they who are to lead others on the way to salvation will not themselves perish. Hear us, merciful Father, as we call upon you for them and for ourselves and for your Christian Church, so that your light will always shine brightly for us and your name be praised now and forever.[23]

The Epistle read is Heb. 13.17-18 as proposed by Mynster (*Helgisiðabók* 1910, 107; Mynster 1839, 90).

After the presentation, the ordinands, assisting priests and the bishop proceed into the church where the ordinands are vested in chasubles. During the procession a special hymn is sung, a hymn written in the seventeenth century and based on Ps 117. The author was Jón Þorsteinsson called a martyr, though in fact he was killed by Algerian pirates who plundered his parish of Vestmannaeyjar in 1627. The verse was rewritten by Helgi Hálfdánarson in 1886 and a melody composed by Cathedral organist Pétur Guðjonsen (1812-1877). There follows the traditional versicles and responses, beginning *Veni, sancte Spiritus* and the collect. The rite suggests that this is to be chanted in Icelandic and gives the Latin original in an appendix. Then the bishop reads the mandatory ordination text which is Titus 1.5-9 and thereafter his own text for his sermon. No other scriptural texts are read.

After his sermon, the bishop reads the ordination oath:

> I now exhort you seriously to preach the Word of God purely and correctly as it is found in the prophetic and apostolic writings and in the spirit of our

---

22. In Icelandic, the assisting priests are called ordination witnesses, *'vígsluvottar'*.
23. *Helgisiðabók* 1910, 106; cf. Mynster 1839, 90. This collect, in turn, is based on the one in the rite for the ordination of bishops by Bishop Münter, 1830.

Evangelical-Lutheran Church; to administer with deference the holy sacraments as Christ Himself instituted them. I ask you to admonish your hearers with love and with seriousness, that you teach the youth dutifully the holy truths of the Christian Faith, that you show compassion to those who are weak, and that in all things you serve your congregations with love. Try as you can to be to them of good example in true faith and sincere love and in all Christian virtues.[24]

The following question is more extensive than the one in the Danish Service Book:

> By virtue of my office I ask you now if you with a sincere heart promise me to do this and at the same time fulfil all the duties that may be bestowed upon you together with the ministry according to the grace that God will give unto you?

When the ordinands have confirmed their promise by joining hands with the bishop and the assisting priests they kneel and the bishop bestows the ministry upon them by the traditional Danish formula. The call to prayer is, however, different from the version in Mynster's proposal and the Danish rite. Here it has the form of a blessing:

> The Almighty, all loving God *grant to you* through Jesus Christ strength to perform this holy ministry with all vigilance and diligence in uprightness and saving teaching to the glory of Jesus' name and to the building up of His church among us. Let us now together pray for this with Jesus' own prayer:

There follows the Lord's Prayer with the laying-on of hands and the ordination prayer. This is the old prayer from the 1685 Rite. The one in Mynster's proposal (and also the prayer in the Danish ordination rite of 1898) refers to the ordinand as being ordained to N.N. congregation which reduces the universal significance of the act of ordination. The Icelandic rite retains the more universal outlook of the original prayer: 'Therefore, we pray your bounteous goodness that you will regard as your minister, the priest N.N. etc. whom we

---

24. It is interesting that the oath does not mention obedience to secular authorities as does the Danish original. On this and the phrase 'the spirit of our Evangelical-Lutheran Church', see below.

in your name have ordained to the holy pastoral and preaching ministry in your congregation'.[25]

After the ordination, one of the newly ordained priests preaches a sermon and the service ends with Holy Communion 'where the newly ordained take communion from the priest who celebrates'.

On the whole, this rite is a translation of Mynster's proposal of 1839 except for the ordination prayer which is from the 1685 Rite. In all probability the rite in the 1910 Service Book is a printed version of the rite used by the Bishops of Iceland since the publication of Pétur Pétursson's Manual in 1869. The influence of purism is very clear. There are no traces of foreign words like *'ordination'*, *'ordinerast'*, *'ordinandus'*, and *'ordinator'*. Instead Icelandic words are used: *'vígsla'*, *'vígja'*, *'kandidat'* and *'biskup'*. As in the Danish tradition, there is no creed – and in view of the liberal influence in Iceland at the time, this would not have been introduced. The rite makes it clear that the ordinands are not ordained priests until after the handing over of the ministry. The rubrics refer to them as *'kandidatar'* ('candidates', 'ordinands') but the rubric introducing the prayer refers to them as *'prestar'* (priests). Yet, the ordinands are vested when they enter the church which corresponds to Danish usage at that time.

The 1910 Service Book: The Ordination Oath

The ordination oath in the 1910 Service Book is based on the Danish oath in the 1685 Rite as it had been used in Iceland until then, but here we notice some interesting omissions and changes. First, the priests are no longer to exhort their congregations to true penitence or conversion and obedience to the correct secular authorities! Secondly, the oath omits the word 'chastity' in the final sentence. Thirdly there is the sentence that preaching is to be consistent with 'the spirit of our Evangelical-Lutheran Church'. This phrase deserves mentioning. From the publication of the 1685 Rite, newly ordained priests had to sign an oath in Latin in which they promised to preach the Word of God purely and correctly according to the Scriptures and in accordance with the Confessional Books of the Danish Churches (*'ecclesiarum danicarum'*). In 1888 this oath was translated into Icelandic and in the translation the expression 'Danish Churches' was in the spirit of nationalism rendered as 'our Church' (Stjórnartíðindi 1888, 124-125). In Iceland, theological liberalism became very strong at the beginning of the twentieth century, drawing a radical

---

25. *Helgisiðabók* (1910), 111. Contrast Mynster 1839, 100 and the Danish rite of 1898, Udtog 1899, 21.

distinction between the Gospel of Jesus Christ and the dogmas and confessions of the Church (Haraldur Níelsson 1908). In 1909, at the annual general meeting to which the bishop calls the priests of the diocese (in Iceland this meeting is called the Synod), Jón Helgason (1868-1941), then professor of theology and later Bishop of Iceland, lectured on the Confessions of the Church and concluded that these in many ways were in opposition to the Gospel of Christ and, moreover, and in particular the Confessions of the Lutheran Church, had been forced upon the nation by an alien authority, the King of Denmark. Besides, since the 1685 Rite had never been formally authorized in Iceland, the bishops had had the oath signed illegally because 'our church' did not have any Confessions at all.[26] The Synod thus concluded that the priests' oath should be abolished. At the same time it was suggested that the phrase 'in the spirit of our Evangelical-Lutheran Church' should be added to the ordination oath as an explanation of the promise to preach the word of God purely and correctly. The spirit of the Evangelical-Lutheran Church was defined as 'the Spirit of Worms', that is, Luther standing up against all authorities and appealing only to his conscience. Thus the liberals concluded that priests were to preach the Gospel of Christ as their conscience allowed them, unbound by any other authority (Sigurður P. Sívertsen 1925, 2-4).

The 1910 Service Book: Ordination of Bishops

The rite for the ordination of bishops is the same as had been used at Þórhallur Bjarnason's ordination in 1908 and is a faithful translation of the Danish Rite of 1898 with the exception of the hymns.[27] The cantata which had been written for that occasion by Valdimar Briem and Sigfús Einarsson was not used. Instead another hymn is used, 'Andinn Guðs lifanda af himnanna hæð', a translation by another priest-poet, Stefán Thorarensen (1831-1892) of a hymn by Grundtvig, 'Du som gaar ud fra den levende Gud' which, in turn, is a translation of an English missionary hymn by James Montgomery (1771-1854), 'O, Spirit of the Living God'.[28]

As in the Danish original, the prayers and addresses in the rite for the ordination of bishops emphasize that the first duty of a bishop is to be 'pastor pastorum'. When in the ordination prayer, the Danish original says: '. . . accept

---

26. Jón Helgason 1909. This conclusion by theologians was contradicted by jurists, cf. Gísli Sveinsson 1914 and Einar Arnórsson 1912, 11. See also Einar Arnórsson 1951.
27. Udtog 1899, 24-48. Cf. Iversen (Part II.6).
28. See Einar Sigurbjörnsson (Part II.6).

this your servant who is appointed to the ministry of bishop in the congregation/church', the Icelandic translation reads 'our church' as if to emphasize the national character of the episcopal ministry. As is the case in the ordination of priests, the ordaining bishop does not hand over to the ordinand any symbol of his ministry, such as cope or pectoral cross. The ordinand is wearing a bishop's cope already at the entry-procession into the church. This might suggest that it is the call but not the ordination that 'makes' the bishop (or the priest) Yet, the rubrics make it clear that the person changes from an ordinand ('*vígsluþegi*') to an ordained bishop when it says that 'the newly ordained bishop' is to preach the sermon. The influence of purism is also apparent in that the verb '*innvígjast*' disappears in favour of '*vígja*', and '*ordinand*' changes to '*vígsluþegi*'.

The 1934 Service Book

In 1931 a law was passed establishing a governing Council of the church ('*kirkjuráð*'), under the presidency of the Bishop of Iceland and consisting of four other members: two lay members, chosen by a rather complicated procedure and two priests chosen by the Synod.[29] This Council was to have authority in so called internal matters of the church, including liturgical matters. Already in 1925, the Synod had appointed a commission which was to revise the Service Book. The commission introduced its proposals to the Synod and Church Council in 1932 and a new Service Book was authorized by the Church Council in 1933, having been accepted by the Synod (*Prestafélagsritið* 1933, 163). This Service Book was a very thorough revision of all church rites. All collects, prayers and rites were rewritten and they bore very obvious marks of liberalism. Consequently the rites of ordination are new even if their formal structure is based on the older rite of 1910 and the Danish tradition.

The ordination rites are in the fourth chapter of the book under the heading '*Vígslur*' but, as already mentioned, '*vígsla*' is the common word for ordination, consecration, dedication, and blessing in Iceland (*Helgisiðabók* 1934, 135-168). The first item in this chapter is the order for marriage (*hjónavígsla*), followed by the rites for the ordination of priests (*prestvígsla*) and bishops (*biskupsvígsla*) (Helgisiðabók 1934, 146-152, 154-160) and the chapter ends

---

29. Since 1958, when the Church Assembly consisting of lay and ordained members was established, the Church Council has been elected by the Assembly. Since 1998, the Church Assembly and Church Council have authority in external as well as internal matters of the church. See Einar Sigurbjörnsson 1996, 34-48.

with the rite for the dedication of a church (*kirkjuvígsla*) and of a cemetery (*vígsla kirkjugarðs*).

The 1934 Service Book: Ordination of priests

The ordination of priests is to take place on a Sunday. The service is to begin with an organ prelude: between 1910 and 1934 organs had become common in Icelandic churches and their role is therefore mentioned in the 1934 Service Book as part of the liturgy. The hymn is the same hymn as proposed for the ordination of bishops in the 1910 Service Book: '*Andinn Guðs lifanda af himnanna hæð*', verses 1-4. There is a special collect for the occasion:

All loving, heavenly Father, we thank you that you have had your Son reveal your love to us and that you have given us life in him. Send your Holy Spirit to your Church that she may be able to expand your Kingdom from generation to generation. Be with the ministers of the word, increase their faith, give them the power of your Spirit and preserve them from evil, sanctify them in your truth and help them to proclaim your Gospel with their words and their whole lives. Let your light always shine clearly over us so that your name may be praised for ever and ever.

There is no Epistle reading but the collect is followed by the remaining verses of the hymn '*Andinn Guðs*'. There follows the presentation, prayer and the hymn based on Ps 117 as in 1910 and during the hymn the bishop leads the procession of ordinands and assistants from the sacristy. The bishop is robed in cope, the ordinands wear albs and chasubles, the assisting priests wear albs. The bishop goes to the altar. The candidates stand before him and the assisting priests. There follows the Latin versicles and responses, beginning *Veni, sancte Spiritus*, and collect. In the 1910 Service Book, it was suggested that the versicles be sung in Icelandic, since the Latin is only in an appendix. This suggestion was probably not accepted and in 1934 Latin was to be the rule and the translation is in an appendix (*Helgisiðabók* 1910, 107, 112; *Helgisiðabók* 1934, 148, 152). The bishop reads his text and delivers his sermon. The sermon ended, the bishop reads the ordination oath which is the same as in the 1910 Service Book followed by the joining of hands.

The formula of conferral is new:

Bishop: Then I hand over to you the noble ministry in the Church of Christ, to preach the word of God, to administer the holy sacraments and to proclaim in the name of Jesus repentance and absolution, and I (*here the bishop and assistants lay their hands on the head of the ordinand*) ordain you to the holy ministry of priest, in the name of the Father, and of the Son, and of the Holy Spirit. Amen.

The ordination prayer is also new:

Bishop: Almighty, eternal Father, send labourers to your harvest because we know that the harvest is still great and the labourers few. Grant to the church of our country as many good servants as possible.

Give to your minister (*the bishop and the assistants lay their hands on the head of each candidate.*) the priest, NN the Holy Spirit to work with faithfulness in your church.

Give him your strength and grace. Sanctify him in your truth. Strengthen his faith and love to you so that he may do his duty with joy and propagate your Kingdom. Be his strength in his weakness, in Jesus' name.

The Lord's Prayer follows. Then the bishop and the other priests kneel in prayer and a hymn is sung while the bishop leads a procession to the sacristy where they take off their robes. One of the newly ordained priests preaches, 'if the bishop wishes there to be a sermon'. After the sermon there is a service of Holy Communion and one of the assisting priests celebrates.

What is striking about this rite is the absence of scriptural readings except for the text read by the bishop and the text (usually the Sunday Gospel) read by the newly ordained priest who was to preach the sermon. Neither is there any creed. Another factor is the double laying-on of hands, first at the handing over of the ministry, and again in the ordination prayer. Finally, the beginning of the ordination prayer is strange. It leaves out the *anamnesis* completely and says instead: '[...] Send labourers to your harvest *because we know* that the harvest is still great and the labourers few. Grant to the church of our country *as many good servants as possible*'. God does not have to be reminded what we know and it is no use praying for too much as far as good servants are concerned! The prayer also is only for ministers of 'our church'. However, there is an explicit *epiclesis* in the laying-on of hands in the prayer: 'Give to your minister [...] the Holy Spirit [...]'. As had been the case in Iceland, the ordinands proceed to the church vested in chasubles so that there is no symbolic action in connection with the handing over of the ministry except the laying-on of hands.

The 1934 Service Book: Ordination of Bishops

The ordination of Bishops takes place on a Sunday.[30] The ordaining bishop and the ordinand put on their robes in the sacristy. They wear copes but there is no mention of a cross. The four assisting priests wear albs. All the other priests invited to the ordination wear cassocks. In the rubric it says that if there are many priests present it would be preferable that they follow the bishops and the assistants in a procession to the church vested in cassocks. A possible participation of bishops from other Lutheran Churches is not mentioned. The service begins with an organ prelude, hymn followed by salutation and collect, special for this occasion:

> Almighty, eternal God, the Father of our Lord Jesus Christ, we thank you for those leaders and teachers whom you have given strength and courage to proclaim the Gospel of your Son in word and deed. We pray you to send your Spirit upon us all and strengthen this your servant who on this day will be ordained bishop in your Church. Preserve him and increase his faith and love in your communion. Let this holy ceremony which we are now beginning be to your glory and to the increase of your Kingdom. Watch over your Church and support it in its work, in the name of Jesus for ever and ever.

Another hymn is sung and after that there is the presentation and the reading of the ordinand's CV and prayer.

After the prayer, the hymn based on Ps 117, 'Lofið Guð, ó, lýðir' is sung and the bishop, ordinand and assisting priests proceed to the altar. There follow the traditional Latin versicles and responses, the collect and the ordination sermon delivered by the ordaining bishop.

There are scriptural readings and between each reading verses from the hymn 'O, Spirit of the living God' are sung as in the 1910 rite. The readings are Matt. 28.18-20; John 15.4-9; 1 Cor. 12.4-6 and Eph. 4.3-6.

The bishop then reads the ordination oath:

---

30. From 1909, when the first suffragan bishops were ordained, it was the custom for the Bishop of Iceland to be ordained in the Cathedral in Reykjavik, the suffragan of Hólar in the old Cathedral of Hólar and the suffragan bishop of Skálholt in Reykjavik until a new cathedral was erected in Skálholt in 1963. Since then the Skálholt suffragan bishops have been ordained there.

You have now, dear brother, heard the commands and promises of God's word. They shall be the lights on your path in your holy work to which you have now been called as a bishop in our church. God requires of you that you be found faithful and awake in your calling and that you build upon the only sure foundation which is laid, our Lord Jesus Christ. You are to live both privately and publicly according to God's will so that you can proclaim his Gospel both in word and in deed. Support as well as you can the church of our country and consecrate your life to the ideal that the Spirit of Christ may work there ever more mightily to the blessing of the life of the nation. But if you are afraid that the path of God's Kingdom is difficult and that you yourself are weak, let it be your comfort that it is God's work that you perform and that our Lord Jesus Christ has promised to be with his ministers always, even to the end of the world and that through his grace and strength they shall bear much fruit.

Do you promise me in the presence of the all knowing God to perform all your duties with diligence and faithfulness according to the grace that God grants you?

The ordinand answers, 'Yes', and there is the traditional joining of hands, after which the ordaining bishop says:

Then I hand over to you the holy ministry of bishop (*and with the laying-on of hands by the bishop and the assistants*) and ordain you a bishop, in the name of the Father, and of the Son, and of the Holy Spirit. Amen.

Almighty and all loving God and Father, accept in your grace this your servant who is now ordained bishop in your Church. Give him your Holy Spirit that he may perform his calling well and faithfully and that it be to your glory and to the building up of the congregations in the country. Strengthen him by power from on high that he may work for the victory of good, the expansion of your Kingdom. Help him to be in all his life and work the true disciple of your Son, Jesus Christ, to the strengthening of your Church among us.

The prayer is followed by the Lord's Prayer. The hymn to be sung is Luther's 'To God the Holy Spirit let us pray' (*Nun bitten wir den Heiligen Geist*) in accordance with the tradition which can be traced to the 1537 Church Order, or another hymn. The newly ordained bishop preaches a sermon and the service ends with Holy Communion.

As is the case with the ordination of priests there is some strange wording in the prayers here. Perhaps the strangest is the one in the ordination oath:

'Support as well as you can the church of our country and consecrate your life to the ideal that the Spirit of Christ may work there ever more mightily to the blessing of the life of the nation'. It is possible that 'church' here means 'ordained ministers', the clergy, since this wording corresponds to the older wording which asks the bishop to support the ministers of the word, but clericalism was very strong in liberalism. There are scriptural readings here as in the older rite but all the older ones have been changed except for Matt. 28.18-20. There is no creed at all. And lastly, there is no symbolic handing over of the ministry, either by robing in a cope or handing over a pectoral cross: the ordinand enters the church in full episcopal robes.

The 1981 Handbook

When Sigurbjörn Einarsson (born 1911) was bishop, 1959-1981, he made some changes in the ordination rites especially as regards the prayers and addresses. In the final year of his episcopate a new Service Book was authorized by the Synod and the Church Assembly and published under the title, Handbook (*Handbók íslensku kirkjunnar* 1981). As mentioned above, this Handbook contained in addition to the rite for the ordination of priests, a rite for the ordination of deacons.[31]

The 1981 Handbook: Ordination of Priests

The Ordination of priests is to take place on a Sunday in a cathedral. It is possible for ordination to take place on a weekday. The bishop, the ordinands, four assisting priests at least, and others, if needed, meet in the sacristy. The ordinands wear albs, the assisting priests wear albs and a stole, the bishop wears a cope.

The service begins with an organ prelude during which the assistants, ordinands and bishop proceed into the church and not after the presentation as had been the case earlier. One of the assisting priests goes to the altar, the others take their places. A hymn is sung, the first part of an ordination hymn by Bishop Sigurbjörn Einarsson, *'Kristur sem reistir þitt ríki á jörð'* ('Christ, who established your Kingdom on earth'), to the same tune as 'O, Spirit of the living God'. There is a special collect, in which the church prays that God may give true and steadfast ministers of the word to the church and strengthen them with his Holy Spirit, followed by the second part of the ordination

---

31. *Handbók* 1981, 183-190 (ordination of priests), 194-201 (ordination of bishops), 202-206 (ordination of deacons). On the ordination of deacons, see Olsen (Part II.3).

hymn. Then follow the presentation and prayer. The first assisting priest reads the Gospel: Matt. 9.35-38, then reads the names of the ordinands and says a prayer. During the singing of the traditional hymn, 'Lofið Guð, ó, lýðir göfgið hann', based on Ps. 117, the bishop goes to the altar, the ordinands and the assisting priests stand before him. The traditional Latin versicles and responses, beginning *Veni, sancte Spiritus,* and the collect are followed by the ordination sermon by the bishop.

The Creed then follows, either the Apostles' Creed or a credal hymn. This is new in ordination services in Iceland. The reading from Scripture that follows is also new. Each assistant reads from the Scripture and sometimes lay people, representatives of the respective congregations, have taken part in this part of the service and also in the laying-on of hands. The readings are: Matt. 28.16-20, John 15.1-9, 2 Tim. 4.1-5 and 2 Cor. 5.14-21.

The ordination oath has been changed:

> Bishop: You have heard the admonitions and promises of the Lord and his apostles. Now I seriously urge you: to preach the Gospel purely and correctly as it is found in the Prophetic and Apostolic Writings and according to the witness of our Evangelical-Lutheran Church in its Confessions; to administer the holy sacraments according to Christ's institution and with reverence, to instruct the young and all your congregation in the holy truths of the Christian faith, to direct, admonish and strengthen in love and with seriousness, publicly and privately, to watch over the salvation of those who are entrusted to your care, support the weak and help the needy. I admonish you to search the Scriptures and meditate on the doctrines of our faith in prayer and with humility and be faithful to the truth in love. Remember always that you are to be an example to others in true faith and good living to the glory of God.
>
> On behalf of holy church I ask you in the name of Jesus: Do you promise me in sincerity to do this according to the grace God grants you?

The ordinand, having said 'Yes,' confirms this by the traditional joining of hands with the bishop and the assistants. Then the ordinand is vested in stole and chasuble and kneels before the altar. The bishop and assistants lay their hands upon the head of the ordinand and the bishop says:

> NN I confer upon you the holy ministry of priest and preacher: to preach the word of God to repentance, conversion and salvation; to administer the holy sacraments of Baptism and Holy Communion; to hear confessions

and proclaim in Jesus' name the forgiveness of sins, in the name of the Father, and of the Son, and of the Holy Spirit. Amen.

Let us pray: Almighty God and Father, who through the mouth of your Son has taught us to pray for labourers for your harvest, we pray you to give to your church true ministers according to your will. Give to your minister (*here the bishop and the assistants lay hands on each ordinand*) the priest NN the Holy Spirit that he/she may be a faithful and true labourer in your vineyard. Give them grace. Let them be strengthened in your communion and in the power of your might. Sanctify them in your truth that, in word and deed, they may witness to your salvation in our Saviour Jesus Christ and may praise his holy name.

There follows the Lord's Prayer with the laying-on of hands. The service ends with the celebration of the Eucharist where the bishop celebrates and the newly ordained assist. There is always a very general participation in the Eucharist by the congregation present.

What is new in the rite is the inclusion of the Creed and the readings from Scripture. In the ordination oath the wording that preaching is to be 'according to the witness of our Evangelical-Lutheran Church in its Confessions' replaces the former wording 'in the spirit of our Evangelical-Lutheran Church'. In the ordination oath the admonition to study is interesting and is similar to an admonition which is found in the old oath for priests in the 1685 Rite. Furthermore, the ordinands are first vested at the ordination proper and do not process already vested into the church. Finally, there is no longer a sermon by the newly ordained which had become the rule even if this was always optional in the older rites. The double laying-on of hands which was introduced in the 1934 Service Book is retained.

The 1981 Handbook: Ordination of a Bishop

The ordination of a bishop takes place on a Sunday in a cathedral. The ordination service starts with a procession. The priests present wear cassocks, the assisting priests and the ordinand wear albs and stoles, the ordaining bishop and assisting bishops wear copes. In the procession the bishop walks last, the ordinand is next in front of him. The two most recently ordained priests ('*famuli*') lead the procession, and stand on the left and the right side of the altar, facing the congregation, during the service. At the end of the service the bishop leads the procession out, but the '*famuli*' go before him.

The service begins with an organ prelude while the procession enters the church. The first part of the ordination hymn, '*Kristur sem reistir þitt ríki á jörð*', is sung as in the ordination of priests. The ordination collect is almost the same as in 1934, and this is followed by the reading of the Epistle (1 Cor. 4.1-5) and Gospel (John 21.15-17). There is the traditional presentation, the ordinand's CV and prayer for the ordinand, followed by the hymn 'Lofið Guð og lýðir göfgið hann' and the Latin versicles and responses, beginning Veni, sancte Spiritus, and collect. The ordination sermon by the ordaining bishop is followed by the Creed and scriptural readings which are the following: Matt. 28.18-20, John 15.1-9, 1 Pet. 5.1-4; Acts 20.27-32).

The ordination oath is revised:

Bishop: You have heard, brother, the Word of the Lord and his apostles. God desires that all humankind be saved and come to the knowledge of the truth. Therefore, he has instituted the ministry of his word and sent his church to proclaim it. He has called you by his grace (or, *if the ordinand is not ordained priest: by his grace he calls you*) to this ministry and bestows upon you an increased pastoral ministry in his church. He requires of you that you be faithful and awake in your calling and build upon the only foundation that is laid, our Lord Jesus Christ, that you guard yourself and all the flock which is entrusted to your care, that you remain in the truth of God's word as it is found in Holy Scripture and according to the witness of our church in its Confessions. In humility and yet with firmness, you are to lead your church, defend it against errors and confirm it in the faith that has been once for all delivered to her. Be of good advice to your fellow ministers, support the weak and correct those that go astray. Be mild without tolerating evil, admonish without forgetting mildness. And when you suffer because the world does not endure sound teaching, then re-member with thanksgiving that it is God's work, not your own, which you are doing, and that our Lord Jesus Christ says: Be of good cheer, I have overcome the world. The work is his, his grace is sufficient for those who follow him and trust in him.

Do you in the presence of the all knowing God promise me to perform the duty of the episcopal ministry with vigilance, fairness and faithfulness according to the grace God grants you?

When the ordinand has answered, 'Yes' and confirmed this 'yes' by joining hands, the ordaining bishop puts the pectoral cross on the ordinand with the words: 'The Lord Jesus Christ says: 'If anyone would come after me, let him deny himself, take up his cross and follow me'. Then the ordinand is robed in a cope, the ordaining bishop saying: 'Put on the Lord Jesus Christ and be renewed in the spirit of your minds and put on the new nature, created after the likeness of God in true righteousness and holiness'. Thereafter the ordinand kneels and the bishop and those Icelandic bishops who are present (see below) lay their hands upon the ordinand's head, and the ordaining bishop says:

NN I bestow upon you the holy ministry of bishop, in the name of the Father, and of the Son, and of the Holy Spirit. Amen.

Ordaining bishop at the laying-on of hands by the bishops present: Almighty, everlasting Father, accept in grace your minister NN. Give him your Holy Spirit rightly to live out his vocation to the glory of your holy name. Make him steadfast in your word and make him proclaim your Son, crucified and risen, as the only Saviour and Lord. Strengthen him to shepherd your congregations with love and watchfulness, to teach, admonish and guide in humility, steadfastness and wisdom and seek as his only glory to be faithful to you and to your holy will, to the blessing of your church and to the salvation of your children. Through your Son, Jesus Christ, Our Lord. Amen.

There follows the Lord's Prayer. A hymn or the Te Deum is sung. The newly ordained bishop preaches a sermon and thereafter the Eucharist is celebrated.

The rubric that only Icelandic bishops are to lay hands on the ordinand deserves mentioning. The first time a visiting bishop was present at an Icelandic episcopal ordination was in 1959 on the occasion of Bishop Sigurbjörn Einarsson's ordination. Bishop Halfdan Høgsbro from Denmark was present then and participated in the laying-on of hands. In the 1960s it became common for the Bishop of Iceland, or a suffragan bishop to represent the Icelandic Church at episcopal ordinations in the Nordic countries and Nordic bishops represented their churches at Icelandic ordinations and installations. The laying-on of hands was a difficult matter since Swedish and Finnish bishops were not allowed to participate in it in 'the Danish Churches' of Iceland, Norway and Denmark. When the Icelandic Church replied to BEM in 1985, it said that it would consider the question of apostolic succession when the time came 'as a sign but not a guarantee' of unity (Churches 1987, IV: 68). This time came when the Porvoo agreement was accepted by the Synod and Church Assembly and it was ruled that visiting bishops from the Porvoo communion would participate in the ordination of Icelandic bishops. When Karl Sigurbjörnsson (born 1947) was ordained Bishop of Iceland in 1997, there were visiting bishops from all the Nordic countries and the Church of England and all participated in the laying-on of hands.

Note on Installation

In accordance with Danish tradition there is a distinction between ordination and installation in the Evangelical-Lutheran Church of Iceland. The area dean installs the priest in his or her parish after he or she has been ordained or changes parish. The installation is a very simple ceremony, the dean reading the letter of appointment and urging the congregation to accept its minister with prayers and in gratitude (*Helgisiðabók*, 1910, 129-130; 1934, 153; *Handbók* 1981, 191). Area deans are installed by the bishop either at their annual meeting or in their respective churches (*Handbók* 1981, 191-193). The ceremony is somewhat more elaborate than is the case with the installation of priests. In cases when suffragan bishops have been appointed Bishop of Iceland, as happened in 1981 and 1989, they were not re-ordained but installed. The service resembled the ordination liturgy with prayers and scriptural readings but there was no imposition of hands.[32]

Conclusion

In structure and form the Icelandic ordination rites follow the Danish tradition. For 300 years they were translations of the Danish rites. The rite for the ordination of a bishop in the 1910 Service Book is a translation of the then official Danish rite, but the rite for the ordination of priests is based on a proposal by J.P. Mynster in 1839, which was never officially adopted in Denmark. The rites in the 1934 Service Book follow the Danish structure but in content they reflect the theological views of the liberal theology that was in vogue at the beginning of the twentieth century. This appears in the terminology used and in the absence of readings from Scripture except for the ordination of bishops. What is structurally new in the 1934 rite is the double laying-on of hands, at the conferral of the ministry and in the prayer of ordination. The rites in the 1981 Handbook retain this special feature but are characterized by the introduction of both scriptural readings in the ordination of priests and by change in terminology. In 1981, ordination to the diaconate was introduced as part of the official liturgy of the church.

In theology the Icelandic rites emphasize that the ministry of priests and bishops is the ministry of the word. The ministers, both priests and bishops, are to preach the Gospel and administer the sacraments. The bishop is regarded above all as '*pastor pastorum*' and as such the chief pastor of the church at large. In the 1910 rite – and also in 1934 – a somewhat national outlook

---

32. Special orders of service were printed on both occasions.

appears in the terminology of the ordination prayer where the bishop of 'our church' is prayed for. The universal or catholic outlook is retained in the 1981 rite. Whereas the Danish rites of the nineteenth century reflect a somewhat congregationalist view of the ministry of priests when they mention in the prayer that priests are ordained to a particular parish, the Icelandic rites retain the universal or catholic view of the rites as in both the Church Order and the 1685 Rite.

References

Please note that the Icelandic references are given according to Icelandic custom.

Arngrímur Jónsson. 1993, *Fyrstu handbækur presta á Íslandi eftir siðbót.* Reykjavík: Háskólaútgáfan.

Björn Magnússon. 1954. 'Þróun guðsþjónustuforms íslenzku kirkjunnar frá siðaskiptum.' *Samtíð og saga. Safnrit háskólafyrirlestra.* 6: 92-116. Reykjavík: H.F. Leiftur.

Churches Respond to BEM. Official Responses to the Baptism, Eucharist and Ministry Text. Vol. IV (Faith and Order Paper no. 137, Geneva: World Council of Churches, 1987).

Danmarks & Norgis Kirkeritual 1685-1985, 1985. Skarrild: Udvalget for Konvent for Kirke og Theologi.

Diplomatarium islandicum –Íslenzkt fornbréfasafn X (DI). 1911-1921. Reykjavík: Hið íslenzka bókmenntafélag.

Ein Kyrkiu Ordinantia epter hvörre ad allir Andlegir og Veraldlegir í Norvegs Ríki skulu leiðrietta sig og skicka sier. 1635. Hólar.

Einar Arnórsson. 1912. *Íslenzkur kirkjuréttur,* Reykjavík. Gefin út á kostnað höfundarins.

– 1951, *Játningarit íslensku kirkjunnar.* Reykjavík. (Studia islandica 12). København/Reykjavík: Einar Munksgaard/Leiftur.

Einar Sigurbjörnsson. 1979a. 'Islandsk gudstjeneste fra reformationen til vore dage.' *Præsteforeningens blad* 4: 5ff.

– 1979b. 'Islandsk salmedigtning - en historisk oversigt.' *Hymnologiske meddelelser* 8.4: 181-192.

– 1987. Das Abendmahl nach der isländischen Ordnung 1594. In *Coena Domini I: Die Abendmahlsliturgie der Reformationskirchen im 16./17. Jahrhundert.* Ed. Irmgard Pahl, 160-180. Freiburg: Universitätsverlag Freiburg, Schweiz,

– 1996. *Embættisgjörð. Guðfræði þjónustunnar í sögu og samtíð.* Reykjavík. Skálholtsútgáfan.

- 2000a. Handbók fyrir presta. In *Þórunn Valdimarsdóttir, Pétur Pétursson*, 28-30. Reykjavik.
- 2000b. Sálmabók 1886. In *Þórunn Valdimarsdóttir, Pétur Pétursson*, 31-33. Reykjavik.
- 2000c. Helgisiðabókin 1910. In *Þórunn Valdimarsdóttir, Pétur Pétursson*, 233-236. Reykjavik.

Frumvarp til endurskoðaðrar handbókar fyrir presta á Íslandi og til breytinga á kirkjurítúalinu. 1897. Reykjavík: Ísafoldarprentsmiðja.

Gísli Sveinsson. 1914. Trúfrelsi og kenningarfrelsi. *Eimreiðin* XX: 200-210.

Guðni Jónsson, ed. 1948. *Byskupasögur Annað bindi - Hólabyskupar.* Reykjavík: Íslendingasagnaútgáfan.

Graduale. Ein almennileg messusaungs- og psalmabok. First published in 1594, reprinted in 19 editions until 1779.

Guðrún Kvaran. 1990. 'Biblíuþýðingar og íslenzkt mál.' *Biblíuþýðingar í sögu og samtíð. Studia theologica islandica* 4: 39-56. Reykjavík: Guðfræðistofnun Háskóla Íslands.

Íslands biskupsdæmis bréfabók 30. ágúst 1866- 30. júlí 1867.

Jón Halldórsson I. 1903-1910. *Biskupasögur Jóns prófasts Haldórssonar í Hítardal með viðbæti I: Skálholtsbiskupar 1540-1801*, Reykjavík: Sögufélag.

Jón Helgason. 1909. Prestarnir og játningarritin. *Skírnir* LXXXIII: 193-224.

- 1922. *Islands Kirke fra Reformationen til vore Dage.* Copenhagen: G.E.C. Gads Forlag.

Jón Pjetursson. 1890. *Kirkjurjettur.* Reykjavík: Prentsmiðja Sigf. Eymundssonar.

Handbók fyrir presta á Íslandi. Endurskoðuð, 1869. Reykjavík. (published several times from the end of the 16th Century until 1879).

Handbók íslensku kirkjunnar 1981. Reykjavík: Kirkjuráð hinnar íslensku þjóðkirkju.

Haraldur Níelsson. 1908. Trúarjátningarnar og kenningarfrelsi presta. *Skírnir* LXXXII: 211-236.

Helgisiðabók íslenzku þjóðkirkjunnar 1910, Reykjavík: Ísafoldarprentsmiðja.

Helgisiðabók íslenzku þjóðkirkjunnar 1934, Reykjavík: Ísafoldarprentsmiðja.

Kirkeordinansen av 1607 og Forordning om ekteskapssaker gitt 1582. 1985. Oslo: Den rettshistoriske kommisjon.

Kirkeordinants for Norge. Kjöbenhavn 2. Juli 1607. In *Lovsamling for Island* 1, 1096-1720. 150-170. Kjöbenhavn: Forlagt af Universitets-Boghandler Andr. Fred. Höst 1853.

Kirkjuordinanzía Kristjáns konungs hins III. – Ordinatio ecclsiastica Regnorum Daniae et Noruegiae et ducatum Slesuicensis, Holsatiae et cetera. In

Íslenzkt fornbréfasafn – Diplomatarium islandicum X, 1911-1921, Reykjavík Hið íslenzka bókmenntafélag, 117-328.

Lagasafn. Íslensk lög 1. október 1999, Reykjavík. Dóms- og kirkjumálaráðuneytið.

Lausten, M. S. 1989. *Kirkeordinansen 1537/39*. Copenhagen: Akademisk forlag.

Lovsamling for Island 5. 1855. Copenhagen: Universitets-Boghandler Andr. Fredr. Høst (& Søn).

Magnús Jónsson. 1952. *Alþingi og kirkjumálin 1845-1943*. Reykjavík: Alþingissögunefnd.

Magnús Már Lárusson. 1949. Drög að sögu íslenzkra biblíuþýðinga 1540-1815. *Kirkjuritið* 15.4: 336-351.

– 1957. Ágrip af sögu íslenzku Biblíunnar. In E. Henderson, *Frásagnir um ferðalög um þvert og endilangt Ísland árin 1814 og 1815 með vetursetu í Reykjavík*. 391-437. Reykjavík: Snæbjörn Jónsson.

Münter, F. C. 1830. *Ritual for Bispevielse. Allnaadigst approberet den 17. Mai 1830*. Copenhagen.

Mynster, J. P.1839. *Udkast til en Alterbog og et Kirkeritual for Danmark I-III*. Copenhagen.

Nýtt kirkjublað. Hálfsmánaðarrit fyrir kristindóm og kristinlega menning 20. 1908. Reykjavík. 15. október.

Páll Eggert Ólason. 1924. *Upptök sálma og sálmalaga í lútherskum sið á Íslandi*. Reykjavík: Fylgirit Árbókar Háskóla Íslands.

Steingrímur J. Þorsteinsson. 1950. Íslenzkar biblíuþýðingar. *Viðförli. Tímarit um guðfræði og kirkjumál*. 4.1-2: 48-85.

Prestafélagsritið. Tímarit fyrir kristindóms- og kirkjumál 15.1933.

Svavar Sigmundsson. 1990. Samanburður á Nýja testamentinu 1813 og 1827. *Biblíupýðingar í sögu og samtíð. Studia theologica islandica* 4: 175-202. Reykjavík: Guðfræðistofnun Háskóla Íslands.

Sigurður P. Sívertsen. 1925. *Fimm höfuðjátningar evangelísk-lúterskrar kirkju. Með greinargjörð um uppruna þeirra*. Reykjavík: Bókaverslun Sigfúsar Eymundssonar.

Stefán Karlsson. 1985. Samfellan í íslensku biblíumáli. *Bókaormurinn* 14. Reykjavík.

– 1990. Drottinleg bæn á móðurmáli. *Biblíupýðingar í sögu og samtíð. Studia theologica islandica* 4: 145-174. Reykjavík: Guðfræðistofnun Háskóla Íslands.

Stjórnartíðindi B nr. 88/1888.

Stjórnartíðindi fyrir Ísland árið 1910 – Regjeringstidende for Island 1910. Reykjavík. Nr. 89/1910.

Tíðindi um stjórnarmálefni Íslands 1870-1875. Vol. 3. Copenhagen.
Udtog af det forordnede Kirke-Ritual i Danmark. 1899. Copenhagen: Det Kongelige Vaisenhuses Forlag.
Þórir Óskarsson. 1990. Sundurgreinilegar tungur. Um mál og stíl Nýja testamentis Odds Gottskálkssonar. *Biblíuþýðingar í sögu og samtíð. Studia theologica islandica* 4: 203-222. Reykjavík: Guðfræðistofnun Háskóla Íslands.
Þórhallur Guttormsson. 1973, *Brynjólfur biskup Sveinsson ævi og störf.* Reykjavík: Ísafoldarprentsmiðja.
Þórunn Valdimarsdóttir and Pétur Pétursson. 2000. *Til móts við nútímann. Kristni á Íslandi* IV. Reykjavík: Alþingi.

Unpublished sources
In the Archives of the University-National Library of Iceland, Reykjavík:
JS 13. 4to. (Manuscript containing a translation of the 1685 Rite of the Danish-Norwegian Church)
JS 165. fol. Manuscript in 29 parts. Part 7: 'Danmerkur og Norvegs Rikia kyrkiu Ritual'. Part 8: 'Eyn Kyrkiu Ordinantia.'
Lbs 5 fol. On pp. 16-17: 'Nogle Obeservationer ved den Islandske Alterbog.'
Lbs 381.8vo. (Untitled Manuscript containing the Rite for the ordination of priests from the
Danish-Norwegian Church Rites of 1685)
Lbs 401.4to. On pp. 58-73: 'Kongs Kirstjans fimta Kirkju Ritual. Kap. X Um biskupa- og prestavígslur.'
Lbs 410 4to. 'Rituale Edur Kyrkiu Ceremoniu Bök. Samanntekenn af Biskupunum Mag. Jone
Arnasyni og Mag. Steine Jonssyni. Skrifad ad nýu á Mýrum í Alftavere Anno 1792.'.
Lbs 496.4to. 'Danmerkur og Norvegs Kirkiu-ritual.'

Rites for the Ordination of Pastors in the Evangelical-Lutheran Church of the Faeroe Islands

Jákup Reinert Hansen

On my 27th birthday I received a peculiar present. It was two days before my ordination as a pastor in the Lutheran Church, so the day was spent in the bishop's residence, where the bishop's examination took place, and it was he who gave me the booklet. It consisted of two sheets of printed paper, folded to make a total of 32 pages, but not sewn, let alone bound. According to the title page here were the rites for the consecration of a church and the ordination of a pastor. In both cases the word *'vígsla'* was used. Other information that might have been expected in a book of this type was not given: publisher, year of printing, authorisation. The preface, however, read:–

> The rite for the consecration of a church was translated by J. Dahl and first used in 1929 for the consecration of the church in Gjógv. The rite for the ordination of a pastor in this form was first used on 2nd July 1967, when the first pastor was ordained in the church of Tórshavn, this being the first ordination in the Faeroes since the Reformation.
>
> Tórshavn at Yuletide 1968
> J. Joensen (Ritual 1968: 3)

Answering some of my questions the preface at the same time raised new ones. Names and dates were given that were not immediately transparent to me. In this paper I shall attempt to present the history of the rite in question, the ordination of a pastor, before taking a closer look at the rite or rather rites, for although this is still the only published rite another has been in use since 1993. They differ so much in content that they cannot go back to the same original, and they vary enough in terminology to make it worthwhile discussing the understanding of ordained ministry behind the vocabulary used.

Historical Background

Today J. Dahl (1878-1944) is generally considered to be the father of Faeroese church language. A pastor in Tórshavn from 1912 and the dean of the Faeroes from 1918 until his death, he was entitled to use the seal bearing the inscription *'Sigillum præpositi, olim episcopi Færoensis'*. The Faeroes had been a diocese under the Archbishopric of Nidaros in Norway, but were shortly after the Lutheran Reformation reduced to a deanery, at first under the Bishop of Bergen and from about 1620 under the Bishop of Copenhagen. Therefore all pastors would be ordained, before they were shipped to the Faeroes and installed in their office by the dean. The official language used in the church as elsewhere was Danish, the language of the King. The islanders had a native tongue of their own, but that being only an oral language, no one questioned the supremacy of Danish. Faeroese was for everyday use including storytelling, legends, and ballads, but not even for the Lord's Prayer! From the dawn of the nineteenth century, with the rise of enlightenment, humanism and romanticism, scholars began to find the Faeroese language an interesting object of study, and when Faeroese students towards the end of the century were attracted to the nationalist movement, it resulted in the formulation of fierce demands for the rights of their own language in school, church, and parliament. Perhaps Dahl was not the first pioneer, but he certainly felt called to provide the necessary means to bring the Faeroese language into the church. Single-handed, he translated the New Testament, the rites, the service book, and nearly 100 hymns; he preached in Faeroese and published two complete collections of sermons along with a number of smaller devotional volumes. After the necessary consultation with experts and committees, the first series of authorised liturgical books appeared: rites for baptism, Holy Communion, confirmation, weddings and funerals in 1930, the New Testament in 1937, the Service Book in 1939 (Rasmussen 1987: 271-295). Dahl's hand could still be observed, when the next authorised books were issued some 20 years later: the Hymnal in 1956, and the Old Testament in 1961. If these books were not authorised by the King himself, they would be authorised by the Bishop of Copenhagen in accordance with a resolution by the state authorities. Dahl translated the rite for the consecration of a church in 1929, responding to the desire of the local congregation and with the permission of his bishop (Rasmussen: 366). The Danish rite had never been authorised, so this did not present any problem.

In 1963 Jákup Joensen, the dean and pastor of Tórshavn, was appointed vice-bishop in the Faeroes[1], and it was only then that the need for an ordination rite arose. The announcement of the regulations for the vice-bishop in the Faeroe Islands (*Bekendtgørelse* 1963) states that he will continue to retain the obligations he has had as dean. He may make decisions and grant dispensations in questions related to baptism, confirmation, and election to the congregational boards. The fourth paragraph deals with ordination:

> With the authorisation of the Bishop of the Diocese of Copenhagen the vice-bishop may ordain pastors who have been called to an office in the Faeroes. With the agreement of the bishop the vice-bishop may hold such an ordination in the cathedral of Copenhagen. The letter of appointment (*'kollats'*) for the pastors appointed to a ministry in the Faeroes will be issued by the Bishop of Copenhagen but countersigned by the vice-bishop.

Thus it is made perfectly clear, that the right to ordain is only delegated to the vice-bishop. When an ordination finally came into prominence with the election of a new pastor for the island of Suðuroy in 1967, the regulations were not followed entirely. The ordination took place in Tórshavn, the capital of the Faeroes, in the parish church where the vice-bishop still had his ministry as a pastor. No doubt this event was seen as a step towards an independent Faeroese diocese, and therefore it would have been a regression in relation to what had been achieved on the road to full recognition of Faeroese, if the ordination could not be carried out in the local language. Only two documents dealing with the case have been found in the episcopal archives in Copenhagen and neither of them reveals anything about the rite. One is a letter of 29th May, 1967 from the Ministry for Church Affairs to the Bishop of Copenhagen, informing him that a certain candidate in theology has been appointed pastor in the relevant office. The other document is a draft of the bishop's letter to the candidate with certain papers, some of which he has to sign and return. This letter is sent through the vice-bishop in the Faeroes, who in a covering

---

1. The Faeroe Islands were not at this point constituted as a diocese with a diocesan bishop. The Danish legal title used was 'vicebiskop', which indicates a deputy or auxiliary bishop. The literal translation 'vice-bishop' has been used here, as the position of the bishop in the Faeroes is not entirely equivalent to that indicated by the English terms 'suffragan bishop', 'area bishop' or 'auxiliary bishop'. The bishops appointed in the Faeroes had no deputising duties in the Diocese of Copenhagen or anywhere else outside the islands. The same applied to the vice-bishops appointed in Greenland (Langgård, Part II.2).

letter dated 30th May, 1967 is advised about the procedure following the ordination:

> When the candidate M has been ordained, you are asked to install him in his office and on that occasion recommend him to the congregation. You are asked to pass on to him the enclosed dispatch, the letter of appointment, however, only after the ordination and with your countersignature.

Presumably the vice-bishop himself – after proper consultation (on the telephone?) with his bishop – did the translation, which he then proudly published eighteen months later. Joensen, who had worked with J. Dahl, had some experience in liturgical language; he had edited a small volume of hymns for Christmas and New Year in 1943 and translated Bishop Balslev's expanded version of Luther's *Little Catechism*. It is my guess that the question of which Danish rite to use would also have been settled between the vice-bishop and his superior, for Jákup Joensen did not translate the authorised Danish rite of 1898, not even in its last revised form of 1955 (*Vejledning* 1955). Instead he chose to carry out this historic first Faeroese ordination according to the 'Proposal for a Book of Rites for the Danish Evangelical-Lutheran Folk Church' of 1963 (*Forslag* 1965). As a proposal these rites were not authorised, and that could explain why the Faeroese translation lacks any information on authorisation. In the introduction the fathers of the proposal present the critical viewpoints they have had as criteria for their 'correction' of the rite (*Forslag*: 15-16): The authority of the ordained ministry, its confessional and nationalist character are more strongly emphasized in the existing Danish than in the other Nordic rites.

Having been in use in the Faeroes under two vice-bishops, this rite was set aside, when the islands were made a diocese again in 1990. When the new bishop, Hans Jacob Joensen, held his first ordination on 27th June, 1993, it became clear to all those present that he had brought with him a new rite not witnessed before in the islands. This was not the new Danish rite, authorised by the Queen in 1987, but the older rite, taken from the Bishops' Handbook of 1955. Hans Jacob Joensen's rite has still not been published and is only available in the printouts handed out to the pastors participating in this or one of the following ordinations. The object of this investigation stems from an ordination on 16th January, 1994. As Hans Jacob Joensen had taken a great interest in a fresh formulation of the liturgical texts, the biblical readings included in his rite also differ from the authorised Bible. Our main concern, however, is not the texts themselves, nor shall we pay attention to the hymns sung during this individual ordination, or try to evaluate the various Danish rites. Instead we shall undertake a synoptic reading of the two Faeroese rites of 1967 and 1993 and concentrate on the terminology.

The Faeroese Rites of 1967 and 1993

Terminology

Translations must be taken seriously. 'Communication is fundamental to clear thinking, opening and releasing maximum powers of mind and heart' (Craddock 2001: 100). If this is true in all preaching, if rethinking and formulating your Christian faith in your native language can be such a breakthrough and renewal that it must manifest itself in a hymnbook (Hansen 2001: 26), then you can also argue that the process of transferring fixed religious expressions from one language to another can prove fruitful. In the Faeroese rites we face hard labour to express the understanding of the ordained ministry in a language never so used before.

The rites are so close to each other that we can easily take them apart and look at the various elements in both rites simultaneously. The bishop is always called a bishop. That is his ministry in this connection, even though he is only a vice-bishop.

Entrance

No information is given about the entrance and the beginning of the service in 1967. A hymn is sung and one of the pastors enters before the altar for the salutation. At the end of the 1967 rite it is, however, mentioned that, if the ordination takes place during a high mass, the normal rite is followed up to and including the sermon. The 1993 rite begins with the procession of the clergy during the organ prelude followed by the normal opening prayer of the Danish Lutheran service, the first hymn, and the salutation.

Collect

The collect is one of the points where the Danish rite proposed in 1963 deliberately departs from the old tradition. 1967 makes use of the collect in the service book for the 13th Sunday after Trinity. Jákup Joensen could then have imported the text translated by J. Dahl, but brings his own instead. Dahl goes along with the Danish original which thanks God because he has let us live in this time of grace, when we can hear his holy gospel and through it see his fatherly will and his Son, Jesus Christ. Thus we are able to hear because of God's self-revelation to us. This objective understanding is not preserved in J. Joensen's translation. He calls the time blessed because God has given us the opportunity (*høvi*) to hear, and so on. Whether we hear is then not a matter of grace, but of our own listening.

1993 renders a shortened version of the collect for the 8th Sunday after Trinity. The Danish original combines the kerygmatic and didactic side of service of the Word, praying for preachers and teachers. The Faeroese translation confuses the two sides, praying for preachers of Christianity ('kristniboðarar') who teach the Word. In both versions God is asked to preserve the preachers in the right doctrine, educate them and give them openness, and let them be a good example to the congregation. At this point a few remarks about the style in the latter translation may be appropriate. This translator is not fond of long sentences. Instead of saying: 'We ask you to...' and continuing with a long consecutive chain of infinitives, he breaks up the chain into short sentences all beginning with imperatives. Apparently this collect is not intended to be sung.

Epistle

Both rites continue with the first biblical reading, the Epistle (Eph. 4.7-13). Again the 1993 rite does not follow the authorised Faeroese translation. Verse 11 mentions different ministries, explaining how God gave us ('édōken') some as apostles, some as prophets and so on. Christ's giving is a keyword in these verses. 1993 lets God *place* some as apostles, and so on, changing the focus from the congregation to the ministers. In both rites at this point, another difficult word is knowledge ('epígnōsis'), in Danish 'erkendelse', in Faeroese 'kunnleiki'. Later on, in the prayer after the presentation, the 1967 rite renders it as 'sannføring' ('conviction').

Presentation and Prayer for the Elect

In the 1993 rite, the Apostles' Creed is recited before the next hymn; the 1967 rite does not mention the creed. Now one of the pastors enters the pulpit (if this is a high mass, he will, according to the final rubrics in 1967, read the Gospel of the day and preach a sermon) and presents the ordinand(s) to the congregation, giving name, educational qualifications and appointment, even stating if this is permanent or temporary!

The 1967 rite simply appeals to the congregation to receive these men/women in love and bring them and their service to God in prayer, while the 1993 rite gives a long motivation for the prayer based on God's admonition to respect them for their service. Love is mentioned twice in the Danish, but only once in the Faeroese version.

The first parts of the prayer are not identical. The 1967 rite begins with thanks to God for preserving the gospel and the sacraments among us in spite of our sin and for calling servants of the Word. Before that the 1993 rite repeats Eph. 4.11, but at this point the Faeroese translation differs from the previous versions, making the various ministries a gift from God, not to the congregation as in the Danish original, but to the church. Both prayers ask God to continue his grace and strengthen not only the ordinands but all the servants of the Word to be faithful stewards of the mysteries of grace. Historically the word 'steward' derives its origin in this liturgical context from Titus 1.5-9. It is faithfully rendered in the 1967 rite, which deliberately avoids the very same reading. In 1993, where the reading is due shortly afterwards, the perhaps somewhat old fashioned word is omitted from the prayer, which then asks simply that ministers deal faithfully with the mysteries, thereby regretfully weakening the sense of responsibility normally associated with the steward's commission.

Invocation of the Holy Spirit

During the following hymn the persons involved in the ordination take their places. According to the 1967 rite it is not until now that the bishop, dressed in his cope, the ordinands, in albs, and the pastors proceed to the choir, where the bishop goes before the altar and the ordinands kneel down on the kneeler. The bishop should intone the hymn, *'Veni, sancte Spiritus'* which would then be continued by choir or congregation, but this element is completely omitted in 1967! Latin could not be sung, and since there was no translation of the Danish *'Gud Helligånd opfyld med lyst'* it was simply left out. The following invocation: 'Lord, send out your Holy Spirit, to create yourself ministers and renew your congregation day by day!' is broken up into short sentences: 'Send out your Holy Spirit. Create yourself ministers. And renew your congregation day by day!' This is altogether a most serious weakening of the role of the Holy Spirit. But it does correspond well enough with the subjectivity we have found in the collect.

Here the 1993 rite is clearly an improvement. In 1991 a new post of dean and pastor of the church – now cathedral – of Tórshavn was established, and Rólant Lenvig, translator of many of Grundtvig's hymns, was asked to write a Faeroese version of *'Veni, sancte Spiritus'* for the installation of the dean. Here the hymn was followed by a more faithful translation of the invocation, and this element also found its way into the later ordination rite – the Holy Spirit was brought back to the proper place! The prayer that concludes this part is one of the few texts that are almost identical in both rites.

Homily

With the ordinands back on their feet, the bishop introduces his homily: 'The holy words that I on this day of your ordination lay on your heart are written in...' The 1993 rite omits that the words are holy, and both rites rather advise/ pray that the ordinands themselves will lay them on their hearts.

Biblical Readings

After the homily the bishop introduces the biblical readings: 'Let us hear the witness of the Word of God about the service of the Word'. Four pastors step forward to read. Now comes the part where it becomes most evident that the rites are different, for the 1967 rite follows the proposal of 1963. The authorised 1898 rite which came back into favour again in 1993 has these readings: Matt. 28.18-20, Titus 1.5-9, 1 Pet. 5.2-4, 2 Tim 4.1-5. However, Hans J. Joensen has consulted the Danish 1997 rite and includes verses 16 and 17 in the first reading. The proposal replaces the second reading with 2 Cor. 3.4-6. In the Danish preface the committee freely admits that Titus 1.5-9 is the oldest reading and has often been considered the most important one. But it cannot claim to be sacrosanct any more than any other text can, and the committee finds it rather obscure and of temporary validity (*Forslag*, 16). Again the 1967 rite uses the authorised texts while Hans J. Joensen gives his own translations. A few problematic sentences ought to be mentioned. In Matt. 28.19-20 the parallelism between baptism and teaching is not properly shown, since the usual construction with two consecutive sentences is limited to one. In Titus 1.9 the verb '*eléngkhein*' ('convince', 'refute') is rendered by the Faeroese '*teppa*', which means 'to silence' somebody. The dialogical aspect of the sermon disappears. In the last of the readings, 2 Tim. 4.2 the same Greek verb is translated '*sannføra*' ('convince') where it might be better to say 'rebuke'.

Commitment/Examination

The commitment is based on the biblical readings. The proposal of 1963, with a reference to Matt. 28, stresses the missionary aspect of the service of the Word, while the 1898 rite underlines how necessary this service is for God's 'congregation' (the Faeroese translation says 'church') on earth. Apart from that there are only minor differences between the two Faeroese rites and their vocabulary. The ordinands are committed to preach, administer the sacraments, exhort and to be an example – to everyone (in 1967), to the entrusted flock (in 1898), but in 1993 to the congregation of God. *Ex officio* the bishop asks the ordinands if they will promise (in 1993: 'Do you promise me...?') to do this faithfully and honestly with the grace of God. The answer is 'Yes', and is at the bishop's request confirmed with a handshake not only with him, but also with the four readers. The Danish original behind the 1993 rite does not mention any number. Could the limitation of the handshake be due to the limited amount of space in Tórshavn church?

Declaration of Conferral

The declaration of conferral, with the ordinands kneeling again in front of the bishop, seems so laden with importance (apparently it is what makes the ordinand a pastor), that the terminology becomes crucial. With what word does the bishop give the ordinand the holy ministry as a pastor and preacher? In 1967 the bishop says: *'So handi eg tær'*, and in 1993 he says: *'So lati eg tær'*. These words both belong within the sphere of synonyms for 'giving', but there is quite a difference in the way they are used in everyday Faeroese. Therefore one can assume that they also reveal two different understandings of the ordained ministry.

The word *'handa'* literally means to hand something from one person to another, but it is also used to indicate an official presentation, even to such an extent that the verb has been turned into a noun, *'handan'*. It can be a new school that is handed over to the village or a new fishing vessel handed over from the shipyard to the owners. But let us look at one of the most common *'handan'*, a graduation. Various elements can be observed: for example, an invited audience, a certain dress code, a musical feature, a speech. We zoom in on the real incident and find three elements: one person who is to hand over, the object that is to be transferred, and the person who is to receive it with his hand. The first of these persons is someone important, the school director or the minister of education. The second person is also important, for he or she has followed the course, done the homework, passed the final examinations. And the proof is important, this signed and sealed list of marks achieved gives admission to higher education or qualifies for a certain job.

The word *'handa'* in the ordination rite thus indicates a mutual recognition between the persons on each side. The bishop in his superior ministry is the right person to confer the ministry of a pastor on the ordinand. And the ordinand, with his theological education, his call to a certain office, and his examination before the bishop, the clergy, and the congregation, is the right person to receive this valuable ministry. There is a fine balance in the picture.

The word *'lata'* literally means 'to let'. It is used as an auxiliary verb and can mean to give permission to somebody to do something, to pay. But when it really means to give, it will usually be connected with a feeling of loss, of letting something go out of your grasp. There exists no corresponding noun *'latan'*. What you let go can be of small value or of significance: They asked me for a donation to the scouts' bazaar and of course I 'let go' ('parted with') a few *krónur.* Or it means so much for you, that the loss is most painful, even if you get paid for what you let go. Imagine: the old farmer had to let his land go!

When such a word is used in an ordination it indicates an absolute supremacy of the bishop's ministry over against the pastor's, which is hardly consistent with the Lutheran understanding of ordained ministry. It even tends to mean that the right to preach and administer and give pastoral care somehow belongs to the ministry of the bishop, and that he is about to give away a share of it. Certainly it makes the ordinand feel humble, not only towards God and the ordained ministry, but also towards the bishop. There is not the same balance in this picture.

With the ministry thus conferred follows the right and authority – in 1993 the power and authority – to preach the Word of God, administer the sacraments, and take care of the congregation. We note that preaching, whether in public or in private, in 1967 is given a certain therapeutic touch. The explicit mention of remission of sins for the penitent, points in the same direction. Following the Danish original the 1993 rite likewise ought to spell out the *potestas clavi,* but this is replaced by general pastoral care.

Imposition of Hands and Prayer for the Ordinand
The conferral is not complete without a prayer. In the 1967 rite the wish is uttered that God himself for his grace and for the sake of Jesus Christ will shape the ordinands and make them able to accomplish this service to the glory of God and the promotion of his Kingdom. In 1898 the prayer is based on a long and fervent wish, but in the 1993 version it is difficult to tell whether the wish really is optative or rather imperative: 'And God himself make you able for this service so that you may be satisfactory in it...'

The bishop and the clergy all place their hands on the head of the ordinand(s). The bishop prays that the almighty Father will accept, preserve, and strengthen the new servant in the ministry once again described. The 1993 prayer is somewhat shortened in comparison with the original of 1898, leaving out quite a few words that can, however, be heard as sheer pleonasms. In both Faeroese rites the prayer eventually leads on to the Lord's Prayer. The bishop says, 'Amen'; the pastors (in 1993 the congregation) say, 'Amen'; the bishop says, 'In the name of Jesus, Amen'. Before retiring to the sacristy the bishop and the ordinands remain for a while on their knees. A hymn is sung before the Eucharist takes place.

Conclusion
The two Faeroese rites are connected with two important incidents in the Lutheran Church in the islands: the appointment of a vice-bishop in 1963 and

of a diocesan bishop in 1990. These two men carried out their own translations of the rite, and I think I have found sufficient terminological evidence to argue that their conception of the ministries of a bishop and a pastor were not quite the same.

In the rite first used in 1967 the role of the Holy Spirit is more limited, in the collect at the beginning of the service as well as in the invocation after the presentation of those to be ordained. The subjective listening prevails over the utterance of the Word, the heart over the Spirit. This is not good for the confidence of those who are called to the ministry of the Word. Could this have been corrected or did it justify the introduction of another rite?

The damage was certainly corrected in the rite that could be heard in the cathedral of this new diocese in 1993. But here the effort to loosen the grip of the all-dominant father of Faeroese church language, leaving the literal course of translation in favour of the more hazardous waters of the idiomatic mode (Funding: 177), resulted in a terminology that is not exact enough. For example, when prayers are based on biblical texts read shortly before or afterwards, the terminology should attempt to be the same to make the coherence as obvious as possible. Too little effort seems to have been made to clarify the various homiletic positions, and so the kerygmatic, didactic, therapeutic, and dialogical aspects are blurred.

The declaration of conferral is, in its gentle as well as in its harsh form, so strong and dominant an element in the whole rite that it leaves little for the final prayer. The conferral has taken place with the bishop's declaration: all God now has to do is to give his blessing. In the new Danish rite of 1987 the conferral is no longer an element in its own right. The ministry is entrusted to the ordinands at the prayer of all those present at the ordination, the bishop, the pastors, and the congregation. Here all depends on the grace of God. In the Faeroe Islands it is still not quite so.

After the ordination the new pastors will still be shipped to their parishes in the archipelago, where they will be properly installed and soon be busy serving the members of their congregations from baptism to funeral. With many small villages scattered on various islands this ministry can include as many as three islands and as many as six churches. The pastors should not despair, even if they find it impossible to visit all their churches every Sunday, for with solid books of homilies and good lay readers the congregations are perfectly able to carry out a service of the Word on their own. If the ordination takes place in Tórshavn Cathedral on a Sunday, this is probably what the pastors' future flocks will be doing meanwhile, although the congregational boards will be invited to the ordination.

None of this is reflected in the rites we have examined. Even though the everyday context of the Faeroese pastors is far from being similar to that of their Danish colleagues, rites used in the Faeroe Islands in general must be either Danish or simply 'mere translations' of the authorised Danish rites. Whether they are translated or not, how they are translated, and whether they in their turn have been authorised – seems to depend nowadays on the bishop and him alone.

So why bother to translate an old rite when new issues are at hand? May we assume that the authoritarian, confessional and nationalist concept of ordained ministry is still as much a reality in the Faeroes as it was in Denmark a century ago?

References

Bekendtgørelse af regulativ for vicebiskoppen for Færøerne. 1963. BEK nr 198 af 31/05/1963.

Craddock, Fred B. 2001. *As One Without Authority.* Revised and with New Sermons. St. Louis, Missouri: Chalice Press.

Forslag til ritualbog for den danske evangelisk-lutherske folkekirke. Gudstjenester og kirkelige handlinger. 1965. Copenhagen: Det Kgl.Vajsenhus' Forlag.

Funding, Elsa. 1998. *Føroyskar bíbliutýðingar og týðingarroyndir. Søga og másligar samanberingar.* Manuscript.

Hansen, Jákup Reinert. 2001. Færøsk salmedigtning. *Hymnologiske Meddelelser* 30. árg. Nr. 1, ed. Peter Balslev-Clausen, 3-26. Copenhagen: Salmehistorisk Selskab og Nordisk Institut for Hymnologi.

Papers from the episcopal archives. 1967. Copenhagen.

Prestavígsla í Dómkirkjuni 16. jan. 1994.

Próstainnseting 1991.

Rasmussen, Petur Martin. 1987. *Den færøske sprogrejsning med særligt henblik på kampen om færøsk som kirkesprog i national og partipolitisk belysning.* Í Hoydølum.

Ritual til kirkjuvígslu og prestavígslu. 1968. Tórshavn.

Vejledning i Den danske Folkekirkes gudstjenesteordning. Med de autoriserede ritualer. 1955. 2d ed. Copenhagen: P. Haase & Søns Forlag.

The Ordination of Pastors and Bishops in the Evangelical-Lutheran Church in Greenland

Karen Langgård

The Inuit forefathers of the Greenlanders immigrated to Greenland about 900 AD and at the same time the Norse population came to Greenland. The Norse population were Christianised soon afterwards. They somehow disappeared during the fifteenth century, but the Inuit remained. In 1721 Hans Egede started the Danish Mission – and colonisation of Greenland – near the place that is now the capital of Greenland, Nuuk (formerly Godthåb in Danish). In 1733 the Moravian Brethren also came to Godthåb. They left Greenland in 1900 – and their congregations became part of the Danish Mission. In this article only the Danish Mission and the Greenlandic Church will be considered. In 1905 the Mission became by law the Church of Greenland. This remained part of the Evangelical-Lutheran Church of Denmark and it is today a diocese within that church. During colonial times Greenland was a closed country. The Mission took care of education. When the country was opened up in 1950 other denominations (and religions) came to Greenland. In 1953 Greenland was decolonised and became part of Denmark. In 1979 Greenlandic Home Rule was established. By a law of 1993 the Greenlandic Church was given its own bishop (1994), appointed by the Danish state. The administration of the Greenlandic Church, however, comes under the Home Rule Administration.

Hans Egede charted the course of the Danish Mission. Its work was to be carried out in Greenlandic; the Greenlanders were to learn how to read and write and he had to make some of them do part of the missionary work. Ever since then economic resources have mostly been too scarce and there was a lack of educated people to do the job, whether Danish missionaries, or Greenlandic national catechists (as they were called), not least as the Mission spread all over the country. A crisis came during Denmark's war with England (1807-1814).

All the missionaries had left Greenland except one. The Danish authorities therefore felt obliged to ordain a Greenlander for the first time. This took place in 1815, in Greenlandic. However, the Greenlandic wording has not been preserved. With this ordination the tradition that the ordained person should immediately preach during the same service was inaugurated in Greenland. Authority was implanted into the ordained by letting him preach to the Danes too. At that time it might have been seen as a step forward in nation building; today it looks more like a significant sign of colonial power.

Not to ordain except when there was a lack of Danish missionaries became the policy of the Danish authorities until the law that transformed the Mission into the Greenlandic Church, and even longer than that. The distinction was drawn very sharply between those who were ordained and those who were not. This being so, the Greenlanders accepted this, but then they wanted some catechists to have more education in order to become ordained. However, during the nineteenth century the Danish authorities let very few Greenlanders (four to be precise) have more education. During the twentieth century the Greenlanders were sent as missionaries to East Greenland and Thule and they increasingly replaced the Danish priests, but the problem of how to serve the vast coastline in an effective way remained. It remains even today, and the solution now is to operate with *ad hoc* permission to officiate at the Eucharist. There was and is no ordination rite for catechists.

The official forms of ordination liturgy in Greenland are shaped in relation to the Danish rites. As in Denmark, there exists an ordination liturgy only for the pastor and the bishop. That there are only these two rites in Denmark is described as remarkable (Iversen, Part II.6 below). It is even more remarkable in Greenland, considering the very permeating and overwhelming part played by the 'national catechists' from the time of Hans Egede until now. Because of the conditions in which the Mission worked in Greenland, with the language and the size of the country, the missionaries realized that they had to rely on training the Greenlanders in order to make them capable of serving as catechists (teaching their fellow Greenlanders about Christianity as well as some educational subjects). As a consequence, the basic composition of the group who served the Danish Mission has been a large number of catechists and a few ordained ministers. In the eighteenth century, this meant a very small number of Danish pastors, some Danish catechists (the last one left Greenland in 1796) and a growing number of national catechists, that is, Greenlanders. The Greenlandic Church still relies on a large number of Greenlandic catechists, but now together with Greenlandic pastors.

The first ordination rite of which wording has been preserved is from 1902 and with some changes in the wording – especially in 1974 – this is still the one in use. The versions of the rite have not been authorized since 1902. Other rites – the rites of baptism, marriage and the Holy Communion – were translated into Greenlandic by Hans Egede and his sons (Hans Egede, 1742; Poul Egede 1756). In time, they were gradually improved and changed. In 1783 the Danish Mission published a book containing the rites. Poul Egede was one of the people behind it, and in 1819, Otto Fabricius reedited and enlarged it. The next version came in 1887, but none of these includes any ordination rite.[1]

The 1902 Rite for the Ordination of Pastors

There is no single word or concept for 'ordination' in Greenlandic. For the ordination of ministers *'palasinngortitsineq'* is used, meaning literally, 'the act of making someone a *"palasi"*. *'Palasi'* is originally a loan-word (*'præst'*) and is the word that in the Danish Mission and the Greenlandic Church has always meant 'the one who serves as ordained in the Church', not considering whether a person would be called in Danish a missionary (*'missionær'*), rector (*'førstepræst'*), catechist supervisor (*'overkateket'*), who was given responsibility for a number of other catechists, and so on.

The Structure of the Rite

In the 1902 rite, the directions cover only part of what is going on overall in the church, when an ordination takes place. In the list below the parts written in capital letters are not printed in the liturgy book:

1. PRELUDE (organ) and/or INTROIT HYMN (during which the Procession of the ordinand, the ordaining minister and other ministers of the Church takes place)
2. Hymn (Greenlandic version of Grundtvig's version of Nordal Brun's *'Ånd over ånder'*)
3. Greeting (salutation)
4. Introductory collect
5. Epistle (Eph. 4.7-13)
6. Hymn

---

1. One or two books have been published about the history of the Danish Mission and later the Church in Greenland (Ostermann 1921, Lidegård 1999). The substantive history still has to be written. For references and further information on the historical development hinted at above, see an enlarged Danish edition of this article in *Kirkehistoriske Samlinger* 2004, Copenhagen.

7. Presentation sermon
8. Presentation
9. Ordination hymn.
10. Antiphon: ordaining minister – congregation: the wording is written in the rite (a Greenlandic version of *Veni, Creator Spiritus*)
11. Ordination prayer
12. Ordination address
13. The four readings (Matt. 28.18-20; Titus 1.5-9; 1 Pet. 5.2-4; 2 Tim. 4.1-5)
14. Ordination (with handshake)
15. Ordination prayer for the laying-on of hands (concluding with the Lord's Prayer)
16. The newly ordained and the ordaining minister kneel and pray in silence
17. Hymn (Greenlandic version of *'Aleneste Gud'* – *'Gloria in excelsis Deo'*)
18. The newly ordained pastor preaches.
19. Hymn with eucharistic theme
20. Eucharist, prayer and blessing
21. HYMN
22. FINAL PRAYER
23. POSTLUDE (organ)

The rite follows the Danish rite authorized in 1898. The translation into Greenlandic was made by former missionary, later lector, Christian Rasmussen. It was published, with a re-translation of the Greenlandic text into Danish, as a parallel text.[2] This text does not differ from the wording of the 1898 Danish rite, except in the following points:

The hymn that is printed in the rite is a revised version of Peder Egede's translation of *Veni, Creator Spiritus* into Greenlandic, published in 1756 (Poul Egede 1756).

---

2. It is not explicitly recorded that this is a re-translation into Danish. However in a report from the first plenary meeting of pastors and other church ministers (i.e. including both North and South West Greenland) in 1910, it was noted that a new service book had been discussed, and among other things it had been decided that not the Danish translation of the Greenlandic wording, but the Danish rite itself should be published, together with the Greenlandic wording. From this it appears that re-translation was the norm and that this is what we have in the 1902 Service Book.

The Danish wording of the presentation in the 1898 version has the following wording (in my translation): 'Those men who today, according to apostolic custom, by prayer and laying-on of hands shall be ordained to the service of the Word, are the *candidati theologiae* NN, who have been called to ..... (Here the names of the ordinands and the places where they are to serve are read aloud)'.

In the Greenlandic rite the following parallel text in Danish is written (in my translation): 'The man who today, according to apostolic custom, shall be ordained minister by our prayer and laying-on of hands, is a catechist supervisor, who according to the royal admission to ordination from the Ministry of Church Affairs is appointed to be minister at ...'. In the Greenlandic text Christian Rasmussen used the form also used in administrative documents in those days and therefore containing an expression normally used for a government minister: 'whom the one next to the king (i.e. the government minister) has appointed as minister in ..., because the king ordered him to do so'.

As seen already in 1815, it was the custom from the very beginning for catechists who (often after further education) were ordained to preach immediately after the ordination act in the presence not only of Greenlanders but also of attending Danes, in order to enhance their authority among their fellow Greenlanders. This custom is reflected in the rite.

The Wording of the Rite

When considering the wording of the rite, it is necessary to look at the Greenlandic terms used for some key Christian concepts around the turn of the century.

Nic E Balle, missionary and Principal at Ilinniarfissuaq, was a very masterful person. His strong feelings about what terms to use for some of the key concepts played a role in every discussion and every text printed in the late nineteenth century and of course also when the 1887 Service Book was published. This came out full of footnotes containing alternative expressions. Balle died in 1900 but the discussion continued. Indeed, there are still some people today who would like to continue the debate about exactly the same terms that were discussed all that time ago in Nalunaarutit.

The Spirit and the Devil: Balle adamantly insisted that the Spirit should be called '*anersaaq*' and not '*anerneq*' (last described in Wilhjelm 1997; 2001). Both of the words are derived from the same stem '*aner-*', which means 'to breathe' (by then extinct, however, as a verb in itself). With a suffix '*-saar-*' ('try to make it happen ...') added, '*anersaarpoq*' means 'he breathes'. This choice cannot be based on meaning or etymology, but could be based on what was used in a particular person's own part of Greenland. Samuel Kleinschmidt wanted to use '*anerneq*' arguing that this was used by most people (and he does not mention '*anersaaq*' at all in his dictionary).[3] The choice could also be based on what had been used, for example, by the Egede family: they used '*anersaaq*'.

'*Anerneq*' was the term used in the 1902 rite, '*anersaaq*' the term used in the 1974 rite.

Balle further insisted that the Devil should be '*Djaavulu*' in Greenlandic while Kleinschmidt continued to use the name that the Egede family had used, that is, the Inuit name for the best helping spirit: '*Toornaarsuk*', because this was firmly established.[4] The outcome seen from the perspective of the Church was that the Devil was called '*Djaavulu*'. However, the most powerful swear-word in Greenlandic, often said by drunkards, has rather swallowed the whole set of terms that have been used: '*Djaavulu Toorngaarsuk Satani*'. As no term is left out it ought to be effective!

Holy: Balle also thought that the term used for 'holy' was inadequate. A discussion in the early twentieth century shows that the terminology must still have been unsettled in 1902.

When the Mission started, loan-words had to be used, for example, for animals that were not known (Kleivan 1978). Moreover, Egede and his sons were very cautious about translating key concepts such as 'God', 'holy' and 'sin' when they did not find any obvious expressions for them. It is often mentioned that the Lord's Prayer in the first rendering in Greenlandic had 'our daily seal meat' instead of 'our daily bread'. However, I want to draw attention to the fact that as early as 1756 the expression had changed to: 'our needs' ('*pissatsinnik*'). The loan-word for 'sin' stands out in the texts (including the hymns), but by 1756 Poul Egede was using '*ajortuliaq*' (which happens to be the term used now and in the most recent translation of the Bible) and other words with the stem '*ajor-*', meaning 'is bad, wicked, evil' (Poul Egede 1756).

---

3. Kleinschmidt (1814-86) was born in Greenland of a German father and a Danish mother in the Moravian Mission. Later after a conflict with the Moravian Brethren, he was a teacher at Ilinniarfissuaq, translator of the Bible, creator of a Greenlandic grammar based on the language's own typological features. As a lexicographer, he devised the standardized orthography that was used until the 1970s and worked together with Balle for many years, despite all their permanent controversies. (See Wilhjelm 2001 for a substantial description.)

4. Jens Chemnitz (one of the Greenlanders ordained in the later part of the eighteenth century) even published an article in the newspaper about what the Devil should be called (Atuagagdlitutit 1890/91, col 82 ff).

The loan-word for 'holy' was still used in 1756, but as a translation of 'to be true believers'. Poul Egede used *'iluartumik upper'* ('to believe in a right way'), and for a long time *'iluar-'* was the stem used for 'holy'. The rendering of 'the Holy Spirit' is seen in Fabricius' hymnal as *'anersaaq iluartoq'*. This was used in the hymnbooks and in the 1819 Service Book (Fabricius 1819) until the hymnbook published in 1876 in which *'anerneq iluartoq'* is used both in the hymns and in the rites. In the 1885 hymnbook the wording in the rites is changed back to *'anersaaq'*, while *'iluartoq'* is unchanged in the texts of the rites, but with footnotes added in which the alternative *'anerneq illernartoq'* is listed as permitted. The very same procedure is followed in the 1887 Service Book, a fact that indicates that the debate was vehement or it would not have been considered necessary in colonial times to print alternatives in a mission that was otherwise always determined to preserve a semblance of internal consensus in front of the congregation. In the 1876 hymnbook *'anerneq'* is used in most instances. However, in hymn no. 1, the Greenlandic version of the Danish rendering of Luther's hymn, *'Wir glauben alle ...'*, a compromise is seen. In verse 3 both *'anerneq'* and *'anersaaq'* (in the stem used in *'anersaarisaanut'*) are used: *'Upperpugut Anernermut / Guutip anersaarisaanut'* ('We believe in the Spirit, the one that God has as his spirit'). The vehemence of the discussion was mirrored in the hymnbooks and the rite. Even today some would like to discuss which version to use.

The choice of term for 'holy' was a matter of meaning and dialects: *'iluartoq'* meant 'to be right';[5] *'illernartoq'*[6] in the northern part of West Greenland

---

5. In the dictonaries we find the following glossing of *'iluarpoq'* (Poul Egede 1750), *'er bekvem, passer godt'*; (Fabricius 1804), 1. *'er bekvem; passer godt'* 2. *'er ret, er som den bør være'* 3. *'er retskaffen, er hellig'* 4. *'opfører sig tilbørlig, lever anstændig'*, 5. *'er fuldkommen, er som han bør'*, 6. *'er retfærdig , handler som han bør'*; (Kleinschmidt 1871), 1. *'er ret, er i sin orden, er som den bør være (fx passende til sin brug, sømmelig etc)'* 2. *'er retskaffen, lever og handler som han bør'* 3. *'er retfærdig, kendes ikke med synd eller tilregnes ikke synd.* [S.v. *iluartoq*: 1. *'det som er ret (som det bør være) ...'* 2. *'en retfærdig. Desuden bruges det passende for ...'* 3. *'hellig (ret i absolut forstand) i 'allakkat iluartut den hellige skrift'*; *'anerneq iluartoq'* *'den hellige ånd'*.]; (Schultz-Lorentzen 1926), *'er ret, er rigtig, er i sin orden, er som det skal være, er retskaffen, er retfærdig, er hellig'*.

6. In the dictionaries we find the following glossings of *'erlinnartoq / illernartoq'*: (Poul Egede 1750), *'erlinnartoq: dyrebar'*; (Fabricius 1804), *'erlinnartoq': 'kostbar, rar, dyrebar'*; (Kleinschmidt 1871), *'illernarpoq*: 1. *'man holder hævd over det'* 2. *'det er ikke til almindelig brug'* 3. *'især: er hellig'* [while s.v. *'erlinnartoq*: et klenodie (*'ujaqqat erlinnartut'*: *'ædelsten'*)]; (Schultz-Lorentzen 1904), *'illernarpoq': 'er værdifuld, er ikke for alle og enhver, er hellig'* [he too refers to *'erlinnar-'*]. Oqaatsit (1990) divides it into two lexemes: *'erlinnarpoq': 'er dyrebar, er kostbar'*, as opposed to *'illernarpoq': 'er hellig'*.

meant that something is precious for one, but in the southern part it meant that something is special and very precious, like gold or something similar. In the latter area it has a connotation of being separated from other things. Each expression covers one of the two meanings of 'holy': the right versus the separated that is seen as something special.

Although the term *'iluartoq'* had been used for a century (for example, in the expression for 'Holy Spirit'), it caused a very long discussion. Some found that it could not be used for the divine, because it was also used for very earthly matters. For example, the word could be used to express whether a pair of moccasins fitted.

'Illernartoq' presented some people with the same kind of problem. It could be used about something that someone owned and appreciated. It was not used just in religious contexts. The ordained catechist supervisor, Andreas Hansen, then turned to *'iluaatsuitsoq'*, an expression Balle had used. This is derived from the stem *'iluar-'*, but the stem is negated to *'iluaappoq'* and then negated once more to *'iluaatsuitsuuvoq'*, which literally means 'it is not anything that is not right' that is, 'it is holy'.

Christian Rasmussen chose to use *'illernartoq'* and not *'iluartoq'*. In the Danish re-translation he translates *'illarnartoq'*, when used in connection with the expression for the Holy Spirit as *'hellig'*, but uses *'højværdige'* instead of *'hellig'* when it is used in connection with the sacraments. This might be related to the discussion at that time.

In the 1902 rite, *'anerneq illernartoq'* is used. By the next rite (1974), the usage had in the meantime been fixed to *'anersaaq illernartoq'*.

The Lord's Prayer and the concepts of glory and honour and obedience: In the Lord's Prayer Hans Egede and sons rendered the first petition by the stem *'usore-'* ('to glorify').[7] The same stem is used at the end to render 'the honour'.[8] However, over time the meaning has changed through 'to praise some as lucky'

---

7. Egede's re-translation was *'Dit navn være lovet af menneskene'* ['Your name be praised. ..']. *'usore-'* meant according to Poul Egede's dictionary: *'berømmer, roser, nogen'* ['laud, praise, glorify'], and *'usornartoq'* meant *'berømmelig, rosværdig'* ['laudable, praisewor-thy']. Fabricius's dictionary gives: 1. *'berømmer, beundrer, priser lykkelig, lover'* 2. *'taler prægtig om en ting, skatter højt, agter stort, anser med beundring'*. Even Kleinschmidt's dictionary has: *'misunder ham (i god betydning), ønsker sig i hans sted, priser ham lykke-lig'*. Schultz-Lorentzen likewise. But since then the meaning seems to have developed more towards 'envy'. In a discussion that I had with some students at the Department of Theology at Ilisimatusarfik, and in which Bishop Sofie Petersen also participated, the general view on *'usore-'* was that it now only means 'to envy someone' and has thus become totally unsatisfactory in our context.

to become in the language today 'to want to be in someone's place'. Fabricius also uses *'usore-'* (Fabricius 1801). The same applies to the hymns in Kjer's hymnbooks (1834, 1838 & 1856). However, in the 1876 hymnbook the usage is changed and another stem predominates: *'naalaC-',* 'to obey', 'to listen in order to obey'.[9] In the dictionaries of Poul Egede and Fabricius, when *'at ære'* ['to honour'] is part of the meaning of *'naalaC-',* it is presumably more like the meaning in the Fourth Commandment. *'Naalagaq'* is the passive nominalization of the transitive part of *'naalaC-'.* It acquired the meaning of 'master' and 'lord' both in a secular meaning as 'authority', and in a Christian meaning as 'God the Lord'. In his dictionary, Kleinschmidt accentuates the reverence and the obedience in the verb stem *'naalaC-'.*

The verb stem *'naalannar-'* is derived from *'naalaC-'.* Kleinschmidt's dictionary is the first one to include it. It is glossed: 'one has to listen to him or obey him', 'one has to acknowledge him as one's superior', 'one subjects oneself to him', 'his ways deserve to be obeyed or oblige one to obedience'. Kleinschmidt adds the nominalization *'naalannarsuseq'* glossed as 'his glory, the essence in him that causes you to submit' when inflected to indicate the possessive 'his'. It appears that the stem *'naalannar-'* at the time of Kleinschmidt had a general meaning which could be used in secular matters too, and then had / was acquiring a more specific Christian meaning that covered by its derivatives concepts such as 'glorious', 'glory', 'glorify', 'glorifying'.[10]

The question is what were the connotations of *'naalannassuseq'* in the nineteenth century when it was introduced into the usage of the Mission and how

8. In the phrase, 'the Kingdom, the power and the glory', Danish has *'ære'* ('honour' not 'power').

9. In the dictionaries, Poul Egede has: *'adlyder, ærer, giver agt på';* Fabricius: intr: a. *'er lydig, er hørig',* b. *'er agtsom, giver agt';* trans: a. *'adlyder';* b. *'ærer';* c: *'giver agt på'.* Kleinschmidt: intr: 1. *'lytter, giver agt, er agtsom, hører efter det, som siges';* 2. *'adlyder, er lydig, er hørig, lystrer';* trans: 1 *'lytter a. til ham: venter på, at han skal sige noget, for da at gøre det';* b. *'til noget fra ham eller det: venter på at opfange en lyd derfra eller at høre noget om ham eller det, hvoraf man da kunne slutte sig til videre';* c. *'til det (et ord eller et bud) for at tage sig det til hjerte eller gøre derefter';* 2. *'adlyder ham'.*

10. Some 50 years later, in the dictionary compiled by Schultz-Lorentzen both of the meanings still seem to be used, i.e. both the more etymological and the more specifically Christian. For stem *'naalannar-'* he has: *'må adlydes, er myndig, er herlig'; 'naalannassuseq', 'herlighed'; 'naalannassusia', 'hans herlighed, hans majestæt'.* The derivatives of the stem seem still to be used not only about God, but could apparently also be used about secular authority.

was it introduced?[11] In the 1876 hymnbook, the rites still used 'usore-' in their wording of the Lord's Prayer. However, an almost 100% revision has taken place in the first two sections (The essence of God the Trinity and God the Father, Creator and his providence) of the 1876 hymnbook (ca 40 hymns), where the transitive stem 'naalaC-' and the stem 'naalannarsi-' have replaced 'usore-', resulting in a manifest change from praise and glorifying to obedience and the accentuating of God's authority. The way this shift towards 'naalaC-' took place is interesting because it shows that 'naalannassuseq' was not introduced as a lexicalised lexeme meaning 'glory', without a salient etymology. On the contrary, the shift is backed up by the verb 'naalaC-', 'to obey'.

The concept of 'herlighed' [glory] signifies the power of God that must be obeyed and also extreme effulgence (Kirkeleksikon for Norden s. v. Herlighed). But when using the Danish or English term, it is, so to speak, up to the faithful believer to act in accordance with it without having to be told to obey. In the Greenlandic term the focus is not on the essential feature of God, but on how this essential feature works on the believer. The Danish / English term speaks to us through its connotations of power and effulgence, while the Greenlandic term orders us how to respond, and thereby renders the mood passive.

When the expression 'naalannassuseq' was introduced and the trend was to use 'naalaC-', the setting was colonial. Furthermore, the Mission was strongly focused on being in control. It had some experience of separatist movements, and some members of the Mission seemed anxious about what would happen if Greenlanders gained more access to education and through this also to wider knowledge and thus competence to become more critical. Moreover, as part of the prevailing Victorianism, the Mission tried to improve the chastity of the Greenlanders. Balle grew more and more fixed on that point, especially after some events at Ilinniarfissuaq, the Catechists' Training College, now a Teacher Training College (Wilhjelm 1997). Moreover, the loose morals of the women rowers of the Women's Boat Expedition to the East coast of Greenland in the 1880s, made Balle block all plans for letting West Greenlanders become missionaries there (Langgård 1999). This might have been a further reason to stress obedience. Another difference between the 1902 rite and the Danish rite of 1898 is perhaps part of the same shift of discourse. In the Danish rite the ordained minister is to be the role model in, for example, purity, while the Danish re-translation has 'chastity', a very precise rendering of the Greenlan-

---

11. The Moravian Brethren also used 'usore-' in the Lord's Prayer, as is seen in their 1772 hymnbook (e. g. 268). In their 1878 hymnbook, they too use 'naalannar-' in the hymns. More research has to be done on their development of terminology.

dic *'piitaajuillutit'*.[12] In the 1974 rite, the expression used is: *'minguissutsikkut'*, derived from *'minguiC-'*, ('being pure, unblemished, without dirt').

Because a word like *'naalannassuseq'* has a very easily accessible etymology for speakers of Greenlandic as a mother tongue, it has not lost this through lexicalization, though used only as a Christian term. It is not an exact match for *'herlighed'* in Danish, which can be used about a landscape, an event, in a way that *'naalannassuseq'* cannot.[13] The etymology still gives it some of its connotations. Furthermore, obedience is a troublesome concept in Greenland today. This has partly to do with the de-colonization of the mind that is going on. Partly, and much more difficult, it has to do with a necessary debate on the realities of contemporary society versus the traditional way of upbringing and education, which considered silent and passive obedience as a major virtue to be inculcated into children.

The Hymns of the Rite

The 1902 rite prescribes the hymn, *'Annerussaartutit uumaa'* (no. 393 in the appendix of both the 1876 and the 1885 hymnbooks) to be sung at the beginning of the ceremony: *'Annerussaartutit uumaa*[14] is based on a version of the first of the three stanzas of Johan Nordahl Brun's hymn for Pentecost, a

---

12. How severe the Mission deemed what it considered to be loose morals is seen in the fact that if a student at Ilinniarfissuaq was caught having a sexual relationship he would be relegated. If a servant of the Mission was caught in adultery, he was dismissed. This procedure caused a lot of problems for the Mission and after 1905 for the Church, because there was always a lack of catechists, and the ones who had been dismissed went to the Royal Greenland Trading Company and got jobs there with a higher salary than they had had in the Mission/ Church. At the beginning of the twentieth century it was discussed whether and how the sinner might be kept in the service of the Church but as a teacher.

13. By contrast most Danes would not have any idea that *'herlighed'* (glory) has anything to do with *'herre'* ('master', 'lord'). The Greenlandic word is built of elements that are productive in the all-permeating derivational process found in Greenlandic. In addition to that, they are found in frequently used lexicalized expressions. This feature of the language means, that if some of the young people today who are not familiar with the Christian terminology, are asked about the meaning of *'naalannassuseq'*, they will have some vague idea that 'it is about God, isn't it? And he is such that one has to obey him'.

14. In the 1876 hymnbook it is annotated as rendered into Greenlandic by Thøger Sørensen (a Danish missionary), but revised by H F Jørgensen (a Danish missionary, one of the two editors of the hymnbook). In the 1885 hymnbook it is listed as translated by the two editors Jacob Kjer and H F Jørgensen. In the 1907 hymnbook

version that Grundtvig wrote in 1854 and published in the *Kirke og Hjem* hymnbook, 1897 (Malling, *'Ånd over ånder'*). The Greenlandic version does not cover the whole of the content: 'Spirit of spirits' is changed to 'that the spirit is the greatest one'. [15] The Trinity is not mentioned. The binding of souls is mentioned, but there is nothing about the heavenly bride. Only the preparation of souls for God is mentioned.[16] The Greenlandic version has: 'You usually gather those who have gained faith in Jesus', but it has nothing equivalent to the Danish expressions 'to explain Jesus', 'to build up his church', 'to enlighten his people' or 'that is your work'. Instead of '...let us experience that (i. e. your work), / and be in our heart the interpreter of God's love', the Greenlandic version has: 'you have many things to do / make us blessed/saved, too'. However, the main content about the Holy Spirit as the one who will be a father and bind souls to God is retained.

In the Danish rite the versicle and response sung by the officiant and the congregation is hymn no. 262 in the 1953 Danish Hymnbook, i.e. Grundtvig's version of *Veni, sancte Spiritus* (based too, on Luther's version of it), characterized by fine rhymes and by a vocabulary using words like 'joy, fire, light, love, burn, enlighten, praise', finishing the stanza with: 'and singing as if in the choir of angels: hallelujah, hallelujah, hallelujah!'. It is not exactly the same fanfares that sound in the Greenlandic rite, where the hymn chosen is based on *Veni, Creator Spiritus* (Malling, s. v. *Kom, o Gud skaber, helligånd* and s. v. *Kom, Gud Faders ånd fuldgod*) and rendered by Christian Rasmussen as follows (in my English translation):

1. Oh, Holy Spirit, come to us / and visit our souls; / we who know so little, / present for our eyes the right goal.
2. Renew truly / all thought of ours; / and remove us away / from everything that is evil.

---

the wording is retained unchanged, but it is noted that the hymn was written by Nordahl Brun and then the Greenlandic version is attributed to Thøger Sørensen.

15. On the translation of Danish hymns into Greenlandic, see Nielsen, 1936; Langgård, 1994 and 2002.

16. A cautious attitude towards the bridal theme (especially towards the eroticizing perspective found in Brorson's hymns) is evident in the hymns of the Danish Mission, and with good reason: it was a difficult matter to present in the restricted Greenlandic of the missionaries, in a mission field where the missionaries had at the beginning to struggle against polygamy, and continuously against sexual customs that differed from the Mission's moral code.

3. Give us the true faith / in our Father on high, / who for his love of mankind / gave them his Son.

4. Let our great Saviour / make us truly his own; / make us first and foremost obedient towards him / who saves sinners.

5. You, Spirit, who yourself are God, / holy, completely holy, / be highly praised among all / who live on the wide earth!

A good reason to choose this hymn was that it had already been translated into Greenlandic by Peder Egede, and it was the first hymn in Greenlandic specifically about the Holy Spirit.[17] It had seven stanzas (in the original) and followed the content of the Danish version quite closely, though the wording was changed in later revisions. In Kjer it is cut down to 6 stanzas, and its content changed by leaving out the Devil and instead stressing that we have been saved and therefore wish to love the Saviour more than anyone else (Kjer1856 no. 136). The praise of God the Father, the Son and the Holy Spirit is retained.[18]

The shift from 'usore-' to 'naalaC-' in the first sections of the 1876 hymnbook, was not carried through in all sections, and not in no. 136. On the contrary the revision removed an ungrammatical use of 'naalaC-' in the third stanza (the stanza not included in the rite). Furthermore, 'usornarsiit' ('be praised / glorious') is not replaced by 'naalannarsiit' ('be so masterly that one has to obey you / be glorious') until the 1885 hymnbook where 'asalarput' ('let us love him') is also replaced by 'naalallarpullu' ('let us deeply [listen to him] and obey him').

The 1885 hymnbook version is the one used in the 1902 rite, but leaving out the third stanza, while the 1974 rite has 6 stanzas. The version of *Veni*,

---

17. Published as no. 39 among the 42 hymns in Poul Egede's *Catechismus Mingneq* (*The Smaller Catechism*) (Egede, 1756). Hans Egede had already written about the Trinity in his translation of Luther's hymn, *'Vi troe alle paa een Gud'* and of *'Aleneste Gud'* (*'Gloria in excelsis Deo'*, originally Greek), both of them published in Egede 1742.

18. Kjer revised the Greenlandic hymnbook in the period when the *Evangelisk-Kristelig Salmebog* was used in Denmark. He shortened and simplified the Greenlandic hymns, but he did not transform the hymnbook into an exact equivalent of the Danish one, still less translated it into Greenlandic, as some sources in Denmark have thought (e. g. Thuesen 1988, cf Langgård 2001). For example, the *Evangelisk-Kristelig Salmebog* left out *'Kom Gud Skaber..'*: Kjer did not.

Creator Spiritus in the 1902 rite demonstrates the tendency of the period to focus on *'naalaC-'* and to introduce *'naalannar-'*.[19]

Conferral of Ministry accompanied by Prayer as constitutive of Ordination

Based on the 1898 Danish Rite, the Greenlandic rite of 1902 is a conglomerate of ordination as prayer and ordination as conferral or handing over of ministry.[20] In the 1902 rite, the conferral was expressed as follows: 'I ask you then in accordance with the duty that has been given to me: Do you promise ......?'. The fact that the officiant asks this question *ex officio* is emphasised by the use of both of the words for job (*'kiffartuut'* as well as *'atorfik'*. Of these *'kiffartuut'* has a stronger connotation of service, while *'atorfik'* is the word for a job as an employee). The shaking of hands takes place after the ordinand has stood up and before he kneels again to hear the words of conferral.

The wording of the conferral itself was in the Danish re-translation *'overantvorder'*: 'I now then hand over this holy duty, the duty of minister and preacher, following the apostolic custom, in the name of God, the Father, the Son and the Holy Spirit, ...'. However, the Greenlandic rendering of the conferral uses *'illernartumik kiffartuuteqalersippakkit'* which has none of the archaic tone of the Danish *'overantvorder'*. It simply means: 'I let you begin to have a holy duty'. This wording has been changed in the 1974 rite to *'tunniuppara'* which is the everyday word for 'to give something to somebody'. The duty is now expressed only through *'atorfik illernartoq'*, that is, the word that has no connotations of service in it. It is reduced to an appointment.[21] However, this word is followed by 'holy'. The prayer at the laying-on of hands follows this. The *'uagut'* ('we') and *'tamatta'* ('we all') turn out explicitly to include only the person who is ordaining and, when the prayer is finished, the assisting ministers, who are supposed to say 'Amen'. This was not changed in the 1974 rite and is still unchanged in the latest rite.

According to the 1902 rite, the ordained and the ordaining minister will

19. In his Danish re-translation, Christian Rasmussen uses *'højlovet'* ('highly praised') which is the word he otherwise uses in order to render the stem *'illernar-'* in connection with the sacraments.
20. For such a description of the Danish rite, cf. Eckerdal 1989, 47, 53.
21. Some would say that this shift from *'kiffartuut'* to *'atorfik'* has been requested by the Greenlanders, because they see *'kiffartuut'* as not equivalent to *'embede'* and therefore signifying their generally inferior education compared with that of the Danish pastors.

pray a silent prayer and then after the Greenlandic version of *Gloria in excelsis Deo*, the newly ordained is to preach. After the sermon the Eucharist is celebrated and he is to receive the Holy Communion. This is followed by the prayer of thanksgiving for the Eucharist, the blessing and a hymn. It is unclear whether only the newly ordained received the Holy Communion, but the reports about ordinations at the beginning of the twentieth century indicate that the ordinand and some of his family received. This is different from the ordination in 1815, where it was an important part of the ceremony that both the Danes and the Greenlanders and the ordinand communicated together.

In the 1974 rite the directions after the last amen are much shorter and fewer and with no mentioning of the newly ordained preaching. Moreover, the direction given about the Eucharist is an impersonal expression: '....and after this the Eucharist shall be officiated'. I have received two copies of the latest rite in the new orthography, and they differ in the directions given after the final 'Amen'. Both of them include a sermon, but in one of them it is not said by whom; in the other the sermon is to be delivered by one of the newly ordained (it is now usual for more than one to be ordained at the same time, after they have completed the education programme together). Finally, in both the rites there is to be a Eucharist, and one of the newly ordained is to assist at the Eucharist.

Ordination Hymns

In 1907 a new hymnbook was published.[22] This had a new section, *'palasinngortitsineq'*, 'ordination of pastors', containing one hymn, Andreas Hansen's version of Grundtvig's *'Du som går ud fra den levende Gud'* (based on 'O Spirit of the living God', written by Montgomery). [23] In the 1971 hymnbook it was placed in the Pentecost hymns section (as no. 231).

In 1937 an appendix was published (Tapii, 1937). This included among its hymns for Pentecost a hymn written by Pavia Petersen, which was moved to the section *'palasinngortitsineq'* in the 1971 hymnbook (the next, and till now

---

22. This hymnbook was the first one after the Danish Mission had become the Greenlandic Church and had absorbed the Moravian congregations after the Moravian Brethren were made to leave Greenland in 1900. It was also the first hymnbook that included the work of many Greenlandic hymn writers.
23. Andreas Hansen (1860-1909) was an ordained catechist supervisor and hymn writer. On the translation of hymns, see Nielsen 1936; Langgård 2002.

latest hymn book) as no. 267.[24] Further, an ordination hymn written by his father, Jonathan Petersen and a translation by Gerhard Egede of Grundtvig's hymn, *'I dag på apostolisk vis'* (DS 1953, no. 294) were published in it (as no. 268 and no. 266).[25] It is worth comparing Jonathan Petersen's ordination hymn with Pavia Petersen's. Jonathan Petersen was deeply influenced by the tendencies prevailing around the turn of the century. In both his two stanzas, obedience (stem *'naalaC-'*) to God's will and commands are mentioned as the key terms to become a good servant of God. In Pavia Petersen's hymn God is asked instead – in metaphorical language – to open the door to the Word and to let the Word sound beautiful on the tongue of those who are in the service of God and, through this, ripen in the hearts of the listeners. It is Pavia Petersen's hymn that has been used in those two services of ordination for which I have seen the order of service, not the one written by Jonathan Petersen.[26]

Gerhard Egede's 'transferred' hymn is used too. It has all the usual losses as most often found in such a process in the Greenlandic hymnbooks (Langgård, 2002), but one or two expressions are of more direct bearing on the message of the hymn. In the first stanza he emphasizes the congregation by using the word *'ilagiit'* ('congregation') when he is translating *'Herrens små'* ('the Lord's little ones'). In the second stanza he has *'ajortilikuluusugut'* ('us poor sinners') with connotations of misery. In Grundtvig's text we find the idea that we came yesterday, tomorrow our days are numbered. The attitude is changed towards a more conservative idea about the relationship to God as centred in the congregations, and towards a more condemnatory attitude.

---

24. Pavia Petersen (1904-1943) was the son of Jonathan Petersen. He was a catechist supervisor and author.
25. Jonathan Petersen (1871-1961) was educated as catechist, organist, teacher at Ilinniarfissuaq, poet, composer, lexicographer. Gerhardt Egede (1892-1969) was ordained and was *'visitationsprovst'* ('visiting dean').
26. Jonathan Petersen often uses the stem *'naalaC-'* in his hymns and differs in this from the other great poet, Henrik Lund, who avoids the use of this stem. Henrik Lund also gave a presentation at the South Greenlandic pastors' meeting in 1911, where in full accordance with the message of his poems he spoke about *'Ivangiiliu', 'inatsisit' 'pinnagit'* (The Gospel, not the Law) (Langgård, [1984] 87 chap. 6). The same difference is seen in their national songs, in their attitude to the colonial Danish authorities (e. g. Langgård 2000). It seems reasonable to me to see a political meaning in the use of *'naalaC-'* around 1900. However, it should be stressed, that even with the strong politicizing mobilization that took place during the establishment of Home Rule, at no time has the origin of the hymns affected their use.

The Rite for the Ordination of Pastors from 1974 onwards

The 1902 rite for the ordination of pastors was revised in 1974, and this revised version is the one that is still used, with minor revisions and with the new orthography. The latest version is undated, but as Home Rule is mentioned, it must have been done after 1979. Although Greenland has Home Rule, there still exists a confessional community between Denmark and Greenland, which means that the rites in use in Denmark are also valid in Greenland. It is presupposed that there can be some adjustments to Greenlandic conditions (including translation into Greenlandic). Although a new Danish rite was authorised in 1987 (with the creed inserted, with alternative readings, with no conferral of ministry and with the last 'Amen' said not only by ministers, but by the congregation), the Greenlandic Church still uses what is essentially the 1898 rite. The changes made since 1902 consist partly of some formalities, partly some terminological developments, partly an updating of the language in general, and finally, a change related to participation in the Eucharist.

I will not try to evaluate the general updating of the language, as to whether it has become smoother in all details. The new translation of the Bible published in 2001 means that at least the biblical readings now have to be adjusted to the new wording.

The formalities mentioned above are that the 1974 rite speaks about the Ministry of Church Affairs as did the 1902 rite, but in 1974 the text states that 'NN will become a pastor in Greenland' (which in 1902 might have been too obvious to be mentioned). In the latest version Greenland's Home Rule Administration is mentioned as the appointing authority.

Viewed from a terminological perspective, the 1974 rite and thereby also the latest one uses the terminology that resulted from the vehement debate before and after 1900. The spirit is *'anersaaq'*, 'holy' is *'illernartoq'*. Glory (for Danish *'herlighed / ære'*) is fixed as derivatives of the stem *'naalannarsi-'*.

However, the tendency to stress obedience and obeying through listening with the use of the verb *'naalappoq'* has stopped. The translation of *Veni, Creator Spiritus* is again a hymn with 6 stanzas. In the fifth stanza, which is the fourth one in the 1902 rite, the wording has been revised to be similar to the one in Kjer's old version, encouraging us to believe sincerely in (God's) Son, our Saviour, and to love him more than anyone else. In the final stanza we find *'anersaaq illernatutit'* ('you spirit who are holy') –and a repetition of *'illernar-'* in *'illernarsiit'* ('become holy'). This means that all words derived from the stem *'naalaC-'* have been removed. In the Lord's Prayer the wording is as it is nowadays: *'naalannarsi-'* is used at the end of the prayer for glory, while to render 'hallowed be' in the first petition *'illernarsili'* is used.

As already mentioned in relation to the 1902 rite, the conferral is found in all the versions of the rite. However, the wording changed a little between 1902 and 1974, as shown in the description of the 1902 rite. The handshake is done (standing as already in 1902, followed by the laying-on of hands while the ordinand is kneeling). The prayer is still just clerical, the last 'Amen' only uttered by the ministers.

In the 1974 rite the old tradition that the ordained should preach as soon as he has received ordination has remained unchanged, while it is sometimes cut out of the latest undated rite, depending on the actual ordination. The additional authority that it was thought necessary to obtain through this in colonial times is no longer felt to be needed. Furthermore, in recent years more education has been delivered in groups, and several people have been ordained at the same time. However, in some instances at least the old tradition is preserved. If several are ordained, one of them preaches.

Finally, the Eucharist is now for everyone, with the newly ordained, or one of them, as assistant. After the Eucharist the service is to be finished in the usual way. However, nothing is said at the beginning about what should be done before the rite starts.

Since there is community of confession between Greenland and Denmark, and the Greenlandic rites are not authorized separately, there is nothing to prevent the rite from being adjusted to follow the 1987 Danish rite. This might even be expected, since that is what had happened to the rite for the ordination of bishops.

The Rite for the Ordination of Bishops

The ordination of bishops is called *'biskopinngortitsineq'* (literally: 'the act of letting someone become a bishop').[27] As is the case in Denmark the ordination rite for bishops is very much like the one for pastors. In Greenland there has in principle not been a special rite developed and published. However, in practice the bishops' ordinations have differed from the pastors' ordinations, and since the 1987 Danish rite was authorized, the ordinations of bishops have been performed in accordance with that. No Service Book has been published, only the orders of service and the wording of the rite used on the four occasions when ordinations/inductions have taken place: two ordinations of a

---

27. By analogy with *'palasinngortitsineq',* the term used for pastors.

vice-bishop,[28] one induction of a bishop, and finally, one ordination of a bishop.[29]

The printed orders of service do not show whether there was a procession or when it took place, though, of course, there was a procession, and it did not enter the church during the prelude, as the procession at a pastor's ordination did, but after the prelude while the congregation sang a hymn (which seems to be different from the Danish usage).

It can be seen from the printed orders of service that the ceremony was carried out partly in Greenlandic partly in Danish.

In all of the three ordinations the Creed was inserted after the Epistle (Eph. 4.7-13), as is the case in the 1987 Danish rite.

The antiphon used at the ordination of pastors and based on *Veni, Creator Spiritus*, is replaced here by the one used in Denmark, i.e. Grundtvig's translation of *Veni, Sancte Spiritus* and a rendering of this into Greenlandic.

There are four readings from the Bible. The same texts were not used in all the ordination services, but the texts chosen were all taken from those given as alternatives in the Danish rite.[30] In all three services, verses of hymns have been sung by the congregation between the scriptural readings, in full accordance with the current Danish rite. Similarly the newly ordained bishop is supposed to preach after the ordination, but no Eucharist is celebrated – both elements in accordance with the Danish rite.[31]

Even more important is the development of the conferral: in the 1980 order

---

28. The Danish legal title used was 'vicebiskop', which indicates a deputy or auxiliary bishop. The literal translation 'vice-bishop' has been used here, as the position of the bishop in Greenland was not entirely equivalent to that indicated by the English terms 'suffragan bishop', 'area bishop' or 'auxiliary bishop'. The bishops appointed in Greenland had no deputising duties in the Diocese of Copenhagen or anywhere else outside Greenland. The same applied to the vice-bishops appointed in the Faeroe Islands (Hansen, Part II.2).

29. On 17th February 1980 Jens-Christian Chemnitz was ordained as vice-bishop (after the establishment of Home Rule; for a comment on the establishment of this post, see Wilhjelm, 1978); on 16th September 1984 Kristian Mørch was ordained as vice-bishop, and on 19th June 1994 he was inducted as diocesan bishop (once Greenland had become a diocese in its own right); on 28th May 1995 cand. teol. Sofie Petersen was ordained bishop.

30. In 1980 and in 1984: Matt 28.18-20; Titus 1.5-9; 2 Tim 4.1-5; Acts 20.28-32. In 1995: Matt. 28.16-20; John 15.1-5; 2 Cor 5.14-21; Acts 20.28-32.

31. Bishop Sofie Petersen declined to preach when she was ordained (source: conversation with Sofie Petersen).

of service it is found with *'atorfik'* and *'tunniuppara'* (Cf the section above on the 1974 rite for pastors). However, there is a change in the ensuing prayer: the ministers will still say 'Amen' but then the congregation will sing 'Amen. The same was done in 1994. In 1995 the 1987 Danish rite was followed: no conferral, no separate 'Amen' from the ministers, but an 'Amen' from the congregation.

It is not at all surprising that the ordination of a bishop follows the Danish rite. Although the community of confession holds for both of them, the bishop's appointment differs from the pastor's appointment, because while the Church is administratively under Home Rule, the bishop is still appointed by the Danish authorities.[32] However, in the orders of service there is no mention of the appointing authority, but only of the post to which the ordinand is to be appointed. This is probably so because of decolonisation, as is the fact that although the decentralization of bishops' ordinations did not become part of the Danish rite until 1987, already in 1980 the ordination of a vice-bishop took place not in Copenhagen, but in Nuuk, where he was to serve. On the other hand this is not surprising, considering that the establishment of a vice-bishop in Greenland was part of the implementation of Home Rule.

The choice of hymns has differed. The only hymns that were sung at all the services were the Greenlandic version of Nordal Brun's *'Ånd over ånder'* (as it is at pastors' ordinations) and the Greenlandic version of *Gloria in excelsis Deo*, translated by Egede (Egede 1742), which can symbolize both the roots of the Christian Church in general and also the roots of the Greenlandic Church.

Since the ordination of a bishop does not take place entirely within the Greenlandic Church, as the ordaining bishop comes from Denmark and bishops from Denmark and the other Nordic countries attend, and some of them read one of the biblical readings, the ceremony is carried out partly in Greenlandic partly in Danish. This makes the ordination of a bishop different from the ordination of a pastor, which is nowadays an internal service of the Greenlandic Church with the Bishop of Greenland as ordaining bishop.

In this way, though the tradition in Denmark is not to stress the difference between pastors' and bishops' ordinations, there are more differences between the ordination of a pastor and the ordination of a bishop for a number of

---

32. The Greenlandic politicians may make laws about the Church. However, the laws are to be within the framework given by the Danish laws. The reason for the Danish appointment of the bishop is to underline the fact that the Church is inside the *Rigsfællesskab* (the Danish commonwealth, including Denmark, the Faeroe Islands and Greenland) and to emphasise the community of confession.

reasons: first, in recent years because of the lack of revision of the ordination rite for pastors; secondly, and more permanently, because of the differences seen in an ethno-national perspective, as the bishop's ordination is inter-Nordic. Finally, the festivity is much greater when ordaining a bishop. The ordination of a bishop will be transmitted on television, and the Church plans to have the ordination of pastors transmitted on the radio.

Summary and Conclusion

It was hard work for the missionaries (and for the Greenlanders) to develop the language for Greenlandic Christianity. However, a Christian terminology grew steadily, the people were Christianized. They were finally ready to become missionaries themselves in Thule and on the East coast; and to participate in discussion about some of the key concepts and how to express them in Greenlandic.

Simultaneously with the debate about some of the terminology, there also came a tendency to greater use of the verb 'naalaC-', and part of this was a terminological shift that took place during the last decades of the nineteenth century, changing the translation of 'glory' from a stem meaning that one 'has to praise' to a stem meaning that one 'has to listen and obey' ('naalannar-'). The tendency to focus on obedience lapsed in the twentieth century, but the term for 'glory' had become lexicalized and is still used. This development was mirrored in the first ordination rite (1902). The prior discussion of some key terms is also reflected in that rite.

Beside the terminology, the 1902 ordination rite was based on the Danish rite of 1898. This means that it can be characterized as 'conferral accompanied by prayer'. In 1974 a revised version was printed. In the 1970s a new Greenlandic orthography was introduced and Home Rule began. Both events are reflected in the rite published later on, though undated. This latest version is not in fact fixed, but it has not been revised on the basis of the 1987 Danish rite. This means that it still operates with a conferral, though it can easily be changed, because of the community of confession that Greenland has with Denmark and the Faeroe Islands in the *Rigsfællesskabet* (the commonwealth). One of the questions in connection with an ordination is who takes part in the Eucharist. The tradition since 1902 that it was the ordinand (together with some of his close family) has gradually changed into the congregation and the ordinand (or one of the ordinands, where there are several) assisting.

In 1980, one year after the establishment of Home Rule, a vice-bishop was appointed. Since 1994 a diocesan bishop has been installed in Nuuk. The most recent episcopal ordination took place in 1995. In the orders of service (there exists no printed rite) from these ordinations it can be seen that even in 1980, the ordination took place in Nuuk, where the vice-bishop was to serve. Apart from this decentralizing, the Danish development from conferral of ministry accompanied with prayer, to prayer alone is followed by the Greenlandic development. In 1980 conferral was still there. But in 1994 and 1995 (that is after 1987), it was cut out. Furthermore, in both 1980 and 1994, the ministers would still say 'Amen' and the congregation would then sing 'Amen'. In 1995 the 1987 Danish rite was followed: no conferral, no separate 'Amen' from the ministers, but an 'Amen' from the congregation.

The reason why these developments can take place easily is the community of confession between Greenland and Denmark and the Faeroe Islands. It therefore seems odd that the pastor's ordination rite has not been revised and adjusted to the developments towards prayer, away from conferral. Although, according to Iversen, there is not much of a difference to be experienced in the rite, as almost none of the congregation succeed in participating in the 'Amen', which is the part that would indicate the difference, there is still a difference (Iversen 1999, 6, opposing Eckerdal 1983). A further difference lies in the fact that the ordained minister is not said to be given the office by the ordaining minister acting by virtue of his own office.

The ordination of a pastor is nowadays an act within the Greenlandic Church, and is carried out in Greenlandic. When a bishop is ordained the outer festivity is greater than at a pastor's ordination. The ordination of a bishop also has another atmosphere, since the ordination ceremony will be carried out in both Greenlandic and in Danish. The Nordic participation instead of just Danish participation from outside Greenland is changing the setting from a post-colonial one to a more global or at least an international setting.

References

Atuagagdliutit. 1861-. Nuuk.
Avangnâmiok'. 1913-. Qeqertarsuaq
Bertelsen, Alfred. 1945. Grønlændere i Danmark. Bidrag til Belysning af Grønlandsk Kolonisationsarbejde fra 1605 til vor Tid. *Meddelelser om Grønland. Vol. 145.* Copenhagen: C. A. Reitzels Forlag.
Berthelsen, Fr. 1815. Brev til Mission Colligiet. In *Grønlandske missionsberetninger,* generelt 1814/15
Berthelsen, Rasmus. 1863. In *Atuagagdliutit,* col.19+ 336.
– 1877. In *Atuagagdliutit,* col. 186 ff

Bugge, Aage. 1928. Godthaab seminarium (1845-1928). In *Træk of Kolonien Godthaabs Historie 1728-1928.* ed. K Honoré Petersen. Nuuk.

Chemnitz, Jens. 1890/91. In *Atuagagdliutit* col.40.

Eckerdal, Lars. 1989. Den danske folkekirkes indvielsesliturgiske tradition i et luthersk liturgisk fællesskab. In *Under bøn og håndspålæggelse. Indvielse af missionærer, diakoner og præster,* ed. Hans Raun Iversen and V. Tranholm-Mikkelsen. Frederiksberg: Anis.

Egede, Hans. (1721-36)1925. Relationer fra Grønland. In *Meddelelser om Grønland.* Vol. 54, ed. Louis Bobé. Copenhagen.

Egede, Poul. 1750. *Dictionarium grönlandico-danico-latinum.* Hafniæ.

Fabricius, Otto. 1804. *Den grønlandske Ordbog.* Copenhagen.

Fenger, H. M. 1879. *Bidrag til Hans Egedes og den grønlandske Missions Historie 1721-1760 efter trykte og utrykte kilder.* Copenhagen.

Gad, Finn. 1976. *Grønlands historie III 1782-1808.* Copenhagen: Nyt Nordisk Forlag.

– 1984: Grønland. *Politikens Danmarkshistorie.* Copenhagen: Gad.

Grønlands præstekonvent. 1906-62. (1-29. konvent) 2 volumes. Greenland's National Library, Oldendow Samlingen kat. nr. 336-37.

Iversen, Hans Raun. 1999. The Ordination of Pastors and Bishops in the Evangelical-Lutheran Church of Denmark. Given at the Symposium on the Theology and Terminology of Ordination, Filadelfia, Denmark, October1999 (unpubl.).

Kanstrup, Jan. 1995. Kampen om Kikkik i København. De udviklingspolitiske mål bag seminarieoprettelsen i Grønland. In *Ilinniarfissuaq ukiuni 150 ini.* (Festskrift i anledning af Ilinniarfissuaqs 150-års jubilæum i 1995).

Kleinschmidt, Samuel. 1851. *Grammatik der grönlandischen sprache mit theilweisem einschluss des Labradordialects.* Berlin.

– 1871. *Den grønlandske ordbog,* re-edited by Sam. Kleinschmidt. Copenhagen: H F Jørgensen.

Kleivan, Inge. 1978. 'Lamb of God' = 'Seal of God'? Some semantic problems in translating the animal names of the New Testament into Greenlandic. In *Papers from the Fourth Scandinavian conference of Linguistics, Hindsgavl,* 339-345. Odense: Odense University Press.

Langgård, Karen. (1984) 1987. *Henrik Lunds verdslige digtning.* Ilisimatusarfik.

– 1994. Henrik Lunds brug af forlæg i sin religiøse digtning. In *Kultur- og samfundsforskning 94* Ilisimatusarfik / Atuakkiorfik.

– 1999. Vestgrønlændernes syn på østgrønlænderne gennem tiden. In: *Kultur- og samfundsforskning 98/99.* Ilisimatusarfik / Atuakkiorfik.

– 1998. An examination of Greenlandic awareness of ethnicity and national self-consciousness through texts produced by Greenlanders, 1860s-1920s. In *Études / Inuit / Studies*, Vol. 22(1).

– 1999. In *From Sealing to Fishing. Social Economic Change in Greenland, 1850-1940*, ed. Ole Marquardt, Poul Holm and David J Starkey. *Studia Atlantica* 4. Esbjerg.

– 2000. Natursynet i den grønlandske litteratur. In *Nordisk litteratur og mentalitet*, ed. Malan Marnersdóttir og Jens Cramer. *Annales Societatis Scientiarum Færoensis Supplementum XXV*. Torshavn.

– 2001. Påskesalmen i den grønlandske salmetradition. In *Luthersk påskpredikan i Norden*. Forskningsprogrammet Norden og Europa. Nordisk Ministerråd.

– 2002. Jonathan Petersen og Grundtvig. In *Nordica* vol 19. Odense.

– 2004. Ordination af præster og biskop i den evangeliske-lutheranske kirke i Grønland. In *Kirkehistoriske Samlinger 2004*. Copenhagen: Selskabet for Danmarks Kirkehistorie.

Lauritsen, K. 1976. Salmesangen i Grønland. *Hymnologiske meddelelser.* 5. year.

Lidegaard, Mads. 1986. Profeterne i Evighedsfjorden. Temanummer i *Tidsskriftet Grønland*. No 6-7, 1986.

– 1993: *Grønlændernes kristning*. Nuuk: Atuakkiorfik.

Ludwigs, Chr. 1921. *1721-1921. Tohundredeaarsdagen for den grønlandske Mission*. Copenhagen.

Malling, A. 1962-78. *Dansk Salmehistorie*. Salmerne. København: København: J. H. Schultz.

Møller, Lars. 1890/91. In: *Atuagagdliutit* col.150

Nielsen, Frederik. 1936: Tussiutivut. In *Nalunaarutit*.

Oqaatsit. 1990.

Ostermann, H. 1921. *Den grønlandske Missions og Kirkes Historie*. Copenhagen: Lohse.

– 1936a. Den første Ordination af en Indfødt i Grønland. *Det grønlandske Selskabs Aarsskrift 1936*. Copenhagen: Gad.

– 1936b. Uddrag af breve fra pastor Tobias Mørch. *Det grønlandske Selskabs Aarsskrift 1936*. Copenhagen: Gad.

Report on Pastors Meetings. In *Nalunaarutit*, e.g. 1906, 1908, 1910, 1911, 1923, 1927.

Sammendrag af statistiske oplysninger om Grønland I-IV. *Beretninger og Kundgørelser* 1942-47.

Schultz-Lorentzen, C W. 1904. Ordbog.

– 1921. Fra Mission til Kirke. In Ludwigs 1921.

– 1926. *Den grønlandske Ordbog*. Grønlandsk –dansk. Copenhagen.

– 1938. Et Besøg i Grønland 1938. *Medd. om Den grønlandske Kirkesag.* Copenhagen.

Sørensen, Axel Kjær. 1983. *Danmark – Grønland i det 20. århundrede – en historisk oversigt.*

Thuesen, Søren. 1988. *Fremad, opad. Kampen for en moderne grønlandsk identitet.* Copenhagen: Rhodos.

Wilhjelm, Henrik. 1978. Kirke og Hjemmestyre i Grønland. In *Dansk kirkeliv 1978-79*, 86-102. Aarhus: Aros.

– 1997. De store opdragere. Grønlands seminarier i det 19. århundrede. *Det grønlandske Selskabs Skrifter XXXIII.* Copenhagen: Det grønlandske Selskab.

– 2001. 'Af tilbøjelighed er jeg grønlænder.' In Samuel Kleinschmidts liv og værk. *Det grønlandske Selskabs Skrifter XXXIV.* Copenhagen: Det grønlandske Selskab.

Greenlandic Hymnbooks (Danish Mission).

Below I have followed the titles given in '*Groenlandica*' published by Greenland's National Library / Atuagaateqarfia, Nuuk (ed.: Benny Høyer) and their electronic catalogue, and for those books that are not in that collection I have used the catalogue of The Royal Library in Copenhagen.

1742: Egede, Hans: Elementa Fidei Christiana. Hafnia.

1756: Egede, Poul: Catechismus Mingneq (Lille Katekismus). Kiøbenhavn.

1761: Bruun, Rasmus: Ivngerutit okko 119. Arsillyput. Kiöbenhavn.

1801: Otto Fabricius: Ivngerutit tuksiutidlo. Kiöbenhavnime.

1834: Knud Kjer: Tuksiautitait. Odensime. (Salmer)

1838: Knud Kjer: Ivngerutit. Kjöbenhavnime. (Salmebog med tekst og bønnebog)

1856: Knud Kjer: Tuksiautit kikiektugaursomik. Frederikshavnime. (Salmer om den korsfæstede)

1876: Kristumiutut Tugsiautit. Kjøbenhavn. (Salmebog med tekst og bønnebog)

1885: Kristumiutut Tugsiautit. Kjøbenhavn. (Salmebog med tekst og bønnebog)

1907: tugsiutit ilagît kalâtdlit nâlagiane igdlunilo atugagssait. Kbh.: A. Rosenberg-ip naqiteriviane, 1907. –VIII, 276, 237 sider (Salmebog, med tekst- og bønnebog, redigeret af Chr. Rasmussen, C.W.Schultz-Lorentzen og Jens Chemnitz./ Grønlandsk salmebog)

1937: tapê: tugsiutit ilagît kalâtdlit nâlagiane igdlunilo atugagssaisa tapê.

–Nûk: sineríssap kujatdliup naqiteriviane naqitigkat, 1937. – 151 sider (Salmebog, tillæg til salmebog. / Den grønlandske menigheds salmer.) 1971: tugsiutit ilagît kalâtdlit atugagssait. –[S.1] : [s.n], 1971. – 524, 396 sider. (Salmebog, med tekst- og bønnebog, godkendt af Grønlands landsprovst)

Greenlandic Service Books
Apart from rites printed in hymnbooks:
1783: ajokærsoirsun Atuagekseit Nalegbingne Grönlandme. Ritual over Kirke-Forretningerne ved den Danske Mission paa Grønland. København.
1819: arkiksutiksak Pellesinnut Ajokærsóïrsunnudlo, kannong-illivdlutik pirsaromarput Naalegiartorbingne, Kaládlit Nun'ænne. Ritual over Kirke-Forretningerne ved den Danske Mission i Grønland. Omarbeidet og forøget ved Otho Fabricius. København.
1887: maligtarissagssat palasit suliokataisalo nâlagiartitsissarneráne. Ritual for den grønlandske Kirke. København.
1891: palasit suliok'ataisalo nâlagiartitsissarneráne maligtaríssanut ilángússagssat. ilagîngnit pârssissûssok sujunersiork'ârdlugo ilánguterk'ussissok' palainik misigssuissok', kúngip tugdlia. Tillæg til Ritualet for den grønlandske Kirke, efter Forhandling med Biskoppen forordnet af Ministeriet for Kirke- og Undervisningsvæsenet. København
1902: palasíngortitsissunut maligtarissagssiat. Grønlandsk Ritual ved Præstevielse. Ved Chr. Rasmussen, godkendt af Sjællands Biskop Skat Rørdam.
1935: maligtarissagssat ilagîngne kalâussune atorfigdlit nâlagiartitsissarneráne. Ritual for den grønlandske Kirke. København.
1974: palasíngortitsinek' (dating according to Det kongelig Bibliotek).

3. The Development of Rites for the Ordination of Deacons in the Lutheran Churches

Deaconesses have been admitted to their ministry for 150 years, and deacons for 100 years, by rites in which some elements are similar and some quite different from those found in the rites for the ordination of pastors in the Nordic Evangelical-Lutheran Churches. Although pastors, as principals of diaconal institutions, or even bishops of the official churches have officiated, these rites have for many decades been considered private, belonging only to the deaconess houses and deacon schools in which they were used. In recent years, for ecclesiastical, socio-historical and ecumenical reasons, a development has taken place, in which the ordination of deacons has more and more come to look like ordination to a full and equal order within the ordained ministry of the churches. Traces of the differences between the churches, outlined in the earlier section of this book, are, however, also found here.

Ghita Olsen outlines the recent development and current rites of admission to diaconal ministry in the five Nordic Evangelical-Lutheran Churches. According to these rites the churches in Iceland and Sweden have introduced the threefold ministry, placing deacons alongside bishops and pastors, sharing in the ordained ministry of the Church. Although the Church of Norway and the Evangelical-Lutheran Church of Finland have signed the Porvoo Common Statement between Anglicans and Lutherans (together with the Evangelical-Lutheran Church of Iceland and the Church of Sweden), and are tending to move in the same direction, the situation in relation to deacons is not at all clear in these churches. Moreover, the Evangelical-Lutheran Church of Denmark, which has not signed the Porvoo Common Statement, may move in the same direction. So far, there have, however, been no official theological and liturgical discussions on this issue.

Liselotte Malmgart outlines the history of rites for the consecration of deaconesses and deacons in the Evangelical-Lutheran Church of Denmark. She deals with 48 different rites, found in the archives of four different diaconal institutions, covering the period from the first consecration of deaconesses in 1867 to the bishops' recommendation in 2001 that there should be a common rite for the consecration of deacons in the Danish Church. As nobody else took responsibility, the pastors and directors of the diaconal institutions considered that they were in charge of the rites, and each new director thought it proper to devise his own version of the rite – with or without any resemblance to the church's official rite for the ordination of pastors.

Helena Inghammar recounts the Swedish history of rites for diaconal consecration placing it in a wider socio-historical context. Like other groups of female professionals, such as nurses, deaconesses found their personal and vocational legitimacy – and emancipation – through installation or consecration in the national church. During the first part of its history the rite for deaconesses took the form of a private process of adoption of the new sisters into the fellowship of the mother house, whereas today the rite mirrors a public agreement between the individual deacon and the Church. Deacons have gained a place within the ordained ministry of the church, even though not yet in a fully equal way. In the process they seem to have lost their collective sense of diaconal ministry.

Rites for Admission to Diaconal Ministry in the Nordic Evangelical-Lutheran Churches

Ghita Olsen

In the twentieth century there has been an increasingly intensive debate in the Nordic Evangelical-Lutheran Churches on the introduction of the diaconate, its place in the Church and its theological identity. In all five churches a rite for admission to diaconal ministry exists, though these rites are quite diverse. The following is a comparative study.[1]

The rites compared are the Church of Iceland's authorised rite of 1981 (*Handbók íslensku Kirkjunnar* 1981, 202-206), the Church of Sweden's authorised rite of 1987 (*Den Svenska Kyrkohandboken* 1988, 30-40), the Church of Norway's authorised rite of 1987 (*Gudstjenestebok for den Norske Kirke* 1996, II, 185-196), the Evangelical-Lutheran Church of Finland's authorised rite of 1984 (*Kyrkohandbok för den Evangelisk-lutherska Kyrkan i Finland* 1995, III, 151-156)[2], and a rite recommended in 2001 by the Bishops of the Evangelical-Lutheran Church of Denmark (Nissen 2001, 249-251).[3]

Not all of these rites can be said to be rites of ordination. Some of the churches consider deacons to be part of the ordained ministry, some do not, and some are in the process of clarifying this matter. Without a doubt it is

---

1. The primary source for this article is my prize dissertation on the theological debate on the diaconate in the Nordic Evangelical-Lutheran Churches (Olsen 2000).
2. This is the authorised Swedish language version of the rite. A new rite is expected in Advent 2004.
3. In Denmark several rites exist and have been used for a number of years. The Service Book only includes the rites of ordination for priests and bishops. The rite in question is the most recent and is a result of discussion in committee. In a letter dated 9th January 2002 and written on behalf of the Danish bishops to all deacons' colleges, Bishop Karsten Nissen recommended the use of the new rite.

common for these Nordic Churches to authorise rites for new vocational groups without prior theological clarification of the significance of these acts. This fact is reflected in the ambiguous names of the rites. They are called by the same term '*vigsling/vigning*', a term used for ordination, dedication, marriage and the consecration of a church building. For the purpose of this article the terms '*vigsling*' and '*vigning*' will be translated as 'ordination', as there is no agreed equivalent in English.

The method of this article is inspired by Puglisi (1996, 200; 2001, 226ff). He sees three main elements as constitutive of a rite of ordination or commissioning to ministry in apostolic tradition. These are '*vocatio*', '*benedictio*' and '*missio*'. At ordination the ordinand is called to a certain function in the Church, blessed for this function by prayer and the imposition of hands, and sent out to perform it.

After a presentation of the rites, a comparative analysis will focus on how their structure, constitutive parts and wording define diaconal ministry and its relation to ordained ministry. Then we shall examine to what extent the three components referred to above are present in these five Nordic rites. The analysis focuses on the rites as liturgical texts in the various service books. However, information on practical aspects of the celebration of the rites will be included where these are known and relevant.

Presentation of the Rites

Having briefly established the historical background we shall see how each rite is presented in the light of the following questions: the title of the rite, its place in the Service Book, where the ceremony takes place, and so on.

In addition to the officiant and the ordinand(s) a group of assistants normally participates actively in the ceremonies in all five churches. They participate as readers of biblical texts and in the imposition of hands during the Ordination prayer. One issue is whether the rite has a collegial or congregational dimension by involving other deacons or people from the parish or diocese, where the new deacon is to be employed.

Church of Norway

In the Church of Norway a liturgical commission worked from 1965 to1991. Its work was complicated because of divergent views on ordained ministry. As part of its work, new rites of ordination were sanctioned in 1987 by the Bishops' Meeting. Five rites were defined: for bishop, priest, deacon, catechist and other church ministry.[4] The rites for priest, deacon and catechist, run parallel in their content. There is no definition of the relation between these ordinations or their relation to the ordained ministry. The term 'office' is not used. Instead the rites speak of different 'ministries' or 'services'. It is clear from the ordination rite for priests that the priest is explicitly part of the ordained ministry, but it is not correspondingly clear that the ministries of deacon and catechist do not belong to the ordained ministry. The reason for this arose from a pragmatic wish to keep the rites of ordination as open as possible to the varying theologies of ministry existing in the Church of Norway. (Olsen 2000, 136) When the cantors also got their own authorised rite in 1999, the question of the theological definition of the ordained ministry became urgent in the Church of Norway. In 1999 a committee was set up in order to reach clarity on the subject, and in March 2001 it issued its consultative report. The majority of the committee members considered deacons to be lay people and not part of the ordained ministry. The consultative report was circulated for consideration in the Church of Norway and gave rise to an ongoing debate. (Olsen 2001, 226)

The title of the rite is 'Ordination to the Ministry of Deacon' ('*vigsling til diakontjeneste*'). The 1987 Service Book uses the term '*vigsling*' as an 'umbrella term' for ordination or commissioning for all ministries in the church.

The service book associates the three officeholders, priest, deacon and catechist, and in the 'Common Regulations' (*Gudstjenestebok* 1996, 159), they appear as one common group. The ceremony takes place in the cathedral of the new deacon's diocese, and the bishop of the diocese officiates and ordains. *Vocatio externa* – the church's calling to a specific ministry – is required.

According to the rubric assistants are chosen by the bishop and they are to be ministers together with lay people. It is not specified whether they should be from the new deacons' places of employment.

Church of Sweden

In the Church of Sweden, on the recommendation of a liturgical commission and under the influence of the document agreed in Lima by the Faith and Order Commission, *Baptism, Eucharist and Ministry* (BEM, published 1982), the General Assembly in 1987 discussed new rites for the ordination of bishops, priests and deacons. During the preliminary work, there was a vehement theological debate on the position of the diaconate in the church and the

---

4. These other ministries could be youth leader, secretary of a congregation or some other form of ministry.

significance of the ordination of deacons. In the light of the debate the General Assembly agreed on a preamble to the Service Book. The preamble reads:

> The church's ordination acts give expression to the idea that from among God's people Christ through the Spirit calls people to lifelong service for the sake of the gospel. This calling is confirmed by the church's ordination. The ordinations of bishop, priest, and deacon are equal expressions of the fullness of the gospel and of the church's commission from this gospel, to be performed both in word and deed. Traditionally the word office is used for the tasks of bishop and priest. Other terms like commission, calling and service express the same calling from Christ to be the servant of his gospel. (*Den Svenska Kyrkohandboken* 1988, 5) [5]

A substantial part of the debate in committee and *plenum* was concerned with if and when to use the term 'office' (*'ämbete'*): the preamble expresses a compromise. However, in 1999 the General Assembly of the Church of Sweden closed the debate on the relationship of the diaconate to the ordained ministry, when a new Church Ordinance was authorised. The term 'office' is supplemented by the term *'vigningstjänst'*, ordained ministry, and the new Church Ordinance clearly states that this ordained ministry of the church consists of three offices: bishop, priest, and deacon.

The title of the Swedish rite is 'Deacon's Ordination Mass' (*'diakonvigningsmässa'*) and the word *'vigning'* is used for the ordination of bishop, priest, and deacon. As seen above, according to the preamble of the service book the three ordinations are defined as equal and of the same standing. The ordination takes place in the cathedral of the new deacon's diocese. Often priests are ordained in the same Mass. The bishop ordains. *Vocatio externa* – the church's calling to a specific ministry – is required.

According to the rubric the assistants are chosen by the bishop, and among them there are to be deacons and preferably priests and lay people. Collegial and congregational dimensions are thereby clearly present in this rite.

---

5. Translated from the original text in Swedish: *'Kyrkans vigningshandlingar är ett uttryck för att Kristus genom Anden inom Guds folk för evangeliets skull kallar människor till livslång tjänst. Denna kallelse bekräftas genom kyrkans vigning. Vigningarna till biskop, präst och diakon är likvärdiga uttryck för evangeliets fullhet och för kyrkans uppdrag utifrån dette evangelium, som skall gestaltes i såväl ord som handling. Av tradition används ordet ämbete i vår kyrka för uppgifterna att vara präst och biskop. Andra termer som uppdrag, kall, tjänst avser att i sak uttrycka samma Kristi kallelse att vara tjänare åt hans evangelium'.*

Evangelical-Lutheran Church of Iceland

In 1981 a new Service Book was authorised in the Evangelical-Lutheran Church of Iceland, and for the first time an ordination rite for deacons was included. The service book includes two types of deacons: parish deacons and diocesan deacons. In recent times the Icelandic Church has had few ordinations of deacons.[6] They have all been conducted according to the same rite and this rite was included in the Service Book. In its structure the rite is very similar to the rite for the ordination of priests. Since 1991, on the recommendation of a working party on the deacon's ministry, ordination has taken place in the cathedral instead of the parish church.[7] Ordination in the cathedral is meant to underline the fact that ordained deacons are under the authority of the bishop and are accountable to him.

The title of the Icelandic rite is 'Ordination of a Deacon' ('djaknavigsla'). 'Djakní' is the Icelandic term for 'deacon', and the word 'vigsla' is also used for the ordination of bishop and priest. A calling from a congregation or a diocese is required. The ordination takes place in the cathedral, and the bishop ordains.

The rubric is quite clear about the four assistants, who are called 'ordination witnesses'. They are the local priest, the chairman of the parish council, another priest and a lay worker or deacon from the parish where the new deacon is to be employed. Thus collegial and congregational dimensions are present.

Evangelical-Lutheran Church of Finland

Ever since diaconal ministry was fixed by law in 1944 in the Evangelical-Lutheran Church of Finland, it has been common practice at all diaconal colleges for all fully qualified deacons and deaconesses to be offered a blessing connected with the graduation ceremony from the college.[8] Usually the bishop of the diocese, where the deacons' college is situated, is the officiant, but no rite for this ceremony was included in the Service Books until 1964. In 1984, after debate in committee, the General Assembly of the Evangelical-Lutheran Church of Finland authorised the existing rite for the ordination of deacons and deaconesses. The committee suggested that the ordination should take place in the cathedral and should depend on the candidate's calling to ministry

---

6. It should be noted that there have never been diaconal institutions such as mother houses in Iceland.
7. The influence of BEM has been evident in the Church of Iceland's understanding of the diaconate (Olsen 2000, 39).
8. The 1944 law required every parish to employ a deacon or deaconess.

as a deacon. These suggestions were turned down by the General Assembly, the latter by only one vote.

The title of the Finnish rite is 'Ordination of a Deacon and a Deaconess' ('*vigning av diakon och diakonissa*'), but most people understand the rite as an act of blessing and not as an ordination. The Evangelical-Lutheran Church of Finland has three more rites of ordination: bishop, priest, and lector. Like the deacons, the lectors are not considered part of the ordained ministry.[9]

In the (Swedish-speaking) diocese of Borgå/Porvoo the ceremony takes place in the cathedral, and the bishop is the officiant. A calling to a specific ministry in the church is normally required. In the other (Finnish-speaking) dioceses, the bishop is the officiant, but the ceremony takes place in a church at the deacons' college, independently of actual employment in the church.

According to the rubric the assistants are chosen by the bishop, but no instructions are given about who they should be.

Evangelical-Lutheran Church of Denmark

The Danish rite is not authorised or part of the Service Book of the Evangelical-Lutheran Church of Denmark, but is part of a consultative report drawn up by a working party on the deacon's ministry, set up by the bishops in 1999. The rite was subsequently recommended by the bishops in 2001. Its shape and wording are inspired by older Danish rites used at the various diaconal colleges, as well as by the authorised rites from the other Nordic Evangelical-Lutheran Churches.[10]

The title of the rite is '*indvielse*' of deacon or deaconess. The term is also used for the consecration of a new church or churchyard, while the authorised rites for bishop and priest are called '*vielse*', 'ordination'. As in the Finnish Church the ceremony is offered by the deacons' colleges to all who are fully qualified. The ceremony takes place in a nearby parish church, and normally the director or chaplain of the college is the officiant.[11] The rite includes no instructions on the choice of assistants, but assistants are mentioned in connection with the biblical readings and the imposition of hands.

---

9. There are few lectors in the church today. It was originally a ministry meant for female theologians, before 1988, the year when the church allowed women to be ordained as priests.

10. For further information on the history of the Danish rite, see Malmgart (Part II.3).

11. Often the director is an ordained minister. If a bishop participates in the ceremony – as is usually the case at one of the institutions – he will normally preach a sermon and/or celebrate the Eucharist, but not say the prayer with the imposition of hands. This is done by the director/minister.

Conclusion

According to the texts themselves and the terms used, the ministry of deacon seems to be parallel to or equal with the other officeholders in the four churches that have an authorised rite for admission to diaconal ministry. The fact that the ceremony takes place in the cathedral with the bishop officiating and ordaining also points to this interpretation.

The Structure of the Rites

Normally the ordination rite forms part of a Sunday service or High Mass. The ordination part of the service or Mass has a structure that can be broken down into seven main sections. These are:

> Presentation
> Introductory Prayer
> Scriptural Readings
> Exhortation
> Commitments
> Ordination Prayer with the imposition of hands
> Reception/Sending out

Yet there are variations of this pattern, as shown in figure 1.

Diaconal Ministry According to the Rites

We shall go through the various sections of the rites to see how diaconal ministry is identified: What is the deacon ordained to, what is the biblical basis of the diaconal ministry, what is said of the ecclesiastical authority and responsibility of the deacon and which gifts and abilities are prayed for?

The Presentation and the Introductory Prayer

The Norwegian Presentation and Introductory Prayer use phrases such as:

- a new worker in our church
- minister as a deacon in/at a specific place
- the ministry of care, so that the love of Christ may be visible amongst us
- today this co-worker is ordained as a deacon after the manner of the apostles during the laying-on of hands with prayer
- with responsibility to organise the congregation's care for people in need
- make him and all your (Christ's) Church's servants faithful stewards of God's mysteries

Figure 1

Church of Norway	Church of Sweden	Church of Iceland	Evangelical-Lutheran Church of Finland	Danish recommended rite
Presentation	Introductory Prayer	Introductory Prayer with Presentation	Introductory Prayer	Presentation
Introductory Prayer	Presentation		Presentation	Introductory Prayer
Scriptural readings	Scriptural readings	Scriptural readings	Scriptural readings	Scriptural readings
Exhortation	Exhortation	Exhortation	Creed	
Commitments	Commitments	Commitments	Commitments	Commitments
Ordination Prayer with the imposition of hands	Ordination Prayer with the imposition of hands	Ordination Prayer with the imposition of hands	Conferral of office Prayer	Ordination Prayer with the imposition of hands
Reception	Reception			
Sending out	Sending out		Sending out	Sending out

A definition of *diakonia* found in a Plan for *Diakonia* in the Norwegian Church (*Kirkerådet* 1988, 8) is used directly in the rite. *Diakonia* is defined as 'the congregation's care for people in need'.

The Swedish Presentation states only that the ordinands :
– are called to the deacon's ministry

According to *the Icelandic rite*:
– the ordinand is appointed to ministry in a specific congregation
– to bear witness to Christ in word and deed
– and be a blessing to God's children

The introductory sentence to *the Finnish rite* is 'In the name of the Father, the Son and the Holy Spirit'. An alternative is: Matt. 25.40, 'Just as you did it to one of the least of my brothers, you did it to me'. The choice of the latter introduction to the ceremony will concentrate the attention on the content of diaconal ministry right from the beginning.[12]

The Introductory Prayer says that:

- God sends his disciples to carry out the service of love
- the ordinand is set aside for his office as servant

The Introductory Prayer of *the Danish rite* speaks of:

- the ministry of care
- caring for each other and our neighbour
- believing in Jesus Christ and being his followers in the service of others
- the ordinand following Christ's calling and being a sign of his love amongst us

Conclusion

According to the Presentations and the Introductory Prayers two elements describing this ministry are particularly emphasised. The first one is that the diaconal ministry is a special ministry for which one is set aside. The Norwegian, Swedish and Danish rites include a reference to apostolic tradition. In the Church of Norway and the Church of Iceland the *vocatio externa* is emphasised – the specific congregation is mentioned. In the Evangelical-Lutheran Church of Finland God's call is explicitly stressed, probably because of the fact that the basis of the ordination in most dioceses is *vocatio interna*.

The other element is that the primary content of the diaconal ministry is described as service – meaning care for people in need – and bearing witness to Christ in life and deeds.

Scriptural Readings

The Scriptural Readings in an ordination rite are expected to express the biblical basis of the specific ministry, the responsibility involved and the blessing to undertake it.

In the Church of Norway the rite provides three readings. The deacon's ministry is first of all set within the general commission to bring the gospel to all people by the reading of Matt. 28.18-20. The second reading is Matt. 25.34-40 on the final judgment. There follows a reading from 2 Cor. 5.17-20 on the ministry of reconciliation and on being ambassadors of Christ. These

---

12. It must be noted that the exegetical view on this pericope varies. The classical interpretation of the phrase 'the least of my brothers' points to the disciples, i.e. to Christians, and not to humanity in general as in a 'diaconal' interpretation.

three readings form a 'sandwich structure'. The first and the third texts are paralleled in the rite for the ordination of a priest and a catechist. They both express the general calling to ministry. The central text is chosen to express what is distinctive for the particular ministry, here Matt. 25 with its clear diaconal content.

In continuation from the readings the bishop gives an address based on an appropriate biblical text.

The Swedish rite provides five series of biblical readings, but the Swedish practice is to ordain deacons on a Sunday using the texts of the day. I will not therefore go into details about these series of readings, but it is noticeable that the Swedish rite is the only one in which all the series of readings have an Old Testament reading, all of them from one of the Prophets. It is remarkable, however, that in all the readings offered there is not one text that has also been chosen for some of the other Nordic rites as the biblical basis for the diaconal ministry, such as Matt. 25, Acts 6, Matt. 20 or Mark 10. Just after the readings the bishop gives the address, possibly based on an appropriate biblical text.

In *the Church of Iceland* the bishop gives the address just before the scriptural readings. The readings emphasise ministry in general and the mutual ministering of the gifts of grace within the congregation – 1 Pet. 4.10-11, 2 Cor. 5.14-21, Mark 10.42-45. Specific to the readings in the Icelandic rite is the choice of Luke 12.35-37a. The reading stops in the middle of the verse with an exclamation mark: 'Blessed are those servants whom the master, when he comes, finds watching!'

The rite from the Evangelical-Lutheran Church of Finland provides seven readings and alternative readings as well. Service, both generally and within the congregation is stressed in the reading of 1 Pet. 4.10-11 and Mark 10.42-45. The verses chosen from Acts 6, verses 2 and 4-6, point to the apostolic tradition of prayer and the imposition of hands. The final part of the story of Jesus washing the disciples' feet from John 13.15-17 stresses the imitation of Christ; Mark 2.16-17 emphasises the mission perspective, and 1 Cor. 13.1-3 points to love as the qualifying factor for service and the foundation of all charisms. Heb. 13.2-3 speaks of specific diaconal acts.

In *the Danish rite* the officiant gives the address before the readings on an optional biblical text. The first reading is Matt. 20.25-28 – the greatest is the one who serves, and Christ giving his life as a ransom for many. The second reading is Matt. 25.31-40, then Acts 6.1-6 and Rom 12.4-12 on the different gifts of grace. Other text suggestions are given.

Conclusion

The readings provided in the rites show that the principal category of diaconal ministry is service. It is emphasised that the basis for ministry is love and the reconciliation of God through Christ, and it is stressed that true greatness consists in serving.

Considering the purpose of the readings – to express the biblical basis of the deacon's ministry – it is striking how many variations of texts we see in these rites. The reason for this could be the richness of biblical texts on service, but on the other hand the explanation could be that there are different exegetical traditions in the five churches and/or different opinions on the biblical basis for *diakonia*. As an example, note that only some of the rites use Acts 6. This could reflect the way in which this text was interpreted at the time of the rite's formation, as the exegetical view on it has varied over time.

Exhortation and Commitments

The Exhortation admonishes the new deacons to personal faith and obedience, but terms describing the diaconal ministry are also present.

In all the rites the ordinands are expected to commit themselves verbally to the ministry by giving one or more promises. The commitment may be sealed with a handshake of fellowship.

In *the Church of Norway's rite*, deacons are exhorted to present the word of God purely and clearly in witness and pastoral care, to care for the life and well-being of their neighbour, to work to improve the living conditions of the weak, to pray for the weak and to live their own lives according to the Word of God.

The single promise refers to the context of the preceding exhortation. It is emphasised that the congregation is witness to this commitment, which is sealed with the traditional handshake of fellowship. The response is a simple: 'Yes'.

In *the Church of Sweden's rite*, the deacon is exhorted to reach out to help and support those in physical and mental need, to teach the Christian faith, live as a servant of Christ and be a sign of mercy in parish and society. The deacon must defend the rights of the weak and encourage and free God's people for good, so that God's love may be visible in the world.

The Swedish rite has the most extensive commitments with four questions/promises and a final confirmation. The first promise is identical with the first promise in the ordination rite for priests, and it expresses the purpose of the ministry and places the deacons as part of the spiritual leadership of the church. The second promise is a commitment to the faith of the church, and the third is a commitment to the Swedish Church Ordinance and a wish to imitate Christ. In the fourth promise the deacon has to accept commitment to a life witnessing to the love of God and the mystery of reconciliation. In the final confirmation the congregation is taken as witness to the ordinand's commitments. To every question the ordinand answers with a 'Yes', and to the final confirmation: 'I, NN, by the help of God and trusting in the grace of God, will live according to these promises'.[13]

In *the Icelandic rite*, deacons are exhorted to walk wholeheartedly and humbly in the footsteps of Christ and to invite others to follow them by the power of the word and personal example.

In this rite, as in the Norwegian one, the content of the promise is a reference to the preceding exhortation, the response is 'Yes', and the promise is sealed with a handshake of fellowship.

The Finnish rite includes no specific Exhortation, but at the same place in the rite – just before the commitments – the ordinands recite the Nicene Creed alone without the participation of the congregation, and the bishop prays for them to be firm believers. By having the Creed in this place in the rite, it is stressed that the basis of the diaconal ministry is the faith of the Church.

The rite has two promises, the first one characterising the deacon's ministry as a stewardship according to the Word of God and the Finnish Church Ordinance. In the second promise deacons have to commit themselves to live as examples to the congregation. The response to both questions is: 'Yes'.

In *the Danish rite* there is no Exhortation, but there is a reference to the preceding biblical readings in the words: 'The Lord has, as we have just heard, ordered us to undertake this ministry of service and through his apostles transferred it to his congregation'.[14]

The promise is formulated rather prosaically: 'Is it your sincere intention and wish to serve as a deacon in the Christian Church?'[15] It is possible to mention here an actual congregation or place where the deacon's ministry will be exercised, instead of 'the Christian Church'.

---

13. Translated from the original Swedish text: *'Jag, NN, vill med Guds hjälp och i förtröstan på Guds nåd leve enligt dessa löften'.*
14. Translated from the original Danish text: *'Herren har, som vi nu har hørt, pålagt os tjenestens opgave og gennem sine apostle lagt den hen til sin menighed'.*
15. Translated from the original Danish text: *'Er det dit oprigtige forsæt og bøn at tjene som diakon i den kristne kirke'.*

Conclusion

The Exhortations give a general description of the content of diaconal ministry in the Church, emphasising the deacon's commitment to his needy neighbours. It is noteworthy that both the Norwegian and the Swedish rite exhort the deacon to work for improvement in the living conditions of the poor and weak and to defend their rights.

The commitments express the personal commitment to be a servant in the Church. In most of the rites the commitments do not only encompass the job in hand, but also the personal life of the deacon, as he or she is asked to conduct their personal life as an example to others.

The Ordination Prayer with Imposition of Hands

One of the characteristics of an ordination rite is the prayer with imposition of hands. This prayer normally invokes the Holy Spirit, praying that he confer charisms for the specific ministry on the ordinand. Moreover it is an act of intercessory prayer for God's blessing on the ordinand and his ministry.

All of the five rites have this prayer in some form, though as shown above not all rites mention apostolic tradition.

In *the Church of Norway* this section is strong on indirect biblical references and missionary and eschatological overtones. Present is a reference to Matt. 9.38 or Luke 10.2 – 'the harvest is great, but the workers are few'.[16] 1 Pet. 4 on stewardship, and 2 Cor. 12.10 shows through, when the bishop prays that the strength of Christ must be known in the weakness of the ordinand. The bishop prays during the laying-on of hands that the new deacon will be granted the necessary gifts for ministry, and the prayer points to a lifelong ministry. In the Church of Norway this section includes an *epiclesis*: 'Send him your (God's) Spirit with the gifts for ministry ... that he may become a fitting worker in your harvest'. The congregation is invited to recite the Lord's Prayer with the bishop. Finally the congregation sings a verse of an epicletic hymn.

In *the Church of Sweden's rite* the section begins with a description of the ministry of the whole congregation and moves on to the special ministry with the phrase 'You (God) select from among us ...' The universal purpose of ministry (not only the diaconal ministry) is stated as the faith of mankind, the renewal of the Church and the maintenance of creation. The *epiclesis* follows: 'Lord, come to *NN* with your Holy Spirit and take him into your service as a

---

16. This prayer for workers for the harvest goes back to the Ordination Prayer in Martin Luther's ordination rite in the Wittenberg Ordinal 1537/1539 (Puglisi 1998, 4f).

deacon in your (Christ's) Church'.[17] The ministry is given a universal perspective with the words 'deacon in your Church', and the prayer has Christological overtones. After the laying-on of hands, the bishop and the assistants pray for the equipping of the deacon with frankness, perseverance and other gifts. Finally the congregation sings *Veni, sancte Spiritus*.

The Icelandic rite states very clearly the special vocation to the ministry and has an invocation of the Holy Spirit with Christological aspects. The beginning says: 'Give him/her your Holy Spirit that he/she may be constant in his/her holy decision, strong and whole in the holy faith and able to increase in wisdom and grace and become an instrument of your blessing, through Jesus Christ, our Lord and Saviour'. The section ends with The Lord's Prayer recited by all together. Nothing particular is said of the diaconal ministry in this section, except the overall objective above: 'be an instrument' of God's blessing. But just before the Ordination Prayer – after the commitments and the handshake of fellowship – the deacon is vested with the stole as a sign of his/her new position.

The title of this section in *the Finnish rite* is 'Conferral of the Office' (*'Ämbetets överlämnande'*). The bishop says that he – in the name of the Father, the Son and the Holy Spirit – entrusts the office of deacon to the ordinand with the authority that is given to him, according to God's will, by Christ's Church. The word *'ämbete'* ('office') is used in this authorised Swedish-language version of the Finnish-language rite. In the Finnish-language version the Finnish word *'virka'* is used at this point. *'Virka'* is an ambiguous word like the English word 'ministry' (Stenberg 1998, 6). It could mean both office and ministry, so it is not clear whether the delegated office is the ecclesiastical office.

There is no *epiclesis* in this section of the rite.[18] During the laying-on of hands done by the bishop and the assistants, the bishop prays a short prayer: 'May God, the triune, bless and sanctify you that you may always and every-

---

17. Translated from the original Swedish text: *'Herre, kom til NN med din helige And och tag honom i din tjänst som diakon i din kyrkan'*.
18. However, in the Introductory Prayer of the rite the bishop prays 'Give them the gift of your Holy Spirit'. And in the new Finnish rite that came into effect in Advent 2004, the epicletic element is considerably strengthened. In the new rite a prayer for the gift of the Holy Spirit is said right after the imposition of hands, cf. para 18, page 7 in the report, *Handboksutskottets betänkande nr 1.3a/2003 med anledning av den av kyrkomötet år 1988 tillsatta handbokskommitténs förslag till ny Kyrkohandbok III (Handbok för kyrkliga förrättningar)*.

where serve Christ's Church. Amen.[19] After the removal of the hands, while the ordinand is still kneeling, the bishop prays the Ordination Prayer. In this prayer witness is stressed, and there is a clear eschatological dimension: 'Let many together with them reach your heavenly Kingdom where all suffering has been defeated, and we together with our Saviour will rejoice in the eternal bliss of God's children'.[20] The section ends with The Lord's Prayer. It is not specified whether the congregation takes part in the recitation.

In *the Danish rite* the officiant, and possibly the assistants, participate in the laying-on of hands. The prayer includes an *epiclesis* reminiscent of the Icelandic one: 'Give them your Holy Spirit that they may be constant in faith, persevere in hope and live in love to become instruments of your blessing'.[21] The prayer asks that the ordinand will receive strength and frankness and 'do a deacon's work for the benefit of his/her neighbour and the advancement of your (Christ's) Church and your Kingdom'.[22] The final 'Amen' said by all is optional.

Conclusion

It is open to discussion whether the five rites include any statement of a precise effect of the Ordination Prayer and imposition of hands. The main implication seems to be personal equipping for ministry with qualities like strength, perseverance and frankness. No specific charisms of the Holy Spirit are prayed for, though in the Icelandic rite it is prayed that the deacon must increase in wisdom. The Icelandic rite is the only one that has a visible change of the ordinand in the form of investiture.[23]

In all churches, except the Finnish, the Ordination Prayer is said during the imposition of hands. In the latter there is a blessing during the imposition of

---

19. Translated from the original Swedish text: '*Må Gud, den treeninge välsigna och helga dig, så att du alltid och overallt tjänar Kristi kyrka. Amen*'.
20. Translated from the original Swedish text: '*Låt många tilsammans med dem nå framm till dit himmelska rike, där alt lidanda är övervunnet och där vi tilsammans med vår Frälsara får glädjas över Guds barns eviga salighet*'.
21. Translated from the original Danish text: '*giv dem din Helligånd, så de kan være stadige i troen, udholdende i håbet og levende i kærligheden, så de må være redskaber for din velsignelse*'.
22. Translated from the original Danish text: '*øve en diakons gerning til næstens gavn og til din kirkes og dit riges fremme*'.
23. Though it is not mentioned in the Church of Norway's rite, in some dioceses of the Church of Norway deacons are vested in a stole. This diversity of practice reflects the ongoing debate as to whether or not deacons are part of the ordained ministry of the Church.

hands, but the Ordination Prayer is said afterwards. The four other churches have a clear *epiclesis* during the imposition of hands.

Constitutive Elements Present in the Rites

Vocatio can be said to be implied as a basis for the whole act regardless of *vocatio externa* or *interna*, but it must be expected that the rite itself express and confirm the vocation verbally. *Benedictio* is implied in the Ordination Prayer, but also present elsewhere in the rites. *Missio* indicates an entrusting of the authority of the diaconal ministry and a sending out to a specifically mentioned ministry. It is present in separate parts called 'Reception' and 'Sending out', but also found in the introductions to the rites.

Vocatio externa is present in the *Norwegian* rite in the Presentation. It is said that the ordinand is called to serve as a deacon in/at a specific place. God's general calling to his church includes, the text says, the ministry of care. The Norwegian Presentation mentions baptism as the basis for the call to be a servant of God. *Vocatio* is also found in the Presentation of the Scriptural Readings: 'Let us listen to the witness of God's word on the service to which God calls [us] in His Church'.[24]

Benedictio is present in the prayer for the ministry of the deacon in the Introductory Prayer, and in the prayer during the imposition of hands.

Missio: The Presentation speaks of 'deacon in/at a specific place'. And the rite has a section called 'A Reminder of the Congregation's Co-responsibility' to support the deacon in the service of reconciliation to which all are called, and the congregation's reception of the deacon is specified. The rite ends with the quotation from John 15.16: 'You have not chosen me, but I have chosen you and appointed you to go and bear fruit, fruit which lasts'.

In the *Swedish* rite *vocatio* is present in the Presentation. The ordinand is said to be called to the diaconal ministry. The Exhortation speaks first of baptism as the foundation of the calling to preach the gospel, and secondly of the deacon's specific commission within this general vocation. The Ordination Prayer says of God: 'You select among us servants of your gospel.'[25] *Benedictio* is primarily present in the Ordination Prayer.

The Swedish rite has a part called 'Reception'. The deacon is entrusted to the receiving congregation. The deacons are said to be 'messengers of Christ'.

---

24. Translated from the original Norwegian text: *'Lad oss høre hvad Guds ord vitner om den tjeneste som Gud kaller til i sin kirke'.*
25. Translated from the original Swedish text: *'Du utser bland oss tjänare åt ditt evangelium'.*

The rite ends with a general blessing and a general sending out to all participants of the service.

The *Icelandic* rite emphasises *vocatio* in the Presentation, speaking of both God's calling and the congregation's calling. The latter is also mentioned in the Exhortation, including the specific location, and it is mentioned again in the prayer during the imposition of hands.

Benedictio: Benediction is asked for in the Introductory Prayer and in the prayer during the imposition of hands. *Missio* is present in the Exhortation, but there is no Reception/sending out.

In the Swedish-language version of the *Finnish* rite the outer calling to ministry – *vocatio externa* – has a specific section called 'Calling to ministry'. Here the name of the ordinand and the ministry he is called to is proclaimed.[26] The calling is also mentioned in the Ordination Prayer, and in the final prayer of the rite.

Benedictio is included in the Introductory Prayer, just after the Creed, in the Conferral of Office, in the prayer after the imposition of hands, and in the sending out.

Missio: As mentioned above, before the Ordination Prayer the rite has a part called 'Conferral of the office'. Here the bishop entrusts 'the office of deacon/deaconess' to the ordinand. The final part of the rite is called 'Sending out'. It mentions vocation to the Church of Christ, includes a biblical reference to John 12.26 – Jesus' promise to be where his servants are – and a prayer for blessing.

The Introductory Prayer in the *Danish* rite contains all three elements. *Vocatio* is seen in the words: 'We thank you for calling us to service for you in caring for our neighbour and each other in the congregation'.[27] This element is also present in the Ordination Prayer. The ordinands are presented as deacons and, after the Ordination Prayer, *mission* occurs when the officiant says: 'Then I send you to live out the ministry of care in your daily work as deacons'.

Conclusion

All the rites include the three constitutive elements *vocatio*, *benedictio* and *missio*. However, there is a variation in how clearly the three elements are present in each rite. A more thorough investigation would have to take into

---

26. In the Finnish-language version this element has been removed (Ahonen 1996:235). *Vocatio externa* is not required in dioceses other than the Swedish-speaking Diocese of Borgå/Porvoo.

27. Translated from the original Danish text: 'Vi takker dig, at du kalder os til en tjeneste for dig i omsorgen for næsten og hinanden i menigheden'.

consideration the historical perspectives of the creation of each of these rites and the compromises of theological views that they may represent.

Final Conclusions

The purpose of this analysis was to identify definitions and descriptions of the diaconal ministry and its relation to ordained ministry in an attempt to clarify whether the rites may be said to be ordinations to ordained ministry. The analysis has shed light on a number of points.

In the *Church of Norway* several features of the rite support the case that the deacon is put on the same footing as priest and catechist and regarded as an equal part of the ecclesiastical office. This is indicated by the fact that both the structure and the wording of the rite is very close to the rite for the ordination of priests. But the picture is ambiguous, because the term *'vigsling'* is used for various functions in the church. The ordination takes place in the cathedral, and the bishop is the officiant. On the other hand some features point to the opposite interpretation, namely that only the priest belongs to the ordained ministry. For instance the terms *'ordinationstale'*, 'ordination address', and *'ordinand'* are used in the ordination rite for priests, while in the rites of ordination for deacons and catechists the terms used are *'vigslingstale'* and the one to be *'vigslet'* (*Kirkemøtet* 1998, 80f). This vagueness and ambiguity reflects the ongoing disagreement on the theology of ordained ministry in the Church of Norway.

The diaconate of all the baptised is emphasised, and the Norwegian rite speaks concretely of the diaconal tasks.

In the *Church of Sweden* the rite contains *vocatio*, *benedictio* and *missio* and, according to the preamble of the service book, considers itself an act of ordination to ordained ministry. The structure of the ordination rites for bishop, priest, and deacon are uniform. Furthermore the deacons are ordained by the bishop in the cathedral. All this reflects that these three officeholders are seen as equal parts of the ordained ministry, as now stated in the Church Ordinance.

The special ministry of the deacon is emphasised. The deacon is defined as a *sign* of mercy. At the same time the rite points to the common priesthood of all the baptised, based on the understanding of the Church as the people of God.

The terms in the rite used in the *Church of Iceland* show that it is considered an ordination: there are, for instance references to 'witnesses of the ordination' and 'ordination address'. Moreover the ordination takes place in the cathedral with the bishop as officiant. The Icelandic rite is the only one where there is a visible 'change' in the ordinand – the vesting with the stole.

In the rite little is said of the tasks of diaconal ministry. The prayers seem to be more connected with the edification of the Christian life in general than with the specific diaconal ministry.

Since the rite of *the Evangelical-Lutheran Church of Finland* in the majority of the dioceses is connected with the graduation from the deacons' college and does not depend on a calling to specific ministry and actual employment in the church, it is not considered to be an ordination. The epicletic element in the rite is weak, as it is only present in the Introductory Prayer. It therefore seems confusing that the terms 'office' and 'conferral of the office' are used in the Swedish-language version. The rite contains all three constitutive elements, *vocatio*, *benedictio* and *missio*. Furthermore the wording expresses a strong connection between the church and the deacon. But this reference to mutual duties, gifts and so on, of the deacon and the church could also be interpreted as a reflection of the substantial role of the diaconate of all the baptised in Finnish theology of *diakonia* (Olsen 2000, 73). The rites in general are in process of reform. A liturgical commission is at work, and the General Assembly of the Evangelical-Lutheran Church of Finland is expected to sanction a new service book during 2004. There is every indication that calling to ministry in the church will be required. It is debated whether there should be one common ordination rite for all vocational groups in the church.

The existing rite stresses that the foundation of the diaconal ministry is love and the faith of the Church.

The rite of *the Evangelical-Lutheran Church of Denmark* is connected with the graduation from the deacons' college and does not depend on a calling to specific ministry in the church. It is a recommended blessing for ministry as a deacon. It is not considered an ordination rite, and it is not an authorised part of any service book. It is the only one of the five rites that does not take place in the cathedral, and the bishop is not the officiant. Danish deacons are not under the authority of a bishop.[28] Yet the rite contains all three constitutive

---

28. The Evangelical-Lutheran Church of Denmark takes up a special position in ecumenical discussions and refused to sign the Porvoo Common Statement. The main reason was a general fear among the congregational councils that Porvoo would lead to an episcopal Church of Denmark (Lodberg 2002, 68f). A Danish bishop is a leader of a diocese, and the Danish bishops take a different view from that of the bishops in the other Nordic countries, as their Bishops' Meeting is an informal institution with no right to speak on behalf of the church. For further information on the Danish situation, see Iversen (Part II.6).

elements, speaks of the 'ministry of deacons in the congregation', includes *epiclesis* and emphasises apostolic tradition.

The diaconal ministry is described as a ministry of care and a life lived as a *sign* of Christ's love.

What we can conclude is that the Church of Sweden and the Church of Iceland clearly ordain deacons. These two churches have a threefold ordained ministry – bishop, priest and deacon. In the three remaining churches there seems to be a discrepancy between the general interpretation of the rite as a blessing and the actual content of the rite. Maybe the existence of a rite recommended by the Danish Bishops since 2001 will raise the question of the diaconate in the Evangelical-Lutheran Church of Denmark. The Church of Norway and the Evangelical-Lutheran Church of Finland are in the midst of a theological clarification as to whether only the priest/bishop or more or all officeholders participate in the one ministry of the church according to Lutheran understanding.

References

Ahonen, Risto A. 1996. Die Entwicklung des diakonischen Amts in den lutherischen Kirchen insbesondere Finlands. In *Erneuerung des Diakonats als ökumenische Aufgabe*, ed. Theodor Strohm, *Diakoniewissenschaftliche Studien* vol. 7, 148-255. Heidelberg: DWI-Verlag.

Baptism, Eucharist and Ministry (BEM). 1982. Faith and Order Paper 111, Geneva: World Council of Churches.

Den Svenska Kyrkohandboken II. 1988. Stockholm.

Die Bekenntnisschriften der Evangelisch-Lutherischen Kirche. 1992. 2nd ed. Göttingen: Vandenhoeck & Ruprecht.

Embetet i Den norske kirke. 2001. Oslo: *Kirkerådet*.

Gudstjenestebok for den Norske Kirke I-II. 1996. Oslo: Verbum.

Handbók íslensku Kirkjunnar. 1981. Reykjavik.

Kyrkohandbok för den Evangelisk-lutherska Kyrkan i Finland III. 1995.Vasa: Församlingsförbundets Forlag.

Lodberg, Peter. 2001. *Dansker først og kristen så*. Valby: Aros.

Nissen, Karsten (ed.). 2001. Diakoni –en integreret dimension i folkekirkens liv. Valby: Aros.

Olsen, Ghita. 2000. *Den teologiske debat om diakonatet i de nordiske folkekirker.* Prize dissertation including short summary: The Theological Debate on the Diaconate in the Nordic National Evangelical-Lutheran Churches. Copenhagen:University of Copenhagen.

– 2001. Diakoniens og diakonatets stilling i de nordiske folkekirker. In *Dia-*

koni – en integreret dimension i folkekirkens liv, ed. Karsten Nissen, 210-227. Valby: Aros.

Plan for diakoni i Den norske Kirke. 1988. Oslo: *Kirkerådet*.

Puglisi, James F. 1996. The Process of Admission to Ordained Ministry, vol I: A Comparative Study –Epistemological Principles and Roman Catholic Rites. Collegeville, Minn: The Liturgical Press.

– 2001. The Process of Admission to Ordained Ministry, vol III: Contemporary Rites and General Conclusions. Collegeville, Minn: The Liturgical Press.

Stenberg, Per. 1998. Ett treledat ämbete. Diskussionen om det diakonale ämbetets förnyande i den evangelisk-lutherska kyrkan i Finland 1982-1997. Extended essay. University of Åbo.

Vigsling av kantorer. 1998:10 Oslo: Kirkemøtet.

The Historical Development of Diaconal Consecration Rites in Denmark

Liselotte Malmgart

The official structure in the Evangelical Lutheran-Church of Denmark (ELCD) does not include posts for deacons or deaconesses. This is reflected in the Service Book of the Church, which contains no rites for ordination or blessing for the diaconal ministry. Since 1989 it has been possible for Danish parishes to employ parish assistants (*'sognemedhjælpere'*) and a number of deacons fill these posts, but the majority of parish assistants are not deacons. Since 1867 the liturgical acts related to deacons and deaconesses have been connected to the deaconess houses or schools for deacons, where the development and use of the rites have been the responsibility of the institutional directors and ministers. The Danish bishops have never taken part in the rites.

The aim of this article is to describe the historical development of the rites, thereby offering an example of a liturgical development in which rites are formed in close context with the people concerned. However, it is not the purpose to analyse the rites in detail here. There is not much historical source material to illuminate the (theological) reasons for the many changes in the different rites, but the wish for more modern language seems often to be the reason, and the changes frequently seem to take place one or two years after the appointment of a new institutional director.

This article is based on 48 different versions of the rites, found in periodicals, books and archives, and used at the institutions from 1867 to 2001, on historical books and material from the private archives of the institutions concerned and from the archives of the Bishops of Copenhagen and Viborg. Due to the number of rites, not all the elements in them will be discussed here. The emphasis will be on the promises and the prayer accompanying the laying-on of hands.

The Danish term used for the liturgical act that creates ministers is *'vielse'* or 'ordination' and the term used for the similar rite for deacons is *'indvielse'* for which there is no agreed equivalent in English (Rogerson 2001, 213-214). In this article the term *'indvielse'* will be rendered by the term 'blessing' because it would be a misrepresentation of the Danish situation on the question of the position of deacons in the ELCD to use the word 'ordination', and the word 'blessing' comes close to the content of the rites. In the rites the word *'indvie'* is also used as a verb and for linguistic reasons it is rendered by the word 'consecrate'.

The Institutions

The German development of Christian social institutions and hospitals in the middle of the nineteenth century also influenced the development of diaconal institutions and organisations in Denmark, resulting in three Danish deaconess houses and two schools for deacons.

Den danske Diakonissestiftelse was established in 1863 in Copenhagen. It was structured along the lines of the German deaconess houses (most notably Kaiserswerth) and engaged in the same kind of work: a private hospital and the first Danish nursing school, institutions for children and the elderly and the sending out of sisters, trained as nurses, to work in local parishes and social institutions all over the country. In most cases, the sisters who worked in parishes were not employed by the ELCD, but by small parish aid associations organised independently of the official church structure. The first deaconesses were blessed in 1867, and since 1979 it has been possible for men and women to be blessed as deacons at *Diakonissestiftelsen.*

The second Danish deaconess house *Sankt Lukas Stiftelsen* was founded in 1900 in an inner-city parish in Copenhagen; the first blessing of deaconesses took place in 1906 and the last in 1996. A very small intake of new sisters means that today the majority of the sisters are retired and the rules for admission are currently being changed to support new recruitment, but primarily still aimed at women.

Kolonien Filadelfias Diakonissehus was established around 1900 in the western part of Zealand as part of an institution for epileptic and psychiatric patients, inspired by the German diaconal institution Bethel bei Bielefeldt. The sisters mainly worked inside the institution, and this deaconess house remained by far the smallest of the three. The first blessing of deaconesses took place in 1913 and there have been no new deaconesses since 1969. Thus, today only a few sisters remain, none of them working.

Deacons have been educated and blessed at two schools, *Diakonhøjskolen* (the Diaconal College), in Århus, founded in 1920, and *Kolonien Filadelfias*

Diakonskole, formally established in 1907 and continuing today as the *Institut for Diakoni og Sjælesorg* (Institute for Diaconal Service and Pastoral Care). The schools only had male pupils until the early 1960s, when women were accepted. In Denmark, the term 'deacon' has mainly referred to a person with an education as a care worker from the two schools. The term has not been related to the specific work functions or the blessing. Until the 1960s the blessing took place after a few years of work experience, which resulted in only around half of the deacons being blessed (but still calling themselves deacons). However, today the blessing is connected to the completion of the education programme. Almost everybody accepts the offer of blessing and they will normally only use the title 'deacon' if they do so.

Being a deaconess has traditionally (until the 1960s) implied a lifelong commitment to the community of sisters, living together in celibacy, sharing financial resources and work and receiving sufficient to meet personal needs. Being a deacon has never had the same practical consequences, and the main function of the two associations for deacons seems to be supporting the schools and publishing a monthly magazine.

The Deaconesses 1867-1960

In 1867 *Diakonissestiftelsen* wanted to bless the first deaconesses, inspired by the tradition in Kaiserswerth. The matter was discussed with the Bishop of Copenhagen, who at first would not allow the ceremony to take place in a church. He suggested it should be performed in the living room of the deaconess house, but later agreed to the ceremony taking place in public. The ceremony was held in the local parish church and the central elements were the promises of the sisters (two questions), followed by a laying-on of hands and a prayer (characterised in the original source as a blessing).[1] Compared with the ordination of ministers in the ELCD, the rite did not include nearly as many parts and only the main structure (promises, laying-on of hands and

---

1. Even though the constitutive elements were the same, it is notable that the promises did not mirror the Kaiserswerth tradition of mentioning the triple duty of the sisters to be the servants of 1) the Lord Jesus, 2) the poor, children and the sick and 3) each other. Louise Conring, the first directress of *Diakonissestiftelsen*, had been blessed in Kaiserswerth in 1863 and the minister who performed the act in 1867 had attended the second Kaiserswerth Conference in 1865, where the question of the ordination of deaconesses was discussed. He was most probably aware of the German tradition but chose not to copy it directly. The first Swedish blessing of deaconesses in 1855 was closer to the German rite, but did not include the laying-on of hands (Elmund 1983, 224).

prayer) was the same. The next blessing of sisters took place in 1870 and not only the minister, but also the rite had changed. The promises had altered and were preceded by the confession of the creed, asking the sisters to affirm their sharing of this faith.[2] The two questions were longer, the first one asking the sisters to take on the work of a servant in the congregation.[3] The second question stated the way to do it: not proudly, but with sincerity of heart, love, gentleness and patience, and how long to do it: as long as God does not indicate another vocation.[4] The promises were confirmed with a handshake. During the laying-on of hands the Lord's Prayer was now included, probably an element adopted from the rite for ordination of ministers in the ELCD.

Another new element after the laying-on of hands was the prayer, known as the 'Deaconess Prayer of the early Church', from the Apostolic Constitutions (dating from the second half of the fourth century). This prayer stresses the importance of women in the history of Israel and invokes the Holy Spirit. It was part of the rite until 1962. It was also used in deaconess houses in Norway and Sweden (Elmund 1983, 226; Bloch-Hoell 1968, 72-73) and it seems to have been widely used in the European deaconess houses.[5]

The next rite available is from 1886 and shows some changes. Most noteworthy, the sisters are no longer asked to affirm their faith. This affirmation returned again at some point (after 1941), for in 1962 the sisters had to recite the Apostles' Creed before the promises. In 1886 the two questions are reduced to one, and the term 'work of a servant in the congregation' has been replaced by 'work and position of a deaconess'.[6] The work of a deaconess is said to be done 'for the sake of Jesus Christ, for the benefit of his congregation, with his compassion for the suffering and poor, with obedience to superiors and faithfulness to the vocation'.[7] The promise was followed by a collective blessing (based on 1 Cor. 15.58) and then the individual laying-on of hands with a blessing, based on a biblical quotation chosen for each woman.

In a later rite of 1916, the congregation is no longer mentioned as the object

---

2. '... dele i vedvarende denne Tro med os?'.
3. '... overtage og udrette en Tjenerindes Gjerning i Menigheden'.
4. '... ikke med Øienstolthed, men i Hjertets Oprigtighed, med Kjærlighed, Sagtmodighed og Taalmodighed ... saalænge Gud ikke klarligen anviser Eder andet Kald for Eders Liv'.
5. Theodor Schäfer stated in 1883, 'Es ist schön, daß in die meisten Einsegnungsliturgien der Gegenwart dies nun 1500 Jahre alte Gebet aufgenommen worden ist' (Schäfer 1883, 53).
6. 'Om I ville overtage en Diakonisses Gjerning og Stilling ...'.
7. '... for Jesu Kristi Skyld til hans Menigheds Gavn, i hans Barmhjærtighed mod de lidende og fattige, i villig Lydighed mod Eders foresatte, i Troskab mod Eders Kald?'.

of diaconal work, in fact the word 'congregation' is not used at all in the rite. Instead the work of a deaconess is said to be done in the Name of Jesus Christ and to further his Kingdom.[8] The laying-on of hands has a new prayer, asking in various ways for the help and strength of God, characterising the work of a deaconess as the work of love, the relief of suffering, healing the sick and bringing salvation to people bound by the power of darkness.[9] The prayer was still concluded with the Lord's Prayer, mirroring the ordination of ministers.

In 1900 another Danish deaconess house was established, and the first deaconesses from *Sankt Lukas Stiftelsen* were blessed in 1906. In 1901, there had been a prior discussion with the Bishop of Copenhagen, who declined to be involved in the blessing ceremony, because it would connect this private institution to the official church structure and give it an undesirable official standing (Malmgart 2001, 264). For the blessing in 1906, it seems that the minister chose to use the rite from *Diakonissestiftelsen*. This rite was used again in 1910, but for the blessing of deaconesses in March 1911, the rite was changed and elements introduced from the Norwegian rite used at the deaconess house in Oslo.[10] The motive for this decision is uncertain. Representatives from the Nordic deaconess houses had met in the spring of 1910, but neither the rite at *Diakonissestiftelsen* nor the Norwegian or Swedish deaconess houses seem to have been altered. Thus, it was probably not a question of a Scandinavian decision to harmonise the rites.

One of the new elements was another wording of the promises, now divided into three questions. In 1911 the wording was not word for word the same as the Norwegian, but in the next version of the rite all three questions were exactly the same. This version was used until the 1960s with a minor adjustment at the beginning of the 1950s. The words of the promises were, 'Do you of your own free will choose the vocation of a deaconess? Will you attempt to accomplish this work in loving and ready obedience, for the sake of the glory of God and the true benefit of your fellow human beings, as long as God allows you to carry it out? Will you seek and preserve the right disposition of a deaconess with prayer and self-denial?'[11]

---

8. '... i Jesus Kristi Navn og til hans Riges fremme'.

9. '...Staa dem bi i Kærlighedens Gerning, at der ved dem maa bringes Lindring til de lidende, Helbredelse til de syge og Frelse til dem, der er bundne af Mørkets Magt!'.

10. The Norwegian rite had been formulated by the first chairman of the board, the minister Julius Bruun. It was printed for the first time in 1889, when it is said that it had been used for several years (Bloch-Hoell 1968, 72-73); perhaps it was used in 1871 for the first Norwegian blessing of deaconesses.

11. 'Er det med din frie Vilje, du vælger en Diakonisses Kald? Vil du, saa længe Gud

Another Norwegian element, introduced in 1911, was the replacement of the prayer during the laying-on of hands with a word of commission: 'I consecrate you to be the Lord's deaconess in the name of the Father, the Son and the Holy Spirit. Amen'.[12] While the sisters were still kneeling, the Deaconess Prayer of the early Church was said. Some years later this prayer was moved to the introduction of the blessing act, before the promises and in the 1950 version it was replaced with another prayer. The 1950 version also includes another new element after the word of commission (while the sister knelt): the blessing based on 1 Cor. 15.58, which was also used at *Diakonissestiftelsen.*

The same type of commission is found in the rite used at the third Danish deaconess house at *Kolonien Filadelfia.* Here the first blessing took place in 1913, but unfortunately there is no recorded version of the rite earlier than 1947. In 1947 the wording of the commissioning was, 'In the name of the Father, the Son and the Holy Spirit, I consecrate you to be a congregational deaconess in the Danish Evangelical-Lutheran Church'.[13] A prayer with invocation of the Holy Spirit was also said during the laying-on of hands, asking for help to accomplish the work with dignity and faithfulness for the benefit of the church and the furthering of the Kingdom.[14]

Comparison of the rite for deaconesses and the rite for deacons at *Kolonien Filadelfia* makes it plausible to argue that the 1947 rite is not the original rite of 1913, because the wording of the promises for deaconesses is very close to the promises for deacons and the versions of the rite for deacons show that it was changed between 1944 and 1951, probably because a new director took over in 1944. It seems logical that he made similar changes in both rites. In 1919 the first directress of the small deaconess house at *Kolonien Filadelfia*

---

forunder dig at staa i denne Gerning, i kærlig og villig Lydighed søge at fuldbyrde den til Guds Navns ære og dine Medmenneskers sande Gavn? Vil du under Bøn og Selvfornægtelse søge at vinde og bevare det rette Diakonissesind?'.

12. *'Saa indvier jeg dig da til at være Herrens Diakonisse i Faderens, Sønnens og Helligaandens navn. Amen'* The expression 'word of commission' is used for want of a more precise description, because this is not a blessing or a prayer with invocation of the Holy Spirit as found in many ordination rites at this point in the rite. The renewed rite at Lovisenberg from 1945 refers to this part of the rite as 'the promise and the commission' (*'løftet med overdragelsen'*), (Bloch-Hoell 1968, 140).

13. 'Saa indvier jeg dig da i Faderens, Sønnens og Helligåndens navn til at være Menighedens Diakonisse i Den danske evangelisk-lutherske Kirke'.

14. '... giv hende ved din Helligånd værdigt og med Troskab at øve den hende betroede Gerning til din Kirkes Gavn og dit Riges fremme ...'.

died, and the chairman of the board asked the directress at *Diakonissestiftelsen* about the possibility of having a directress from this larger house. She declined, giving as her reasons the lack of a suitable sister and the difference between the blessing at *Diakonissestiftelsen* and the blessing at *Kolonien Filadelfia* (Malmgart 1997, 46). The absence of source material makes it impossible to determine whether this referred to the rite of blessing or the rules of admission for new deaconesses. One theory on this discrepancy is that the rite at *Kolonien Filadelfia* was influenced by the eccentric founding father of the institution, Dr. Adolph Sell, who had quite his own interpretation of pietistic Christianity and who remained very much the religious authority at the institution even after appointing a theologian to be the minister.[15]

The different structures of the three rites for deaconesses about 1960 are outlined in figure 1 (not all elements of the service included).

Figure 1

Diakonissestiftelsen	*Sankt Lukas Stiftelsen*	*Kolonien Filadelfia (sisters)*
The Deaconess Prayer of the early Church	Introductory Prayer	Introductory Prayer
Scriptural reading Rom. 16.1-2	Scriptural reading Rom. 16.1-2	Scriptural reading Matt. 20.25-28, Matt. 25.31-41, 2 Thess. 1.11-12.
The sisters recite the Creed		
The promise – one question	The promises – three questions	The promises – three questions
Confirming handshake	Confirming handshake	Confirming handshake
Blessing (1 Cor. 15.58)		
The laying-on of hands Prayer	The laying-on of hands Word of Commission Prayer	The laying-on of hands Word of Commission Invocation of the Holy Spirit
The Lord's Prayer	Blessing (1 Cor. 15.58)	Blessing (1 Cor.15.58) The Lord's Prayer

15. For instance, one of the reasons why the 1947 deaconess rite cannot be the original is that Dr. Sell would never have accepted the use of the expression 'the Evangelical-Lutheran Church', believing that the church could never be named after a person (Malmgart 1997, 35). Instead he used the word 'congregation', and it is notable that this word is found more often in the rites of '*Kolonien Filadelfia*' than in the rites of the other institutions.

None of the questions in the promises or the prayers were identical, and the blessings, formed from 1 Cor. 15.58, were not word for word the same. At *Sankt Lukas Stiftelsen* the form was: 'May the Lord strengthen and bless you for what you now have been consecrated to, that in the word of his apostles you may be firm, unshakeable, rich in the work of the Lord, knowing that your work in the Lord is not in vain'.[16]

The expressions used in the rites for the blessing of deaconesses are characterised by the inclusion of many of the distinctive qualities often presented as ideals for the sisters. They are to be humble, obedient, loving, dignified, faithful, obedient to their superiors, self-denying, faithful to their vocation, firm and unshakeable. In the rites, the service of the deaconess is characterised as the work of love, the imitation of the mercy of Christ, the relief of suffering, healing of the sick and bringing salvation to people bound by the power of darkness. Their task is to help the body and soul of the young and the old, the sick and the healthy, the poor and the needy.

The vocation of the individual woman to be a deaconess has always been a cornerstone in the theology in the deaconess houses and consequently many references to personal vocation are found in the rites.

The Deacons 1917-1960

The first Danish blessing of deacons took place in 1917 at two different schools. The small private association *Stefansforeningen* had established a school in 1912 and held a blessing for three deacons in Copenhagen in September 1917; a few weeks later, the first deacons were blessed at *Kolonien Filadelfia*.

The Copenhagen rite was written by a theologian teaching at the school, and it seems that he wrote it quite independently, not seeking advice from the directors of the deaconess houses. Shortly afterwards, *Stefansforeningen* had to close their school and asked the Danish Inner Mission association ('*Indre Mission*') to take over the responsibility of educating deacons. The new school, *Diakonhøjskolen*, was located in Århus and welcomed the first pupils in 1920 for a three-year education programme. In 1925 the time came to organise the blessing of the first deacons. Nearly all the board members (including several theologians) contributed to the first version of the rite. As references they read

---

16. 'Så styrke og velsigne Herren jer i det, som I nu er indviet til, så at I efter Hans apostles ord må blive faste, urokkelige, altid rige i Herrens gerning, vidende, at jeres arbejde i Herren er ikke forgæves.'

the rite from *Kolonien Filadelfia*, the Church Army and the Swedish and Norwegian rites for deacons, but they chose the rite from *Stefansforeningen* as the main starting point. It seems that the rite for ministers from the authorised Service Book was not taken into consideration, and the final rite did not reflect the ordination of ministers in the ELCD, as it was lacking in several elements, such as the invocation of the Holy Spirit and the corporate dimension of the laying-on of hands.

When the rite was finished, the Danish Bishops were asked to approve it, which they did at their meeting in January 1927, after having made several corrections to it (Malmgart 2001, 265-266). The approval of the rite did not give the rite or the deacons an official standing in the ELCD, but the school saw it as an unofficial endorsement, legitimating the deacons in the church, even though very few deacons were actually employed within the ELCD.

As a consequence of one of the comments made by the bishops, the Århus rite was the first and for many years the only rite which referred to the candidates as 'deacons in the Danish Evangelical-Lutheran Church'. At a later point, the word 'Danish' was omitted. The words were for instance used in the promises, where the candidate had to promise to 'practice the work of a deacon in our Danish Evangelical-Lutheran Church with obedience, love for [our] heavenly Father and [our] Saviour Jesus Christ, with love for your fellow human beings and faithfulness to [your] vocation'.[17] The expression was repeated in the word of commission during the laying-on of hands, 'In the name of the Father, the Son and the Holy Spirit, I consecrate you to be a deacon in the Danish Evangelical-Lutheran Church'.[18]

Until the 1960s the rite at *Diakonhøjskolen* seems not to have been subject to many changes, perhaps out of reverence for the episcopal approval or because the directors in Århus did not take an interest.

At *Kolonien Filadelfia*, the rite for the blessing of deacons took place for the first time in 1917 and was repeated in 1924 and 1931 (it was quite a small school). In some ways, this rite stands out from the rites at the other institutions, probably because of the influence of the above mentioned Dr. Sell. The promises had three questions. In the first question, the deacon was asked to confirm the intent and wish in his heart to continue as a deacon. Secondly he

---

17. 'Erklærer du dig af hjertet villig til altid at udøve din Diakongerning i vor danske, evangelisk-lutherske Kirke i Lydighed og Kærlighed til din himmelske Fader og din Frelser Jesus Kristus, i Kærlighed til dine Medmennesker og i Troskab mod dit Kald?'
18. 'Saa indvier jeg dig da i Faderens, Sønnens og Helligåndens navn til at være Diakon i den danske evangelisk-lutherske Kirke.'

had to promise by the grace of God to try to acquire and preserve the right disposition for a deacon and thirdly, he was asked to love the deacon school and his brother deacons.

The word of commission during the laying-on of hands was special, because it was the only rite that mentioned 'the office of the deacon'. The wording was, 'In the name of the Father, the Son and the Holy Spirit I entrust you with the holy office of deacon'.[19]

The rite at *Kolonien Filadelfia* was revised in the late 1940s by a new director, who omitted the expression 'the office of deacon' in the word of commission and substituted it with a phrase closer to the form used at *Diakonhøjskolen*, 'In the name of the Father, the Son and the Holy Spirit, I consecrate you to be a congregational deacon in the Danish Evangelical-Lutheran Church'.[20] The promise was reformulated into two questions and the first one went on to be the model for the united rite for deacons in the 1960s, 'Is it your sincere intention and prayer to serve in the Danish Evangelical-Lutheran Church as a deacon, being the servant of the congregation, helping the sick and poor and needy?'.[21]

The next director at *Kolonien Filadelfia* revised the promises again and added a final exhortation to the rite: 'I command you to fulfil this service in your daily work, to educate yourself and to mark your work with justice, truthfulness and love'.[22]

The structures of the two rites for male deacons are compared in figure 2 (not all elements included). For comparative purposes, the main structure of the rite for the ordination of ministers in the ELCD is also included.[23]

---

19. 'Saa betror jeg dig, N.N., det hellige Diakonembede i Faderens og Sønnens og Helligaandens Navn.'
20. 'Så indvier jeg dig da (navn) i Faderens, Sønnens og Helligåndens navn til at være menighedens diakon i den danske evangelisk-lutherske kirke.'
21. 'Er det dit oprigtige forsæt og din bøn at tjene i den danske evangelisk-lutherske kirke som diakon ved som menighedens tjener at hjælpe de syge og fattige og nødlidende til legeme og sjæl?'
22. 'Så befaler jeg jer da at virkeliggøre denne tjeneste i jert daglige arbejde, stedse at dygtiggøre jer og i jeres gerning at være præget af retfærdighed, sanddruhed og kærlighed.'
23. See Iversen (Part II, 6) for further material on the ordination of ministers in the ELCD.

Figure 2

Kolonien Filadelfia	Diakonhøjskolen in Århus	Rite for ministers (1898)
From the pulpit: The names of the future deacons are read	From the altar: Prayer for the future deacons, their names are read	From the pulpit: Presentation of the candidates Prayer for the ministry
		Invocation of the Holy Spirit
Three scriptural readings	1-3 scriptural readings	Four scriptural readings Exhortation
	Prayer	
The Promises (three questions) *	The Promise (one question)	The promise (one question relating to the exhortation)
Confirming handshake		Confirming handshake
The laying-on of hands Word of commission Invocation of the Holy Spirit	The laying-on of hands Word of commission	Ordination prayer with invocation of the Holy Spirit, concluded with the Lord's Prayer during the laying-on of hands
Blessing * (1 Pet. 5.10b; Heb. 13.21)	Blessing	
Exhortation (after 1958)		

Between 1944 and 1951 the promises were revised considerably, shortened to two questions and the final blessing omitted. Some time around 1960 the promises were reduced to one question.

The distinctive qualities indicated for the deacons in the rites are humility, obedience, love, justice, truthfulness, faithfulness, dignity and humble frankness.

In the rites, the work of the deacon is characterised as a holy service and as a help to the body and soul of the young and the old, the sick and the healthy, the poor and the needy. This last form of words was used in the rites for both deacons and deaconesses at *Kolonien Filadelfia* and later came into the united rite for both deacon schools.

Aiming for Unity

At the beginning of the 1960s the directors of the three deaconess houses decided to co-operate and co-ordinate the rites for the blessing of deaconesses. The reason behind this was a question from the Liturgical Commission, appointed by the bishops in 1953 to revise the Service Books of the Danish Church. In 1961 the Commission asked to see the rite for the blessing of deaconesses, clearly assuming there was only one rite: the directors decided to provide one. The rite was finished in June 1962 and was approved by the boards and sisters' councils in all three deaconess houses. There was general disappointment when the rite was not included after all in the proposal for new liturgies, published in 1963. One of the three directors of deaconesses was also the head of the school for deacons at *Kolonien Filadelfia*, and in 1964 he and his colleague from Århus also decided to rewrite and co-ordinate the two rites for deacons into one rite. The rite was not sent to the Danish Bishops as was the case in 1925, partly because the directors did not think it was necessary or possible to ask for the bishops' approval.

The two new rites were a mixture of elements from the five existing rites and some choices were still left to the individual institution, for instance the choice of scriptural readings. The two rites did not match each other, perhaps because the traditional life of the sisters in the deaconess houses and the life of the (male) deacons were still very different. Perhaps the need to consider all the different traditions of rites made it too complicated – or perhaps it was not seen as an option at all to have the same rite for both groups.

The directors, who had agreed the rites, soon began to change them or to retain elements from their own tradition. An example is the deaconess rite used at *Kolonien Filadelfia* in 1969, where the first question in the promises was identical with the question from the rite for deacons (originating in the earlier rite from *Kolonien Filadelfia*) and the second question was the one recommended in the new deaconess rite of 1962.

Subsequent generations of directors at the diaconal institutions did not feel bound by the decisions made by their predecessors, and during the next four decades the rites underwent minor adjustments again, mostly in the precise wording of their component parts. An example of a more radical change was the disappearance of the traditional prayer from the early Church, used only at *Diakonissestiftelsen* and replaced by another prayer in the early 1970s.

Conclusion

All the Danish private rites for the blessing of deaconesses and deacons were originally formulated at the individual institutions, sometimes inspired by rites from other institutions, but never directly copied. The unofficial status of the rites made it quite easy to make minor or major changes to them, and nearly every director has taken this opportunity, sometimes inspired by other rites

(Danish or foreign) and sometimes according to their own theological opinions (for instance in the specific wording of prayers).

The debate on and changes to the rite for the ordination of pastors in the ELCD do not seem to have influenced the development of these private rites. The blessing of deaconesses and deacons has not been related to an office or a diaconate in the ELCD. Consequently, the rites have often been interpreted as a personal blessing for the future work of the diaconal workers, and their significance has been related to the individual deaconess or deacon on a personal level.

The Future

In September 2001 the first report on Diaconal Service in the ELCD was published. It also included a proposal for a new rite for the blessing of deacons (Nissen 2001, 249-251).[24] The promise in this rite is a short version of the question from the earlier rite for deacons, and it is notable that the new proposal replaces the commission during the laying-on of hands with an invocation of the Holy Spirit.

In January 2002 the four diaconal institutions received a letter from Bishop Karsten Nissen, who wrote on behalf of all the Danish Bishops. The bishops had decided to approve the rite and recommended that all the institutions use this rite in the future. All the institutions appear to have complied with this recommendation.

References

Bloch-Hoell, Nils. 1968. – *at vi skulle vandre i dem. Diakonissehusets første hundre år 1868-1968.* Oslo.

Elmund, Gunnel. 1983. Synen på diakonatet och vigningen till detta vid de svenska diakonianstalterne från 1851 – omkr 1950, in *Vigd til tjänst. Betänkande av Svenska Kyrkans diakoninämnds vigningsutredning,* 222-244. Stockholm.

Hauge, Svend. 1963. *I troskab mod kaldet. Den danske Diakonissestiftelse 1863-1963.* Copenhagen: Lohse.

Malmgart, Liselotte.1997. Kærlighedens liv er handling. Diakonitænkning og diakoniuddannelse på Kolonien Filadelfia 1897-1987, in *Bær hinandens byrder ...,* eds B.B. Mortensen and L. Malmgart, 32-96. Dianalund.

---

24. The new Danish rite is analysed in Olsen's article on the Nordic rites for deacons (Part II.3).

– 2001. Indvielse af diakonisser og diakoner i Danmark. In *Kirkehistoriske Samlinger 2001*, 259-277. Copenhagen: Selskabet for Danmarks Kirkehistorie.

Müller, Johannes. 1950. *Tjene vil jeg: Nogle Blade af Diakonissehuset Sankt Lukas Stiftelsens Historie 1900-1950.* Copenhagen.

Nissen, Karsten (ed.). 2001. *Diakoni –en integreret dimension i folkekirkens liv.* Valby: Aros.

Rogerson, Barry. 2001. A Translation of the Church of Norway's Ordination Rites, in *Studia Liturgica* 31:211-240.

Schäfer, Theodor. 1883. *Die weibliche Diakonie III. Die Diakonissen und das Mutterhaus.* Altona.

Svalander, Ulla and Palmgren, Bo. 1962. De svenska diakonianstalternas diakon- och diakoniss –vigningar, in *Kyrkohistorisk Årsskrift 1962*, 110-137. Stockholm.

The versions of the rite from the various institutions are dated:
Den danske Diakonissestiftelse: 1867, 1870, 1886, 1909, 1916, 1925, 1934, 1941, 1962, 1972, 1982, 1987, 1992, 1999, 2001.
Sankt Lukas Stiftelsen: 1906, 1911, 1934, 1950, 1955, 1962, 1971, 1982.
Stefansforeningen: 1917.
Kolonien Filadelfias Diakonissehus: 1947, 1959, 1969.
Kolonien Filadelfias Diakonskole: 1925, 1937, 1944, 1951, 1955, 1963, 1966, 1976, 1988, 1995.
Diakonhøjskolen i Århus: 1925, 1927, 1949, 1951, 1954, 1960, 1964, 1975, 1983, 1988, 1999.

The Development of Diaconal Ordinations in Sweden in the Light of Social History

Helena Inghammar

The organ plays as the newly ordained deacon leaves the cathedral, accompanied by fellow-deacons, assistants (either deacons or priests), and the ordaining bishop in a procession. The ordination liturgy they have taken part in is officially published in the Service book of the Church of Sweden. All new deacons wear an alb and the stole over their left shoulders. They also wear the necklace with the deacons' emblem; the dove in a cross, surrounded by a circle. After the ordination, they will all be employed in the Church of Sweden. Most of them are trained nurses or social workers and all have gone through a one-year diaconal training programme, after which they were examined by their bishop and the diocesan chapter of their diocese. The majority of the newly ordained are women. The situation as described here is typical for Sweden in 2004.

Presently most would agree that the Church of Sweden has a three-fold ordained ministry of bishop, priest and deacon. Even so, the recent Church Order does not stipulate that the parishes have to employ deacons, though it does stipulate that the bishop should ordain deacons. Paradoxically, it states that only those who are going to be appointed to posts within the diocese after ordination may be examined for ordination (*Kyrkoordning* 1999, ch. 2, §1-7; ch. 32, §1-6). Ever since the Reformation there has been a latent discussion on the Church's ordained ministry in the Church of Sweden (Askmark 1949, 250-251, 260-263). There has been a quest for a common pattern of ordained ministry, valid for all times. But, the question is whether such a pattern exists in either the New Testament or the tradition. And, if it does, should it be considered normative? When it comes to the threefold ministry of bishops, priests and deacons, it is uncertain whether such a pattern exists in the Swedish tradition (*Diakonens ämbete* 1995, 18; Askmark 1949, 232.).

The first Swedish deaconess house, *Diakonissanstalten* (later *Ersta*) was founded in Stockholm in 1851, and the first ordination also took place there four years later. Already at this point, there were problems to be solved: Were the early ordinations intended to be ordinations? If the deaconesses were ordained, to what were they ordained? There were no ecclesiastical regulations on deaconesses. There were not even posts for them to hold within the Church of Sweden. In fact, they were completely dependent on the mother houses for economic and social security as well as for ecclesiastical identity.

This article focuses on two periods of primary importance in order to bring to light the relationship between social and liturgical changes. The first is the foundational period, from c. 1850 until c 1920, when all modern Swedish diaconal institutions began their work. The second period, a period of reorientation, covers the last two decades, focusing on attempts to secure the identity and role of deacons through ordination. Since 1987, there has been one single ordination rite for both sexes. Ordination rites for deacons and deaconesses are interesting because of their relatively short period of existence and the considerable changes they have undergone during that time. The aim here is to highlight some factors that might have influenced the ordination rites. Over time, the concept of ordination has changed. The words actually used indicate the changes. What the ordinations were and are called is therefore interesting, and, in a third part, this article focuses on the official liturgies of the Church of Sweden. It is in no way self-evident that what we are looking at are actual 'ordinations'. The most frequent term used in the early period, from c1850 to1900 is 'acceptance' or 'enrolment' ('*upptagning*').[1] After 1920, when the first official liturgy was agreed, the words 'install' ('*inställa*') and 'bless' ('*inviga*') were used simultaneously (*Handbok* 1917, 261-279). Since 1942, 'ordination' ('*vigning*') has been the official term (*Kyrkohandbok* 1942, 366-382). In Swedish vocabulary, the use of the word 'deacon' is no longer restricted to men. All deacons (male) and deaconesses (female) are usually called deacons. For clarity, in this article, women ordained to the diaconal ministry will be referred to as deaconesses, when reference is to the period in which there were different ordination liturgies for men and women, that is, until 1987.[2] Since then, diaconal ordination has been one and the same for men and women, whether they are ordained separately or together.

---

1. Accounts about ordinations in *Olivebladet* (1885-1904) use the word 'acceptance' ('upptagning').
2. There are exceptions: women ordained at the Swedish Deacons' Institute in the late 1970s are sometimes mentioned as 'deacons'.

This article is based on material found in periodicals and books from the diaconal institutes and on official rites of ordination found in Service books. These in turn relate to the situation in society in general and to changes that have taken place over the years. The thesis of the article is that the ordination rites for deacons and deaconesses in Sweden have developed as they have done for a number of social historical reasons. Several examples of secular or civil changes influencing opinions on the diaconate, and thence its ordination rites, could be mentioned; for instance, the growing possibilities that women had of holding salaried posts and of receiving higher education. In addition, the rise of the welfare state in the mid-twentieth century made it possible for deaconesses to take on new fields of responsibility, thereby changing the view of the diaconate. Nurses and social workers had taken over many of the deaconesses' previous tasks. The fact that deaconesses gained the right to marry and receive their own incomes influenced the ordination rites. The ordination liturgy had to change to comply with these and other changes in society and church.

The changes mentioned above have civil parallels, such as the initiation rituals for nurses. It is still common for nurses who have just completed their training to receive the emblems of their profession at an examination ceremony. The brooch signals where the nurse received her, or his, education. Moreover, the emblems of many schools of nursing still have the sign of the cross on them. The title 'sister' is reminiscent of the time when being a nurse was equal to being a deaconess or a nun (*Sjuksköterskan* 1969, 196). The secularisation of medical care has probably influenced these initiation rituals and processes. Until 1969, nurses trained in Linköping were 'installed' at ceremonies in the cathedral, at which they also received their brooches. In the middle of the 1990s the ceremonies were moved back to the cathedral.[3] It is still quite common for newly qualified nurses to receive their brooches at ceremonies held in a church. Also other categories of professionals have had ceremonies similar to ordinations or installations. At *Samariterhemmet*, the diaconal institution founded in Uppsala in 1882, parish sisters were educated and 'ordained' between 1906 and 1946 (*Betänkande* 1948, 22). For quite a long period of time *Vårsta*, the diaconal institution founded in Härnösand in 1912, offered a training programme for 'domestic helpers', who cared for the

---

3. The nurses in Linköping were blessed at ceremonies in the cathedral, where they also received their brooches, until 1969, and in 1995 the ceremony moved back to the cathedral. From the beginning, in 1895, the brooch has had the sign of the cross on it (Boman 1995, 69-76).

housebound in their own homes.[4] Their programme ended with a blessing ('*invigning*'), as did that of the deaconesses. A ceremony described in 1958 resembles a deaconess blessing and was held in the cathedral of Härnösand. The domestic helpers walked side by side up the aisle of the cathedral wearing their uniforms. After the singing of a hymn the dean of the diocese spoke and the women received their grades and brooches. Thereafter another hymn followed and the domestic helpers walked up to the altar rails where intercession for them took place and they received the Lord's blessing (*I beredda* 1962, 113). Obviously, deaconesses were far from the only professionals to be blessed or installed in Sweden during the nineteenth and twentieth centuries. The words 'blessing' or 'installation' were used simultaneously for several other categories of professionals.

The Foundational period
The First Deaconesses
In the mid nineteenth century, charitable work not only seemed a proper task for unmarried women, but could also be seen as a solution to the problem of their financial support and possibly as a way of giving a sense of meaning to the women involved. Over and above the benefits to the needy, the diaconal idea seemed a win-win situation.

When *Diakonissanstalten* was founded in Stockholm in 1851, men and women from revivalist pietistic movements were behind the institution. Forming associations had become common at the time, and the diaconal association parallels other philanthropic associations. *Diakonissanstalten*, later *Ersta diakonissällskap*, was and is the largest school for deaconesses, now deacons. It followed the Kaiserswerth tradition, forming a sisterhood and mother house. The first two women were accepted into the newly founded mother house in 1855. They were called sisters and were 'adopted' as daughters in the mother house. The leader of the mother house was a priest, the father, on some occasions even explicitly referred to as the deaconess-father (Lönegren 1901, 88-89; *I beredda* 1962, 20). In the mid-nineteenth century, there was an excessive number of single women[5] in the capital of Sweden, so many that it had become a problem, especially for the upper classes (Elmund 1973, 37;

---

4. In Sweden, until not very long ago, these 'domestic helpers' were called 'hemsamariter' ('home Samaritans').
5. According to Qvist (1978, 101-102), the excessive numbers were brought about by the emigration of men to foreign countries and the migration of women to the cities. Women left the countryside in greater numbers than men did. Qvist (1978, 177-180)

Andersson 1997, 53). A woman needed a family in order to secure her economic support and provide a stable platform for her social life. Most researchers seem to agree that at this time the Lutheran idea of female subordination founded in creation was still dominant among theologians, as was the thought that a woman's primary mission in life was her home (Hammar 1999, 7; Martinsen 1984, 81-82; Elmund 2001, 27). The founders of the mother house considered this notion. The homelike structure of the diaconal institutes gave the deaconess what she needed to perform her work. When she died, she was buried in a sister-grave (Lönegren 1901, 164-165).

The deaconesses-to-be took vows, in three main parts, based on the Kaiserswerth tradition. At *Diakonissanstalten* in the 1850s, the ceremony was influenced on the whole by Kaiserswerth but without the imposition of hands (Elmund 1973, 99-102). First, a vow to serve the Lord Jesus was taken. This vow seems to have been the first in all cases. The second and third vows concern serving the fellow sisters in the sisterhood and serving the needy. The order of these two vows varies. The leader of the diaconal institute posed the questions, with smaller variations, as closing remarks in his addresses at the ceremonies: 'Will you be the praying servants of the Lord, your fellow sisters' servants and the servants of the wretched?'[6] The fellowship between the sisters seems to have been important. The other sisters, through a referendum, recommended whether a new sister should be accepted into the sisterhood, or not. The leaders of the mother house then took the final decision. Apparently, the collective aspect of sisterhood was emphasised more in the early ordinations than it is now.

Some texts state that acceptance into the diaconate was valid only as long as God did not explicitly call the sister to something else, presumably marriage.[7]

---

also argues that the large number of children who were born about 1820 were of marriageable age at the middle of the century; then the number of marriages decreased, causing problems for women. The problem was particularly acute for women in the middle levels of society (Qvist 1978, 96-97). The foundation of a diaconal institution, where such women could make a living and at the same time be of help to the many single mothers of the capital, seems therefore a logical solution to the problem.

6. 'Wiljen i så blifwa bedjande Herrens tjenarinnor, Edra medsystrars tjenarinnor och de eländas tjenarinnor?' *Olivebladet* (1895, 129). See also *Olivebladet*, (1887, 69); (1888, 73); (1889, 81); (1890, 81); (1891, 73); (1892, 97); (1894, 131); (1896, 141); (1897, 135); (1898, 133) and (1900, 140).
7. For example *Olivebladet* (1877, 3). *Stadgar för Diakonissorna vid Diakonissanstalten i Stockholm antagna 1867, med förändringar gjorda 1885 & 1890*, in Lönegren 1901, 100-103.

The acceptance of deaconesses had an economic and collective character, assuring the deaconess life-long social security.

Samariterhemmet in Uppsala was founded with no explicit aim to become a deaconess house. Its founder and first leader was Ebba Boström, a wealthy upper class woman. She gathered around her women who wanted 'to follow Jesus' and become 'Jesus-like' and set out on her mission of charity in 1882 (Koivunen Bylund 1994, 141). As at *Diakonissanstalten*, a hospital was built and nurses were trained and in due time they formed a sisterhood.

The first women were accepted into the newly founded sisterhood in 1893. At the ceremony they gathered in the private home of the principal, Ebba Boström, and were called one by one into her private room, where they received the deaconess's bonnet and brooch. Thereafter all joined in the Lord's Prayer and the blessing. The ceremony was held in private and was led by Boström (Palmgren and Svalander 1962, 115). No priest seems to have been present, or any other representatives of the official church. The word 'blessing' ('*invigning*') seems to have been used at *Samariterhemmet* at this point (Koivunen Bylund 1994, 148). One might ask if this first blessing was ever meant actually to ordain deaconesses. A few years later, when *Samariterhemmet* became more closely linked to the Church of Sweden and its leadership was taken over by a priest, the issue was addressed. Did the first deaconesses need to be re-ordained, or not? In the end they were not re-ordained. Tuulikki Koivunen Bylund concludes that it was never the primary aim of *Samariterhemmet*, in the early period, to ordain deaconesses, but rather to educate sisters who could work as deaconesses (Koivunen Bylund 1994, 180). The statutes of *Samariterhemmet* in 1900 stated that the assignment of the institution was primarily to minister to the needy and secondly to educate deaconesses (*Årsberättelse* 1900, statutes §1). Neither deaconesses nor deacons have been educated at *Samariterhemmet* since the mid 1990s, but it runs a centre for diaconal research in association with Uppsala University.

Earliest Recruits

Initially, the diaconal institutions appeared to adjust to upper class values, which those who directed them seemed eager to safeguard. For instance, no applicant receiving charity from society could be accepted at *Diakonissanstalten*. The aspiration to attract women of different classes did not initially succeed. The working classes as well as the upper classes are infrequently represented among the 53 deaconesses who were educated at *Diakonissanstalten* until 1862 (Elmund 1973, 115). A few years later, the periodical *Olivebladet* mentioned as a problem that relatively few well taught and educated women joined the diaconal institution.[8] A few years later, conditions seem to have changed slightly. More women from the lower middle stratum of society than from other classes were accepted at *Diakonissanstalten*, but women from other classes also began to come. In due time, the writer of the article hoped, diaconal work would be considered suitable for anyone.[9] The ordination, together with the mother house system, guaranteed the social status of the deaconesses and gave them a stable base. Women of the upper classes could, under the banner of philanthropy, undertake tasks previously regarded as unacceptable. That women from upper class families took part in caring for sick and poor people outside their own homes was radical, but it became more easily accepted 'in veils'. It appears that bourgeois women who wanted to work outside their homes and families had to accept a patriarchal system and take the role of a sister. The sisterhood seemingly offered a rather neutral position in terms of relations between men and women. Only by accepting this, could they go public. In the long run, their acceptance of the rules and expectations of a patriarchal society opened up the way for emancipation (Wendel 1999). In the case of nurses, this is evident. Becoming a nurse was becoming a professional, but initially it had to take place within certain boundaries, those of a mother house.

Later Deaconesses

A period of strategic planning followed the initial period in which Ersta and *Samariterhemmet* were founded. In the years around the turn of the century an institute for training deacons[10] had been started in Gävle, but shortly thereafter it moved to Stockholm. All three existing diaconal institutes were concentrated in the capital and its surroundings. The pietistic northern part of Sweden as well as the spiritually more severe western part were both without possibilities for the training of deaconesses and deacons. When Vårsta, the diaconal educational institute in Härnösand, a northern town in the 'forgotten' remote part of the country, was founded in 1912, the new institution built on the Kaiserswerth tradition and on that of one of the institutes in Stockholm: in its early years, Vårsta was a branch of Ersta (Jonsson et al 1987, 11-13). Installations took place in the cathedral of Härnösand diocese, with the bishop officiating (Lönegren 1937, 17).

The youngest of the five diaconal educational institutions is *Bräcke* in the

---

8. *'af den bildade klassen'; 'med mera kunskaper och bildning'* (*Olivebladet* 1870, 68).
9. Appendix to *Olivebladet* (1872, no. 3,2).
10. *Svenska Diakonanstalten* (the 'Swedish Deacons' Institute'), later *Stora Sköndal*

western city of Gothenburg, founded in 1923 at the initiative of the diocesan bishop. Bräcke was initially led by a deaconess trained at *Diakonissanstalten* and also built on the mother house system. In 1928 the first deaconesses were installed. Installations at Bräcke were generally held in the parish church where the institute is situated (Hellman 1948, 135). On some occasions, they were held in the cathedral. Bräcke was the first diaconal institute to abandon the mother house system. Nowadays both deaconesses and deacons are educated there.

Deacons

The first deacons were educated at *Svenska Diakonanstalten* and were blessed in 1902 (Kjell et al 2000, 37). Their training consisted of theoretical work as well as practical training and caring for the poor. Deacons were usually blessed in the chapel at the institution or in a church nearby. The earliest rite of 'blessing' ('*invigning*') of deacons dates from 1902, and states that the act should be held in a church. The vow that the first deacons made was to declare themselves willing, 'out of love to [your] God and Saviour and trusting his grace and help, to commit [yourselves] to the deacon's ministry within our Swedish Evangelical-Lutheran Church in obedience to her teachings and or-der'. Hereafter the Lord's Prayer was read for each individually during the laying-on of hands.[11] Deacons have never been expected to live in celibacy and have had only loosely knit ties to their school. Nor did they have anything similar to a mother house.

In 1989, the last ordination took place at *Stora Sköndal*: from then, all deacons trained there were ordained in the cathedrals of their respective dio-ceses (Kjell et al 2000, 80). Deacons have not been educated at *Stora Sköndal* since 1996. (Kjell et al 2000, 77). The institute has a function similar to that of *Samariterhemmet*, but in cooperation with Ersta.

Period of Reorientation

Since 1987, when a new Service Book was published, the word deacon may be used for both male deacons and female deaconesses. The word deaconess has practically fallen out of use. From that time, there has been one single ordi-nation rite, the same for men and women. However, ordinations of men and women together have taken place for longer than that. Once all institutes had

---

11. '[...] att af kärlek till eder Gud och Frälsare och i förlitande på hans nåd och hjälp egna eder åt diakontjänst inom vår svenska evangelisk-lutherska kyrka i lydnad för hennes lära och ordning?' *Diakonen* (1902, 125).

been opened to both sexes during the 1970s it seemed strange that those who had studied together should be separated and ordained in different ways on different occasions. As early as 1975, a proposal was put to the General Assembly of the Church of Sweden to construct a common ordination rite. A decision enabling each bishop to adjust the current ordination rite to each ordination was taken. Nevertheless, there were still differences as to how deacons and deaconesses, as they may still be called, were ordained. Most women still wore the traditional deaconess dress and some men wore liturgical robes, including the stole that was given to them during the ordination. The first ordination of female deacons took place at *Stora Sköndal* in 1978. At that ordination, at which four women and one man were ordained together as deacons, the women wore the deaconess dress and the man was liturgically dressed (Kjell et al 2000, 80). In 1978, all diaconal institutes had opened their education programmes to both sexes (Jonsson et al 1987, 70).

Among deacons and deaconesses there was an ongoing discussion about what dress to wear, especially in the 1980s, and the quest for a common symbol to be used by deacons and deaconesses had begun a few years earlier. A proposal was put forward to use the deaconesses' brooch, made in a slightly smaller variant for men (*Tidskrift f. information och debatt* 1977, 1:13). A year later the common symbol was ready. It was the former deaconess symbol with a dove on a cross surrounded by a circle (*Tidskrift f. information och debatt* 1978, 2:12). In the 1970s deacons and deaconesses had also formed a common association without ties to any specific diaconal institution. It is possible that this paved the way for a common liturgical dress and for the common green shirt that both deacons and deaconesses have used since 1994.

Official Liturgies

There have been several ways of expressing the diaconal responsibility of the church in its ordination liturgies. In the official Service Books of the Church of Sweden, on which the following is based, this responsibility was first laid on priests.

1894 and 1917. The Service Books accepted by the Church of Sweden in these years contained a diaconal vow made by priests at their ordination. Priests, through ordination, took on a responsibility for diaconal work. Beside the obligation to preach, teach and comfort, they also promised to care for the poor, sick and helpless.[12]

1921. Before 1920, there were no official liturgies for 'ordaining' deacons and deaconesses. In 1921 an official liturgy was included in the revised edition of the Church of Sweden Service Book (*Handbok* 1917, 261-279). In fact, there were two liturgies, one for each sex. They were placed after the other 'ordination' liturgies, which were, in order: installation of bishops, ordination of priests, and liturgies for installing vicars and missionaries.[13] The liturgy for 'installing' (*'inställa'*) deacons is similar to that of priestly ordination. A bishop, invited by the board of the diaconal institute, was to officiate and ordain – or a priest, whom the bishop asked to take his place. Other priests and members of the board of the diaconal institute and some older deacons were to assist the ordaining bishop or priest. The deacons made a vow of obedience to the teaching and order of the Church of Sweden.[14] According to the Service Book, the deacons to be ordained knelt, and the bishop and his assistants laid their hands on each one of them saying the Lord's Prayer for each specifically (*Handbok* 1917, 268). There is no mention of the content of the deacons' service, and the poor, the sick or those in any other need are not mentioned.

The part of the rite containing the vows varies, when compared with the installation of deaconesses. The deaconesses' installation liturgy did not mention loyalty towards the Church of Sweden. The tradition of making vows of service to the Lord, the needy and one another remained and the question posed by the bishop was 'Will you, by the help of God, be the Lord's and his congregation's servants, serving each other and the needy in the love of Christ?'[15] At the time, the mutual agreement between the sisters to serve each other was still made, though the system of mother houses for nurses was still in force but questioned by some. After a new pension scheme was launched in

---

12. '[...] bära kristlig omvårdnad om de fattiga, sjuka och värnlösa [...]' (Handbok 1894, 228). 'Viljen I ock vid utövandet av prästämbetet [...] bära kristlig omvårdnad om de fattiga, sjuka och värnlösa [...]' (Handbok 1917, 234-235)
13. 'Huru biskop skall inställas i sitt ämbete', 'Om invigning till prästämbetet', 'Huru kyrkoherde skall inställas i en församling' and 'Huru missionär inställes i sitt kall' (Handbok 1917, VIII)
14. 'Inför Gud och denna kristna församling frågar jag: Förklaren I eder villiga att i förlitande på eder Guds och Frälsares nåd och hjälp och av kärlek till honom vara diakoner inom vår kyrka i trohet mot hennes lära och ordning?' (Handbok 1917, 267)
15. 'Inför Gud och denna kristna församling frågar jag: Viljen I med Guds hjälp vara Herrens och hans församlings tjänarinnor, i Kristi kärlek tjänande varandra och de hjälpbehövande?' (Handbok 1917, 276)

1919, the mother houses no longer needed to guarantee the sisters' pensions in their old age. The Swedish diaconal institutions hesitated to decide to grant the sisters their whole salary (*Betänkande* 1948, 16-17). In the 1921 installation liturgy, the relation to the Church of Sweden or the Church at large is vague though at least for deaconesses the relation to the mother house seems stable. The mother house and its board seem to have had the function of a diocese. The actual 'ordination' was not related to a specific service or task (Eckerdal 1985, 434-435).

As for the deacons' ordination liturgy, a bishop invited by the board of the diaconal institute was to officiate at the liturgy for installing deaconesses – or a priest whom the bishop invited. There was no mention of deaconesses assisting the bishop. Only priests and members of the institute's board could assist. In the deacons' installation liturgy, other deacons were active in the liturgy as assistants. Deaconesses seem to have taken no liturgical part in installing new sisters. The sisters did, however, get to vote on who should be accepted into the sisterhood. The priestly diaconal vow remained in the Service Book.

1942 The Service book of 1942 stated that a bishop who was a member of the board of *Diakonanstalten* should officiate at ordinations of deacons. If no bishop was a member of that board, the bishop of the diocese or a priest whom he sent in his place could officiate at the ordination. Members of the board, priests and some older deacons were to be summoned as assistants. The deacon candidates made a vow, 'with the help of God, out of love to the Saviour and in loyalty towards the teachings and order of our Church', to 'accept the deacon's office in the congregation of Christ'. The candidates knelt and the Lord's Prayer followed during the laying-on of hands.[16]

The bishop of the board was likewise to officiate at the ordination of deaconesses; in his absence a priest was invited to deputise for him. The bishop of the diocese or a priest acting on his behalf could also officiate. Assistants might be invited, but need not be. Those summoned should be members of the board, priests or lay people, men or women. There was no mention of deaconesses being invited to assist.

The vow made by the deaconesses-to-be was, 'with the help of God, in loyalty towards the teachings and order of our Church', to 'be the servants of the Lord and his congregation, always prepared to follow Christ and stand by

---

16. 'Viljen I, med Guds hjälp, av kärlek till Frälsaren och i trohet mot vår kyrkas lära och ordning, åtaga eder diakontjänsten i Kristi församling?' (*Kyrkohandbok* 1942, 369)

anyone in need of your service'.[17] The laying-on of hands during the Lord's Prayer followed. At the ordination of deacons, assistants read several texts from the Bible, but when deaconesses were ordained there was only one Scripture reading, from 1 Cor. 13. It was read by the bishop or by one of those assisting him (*Kyrkohandbok* 1942, 368, 377-378). In this liturgy for the first time the mutual service between the sisters is not mentioned. The deaconesses are only obliged to serve the Lord and his congregation, not, as in previous rites, each other. In the Service Book the ordination liturgies for deacons and deaconesses followed after the rites for ordaining and installing bishops, priests, vicars and missionaries. The diaconal vow made by priests was retained.

1975. In time, there were social changes related to gender issues. Men and women were given the same opportunities to take part in higher education and to hold positions within the state. Overall, the level of education in Sweden rose during the twentieth century. That century faced previously unseen demands for equality, a fact that had consequences for the diaconate in the Church of Sweden. When men and women began to study together, they also wanted to be ordained together. A proposition to change the ordination rites was raised in the General Council in 1975 (*Allmänna* 1975, 21: 2 Oct., §18). In 1958, the Church of Sweden decided to allow women into the priesthood, and the first female priests were ordained in 1960, hence the diaconate was no longer the only ecclesial position open to women. Liturgical dress had until then been exclusively male, but in the 1970s, deaconesses' and deacons' liturgical dress was debated.

In 1979, a woman ordained at *Stora Sköndal* received the stole at her ordination as a sign of the diaconate. The giving of the stole was an ancient practice at the ordinations of deaconesses, it was said. Deacons and deaconesses acted through their association to strengthen their position. Though the actual liturgy of ordination was officially set at this time, they considered it open to certain modifications: 'The content and procedure of the ordination is basically stated in the regulations of the Service Book. But liturgy is living and changeable, giving room for some variations' (*Tidskrift f. information och debatt* 1979, 4:11). Yet years after that, the traditional deaconess dress seems most common at ordinations (*Tidskrift f. information och debatt* 1982, 1:15, 19-20). Though it cannot be conclusively proved, it is possible that the reform of the diaconate in the Roman Catholic Church following the Second Vatican

---

17. '[...] med Guds hjälp, i trohet mot vår kyrkas lära och ordning, vara Herrens och hans församlings tjänarinnor, alltid redobogna att efter Kristi sinne bistå var och en som behöver er tjänst?' (*Kyrkohandbok* 1942, 379)

Council in the 1960s influenced this development. The reform demonstrated that a permanent diaconate is possible and that deacons are part of the clergy and should wear liturgical dress and take on liturgical tasks. The priestly diaconal vow in the Service Book of the Church of Sweden was not altered at this point.

1987 In 1987, when a complete new Service Book was published, society had changed even more. A welfare state had developed and society had taken over many of the former diaconal tasks. Deacons and deaconesses were left with their ordinations and a mission to perform tasks that had partly been taken over by society and that were perhaps better handled by it. The obligation to care for the poor and needy was no longer solely a diaconal task. In addition, a new and rather lively ecumenical discussion had taken place resulting in *Baptism, Eucharist and Ministry* (BEM), the document agreed at the Faith and Order Commission meeting in Lima in 1982. The document was signed by churches that had decided to recognize each other's baptism, Eucharist and ministries. It recognized a threefold ministry including deacons and deaconesses.

The 1987 Service Book contains three ordination liturgies, for bishops, priests and deacons. A preamble to the liturgies states that all three are equal expressions of the one threefold ministry of the Church of Sweden, but that the word ministry is traditionally used in relation to bishops and priests (*Kyrkohandbok* 1987, 235). Nevertheless, there is a minor but important difference relating to the diaconate. Bishops and priests are called through ordination to live in their 'ministries' ('*ämbete*')[18] as servants of Christ. Deacons on the other hand are told to live as Christ's servants, without being mentioned as bearers of a ministry (*Kyrkohandbok* 1987, 242). The difference is significant. It shows that the matter of the deacons' role in the ordained ministry had not been clarified. The ordination liturgy is ambivalent when it comes to deacons. The call to live as the servants of Christ is in no way exclusive to deacons but applies to all Christians. It is, however, exclusive, when priests and bishops are told to live in their ministries as the servants of Christ. All three ordination liturgies follow the same pattern and most of the vows made by the candidates are the same for all three ministries. In 1987, the priestly diaconal vow was removed, and instead deacons give the diaconal vow, identical for all deacons: 'Will you stand firm in the faith of the church, help those in need of your service and

---

18. In Swedish '*ämbete*' (*Kyrkohandbok* 1987, 240-241).

stand by the side of the oppressed?'[19] A strictly individual affirmation is introduced after the giving of the vows: 'I, NN, with the help of God and trusting in God's grace, will live in accordance with these vows'.[20] In a new Church Order, in force from 2000, the issue of diaconal ministry was partly solved. Bishop, priest and deacon are referred to as equal expressions of the ordained ministry. The ordinance introduced the new term *'vigningstjänst'* ('ordained ministry'), to which all three are meant to belong.[21] This change has not had any effect on the Service Book. The small difference, related to the word 'ministry', between the deacon's ordination liturgy and the other two rites remains. *'Ämbete'* (*'Amt'*, perhaps better translated into English as 'order') is still not used when deacons are ordained.

Dress has been an issue of debate. The dress that deacons adopted became a means of changing opinion on the diaconate. After the introduction of the green shirt with white clerical collar, currently the official dress for deacons, deacons encouraged each other to wear it in order to get the diaconate recognised as part of the ordained ministry (*Diakoni och diakonat 1988*, 1:4-5). Men were often ordained wearing liturgical dress, thereby signalling a liturgical mission. For some time, in the 1980s and early 1990s there was great variety and confusion about the ordination of deacons. Ordinations took place in cathedrals as well as in the diaconal institutes, and in some places deaconesses wore their traditional black dress with a white bonnet, together with the deaconess's brooch. In other places at the same time, deaconesses were given the stole. There are articles and photos describing ordinations where the deaconesses are in their black dresses and the deacons wear the alb and the stole in a joint ordination service (*Tidskrift f. information och debatt* 1980, 2:11). It seems that no one knew what proper dress was. These conditions might seem of minor interest, but are in fact indicators of how the diaconal task has been understood. The 1987 rite states that the newly ordained deacons should receive a letter of ordination, but does not mention the stole or the brooch or necklace (*Kyrkohandbok* 1987, 248). Nevertheless giving the brooch or necklace and the stole to the ordinands has become customary (*Diakonvigning*, 2 September 2001 and 1 September 2002). Diaconal ordinations are regularly

---

19. 'Vill ni stå fasta i kyrkans tro, hjälpa dem som behöver er tjänst och stå på de förtrycktas sida?' (*Kyrkohandbok* 1987, 244).
20. 'Jag, NN, vill med Guds hjälp och i förtröstan på Guds nåd leva enligt dessa löften' (*Kyrkohandbok* 1987, 245).
21. See Olsen (Part II.3).

held in the cathedrals. The bishop of the respective diocese now officiates and ordains.

Conclusion

The ordinations of deacons and deaconesses provided 1) social legitimacy, 2) ecclesial legitimacy and 3) personal identity and sense of belonging. In other words a transition has taken place from a family-oriented ceremony, through stronger bonds to the official church, to a more individual statement and an ecclesial office. Accordingly, the early liturgies for accepting deaconesses into the mother house were 'adoption ceremonies' that were not of lifelong character. They aimed to equip the deaconesses with human authority, in the sense of making them socially accepted. Additionally, the early liturgies aimed to introduce the deaconesses to an office instituted by God. The latter is true also about the liturgies for ordaining deacons. In the nineteenth century advocates for deaconesses pointed to older traditions and heritage from the early Church, where, as they said, the deaconess's office was an accepted ministry (*Oliveblade* 1870, 9). Through serving as deaconesses, women of all social classes were able to have a socially legitimate occupation. Ordinations have two main constituents: vocation and sending. In the case of the deaconesses, these two were intertwined in the mother house. The sisterhood was the calling agent. Together the sisters decided who should be accepted as a new sister. Becoming a deaconess was also becoming an equal part of the deaconess family. The ordination rite expressed a collective spirit. Initially, there were no legal ties between the sisters and the Church of Sweden. The agreement was between the mother house and the sister. As time changed, sisterhood and mother house became burdens rather than keys to freedom. The mother house system was finally abandoned in 1967 (Bromander and Bäckström 1994, 14). Deaconesses never made vows to live in celibacy, but it was presupposed that if they married they would leave the mother house, and the mother house would no longer have economic obligations towards the sister. The diaconal institutions survived, however, and left deaconesses of the late twentieth century in an awkward position, serving the Church of Sweden but not being ordained or sent by it.

The early ordination rites focused on legitimising diaconal work in general and women's work outside their homes in particular. The liturgies stressed the ties to older traditions, as a means of legitimising *diakonia*, for instance by referring to the Apostolic Constitutions (Lönegren 1901, 103-106). The whole idea of *diakonia* was new to the nineteenth century Swedish Lutheran context.

Circumstances changed, and from the 1940s deaconesses and deacons were sent and ordained by the diaconal institutes, using an official Church of Sweden liturgy. Nevertheless, most deacons and deaconesses did not hold posts in the Church. It was not until in the 1980s that most of them did. At the same time, ecumenical discussions had taken place and influenced the Swedish debate on the ordained ministry. At present, the Church of Sweden ordains and employs deacons, male and female. Their ordination is life-long, personal and independent of whether the deacon holds a post as deacon or not. Ordination for women deacons does not involve celibacy. Equality between the sexes has enabled equal conditions for male and female deacons. The vows they make and the liturgical dress they wear during ordination are the same.

A transition to ordinations that have the intention of admitting deacons (male and female) into the fellowship of ordained ministers has taken place. The element of introducing the deacon to an office instituted by God is stressed, not only by deacons themselves, but also by the Church of Sweden in the contemporary Service Book. But, though it is emphasised, it is not as clearly emphasised as when bishops or priests are ordained.

Overall, the ordination of deacons has become a public act. It is no longer limited to the diaconal institutes, but takes place in the cathedrals with the bishop officiating and ordaining. The liturgy is included in the official Service Book, side by side with the liturgies for ordaining bishops and priests. The fact that the diocesan chapter of the respective diocese calls and examines each deacon stresses the public character of the diaconal task and ordination. The Swedish ordination of deacons is today an agreement between the deacon and the church – an individual act. The vows made in the ordination are between the individual and the church and do not concern the deaconesses as a collective. What used to be private has become public and what used to be collective has become individual.

References

Allmänna kyrkomötets protokoll. 1975.

Andersson, Åsa. 1997. Livsideal och yrkesetik: Om kalltankens betydelse i det kvinnliga vårdarbetets idéhistoria. In *Svensk Medicinhistorisk tidskrift*, 1: 53-71.

Askmark, Ragnar. 1949. *Ämbetet i den Svenska kyrkan.* Lund:Gleerups.

Baptism, Eucharist and Ministry (BEM). 1982. Faith and Order Paper No. 111. Geneva: World Council of Churches.

Betänkande angående utbildning av sjuksköterskor och annan sjukvårdspersonal. 1948. SOU 1948:17. Stockholm: Inrikesdepartementet.

Boman, Gunilla. 1995. *Av din gärning beror det...* Linköping: Hälsouniversitetet.

Bromander, Jonas and Bäckström, Anders. 1994. *För att tjäna.* Svenska Kyrkans Utredningar 1994:1. Uppsala: Diakonistiftelsen Samariterhemmet.

Den svenska kyrkohandboken. 1942. Published 1943. Stockholm: Svenska kyrkans diakonistyrelses bokförlag.

Den svenska kyrkohandboken. 1987 (I) and 1999 (II). Stockholm: Verbum.

Diakonen (periodical).

Diakonens ämbete. Betänkande av den av centralstyrelsen tillsatta utredningen om diakonatet. 1995. *Svenska Kyrkans Utredningar* 1995:1. Uppsala: Svenska kyrkans centralstyrelse.

Diakoni och diakonat (periodical).

Diakonvigning. Göteborgs Domkyrka 2 September 2001 (unpublished).

– 1 September 2002 (unpublished).

Eckerdal, Lars.1985. *Genom bön och handpåläggning. Vignings- jämte installationshandlingar - liturgiska utvecklingslinjer.* SOU 1985:48. Stockholm.

Elmund, Gunnel. 1973. *Den kvinnliga diakonin i Sverige 1849-1861.* Lund: Gleerups.

– 2001. Johan Christoffer Brings syn på det kvinnliga diakonatets uppgift och form. In

Kyrkohistorisk Årsskrift 2001, 25-29.

Hammar, Inger. 1999. Det förargliga sexualsystemet. In *Aktuellt om genusforskning* no 2, 6-8.

Handbok för Svenska kyrkan 1894. Revised edition 1904. Lund:C. W. K. Gleerups förlag.

Handbok för Svenska kyrkan 1917. Printed 1930-1931. Stockholm: Svenska kyrkans diakonistyrelses bokförlag.

Hellman, Axel. 1948. *Västsverige och diakonien.* Stockholm: Svenska kyrkans diakonistyrelses bokförlag.

I beredda gärningar. Vårsta diakonissanstalt 1912-1962. 1962. Stockholm.

Jonsson, Folke; Melin, Agneta, and Nilsson, Ester (eds). 1987. *Vårsta diakonigård 75 år 1912 -1987.* Härnösand: Diakonigården.

Kjell, Sixten; Ramström, Sture, and Säfström, Lotta (eds). 2000. *Stora Sköndal, diakonerna och Svenska kyrkan 1898-1999.* Stockholm: Stiftelsen Stora Sköndal.

Koivunen Bylund, Tuulikki. 1994. *Frukta icke, allenast tro. Ebba Boström och Samariterhemmet 1882-1902.* Stockholm: Almqvist & Wiksell.

Kyrkoordning för Svenska kyrkan. 1999. Stockholm: Verbum.

Lönegren, Ernst. 1901. *Minnesskrift till Svenska Diakonissanstaltens femtioårsjubileum.* Stockholm.

-. 1937. *Vårsta diakonissanstalt, Härnösand 1912-1937.* Härnösand.

Martinsen, Kari. 1984. *Freidige og uforsagte diakonisser.* Oslo: Aschehoug/ Tanum-Norli.

Palmgren, Bo and Svalander, Ulla. 1962. De svenska diakonianstalternas diakon- och diakonissvigningar. In *Kyrkohistorisk årsskrift 1962,* 110-137.

Olivebladet (periodical).

Qvist, Gunnar. 1978. *Konsten att blifva en god flicka.* Stockholm: Liber Förlag.

Sjuksköterskan genom tiderna. 1969. Helsinki: Söderström.

Tidskrift för information och debatt (periodical published by *Svenska Kyrkans Diakon och Diakonissförbund*).

Wendel, Lotta. 1999. Kön, religion och kvinnor i rörelse. In *Aktuellt om genusforskning,* no. 2, 18-19.

Årsberättelse för Samariterhemmet i Uppsala 1898-1899. 1900. Uppsala.

4. Rites of Ordination and Commitment: Intention and Effect

The question behind the articles in this section concerns the action of the rites (who is doing what to whom and in what way?), that is their intention and effect. One basic distinction seems to come out clearly: in ordination rites there are *expressive* elements, in which the officiant in the liturgy and the congregations (and to some extend the ordinands) make declarations, express their wishes, say prayers and give blessings, but at the same time there are also *instrumental* elements, in which, according to the rite, the ordinand receives a specific equipping for ministry, grace from God through the work of the Holy Spirit and/or a specific *'potestas'* in the life of the Church. By contrast, in rites of commitment, the central elements are the profession and vows, by which people commit themselves to life in the imitation of Christ.

Bjørn Øyvind Fjeld confines his first article to Lutheran rites, comparing rites for the ordination of pastors and installation of overseers in the Church of Norway with the rites of two free Lutheran Churches in the same country. He pays special attention to variations in terminology and their connection (not always direct) to variations in the theology of ordination and ministry as it appears in the rites. He finds (historically related) differences in terms of Trinitarian and ecclesiological foundation and not least in the balance between expressive and instrumental elements in the rites of the three churches he examines.

In his second article, *Bjørn Øyvind Fjeld* undertakes a comparative theological study of rites for the ordination of pastors and installation of overseers in seven Protestant, non-Lutheran churches in Norway. The general tendency seems to be, that the rites of 'low church' and congregationalist traditions are more independent in terminology and more inclined to favour expressive rites than those from a more 'high church' background such as the United Methodist Church in Norway, where there is a highly instrumental ordination rite.

On the other hand instrumental theology also appears in the rites for the ordination of pastors in a congregationalist church such as the Pentecostal Movement of Norway, where there is a strong invocation of the Holy Spirit to equip the ordinand. It might be generally concluded that ordination rites may only rarely be placed on a one-dimensional scale between an expressive and an instrumental theology of ordination.

Sven-Erik Brodd deals with the theology of ministry and ordination in the Swedish Mission Covenant Church as found in its old handbook from 1983. He asks whether the various rites of that church are to be interpreted as 'ordination', 'setting apart', 'installation' or 'acts of intercessory prayer'. The result seems to be that this handbook representing a transitional stage of the churches using it, does not allow a clear theological distinction between the various rites in the handbook.

Else-Britt Nilsen analyses 40 rites of perpetual commitment to religious life in the Nordic Countries. Surprising as it may be to 'low church' Protestant prejudice these rites do not place brothers and sisters of the religious orders in a special position above the priesthood of all believers. Firstly rites for perpetual commitment are used across denominational borders in the Nordic Churches. Secondly they are ecumenically open, emphasising the *sequela Christi* rather than a particular confessional adherence. Thirdly the core of these rites is the commitment of a person within the sacramental life of baptism. Rather than as a threat to the priesthood of all believers they may thus be seen as a challenge to the self-understanding of ordained ministers.

Rites for the Ordination of Pastors and the Installation of Overseers in three Lutheran Churches in Norway: A Comparative Theological Perspective

Bjørn Øyvind Fjeld

Objectives of the Research Task

The task is to present and compare the different terms used in three Lutheran Churches in Norway in connection with the ordination of pastors and installation of overseers. The aim is then to clarify the theological understanding behind the terminology and the liturgical celebration of ordination in the different churches. To some extent the intention is also to analyse and evaluate similarities and dissimilarities within the Lutheran church family.

There are four Lutheran Churches in Norway. The question is whether churches that belong to the same confession and work in the same cultural and linguistic setting, develop over the years different rites for ordination and installation, or whether they all retain the same terminology and liturgy. The main question is: 'What are the similarities and dissimilarities within the Lutheran churches with regard to the ordination of pastors and installation of overseers?'

The Three Lutheran Churches

The comparison undertaken here is limited to three Lutheran Churches in Norway: the Church of Norway (CoN), the Evangelical-Lutheran Church

Community (ELCC) and the Evangelical Lutheran Free Church (ELFC).[1] Appendix 1 (page 260 below) gives in Norwegian and English the official names of the ten churches dealt with in this and the following article and their acronyms.

The Church of Norway

The Church of Norway (CoN) is a state and folk church with a ministerial and synodical structure: it is an episcopal church with eleven dioceses, and the Reformation in Denmark-Norway (1536) forms its historical background. The state church was the only legal church in the country until the law on dissidents was introduced in 1845. Today 86% of the population belongs to the CoN (Sødal 2002, 99ff). With a common theological focus on baptism as the main route of entry into the church, the CoN encompasses a broad spectrum of movements and theologies from conservative revivalists to liberal folk religiosity. During 2001 a proposal for the alteration of terms and a new terminology for specific ministries was put forward (it is discussed later in the article). However, in this project, the present terminology, based on the current CoN handbook, is taken as the point of departure. The CoN consecrates ('vigsler') pastors, catechists, deacons, cantors, bishops and some other specialised ministries, such as youth leaders and missionaries (the terminology will be discussed later in the article). All who are consecrated by the bishop or his substitute will later be locally installed for their particular ministry.

The Evangelical-Lutheran Church Community

The smallest of the three Lutheran Churches, the Evangelical-Lutheran Church Community (ELCC) ordains pastors to the ministry of its larger church body, installs the (one) overseer and installs pastors and elders in the local congregations.[2] Only males are ordained as pastors and installed as elders. The ELCC is rooted in the orthodox-pietistic tradition, considers itself conservative and puts emphasis on avoiding liberalism in theology and secularism in church and society. Historically, the ELCC was established as a separate Lutheran church body in specific protest against secularisation in public schools (Sødal 2002, 135). A new law for public schools, which broadened the curriculum to more than Christianity, was put into effect in 1860. The edu-

---

1. There is also a fourth Lutheran Church in Norway, the Church of Fellowship (*Menigheten Samfundet*). This church is small and has not been included in the project.
2. The ELCC, established in 1872 with an episcopal and Presbyterian structure, has 16 local congregations and 3,791 members. Figures for church membership in this footnote and the following footnotes are taken from *Statistisk Sentralbyrå*, 2002.

cational issue is still important for this church today.[3] The conservative profile is visible in liturgy: for example, the Lord's Prayer is taken from the 1930 translation of the Bible, even though the most recent Bible translation is now authorised for liturgical use.[4] The liturgy takes its main structure from the older High Mass of the CoN (1920).

The Evangelical-Lutheran Free Church

The Evangelical-Lutheran Free Church (LFCN) is a growing church and among the larger churches outside the CoN.[5] The church presents itself as open in style, but conservative in theology. Currently the LFCN is discussing the gender question in relation to ordination. Only males are ordained as elders and pastors. The LFCN emphasises the confession of faith, the community of believers and a church leadership elected by confessing members only.[6] The church structure is Presbyterian as a result of the historical influence of the Scottish Presbyterian Church (Sødal 2002, 139). During recent decades the church has welcomed a moderate charismatic influence in leadership and church life. The act of ordination normally takes place in the local congregation and is followed by an act of installation in the same service. The current liturgy of ordination, introduced in 1988, is a rearrangement of the former liturgy of ordination, in part of the liturgy of ordination and part of the liturgy of installation.

Sources

The Primary sources for this study are 1) The Handbook of the Evangelical-Lutheran Church Community, sections on ordination and installation, 2) The Handbooks of the Evangelical-Lutheran Free Church with alterations, and 3) The Church of Norway's Service Book, part II, Liturgical Celebrations of the Church.

---

3. Today the ELCC runs seven private primary schools with a total of 600 students.
4. The Bible translation of 1978 introduced a new version of the Lord's Prayer, which has been in common use for decades in almost all churches.
5. The LFCN, established in 1878 with an episcopal and Presbyterian structure, has 80 local congregations and 21,289 members.
6. Historically, the rites of ordination included a question which required the ordinand to confess his belief that the governance of the church had been transferred from Jesus Christ to the church itself and not to any civil regiment. The negative reference to civil regiment is omitted in the 1988 rites of ordination.

Methodology

The main focus is on the *comparative aspects* of the different rites. The research task is confined to examining the rites for the ordination of pastors and the installation of overseers. The comparison of the different rites is done by creating two *comparative tables,* one for the ordination of pastors and one for the installation of overseers.[7] The method is to present particular rites, to study and compare the different texts, that is, carefully examine the wording and search for theological similarities and dissimilarities.

Furthermore, this method assesses the two dimensions of context and structure by taking into account additional written texts found in general instructions and explanations in the handbooks, which give information about the liturgical celebration of the acts of ordination, including the congregational setting, the symbols used, who carries out the ordination and who assists, and so on.

Before comparing and analysing the different rites, it is necessary to categorise the specific terms used in them.

Categorisation of Terms used for Ordination and Installation

Ordination and Installation

Ordination rites may be arranged as a matrix with two axes, one referring to the time aspect and the other to the different types of ministries. At one end of the time axis are holy acts which are celebrated only once, celebrations which will not be repeated because the validity of the act is for life. At the other end are ceremonies which might be repeated several times. The validity of these acts is limited to a certain ministry, place or time.

The terms 'ordination' and 'installation' correspond to two different entities. Most churches distinguish between these two events, though the liturgical celebration itself, the terms used and the prayers might be different. An act of ordination cannot be repeated, while an installation will take place several times during a person's lifelong ministry. Installation in this sense refers to inauguration for a certain ministry in a local congregation.[8]

---

7. The tables are foundational for the comparison in this and the following article. They may be downloaded free of charge from www.teol.ku.dk/ast/ansatte/Hans%20 Raun%20Iversen-ordination.htm
8. Later in this article the term 'installation' is used in another and major setting, i.e., for the ordination of an overseer.

The Different Ministries

The second axis, referring to different ministries, shows a wide variety among the churches. Different traditions, leadership structures and terminology leave us with a complex situation. The CoN alone makes use of the following titles for different ministries: 'pastor'[9] ('*prest*'), 'dean' ('*prost*'), 'cathedral dean' ('*domprost*'), 'catechist' ('*kateket*'), 'organist' ('*organist*'), 'cantor' ('*kantor*'), 'deacon' ('*diakon*'), 'youth leader ('*ungdomsleder*'), 'secretary' ('*sekretær*'), 'bishop' ('*biskop*') and several non-commissioned ministries, plus members elected to different church boards. The inauguration of these ministries is celebrated in the regular Sunday worship by means of separate rites.

The two other Lutheran Churches do not have all these ministries. However, in these churches there are rites for the following additional ministries: 'elder' ('*eldste*'), 'missionary' ('*misjonær*'), 'pastor' ('*pastor*'), 'evangelist' ('*evangelist*') and 'overseer' ('*tilsynsmann*'). Some of these terms overlap partly or entirely. However, it is possible to recognise some basic structures for specific ministries. The challenge is how to understand, distinguish and compare the many terms and ministries.

Different Terms in Use

Various Norwegian terms are used for the same ministry. The person who exercises the function of a minister of word and sacrament ('*ministerium ecclesiasticum*') is called 'pastor' or 'priest' ('*prest*'), 'pastor' or 'minister' ('*pastor*') and 'elder' ('*eldste*').[10] 'Pastor' has been chosen as the key term for the purposes of this article.

The person who exercises the function of an overseer is called 'bishop' ('*biskop*') and 'overseer' ('*tilsynsmann*'): these titles are found both at national synodical level and at the level of the district or regional presbytery.[11] 'Overseer' has been chosen as the key term for the purposes of this article.[12]

Different terms are used for the act of ordination. This once-in-a-lifetime

---

9. The church glossary (*Kirkelig ordliste*) translates the Norwegian term 'prest' as 'priest' (Orthodox, Roman Catholic, Anglican and Lutheran), 'pastor' (Lutheran) and 'minister' (Reformed). In this article the term 'pastor' has been chosen

10. Rogerson (2001, 211f), translates '*prest*' (in CoN) as 'priest'.

11. Rogerson (2001) translates '*biskop*' as 'bishop' or alternatively as 'superintendent'. The latter reflects '*tilsynsmann*'. (Rogerson 2001, 237)

12. The term 'bishop' would be the most appropriate term for the largest church, the CoN. However, as ten churches are examined in this and the subsequent article, 'overseer' has been chosen as the common term.

event is called 'ordination' ('*ordinasjon*'), 'dedication'[13] ('*innvielse*'), 'consecration' ('*vigsling*') and 'blessing' ('*signing*'). 'Ordination' has been chosen as the key term for the purposes of this article.

The term 'installation' denotes either a repeatable local act of dedication, or an act of 'ordaining' overseers. Only the latter meaning is examined in this project. Presently the CoN uses the term 'consecration' ('*vigsling*'). The term 'blessing' ('*signing*') has been suggested for future use.[14] The two other churches use the term 'installation'. This latter term, 'installation', has been chosen as the key term for the purposes of this article.

To sum up: the terms 'ordination of pastors' and 'installation of overseers' are used in the following discussion. A table of important terms in translation and the use of key terms is found at Appendix 2 (page 261 below).

A matrix has been set up to compare, organise and categorise the different ministries and terms in use in the Norwegian churches examined.[15] The table at Appendix 3 gives the necessary overview.

Terminological Discussions in the Church of Norway

In relation to the table at Appendix 3 one particular comment related to the CoN is required: today the CoN 'consecrates' pastors, catechists, deacons, cantors and bishops.[16] The term 'ordination' is absent in its rites of consecration. The only reference to the concept of ordination is in the terms 'ordinand' and 'ordination address', which are found in the margins, not in the main text of the rites themselves. Furthermore, the same term 'consecration' ('*vigsling*') is used for the act of inauguration of five different ministries. However, the theological content of the acts is not identical. This has caused a lengthy discussion on the theology of ordination in the CoN.[17] The issue is under ongoing debate and is in process of change. A new proposal was put forward in 2001. The issue revolved and still revolves around the question of which ministries or offices are part of the one ministry of word and sacraments.

---

13. The term '*innvielse*' may be translated 'consecration'. However, the term 'dedication' has deliberately been chosen to distinguish '*innvielse*' from the term '*vigsling*', which is translated 'consecration'. The term 'dedication' ('*innvielse*') is not used as an equivalent for ordination within the three Lutheran Churches examined.
14. A broader discussion follows below.
15. This includes all the ten churches examined in this and the following article.
16. Rogerson (2001, 214) translates '*vigsling*' as 'commissioning', both for priests, catechists, deacons, cantors and bishops, 'as there is no agreed equivalent in English'.
17. Rogerson (2001, 214-16) has an excellent presentation of the ambiguity and issues related to the discussion in the CoN in regard to which officeholders participate in the '*ministerium ecclesiasticum*'.

The fact that the catechist is a separate ministry in the CoN represents an ecumenical challenge. The catechetical ministry might be redefined in the future. According to the proposal, pastors are to be 'ordained' (*'ordinert'*), while future catechists, deacons and cantors are to be 'consecrated' (*'vigslet'*) and bishops to be 'blessed' (*'signet'*). The reason is mainly theological, but also practical. (*Kirkerådet* 2001, 9-12).[18] This proposal means that the one 'ministry of word and sacraments' will be confined to pastors alone, including specialised ministries, for example, catechetical pastors, while ordinary catechists, deacons and cantors, important as their ministries are, will not be included in the *'ministerium ecclesiasticum'*. The debate about ministry and ordination has not yet reached a final conclusion.

The terminological discussion reflects different theologies and ways of understanding ordination. The theological content of the concept of ordination, at least in regard to the different ministries, is not settled in the CoN. The proposed differentiation of the terms may to some extent clarify the theology of ordination in the CoN.

As far as the consecration (*'vigsling'*) of bishops in the CoN is concerned, the term 'ordination' is avoided. The term 'blessing' (*'signing'*) has been proposed for future use. The ministry of a bishop is an extension of the ministry already received as a pastor. Even though episcopacy in many respects carries a broader ministerial responsibility, the ministry itself does not represent any additional divine or ecclesiastical responsibility.[19]

Not all Lutheran Churches support the concept of the threefold ministry of bishop, priest and deacon.[20] The CoN emphasises the unity of the ordained ministry by letting the pastor's ministry be constitutive (CA 5 and 14). The ministry of a bishop is basically the same ministry as the ministry of a pastor, that is, *'ministerium verbi'* (Grane 1970, 133). In 1994 the CoN signed the Porvoo Declaration, *Together in Mission and Ministry*. This British Anglican and Nordic and Baltic Lutheran declaration challenges the understanding of ordained ministry in the CoN. According to the working group behind the proposal, the Porvoo Declaration leaves the issue open (*Kirkerådet* 2001, 78-

---

18. See the extensive discussion and broad presentation of the different views in *EMBE-TET i Den norske kirke, en rapport fra en arbeidsgruppe nedsatt av Kirkerådet*, 28th February, 2001(*Kirkerådet* 2001).
19. Rogerson (2001, 214) adds that the preposition used in consecration *of* (*av*) a bishop, instead of consecration *to* (*til*) pastor, catechist etc, 'reflects that the ministry of a bishop is perceived in personal terms', more than the functional view of ministry.
20. The Lutheran Churches of Sweden and Iceland clearly support the threefold ministry.

79). However, this understanding has been disputed. Tjørhom argues that the Porvoo Declaration confirms the threefold ministry and challenges the CoN to reconsider her position (Tjørhom 2001, 387-9).[21] Later, under installation of overseers, we will discuss the consecration of bishops.

Comparison of Rites for the Ordination of Pastors
Context and Structure
In the context of the ordination of pastors, there are some differences: The CoN ordains both women and men. The two other churches ordain men only. In the LFCN a debate about the ordination of women is currently going on, and the officiating ministers at ordinations are male overseers. However, in the CoN female and male bishops ordain pastors. Signed ecumenical agreements such as the Porvoo Agreement (1994) and the *Fellowship of Grace* (1995), which involve the exchange of ministerial service, challenge the CoN in relation to churches which do not accept female bishops, that is, 'other Porvoo churches' (*Kirkerådet* 2001, 73).[22] A similar ecumenical problem arises because of the practice in the CoN of allowing a cathedral dean, as a bishop's substitute, to ordain pastors. Some churches do not regard these pastors as properly ordained (*Kirkerådet* 2001, 81).

The vesting of ordinands is found only in the CoN, where a stole is laid on the shoulders of the new pastor as a visible sign of his/her new authority. This is an integral part of conferral of ministry.

The LFCN and the ELCC have no 'absolute' ordination, that is, ordination in which candidates are ordained to a form of ministry in the wider Church, rather than to a specific ministry in a local congregation (Puglisi 1996, 174f).[23] Neither does the CoN have absolute ordination, unless ordination to specialised tasks such as a ministry in the army, hospitals or prisons, is regarded as absolute ordination. All three churches realise that ordained pastors eventually withdraw from their ministerial duties in the church. In all three churches such a pastor keeps his or her authorisation and may return to the ministry without a new act of ordination (BEM 1983, 51 § 48). Due to ordination, pastors in

---

21. See also a follow-up discussion in *Luthersk Kirketidende* 2001, no. 15, 17 and 19.
22. *Fellowship of Grace* is an agreement on ministerial fellowship between the CoN and the United Methodist Church of Norway (UMCN), signed in 1995. The Norwegian agreement was a follow-up to the international Lutheran-Methodist report, *The Church: Community of Grace* (Geneva 1984).
23. Puglisi emphasises the necessary relationship between ordination and the communal aspect of the body of Christ and the Eucharist.

the CoN will also keep their juridical power of attorney, which allows them to conduct the legal part of wedding ceremonies, even if they have left ministry and may be pursuing a secular profession for the rest of their lives. Pastors in the LFCN and the ELCC lose their juridical power of attorney as soon as they withdraw from their ministerial responsibilities. According to Norwegian law, this applies to all pastors outside the CoN, unless they resume ministry in a particular church.

In the ELCC a candidate for the pastorate will normally start his ministry as an elder. The process of election includes a major test in conversation with the overseer and a recommendation from him: it closes with a final approval given by the National Church Board. The act of ordination starts with a public announcement that the prescribed time for testing the candidate, normally one year, is over. In the ELCC, like the LFCN, theological training is preferred, but not decisive. In the latter church, the confidence of the local leadership is decisive. The request and call from the local congregation, where the faithful members affirm the call by a majority vote, is followed by a final approval by the board of elders. The CoN requires theological training, to the level of *candidatus theologiae* (normally six years of Higher Education) before a candidate is approved for ordination. However, candidates with a different, but proper training and practical church-related experience may be accepted.[24] The final requirement for all candidates is a recommendation from the bishop after several mandatory talks with him or her.

Minor differences are found in the context and structure of ordination: both in the CoN and the ELCC the election of ordinands is announced to the congregations ahead of the act of ordination. In the CoN the announcement, followed by prayer for the candidates, takes place at the latest on the Sunday before the ordination. In the LFCN no rules are found in the rites. However, the election takes place in the local congregation weeks ahead of the ordination, in a similar way to election in the ELCC.

Two of the three churches use liturgical dress for the ordination. In the LFCN clerical dress is not the custom: though collars are common, their use is optional.

Assistants at the act of ordination are normally pastors and belong to the college of ministers in the three churches. In the ELCC two pastors assist. In the LFCN board members of the presbytery assist. All are ordained. However, in the CoN, both pastors and lay leaders assist the bishop in ordination. The

---

24. See Resolution of 19th March, 1999, Royal Department of Church, Education and Research.

lay leaders are not ordained. They take part in prayer and in the imposition of hands on the ordinands.

The context and structures of rites of ordination show some similarities: 1. Ordination in all three churches is administered by the bishop or the overseer.[25] 2. All three churches have their service of ordination on a Sunday, or, in the CoN, 'preferably' on a Sunday. The act of ordination will normally take place in the local congregation in which the ordinand will minister. If several people are ordained on the same Sunday, this may take place in the cathedral of the diocese in the CoN, or in a service during the annual meeting of the presbytery or the synod in the LFCN. 3. All three churches leave open whether or not the Eucharist is celebrated in a service of ordination. It is 'preferable' (LFCN), 'if the Eucharist is to be celebrated' (CoN) and it is often left out 'for a pragmatic reason' (ELCC).[26] This means that none of the Lutheran churches necessarily link the Eucharist and ordination.[27]

The Liturgical Text

Ordination rites in the CoN are comprehensive and detailed. Explanations are numerous and the clarity is evident. Also the ELCC has a comprehensive and detailed ordination rite that is almost similar to the CoN rite. However, explanations are scarce and some questions arise for outsiders. The rite of ordination in the LFCN has its own structure. One is the already mentioned differentiation between the act of ordination and the act of installation. In general, the structure in the LFCN shows similarity to the structure of ordination in the present rites of the Church of Scotland, for example in the installation which follows immediately after the ordination in the same service and the emphasis on *rite vocatus* during the installation, not in the ordination (Puglisi 2001,110-113). The close connection between ordination and installation is also found in the Lutheran Church of the Missouri Synod (Puglisi 2001, 91).

The Trinitarian Perspective

The Trinitarian perspective is found in all three rites. The Holy Trinity is mentioned as part of the conferral of the ministry (LFC N), and the handshake

---

25. In the CoN a cathedral dean may act as a substitute for the bishop
26. Quotations from the explanatory text to the rite of the LFCN; the explanatory text to the rite of the CoN, and a written note to the author from Ulf Asp, the overseer in ELCC, 27th February, 2002
27. This is significantly different from the ordination liturgies of the Roman Catholic Church and the Orthodox Churches.

of fellowship (ELCC). The Trinitarian perspective is expressed in all three churches during prayer and imposition of hands. We find references to the Trinitarian formula in the CoN in the general liturgical sections of the service, such as the opening greeting, the *Kyrie*, the collect and Creed. Also the opening prayer of ordination expresses this perspective in identical formulae in the ELCC and the CoN. In the LFCN the continuing ministry of Christ through his servants is expressed in the installation prayer and the corresponding lay-ing-on of hands.

The pastor's ministry is dependent on the Holy Spirit. The CoN expresses the pneumatological perspective in an opening prayer of ordination, which asks the Lord, through his Holy Spirit, to 'enlighten and guide, comfort and strengthen [your] servant, who today is consecrated to the ministry of a pastor in the church'.[28] This sentence is missing in the otherwise identical opening prayer in the ordination rite of the ELCC. The LFCN has no opening prayer. The CoN has a separate invocation of the Holy Spirit, where the ordaining minister (normally a bishop) sings and prays either 'Come, Holy Spirit' or 'Send out your Holy Spirit'. The ELCC has a hymn of prayer to the Holy Spirit immediately before the ordination, and the LFCN suggests a prayer which focuses on the ministerial gifts of the Spirit.

The christological and pneumatological perspective may be traced in all three rites. The epicletic prayer, however, is not prominent in the LFCN and the ELCC. It is most strongly expressed in the CoN.[29] The congregation participates in the liturgy by singing and listening, not by praying. In all three churches the ordination seems to be an integral part of the ministry of Jesus Christ and his sending out of apostles and disciples through the power of the Holy Spirit.

The Ecclesiological Perspective
The priesthood of all believers is connected to ordination. In the opening prayer of ordination the CoN makes particular reference to baptism and the priesthood of all believers: 'In baptism we were incorporated into the people of God, and we were all consecrated ('*vigslet*') as servants of God. The Scrip-ture states that the whole people of God is a royal priesthood, a holy people ...'. A reference then follows to the pastor's ministry instituted by God for the

---

28. This quotation and all subsequent quotations from the Norwegian rites are translated by the author. All quotations from the Bible are from NIV.
29. Rogerson (2001, 218) states that the ordination rites in CoN 'are uncharacteristic, for the emphasis on the invocation of the Holy Spirit is considerable'.

purpose of faith and salvation. God has given his church 'the task to challenge people to enter into this ministry'.

The ELCC makes no particular reference to the relationship between baptism and ordination. In the LFCN the ecclesiological perspective is expressed in the questions to the ordinand, where the ministry of Word and sacraments is mentioned twice and reference is made to the sacraments as well as to the Lutheran confessional documents. The emphasis is on the building up of the Church and the willingness of the ordinand to serve the Church. One of the questions runs: '. . . Will you, as far as God gives grace, work for the purity, the building up, peace and extension of the Church of Jesus Christ and preach the Word of God in purity and administer the holy sacraments in accordance with the Lord's consecration?' Except for this examination, the ecclesiological perspective is absent in the ordination rites. However, ecclesiological perspectives are found in the rite for the installation of pastors. During the imposition of hands, the Lord is praised for the 'baptism with one Spirit'. The questions and vows as well as the imposition of hands include references to the body of Christ and the extension of his Kingdom. And the final installation reminder runs: 'So I present you (name) as properly called and installed to the ministry of pastor for this church'. Here the *rite vocatus* is expressed.

The two other churches also underline the proper call. In the CoN this is stated in the conferral of the ministry and visibly confirmed by the giving of the stole. In the ELCC it is expressed at the handshake of fellowship: 'So I hand over to you the holy ministry of a pastor'. The questions and responses make it clear that the ordination refers to a ministry in a particular Lutheran church: '. . . will you accept the task of shepherd of souls in our church? . . .'

The ordination of pastors is related to the local congregation as well as to the larger church body. The preaching of the word and administration of the sacraments points to both groups. The ministry relates mainly to the local congregation. The opening prayer in the ELCC and the CoN contains phrases such as: 'so that they may carry out their ministry and your body be built up . . . . to the extension of your Kingdom'. The reference to the Kingdom points to the universal Church.

The ecclesiological perspective is also emphasised in the identification of certain duties to be fulfilled by the church that receives the ministers. All churches emphasise the responsibility of the church community to receive the new worker in love, to support them in prayer and co-operation. This is expressed in general terms in the CoN, ending with the words: 'Let us. . . stand together with him/her in the ministry of reconciliation'. In the LFCN the duties are found in the rites of installation and are more specific: 'Will you receive him with gratitude, share all good things with the one who now shall teach you in the word; will you encourage him, show him reverence and obey him?' The members of the congregation respond in the affirmative by raising their right hands.

The ELCC puts even more emphasis on the responsibility of the believing community: four questions require an affirmative 'Yes' from the congregation. References are made to Heb. 13.17 and Gal. 6.6. The last question runs: 'Will you pledge yourself to give him the necessary support as long as he is in ministry, according to the Word of God?' This emphasis is also related to the financial responsibility of a minority church, where expenditures and running costs, including the salary of the pastor, are to be covered by members' gifts.

The confession, exhortation and vows express the ecclesiological perspectives in all three churches. Above we have referred to the questions raised in LFCN. After three vows the exhortation follows. The same truth is expressed in the CoN and the ELCC as part of the exhortation. In a separate question the latter church emphasises even more strongly the word of the Old and New Testaments and personal responsibility: 'Do you accept the Word of God as it is given us in the Holy Scripture and as our church testifies in its confession, as mandatory for your ministry?' In the CoN the administrator exhorts, 'You have heard the Word of God about the ministry . . . how necessary it is for the Church of God on earth'. The ordination of a pastor is partly grounded in the priesthood of all believers and partly in a particular divine institution (Skjevesland 2001, 429).

The LFCN lacks the 'missio' perspective, both in the act of ordination and the act of installation. The two other churches close the service of ordination by the sending formula: 'Go in peace and serve the Lord with gladness' (partly a quotation from Psalm 100 v. 2). The CoN adds: 'You did not choose me, but I chose you and appointed you to go and bear fruit, fruit that will last' (John 15.16). Ordination to the ministry of Word and sacraments is rooted in the local congregation and the Word of God.[30] At the same time ordination is a sending to the world. The ecclesiological perspective seems most emphasised in the ELCC.

The Instrumental and/or Expressive Perspectives

The instrumental perspective emphasises the objective, lifelong, sacramental and conferred character of the ordination. Does the rite itself have any creative effect on the receiver or does the ordinand receive any gift, power or character

---

30. Skjevesland (2001, 430) confirms the Lutheran position that the ministry of Word and sacraments is primarily expressed in the local congregation.

during ordination? The expressive perspectives emphasise more the subjective, visible and relational side of ordination. Is ordination mainly a proclamation of what has been effected during the process of election, now publicly confirmed by prayer and blessing?

The centre of the ordination is found in the readings, the exhortation and vows, the conferral of the ministry and the imposition of hands.

The readings remind hearers and ordinands of major, ministerial truths. In the ELCC six readings precede the commitments. These are read by two assisting pastors and describe the ministry as a missiological and catechetical task (Matt. 28.18-20); a task of reconciliation on behalf of Christ (2 Cor. 5.17-21); elders as a Christian example (Titus 1.6-9); the shepherding of the flock (1 Pet. 5.1-5); fanning the flame of the God-given gifts (2 Tim. 1.6-12), and a guarding of the flock (Acts 20.28). The emphasis is task-orientated.

The LFCN has no fixed introduction to the reading. Twelve readings are suggested for the ordination of pastors and elders. Only some of these are read for the ordination: others are read at the act of installation. Compared with the passages above, we find three additional passages referring to the gifts of the Holy Spirit, 1 Cor. 12.1-11, 28-30 and Eph. 4.11-16. These passages correspond to the prayer at the imposition of hands. The emphasis is on equipping for ministry and points to an expressive dimension.

In the CoN the readings reflect the missiological and catechetical responsibility (Matt. 28.18-20), the empowering of the Holy Spirit for the forgiveness of sins (John 20.19-23), the ministry of reconciliation (2 Cor. 5.17-20) and the shepherding of the flock (1 Pet. 5:1-5). The emphasis is on the ministerial task and the Holy Spirit.

After a brief address, the ordaining minister, in the ELCC, asks three questions. After the affirmative answers, admonitions concerning the pastoral dimensions of preaching, living and serving are added. The content is almost similar to the three exhortations in the CoN. One detail might be mentioned: the ordinand is exhorted, 'that [you] in love seek to win other people for the Kingdom of God. . . and care for the sick and helpless, comfort those who mourn and instruct those who have gone astray'. This is a rather personal and specific challenge, for example, to gather people into the Kingdom and care for the sick. The emphasis is task-orientated.

Also in the LFCN the ordaining minister asks three questions. One of these runs: 'Do you love our Lord, Jesus Christ? Do you love the community of believers? As far as God gives his grace, will you work for the purity, building up, peace and growth of the Church of Jesus Christ and preach the Word of God in purity and administer the holy sacraments in accordance with the instructions of the Lord?' Reference is made to the purity of the Church. The ecclesiology of the LFCN was originally a protest against the ecclesiology of the broader state and folk church. The 'purity of the church' is not to be interpreted as ecclesiastical purity or Christian sinless-ness. It is an expression of the ultimate objective of the Church of Jesus Christ, not only eschato-logically, but also here and now. The personal character of the above questions and the emphasis on the purity of the Church points to expressive dimensions of ordination. The emphasis is on the ordinand, his gifts and participation in the Christian fellowship.

The CoN does not ask any questions of the ordinands, either about the Holy Scripture or any personal exhortation, except a final, comprehensive question: '(name), standing before the face of the Lord and in the presence of this church, do you promise to serve with fidelity, by the grace God gives you?' (Yes). The exhortation makes a general reference to the Bible readings and an affirmation that the Lord is entrusting the candidate(s) with the pastorate in his church: 'When the Lord entrusts you with the pastor's ministry in our church, I instruct and admonish you. . .' The ordinand is admonished to show compassion to every single person and to hold them before God by prayer and petition, with thanksgiving. The CoN alone has an explicit reference to the use of hearing confession as part of the pastor's duties.[31] Unlike the ELCC, spe-cific exhortations are fewer in the CoN. Admonitions are more general and the emphasis is on the spiritual authority and the instrumental perspectives.

The ELCC has a clear terminology about conferring a ministry, explicitly mentioning the term '*ministerium*'. The promise is confirmed by the hand-shake of fellowship. The CoN does not use the term 'confer', even though the expression 'we now leave you to God' points to the same reality. The hand-shake of fellowship is a visible confirmation in the CoN. The LFCN refers orally to a conferral of the ministry, but does not refer to any ministerial office. Neither do we find the handshake of fellowship as a visible sign in the LFCN.

There are multiple similarities. All the ordinands kneel. The ordaining minister and the assistants put their hands on the head of the ordinand(s). The ordaining minister prays for the candidate(s) and the imposition of hands is closed with the Lord's Prayer.

Nevertheless some differences are evident: in the LFCN the assistants are challenged to lead in spontaneous prayer; the ordaining minister is recom-mended to follow a written prayer. He and his assistants close the prayer with the Lord's Prayer, followed by the benediction. The ELCC makes use of the older version of the Lord's Prayer. When several candidates are ordained, the

---

31. Confession is not regarded in CoN as a sacrament like Baptism or the Eucharist.

presiding bishop in the CoN is particularly instructed to put his or her hand on all the heads of the ordinands. The Lord's Prayer follows and is said with the congregation. Lastly, the bishop and his assistants kneel down, while the congregation sings a hymn to the Holy Spirit.

The content of the prayers is almost the same in the ELCC and the CoN.[32] A reference to Matt. 9.37-38, about the plentiful harvest and few labourers, is followed by a prayer for the ordinand: 'Hear our prayer for the one we today "install" ("*insette*"/ELCC), "consecrate" ("*vigsle*"/CoN)'. The CoN has a reference to 1 Pet. 4.10, 'to be a good steward of the manifold grace of God', while the ELCC has a special prayer for the ordinand's family. Both prayers close with allusions to John 9.4; Eph. 1.18 and the eschatological perspective.

The LFCN has a shorter prayer. God is praised for the act of redemption through his Son, Jesus Christ, for the presence of the Son as the head of his Church, for his outpouring of the gifts of the Holy Spirit, and for his building up of the body of Christ today. Then follows a prayer for the ordinand: 'Equip (name) with the gifts of your Holy Spirit. Bless him in his ministry so that your people may grow and be strengthened in the ministry. . . .'

The LFCN focuses on the divine work in the Church of Christ in general. The two other churches are more focused on the ministry of the labourers, from the day of Jesus onwards. The LFCN focuses on the spiritual equipping of the candidates for ministry, the renewal of the church and the glory of God. The two other churches focus on serving with faithfulness, 'so that your power may be made perfect in his weakness'. The expressive perspective is most evident in the LFCN, while the instrumental perspective is closer in the two other churches (cf. the eschatological perspective). The emphasis in the CoN is that the power of God is working anyway, through the ordained pastor.[33] This is visibly expressed in the CoN by the kneeling of the bishop and his assistants. They are all a part of the same ministry of Word and sacraments.

---

32. The linguistic differences are due to the use of different translations of the Bible.
33. Rogerson (2001, 221) interprets the use of the Norwegian preposition '*under*' as meaning 'during', before the laying- on of hands: 'It is intended to reduce the instrumentality of the action, conveying a combination of instrumentality, sign and symbol'.

Comparison of Rites for the Installation of Overseers

The Context and Structure of the Installation of Overseers

The terminology reflects some differences. For the purposes of this article the terms 'installation' and 'overseer' have been chosen as the key terms,[34] though when referring to *installation* and *overseers* in the CoN the proper terms, 'consecration' and 'bishop' are used.[35]

Puglisi finds it curious that the same term is used for the ordination of pastors and consecration of bishops in the Lutheran churches in Norway and Sweden (Puglisi 2001, 52). According to the Lutheran understanding of the pastor's ministry as constitutive, the rite for the consecration of bishops in CoN does not add any theological content to the rite for the ordination of pastors. Neither is the consecration of a bishop a repetition of the ordination.[36] I agree that the use of identical terms sounds curious when the content of the rites is not identical.[37] The two other Lutheran Churches in Norway differentiate the terms for 'ordination' and 'installation'.

In 1975 Per Lønning, diocesan Bishop of Borg, resigned from his episcopacy as a protest against a new abortion law. In 1987 he was again appointed bishop, this time of the diocese of Bjørgvin. His re-instatement as bishop was not a second consecration. His understanding was that his consecration as bishop should not be repeated. His second inauguration was consequently confined to a handing over of the ministerial cross by the former bishop of Bjørgvin, followed by a brief prayer.[38]

The gender issue for the installation of overseers reflects the same differences as for the ordination of pastors. The consecration of women bishops in the CoN has created an ecumenical challenge. The exchange of ministerial services, in accordance with ecumenical agreements like Porvoo, may be hindered in churches which do not accept women bishops. This applies to women bishops and pastors ordained by them (*Kirkerådet* 2001, 81).

The election of overseers is rather different in the three churches. The

---

34. 'Installation' includes the term 'consecration' ('*vigsling*') of a bishop in the CoN. 'Overseer' is used as a common term for bishops and overseers.
35. The term 'overseer' is also used in CoN. Cf. during the word of introduction: 'Today a new overseer ('*tilsynsmann*') is presented in our church'.
36. This is the main reason for the proposal mentioned above to differentiate the terms (*Kirkerådet* 2001).
37. The argument above can also be turned around, i.e. a consecration of a bishop means a real ordination
38. Private conversation with Per Lønning, 30.01.02

ELCC members elect their overseer for a five-year term at their annual meeting by simple majority vote. Candidates must be ordained pastors. Re-election may take place once.

The LFCN elects regional overseers and their substitutes at presbytery meetings, and the national overseer and his substitute at the meeting of the synod. Both meetings only consist of pastors and male elders from local congregations. During the 1999 Synod, however, women delegates representing their local congregations were accepted as full members of the synod. Still candidates for election as overseers are limited to ordained pastors or elders. However, in the future a majority vote in the Synod may decide to accept women elders and pastors and, by so doing, also women candidates for leadership positions. It is of major importance in LFCN that elders, pastors and overseers are elected by the church itself, that is, by believers who confess the Christian faith.

The CoN has a longer election procedure. The structure is partly democratic, with all members of the church eligible to be elected at quadrennial elections to the many different boards at all levels from the local to the national. For the episcopate, the diocesan board nominates five candidates. Several church bodies and church leaders give their ranking of the candidates, sometimes by adding more candidates and always by choosing their three preferred candidates. The bodies and leaders involved are: all the deans of the diocese, the professors of the three Lutheran Faculties of Theology and deans of the corresponding Theological Seminaries, the bishops and the national board of the CoN. All nominations and rankings are forwarded to the King, that is, the Government, who finally appoint the new bishop.[39] According to the National Constitution the King's final decision requires that at least half of the Government Ministers should be members of the CoN. A bishop may be appointed even though he/she has not previously been consecrated as a pastor. However, in such a case the consecration as bishop also includes a consecration as pastor.[40] During the introductory prayer, the presiding bishop says to the one who is to be consecrated: 'As the Lord entrusts you with the continuing ministry of Word and sacraments. . . .' The word 'continuing' is omitted in cases where the new bishop has not been previously consecrated as a pastor. The age limit for appointment as a bishop is 70.

---

39. The procedures for nominating and appointing bishops in the CoN are currently under discussion
40. This was the case with the present Bishop of Stavanger, who was formerly a professor of theology.

Only in the CoN, after the imposition of hands and the affirmation of his new responsibility, is the ceremonial cross put on the new bishop.

In the ELCC and the CoN the sermon follows after the installation. In the LFCN the sermon takes place before the installation. No instruction is given about who is to preach the sermon in ELCC and LFCN. When the new bishop in CoN has received the ministerial cross, he or she moves to the altar and professes the Nicene Creed. The new bishop also preaches the Word of God from the text of the day. The bishop enters his/her new responsibility immediately after the rite of installation is completed by presiding over the rest of the service.

The consecration of bishops in the CoN is administered by the presiding bishop or his/her substitute. In the ELCC the former overseer officiates at the installation of the new leader. This is also the normal order in the LFCN. However, the leader of the meeting of the synod or presbytery may also officiate at the inauguration of a new overseer.

Those who assist at the act of installation are members of the college of leaders in the three churches. In the ELCC two pastors assist at the installation. In the LFCN, colleges of pastors and elders assist. In the CoN the presiding bishop appoints those who assist, normally other bishops and leaders of the diocese. The participation of bishops from other Nordic Lutheran folk churches emphasises the wider context of the episcopal ministry. Following the signing of the Porvoo Agreement and the *Fellowship of Grace,* bishops from the Anglican Church and the United Methodist Church of Norway take part in the consecration ceremonies in the CoN. The presence of the King and other dignitaries emphasises the public importance of the consecration of a bishop.

The act of installation of overseers takes place in the cathedral of the diocese in the CoN and at the annual meeting or the meeting of the synod or presbytery in the two other Lutheran Churches.

The Liturgical Text

The structure of the three liturgical texts is different.[41] The CoN has the most comprehensive liturgy and is the only church with a special ordination address and a vow. The ELCC has sections which are almost identical with the CoN rite, for example, the opening prayer and the prayer for the new overseer. The LFCN lacks the opening prayer and has a different prayer for the overseer. The

---

41. A comparison of the liturgical texts used at the installation of overseers may be downloaded free of charge in synoptic tabular form from www.teol.ku.dk/ast/ansatte/hri. htm.

latter church also lacks the introduction to the main prayer as well as the exhortation. By contrast, the same church alone lets the new overseer give a brief personal address.

The handshake of fellowship is found only in the CoN. The same applies to the Creed and also to the vesting and the putting on of the ministerial cross. There is no imposition of hands in the ELCC. This takes place only in the LFCN and the CoN. However, the ELCC alone has an explicit sending out.

The Trinitarian Perspective

The Trinitarian perspective is found in the main prayer in all three rites. In the LFCN the prayer refers to the Son and the Holy Spirit, not to the Father. However, the LFCN alone includes the Lord's Prayer as part of the rite. The reading from Matt. 28.18-20 also refers to the Holy Trinity. The text is read both in the LFCN and the CoN. In the CoN the Trinitarian perspective is also expressed through the Nicene Creed.

There is a christological perspective in all three rites. The ELCC and the CoN close the opening prayer with: '. . . that we together may build our church on the only true foundation, Jesus Christ, our Saviour'. The LFCN introduces the readings: 'Let us hear how the Lord Jesus calls to the responsibility as shepherds'.

Furthermore, the pneumatological perspective is found in all three rites. In prayers for the new overseers, there are almost identical expressions in the ELCC and the CoN, except for the gender issue: 'Give him (her) your Holy Spirit, that he (she) may carry out his (her) ministry. . .'. The LFCN prays: 'By your Holy Spirit, give him power to continually encourage the churches. . .'. There is no separate invocation of the Holy Spirit in any of the rites for the installation of overseers. However, in the CoN, a pneumatological hymn (*'Kom, Hellig Ånd med skapermakt'*) is sung by the congregation between the readings.

The Ecclesiological Perspective

The priesthood of all believers is also connected with the ministry of overseers. At the imposition of hands the LFCN has a particular reference to baptism by one Spirit into the one body (1 Cor. 12.13). In the ELCC and the CoN the opening prayer refers to the building up of the Church. The CoN follows: 'You have heard the Word of God about the ministry of overseers . . . . and how important it is for the Church of God on earth'. In the prayer of installation both churches pray: '. . . that he (she) may carry out his (her) ministry so that your church may be built up and your holy name honoured'.

The ministry of overseers is a continuation of the ministry of Jesus Christ and his sending of apostles and his ministry as the Chief Shepherd (1 Pet. 5.4). The CoN and the ELCC both make an allusion to 1 Thess. 5.12-13 and emphasise the shepherding role of the overseer. In the opening prayer, a general reference is made to the ministry of the apostles, the ministry of all believers and the continuing ministry until today. Both churches introduce the reading by: 'Let us hear what the Word of God testifies about the ministry of an overseer'. In the ELCC the ministry of shepherd is added, followed by four scriptural passages which all make explicit reference to shepherding the flock (John 21.15-17; Acts 20.28-32; Titus 1.6-9; 1 Pet. 5.1-3). The CoN readings emphasise the same themes, but add the responsibility of global mission (Matt. 28.18-20; 1 Cor. 15.1-11; Titus 1.7-9; 1 Pet. 5.1-4).

The LFCN also uses the term 'overseer' and refers to the calling of overseers by the Lord and their service as shepherds. Both the LFCN and the ELCC refer to the responsibility of a shepherd in their introduction to the reading. Also the main prayer of the LFCN refers to the responsibility of an overseer. 'Give (name) strength to take responsibility for his ministry as overseer. . . . Give him boldness to lead our churches in faithfulness to your word'. The task of leadership is explicitly mentioned. We find the same in the confirmation of the new overseer: 'You are now entrusted with the responsibility as an overseer in . . .'.

The exhortation in the CoN underlines the continued '*ministerium ecclesiasticum*': this term, mentioned above, continually refers to the theological concept that episcopacy is a continuation of the pastor's ministry. 'It may, however, be concluded that a bishop is a priest with a special set of functions' (Rogerson 2001, 217). This relation between the pastoral and episcopal ministry may come close to the position of Miroslav Volf (1998, 247) when he agrees 'on a threefold (not three-level) understanding of the office . . .'.[42]

However, some new dimensions are added. Episcopacy is a ministry of unity in the church. '. . . together with your co-servants you must emphasise the enhancement and maintenance of unity in the Church of God, to the glory and honour of his holy name (BEM 1983, 43 § 23). The new bishop promises to work faithfully toward this and other truths and confirms his vow by a handshake of fellowship. The following prayer and imposition of hands repeat the importance of unity: '. . . that the holy gospel may be kept clearly and purely among us and the unity of your church be enhanced among us by your

---

42. The difference is that Volf strongly underlines the importance and independence of the local congregation versus a church with a denominational or national structured leadership.

Son, Jesus Christ'. The ELCC has an almost identical prayer, while the concept of the overseer as a minister of unity is not clearly expressed in the LFCN. The ELCC closes the act of installation by a sending: 'Go in peace and serve the Lord with gladness'. The ecclesiological perspective is clearly expressed in all three churches. However, the issues of episcopacy and the unity of the Church bring the concept of the representation of Christ into focus.

The Instrumental and/or Expressive Perspectives

A key term in all three rites is 'entrust with'. 'Now the Lord entrusts you with the ministry of overseer in the ELCC'. 'Now you are entrusted with the responsibility of an overseer in the synod of the LFCN'. The same expression in the CoN is referred to above.

Another key term, 'deliver', is found in the rites of the ELCC. 'Today we shall deliver to him the task. . .' In the CoN, '. . . we will deliver you to God. . . '. In the ELCC the ordinand is delivered to the call, the task and the responsibility as overseer. In the CoN the person is delivered to God. The latter church also has the laying-on of hands for the consecration of a bishop, while the former church has no laying-on of hands for the installation of an overseer. The LFCN practises laying-on of hands, but the term 'deliver' is not used.

The readings for the installation describe the ministry of the overseer. In the ELCC: (1) He is to look after and feed the flock, John 21.15-17; (2) He is the guardian/shepherd who watches over the flock, Acts 20.28-32; (3) He is an elder and an example in faith and conduct, Titus 1.6-9, and (4) he is a caring and humble shepherd of the flock, 1 Pet. 5.1-3. In the LFCN readings are the same as at (1), (2) and (4) above. Readings at (3) above are replaced by Matt. 28.18-20, a reminder of the command to go out to baptise and teach people. In the CoN readings at (3) and (4) are the same, plus Matt. 28.18-20. However, John 21.15-17 is replaced by 1 Cor. 15.1-11, which points to the resurrection of Christ and new life in the Church.

On examination, the texts are seen to have promises from the Word of God, prayers and challenges related to the ministry of overseers. An overseer represents Christ and is dependent on God and his grace to serve according to his/her ministerial call as leader, comforter and shepherd. The Trinitarian perspective is evident in all three churches. Compared with the ordination of a pastor, the ordination of an overseer represents an extension of the ministry, but no additional dimension is added.[43]

Conclusions on Terminology and Theology in the Liturgies
The Ordination of Pastors
In structure and context, the ordination rites of the CoN have several traits that are different from the two other churches. The CoN alone ordains both women and men, uses the symbol of the stole, makes use of non-ordained lay people during the prayer and imposition of hands, requires a comprehensive theological training, or an equivalent training and/or practice, and her ministers keep the power of attorney if they leave the church ministry. This is no surprise when we recall the dominant role that the CoN, both past and present, plays as a state church.

In all three Lutheran Churches there is no necessary connection between the celebration of the Eucharist and the act of ordination. The Eucharist is normally, but not necessarily celebrated during the consecration of pastors in CoN. In the ELCC and the LFCN the Eucharist may be celebrated during a service of ordination, but is most often left out for practical reasons, time constraints or other reasons. The difference between this and the 'eucharistic ecclesiology' of the Roman Catholic Church is evident (Volf 1998, 43), and the distance is even greater from the ecclesiology of the Orthodox Churches, where 'the Eucharist constitutes the Church' (Volf 1998, 98).

All three Lutheran Churches express Trinitarian and pneumatological perspectives. Prayers about the Holy Spirit are underlined. The LFCN emphasises equipping with the gifts of the Holy Spirit as a necessity for the pastorate. Being ordained as a pastor is an integral part of the ministry of Jesus Christ through the power of the Holy Spirit. The ordinand is authorised for the ministry of the triune God and his Kingdom. The equipping with the gifts of the Spirit is a prerequisite for the carrying out of the pastor's ministry in all three churches, most evidently in the LFCN. The sending to the world is underlined in the CoN and the ELCC, but missing in the LFCN. We understand that the triune God is at work during ordination. The ordinand is thus drawn into the ministry of the triune God and his Kingdom by being sent out to the world. However, it is not clearly expressed whether this sending is a

---

43. The Lutheran understanding of the relationship between the Trinitarian and ecclesial structures is different from the hierarchical structure of Ratzinger and the asymmetrical structure of Zizioulas and more like the symmetrical structure of Miroslav Volf (Volf 1998, 214ff).

function of an office or a Trinitarian sending to a communal and ecclesio-logical ministry.

The ecclesiological perspective is also found in all three churches, that is, the connection between the priesthood of all believers and baptism and the proper call to the pastor's ministry. Rogerson concludes that the way the CoN rites 'are set in the framework of the common baptism of the people of God' ..... is 'worth pinpointing' (Rogerson 2001, 219). Emphasised in all churches is also the responsibility of the faithful in the congregation to receive the new min-ister. The mutual dependence between congregation and ordinand is most clearly expressed in the ELCC, due to the strong commitment testified by the four affirmative responses from the believing community. The relation be-tween the ordinand and the faithful of the local congregation seems weakest in the CoN. This results from a weaker participation in the process of calling, a more general rite of reception and the fact that the act of ordination often takes place in the cathedral. All together, this may contribute to a stronger clerical-isation in the CoN than in the two smaller Lutheran Churches.

The terms 'believer' and 'personal confession of faith' are differently un-derstood in a major folk church compared with the understanding in minority churches. The emphasis on the confessed faith among members is different. The ELCC and the LFCN base membership equally on baptism and personal confession of faith. Baptism alone is not satisfactory. Personal confession of faith is required to obtain full membership and the right to vote. This means that the believing communities in the two smaller churches are directly in-volved in the process of election. This is not so clear in the CoN, where baptism is the only prerequisite for membership and voting rights. Participa-tion in the Lord's Supper and personal confession of faith are encouraged, but not required. The believing community, as the calling agent to the ministry of Word and sacraments, is obscured in the larger folk church.

The rites in the CoN and the ELCC are almost alike. The LFCN is influ-enced by the Scottish Presbyterian Church. The rite of ordination and the rite for the installation of pastors must be interpreted together. When they are, we may conclude that liturgically the ecclesiological perspective is weaker in the LFCN, where the closing *missio* is lacking in both rites.

The exhortations to the ordinands are general in the CoN, while the chal-lenges and examination in the ELCC and the LFCN are more specific and personal. The expressive perspectives, such as the ordinand's gifts, status and personal participation in the ministerial acts, are most evident in the LFCN. The CoN alone mentions the task of hearing confessions and giving penance to sinners. All three churches state that ministry is conferred on the ordinands. Although the conferral is done by the officiating minister, the overseer him/

herself is somehow reduced to a channel of the Holy Spirit, who is the real agent of divine authority, enabling pastors to serve their fellow men in the name of Christ. The CoN liturgy does not reflect any substantial conferral upon the ordinand: however, he or she is given a new authority. The act of conferral is most clearly expressed in the ELCC, while the confirming hand-shake of fellowship is found in the CoN and the ELCC. The epicletic prayer is weak in ELCC and LFCN, stronger in CoN.

The rites of all three churches have imposition of hands while the ordinands are kneeling. The LFCN focuses on spiritual equipping, the renewal of the Church and the glory of God, while the two other churches focus more on power realised in weakness. All churches emphasise the instrumental perspective that ordination and ministry today are a continuation of the ministry of the Lord Jesus and his apostles. Ordination is for life and not to be repeated: the ordinand must therefore have received an authority different from the believing community. Both the scriptural reading, questions, vows and lay-ing-on of hands emphasise that the pastor's ministry is rooted in the ministry of the Lord Jesus Christ, based on the Word of Scripture and conferred by the Holy Spirit. In ministry, the ordained person represents Christ. However, none of the rites indicate that the act of ordination creates a new character or an ontological change in those who are ordained.[44]

It may thus be concluded that the instrumental perspectives in the pastor's ordination are most evident in the ELCC, while the expressive perspectives are most evident in the LFCN. In the CoN the representative perspective is most evident, that is, that ordination gives authority to act on behalf of the triune God. The main conclusion that follows is thus that the different terminology and structure among the three Lutheran Churches in Norway in their rites for the ordination of pastors uncover, not an identical but a very similar theology.

Installation of Overseers

In structure and context, similar differences are to be found in the installation of overseers as in the ordination of pastors. The ELCC and the LFCN are also democratic in their election of overseers. In the CoN the King – in reality the

---

44. This conclusion confirms the ideas put forward in some comments on ecumenical agreements, i.e. a complaint that Lutherans have 'a highly critical attitude towards and even a repudiation of ontological conceptuality' (regarding Catholic-Lutheran Dialogue, Meyer 1995, 56) or the challenge to Lutheranism 'on its emphasis on the necessity to convert achieved agreement into concrete fellowship and its application of a largely instrumental but by no means purely functional approach to the church and its structures' (regarding the Porvoo Report) (Tjørhom 1995, 36).

Government – appoints bishops. Also the issues of terminology, consecration of women, ministerial cross and ecumenical presence are particularities for the CoN. Immediately after the installation, the consecrated bishop leads the congregation in the Nicene Creed. This is the first visible duty in his/her new ministry, before he/she enters the pulpit and preaches his/her sermon. The new responsibility as a leader of the church is immediately expressed.

The same Trinitarian, pneumatological and ecclesiological distinctiveness is to be found here as in the rites for the ordination of pastors. The CoN and the ELCC underline the importance of the ministry of an overseer and particularly that the episcopacy is a sign of the unity of the church. But none of the churches expresses the view that the installation of an overseer implies any transmission of a new character, gifts or *potestas per se*. Most important of all, installation means that the overseer has become *'pastor pastorum'* and has been given a kind of regional pastor's ministry. However, some theologians will emphasise the view that episcopacy is a continuation of the apostolic teaching. A bishop has authority and expresses the unity of the Church of Christ. This is closer to Catholic theology where episcopacy is the major ministry and priests and deacons have their authority delegated from the bishop. The difference between theological minimalism and 'the sacramentality of episcopal consecration' (Volf 1998, 57) is evident. The texts of the rite do not imply any objective ontological reality being conferred during installation. The laying-on of hands in the CoN and the LFCN may be interpreted as the giving of additional ministerial gifts to the person him/herself. It is, however, difficult to state that the absence of the imposition of hands in the ELCC should lead to the opposite conclusion.

We conclude that the expressive perspectives are most visible in the LFCN, while the ELCC and the CoN have a stronger instrumental emphasis. The instrumental perspectives in Lutheran Churches are mostly linked to the ministry of the creative Word of God and the administration of the sacraments, while the expressive perspective is more related to the ministers and the ministry *per se*. This most probably results from the Lutheran emphasis on a single *'ministerium ecclesiasticum'*. The pastorate is the major ministry. The ministry of an overseer is primarily an extension of the pastorate.

References

Baptism, Eucharist and Ministry. 1983. Faith and Order Paper No. 111. Geneva: World Council of Churches.
Den Evangelisk Lutherske Frikirkes håndbøker med endringer fra 1877-1995.

Received as electronic file from Terje Solberg, LFCN headquarters in Oslo, 5th October, 2001. (especially chaps. 9-10: 237-244).

Grane, Leif. 1970. *Confessio Augustana*. Copenhagen: Gyldendal.

Gudstjenestebok for Den norske kirke 1-2. 1992. Oslo: Verbum.

Håndbok for Det Evangelisk-lutherske Kirkesamfunn, ordinasjon og innsettelse. Received as an electronic file from Ulf Asp, ELCC headquarters, Tønsberg, 5th November, 2001.

Kirkerådet. 2001. *EMBETET i Den norske kirke*. (28.02.2001)

– 1998. *Vigsling av Kantor. Forslag til ordning for vigsling av kantor.* Oslo.

Meyer, Harding. 1995. What does unite Catholics and Lutherans? In *Studia Oecumenica Farfensia* I: 47-57.

Puglisi, James F. 1996, 1998, and 2001. *The Process of Admission to Ordained Ministry*, vols. I-III. Collegeville, Minn: The Liturgical Press.

Rogerson, Barry. 2001. A Translation of the Church of Norway's Ordination Rites. In *Studia Liturgica* 21:211-40.

Skjevesland, Olav. 2001. Fra embetsteologisk 'blindvei' til 'highway'? In *Luthersk Kirketidende* 15: 428-30.

Stange, Dag (ed.). 1995. *Kirkelig ordliste, norsk-engelsk.* Kirkens Informasjonstjeneste.

Sødal, Helje Kringlebotn ed. 2002. *Det kristne Norge. En innføring i Konfesjonskunnskap.* Kristiansand: Høgskoleforlaget.

Tjørhom, Ola. 2001. Embetsteologisk blindvei? In *Luthersk Kirketidende* (LK) 14: 387-9.

– 1995. The Catholic-Lutheran Dialogue: Status and Challenges. In *Studia Oecumenica Farfensia* I: 21-36.

Vigsling til Kantortjeneste, tillegg til Gudstjenestebok for Den norske kirke. 1999. Oslo: Verbum.

Volf, Miroslav. 1998. *After our likeness: The Church as the Image of the Trinity.* Grand Rapids, Michigan and Cambridge, UK: Eerdmans.

Appendices

Appendix 1: Table of Official Names of Churches in Norwegian and English and their Acronyms.

Appendix 2: Table of Translation of Important Terms and the Use of Key Terms.

Appendix 3: Table of Terms for Ordination and Installation in Norwegian Churches.

Appendix 1: Table of Official Names of Churches in Norwegian and English and their Acronyms

Norwegian name	Acronym	English name	Acronym
Den norske kirke	DNK	Church of Norway	CoN
Det Evangelisk-lutherske Kirkesamfunn	DELK	Evangelical-Lutheran Church Community	ELCC
Den Evangelisk Lutherske Frikirke	DELF	Evangelical-Lutheran Free Church of Norway	LFCN
Det Norske Baptistsamfunn	DNB	Baptist Union of Norway	BUN
De Frie Evangeliske Forsamlinger	DFEF	Free Evangelical Assemblies of Norway	FEAN
Det Norske Misjonsforbund	DNM	Mission Covenant Church of Norway	MCCN
Pinsebevegelsen i Norge	PB	Pentecostal Movement of Norway	PMoN
Frelsesarmeen i Norge	FA	Salvation Army in Norway	SAN
Syvendedags Adventistsamfunnet	SDA	Seventh-day Adventist Church in Norway	SDAN
Metodistkirken i Norge	MK	United Methodist Church in Norway	UMCN

Appendix 2: Table of Translation of Important Terms and Use of Key Phrases

Norwegian terms	English translation	Key phrases in this project
Ordinasjon/ordinere	Ordination/ordain	
Innvielse/innvie	Dedication/dedicate Commissioning/commission	Ordination/ordain
Vigsling/vigsle	Consecration/consecrate Commissioning/commission[1]	
Signing/signe	Blessing/bless	
[Innsette/innsettelse][2]	[Installation/install]	
Prest	Priest, Pastor	
Pastor	Pastor, Minister	
Forstander	Pastoral leader	Pastor
Hyrde	Shepherd	
Offiser	Officer	
Eldste	Elder	
Innsettelse/innsette Vigsling/vigsle Innvielse/innvie	Installation/install Consecration/consecrate Commissioning/commission Dedication/dedicate	Installation/install
Tilsynsmann, (synode, presbyteriet eller distrikt)	Overseer Superintendent District Superintendent[3]	
Biskop	Bishop Superintendent General Superintendent[3]	
Prost, Domprost	Dean, Cathedral Dean	Overseer
Generalsekretær	General Secretary	
Distriktsforstander	Superintendent	
Misjonsforstander	Mission leader	
Kommandør	Territorial Commander	

1. Rogerson's term both for ordination of pastors and installation of bishops in CoN (Rogerson 2001, 214)
2. 'Installation' ('*innsettelse*') is used in local congregations of independent churches with a meaning almost similar to 'dedication' ('*innvielse*')
3. Applies only to UMCN

Appendix 3. Chart of Terms regarding Ordination and Installation in Norwegian Churches

Kirker Churches	Vigsling/consecration, Ordinasjon/ordination, Innvielse/dedication og/and lokal innsettelse/local installation				Vigsling/consecration Signing/blessing Innsettelse/installation	Kirkeforfatning/Church structure
Den norske kirke Church of Norway	Prest (pastor) Vigsles (consecrated)	Kateket (catechist) Vigsles (consecrated)	Diakon (deacon) Vigsles (consecrated)	Kantor/andre tjenester (Cantor/ other ministries) Vigsles (consecrated)	Biskop (bishop) Vigsles (consecrated)	Statskirke Episkopal-synodal (State church Episcopal-synodal)
Den norske kirke, forslag Church of Norway; proposal	Prest (pastor) Ordineres (ordained)	Kateket (catechist) Ordineres eller vigsles (ordained or consecrated)	Diakon (deacon) Vigsles (consecrated)	Kantor (cantor) Vigsles (consecrated)	Biskop (bishop) Signes (blessed)	
Den Evangelisk Lutherske Frikirke Evangelical Lutheran Free Church of Norway	Forstander (Pastoral leader) Ordineres (ordained)	Eldste (elders) Ordineres (ordained)	Evangelist (evangelist) Ordineres (ordained)	Misjonær (missionary) Ordineres (ordained)	Tilsynsmann (overseer) Innsettes (installed)	Synodal-presbyteriansk (synodal-presbyterian)
Det Evangelisk-lutherske Kirkesamfunn, Evangelical-Lutheran Church Community	Prest (pastor) Ordineres (ordained)				Tilsynsmann (overseer) Innsettes (installed)	synodal-presbyteriansk (synodal-presbyterian)
Syvendedags Adventistsamfunnet Seventh-day Adventist Church, Union of Norway	Forstander (Pastoral leader) Ordineres (ordained)	Eldste (elders) Ordineres (ordained)	Diakon (deacon) Ordineres (ordained)		[1])	Nasjonale unioner (national unions)

Kirker / Churches	Vigsling/consecration, Ordinasjon/ordination, Innvielse/dedication og/and lokal innsettelse/local installation				Vigsling/ consecration Signing/blessing Innsettelse/ installation	Kirkeforfatning/ Church structure
Det Norske Baptistsamfunn Baptist Union of Norway	Pastor (pastor) Innvies (dedicated)			Misjonær (missionary) Innvies (dedicated)	Generalsekretær (General Secretary) Innsettes (installed)	Kongregasjonalistisk (Congregational)
De Frie Evangeliske Forsamlinger, Free Evangelical Assemblies of Norway	Pastor (pastor) Innsettes lokalt (Installed locally)			Misjonær (missionary) Innvies (dedicated)		Independistisk (Independent)
Frelsesarmeen i Norge Salvation Army in Norway	Offiserer (officer) Ordineres (ordained)				Divisjonssjef (leader of division) Innsettes (installed)	Territorier og divisjoner (Territories/ divisions)
Metodistkirken i Norge[2] United Methodist Church in Norway	Eldste (elder) Ordineres (ordained)	Lokalpastor (pastor locally) Innvies (dedicated)	Diakon (deacon) Ordineres (ordained)	Misjonær (missionary) Innvies (dedicated)	Biskop/Tilsynsmann (Bishop/ Overseer) Innvies (dedicated)	Episkopal (Episcopal)
Det Norske Misjonsforbund Mission Covenant Church of Norway	Pastor (pastor) Innvies (dedicated)			Misjonær (missionary) Innvies (dedicated)	Misjonsforstander/ tilsynsmenn (Mission leader(overseers) Innsettes (installed)	Kongregasjonalistisk (Congregational)
Pinsebevegelsen Pentecostal Movement of Norway	Pastor (pastor) Innsettes lokalt (Installed locally)			Misjonær (missionary) Innvies (dedicated)		Independistisk (Independent)

1) SDA has elected for the three districts. These are installed by prayer. There is, however, no rituals.
2) The Methodist Church has the (final) ordination efter a test period of (normally) Three years of ministry. The test period starts with an installation af a first 'ornidation't

Rites for the Ordination of Pastors and Installation of Overseers in seven Protestant, Non-Lutheran Churches in Norway: A Comparative Theological Perspective

Bjørn Øyvind Fjeld

Objectives of the Research Task

The task is to present and compare the different terms used in certain Protestant, non-Lutheran Norwegian churches in connection with the ordination of pastors and installation of overseers. The aim is then to clarify the theological understanding behind the terminology and the liturgical celebration of the ordination of pastors and the installation of overseers in the different churches. To some extent the intention is also to analyse and evaluate similarities and dissimilarities between the churches.

The Protestant, non-Lutheran churches in Norway are minority churches and several of them are rather small. Seven churches will be examined. Many of them are rooted in an Anglo-American and Reformed tradition. However, the national setting is Norwegian and the religious setting is the Lutheran folk church tradition. The main question is: 'What are the similarities and dissimilarities within this group of churches with regard to the ordination of pastors and installation of overseers?'

Presentation of Seven Protestant, non-Lutheran, Churches

The comparison undertaken here is confined to: the Baptist Union of Norway (BUN), the Free Evangelical Assemblies of Norway (FEAN), the Mission Covenant Church of Norway (MCCN), the Pentecostal Movement of Norway (PMoN), the Salvation Army in Norway (SAN), the Seventh Day Adventist Church in Norway (SDAN), and the United Methodist Church in Norway (UMCN).

Abbreviations are used because of the frequent use of names of churches, and a table of official names of churches in Norwegian and English and their acronyms is at Appendix 1 (page 258 above).

The Baptist Union of Norway

BUN has its roots in 1860 and is among the oldest free churches in Norway.[1] Its Anglo-American heritage is evident. It is congregational and democratic in structure. Members confess their faith in Jesus before they are baptised (Sødal 2002, 177-190). BUN ordains men and women as pastors and missionaries and installs the general secretary as overseer. There are few liturgical elements in their services. BUN is a member of The Baptist World Alliance and runs its own Theological Seminary, which offers a four-year theological training for the pastorate.

The Free Evangelical Assemblies of Norway

FEAN is a loose congregational and independent fellowship of local congregations.[2] It is often included in the broader Pentecostal stream, though it has its own distinctiveness. Its historical roots go back to the eighteenth century and are linked to the Mission Covenant Church of Norway and the Plymouth Brethren, as well as to the growth of the Pentecostal movement. Their most distinct character is the resistance against any form of public registration and listing of membership. FEAN has a strong emphasis on mission and consecrates missionaries. It offers a one-year pastoral training, though this is not a requirement. Elders and preachers are installed locally. Missionaries are dedicated to ministry, partly on behalf of the movement, partly on behalf of the local congregation.

---

1. *Det Norske Baptistsamfunn* was established in 1879. The first congregation was established in 1860. Today BUN has 69 local congregations and 10,288 members. It has a modified congregational structure. Figures for church membership in this footnote and the following footnotes are from *Statistisk Sentralbyrå*, 2002.
2. *De Frie Evangeliske Forsamlinger* was established in 1890 with a congregational structure. Today it has 70 local congregations and 4,057 registered members. Not all local congregations are legally registered as churches. It is surprising that FEAN is not mentioned in Sødal, not even under the Pentecostal movement.

The Mission Covenant Church of Norway

MCCN has its roots back in 1856 and was influenced historically from Sweden and by the international Evangelical Alliance.[3] The distinctiveness of MCCN is its emphasis on personal faith and freedom of conscience with regard to baptism, the Lord's Supper and membership in the CoN. Children of believing parents are baptised as well as adult believers who confess their faith. Half of the members are also members in the CoN. MCCN has a democratic and congregational structure (Sødal 2002, 231-241). MCCN ordains both women and men as pastors and missionaries and installs superintendents and a mission leader as overseer. It offers a four-year theological training at Ansgar Theological Seminary. MCCN is a member of the International Federation of Free Evangelical Churches (IFFEC).

The Pentecostal Movement of Norway

PMoN traces its roots back almost a hundred years.[4] It emphasises the Holy Spirit and the gifts of the Spirit. It is a loose congregational and independent fellowship. (Sødal 2002: 255-285). The structure is democratic, though with a strong emphasis on the pastor's leadership. Emphasis is also put on mission, evangelisation and social work. PMoN installs pastors, missionaries and elders. It offers one or two years of practical and theological training for the pastor's ministry in various schools based in local congregations. It has no appointed national leadership. The pastor's ministry is based in the local congregation.

The Salvation Army in Norway

Traditionally SAN has been more like an organisation than a church.[5] Its social work and concern for the poor are outstanding. The old slogan 'Soup, Soap and Salvation' is still valid. About 200 officers are serving as pastors. Both women and men are ordained as officers and the Territorial Commander is installed as overseer and leader. SAN belongs to the international organisation

---

3. *Det Norske Misjonsforbund* was established in 1884 with a modified congregational structure and has today 110 local congregations and 8,503 members
4. *Pinsebevegelsen i Norge*, started in 1906, developed a congregational structure over some years and has today 240 local congregations and 44,441 members. The broader charismatic Pentecostal movement in Norway may include an additional 80 local congregations and 12,000 members in the so called faith movement.
5. *Frelsesarmeen i Norge* was established in 1888 as part of the international Salvation Army. According to Sødal 2001, 220, SAN has 25,000 members, 120 corps and 60 social institutions and is at the beginning of a process of legal registration as a church body. The vast majority of its soldiers are members of the CoN. This is the reason for not finding any SAN figures in *Statistisk Sentralbyrå*.

of the Salvation Army, which has 50 territories world-wide. Together with the Faeroe Islands and Iceland, Norway is a separate territory (Sødal 2002, 219-229). Practical and theological training for the ministry takes place at the Training School, which offers two-year courses.

The Seventh-day Adventist Church, Union of Norway

SDAN celebrates the Sabbath and is known for a healthy life and simple lifestyle.[6] SDA, Union of Norway, is one of 904 unions internationally, all linked to the General Conference of Seventh Day Adventists through 12 regional Divisions (Sødal 2002, 211-18). SDAN is organised in three districts, is democratic in structure and ordains men only to the pastor's ministry. However, women may be commissioned to a local pastorate for a five-year term, but not ordained. Theological training normally takes place abroad. SDAN has few liturgical documents translated. The written rites are in English and are more like instructions. Prayers are spontaneous and seldom written.

The United Methodist Church in Norway

Outside the CoN, UMCN is the oldest organised Protestant Church in Norway.[7] Liturgically, it is influenced by the Anglican Church and has a strong structure, in which theology and leadership are developed at conferences, from the local congregation upwards via a national Annual Conference, regional Central Conference and the world-wide General Conference (Sødal 2002, 199-210). UMCN ordains men and women to the ordained ministry of deacons and presbyters. It installs district superintendents and consecrates its bishop.[8] In 1996 UMCN signed an agreement with the CoN, entitled *Fellowship of Grace*, which includes mutual acceptance of each other's ministries. Theological training is normally four years. Today this is offered as a joint study programme between UMCN and the Norwegian Lutheran School of Theology.

---

6. *Syvendedags Adventistsamfunnet, Den norske Union*, was established in 1879 within the international structure. Today the SDAN has 70 local congregations and 5,732 members.

7. *Metodistkirken i Norge* was established in 1856 with an episcopal structure. Today the UMCN has 60 churches and 12,766 members.

8. There are two superintendents in UMCN. The bishop's conference covers the Nordic and the Baltic countries.

Sources

Our primary sources are the Handbooks and liturgies of the seven churches examined. Several of these, namely the Handbooks of UMCN, SAN and SDAN, are translated and adapted from their international denominational structures. Others are developed in a Norwegian or Scandinavian context (cf. the references at the end of this article).

Methodology

The main focus is on the *comparative aspects* of the different rites. The research task is confined to examining the rites for the ordination of pastors and installation of overseers. The comparison of the different rites is done by creating two *comparative tables*, one for the ordination of pastors and one for the installation of overseers.[9] The method is to present particular rites, to study and compare the different texts, that is, carefully examine the wording and search for theological similarities and dissimilarities.

Furthermore, this method assesses the two dimensions of context and structure by taking into account additional written texts found in general instructions and additional explanations in the handbooks, which give information about the liturgical celebration of the acts of ordination, including the congregational setting of the ordination, the symbols used, who carries out the ordination and who assists, and so on.

Before we can compare and analyse the different rites, we must categorise the specific terms used in them.

Categorising the Terms used for Ordination and Installation

Ordination and Installation

Ordination rites may be arranged as a matrix with two axes, one referring to the time aspect and the other to the different types of ministries. At one end of the time axis are holy acts which are celebrated only once, celebrations which will not be repeated,[10] because the validity of the act is for life. At the other end are ceremonies which might be repeated several times. The validity of these acts is limited to a certain ministry, place or time.

---

9. The tables are foundational for the comparison in this and the previous article. They may be downloaded free of charge from www.teol.ku.dk/ast/ansatte/Hans%20 Raun%20Iversen-ordination.htm.

10. Miroslav Volf objects to this. Referring to Scripture (Acts 6.6; 13.13; 1 Tim 4.14;

The terms 'ordination' and 'installation' correspond to two different entities. Most churches distinguish between these two events, though the celebration itself, the terms and prayers might be different. For some independent churches, however, the distinction is unclear.[11] Normally, an act of ordination cannot be repeated, while an installation will take place several times during a person's lifelong ministry. Installation in this sense refers to inauguration for a certain ministry in a local congregation.[12]

The Different Ministries

The second aspect, referring to different ministries, shows a wide variety among the churches. Different traditions, leadership structures and terminology leave us with a complex situation. The terms referring to different ministries are: 'elder' ('*eldste*'), 'missionary' ('*misjonær*'), 'pastor' or 'minister' ('*pastor/prest*'), 'pastoral leader' ('*forstander*'), 'evangelist' ('*evangelist*'), 'overseer' and 'district superintendent' ('*tilsynsmann*'), 'superintendent' ('*distriktsforstander*'), 'mission leader' ('*misjonsforstander*'), 'general secretary' ('*generalsekretær*'), 'local lay pastor' ('*lokal legpastor*'), 'shepherd' ('*hyrde*') and several ranks of SAN 'officers' ('*offiserer*'). Some of these terms overlap partly or entirely. However, it is possible to recognise some basic structures of specific ministries. The challenge is how to understand, distinguish and compare the many terms and ministries.

Different Terms in Use

Various Norwegian terms are used for the same ministry. The person who exercises the function of a minister of word and sacrament ('*ministerium ecclesiasticum*') is called 'minister' ('*prest*'), 'pastor' ('*pastor*'), 'pastoral leader' ('*forstander*'), 'shepherd' ('*hyrde*'), 'officer' ('*offiser*'), and 'elder' ('*eldste*').[13] 'Pastor' has been chosen as the key term for the purposes of this article.

The person who exercises the function of an overseer is called 'bishop' ('*biskop*'), 'district superintendent' ('*tilsynsmann*'), 'superintendent' ('*distrikts-

---

2 Tim 1.6) he argues that the charismata of office are not necessarily life-long and therefore 'ordination, in contrast to baptism, can be repeated, and is not necessarily a one-time event' (Volf, 1998, 251).

11. The ecclesiology of these independent congregations, i.e. the PMoN and the FEAN, is quite similar to the Free Church concept advocated by Miroslav Volf 1998, 137f.

12. Later in this article the term 'installation' is used in a different setting, i.e., for the 'ordination' of an overseer.

13. According to Stange 1995, the Norwegian word '*prest*' may be translated as (1) '*priest*' (Orthodox, Roman Catholic, Anglican and Lutheran), (2) '*pastor*' (Lutheran) or (3) '*minister*' (Reformed).

forstander'), 'general secretary' ('*generalsekretær*'), 'mission leader' ('*misjonsfor-stander*') and 'territorial commander' ('*kommandør*'). 'Overseer' has been chosen as the key term for the purposes of this article.

Different terms are used for the act of ordination. This once-in-a-lifetime event is either called 'ordination' ('*ordinasjon*') or 'dedication' ('*innvielse*').[14] 'Ordination' has been chosen as the key term for the purposes of this article.

The terminology of the act of installation seems to be consistent in most of the churches. The term 'installation' denotes both a local act of dedication, which might be repeated, and also an act of 'ordaining' overseers. The former meaning is not examined here.[15] 'Installation' in the latter meaning has been chosen as the key term for the purposes of this article.

To sum up: for reasons of simplification, the terms 'ordination' of pastors and 'installation' of overseers are used in the following discussion. A table of important terms in translation and use of key terms is found at Appendix 2 of the previous article. A matrix has been set up to compare, organise and categorise the different ministries and terms in use in the Norwegian churches examined. The table at Appendix 3 of the previous article gives the necessary overview.

A Comparison of Rites for the Ordination of Pastors
The Context and Structure of the Ordination of Pastors
The context of the rites reflects the fact that BUN, MCCN, SAN and UMCN ordain male and female pastors and that FEAN, PMoN and SDAN ordain men only. Some nuances are found in the last group: SDAN commissions women as local pastors and the PMoN may dedicate women as elders and pastors on the local level. All seven churches dedicate women as missionaries.

With regard to the terminology of ordination, three churches, SDAN, UMCN and SAN, use the term 'ordination'. These churches have a strong centralised leadership. The two congregational churches, BUN and MCCN, normally use the term 'dedication', though the term ordination is also used.

---

14. The term '*innvielse*' may be translated 'consecration'. However, the term 'dedication' is deliberately chosen to distinguish '*innvielse*' from the term '*vigsling*', which is translated 'consecration'.
15. An exception to this use is found in the episcopally governed UMCN, where the act of ordination at the Annual Conference, called a 'dedication', also covers the local installation. A later, local installation of a new minister in the UMCN is possible, but not common.

FEAN and PMoN use the term 'installation'.[16] In these two independent churches the act of installation will always take place in a local congregation.[17] This position seems close to Miroslav Volf, who emphasises the importance of independent churches and, by pointing to Scripture, defends a view that the charismata of office and ordination are not necessarily life-long. Ordination may be repeated (Volf 1998, 251).

In SDAN, UMCN and SAN the process of election includes general requirements which have to be met by the candidates. Certain tests and a degree of theological and/or practical training must be completed before ordination. SDAN and UMCN have a probationary term of three years before the final ordination takes place. A recommendation from the board responsible is required in all three churches before the final ordination. In UMCN the recommendation from the local congregation is basic for ordination. Ordained pastors are appointed to a specific ministry and a specific place, though personal and congregational preferences are taken into account.

Among the independent and congregational churches the decision to enter a particular ministry is anchored in the believing community of the local congregation. A meeting of the local congregation votes for a particular candidate to be called as their pastor. PMoN and the FEAN emphasise the call from the local congregation only. BUN and MCCN have additional requirements for the ordination of pastors, which takes place on behalf of all member congregations. Requirements normally include a four-year theological training, acceptance of the doctrinal position of the respective church and presentation of 'a written recommendation from the leadership' of the local congregation confirming that the candidate may 'be regarded as worthy of the pastor's ministry in terms of life and conduct'.[18] At least one year of practical internship is also required in MCCN. We may conclude that all churches regard the confidence of the official leadership, either on the local, regional or national level, as decisive before the act of ordination takes place.

---

16. 'Installation' ('*innsettelse*') in this sense is used about a new pastor being installed in a local congregation, and may thus be repeated in the next local congregation. However, a pastor in PMoN and FEAN is somehow 'ordained' to each local congregation, which within PMoN is legally organised as a separate denomination. 'Installation/ordination' in PMoN and FEAN is not really understood as a once-for-all event. The understanding is the same as Volf's (1998, 251). The terms are therefore put in brackets in the table at Appendix 2 of the previous article.

17. FEAN uses the term 'installation' for pastors, but the term 'dedication' when missionaries are being set apart

18. Requirements for ordination in MCCN (translation by the author)

SAN uses the flag as an important symbol. UMCN presents a Bible and stole to new deacons and presbyters. In MCCN new pastors receive a Bible and a pastor's handbook. SDAN gives flowers. Most churches issue a certificate of ordination (SDAN, BUN, SAN, UMCN and MCCN.) Only the two independent movements (PMoN and FEAN) have no kind of visible symbols. SAN and UMCN have uniforms or albs. Clerical collars are in use in BUN and MCCN on an optional basis. The ordination service starts with a procession in BUN, MCCN and UMCN.

PMoN and FEAN have no regional or national structure of authority and, accordingly, the ordaining minister is a local leader, most often an elder or a former pastor in the local or a neighbouring church.[19] The five other churches have elected leaders on a regional or national level and ordination takes place at national or regional conferences or the annual congress. The elected leaders are the responsible ordaining ministers, that is, the leader of the Union or the District (SDAN), the general secretary (BUN), the territorial commander (SAN), the bishop (UMCN) and the mission leader (MCCN).

The assistants at ordination are elders of local congregations, former pastors or travelling evangelists (PMoN and FEAN). In BUN and MCCN, they are the principals of seminaries, members of the college of pastors or members of the boards at national, district or local level. In SDAN ordained pastors assist; in UMCN presbyters assist together with lay leaders and in SAN several officers assist. In all churches (except SDAN) the ordination service takes place on a Sunday. SAN may also use a weekday during the annual congress.

All seven churches ordain ministers to ministry in a specific congregation. The practice of absolute ordination, that is ordination not related to the fellowship in the body of Christ, is not found (Puglisi 1996, 174f). However, the lack of financial resources in many of the small congregations requires a dual pastoral responsibility, where some pastors need to practise as tent makers. For this reason, it may happen that a candidate is ordained as a pastor, even though their ministry in a particular congregation has not yet been agreed. The national church body – the local congregations through their representatives at the annual conference – serves as the believing community in relation to ordination. This may apply to several of the churches (MCCN and BUN, for example).

For the same financial reason ordained ministers in some of these churches

---

19. FEAN has a national structure for international missionary work. Missionaries are dedicated at the annual conference and their mission secretary is 'the ordaining minister'.

will from time to time leave the church ministry for civil professions. After some years, many re-enter the ministry. Except for the legal power of attorney, these ministers will normally maintain their rights as pastors.[20] However, if an ordained minister for some reason, doctrinally or morally, breaks some of the vows, he or she will lose their rights as ordained pastors and must return their certificate of ordination (MCCN and UMCN), or a two-year probationary period is required before the ministry can be resumed (BUN).

The Liturgical Texts

In general, there are few liturgical texts, and they are not very prominent in most of the seven churches examined. Because of their international heritage, SDAN and UMCN are exceptions to this. The official liturgy of SDAN is in English and their certificate of ordination is valid globally. Most of the seven churches have a revivalist history and an emphasis on personal salvation, evangelism and mission. The priesthood of all believers is emphasised. However, all churches need somebody to govern, to preach and to exercise leadership in the church. Thus the issues of *electio*, *ordinatio* and *missio* arose quite soon in the historical growth and development in these churches.

A comparison of liturgical texts has been made in a separate table entitled 'A comparison of Rites for the Ordination of Pastors in seven Protestant, non-Lutheran churches in Norway'[21] The table compares sections on the context and structure of the ordination rites and continues with a comparison of the different texts. It makes use of almost the same sections as in the previous article on three Lutheran churches in Norway. However, several of the sections have a different number or order, several sections are left out and the content of each section is not always the same.

The Trinitarian Perspective

The Trinitarian perspective is evident in the comprehensive rites of UMCN; for example, in the opening prayer, the vows, the prayer for the ordinands after the conferral of the ministry, and the closing apostolic benediction. In BUN the Trinitarian perspective is explicitly mentioned under vows: 'Do you believe

---

20. In UMCN the pastors' rights are limited to their local congregation. See also the discussion on the legal power of attorney in the previous article (pages 241 and 255 above).
21. This table may be downloaded free of charge from www.teol.ku.dk/ast/ansatte/hri. htm.

in the Triune God?'.[22] There is the same mention at the prayer and laying-on of hands (SAN and MCCN), and in the exhortation (PMoN), which refers to the Father, the Son and the Holy Spirit. In SDAN and FEAN there are no references to the Trinity.

Christ is central to the exhortations (SDAN, where this is made clear in a rubric, not included in the rite, and PMoN), in the vows (BUN, SAN, UMCN, MCCN and PMoN) and in the prayer and imposition of hands (BUN, SAN, FEAN and UMCN). The christological perspective is indicated in all seven churches.

The Holy Spirit is not explicitly mentioned in all the liturgies, however the perspective is present. This is most clearly expressed in UMCN, both in the introduction, the invocation of the Spirit (by singing a hymn), the vows, and at the prayer and imposition of hands. PMoN refers to the Holy Spirit in the exhortation and the introduction to the imposition of hands. SDAN has a reference to the Holy Spirit at the recommended prayer and imposition of hands, BUN prays for the coming of the Holy Spirit, and SAN and MCCN refer to the Holy Spirit at the prayer and laying-on of hands. FEAN has no reference to the Holy Spirit. The latter fact should not lead to the conclusion that the pneumatological perspective is missing. In most of the churches examined, spontaneous prayers are also offered, not least in FEAN. It may be presumed that the Holy Spirit plays an important role in these prayers.

The meaning of the Trinitarian perspective is not clearly expressed in these churches. However, the ministry of a pastor is basically connected to and dependent upon the authority, sending and empowering of the triune God.

The Ecclesiological Perspective

UMCN makes an explicit reference to the priesthood of all believers and to baptism, in the opening prayer. The bishop says: 'Ministry is the work of God. . . . Through baptism we are all dedicated to the priesthood of all believers, which is made visible through the church. . . . I call upon all people of God, assembled here; confirm your baptism and be thankful!' All: 'We confirm our baptism and give thanks for our common call to ministry!' None of the other churches has a similar section.

The priesthood of all believers is, however, confirmed in PMoN when the officiant exhorts the local congregation: 'As the local congregation we are responsible for the installation of NN as pastor in this church. . . To confirm

---

22. All quotations from the liturgical texts, except the rites of SDAN, are translated by the author

that we, with all our hearts and as best we can, will dedicate ourselves for such a ministry before the face of the Lord. . . . I ask you to lift your hand'. Those present lift their hands or express the same by saying in unison: 'Amen!'[23] The same truth is repeated as a closing exhortation: 'Let us. . . stand together with him in the ministry of reconciliation'.

In MCCN the same responsibility is expressed in an explanatory remark in the exhortation: 'In the act of dedication, the fellowship of congregations requests that God will bless those who dedicate their lives to the ministry of the gospel, takes spiritual responsibility also for them and authorises them as the servants of the gospel'.[24]

Ordination is related to a particular ministry in a specific church. In the opening words of the rite used in BUN, the ministry of BUN is mentioned three times, and repeated in the vows. Also in MCCN and SAN faithfulness to the denominational ministry is underlined. In SDAN the name of the church is found in a rubric, but not in the rites.

The UMCN rite refers to the ministry of the wider church, for example in the prayer of ordination: 'Give your grace to all whom you have called to ministry in your Kingdom, that they may serve your church and the world with gladness and fidelity. . .' At the conferral of the ministry, a presbyter is called to 'lead the people of God in obedience to carry out the mission of Christ in the world. . .' The ecumenical aspect is expressed in UMCN by the presence and involvement in the laying-on of hands of representatives from other churches. However, loyalty to UMCN is also requested. In the vows, the question runs: 'Do you promise to be loyal to the United Methodist Church of Norway, and accept its order, liturgy, doctrine and discipline. . . . to the bishop and those who . . . . oversee your ministry?' The ordination is to a given ministry in UMCN, for example, the ordained presbyters and deacons become co-workers with the bishop.

In PMoN the local congregation is the focus. The same is true of FEAN, where, however, rites are few. It is not possible to point to a particular wording.[25] In SAN the ecclesiological perspective is emphasised in terms of social

---

23. The 'Amen' in unison may be compared to the congregational *axios* ('worthy') in the Orthodox Churches (Volf 1998, 121). The theological distance from the eucharistic context in the Orthodox Church is, however, evident.
24. This dual dedication is similar to the theology of ordination expressed by Miroslav Volf (Volf 1998, 248-249).
25. The difference between the few rites used in FEAN and the comprehensive rites of PMoN is remarkable. In practical church life the differences are few. The reality might

involvement. In the vows, the officers promise to 'serve [their] fellow man according to the word of Jesus, to support the hungry and thirsty, receive the strangers, clothe the naked, visit the sick and those in prison'.

In PMoN the missiological dimension of ministry is emphasised: 'We all desire to dedicate ourselves to a new and extended ministry in your Kingdom. ...Bless the ministry and tasks of the church today, together with NN, that the work may be richly blessed, both at home and in all places where we are involved in mission work'. The emphasis is evident: ministry belongs to the congregation and its pastor. UMCN and MCCN also emphasise the missiological perspective by closing the service of ordination with a sending formula, partly taken from Ps. 100 verse 2, 'Go in peace and serve the Lord with gladness' (MCCN) and 'Go in peace and serve God and your neighbour in all your doings' (UMCN).

The call proper is not explicitly found in any of the rites. However, in the vows MCCN, UMCN, SAN and BUN request the candidates to confirm their belief in and study of the word of God. The pastor's ministry is anchored in the Bible. PMoN refers specifically to what the Bible says about, (1) the responsibility of a preacher, (2) the ministry of the pastor, and (3) the personal call.

Instrumental and/or Expressive Perspectives

The most important parts of the rites are (1) the reading, (2) the exhortations and vows, and (3) the prayer and impositions of hands. Surprisingly, SAN has no scriptural reading in its rites. SDAN has a different use of the readings. A total of fifteen scriptural passages is quoted, to confirm the charge to and welcome of the ordinand(s). This takes place after the ordination prayer. The readings are almost the same as found in the other churches.

UMCN reads both from the Old and the New Testament. Passages are not specified. However, the bishop refers to Eph. 4.11-13, the ministerial gifts and the building up of the church. FEAN reads four passages: Ezek. 3.17-19, a watchman who is to warn the sinner; Mal. 2.4-7, the covenant of life, peace and instruction from a priest; 2 Cor. 3.4-6, the new covenant and the competence given by the Lord, and 1 Pet. 5.1-4, the shepherding of the flock. The PMoN reads the last passage and adds the following passages: Eph.4.11-13; Acts 20.28, the guarding of the flock; 2 Tim. 4.1-2, the preaching of the word,

---

be better understood, by quoting a Pentecostal pastor who commented on their rites: 'We know they are written. I wonder, however, how many local congregations take advantage of them'.

and 2 Tim. 2.1-2, 15, entrusting the ministry to reliable men and approved workers. BUN has two alternatives: one includes Is. 6.1-8, the call of the prophet; Matt. 4.17-22, the calling of the first disciples; Rom.10.8b-17, the necessity of preaching, and 1 Tim. 4.14-16, be diligent in the matters of ministry. The other includes: Jer. 1.4-19, the call of the prophet. John 20.21-23, the empowering of the Holy Spirit and the forgiveness of sins; 1.Tim. 6.12-14, fighting the good fight of faith, and 1 Pet. 5.1-4. In MCCN, four of the following texts are read: Ezek. 3.17-19; Mal. 2.4-7; Acts 9.15-16, a chosen instrument to carry the name of the Lord to the gentiles; Acts 13.47-49, the word of God preached to the gentiles; Acts 20.24 and 28, the task of testifying to the grace of God and shepherding the flock; 1 Cor. 9.19-23, becoming a Jew to the Jews; 2 Cor. 3.4-6; 2 Cor. 5.12,14-21, the ministry of reconciliation; 1 Thess. 2.3-4, men entrusted with the gospel; 2 Tim. 4.2-5, and 1 Pet. 5.1-4.

The majority of these passages are related to the ministry of a pastor, the divine call, the equipping of the saints, the preaching of the word and the shepherding of the flock. It is surprising that Matt. 28.18-20 is not included. The instrumental and representative perspectives are recognised in passages about the divine call, the competence given by God, the power of the Holy Spirit, the ministry of reconciliation on behalf of Christ and the forgiveness of sins. The expressive perspective is underlined in passages that mention serving, preaching, fighting and carrying out the ministry diligently. No conclusion can be reached about which churches put more emphasis on one side than the other. We must recall that the passages used in UMCN are not specified, and no texts are given for SAN.

With regard to the exhortations and vows, the SDAN emphasises the expressive perspective by saying: '. . . no higher honour can come to any person'. The same perspective is visible in the following text, where the ordained is charged to minister as (1) a servant, (2) a shepherd, (3) a watchman and (4) a teacher. The readings confirm the charge. FEAN has no rites for the exhortation or vows.

BUN is the only church with an explicit conferral of ministry, followed by the blessing. The vows consist of four questions, which are to be confirmed, in relation to (1) the Triune God and Christ, (2) a personal call and the duties of a pastor, (3) personal prayer, reading and living a worthy life and (4) the duty of professional secrecy. The emphasis is on the expressive perspectives, for example, the personal call to ministry.

SAN has three questions in the vows, followed by a common declaration of faith read by all cadets. The declaration confirms a personal calling, a dedication to the ministry, the will to serve as well as possible and a statement that the ministry is done as an optional response of appreciation of the love of God. The ministry is given by God, though the expressive perspective is dominant.

In PMoN, the instrumental perspective is stated: '. . . the Lord has entrusted to you the ministry of a pastor. . . . You are to. . .. use the gifts and abilities which God has granted you. . . . and that you, in co-operation with the leadership of the church, will strive to keep the unity of the Spirit and to enhance the Kingdom of God'. The exhortations underline a dynamic co-operation in leadership. The divine calling, the equipping and the uniting role of the Holy Spirit are emphasised for the pastor's ministry.

MCCN has five questions in the vows, confessing (1) the life of faith in God, (2) a personal call to ministry, (3) dedication to preach the infallible word of God, (4) the keeping of professional secrecy and (5) fidelity to the rules and mission of the MCCN, followed by a confirmation that God will help the candidate to keep his or her vows. The emphasis is on the expressive perspectives, even though the reference to faith in God and the word of God is instrumental as well. An explanatory remark confirms the double perspective referred to above: 'The dedication is a confirmation by MCCN and its local congregations of the call to ministry that the individual has already received from God. . . . During dedication the fellowship prays for the blessing of God on those who are dedicated, . . .takes spiritual responsibility for them and authorises them as servants of the gospel'. Ordination is a mutual giving and receiving.

In UMCN the bishop says: 'Ordination is a gift of God to the Church. Ordination is administered in a covenant fellowship with the whole church. . . . The church is confirming your call through ordination'. The emphasis is instrumental. The pastor's ministry is given by God and leads to a covenant fellowship which transcends the personal call. The church is both receiving and confirming the ministry. Five questions are confirmed under the vows, not unlike the five questions in MCCN: (1) personal call to the ordained ministry, (2) personal faith in God, (3) the sufficiency of Scripture, (4) continued renewal of faith and ministry and (5) loyalty to UMCN, followed by a wish that God will empower the ordinands to fulfil their ministries.

With regard to the ordination prayer and imposition of hands, all churches practise the laying-on of hands, except SAN. All candidates kneel, except PMoN, where kneeling is optional. In PMoN, SAN and SDAN married candidates are prayed for together with their spouses. BUN and UMCN explicitly mention the administration of the sacraments, that is, baptism and communion. The main focus of the pastorate in all seven churches is the preaching of the word.

The instrumental perspective is underlined when SDAN prays for the power of the Holy Spirit in ministry. In BUN the focus in the prayer of ordination is the purpose of God, how the minister can please God and serve the Lord. The prayer is completed with the Lord's Prayer. In SAN, SDAN and FEAN the prayer of ordination is not written. FEAN completes the prayer with Heb.13.20-21. The same closing words are used in MCCN, which also makes a reference to the holy vows made and the apostolic manner of dedicating new ministers by prayer and the laying-on of hands in the name of the triune God.

In PMoN the recommended prayer starts with the Lord of the harvest and an emphasis on his Kingdom, his thoughts, his strategy, his equipping and his blessing and it concludes with Jude 24-25 and the Lord's Prayer. In the UMCN the bishop prays for the Holy Spirit to come upon each of the candidates as he lays his hands on them one after the other. The ordinands put their hands on a Bible, and the bishop continues: 'NN, receive authority as a presbyter to preach the word of God and to administer the holy sacraments'. The latter rite is instrumental. The ordinand receives an objective reality through the Holy Spirit by the laying-on of hands.

Miroslav Volf gives a double warning about the pastor's office and ordination when he says that the office is based on the gifts of the Spirit and cannot be based on a delegation from the congregation, nor on a sacramental act of the bishop.[26] Some of the seven churches run the risk of reducing the pastor's office to a 'purely human commission', only stressing the personal call and the activity of the candidate and the congregation (Volf 1998, 249). However, the Trinitarian references and prayers secure the churches concerned against such a misunderstanding, even though the divine reality in the act of ordination remains unclear for some of them. Strongest is the instrumental perspective expressed in UMCN. Here the episcopal conferral of divine authority and gifts to the ordinand seems evident.

A Comparison of Rites for the Installation of Overseers in four Churches

The Context and Structure for the Installation of Overseers

The four churches under consideration here are BUN, UMCN, MCCN and SAN (FEAN and PMoN have no overseers and SDAN has no installation, only a prayer for new overseers at the district level). The terminology is not

---

26. His conclusion is that 'ordination is to be understood as a public reception of a charisma given by God and focused on the local church as a whole'.

identical in all four churches.[27] UMCN uses the terms 'dedication' ('*innvielse*') and 'installation' ('*innsettelse*').[28] The three other churches use the term 'installation' only.[29] The acceptance of women pastors includes also the acceptance of women overseers in all four churches. So far no woman has served as an overseer in any of the churches, except as superintendent within the UMCN.

The processes of election in the different churches reveal some dissimilarity. In SAN leaders are appointed on two levels: the leader of the division is appointed by the territorial commander and the territorial commander is appointed by the general. In UMCN the two district superintendents are appointed by the bishop to assist him or her on the regional level, and the bishop is elected at the Central Conference. The election requires a minimum of 60% majority vote (Nordbye 2002, 129-31). In BUN and the MCCN the election is democratic in the sense that the believers at district level (MCCN) or national level (both churches) elect their leaders by a majority vote. The regional or national boards recommend their candidates. Likewise, several institutions and groups of co-workers are consulted before the voting takes place.

The use of symbols is evident in SAN, where the Bible, flag and the mercy seat are given a prominent place, and where uniforms and clerical collars are used. UMCN uses liturgical robes. In BUN and the MCCN the use of clerical collars is optional during ordination and installation.

In all four churches the installation of overseers takes place at the main worship on Sunday morning during the general conferences or the congress. On the level of districts or divisions, the installation may take place at their annual meetings. In all churches the officiant at the installation is the former leader or someone who is a leader on a national or international level, for example, an overseer or his or her substitute.

There are great dissimilarities between the installation rites of these four churches. In UMCN the rites are detailed and instructive, as a result of its belonging to the international UMC. This is also partly true for SAN. SAN's

---

27. The terms are 'general secretary' (BUN), 'district superintendent' and 'bishop' (UMCN); 'superintendent' and 'mission leader' (MCCN) and 'leader of a division' and 'commander' (SAN). The term 'overseer' is a common term.
28. In UMCN the district superintendents are 'installed' ('*innsatt*'), the bishop is 'dedicated' ('*innviet*'). Even though the proper term in UMC internationally is 'consecrated', for the purposes of this article '*innvie*' is translated 'dedicate'.
29. The CoN uses the term 'consecration' and two other Lutheran Churches use the term 'installation'.

rite for installation of leaders is in process of being drawn up. BUN has no particular rite for the installation of the general secretary: the installation is made up of sections from the ordination of pastors.[30] This is also partly true for MCCN. None of the churches has instructions about installation with the celebration of the Eucharist.

The Liturgical Texts

A comparison of liturgical texts has been made in a separate table entitled 'A comparison of Rites for the Installation of Overseers in four Protestant non-Lutheran Churches in Norway.[31] The table starts with a comparison of the context and structure of installation and follows with almost the same sections as in the previous table for the ordination of pastors. Because rites for overseers in MCCN and the BUN are not very detailed, the comparison is not completely accurate. Differences are evident and some sections are difficult to compare.

Music is played at the beginning of the service in all four churches. Entry processions are only found in UMCN and MCCN. Then all four churches have a hymn. In MCCN the sermon normally comes before the installation, unlike the other churches. UMCN alone has an opening greeting and prayer, followed by a general recognition of the common ministry. In BUN and SAN an address to the new leader follows. If the leader in SAN is married, the address also includes the spouse. After a hymn the reading follows in MCCN. In UMCN the *Gloria*, sermon and response follow.

Then follows the presentation and a statement on the responsibility of the church (UMCN), the presentation of the new leader and a statement on the responsibility of the believers (MCCN), exhortations and vows (UMCN and SAN) and words about the call, challenges and promises (MCCN). Some of these sections may also apply to BUN. Prayer, imposition of hands and the sending follow in the three churches. UMCN places particular emphasis on the new district superintendent who now sends the believers. The closing includes a postlude or benediction in the three churches.

The Trinitarian Perspective

UMCN emphasises the Trinity in the opening greeting and the opening prayer. The Holy Spirit is mentioned in the recognition of the common ministry, and

---

30. BUN is in the process of establishing rites for the installation of the general secretary.
31. This table may be downloaded free of charge from www.teol.ku.dk/ast/ansatte/hri. htm. Note that for UMCN the liturgy for the installation of a district superintendents has been chosen

in the prayer and imposition of hands and the closing greeting. The christological perspective is referred to during the presentation and the sending.

SAN refers to God the Holy Spirit and the message about Jesus Christ in the address to the new leader. Likewise, SAN twice refers to the Holy Spirit in the word about the call, challenges and ministry, and the closing exhortation has a Trinitarian formula.

MCCN puts emphasis on the Holy Trinity by stating that the spontaneous prayer and laying-on of hands are done 'in the name of the Father, the Son and the Holy Spirit'. The pneumatological dimension may also be covered during spontaneous prayers, and most probably is. The confession of Heb.13.20-21 concludes the imposition of hands.

The Ecclesiological Perspective

The ministry and task of an overseer are in focus in all four churches. The UMCN emphasises the ministry of all believers in its opening prayer and recognition of the common ministry. During the presentation, the new servant is described as appointed to the ministry of an overseer, and during the exhortation the new leader is challenged to be a servant and shepherd: 'Will you dedicate yourself . . . . to fulfil the ministry of the church and give priority in terms of time and resources to enhance spiritual leadership?' The growth of the Kingdom of God is focused upon during prayer and imposition of hands; serving God and neighbour is underlined during the sending.

In SAN the ecclesiological perspective is evident during the address to the new leader. The ministry in the church of Jesus Christ is emphasised, in particular the leadership responsibility and the proclamation of the message about Jesus Christ who came 'to the world to seek and save the lost'. Furthermore, the ministry is focused upon in the exhortation and vows, where the closing question runs: 'Will you seek to serve as good shepherds, mentors and counsellors?' If the candidates are married, both spouses give their confirmation.

MCCN focuses on the ministry of leadership and the people of God. After an address to the new leader the congregation is approached: 'Our annual conference has elected NN as mission leader. By so doing, we as a people of mission have given confidence to NN as shepherd and leader. I now challenge you to receive NN, carry him forward in prayer and support and strengthen him in the ministry God has called him to do'. Then an admonition follows, from Heb.13.17, to obey leaders. During the exhortation and vows, the emphasis is put on the responsibility to serve as a shepherd, that is, to 'preach the gospel, do counselling and mentoring, inspire pastors and church leaders, guide and admonish all the children of God to live a worthy life according to their call'. The co-operative dimension of leadership is emphasised. Also the sending underlines the ecclesiological and missiological perspectives of the church.

The Instrumental and/or Expressive Perspectives

The UMCN presentation states: 'Brothers and sisters in Christ, NN, standing here today, will be appointed to the ministry of a district superintendent. . .' MCCN uses the term 'elected'. Later UMCN states that the overseer is set apart for the task as overseer. Prayer and laying-on of hands take place in UMCN and MCCN. UMCN prays, 'Eternal God. . . . empower him/her with your Holy Spirit to act as overseer in accordance with your will' and 'by your grace, give him/her the gift to love you wholeheartedly and serve you with gladness and a willing spirit'. Under the guidance of the Holy Spirit, the episcopal leadership alludes, though not very clearly, to the unity of the church. In SAN and MCCN, prayers are spontaneous. SAN refers to the Scriptures in the exhortation and vows. The leader of the division is asked: 'Will you uphold the Bible as the divine rule for Christian faith and ministry?' Only MCCN reads from the Scriptures. The readings relate to the shepherd who watches over his flock (Acts 20.28); the competence that comes from God (2 Cor. 3.4-6); the ministry of reconciliation (2 Cor. 5.14-21), and the caring and humble leader of the flock (1 Pet. 5.1-4). The texts do not imply any objective reality conferred on the overseer. They express the task of an overseer and refer to the promises of God.

The rites we have examined emphasise the task and responsibility of a leader in the Church of God. UMCN has a stronger emphasis on the aspect of setting apart than the other churches. The acceptance of a threefold ministry of bishop, presbyter and deacon in UMCN is not reflected in the rites for the installation of the district superintendent, though it is found in the rites for the dedication of a bishop.[32] The MCCN leader is reminded to serve God, before whom he/she will one day have to give account of his/her ministry. SAN has a strong emphasis on leadership and obedience (cf. the five questions and responses in the exhortation and vows). The office of an overseer must give apostolic leadership to the churches. However, the office of unity is not emphasised, except vaguely in UMCN.

---

32. 'Among the baptised. . . . some are dedicated by the church. . . . as deacons, presbyters and bishops' (*Liturgi for biskopsinvigning* 2001).

Conclusion on Terminology and Theology

Ordination of Pastors

The contexts and structures of the rites of the seven churches reveal three groups of churches: the independent churches, PMoN and FEAN, place their emphasis on local leadership, use no symbols, are reluctant to ordain women, use the term 'installation' and confine the process of election mostly to the local congregation. The centrally governed churches, UMCN, SAN and SDAN, use similar terminology and have similar processes of election and nationally and internationally governed leadership. SDAN, however, differs from the two other churches with regard to the ordination of women, the use of the Sabbath and little use of symbols. The third group is the congregational churches, BUN and MCCN. The two churches are similar in terms of their congregational structure, an unclear use of terminology, such as 'dedication' or 'ordination', the optional use of clerical collars and in the fact that the act of ordination normally, but not always, takes place during the national annual meeting.

We find the Trinitarian perspective underlined in the rites of all churches, except SDAN and FEAN. The pneumatological perspective is most strongly expressed in UMCN and PMoN. The ecclesiological perspective is found in all seven churches. One surprising fact is that none of the churches reads the central passage from Matt. 28.18-20. The reason for this may be that the passage is reserved for the ordination or dedication of missionaries. In UMCN the ecclesiological perspectives are particularly linked to ecumenical issues, in SAN to social involvement and in PMoN and FEAN to global mission.

In all the churches except FEAN and PMoN, the officiant is a national leader or an overseer. Assistants during ordination are both ordained and lay members of the seven churches. Theological training for the pastorate varies from *candidatus theologiae* to a brief Bible course and some practical theology. All churches emphasise the need for the recommendation or approval of the believing community, locally or nationally, before ordination.

The main issue in the context of this discussion is the question: 'What really happens in the act of ordination?' The structures, contexts and texts make up a whole which communicates a particular message about the act of ordination. The key issue is the correct content of ordination. Is the perspective of blessing more important than the perspective of equipping? It is not easy to find clear answers. Rites that are not very detailed and frequent use of spontaneous prayers are one reason. The theology of revivalist churches is historically not expressed in rites, but more in acts and spontaneous words. Some of the churches were originally determined not to have any confessional books in addition to the Bible.[33]

Classical instrumental expressions are lacking in several of the rites. Expressive features are most frequent. However, we may be led astray if we constrain our interpretation of ordination in these churches to subjectivism, emotionalism and outward acts on a human level. For example, when in a spontaneous prayer during the installation of a new pastor a Pentecostal asks for the power of the Holy Spirit, is it to be interpreted as expressive or instrumental? We do well to understand this prayer as instrumental in content, even though the context is expressive. Behind expressive words and acts on the one hand, and the lack of instrumental terms on the other, we may find strong instrumental thinking, anchored in the belief that the triune God empowers and authorises his servants, be it before, through or after the act of ordination.

From a sacramental and instrumental point of view, the importance of the ordination itself may thus be of a different value. However, the divine reality, before, during or after the act, is there. In an ecumenical context, the issue may be raised, whether or not the matrix instrumental-expressive is proper, or if the matrix itself should be differentiated.

The objective perspectives seem more linked to the ministry itself, to the proclamation in word and deed, than to the ordained person. All churches have in common the view that ordination does not add any new dimension to the character of the ordained. However, the ordained pastor does receive a new authority, partly given him or her by the churches and partly given as ministerial gifts by God. Though this is not explicitly expressed in the rites, most of the churches will confirm that the believing community, or the officiant on their behalf, confers a ministry or a new responsibility on the ordinand on behalf of the triune God. In ordination the divine call is thus confirmed by the people of God, or as 'a complex interaction of mutual giving and accepting (also rejecting) between officeholders and the congregation' (Volf 1998, 256).

This examination concludes that some of the seven churches express the instrumental perspective more strongly than others, for example UMCN and PMoN, the former mostly linked to the conferral of the ministry (the sign of the stole), the latter mostly to the power of the Holy Spirit. But the instrumental perspective in the act of ordination is weakly expressed in the other churches. In general, the expressive perspective is most dominant. This conclusion is confirmed by the emphasis put on the minister him/herself and the practical perspectives of the ministry.

---

33. This applies clearly to MCCN, PMoN and FEAN

All seven churches, except FEAN, underline the divine call. The equipping with gifts by the Spirit are necessary prerequisites for the pastor's ministry in the seven churches, though this is not expressed in SAN, and the sending into the world is expressed clearly in UMCN, MCCN and PMoN. The term 'missio' is not used in the SAN rite, though the concept of 'missio' is evident in the ministry of SAN.

One major difference between the seven churches is found in connection with the ordination and installation of pastors. Episcopal churches emphasise ordination, as an act of the whole church body and the local act of installation is weak or absent (for example, UMCN), while independent churches put all the emphasis on the local installation (for example, PMoN and FEAN). Ordinations in SDAN and SAN are valid globally, because of their international structure, but installation also takes place in local congregations. BUN and MCCN practise ordination on the national level and installation on the local level. The two latter churches are close both in terminology and theology in relation to the ordination of pastors. This was visible during the spring of 2002, when an agreement for the mutual recognition of ordination in BUN and MCCN was proposed.

Installation of Overseers

Only four of the seven churches have separate rites for the installation of overseers. Two different groups are identifiable, UMCN and SAN on the one hand and MCCN and BUN on the other. The importance of structure in the former churches corresponds to the ritual detail in the installation of leadership. This applies in particular to UMCN. The rites for installation of overseers confirm the same differences between the churches as were identified in the ordination of pastors. It is surprising that SDAN has no fixed rite for the installation of overseers in its three districts.

In general, the expressive perspective is strong among these churches, for example, in the rarity of rites and the frequent use of spontaneous prayers, in particular in BUN and MCCN. It seems that ordination to the pastorate is of major importance by comparison with the installation of overseers. This applies also to the district superintendents in UMCN. During the dedication of the bishop, the UMCN rite emphasises the vows given during the ordination to the presbyterate, the unity of the church and servant leadership. In the light of the threefold ministry of bishop, presbyter and deacon, the instrumental perspective is not expressed clearly. The instrumental perspective seems clearer in the rites for ordination of pastors.

The ministry of an overseer is a distinct ministry in all four churches, based on calling and equipping by God, recognition, the confidence and prayer of the churches, the promises of God in his Word and the power of the Holy Spirit. The ministry of an overseer is a ministry of servant leadership. The office of unity is not expressed clearly. None of the churches celebrates the Eucharist for the installation of overseers.

All four churches emphasise that the new leader is called by God, elected or appointed by the churches, needs the power and blessing of the Holy Spirit, and is sent to the world. The sending is not expressed in SAN, but the reality is there. Also for installation of overseers and the dedication of the bishop, UMCN has the clearest and most comprehensive and instrumental understanding in its rites.

Except for UMCN, the main conclusion is that an overseer has received an extended responsibility as a shepherd in terms of the number of local congregations and their pastors, but no divine reality is conferred on the overseer which was not already present before the installation. However, a continual filling with wisdom, love, strength and guidance from the triune God and a corresponding confidence and support in prayer from the believing community, are a prerequisite for an overseer to complete his or her ministry. Miroslav Volf, who advocates the attachment of ordination to a local congregation, also admits that a person may acquire 'recognition' within a territorial church or a denomination (Volf 1998, 251).

References

Baptism, Eucharist and Ministry (BEM). 1983. Faith and Order Paper No. 111. Geneva: World Council of Churches.

Håndbok for Det Norske Baptistsamfunn. 'I menighetens tjeneste'. 1994. (Baptist Union of Norway). Copy received from Billy Taranger, Baptist headquarters in Oslo, May 1997, updated November 2001

Håndbok for De Frie Evangeliske Forsamlinger. 1997. Copy received from Kjell Ohldieck, secretary of the Free Evangelical Assemblies of Norway, May 1997.

Liturgi for biskopsinvigning. 2001. Helsinki: Kristuskyrkan (March 2001).

Liturgi for Metodistkirken i Norge 1) *Ordinasjon til tjeneste som diakon og eldste* og 2) *Kallsgudstjeneste.* 1998. Oslo. Received on file from the headquarters of the United Methodist Church in Norway in Oslo, November 2001.

Menighetshåndbok. 1983. Oslo: Det Norske Misjonsforbund (Mission Covenant Church of Norway).

Nordbye, Lars-Erik. 2002. Den ordinerte tjeneste i Metodistkirken. In *Luthersk Kirketidende* 5,129-31.

Predikanthåndbok. 1995. Oslo: Rex Forlag. (Pentecostal Movement of Norway).

Puglisi, James F. 1996, 1998, and 2001. *The Process of Admission to Ordained Ministry*, vols. I-III. Collegeville, Minn: The Liturgical Press.

Seremonier for ordinasjon/innsettelse av korpsledere i Frelsesarmeen i Norge. 1993. Copy received from the headquarters of the Salvation Army in Oslo, May 1997, updated November 2001.

Seventh Day Adventist Minister's Handbook. 2001. Copy received from Kirsti Bøhmer, headquarters of the Seventh Day Adventist Church in Norway, Røyse, November 2001. Only some of the texts are translated into Norwegian.

Stange, Dag (ed.). 1995. *Kirkelig ordliste, norsk-engelsk.* Kirkens Informasjonstjeneste.

Sødal, Helje Kringlebotn (ed.). 2002. *Det kristne Norge. En innføring i Konfesjonskunnskap.* Kristiansand: Høgskoleforlaget.

Volf, Miroslav. 1998. *After our likeness. The Church as the Image of the Trinity.* Grand Rapids, Michigan & Cambridge, UK: Eerdmans.

Appendices

The following appendices are to be found at page 260-263.

Appendix 1: Table of Official Names of Churches in Norwegian and English and their Acronyms

Appendix 2: Table of Important Terms in Translation and Use of Key Terms

Appendix 3: Table of Terms for Ordination and Installation in Norwegian Churches

A Close Reading of the Rites of Admission to Public Ministry in the Swedish Mission Covenant Church Service Book, 1983

Sven-Erik Brodd

This article addresses the issues involved in reading rites as dogmatic texts. It explores the rites of ordination, setting apart, installation and the acts of intercessory prayer used in admission to public ministry, as they are given in the 1983 Service Book of the Swedish Mission Covenant Church (SMCC). The reader should note that SMCC has now changed its title to the Swedish Mission Church, a change which is mentioned in the article in various places, though the church's contemporary title has been retained in the discussion of its 1983 rites.

Mutual Recognition of Ordained Ministry

One of the most important issues in the ecumenical movement is in different ways related to what has been called the (mutual) recognition of (ordained) ministry. The concept of recognition is in itself problematic, emanating from the sphere of canon law and theologized in various ways.

In the debate about (ordained) ministry, three elements; history, doctrine, and liturgy are seen to interplay. Sometimes the importance of each of these has been unclear and sometimes there are obvious tensions within one and the same church, not only about how to conceive of (ordained) ministry but about the normative and formative role of the three elements mentioned.

In several 'Protestant' traditions, there is a certain amount of confusion about who is ordained and who is not. The reason for this is that historically developed rites for admission to public ministry are similar in structure and sometimes, when compared, demonstrate the same fundamental content as ordination rites. Yet they are interpreted either as ordination or as another form of setting apart, not for the offices of the church but for lay ministries. For example, in the Church of Norway the word '*vigsling*' ('consecration') is used for both bishops and deacons, but the church does not define the character of these offices. On the diaconate the Bishops' Conference of the Church of Norway has even stated that it is equally proper to understand it either as a lay ministry or as an office of the Church (Meland 1999).

This and other kinds of confusing situation, as they seem to be from an external perspective, are often explained either by historical reasons or by doctrinal basis. Very often it seems that history is used tendentiously in doctrinal elucidations.

The theme in this article is rooted in the situation hinted at above. It asks whether it is possible to arrive at an understanding of the various similar rites of admission into the public ministry of a church by a close reading of the liturgical texts as they stand. If the answer to that is negative, the texts in the ordination rites are not by themselves understandable and must be supplemented by either ritual acts or expositions. Usually, however, in 'Protestant' traditions neither rubrics nor explanatory texts are printed in the Service Books, and it seems therefore possible to presume that the rites may be read and understood also as texts that convey a representative message about what ordination and other forms of setting apart mean in a given church Service Book.

Methodological Considerations

The issue here is whether it is meaningful to read ordination rites as dogmatic texts or not. The example chosen, the 1983 rites for public admission into public ministries in the (then) Mission Covenant Church of Sweden, shows a wide spectrum of rites and ministries, all bearing the burden of historical layers (*Handbok* 1983, revised edition published 1990). The issue at stake is if it is possible to understand them even if these layers are unknown to the readers of the rites. Another question is whether rites of this kind are understandable as written texts for those who have never taken part in them.

The problem is thus how to proceed (a) to analyze the cluster of liturgical texts with their different terms, for example, 'setting apart', 'installation', 'blessing', or 'ordination', but with their similar or even almost identical structure and content, and (b) to determine whether it is possible to compare these liturgical texts in a meaningful way.

(a) Initially the texts will be interpreted as they stand. It seems banal to mention it, but this is not frequently done. Interpretations are normally integrated into, or even directed by, the contexts of the rites, their historical development and the teaching documents about them. In reality this presents a mixture of text and context, thereby making it easier for the ecclesial tradition that is the 'owner' of the liturgy to recognize and identify with the result of the analyses. The reading of the texts as they stand might, however, result in the conclusion that clarification is needed.

On the one hand, if it is necessary to demand specific knowledge about the historical context of the rite in order to understand the texts presented in it, this raises questions about distinctiveness and transparency. On the other hand, in all liturgies there are historical layers, reflecting various theologies and ecclesiologies put together and not always properly integrated. It seems also reasonable to expect compromises between different understandings within the *corpus* of texts and even within the individual texts. Nevertheless, the question is what the texts as such convey to the reader.

(b) Comparative studies of rites and texts can be pursued using the different sorts of rites within one church or rites from several different churches. The result can sometimes surprise. A comparison of the texts for the 'setting apart' of missionaries in the Baptist Union of Sweden and the 'ordination' ('*vigsling*') of priests in the Church of Norway is provoking when reading the prayer for 'setting apart'/'ordination'. It is hardly possible in either of them to identify the character of the rite, though one is for a lay ministry and the other for an office of the church.

The task here is, however, to investigate the situation in one church at a given historical time, and try to establish some of the content and character of the different liturgical texts by comparing them, thus supplementing the intratextual possibilities of interpretation.

In the liturgical texts there is some interpretative wording that can be used as a hermeneutical key, for example, 'we ordain' or 'we set apart'. The problem with examples such as these is, however, that they often present new questions. A notable instance of this is the phrase 'according to apostolic example', which appears frequently in many rites.

The most important dogmatic questions to put to the texts are probably found in the tensions respectively between what is instrumental – and thereby in some sense sacramental – and what is expressive, and between what is epicletic and involves transference of power. Does the rite result in a change in the person who is the object of the rite, for example, by a specific gift of the Holy Spirit (instrumental) or is the rite a confirmation of gifts already given by the Spirit (expressive)? From an ecumenical perspective the purpose of prayer with laying-on of hands seems to be crucial.

Dogmatic themes that are not clear in the rites themselves are often focused by the simple question: 'Why?' For example: 'Why is a lay minister inaugurated into his or her ministry by an act of semi-ordination?'

The Purpose of this Research

This study does not aim to describe the present position on ordination of the Swedish Mission Covenant Church (the name changed in 2003 to the Swedish Mission Church). The problem raised is how to understand different rites of admission to public ministry in a 'Protestant' tradition that uses different terms for that. Is it possible, using the texts and rubrics for the liturgical actions, to say something about the content? In order to explore this, I chose the Service Book of the Swedish Mission Covenant Church published in 1983. A new and different Service Book was introduced in 2003 (*Kyrkohandbok* 2003).

Before entering into the actual texts, it seems appropriate to give some indication of the identity of the Mission Covenant Church, the problem of recognition of ministries related to that church and its ministerial structure.

Historical Background

The Swedish Mission Covenant Church was founded in 1878 and originated in the nineteenth century Swedish evangelical revival movement, confronting at the time the monolithic Swedish state church (Walan 1964). The denomination is congregational in character, which makes the local congregation the fundamental unit in the church. Today, however, the Swedish Mission Church has quite a strong structure on the national level; this structure is ecclesiologically significant and is described as a communion of local churches/congregations (*Konstitution* 2002). Originally the idea was to re-establish the orders of the primitive church, what was called 'the view of the church in the New Testament' (Persenius 1987, 127-160). The Church was interpreted as a movement of equal believers, and the role of the laity was stressed. From the beginning a double practice of believers' baptism and infant baptism, including re-baptism, was accepted. In 1982, the Swedish Mission Covenant Church was characterized as a non-credal church.

In Swedish the title of the Swedish Mission Covenant Church is *Svenska Missionsförbundet*, literally the 'Swedish Covenant of Mission'. According to the decision of the Church Conference in 2002, the official name of the denomination from 2003 is, as mentioned, *Svenska Missionskyrkan* (The Swedish Mission Church).

Ecumenical Recognition of Ordained Ministry

The Swedish Mission Covenant Church is the bearer of elements from different traditions. There are Lutheran elements because of its background in nineteenth century Church of Sweden pietist theology. There are also Baptist elements, and during the 1970s and subsequently the Reformed heritage was emphasised. The Swedish Mission Covenant Church is a member of the World Alliance of Reformed Churches and the World Council of Churches (Holmgren 1993). Its pietist background gives ample room for the idea of the common priesthood as interpreted by nineteenth century pietism. The Baptist and Reformed strain fosters democratic ideals but also a growing awareness of the meaning of ordained ministries.

Ecumenically the Swedish Mission Covenant Church is engaged in various local ecumenical congregations. In 1983, about two-thirds of all Baptist Union of Sweden congregations were also members of the Swedish Mission Covenant Church. This happened as old congregations merged and formed a new one, which then became a member of two or more denominations (Bergsten 1995, 165ff, 281-286).

The Swedish Mission Covenant Church thus recognizes the 'ordination' or 'setting apart' of all free churches. In consequence, in 1983, the Swedish Mission Covenant Church had pastors that it had not ordained and who were not even its members.[1] This is not in fact a new phenomenon among the Swedish free churches because in local villages, during vacations, for example, pastors served each other's congregations irrespective of denominational membership.

There has also been a strong demand in ecumenical dialogues for the Church of Sweden to recognize the pastors (and later deacons) ordained by the Swedish Mission Covenant Church. The Church of Sweden has practiced re-ordination of pastors converting from the Swedish Mission Covenant Church (*Guds kyrka* 1995, 84-121; Fagerberg 1987, 172-177).

The 1983 Service Book of the Swedish Mission Covenant Church (*Handbok till den kristna församlingens* tjänst: HB) is an ecumenical manual in the sense that it is common to two free-church denominations in Sweden: The Mission Covenant Church/*Svenska Missionsförbundet* (SMF) and Swedish Al-

---

1. In the 1984-85 Roll of the denomination, there were 42 pastors serving congregations which were members of the Mission Covenant Church but also belonged to other denominations (*Svenska Missionsförbundet* 1984-1985. Matrikel utgiven i maj 1984, Stockholm, 1984).

liance Mission/ *Svenska Alliansmissionen* (SAM). Only in one rite is there a difference between SMF and SAM, and that is in the wording of the vows in the rite for the setting apart of missionaries.

The implications of the fact that the Service Book was made to suit two denominations is a historical question. The Swedish Alliance Mission, however, is much smaller in numbers; it is restricted mainly to one part of Sweden, the county of Småland, and has partly had a common history with the Swedish Mission Covenant Church (Åberg 1972 and 1980). Ecclesially, since 1982, the two denominations have manifested divergent developments, and that will be the focus of this piece of research.

A Brief Background to the Rites of Admission to Public Ministry

As a denomination, the Swedish Mission Covenant Church held its first ordination of pastors during the 1916 General Conference.[2] Gradually, between 1910 and 1950, the title 'pastor' (*pastor*) replaced the title 'preacher' (*predikant*) (Åberg 1972 and 1980). In 1963 the Service Book contained, for the first time, a developed rite for the 'ordination' (*'ordination'*) or 'setting apart' (*'avskiljning'*) of pastors. Before that, there were several instructions containing general directives for 'setting apart' for various ministries in the denomination.[3]

Ordinations and rites of setting apart are presided over by the superintendent of the denomination, who has the title '*missionsföreståndare*', which might be translated as 'director of mission'. This reflects the original self-understanding of the Swedish Mission Covenant Church as a federation of missions (*'missionsförbund'*). By 1983, however, the superintendent exercised *episkopé* over 'the congregation of congregations'.[4] He and the superintendents of inner mission and foreign mission are 'set apart' for their ministries during the General Conference (after 2003 the Church Conference).

The denomination is divided into districts, each led by a district superintendent (*'distrikts-föreståndare'*). He or she usually presides over an installation (*'installation'*) or act of blessing (*'välsignelseakt'*) for people who are received for

---

2. For the history of ordained ministry and ordination in the Swedish Mission Covenant Church, see Eckerdal 1985, 148-170.
3. For the history of the 1983 Service Book, see Onerup 1994.
4. From time to time there have been voices raised in favour of introducing a ministry of bishops in the Swedish Mission Covenant Church (Brodd 1990).

public ministry by the local congregation or a group of congregations (*'för-samlings-krets'*) that share the same pastor.

As the General Conference is the highest decision-making body in the denomination and its mouthpiece, the authority given in ordination or setting apart is obvious. In other matters the authority of the General Conference is restricted to guidelines and recommendations. The rite of ordination, however, has full effect in the whole 'congregation of congregations'. So does the rite of 'setting apart' during the General Conference, even though these may be perceived as entrances into lay ministries.

The Structure of this Article

The structure of this article is comparative in character. Different texts are given in translation and in parallel: first the rites performed during the General Conference, that is, on the denominational level, for example, the ordination of pastors. Thereafter local rites are presented, for example the installation of a pastor. Thus it becomes clear what is common to the rites and what is not. It also becomes obvious that the availability of printed texts for the different rites varies significantly.

The presentation is divided into seven parts:

1. *Introduction of the rites* for admission to public ministry in the Swedish Mission Covenant Church, 1983, firstly the structure of the rites on the denominational level and thereafter their structure on the local level.
2. *The initial texts of the various rites*, that is, introductory texts to rites of ordination and setting apart at the General Conference are followed by introductory texts to the rite of installation and 'acts of intercessory prayer' in the local congregation. An instruction for lay presidency in the introductory text to the ordination of pastors is dealt with as an *excursus* to the ordination of pastors where the text is to be found.
3. *The ordaining minister's address* in the rites of admission and the rest of *the entry* into the ordination and setting apart at the General Conference This is followed by the introduction to the rite of installation and 'acts of intercessory prayer' in the local congregation.
4. The *readings from the Holy Scriptures* in the rites of admission also divided into two subsections in the presentation, namely readings from the Holy Scriptures in ordination and setting apart at the General Conference and readings from the Holy Scriptures in the rites of installation and 'acts of intercessory prayer' in the local congregation.
5. Thereafter follow *questions, vows, assurances and confirmations* in the

rites of admission, first in ordination and setting apart at the General Conference and thereafter in the rites of installation and 'acts of intercessory prayer' in the local congregation.

6. There is a section in all the rites called *Intercessory prayers* ('*Förbön*'). The first section of the presentation of these is intercessory prayers in ordination and setting apart at the General Conference and the second is about the rite of installation and 'acts of intercessory prayer' in the local congregation. I will also examine here the formula 'according to apostolic example'.

7. Lastly, *the conclusion* of the rites of admission, at the General Conference and in the local congregation.

A preliminary analysis of the 1983 rites of admission in the Swedish Mission Covenant Church concludes this article.

Rites for Admission to Public Ministry in the Swedish Mission Covenant Church, 1983

In the Swedish Mission Covenant Church's 1983 Service Book, there are seven detailed rites for admission into the service of the denomination or of a local congregation. To that should be added the short 'instruction' for lay presidency at the Eucharist. It is possible for a local congregation to give permission for that, and the permission should, according to the *prenotanda* to the ordination of pastors, be given by laying-on of hands.

The order of the liturgy is traditional Protestant: (1) It starts with *prenotanda*, which give some explanations of the rites, and are followed by (2) an address which uses different terms for the various orders, (3) readings from the Holy Scriptures, (4) a section containing vows/promises and confirmations, (5) an act of intercession, as it is called in the liturgies and 6) a concluding section.

The various headings of the rites are to be found in figure 1.

There are thus two terms for rites by which the Swedish Mission Covenant Church inaugurates people into public ministry on the denominational or national level, during the annual General Conference: They are (1) ordination and (2) setting apart. The rites for ordination of a pastor and setting apart of a deaconess/deacon are followed by an act of installation in the local congregation. Rites for use locally are called (1) installation and (2) 'an act of intercessory prayer'.

The term ordination is exclusively used for pastors, though, as we shall see, the term 'setting apart' is also used in the ordination rite itself. There seems to be a sort of parallelism between the setting apart of a deacon/deaconess and the ordination of a pastor, since they are both installed in a local congregation after the act at the General Conference.

Figure 1

Rites performed at denominational level	*Ordination av pastorer* (Ordination of pastors)	*Avskiljning av missionärer* (Setting apart of missionaries)	*Ordning vid avskiljning av diakonissor/diakoner* (Setting apart of deaconesses/deacons)		*Avskiljning till särskilda tjänster* (Setting apart for special ministries)
Rites performed in the local congregation	*Installation av pastor* (Installation of a pastor)		*Förbönsakt för diakonissa/ diakon* (An act of intercessory prayer for a deaconess/ deacon)	*Förbönsakt för fritids- ledare* (An act of intercessory prayer for a youth leader)	

The one who is set apart for special ministries in the denomination during the General Conference is normally – as can be seen from history, but not from the rite itself – already ordained pastor. Persons set apart for special ministries in the denomination are, for example, district superintendents, the superintendent for 'foreign mission' and the superintendent for 'inner mission'.

The term 'act of intercessory prayer' seems to be used when a person who has not previously been ordained, is received into a congregation. The same term is used for the deaconess/deacon when she or he is received into a congregation. That makes the parallel with the pastor, who is installed, (both are acknowledged by the General Conference and received locally) uncertain. This could thus indicate that the deaconess/deacon does not necessarily have to be ordained.

As can be seen from the table above, there is not total parity between the rites carried out on the denominational level and those on the congregational level. The discrepancies are that the missionaries have no act of reception at the local level, probably because they are received by the local custom in the church they are sent to. The setting apart to specific ministries during the

General Conference is for service either in the districts or in the denomination nationwide. There is no order for the reception of district superintendents at the regional level. That might indicate that they are the officers sent by the General Conference to the district and not the officers of the district. It is also mentioned, however, in the introductory text of the installation of pastors, that a pastor may be installed for his or her duties in a district. However, the equivalent of the installation of pastors for deaconesses and deacons also mentions the possibilities of their being welcomed to a district by means of an act of intercessory prayer.

Others set apart for specific ministries during the General Conference might – if they were ordained – be thought to be undergoing the equivalent of installation at the local level. Those who were not ordained but set apart for special ministries might find themselves in a situation where there is an act of locally performed intercessory prayer but in this case at the denominational level. This, however, remains uncertain.

Also included in the Service Book is a rite called 'Prayer for co-workers in the congregation'. It is not placed in the section that contains the rites for ordination, setting apart and other rites for admission into public ministries. The co-workers who are prayed for are those who are elected for special assignments by the annual meeting of the congregation. The structure of the rite is the following: (1) Prescribed address including Eph. 6.7, Gal. 6.9-10a, 1 Peter 4.11, (2) Intercessory prayer, (3) the Lord's Prayer, (4) the Aaronic blessing and (5) Dismissal. The president is the local pastor. The text of the intercessory prayer is:

> Heavenly Father, we thank you for taking these people into your service, letting them become your co-workers. Use their gifts and fill them with blessings. Help them when they meet others to find the words and deeds that convey the Gospel of Jesus Christ. Let people through them receive greetings from you, convincing them that you exist and are their heavenly Father. We pray for those who have now taken on various tasks in our congregation: Give them strength, frankness, joy, and eagerness to serve you. Help them to find consolation in the Word and in prayer and to find spiritual renewal. Let your Holy Spirit guide and keep them, now and forever. Amen.

What is interesting in this text is that it seems to have neither reference to the prayer for setting apart at the General Conference, nor to setting apart lay presidents in the congregation. We will return to this.

The Structure of Rites at the Denominational Level

The comparative table above already points to the main problem in this paper, namely who is ordained and who is not. It is neither clear from the terminology, ordination and setting apart respectively, nor from the presentation of the structure. It is arguable that there is a tension between the different headings in the rites and the structure of the rites themselves, which are certainly similar in all rites.

Three of the four rites contain three main parts of the liturgy, namely readings from the Holy Scriptures, some sort of *votum* and assurances, and an intercessory prayer. The only rite that has no *votum* is the rite for the setting apart of special ministers at the denominational level. Even if this could be interpreted as an installation, it also diverges from rites for local installations, which include the *votum*.

Figure 2 gives an overview of the structure of the rites performed during the General Conference:

Figure 2

Ordination of Pastors	Setting apart of Missionaries	Setting apart of Deaconesses/ Deacons	Setting apart for Special Ministries
1. *Prenotanda*	1. *Prenotanda*	1. *Prenotanda*	1. *Prenotanda*
2. Presentation of the candidates			
3. Address	2. Address	2. Address	2. Address
4. Biblical readings	3. Biblical readings	3. Biblical readings	3. Biblical readings
5. *Votum*	4. *Votum*	4. *Votum*	
	5. Assurances from the denomination. Handshake.		
6. Intercessory prayer: Exhortation Ordination prayer Lord's Prayer The Aaronic Blessing	6. Intercessory prayer: Exhortation Prayer for setting apart Lord's Prayer The Aaronic Blessing	5. Intercessory prayer: Exhortation Prayer for setting apart Lord's Prayer The Aaronic Blessing	4. Intercessory prayer: Exhortation Prayer for setting apart Lord's Prayer The Aaronic Blessing
7. Words of sending/ Exhortation		6. Words of sending/ Exhortation	
8. Hymn	7. Hymn	7. Presentation of a Bible to the Deaconess/ Deacon or youth leader	5. Hymn
9. Presentation of a Bible to the pastor	8. Presentation of a Bible to the missionary	8. Hymn	

The fact that one of the rites is called ordination does not alter the impression of similarity.[5] The part called intercessory prayer seems to dominate the rite, but an analysis of the individual rites shows that is not actually the case.

The Structure of the Rites at the Local Level

There are four rites for ordination and setting apart at the denominational level and three at the local level. The setting apart for special ministries has no equivalent at the local level, or for that matter, at the regional (district) level for district superintendents set apart during the General Conference. A prayer for co-workers in the congregation is not part of this structure, nor is the setting apart of lay presidents of the Eucharist. What is new is the act of intercessory prayer for the youth leader.[6]

5. The biggest revision made in the revised Service Book of 1990 was in the setting apart of deaconesses/deacons. At the same time the structure of the rite became less clear in content because the idea was to set apart at the same time and during the same act and by the same rite both deaconesses/deacons and youth leaders. The structure of the rite, however, became more comparable to the ordination of pastors.

6. 'Setting apart for service in the diaconal work of the Christian congregation' (*Handbok till den kristna församlingens tjänst*, rev. ed. Stockholm 1990). The revised edition was common not only to the Mission Covenant Church/*Svenska Missionsförbundet* (SMF) and Swedish Alliance Mission/*Svenska Alliansmissionen* (SAM) but also to the Swedish Salvation Army/*Svenska Frälsningsarmén* that had at that time become associated with the Swedish Mission Covenant Church.

Figure 3 gives an overview of the structure of the rites performed in the local congregation:

Figure 3

Installation of a Pastor	An Act of intercessory Prayer for a Deaconess/ Deacon	An Act of intercessory Prayer for a Youth Leader
1. *Prenotanda*	1. *Prenotanda*	1. *Prenotanda*
2. Hymn		
	2. Address	2. Address
3. Biblical readings	3. Biblical readings	3. Biblical readings
4. Prayer 5. Hymn 6. Installation address 7. Biblical readings		
8. *Votum*	4. *Votum*	4. *Votum*
9. Intercessory prayer: Exhortation Free Prayer Lord's Prayer The Aaronic blessing	5. Intercessory prayer: Exhortation Free Prayer Lord's Prayer The Aaronic blessing	5. Intercessory prayer: Exhortation Prayer for setting apart Lord's Prayer The Aaronic blessing
10. Hymn	6. Hymn	7. Hymn
11. Sermon by the new pastor	7. Personal witness or short address by the deaconess/deacon Exhortation	7. Hymn

Looking into the structure of the installation and intercessory prayers on the local level the structural similarities with the rites used during the General Conference are as striking as the similarities between the rites used during the General Conference.

The Introductory Texts to the Various Rites

The *prenotanda* to the rites are of various length and character. The most extensive text is about the ordination of pastors, followed by the 'setting apart of deaconesses/deacons'. A very short text introduces the order for 'setting apart for special ministries'. This might be so because effectively it had to be possible to use the rite for the admission of the whole leadership of the church. The texts also reveal various features, which indicate different historical layers within them. The following presentation will be divided between rites used at the General Conference that give officers recognition from the whole denomination and rites through which a local congregation recognizes a person's ministry.

In all introductory texts for admission to public ministries, except for lay presidency, youth leaders and the setting apart for special ministries in the denomination, the obligation of secrecy in pastoral care is emphasised. This could give the impression that importance is attached to private confession in this denomination, but in fact this obligation is connected with the Swedish juridical system at the time and made it possible for pastors and others not to reveal to state authorities, for example in courts of law, what they had heard (Onerup 1995).

Introductory Texts for Ordination and Setting Apart at the General Conference

The rites used for admission rites during the General Conference have a more extensive *Prenotanda* than those used locally. These serve to explain and contextualise the rite.

The lengthiest introduction to the four rites is in the rite for the ordination of pastors. This gives the impression that this rite is the most important one to explain. The greatest difference comes with the introductory texts for the rite for deacons in the revised version of 1990. This is important to note since it later became an ordination, namely that like the ordination of pastors in 1983, the name of the act changed.[7]

In the *prenotanda* to the ordination rite for pastors, there is a *dialectic between the common and the specific,* what is common to all Christians ('each of us', Eph. 4.7) and what is for some, what is specific for the ministry ('some', Eph. 4.11), to be shepherds and teachers to all (Acts 20.28). This is then characteristic for the whole rite. Also in the act for the setting apart of mis-

---

7. 'The Christian congregation is commissioned to let the message of God's love for people take shape in both words and deeds. As there is for all Christians a common priesthood, there is a common diaconate. As there is a specific pastoral ministry, there is also a specific diaconal ministry. In Jesus, deeds and words were knit together into one. He taught, preached, and cured all kinds of sickness (Matt. 9.35ff) The congregation of Christ is called, in every age, to give shape to the Gospel of love, in witness, service, and communion. Also in our time, people are oppressed and helpless, like sheep without a shepherd and in need of the service and presence of the congregation. The office (*ämbete*)/ ministry of *diakonia* can be shaped in various ways. It can be focused on children, youth, or adults. It is a ministry that has its centre in service to fellow-human beings ('*det medmänskliga tjänandet*') and it includes witnessing. The diaconal work is to serve people. Various parts of this service compose a common diaconate. It can be carried out by specially set apart and employed persons. The services are performed on the basis of the commission of the congregation ('*Handbok till den kristna församlingens tjänst*', rev. ed. Stockholm 1990).

sionaries and deaconesses/ deacons[8] the dialectics of what is common to all Christians and what is a specific calling is obvious.

If the text in the ordination of pastors and the setting apart of missionaries is stamped by the idea that there is a 'common priesthood' and that all Christians are missionaries, so deaconesses/deacons are placed in a framework of a 'common diaconate'. It is also interesting to note that the rites for deacons/ deaconesses and missionaries, include the triad then in vogue: witness/ *martyria* (*'förkunnelse'*)/ preaching for missionaries; *'vittnesbörd'*/witness for deacons/ deaconesses), service/*diakonia*, and communion/ *koinonia*.

The question is how what is common to all relates to what is committed to those set apart or ordained. What precisely is *the relationship between those set apart or ordained to the rest of the believers*? The headings in the rites are not really comprehensible without going into the texts themselves and are in a way confusing. However, at the same time these same headings imply that the rites are equivalent even if there is a more differentiated content in the texts themselves.[9]

The main character of the rites according to the introductory texts is *juridical*, a covenant established between the denomination and the ordinand or the one who is set apart. The key words are *confirmation* and *authorization*. It is never said in this text that the Mission Covenant Church is 'ordaining' or 'consecrating', but 'confirming'.

> a. The ordination of pastors says that the inner calling is confirmed by the denomination, by the act of ordination. The ordinand promises to take on certain obligations and responsibilities and the denomination gives him or her authorization for that. The juridical character

---

8. In the introduction to the 1990 rite for 'Setting apart for service in the diaconal work of the Christian congregation' nothing is actually said about the meaning of the rite. There is, however, a parallelization of the deacon's and the pastor's ministries that could form the basis of an interpretation of the act as equal to the ordination of pastors. In the rite itself, as we shall see, the text does not speak about diaconal work or ministers in general, but more precisely about deacons and deaconesses. On Deaconesses in the Swedish Mission Covenant Church, see Rimmerfors 1960.

9. The 1983 rite for the ordination of pastors was previously called the 'setting apart of pastors' and one reason for the change in 1983 was to enable the rite to gain a stronger ecumenical legitimacy. Gösta Hedberg, then superintendent of the Swedish Mission Covenant Church and Chairman of the committee that produced the 1983 Service Book, maintains that the 'words "ordination" and "setting apart" are expressions for the same biblical reality through prayer and imposition of hands'. He can therefore also use 'ordination' to refer to the admission rite for deaconesses/deacons and missionaries (Hedberg 1986, 17; Lindberg 1994, 94-98).

of the ordination is underlined by the fact that it is done for the sake of good order, and does not lead to any difference 'in principle' between lay and ordained.

b. In the setting apart of missionaries the text interprets the rite as a blessing and a confirmation of vocation, but it also stresses the mutual obligations and commitments established through this setting apart by the denomination. On the setting apart of missionaries it says: 'By answering the questions put during the act of setting apart, the missionary enters into his work ('*gärning*') with its obligations, and the denomination calls down the blessing of God and confirms its duties and its solidarity'. The sending of missionaries is stressed by the mention in the act itself that it is 'by answering the questions during the act of setting apart, that the missionary enters into his ministry'.

c. The rite for the setting apart of deaconesses/deacons does not have that heavy juridical character in the introductory texts, but it gives a clear mandate by rooting the diaconate in the congregation and restricting the role of the deacon by reminding him or her of the duty of 'cooperation'. That reminder is found in this rite only.

The *Prenotanda* to the rite of setting apart for special ministries in the denomination are very vague. The reason for that is, of course, that they are intended to be used for various purposes and various ministries at the national level.

In the introductory texts it is made clear that the ordination of pastors and the setting apart of deacons/deaconesses and missionaries is the *denomination's confirmation* of the personal vocation of the ordinands. It is the denomination ('*samfundet*') that gives the blessing to those previously called by God and that gives them authorization. Thus it is not the Church that calls: God himself does.

The *inner calling* that is presumed to exist prior to the denomination's confirmation is the pietistic heritage present in the texts, the '*vocatio interna*'. The rite for the ordination of pastors does not mention that there is a process of calling before the ordination rite itself, to which the rite does not refer. That process of vocation starts with the acceptance into the seminary or an equivalent institution: the candidate has to pass through various stages and normally also have an invitation to serve a congregation. Thus, what is confirmed in the rite is obviously the 'inner' calling.

What is said in *the prayers* about the rites of setting apart and ordination?

This is only mentioned in the introductory texts for the ordination of pastors and setting apart of missionaries. In the first case the denomination 'invokes the blessing of God on those who enter the work as ministers of the Word' and in the second case 'on the missionary'.

There is no reference in the introductory texts to any *gifts given in ordination*. The grace, which the rite mentions with reference to Eph. 4.7, in the introductory scriptural readings, refers to a grace already given in the personal calling from God which the individual has experienced. Grace is not given in ordination. The *Prenotanda* explicitly say that no distinctions 'in principle' are drawn in ordination between ordained and lay persons.

In the rite for the setting apart of missionaries, most of the introductory text is about mission. Here it is even more obvious that the grace of God is not given in the rite but has been given as a precondition for the act. However, for this ministry also, the denomination prays for the blessing of God.

It seems impossible to clarify *the relationship between the meaning of setting apart and the meaning of ordination*. If the key word in the ordination act is 'ordination', the equivalent in the setting apart of missionaries is 'sending'. A similar interpretative key concept is not present in the setting apart of deaconesses/deacons.[10]

Introductory Texts to the Rite of Installation and 'Acts of Intercessory Prayer' in the Local Congregation

There are, in the 1983 Service Book, three rites of reception and recognition that take place at the local level. One is for youth leaders ('*fritidsledare*'). The rite is called an 'act of intercessory prayer for a youth leader'. The post is not linked with an act of ordination or setting apart. The rite has the character of welcoming a person into the congregation.

One reservation might be proper in this case. If the youth leader is already set apart as a deaconess/deacon, or even an ordained pastor, then the rite obviously becomes similar to the installation of a pastor and the 'act of intercessory prayer for a deaconess/deacon' because it relates to an earlier act of setting apart for a ministry recognized by the whole denomination. However, this is not indicated in the text.

The other two local rites are more interesting from the perspective of or-

---

10. The 1989 General Conference decided that the title 'deaconess' should be changed to 'deacon' and thereby introduced a gender neutral ministry, the diaconate (*Svenska Missionsförbundets årsberättelse* 1989, Falköping 1990). In the *prenotanda* to the 1990 rite for the setting apart for diaconal ministries, the term 'office' ('*ämbete*') is also used and that is not the case in the other rites.

dination because they are the 'installation of a pastor' and 'an act of prayer for the deaconess/deacon'. In both cases those who are ordained and set apart in these categories are not re-ordained. At the same time the names of the rites differ and the content also seems different. The pastor who is installed is reminded of the obligations undertaken in ordination while nothing is said about the earlier ordination of the deaconess/deacon. This actually gives room for the installation of a non-ordained deaconess/deacon, though the text includes a reminder of the necessity for professional secrecy, something also mentioned in the order for the setting apart of deaconesses/deacons.

The introductions to the rites of installation, reception and prayer, give instructions about how the local rites are to be organised. It is, however, to be expected that these are more flexible in practice than the rites at the denominational level.

The parallel between the rites for the installation of pastors and deaconesses/deacons into local congregations is striking. The Swedish term is '*installera*' ('install') for pastors, but for deaconesses/deacons it is '*insätta*' ('inaugurate'), which may also mean 'install'.[11] However, it is equally clear that there are juridical differences. The deacons'/deaconesses' ordering in relation to the denomination is well grounded in the fact that they are installed on the implicit basis of an act of setting apart for life. The ordering of their ministries is, however, different. The deacons/deaconesses do not have a reference to the Constitution of the congregation in the same way as the pastors.

The act of installation of a deacon/deaconess according to the ordinance of the Swedish Mission Covenant Church may refer not only to a congregation or a group of congregations but also to an ecumenical agency. That actually underlines the fundamental relationship between the 'setting apart' and the denomination. The relation to the denomination is in this case absolute, which indicates the character of ordination.

Instruction for Lay Presidency in the Introductory Text to the Ordination of Pastors

There is one rather interesting passage in the *prenotanda* to the ordination of pastors, which was mentioned earlier. It is about lay presidency at the Eucharist. It is negatively formulated in the text, namely in the assertion that there

---

11. In the installation of pastors in the Service Book of 1963, the term used was 'setting apart'. That is reminiscent of the times in the denomination when all ordinations of pastors took place in the local congregation. There were no rites for the installation of deacons/deaconesses.

is 'in principle' no difference between ordained and non-ordained persons according to the Swedish Mission Covenant Church. Positively, however, it becomes an instruction for the congregations on how to arrange lay presidency. Anyone who has the confidence of the congregation may be entrusted with the ministry of preaching the word and administering the sacraments. But, here comes the instruction: It is 'a good biblical order' that lay persons who have the mandate to serve the congregation by preaching and administration of the sacraments, 'are set apart by imposition of hands and intercessory prayers'. For the sake of good order, however, if possible, those who have been ordained pastors should administer the sacraments.

The implications of this rite are not clear. It presupposes that there is no difference in principle between lay and ordained persons, as is taught in the *prenotanda*. However, that can be questioned. If there is 'in principle' no difference between the ordained and the non-ordained, the act of laying-on of hands for lay presidency seems to be a way of indicating who has the confidence of the congregation. If this act is in fact a parallel to the rites for ordination and setting apart, then what is meant in those rites by 'confirmation' of the personal calling by God becomes uncertain. It is not the call of God that is mentioned in the act of giving permission for lay presidency, but the call of the congregation.

The Ordaining Minister's Address in the Rites of Admission

After the *prenotanda*, the next part is dominated by the president's address. It is variously called in the rites, 'ordination address', and 'welcome', but the intention is the same. In open rites, such as the ones dealt with here, this is, of course, of crucial importance, and these addresses should be interpreted over time in order to follow whether they reflect, for example, a development in the understanding of the rites. The entrance is, however, given in the rites.

Entrance into the Ordination and Setting Apart at the General Conference

One of the rites – that for the setting apart of missionaries – has a very distinct character, which stresses the importance of 'The Great Commission' by placing it right at the beginning (see figure 4). It is not the equivalent of the Scripture readings in the other rites. Its centrality is marked by its own heading in the rite. The personal references to the names of those who are 'ordained' or 'set apart' are not prescribed in the 'setting apart' of deaconesses/deacons.

Figure 4

Ordination of Pastors	Setting apart of Missionaries	Setting apart of Deaconesses/ Deacons	Setting apart for Special Ministries
The Secretary for Inner Mission says to pastors who will now be ordained:	*Address* The superintendent gives an address to those who will be set apart	*Address* (The superintendent will give an address to those who will be set apart)	*Address* Address to those who will be set apart.
The names of those who will be ordained are announced.	*The great Commission* The superintendent says: 'Let us listen to the great commission of Jesus Christ. The Lord says ...'– Matt. 28.18–20 is read. [Printed in the Service Book]		The superintendent names each of them by name and makes some personal remarks on the ministry they will respectively be taking on.
Ordination Address			

There is an understood relationship between the superintendent's address and the readings of the Word. Since the setting apart of deaconesses/deacons is the most open rite, its content becomes logically the most open to interpretation by the superintendent.

The Entrance to the Rite of Installation and 'Acts of Intercessory Prayer' in the Local Congregation

In the act of installation of a pastor the installation address comes immediately after the rather extensive readings from the Holy Scriptures (see figure 5). Therefore the local rites are not wholly compatible. This is of no theological importance but is due to the arrangement of biblical readings.

To understand the rites more fully, it would be necessary to analyze the addresses given by presidents of the rites over a period of years. All rites for use locally have fixed wording for the introduction and conclusion of the address. It gives the impression that the act has the rather juridical character of regulating admission into the local ministry.

Figure 5

Installation of a Pastor	An Act of intercessory Prayer for a Deaconess/ Deacon	An Act of intercessory Prayer for a Youth Leader
Choral singing if that is possible		
HYMN READINGS FROM THE SCRIPTURES Eph. 1.2-3 [full text printed] *Or another suitable word from the Scriptures.*	In the name of the Father and of the Son and of the Holy Spirit.	In the name of the Father and of the Son and of the Holy Spirit.
PRAYER HYMN OF PRAISE		
INSTALLATION ADDRESS *The pastor who is being installed stands to listen to the address. The address begins as follows:* Brother/Sister in Christ! You stand today prepared to make.... your entrance as shepherd and teacher in the Mission Congregation (*Missionsförsamling*)/group of congregations, district of ..... *The address concludes:* As God's word to you today and to all of us, we listen to what the Holy Scriptures say about the ministry of God's word.	ADDRESS *The deacon/deaconess stands to listen to the address. The address begins as follows:* NN, Sister/Brother in Christ! You stand today ready to serve as a deaconess / deacon in the congregation of ...... *The address concludes:* We listen to the word of God to you and to all of us.	WELCOME *The youth leader stands to listen to the address. The address begins as follows:* NN, Sister/Brother in Christ! You stand today ready to serve as a youth leader in the mission congregation (group of congregations) of ...... *The address concludes:* As the word of God to you and to all of us, we now listen to what the Holy Scriptures say about ministries in God's congregation.

The reading from Ephesians in the installation of a pastor opens with praise and corresponds to the Trinitarian formula in the other rites. It is clear from the introduction to the rites that no one 'becomes' anything during the rite and that it presupposes an ordination, a setting apart and/or an appointment.

Readings from the Holy Scriptures in the Rites of Admission

The combination of printed biblical texts and references to the Scriptures gives the impression that some readings are more representative than others. Some texts are to be found in different rites but they are few and of a general nature. It is not possible to draw substantial theological conclusions from them. If any were to be drawn, it would be that the rites differ in content. On the other hand the texts are, as we shall see, rather imprecise in identifying the specific character of the ministries.

Readings from the Holy Scriptures in the rites for ordination and setting apart at the General Conference

The different degrees of importance given to the texts used are indicated, as already mentioned, by the fact that some are printed in full in the Service Book, while other are simply suggested. The multitude of texts suggested for use in the rite of ordination, by comparison with the other rites, is marked (figure 6).

The main readings in the ordination rite start with two texts about the harvest and the need for labourers. Thereafter come two texts about the work of the Holy Spirit, that the disciples have the mandate of Christ to forgive sins and that the Spirit made the elders overseers to care for the Church. Thereafter follow two texts about growth and the building up of the Church, and the texts end with an exhortation to the young pastors.

The alternative texts have almost the same content and the last seven texts are about the duties and especially the virtues of those who witness to the gospel and tend the flock.

The rite for deaconesses/deacons has texts about humble service in love, texts that are rather traditional in Protestant *diakonia*.

The choice of readings for the rite of setting apart for special ministries is left totally open because the content of the rite must cover various kinds of ministries.

Figure 6

Ordination of a Pastor	Setting apart of Deaconesses/ Deacons	Setting apart for specific ministries
The superintendent says: Let us now hear the promises and the admonitions of the Holy Scriptures		*The superintendent says:* Let us now hear the witness of the Scriptures
Some of the following words from the Scriptures may be chosen Matt. 9.36-38; John 15.16; John 20.21-23; Acts 20.28; 1 Cor. 3.7-8; Eph. 4.11-12; 2 Tim. 2.15 (all texts printed in full) Matt. 28.18-20; John 21. 16; 1 Cor. 3.11-13; 1 Cor. 9.26-27; 2 Cor 5.18-20; 1 Tim. 4.12; 2 Tim. 4.2; Luke 17.10; Acts 20.24; 1 Cor 4.1-2; 2 Cor. 5.14-15; Phil. 4.19; 2 Tim. 2.24-25; 1 Peter 5.2-4	The readings of the Scriptures are distributed among those who are assisting. Rom 12.6-15 [full text printed] Another suggested reading: 1 Cor. 13.	Some of the assistants read suitable texts from the Scriptures.
	The superintendent says: May God give you grace faithfully to keep these words in your hearts!	

Coming back to the question of the instrumental versus the expressive character of the rites, there is one interesting feature to note in the choice of biblical readings. Texts referring to gifts given by the imposition of hands are missing (1 Tim. 4.14; 2 Tim.1.6). In 1 Tim. 1.12-16 it says: 'Let no one despise your youth, but be an example to believers, in word, in conduct, in love, in spirit, in faith, in purity' (v.12); 'Until I come, give attention to reading, to exhortation, to doctrine' (v. 13); 'Do not neglect the gift that is in you, which was given to you by prophecy, with the laying-on of the hands of the eldership'(v. 14); 'Meditate on these things; give yourself entirely to them, that your progress may be evident to all' (v.15); 'Take heed to yourself and to the doctrines. Continue in them, for in doing this you will save both yourself and those who hear you' (v.16). In the optional readings v. 12 is suggested for the ordination of pastors and v. 16 for the installation of pastors.

Readings from the Holy Scriptures in the Rite of Installation and the 'Acts of Intercessory Prayer' in the Local Congregation

In almost all the rites other 'suitable' texts or words are referred to as alternatives to those suggested. It is also interesting to see what suitable words are suggested for the inauguration of a youth leader and deaconess/deacon and for the installation of a pastor. Here the suggested readings may be compared (figure 7).

Figure 7

Installation of a Pastor	An Act of intercessory Prayer for a Deaconess/Deacon	An Act of intercessory Prayer for a Youth Leader
Words from the Bible *The assistants each read a word from the Bible.*	Words from the Scriptures *The assistants read suitable words from the Scriptures.*	Words from the Scriptures *The assistants read suitable words from the Scriptures.*
Some of those mentioned below may be used: John 15.16; Eph. 4.11-13; Acts 20.28; 1 Tim. 4.16; Rom. 10.15, 17; Heb. 13.8; 1 Cor. 4.1-2.	*Some of those mentioned below may be used.* Matt. 20.25-28; 2 Cor. 1.3-4; Eph. 6.6-7; 1 Thess. 5.14-22; James 2.14-16; 1 Peter 4.10-11.	*Some of those mentioned below may be used.* John 12.26a; Eph.3.20-21; John 15.16; Heb. 13.8; 1 Cor. 12.4-6; 1 Peter 4.10.

The profile of the ministries is clear for pastors and deaconesses/deacons. The former are shepherds, teachers and preachers, servants and stewards of the mysteries of Christ; the latter are servants doing good deeds. The youth leaders are, necessarily, more difficult to define. Here the imitation of Christ, the one who has chosen people for his ministry, is the basis.

The theme common to all texts in the local admission rites is that of the many gifts and charismata given in the Church of Christ.

Questions, Vows, Assurances and Confirmations in the Rites of Admission

In all the rites, with the exception of the rite of setting apart for special ministries in the denomination, there is quite an extensive section of a juridical nature. Those who are ordained, set apart, installed or received by an act of intercessory prayer thereby have their status in the denomination or the local congregation regulated. The juridical character of the act called 'intercessory prayer' even makes the headings of the rites somewhat misleading.

Questions, Vows, Assurances and Confirmations in Ordination and Setting Apart in the General Conference

This section of the rites describes the functions that are inherent in the various ministries and identifies the position of the ministries in the denomination.

This is the most developed part in all the types of admission to public ministry given in the Service Book (figure 8). The only rite that is not included in this is the rite for setting apart for special ministries in the leadership of the denomination. In some of the rites it is prescribed that the congregation stand and remain standing during this moment in the rite. This underlines the juridical character of the act. The questions that are put to the ordinand are answered by a promise or vow. The commitments are underlined by the subsequent reading from the Bible or words of confirmation. The readings involved are strongly admonitory. Only the 'act of prayer for a youth leader' lacks this admonition and includes instead confirmation of the youth leader's calling by the congregation.

Figure 8

Ordination of a Pastor	Setting apart of Missionaries	Setting apart of Deaconesses/ Deacons
Questions and Assurance: The superintendent says: Before Jesus Christ, the Lord of the congregation, I ask each of you, 1. Will you here confirm anew that you believe in Jesus Christ as your Lord and Saviour? Response	*Questions and Assurance:* The superintendent says to those who will be set apart: Before Jesus Christ, the Lord of the congregation, I ask each of you, [here there is an alternative section for the Swedish Alliance Mission] 1. Will you here confirm anew that you believe in Jesus Christ as your Lord and Saviour? Response	*Questions and Assurance:* The superintendent says: Before God and this congregation, I ask each of you, 1. Will you here confirm anew that you believe in Jesus Christ as your Lord and Saviour? Response

2. Will you abide by the word of God and through the grace of God and in the power of the Spirit proclaim the word and teach, administer the sacraments, practice the cure of souls and serve the congregation and your fellow human beings in the name of Jesus? Response	2. Are you, NN, willing, as a Missionary of the Swedish Mission Covenant Church, to go to ... in order to serve with the gift of grace given to you, faithful to your Lord and Saviour? [If a married couple is set apart at the same time, both should be named and have the possibility of answering at the same time. Response	2. Will you abide by the Word of God and in following Christ ('*i Jesu efterföljd*') seek to carry out your vocation as a deaconess /deacon Response
3. Do you promise not to reveal to anyone what people confide to you during confession? Response	3. Do you promise to observe secrecy about people's personal circumstances? Response	
4. Will you be faithful to your vocation to be a pastor in the Mission Covenant Church/Swedish Alliance Mission and work for Christian unity in accordance with the prayer of Jesus 'that they all may be one' ....? Response	After the questions have been answered, the superintendent gives his hand to each saying: God be with you! [here follows again the common text]	
The superintendent says: 'God will help each of you to keep these vows'.	The superintendent says: 'Be sure that the Swedish Mission Covenant Church/ Swedish Alliance Mission will follow each of you in prayers and support you. Jesus said', [John 15.16 is read]	

The first question in the rites for setting apart and ordination, in which candidates confirm that they 'believe in Jesus Christ as [your] Lord and Saviour', is fundamental for the Swedish Mission Covenant Church. Historically there is behind it, of course, the tradition of the believers' church.

The fourth question, on promoting Christian unity, is in accordance with the Constitution of the denomination. It is combined with the promise to be faithful to the vocation of a pastor in the denomination. It substitutes the question in the 1963 Service Book, where it says: 'Do you desire to be faithful to the view of the congregation (*församlingssyn*) in the Swedish Mission Covenant Church?'

This actually makes a shift in the pastor's obligation from the nineteenth century ideal of the New Testament congregation (*den nytestamentliga församlingssynen*) to a modern ecumenical profile. It also mirrors a shift from a rather closed to an open ecclesiology in the Swedish Mission Covenant Church (Eckerdal 1982; Olofsgård 1973; Bredberg 1962; Sundström 1959).

Questions, Vows, Assurances and Confirmations in the Rite of Installation and 'Acts of Intercessory Prayer' in the Local Congregation

In the rites administered locally – the installation of a pastor and the intercessory act for deacons and deaconesses – the crucial part is called 'Questions and admonition'. In the rites at the denominational level the title of this part is, 'Questions and assurance'. Why this is the case is not clear. The local act for youth leaders has 'Confirmation and admonition', which should presuppose that the person has been called but not previously set apart or ordained. Confirmation seems to be the main content of the rites during the General Conference.

The rites are very different. The inauguration of a youth leader is an act of welcome in which the new co-worker is assured of the support of the congregation. The installation of a pastor and the act of intercessory prayer for the deaconess/deacon has a covenant character. The promises given by the pastor or deaconess/deacon are matched by a declaration of responsibility made by the congregation.

Intercessory Prayers (*Förbön*) in the Rites of Admission

Two rites are entitled 'Intercessory Prayer': the local inauguration of deaconesses/deacons and that of youth leaders. In the Service Book there is a block of various prayers given the name 'Intercessory prayers' (*förbön*). Under this term some types of admission prayers are also subsumed. What is meant by intercessory prayer is not clear. The term is used in a wide range of meanings in the Service Book, which even has a chapter on 'Intercessory Prayer'. It contains a rite for the 'Service of Intercessory Prayer' and a rite for 'Intercessory Prayer with Anointing with Oil'. The main content is, according to the preface of this chapter, 'to bring a person before God'. The meaning of the prayer is, thus, to establish a relationship in the presence of God, between God and a person. In this sense, all types of intercessory prayers are instrumental or effective. However, in the admission rites, that relationship might also be interpreted as already established by the personal calling of the person. One possible reading is that, in as far as the intercessory prayer establishes a relationship between God and a person it is an extension of the personal vocation. Intercessory prayer is a part of all the admission rites.

Intercessory Prayers in Ordination and Setting Apart at the General Conference

In the framework called intercessory prayer there are several sections. They all begin with an introductory reference to the apostolic example of prayer and laying-on of hands. For pastors there is a prayer called 'ordination prayer' and for the other ministers 'setting apart prayer'. No words are given for any of the 'setting apart prayers', and even for the 'ordination prayer', free prayer is possible as an alternative. In the prayer sections in all the admission rites, the Lord's Prayer is obligatory as well as the Aaronic blessing (Num. 6.24-26). The instruction to the president and the assistants to pray the Lord's Prayer together may indicate that this is the moment for the imposition of hands, but that is not explicit in the rite. Whether or not the Aaronic blessing is part of the ordination prayer/setting apart prayer ('*ordinationsbön/avskiljningsbön*') is not clear. However, according to the rubric, all those who are ordained or set apart kneel from the start of the ordination prayer/prayer for setting apart to the end of the Aaronic blessing.

The ordination prayer in the ordination of pastors starts with an invocation followed by a section interpreting the whole rite as confirmation of the personal calling of the ordinands through laying-on of hands and prayer by the congregation, which in this case means the Swedish Mission Covenant Church. The ordinands' vocation is to be the servants of the Word, shepherds and teachers.

The next part of the ordination prayer expresses a form of representational theology: 'Let people hear Jesus' voice when your servants instruct and preach, and see Jesus' hands when your servants baptize and distribute the gifts of the Holy Communion'. It is, however, a functional representation to see the acts of Christ in the acts of the pastor. The pastor is not representing Christ as a person and then consequently exercising the functions mentioned.

In the ordination rite there is also an invocation of the Holy Spirit: 'Give these your servants the strength and gifts of the Holy Spirit so that they, with humbleness and frankness may, together with your congregation, carry the message of joy'. This prayer for the gifts of the Holy Spirit might be interpreted instrumentally rather than in a purely expressive way. However, the gift prayed for is put in the context of the message of joy, that is, the gospel, not in relation to the administration of the sacraments or to the teaching authority. It is possible to ascribe to the rite for the setting apart of missionaries an epicletic nature. The introductory text mentions the congregation sent into the world by the power of the Holy Spirit, the president invokes the blessing of God on the missionary, and the free prayer of setting apart may also include a sort of epiclesis. The only rite found in the Service Book that has a written epicletic prayer is the 'Prayer for co-workers in the congregation', mentioned earlier. Here it says 'Let your Holy Spirit guide and keep them ...'.

The last part of the ordination prayer is formally not an ordination prayer at all. It is an intercessory prayer for 'those people who stand closest' to the ordinand. The concluding words referring to 'ordinands' and those who 'are being set apart' are not what would be expected. Traditionally these persons at this moment in the rite would be considered already ordained or set apart. The description of the deaconesses/deacons at this point is different: they are clearly regarded as set apart by then, and the text explicitly says so. This differentiation seems to be more of a textual accident because it has no support in the text itself, which indicates that the ordinands are by then ordained. On the other hand, the lack of consistency could also indicate that the ordination or setting apart is not complete until the whole worship has come to an end. That indicates that neither the intercessory prayer nor the juridical part is constitutive of the ordination rite or indeed that there is no constitutive element.

In the rites for admission, there is no prayer of thanks to summarize the meaning of the act.

Intercessory Prayers in the Rite of Installation and the 'Acts of Intercessory Prayer' in the Local Congregation

The structure of the intercessory prayer is the same in all the rites of ordination and setting apart. It is threefold with (1) a prayer, freely formulated, (2) the Lord's Prayer and (3) the Aaronic blessing ending with the Trinitarian formula.

The Formula 'according to Apostolic Example'

The most conspicuous feature of the rites is the total absence of any rubric prescribing imposition of hands. It is, however, the normal custom in the rites for ordination and setting apart and, in 1982, the gesture was that the president and the assistants put their right hands on the shoulder of the person who was being set apart or ordained.

Despite this lack of rubric, the laying-on of hands is mentioned in the introduction to the intercessory prayer and in the form 'according to apostolic example, we now wish, by prayer and laying-on of hands, to

'set you apart ('*avskilja dig*') for the ministry ('*tjänst*') to which God has called you'. [at the ordination of pastors]

'install you as shepherd and teacher in this congregation and invoke God's blessing on you'. [at the installation of pastors]

'set you apart ('*avskilja dig*') for the ministry ('*tjänst*') to which God has called you and invoke God's blessing on you'. [at the setting apart of missionaries]

'set you apart ('*avskilja dig*') for the ministry ('*tjänst*') that God has called you to and invoke God's blessing on you'. [at the setting apart of a deaconess/deacon]

'pray for you, as you enter into your work' ('*gärning*'). [in the act of intercessory prayer for a deaconess/deacon]

'set you apart ('*avskilja dig*') for the ministry ('*tjänst*') that God has called you to and invoke God's blessing on you'. [at the setting apart for specific offices]

'inaugurate/install ('*insätta*') you to/in your ministry ('*tjänst*') and invoke God's blessing on you'. [in the intercessory prayer for youth leaders]

The 'apostolic example' seems to refer to the imposition of hands with prayer as an action, not to the content of the liturgical act interpreted from the concept of apostolicity. There are no references in any act at the moment of the prayers to the apostolicity of the Church. All the prayers of admission may be freely formulated by the president or another person (there are no instructions who should pray), which indicates that there is no normative teaching that is decisive for the content of an ordination or installation prayer or its equivalent. The content is left open for the person who is to pray, limited, of course, to the self-understanding and tradition of the Swedish Mission Covenant Church.

The Conclusion of the Rites of Admission

The final moments in the rites consist of hymns in the local rites but, more extensively, of exhortations and hymns in the rites at the denominational level.

The Conclusion of Ordination and Setting Apart at the General Conference

The endings of the rites at the General Conference have two basic ingredients, praise and sending. They do not contribute anything to the understanding of the ordination rites. Another element is the presentation of Bibles to everyone, except for those set apart for special ministries, who do not receive Bibles, a practice that is not explained in the rites. More than as a *redditio symboli* it seems possible to interpret this as confirmation of the Word spoken in the liturgy and given to the person in the admission. That would fit the main function of the rite as confirmatory.

The rite for installation in the local congregation is concluded with a sermon by the new pastor. The rite for a deacon / deaconess ends with a hymn and eventually a personal witness or short address by the deacon or deaconess. The prayer service for a youth leader ends with a hymn.

A Preliminary Analysis of the 1983 Rites for Admission in the Swedish Mission Covenant Church

As mentioned in the introduction, the main issue in this article is to discuss whether it is possible to draw theological conclusions from a series of rites in a denomination that uses different terms for different rites. Another question is whether it is possible, from a reading of the rites themselves, to say anything about the probable differences in content or effect of different rites. For that it should be possible to put various questions to the rites themselves.

We have already tried to distinguish, according to the ritual texts, between rites performed in the local congregation and rites performed at the General Conference and thus for 'the congregation of congregations'. What is not obvious in the Service Book is that the setting apart of deaconesses/deacons and the ordinations of pastors are never repeated in the denomination. It is, however, impossible to say, from the rites themselves, which ordinations are for life and which ordinations are not. The terminology gives no direction on that. However, the fact that there are rites for the installation of deaconesses/deacons and pastors might be an indication of an ordination and setting apart for life for these groups. On the other hand the fact that the deaconess/deacon is installed in the local congregation by an 'act of intercessory prayer' might indicate that he or she is not necessarily ordained.

The difficult question is how to assess the position of youth leaders. Are they already set apart or ordained, as their local reception and authorization is parallel to that of pastors and deacons/deaconesses?

The conclusion drawn from the 1983 rites is that life-long ministry without re-ordination is based on commitments made in the rites of ordination and setting apart. It is an effect of the *votum*, not of charismata given in ordination by means of words and the imposition of hands (Hedberg 1986, 94ff).

The texts for the setting apart of missionaries and deaconesses/deacons and for the ordination of pastors are dominated by the juridical perspective, the confirmation of the calling and the relationship to the denomination. That is also the case for the local rites of installation or acts of intercessory prayer. The juridical view of ordination has in Protestantism led to a confusion of various rites of admission into the public ministry of the Church. The differences between ordination, inauguration, installation, and so on, becomes from time to time in this system more a question of randomly applied terminology than of content, and the different churches define what ordination is and what it is not from the tasks assigned to a person in ordination, not from the ordination as such. Thus the juridical view of ordination focuses sharply on power. It does not necessarily imply that ordination conveys definable gifts of the Holy Spirit. The type of the juridical view of ordination is the public recognition of personal vocation. This idea can be found in Pietism and also in the Congregationalist, Baptist, and Pentecostal traditions. It is based on the teaching that the grace that fits a person for the ministry, is given directly by God and is recognized but not conferred or given in ordination.[12]

The strong emphasis on confirmation in the rites has a positive and a negative side. The positive side is that Christ is the identifiable agent in the vocation. The negative side is ecclesiological and is typical of nineteenth century Protestant theology: Christ is *not* the agent in the rite itself: he is not acting there through his Church and its ministries. The stress is on what Christ has done before the action of the Church takes place. Christ is not directly affecting a person in the rite but before the rite. The calling, not the rite is instrumental, whereas the rite is expressive, that is, a sign that Christ has already acted upon a person in his or her calling and that Christ has already appointed a person to a ministry, which is thus confirmed by the rite. Negatively this indicates a rejection of the transforming role of the Church in the world: positively it affirms the ongoing work of the risen Lord in the Church, though not by the Church.

The word 'samfun' ('denomination') is frequently used in the texts. One of the reasons for that is the dominant character of a rite expressing mutual obligations. From this perspective the rite is instrumental, because it imposes obligations on the persons involved. At the same time this juridical character and the character of confirmation of the personal calling to service in the church makes the differences between the rites unclear. The denomination is

---

12. The question as to whether a special gift is given in ordination or not has, however, been discussed in the Swedish Mission Covenant Church at least since the 1940s (Bjöersdorff 2001, 155ff).

central in the rites for ordination and setting apart. It is actually the subject of the rites. This underlines the juridical character and at the same time restricts the ecumenical importance of the rite. There are no references to the Church universal, and there are no claims to catholicity either for the ordination or for the setting apart.

The terms used in the 1983 rites of the Swedish Mission Covenant Church obviously intend to distinguish between various rites of admission to public ministry in the denomination. The crucial concept seems, however, to be 'setting apart'. In the ordination of pastors the term 'setting apart' still remains in the same place as in the rites for missionaries and deacons/deaconesses. The conclusion is that this interpretative expression indicates that, as rites, the rites carried out are in principle the same, whatever terms are used to designate them.

Ordination rites differ mainly in the fundamental matter of whether they are considered instrumental or expressive. The instrumental view of ordination holds that appropriate gifts of the Holy Spirit are conferred on the ordinand by prayer and the imposition of hands and that thereby the ordained person himself or herself becomes a gift to the Church for life. The expressive meaning of ordination implies that the ordination itself does not convey any specific and lifelong gifts from God: it is recognition by the church and the church's prayer for the person, without itself adding anything to baptism and the preceding personal calling.

The understanding of ordination interpreted as an instrument is reflected in the 1977 Reformed-Roman Catholic dialogue, in which it is conceived as 'a sign and effective instrument through which a person receives the gifts of the Holy Spirit for a specific office or order in the Church and through which a person becomes a gift to the Church for life. The liturgical validation at the time of the act of ordination includes the invocation of the Holy Spirit ('epiclesis') with the laying-on of hands by other ordained ministers. [...]. The laying-on of hands is an efficacious sign, which initiates and confirms the believer in the ministry conferred' (The Presence of Christ 1977, § 98).

In the response to the Faith and Order document *Baptism, Eucharist and Ministry* (1982), the Swedish Mission Covenant Church stated (1986) that it did not find 'that the ordained ministry is constitutive of the Church' (Thurian 1986, 320). The response also asserts that there is a difference between the ordination of pastors and the 'dedication' of deaconesses, deacons, missionaries and youth leaders (Thurian, 321), but 'the relationship of those who are set apart to work as deacons in the church with the ordained ministry is, however, unclear' (Thurian, 322) and will be a task for further study. Furthermore, 'The meaning of ordination is being discussed according to this line of thought:

What is it that necessitates formal ordination? Some kind of confirmation on the part of the church is necessary in order to avoid subjectivity when considering fellow workers, but what is the relationship between the functional and personal authority and the formal one? Should there be a setting apart through the laying-on of hands with prayer of those who perform temporary tasks in the local congregation? If so: 'What is the difference between such a setting apart and an ordination?' (Thurian, 322).

In the 2003 Service Book, the Swedish Mission Church ordains pastors and deacons (male and female), sets apart for special ministries and for missionary tasks, and installs pastors and deacons. In the ordination rites there is an ordination prayer and in the rites for setting apart there are intercessory prayers. The formula 'according to apostolic example' has been reformulated to 'in apostolic manner' and reserved for ordinations.

References

Bjöersdorff, Åke. 2001. *Frihet, mångfald och Enhet. En undersökning av två konflikter i en kongragtionalistisk miljö.* Lund: Teol. Lic. thesis, Faculty of Theology.

Bergsten, Torsten. 1995. *Frikyrkor i samverkan – Den svenska frikyrkoekumenikens historia 1905-1993.* Stockholm: Verbum.

Bredberg, William. 1962. *Sällskap, Samfund, Kyrka.* Stockholm: Missionsförbundet.

Brodd, Sven-Erik. 1990. Biskopsämbete och episkopé. Ett kyrkorättsligt dilemma i ekumenisk teologi. In Brodd, Sven-Erik: *Ekumeniska perspektiv. Föreläsningar,* 113-132. Uppsala: KISA Rapport 1990:4-5. Uppsala: Svenska kyrkans forskningsråd.

Eckerdal, Lars. 1985. *'Genom bön och handpåläggning'. Vignings- jämte installationshandlingar – liturgiska utvecklingslinjer.* Stockholm: LiberFörlag/Allmänna förl.

Eckerdal, Lars. 1982. *Kyrkosyn, bekännelse, liturgi.* Föredrag vid Pastorernas Riksförbunds inom Svenska Missionsförbundet årsmöte i Göteborg den 13 september 1982. Tro och liv 41: 6.

Fagerberg, Holsten. 1987. *Svenska kyrkan i ekumeniska samtal. Evangeliet som förenar.* Stockholm: Verbum.

Guds kyrka och en levande församling. Rapport från den officiella samtalsgruppen mellan Svenska kyrkan och Svenska Missionsförbundet. 1995. Stockholm: Verbum.

Gustafsson, Johan. 1944. Predikanten och hans gärning. In *Tro och gärning. Till Axel Andersson på sextiofemårsdagen.* Stockholm: Sv. missionsförb.

Handbok till den kristna församlingens tjänst. 1983. Älvsjö : Verbum.

Handbok till den kristna församlingens tjänst. 1983. Älvsjö : Verbum. 2:a rev. utgåvan.

Handbok till den kristna församlingens tjänst. 1990. Stockholm: Verbum.. Rev. Ed.

Hedberg, Gösta. 1986. *Budskapet och tjänsten.* Älvsjö : Verbum.

Hedberg, Gösta. 1986. Några liturgiska perspektiv – från slutet av 1960-talet – 1986. *Tro & Liv* 45:1, 13-23.

Hellström, Joh. 1928. Predikoämbetet. In *Tidsbilder. Svenska Missionsförbundet vid 50 år*, ed. J. Nyrén. Stockholm: SMF.

Holmgren, Christian (ed.). 1993. *Reformation pågår. Svenska Missionsförbundet bland kyrkofamiljerna.* Stockholm: Svenska missionsförb.

Konstitution. Svenska Missionsförbundet. 2002. 1. Trons grund och innehåll. En bibelteologisk inledning till konstitutionen, antagen av Svenska Missionsförbundets kyrkokonferens 2000. 2. Grundsatser, Kyrkoordning och Kyrkostadgar antagen vid General/Kyrkokonferensen 1999-2000. 3. Rekommendation till Församlingskonstitution med Församlingsordning och Församlingsstadgar antagen av Svenska Missionsförbundets kyrkokonferens 2000. In *Svenska Missionsförbundet & SMU 2002-2003. Matrikel med konstitution utgiven i augusti 2002.* Stockholm.

Kyrkohandbok för Missionskyrkan – till församlingens tjänst. 2003. Stockholm: Verbum.

Lindberg, Lars. 1994. Tjänsterna/ämbetena i Svenska Missionsförbundet. In *Kallelsen till hela Guds folk – om tjänst, tjänster och tjänande. Ett material för studier, samtal och fortsatt fördjupning från den av Sveriges Frikyrkosamråd tillsatta studiegruppen kring ledarskap och ämbete*, 94-98.

Meland, Roar. 1999. The Deacon in the Church of Norway. In The *Ministry of the Deacon. 1. Anglican – Lutheran Perspectives*, ed.Gunnel Borgegård and Christine Hall, 59-96. Nordisk Ekumenisk Skriftserie 31. Uppsala: Nordiska Ekumeniska Rådet.

Olofsgård, Olle. 1973. *Församlingen en öppen famn. Studiebok om Svenska Missionsförbundets församlingssyn.* Stockholm: Gummesson.

Onerup, Egon. 1995. *Somliga till pastorer. Om tystnadsplikt och pastoral handledning* [1994]. Stockholm; Verbum.

Onerup, Egon. 1994. Handbok blir till. Fragment ur SMF:s liturgihistoria. In *I enhetens tecken. Gudstjänsttraditioner och gudstjänstens förnyelse i svenska kyrkor och samfund*, ed. Sune Fahlgren and Rune Klingert. Örebro: Libris.

Persenius, Ragnar. 1987. *Kyrkans identitet. En studie i kyrkotänkandets profilering inom Svenska kyrkan i ekumeniskt perspektiv, 1937-1952.* Stockholm: Verbum.

Rimmerfors, Einar. 1960. Kvinnlig diakoni. In *Ansgarius. Svenska Missionsför-bundets Årsbok 55*.

Sundström, Erland. 1959. *Förbundskyrkan – nådegåva eller villfarelse*. Stockholm: Missionsförbundet.

Svenska Missionsförbundet 1984-1985. Matrikel utgiven i maj 1984. Stockholm.

Svenska Missionsförbundets årsberättelse 1989. 1990. Falköping.

The Presence of Christ in Church and World. Reformed-Roman Catholic Report 1977. In: The Secretariat for Promoting Christian Unity. Information service, No. 35, 1977/III-IV, 18-34.

Thurian, Max ed. 1986. *Churches respond to BEM, Vol. II. Official responses to the 'Baptism, Eucharist and Ministry' text*. Faith and Order Paper 132. Geneva: World Council of Churches.

Walan, Bror. 1964. *Församlingstanken i Svenska Missionsförbundet. En studie i den nyevangeliska rörelsens sprängning och Svenska Missionsförbundets utveckling till omkring 1890*. Stockholm: Gummesson.

Åberg, Göran. 1972. *Enhet och frihet. Studier i Jönköpings missionsförenings historia*. Lund [With a summary in German].

Åberg, Göran. 1980. *Sällskap – Samfund. Studier i Svenska Alliansmissionens historia fram till 1950-talets mitt*. Lund [With a summary in English].

Rites for Perpetual Commitment to Monastic and Religious Life in the Nordic Countries[1]

Else-Britt Nilsen

Religious life is fundamentally the same everywhere, whatever its confessional provenance.[2] "The call to leave everything in order to follow Jesus echoes in all the churches, and those who hear it recognise each other in the one vocation. Thus religious life is a bridge builder and mediator of unity in a divided church which seeks to find the unity for which Jesus himself prayed."[3]

The steps by which individuals dedicate themselves to God and the Church today in western religious life are the following: noviciate, temporary profession, and perpetual profession. In Orthodox monasticism there is also a period of testing and formation, during which the candidate's fitness is assessed, and he or she is evaluated as to whether they are sufficiently formed. The Byzantine

---

1. The author is indebted to Father Leon Strieder, Professor of Liturgy and Sacraments at the University of St. Thomas School of Theology, Houston, Texas, USA, for his helpful comments on this article at various stages of the research.
2. Here not to be interpreted in the wide sense of the religious life of all people, but in a more technical and limited sense as stated and described, for example, in the *Catechism of the Catholic Church*: 'The state of life which is constituted by the profession of the evangelical counsels, while not entering into the hierarchical structure of the Church, belongs undeniably to her life and holiness' (CR 914). The 'consecrated life' is also a current expression.
3. Sister Eva Dahl, in a sermon given at a profession service in Kolbu Church (Norway) on Ascension Day, 1995. Eva Dahl is prioress of the Norwegian deaconesses' community which has its Mother House in France (*Communauté des Diaconesses de Reuilly*). See her article on monastic life and the Reformation (Soeur Eva 1981). Cf. also Simon 1997.

celebration of monastic profession consists of three parts, which do not necessarily follow one after the other: the *'rasophorate'* (associated with the rite of
one who is beginning monastic life, a 'novice'), the little habit, and the great
habit. Contemporary praxis varies from one local church to another and even
from one monastery to the other.[4] In this article our point of reference for
Orthodox monasticism will be the rite of the little habit. In the Nordic countries only the little habit (or little *'schema'*) is relevant, since there are no nuns
or monks of the great habit (great *'schema'*) here.[5] For western religious it will
be the rite of perpetual profession, theologically the most distinctive and
ritually most complete (Augé 2000, 35).

Our basis for analysis will be approximately 40 different rites, collected
between 1999 and 2002.[6] Their common feature is that they are in current use
in the Nordic countries, and that their text is available in one or more of the
Nordic languages. Such public liturgies manifest and shape the relation of
these men and women to the Church and to the world.

Religious Life in the Nordic Countries

Religious life in the Nordic countries disappeared with the Protestant Reformation in the sixteenth century (Nilsen 1991; Berntson 2003). Several centuries passed before this once important part of church and social life could be

---

4. On Mount Athos today there are only *rasophoroi* and monks of the great habit. This
   means that most of the monks on Mount Athos wear the great habit (which is entirely
   different from the Russian habit). In Russia, the situation is different: The majority of
   monks are of the little habit, and only rarely of the great one. (Source of information:
   Fr. Kliment Huhtamäki, hieromonk in the Russian Parish of St Olga, Norway.)
5. New Valamo and Lintula in Finland adhere to the Russian tradition, and Swedish
   monks receive the tonsure either in Finland or Serbia: the pure Greek or Byzantine
   tradition is not represented in the Nordic countries.
6. These will be our 'primary sources' and are enumerated at the end of this article at
   Appendix 1. Because we have confined this study to perpetual vows, it does not include
   convent-like communities whose members take vows for a limited period of time, as in
   the Swedish Pentecostal Brotherhood, *'Bröderna på Bjärka Säby'*. We regret deeply,
   however, that we have not received the rite of the largest Protestant religious order in the
   Nordic countries, the 'Daughers of Mary' in 'Mariavägen', with communities in Sweden, Denmark, Finland and Germany. This order was founded by the charismatic
   Paulina Mariadotter, who even after her death continues to dominate the ideology and
   practice of her sisterhoods (Laghé 2004). The Little Sisters of Jesus living in a small
   community in Greenland made their profession long ago in Rome; the Franciscan
   Missionary Sisters working in the Faeroe Islands and Iceland make their profession in
   Ireland.

re-established (*Stati del Nord-Europa* 1997; Malchau & Nilsen 2004). In Finland we find the oldest monastery in the Nordic countries, the Orthodox New Valamo Monastery, and Lintula monastery for women a few miles away. After a long period of exile and difficulties, tensions and decline, associated with the changing political conditions in the country, the Orthodox monastic tradition of today is seen as viable, lively and a valuable part of the national culture. In addition to the above mentioned Finnish Orthodox monasteries, there are also a few other small communities in the Nordic countries.[7]

From the middle of the nineteenth century, when civil law opened up opportunities for greater religious liberty, Catholic parishes were re-established in the different Nordic countries, but greater religious freedom did not mean an automatic 'green light' for the foundation of religious houses. In Sweden, the re-establishment of Catholic religious communities was camouflaged as 'convalescent homes' and 'guest houses' (Werner 2002, 10). Contemplative monasteries were founded after 1952, when the law against the foundation of monasteries was abrogated. In Norway, Jesuits were explicitly banned from the country by the Constitution. The so-called 'Jesuit' paragraph was not repealed until 1956. In Denmark, however, there were no such restrictions and Catholic religious life flourished from the early twentieth century.

Within or close to the Lutheran Church of Sweden, some communities – chiefly female – were founded in the 1940s. Most of them remained small and some of them died out. A few of the earlier ones have been successfully adapted to Catholic traditions; some have joined the Catholic Church. The Church of Sweden recognises at present eight religious communities, six of them for women.[8] The Finnish and Norwegian Churches have officially recognised one religious community in each country. Their sources of inspiration seem different from the Swedish ones. This is partly attributable to the relative weakness of the High Church movement and the relative strength of Low Church groups in the Finnish and Norwegian Churches (Sundback 2001, 9; Thorkildsen 1997).

Life dedicated to God by the bonds of religious life has always held a place

---

7. For example, in Norway a '*skita*' with two monks under the Paris exarchate; in Sweden a Serbian Orthodox community of monks, and a small convent ('*metochion*') for nuns belonging to the Old Calendarist Orthodox Church of Greece.

8. Bidalite, a Swedish Free Church community of religious sisters defined itself outside our study by the following response to our inquiry: 'We have no rites and no special ceremony. We just try to do what God says'. Here we face a similar type of challenge as with the 'spontaneous', non-written ordination rites of the Pentecostal churches.

of honour both in the Orthodox and the Catholic Church. From the earliest centuries they have surrounded the act of religious profession with liturgical rites and raised religious life to the rank of a canonical state. This is clearly different from the situation in the Protestant churches. In a statement of 17th January 1960, the Bishops' Conference of the Church of Sweden officially recognised the monasteries that have emerged in their church. The Bishops' Conference of the Norwegian Church issued a similar statement as late as 1991: 'Religious communities may seem alien to our religious practice, but the Bishops' Conference sees the importance of religious communities in an Evangelical context'.[9] The Finnish bishops have also discussed this question. Unofficially they have said that 'community life in the form of monastic life is an organic part of the life of the Church, and the bishop in whose territory such groups are found is the Church's representative in relation to a community of this type'.[10] The presence of religious life seems to offer a chance for the Lutheran Churches to undergo changes contradicting the tendency of passive adjustment to the secularisation process (Sundback 2001, 11).

This presentation of the recent history of religious life in the Nordic countries is by no means complete, but will show that men and women, independently of their different religious traditions, have followed and follow a common vocation. Today, religious communities in the Nordic countries comprise approximately 900 men and women. The great majority of religious are Catholic, as they have been in the past.[11]

A Standard Outline of the Structure of Perpetual Profession

There is an evident methodological challenge in handling a material as comprehensive as that which is presented here, comprising not only a multitude of religious communities with various ecclesiastical traditions, but also a multitude of languages, ranging from Danish through Finnish, Icelandic, Norwegian and Swedish. We shall use the standard outline of the structure of perpetual profession as presented in the *Ordo Professionis Religiosae* of 1970

---

9. *Vårt Land,* 23.03.1991.
10. From a statement made by Archbishop John Vikström during a visitation to Nådendal Parish, as recorded in the parish protocol of 15-17 January 1993. (Source of information: Susan Sundback 04.02.2002.)
11. In addition there are persons who are attached to a religious community or religious family without making the traditional religious profession, but who make a perpetual vow to live according to the spirit of their community, e.g. as an oblate or lay member.

(OPR).[12] The OPR results from the documents of the Second Vatican Council, which called for the creation of a rite that would foster greater sobriety and dignity and re-establish a basic unity in this area (SC 80). The proliferation of religious institutes, and the lack of liturgical order within the Catholic Church, had caused a slow deterioration in the rite of profession, especially in rites composed in the twentieth century. The simplicity of earlier times was gradually lost, with a parallel increase in ascetic subjectivism and spiritual legalism (Augé 2000, 324, Raffin 1970, 152).

We may well ask whether the use of a *Catholic* document as our point of departure will give our analysis a confessional bias from the outset. Generally, we regard the liturgical renewal in the western family of churches as a common effort which has brought us closer, rather than as a movement which has strengthened confessional frontlines (Martola 2001, 10-26). We assert that the OPR represents a positive contribution to this process.[13]

Religious life is not a uniform reality, but one that is marked by a variety of charisms. The OPR respects this variety when it points out that: 'The norms governing the rite of initiation are not of obligation unless this is clearly stated ... Religious families should adapt the rite so that it more closely reflects and manifests the character and spirit of each institute' (12; 14). This means that it presents no obstacles, but is rather a tool to be employed by the different religious families as they see fit. It is our opinion that the open character of the OPR makes it a suitable tool for assessing other rites of profession within other ecclesiastical traditions.

The rite of perpetual profession should take place within the context of the Eucharist, and the following structural elements are indicated (OPR Intr. No. 6):

Introductory Rites
Liturgy of the Word
Religious Profession
    a – Calling or Request
    b – Homily or Address
    c – Examination/Scrutiny
    d – Litany

---

12. In fact we here refer to the revised edition of the text, 'The Rite of Religious Profession' published in *The Rites of the Catholic Church as Revised by the Second Vatican Ecumenical Council*, vol. 2. 1991.
13. This obviously does not preclude criticism of the document.

e – Profession
f – Solemn Blessing or Consecration of the Professed
g – Presentation of the Insignia of Profession
h – Statement of Admission or Sign of Peace
Liturgy of the Eucharist
Concluding Rite
Solemn Blessing

The rites will be compared on the basis of the above structure, either separately, or more often, in categories, though not all elements are clearly present in every rite. They will primarily be analysed as they are presented in the liturgical texts in the various pamphlets or orders of service especially drawn up for the occasion, or as they appear in liturgical prescriptions proper for a religious family or order. Several synopses of texts have been worked out in order to substantiate this work. Information on the practice of the rites will be included where these are available, since 'liturgy is enacted by real people, in concrete situations' (Foley 1989, 73-90).

Titles, Terminology and Language

In the decree presenting the OPR, the Sacred Congregation for Divine Worship leaves it to the conferences of bishops 'to see to the careful vernacular translations of the rite' (Prot.n.200/70). This seems to us to be a significant matter. For example: How do we translate the term 'perpetual profession' within a Nordic linguistic context? Of course different terminologies are used. What is common to the Catholic rites is the term 'perpetual vows',[14] or the term 'perpetual profession' – somewhat artificially construed for the occasion in Nordic terms. This, however, is used indiscriminately across national and linguistic borders. There is a greater need to conform to the original term when the term 'perpetual' vows is replaced by 'solemn' vows according to legislation proper to some monastic families and ancient orders.

In Protestant religious communities the terminology is less clear. The Norwegian deaconesses' community uses the term 'consecration to monastic life',[15] while the Swedish Sisters of the Holy Spirit prefer the laborious term 'great

---

14. *'Evige løfter'* in Danish and Norwegian; in Swedish *'eviga löften'*, in Finnish *'ikuiset lupaukset'*.
15. In Norwegian *'vigsling til klosterliv'*.

profession with final vows'.[16] The Benedictine brothers of the Östanbäck community (Church of Sweden) use both 'solemn profession' and 'monks' consecration' – or 'monastic consecration'.[17] The term 'consecration' of monks and nuns is also found in the Orthodox rites, though the term 'receiving the tonsure' is more in accordance with tradition.[18]

A complete linguistic review of the rites in their totality is outside the scope of this article, but we should like to point out our impression that some of the Catholic rites do not correspond entirely to the recommendation of the 'careful vernacular translation' mentioned above.[19]

In approaching these texts, some of very ancient origin, it is important to keep in mind that the rites are more often expressions in poetic and prophetic language rather than statements of carefully circumscribed legal obligations. 'They are something a person grows into, realities whose significance changes and unfolds as a person matures, and whose understanding is affected by changing cultural conditions over time' (Schneiders 2001, 105).

Context – Participants – Symbols

The profession is a central rite, which comes after the Liturgy of the Word within the context of the Eucharist. The dual instruction in the OPR says; 'The rites should take place on a Sunday or another significant feast, and the faithful should be well informed of the time so that they can attend in greater number' (OPR I: 40, 42; II: 43, 45). The perspective is Catholic, but it is unequivocally echoed in the Protestant rites as well. The level of festivity and publicity has no counterpart in the other rites of profession. In Orthodox

---

16. In Swedish *'stora professen med finalt löfte'*.
17. In Swedish *'högtidlig profess'* and *'munkvigning'*.
18. In the Finnish Orthodox rite, the verb *'vihkiä'* is used. But it is reasonable to assume that the idea of 'consecration' (*'vielse'*) has arrived through translation into the local language. In Russian, the term 'tonsuring of monks' (*'monasheskij postrig'*), is used about 'being tonsured' (*'postrigatsja'*) and 'to tonsure' (*'postrigat'*). It should be possible to translate the Greek word *'koura'* as 'being tonsured'. In the Orthodox rite, the 'tonsuring' itself is the most important element. We may assume that it is expressed in words as well.
19. Prof. Gunnel Vallquist, a member of the Swedish Academy, has pointed out serious shortcomings here after analyzing the collected rites for profession in the Swedish language (Vallquist in a letter to the author 22.04.2002).

monasticism the Divine Liturgy is not – as we shall see further on – always the context of profession or tonsuring.[20]

Is the setting a parish church or a convent chapel? In many cases the profession of vows takes place in chapels or churches belonging to the relevant community or religious family. In female monastic ('contemplative') orders this is always the case, even if exceptions are possible during the founding phase of a new community. In 'clerical' orders, parish church and convent chapel may be identical. When a parish church is preferred to a convent chapel, questions of space and greater public participation of course may play a role.

When the ceremony takes place on a Sunday or another significant feast day, the choice of Scripture readings is given in advance. In a Nordic Catholic setting, where there is usually a significant public turnout for such occasions, it is not unusual for the ceremony to take place on a Saturday, so that the Mass for the Day of Perpetual Profession may be used. In such cases there is great liberty in the choice of Scripture readings.[21]

Who are the *main* participants apart from the person who is going to make his or her profession? They are the local bishop (or another priest) and the superior receiving the vows. In addition there are many different ministries in the liturgy open for additional contributors: the call, the sermon, the readings, songs and music. In rites of profession, a certain ministerial balance is desirable, but not always evident. Some Catholic rites of vows for women show that the reception or witnessing of the vows is the superior's only role.[22] This is at the very centre of the celebration, but risks being drowned out if there is a concelebrated Mass as well. This is less frequent during the religious profession for men, as the superior is often a priest who also participates in the celebration of the Eucharist.

Whilst in the Catholic Church the participation of the local bishop is the exception rather than the rule during the profession ceremonies in male religious communities, the opposite is the case in the two male religious com-

---

20. In New Valamo the monastic rites are public, but in Lintula only the sisters of the community and some of the monks (priests and brothers) from New Valamo will be present.
21. The OPR gives numerous suggestions, but other texts are frequently chosen. Our material is limited, but suggests that the candidates prefer their 'favourite' text. Both men and women often choose John 15.9-17.
22. Sr. Madeleine Fredell, Vice-Provincial of the Roman Dominican Sisters (CRSD) in Sweden, informs us that the sisters have consciously toned down the roles both of the clergy and the bishop.

munities in the Church of Sweden. In one or two of the rites for Lutheran women religious the bishop is not mentioned, but they mention 'the priest' or 'the father confessor'.[23] According to the rubrics of the Orthodox rites, the bishop or the *hegumen* (when he is a priest),[24] assisted by a deacon, presides at the monastic rites of the monks, while the chaplain or the local bishop has the same function at the same rites for nuns. In Finland it is traditionally the *hegumen* who tonsures the monks of New Valamo whilst the local bishop[25] has presided at all these ceremonies for the nuns in Lintula, and this is becoming more and more the custom also for the monks of New Valamo.

Both in Catholic and Protestant celebrations the act of profession usually takes place in the sanctuary, with the candidate kneeling before the person designated to receive the vows, seated in front of the altar or in another suitable part of the sanctuary. In Orthodox celebrations we find approximately the same disposition, in the church in front of the Holy Doors (between the choir and the sanctuary).

What are the symbols or insignia associated with the profession ceremony? Insignia, such as a ring or a cross, are often connected to the profession of women religious, whether Protestant or Catholic. In our material there are no similar insignia in men's rites. An exception is Orthodox monks. A (usually black) veil may also be given to women religious (Lambin 2001, 189). If we extend the question of insignia to include the religious habit, there will be a slightly different and more complex landscape. This will be one of the issues examined in the next section.

Rites of Profession in Different Traditions

It might be opportune to point out that the word 'tradition' in our context does not have any special confessional connotation. It is a well-known fact that in the Catholic Church there are several monastic families with their particular traditions. It would be wrong to exclude possible spill-over effects from the Catholic or Orthodox Churches with their unbroken traditions of religious life to the rites in newer Protestant communities. Here we shall simply look at the existing rites or groups of rites in a chronological perspective. 'Religious life is not a univocal or uniform reality but one that is marked by a variety of

---

23. The Sisters of the Holy Spirit and the Sisters of Mary Magdalene.
24. The bishop may delegate authority to another priest-monk. (Only monks may tonsure others to be monks/nuns).
25. The Archbishop of the Diocese of Karelia

charisms' (Augé 2000, 315). Our approach is chronological, while the reality shows both divergence and complexity.

A common feature of religious professions in the eastern tradition is the character of the celebration. The most important moments are the giving of the tonsure and the clothing, without concentrating on the pronunciation of the vows, as the indispensable core of the profession, an emphasis which happens so often in the West (Raffin 1992, 181).[26] The rites and ceremonies are very rich and expressive in mystical meaning (Robinson 1916, 55).

The rite of *the little habit* in the Byzantine church family[27] may be celebrated during the Divine Liturgy, but this is not necessarily the case.[28] The candidate remains in the narthex of the church until the Little Entrance and the singing of the *troparia*, then is led into the church and stands before the Holy Doors (barefoot, head uncovered, wearing only a simple tunic). The *hegumen* of the monastery (the bishop or chaplain/priest in the case of a community of nuns) gives a preliminary instruction to the candidate then asks a series of distinct and definite questions regarding stability, chastity, obedience, and poverty. The 'vows' are four in number and taken merely by the candidates answering these formal questions.[29] Though the vows are formal

---

26. This view is however strongly contested by the former Archbishop of the Finnish-Orthodox Church, Fr. Johannes Rinne: 'There is no reason to devalue the significance of religious vows in the Orthodox context in this way. Even at my own monastic consecration in the monastery of St. John on Patmos, the *hegumen* emphasised their significance' (Fr. Johannes Rinne in a letter to Gunnel Borgegård 16.11.2003). The two monastic states of the little and the great habit do not correspond to western temporary and perpetual profession. At each stage the monk is fully a monk, so that he may well remain at the first or the second stage without aspiring to reach the following (Raffin 1992, 30, 37, Nin 2000, 308).

27. We actually have two typewritten rites from this family; one in Finnish (New Valamo/ Lintula), the other in Swedish. The two rites are quite similar without being identical. (These rites for monastic profession seem to be very close to the Roman edition of the *Euchologion* 1873) Fr. Johannes Rinne comments: 'The Orthodox Church in Finland has no definite official rite for the consecration of monks and nuns, and thus no written rite. My predecessor, Archbishop Paavali, used a typewritten translation from Russian sources, while I used a translation from Greek'. It is well worth noting that the Eastern Churches do not divide religious life into different monastic orders or congregations. All who are living the monastic life are regarded as members of a great monastic brotherhood of asceticism (Robinson 1916, 1).

28. In Russia it is common to give the tonsure at night, after Vespers or the Vigil, but it may also take place during the Liturgy. Various local traditions are in use.

29. Since the tonsuring is what makes a monk a monk, and a nun a nun, it is imprecise to place these 'vows' on a par with the vows in the western monastic tradition. It is

and explicit, there is no written formula of profession to be signed by the candidates at their admission.

Then the *hegumen* (or bishop or priest) gives the candidates a second instruction, recalling that to which they are committing themselves. This is succeeded by a series of prayers and the tonsuring, in which the candidates' hair is cut in the form of a cross and they are given a new name. Then the newly professed receive the various parts of the monastic habit with a spiritual elucidation.[30] At the end the new monk/nun is given a lighted candle, with the words: 'Let your light so shine before men that they may see your good deeds and glorify your Father in Heaven'. The rite of profession concludes when the newly professed receives his/her brothers'/sisters' greetings of peace.[31]

In Finland the rite of the little habit is not celebrated during the Divine Liturgy but usually in the evening during the Great Vespers or all-night vigil. The nun or monk comes to the church at the end of the service after the Great Doxology. Following the profession they will stay the whole night in the church.[32] In the morning the newly professed receives the blessing from the *hegumen*, bishop or priest and attends the Divine Liturgy with the reception of the Holy Communion.[33]

In the rites of the Benedictine monastic family, the oldest in the western tradition to survive into modern times, we observe a different way of taking the vows. Not only does the candidate read the profession formula, promising stability, conversion of life and obedience, but s/he also signs this written formula on the altar. That is why it is called '*professio super altare*'. 'Profession is the offering of oneself in the one sacrifice of Christ and the Church' (Augé

---

rather a question of a form of examination before the tonsuring, to ascertain whether the candidate is a free agent as regards the forthcoming rite, and whether s/he understands what kind of life is expected of a monk or nun. When the candidate answers: 'Yes, with the help of God, I want to be obedient, live in purity/poverty, etc...' s/he confirms his/her desire to be received into the monastic community through the tonsuring.

30. These are the scapular (a small square piece of cloth with embroidered representations of the instruments of the passion), tunic, belt, *mandyas* (a flowing cloak without a hood, which reaches to the ground in long narrow pleats), *klobuk* (cylindrical hat and veil), sandals, chaplet, and a small pectoral cross.

31. When the Divine Liturgy is not celebrated, a litany and a series of prayers are added to the ceremony, in which case the scriptural readings are Eph 6.10-17, Matt. 10.37-38, 11.28-30.

32. In Finland the rite for the *rasophorate* is always celebrated in church during the Divine Liturgy.

33. Source of information: Mother Igumenia Marina, Lintula.

2000, 319).[34] This act is followed by the singing the 'Suscipe' three times: 'Receive me, O Lord as you have promised...' by the newly professed. The solemn prayer of monastic consecration comes afterwards; it is a long prayer addressed to the Father, the Son and the Holy Spirit. Then follows the clothing: the monastic cowl, supplemented with the black veil for women religious.

Characteristic of the *mendicant* orders (Dominicans, Franciscans, and Carmelites) is the gesture known as '*professio in manibus*': The candidate kneels before the superior, places his/her hands in those of the superior and reads the profession formula. This act expresses the nature of profession as a contract between the religious and the community that receives them.[35] But in these rites we do not only observe a difference in the very act of profession. There is also a shift in content: the Franciscan and Carmelite formulae of profession explicitly mention the so-called evangelical counsels of poverty, chastity and obedience[36] (corresponding to the Benedictine triad of stability, conversion of life, and obedience), while the Dominicans explicitly mention only obedience.

The Jesuits' rite, the so-called '*professio super hostiam*' is different again from the preceding monastic and mendicant traditions. The profession takes place during the eucharistic celebration, before the reception of Communion, while the priest is holding up the consecrated bread. The candidate reads aloud the profession formula and then receives Communion. The ceremony is public, and the vows are pronounced in the presence of the superior, who accepts them (Augé 2000, 322). Suárez, an early Jesuit theologian, has shown the theological meaning of this very simple rite: profession is made into the hands

---

34. The Benedictine promise is supposed to have assumed the interrogative form of the '*stipulatio*'of Roman law (an oral contract with a number of applications). When it was completed, after it had been written out with all its clauses, it was read by the future stipulator to the future promiser and ended with the question: '*Ea quae supra scripta sunt, promittis?*', to which the promiser replied: '*Promitto*' (Augé 2000, 315).

35. The '*immixtio manuum*' was in the tenth and eleventh centuries the most important symbolic gesture of the feudal contract. When the '*iunior*', or vassal, entered into the service of the '*senior*', or lord, of the region, entrusting himself to the latter's protection, he would kneel, place his hands in those of the lord '*immixtio manuum*', and promise him fealty. The '*senior*', as sign of acceptance, would give the vassal the kiss of peace ('*osculum*') (Augé 2000, 320-321).

36. This formula also appears for the first time in the middle of the twelfth century at the Abbey of St. Geneviève in Paris. During the thirteenth century most religious orders followed the example of the Franciscans, even those that had been founded earlier. Thus the three vows came later to constitute the essential element of religious profession.

of Christ himself, rather than into those of the prelate.[37] And Christ, by giving himself, promises to help the professed to remain faithful and accord him the pledge of a special reward. Suárez also points out that since the Eucharist is the 'consummation and perfection of all that is sacred', Communion should be seen as the 'completion of profession'.[38]

Obviously, each type of profession represents clearly defined cultural and spiritual milieus not impervious to change over time (Strieder 2001).[39] Our material shows how the different rites continue to inspire each other today.

The Benedictine branch of monastic life is present in our research thanks to rites from five Benedictine communities and one Cistercian.[40] They all include the early *'professio super altare'*, and some add *'professio in manibus'*. In Sweden the two Catholic female communities exemplify this in different ways: in the first case (Mariavall) a promise of stability, conversion and obedience is made publicly *'in manibus'* of the superior at the end of the 'examination', before the litany and the reading of the hand-written formula. In the second case (Maria-döttrarna) there is an even closer fusion of these two ways since the candidate kneeling and *'in manibus'* of the superior reads her hand-written formula and signs it before rising and putting it on the altar. The Cistercian nuns in Denmark (Maria Hjerte) represent a third modality including a public promise of obedience to the abbess just before the reading of the formula.

It would be wrong to say that *'professio in manibus'* is alien to the Benedic-

---

37. Francisco Suárez (1548-1617) is usually considered the greatest theologian of the Society of Jesus.

38. F. Suárez, *De Religione Societatis Jesu*, book 6, chap. 5, 9-12, *Opera omnia*, t. 16: ed. C. Berton (Paris, 1860), 868-870. Here as summarised by Augé 2000, 323. The origin of *'professio super hostiam'* probably goes a long way back. As early as the third century the schismatic Novatian, before giving communion to his followers, required from them an oath of fidelity (Eusebius, *The History of the Church*, 6, 43.18). For a short time in the high Middle Ages even the Friars Minor pronounced the vows immediately before the reception of Communion (Augé 2000, 323).

39. The development of the many stages in the commitment to religious life is making this extremely intricate. Until the last two decades in the Dominican order, the important act was the clothing as a novice, not the perpetual profession. And even today the clothing in this order contains elements from the rite of profession. (Source of information: Fr. Simon Tugwell OP, Rome, Oct. 2001.)

40. The Birgittine Nuns of Vadstena use the Rite of Profession as it was given originally by Saint Birgitta except for one important modification: 'We have divided up the rite originally made by the sisters in *one single act*, to correspond to the actual stages of religious life'. (Source of information: Sr. M. Karin O.Ss.S.)

tine tradition since it probably dates from the Cluny reform (Strieder 2001, 63), but as it is practised today, it risks obscuring the rite of profession.[41]

Some rites collected from orders belonging to the *mendicant* tradition also include elements of '*professio super altare*'; the Carmelites (both friars and nuns) as well as the Conventual Franciscans include the signing of the profession document and its placement on the altar as part of the rite. However, this is not a double track like the examples taken from actual Benedictine rites. These modern variants (often with the addition of the Litany of the Saints) might be interpreted as an enrichment of the traditional rite,[42] or more negatively as a complication of what it used to be.[43]

Most rites, even those without a direct and unbroken line to the old monastic rites, contain one or several elements from these old traditions. For example we find the act '*professio in manibus*', which is a mendicant tradition, repeated in a new rite such as that of the Little Sisters of Jesus. In the rite of the Protestant deaconesses' community in Norway, we find the same expression as in the ancient Benedictine rite: '*Suscipe me...*' On the other hand in Catholic and Orthodox communities, we do not find the imposition of hands that occurs occasionally in Protestant communities.

Influenced and inspired by the Jesuits, the '*professio super hostiam*' became prevalent in many modern congregations, especially women's. However, the Sacred Congregation of Rites has not, over time, appreciated this develop-

---

41. According to the rites of profession from Vor Frue and Sankt Lioba (both Denmark), and from Östanbäck (Sweden), the vows are recited with the sister/brother simply standing and reading the formula, and then signing it on the altar. This does not necessarily exclude a promise of obedience '*in manibus*' of the superior a few days before or on the same day, before the public ceremony. However there is a tendency today to cut out this supplement to the public act, e.g. in some Cistercian communities in France. It seems meaningless to double up the promise of obedience.
42. Perhaps this is especially relevant for religious (the great majority are of course women) who are not going to be ordained later on. As one Norwegian Cistercian nun comments on the Litany of the Saints: 'By adding this litany (to the rite), we make our commitment, strengthened not only by the prayers of our Sisters but also by the prayers of all the Saints. We need nothing less' (Sr. Ina Andresen, OCSO, Tautra). The Litany of the Saints is included in all Catholic ordinations of deacons, priests, and bishops.
43. This negative aspect has been emphasised by Simon Tugwell *à propos* the Dominican profession originally not located in the Mass or even the church, but in the Chapter Room (Tugwell 1983).

ment.[44] The OPR makes no exception and urges the institutes (religious orders and congregations) using such a rite to discontinue it on the grounds that '...the rite of profession before the Blessed Sacrament, prior to receiving Communion, is not in harmony with good liturgical sense' (OPR, no. 15). This appeal might explain the absence of a *professio super hostiam* in our material, except for the Jesuits.[45] However, there are defenders also outside the ranks of this tradition claiming that the OPR is in danger of reducing all religious vows to the pattern of neo-baptismal *conversio morum*, forgetting the eucharistic and missionary dynamism of profession *super hostiam* (Hausman 1988).

Instead of joining this discussion, we shall re-consider the theological meaning of this rite. Suárez brought our attention to the christocentric character of the Society of Jesus and, by doing so, to its distinguishing feature. And even today when a Jesuit is asked about the 'meaning' of his profession, the answer might be astonishingly simple: 'The newly professed is the companion of Christ'.[46] Actually the Jesuit rite is an exception preventing us from seeing mission and profession too narrowly.

Before concluding this section, we shall also mention a particular and very old tradition: the consecration of virgins. In our material we find this phenomenon even within certain monastic communities. In the liturgy, *Ordo Consecrationis Virginum* is officially approved by the Catholic Church as it states (4b): 'In the case of nuns, it (Consecration of virgins) requires that they have made their final profession, either in the same rite or on an earlier occasion'.[47] The revision of this rite (SC 80) intended it to be a sign of sanctification and service to the Church (SC 37-40) and to preserve the solemnity of the celebration.

Another objective was to strip it of extravagance and omit elements not adapted to our times, particularly those that could be seen as 'downgrading' matrimony. The rite was scripturally enriched, and some prayer texts were restored to their original form, keeping its authentic meaning as the celebration of a marriage between Christ and the consecrated virgin. The minister for

---

44. The taking of vows before the host prior to the reception of Communion was forbidden by the Sacred Congregation of Rites several times during the nineteenth century with reference to their earlier refusal of 1677 (Augé 2000, 324).
45. Pope Gregory XIII approved this practice of the Society of Jesus (Ravasi 1968).
46. Fr. Ulf Jonsson, SJ (Uppsala) in conversation with the author (Oslo 16.11.2002).
47. *Ordo Consecrationis Virginum*, Libreria Editrice Vaticana 1978. From Denmark we have the rite for this consecration given to women living in the world.

consecration is the local bishop, emphasising the relationship between the virgin and the local Church. He establishes the conditions under which she is to undertake a life of perpetual virginity. There is no mention of delegation to a priest, as both tradition and the fullness of the sign require the presence of the bishop, who represents Christ.[48]

Theological Content of the Rites of Profession

The fundamental consecration is that of *baptism* (LG 42). Any other type of consecration can be understood only on the basis of this, and, by analogy, in relation to it (PC 5). This ancient bond is confirmed in the Orthodox rite of the little habit[49] where the allusions to baptism are manifold: the candidate at a monastic profession, a penitent like the candidate for baptism, is presented as for a second baptism, clothed only in a tunic, in the narthex as if going to be baptised by immersion. This is to signify that s/he is to put off the old man and put on the new.[50] The penitent is likened to the prodigal son in the gospel, and the *hegumen* (bishop or priest in the case of a nun) standing and waiting before the doors leading to the sanctuary, symbolises the father of the household. The profession rite of the Benedictine community in the Church of Sweden presents similar perspectives. During the examination the father of the community asks the candidate: 'Do you renounce the devil, the world and your own flesh?'

Though there are parallelisms between initiation into the Christian community and initiation into religious life, it is also true that these are quite different phenomena. 'The former, which can properly be called ecclesial

---

48. The rite of consecration of Virgins can to a certain extent be seen as a female counterpart of the priestly ministry. The minister of the rite is always the bishop who is the local Ordinary. The structure of the rite is very close to the rite for ordination of a priest. The laying-on of hands is substituted by a simple '*Castitatis propositi renovatio*', ('renewal of intention') at the hands of the bishop. The prayers of consecration differ as well as the scriptural readings. Where the priest is vested with stole and chasuble, the virgin receives the insignia of consecration; veil, ring (spousal signs) and the Book of Hours (ecclesial sign). (In the Danish rite, 'women living in the world' are not given the veil.)
49. As well as in the rite of the great habit (but less pronounced in the rite of the *rasophorate*).
50. To this we might add: the vows are taken, as at baptism, in answer to formal and explicit questions. A new name is given. The monastic tonsure is made in the name of the Father, Son and Holy Spirit; the new monastic habit may be compared to baptismal garments. The cross, the lighted candle and the kiss correspond to those given at baptism (Robinson 1916, 57-58).

initiation, is the foundational and definitive act of entry into the whole of the Christian mystery... Initiation into a religious community, on the other hand, is a specifying process that concretely defines a context for living out this baptismal commitment in poverty, chastity and obedience' (Foley 1989, 4, cf. Boisvert 1988). In the rites of the Carmelites the bond between baptism and religious vows is explicit: 'Dear brother/sister; at your baptism you died to sin and were sanctified in God. Do you now want to unite yourself to him more intimately through these solemn vows?'

Or it may be articulated as in the rite of the Norwegian deaconesses' community: 'In baptism we were incorporated into God's people and we were all consecrated to be servants before God. For the Scriptures witness that the whole of God's people are a royal priesthood, a holy people... Today this fellow-worker wishes to dedicate her life to Christ in order to live her baptismal life committed to a common life of prayer, praise and service within the framework of a religious community'.[51]

The term 'fellow-worker' might be a little surprising, but this part of the rite has been identical with the presentation of candidates going to be ordained priest, catechist or deacon in the Church of Norway until now. It is remarkable that the candidate for profession is also presented 'as a new worker in our church'. In terms somewhat unusual within the context of religious vows, this expresses an essential point: Religious are baptised Christians who are given a special service in the *ecclesial* community. As the Second Vatican Council reminded us, consecration to God's service leads to service of the Church (PC 5). Religious life is an eminently ecclesial life.

In this context it is useful to stress a fundamental difference made in recent Catholic theology between ordained ministry and religious life: the ordained ministry is not a state or a status, but rather a functional service in the Church (Legrand 1993, 267). Ordination is not a re-enforcement of the holiness received in baptism, but a gift of the Holy Spirit, a charge to build up the Church and a power to fulfil this task. Religious profession on the other hand joins itself to the baptismal consecration and completes it, being a personal response to the fundamental demand of baptism i.e. to offer one's life to God.

---

51. Fellow-worker translated from the Norwegian: '*medarbeider*'. When we read later in the same paragraph: 'Give her your Holy Spirit and cleanse her from all impurities of body and soul, that she may be worthy to fulfil the task you have given her', it is clear that this rite contains elements that are easily associated with baptism.

This commitment is further realised in a plan structured on the relation to God and the service of the Kingdom (Boisvert 1988, 93).[52]

The Church itself initiates the call to this relationship, and it is none other than the Church itself that receives the vows of those who make profession.[53] In the rite of the Conventual Franciscans, the guardian calls the candidate by name and asks: 'My dear brother, what do you ask of God and his Church?' In response the candidate answers: '... to follow the teachings of Our Lord Jesus Christ and to walk in his footsteps until I die ... ', to which the community responds: 'Thanks be to God'. The introduction made to the Litany of the Saints underlines that no one but God has called the candidate '*to follow Christ* in evangelical perfection'. Thus it is not only the blessing of the Church and the support of the community which is invoked, but the very grace of God.[54]

Every form of religious life is ordered to the following of Christ – the '*sequela Christi*'.[55] Each particular heritage, each community must be in harmony with this central call to the imitation of Christ. As Foley points out, this christological focus has important ritual consequences for perpetual profession as well as for its context within the Eucharistic celebration. 'As the Eucharist is the central sacramental act of the Church, and in its essence is an act of Christ, so does the Eucharist present itself as the paradigmatic context for religious profession' (Foley 1989, 53-69). The sacrifice of oneself, expressed by the religious in his or her profession, is an inner and personal sharing in the sacrifice of Christ. Profession is the offering of oneself in the one sacrifice of Christ and the Church (Augé 2000, 319).

The candidate does not only answer to a call from God, but engages in the

---

52. Paul VI, *Magno gaudio. La Documentation catholique* 1964, 690. It is important to note that a non-ordained monk (or nun) does not belong to the hierarchical structure of the Church.

53. According to present Church law, 'by religious profession members assume by public vow the observance of the three evangelical counsels, are consecrated to God through the ministry of the Church and are incorporated into the institute with rights and duties defined by law' (CIC, can. 654).

54. Actually all these rites of profession are characterised by continuous petitions for grace for the candidates. The observation here is in full accordance with Foley's for the OPR.

55. To follow Christ and become his disciple is a project which concerns everybody (John. 10.4-16, Matt. 28.18-20). Thus, religious life is *a* following of Christ. In religious life one obviously follows Christ, as all his other disciples do, by accepting the basic values which he proclaimed. One follows him, however, above all by choosing some radical activities which amount to a religious 'profession' or a definite 'state' (*De Candido* 2001, 1163).

service of the Church. Even those living secluded lives cannot be separated from its welfare. Profession is an acceptance of the Church's mission to live the gospel in service to others. This is clearly stated in the examination of the Little Sisters of Jesus. One of the questions asked of the candidate is the following: 'Do you wish to engage your whole life in searching for a greater human understanding across all borders, religions, races, social differences, ages and our many different individual differences?' Such a precision is unusual in our material, but the principle is preserved. The forms of service are manifold, and the rites express some of them: 'May his life build up the Church, advance the salvation of the world and stand as a sign of the blessings that are to come'.[56]

The Eschatological Perspective of the Rites of Profession

Religious life is essentially a prophetic vocation, as pointed out by Sandra Schneiders: 'By profession the religious enters into an alternative world whose co-ordinates are pointed towards (not defined) by the vows. The three vows bear on the three fundamental co-ordinates of human experience: sexuality and relationships; material goods and ownership; freedom and power. In regard to each of these co-ordinates, or spheres of human life and endeavour, the religious takes an alternative stance that both announces and effects an approach that calls into question the oppressive arrangements of the status quo' (Schneiders 2001, 109).

The many rites with nuptial allusions are poetic expressions of the eschatological dimension of religious life, but are not devoid of theological meaning. The theological content is rich: The nuptial perspective can be understood in a collective sense (the Church as the bride of Christ)[57] or in an individual sense (the candidate as the bride of Christ). However, virginity for the Kingdom of God as a *mysterium* nevertheless cannot be explained by reason, but only through faith (Emsley 2000, 339). The virgin renounces the sexual element in marriage but seeks to achieve what marriage signifies. The plan of the Father is to unite the virgin with Christ as *'sponsa Christi'*.

This becomes clear when the bishop asks: 'Are you resolved to accept solemn consecration as a bride of our Lord Jesus Christ?' (Cistercian nuns of common observance, Denmark) When giving her the ring, the bishop says: 'Receive this ring, for you are betrothed to the eternal King' (Birgittine Sisters

---

56. Quotation from the solemn blessing of the Carmelite Brethren, Sweden.
57. For example, Bernard of Clairvaux in his *Sermons On the Song of Songs* 12, 11. The Carmelite spirituality and way of life is totally inaccessible, if detached from the nuptial mysticism employed by John of the Cross and Teresa of Ávila.

[Italy], Norway). Even in convents belonging to the Church of Sweden this consecration is practised (the Holy Spirit Sisters). A more 'gender-neutral' rite of profession may even risk rejection: 'At the profession of perpetual vows, no ring is bestowed. We have consciously tried to move away from the bridal mystique. But our younger sisters today seem to want to change this again'.[58] The Orthodox rites of profession are practically identical for nuns and monks, and in this sense 'gender neutral'.

We have already characterised these rites in a general way as coming from different traditions, ages, cultures and churches. Some of them contain counter-cultural elements. Others are more serene and perhaps more easily accessible for people who are not familiar with this kind of celebration. Profession is, however, like the act of marriage, a performative language. 'It is a language that not only expresses, but actually does something' (Schneiders 2001, 101).

It is easy to disregard people's 'understanding' of this language: a Norwegian convert from the Lutheran to the Catholic Church pointed out à propos nuptial allusions, 'In my Low Church tradition, the concept of the bride of Christ was used indiscriminately of men and women and posed no problems'.[59] But even so, these images do not work so well for men. A religious woman can see herself married to Christ. A male priest can see himself married to the Church (this is the other side of this paradigm), but what about a male religious, who is not a priest? The absence of such allusions in men's rites seems to confirm the limits of this symbolism.[60]

---

58. Sr. Madeleine Fredell. The liturgical use of the ring is well known also in male orders, viz. for bishops (and later for abbots). The bishop's ring may have been due to the practical need for a signet ring, but gradually came to be seen as a sign of the bishop's fidelity to the Church. From the thirteenth century, the giving of the ring at the consecration of virgins and at the monastic profession of women was seen as an expression of their betrothal to Christ. But generally, all use of rings relates to the older rites of betrothal and marriage (*Neues Pastoralliturgischer Handlexikon*, Herder, 1999, 448-449).
59. Fr. Torbjørn Olsen, Dr. Can. Iur., Norway.
60. The Orthodox rites of profession are however practically identical for nuns and monks, and this does not exclude a nuptial dimension. The monk as well as the nun becomes 'the betrothed of God'. The verse sung during the clothing of the great habit solves this problem: 'My soul shall rejoice in the Lord, for he hath put on me the garment of salvation...He hath put upon me a crown as upon a bridegroom, and as a bride hath he adorned me with an ornament'. This verse is taken from the website of the Russian Orthodox Church in America – http://www.russianorthodox.org/monast05.html – but we find it also in the Russian *Euchologion* ('*Trebnyk*'). The priest also recites this

However, contrasts of a more principal character appear occasionally between the rites of profession for men and women. The former are more inclined to employ language that emphasises the ministerial, active and ecclesial nature of religious life, while the latter tend to stress the exemplary, receptive and non-hierarchical nature of religious life. 'This disparity is an unfortunate reflection of the Church's past tendency to restrict religious women to a cloistered, exemplary life, receptive to the rules and directions of male ecclesiastics. When women attempted to move outside the cloister, especially after the Council of Trent, ecclesial recognition was sometimes only grudgingly given' (Foley 1989, 46).

The different rites of perpetual profession signify in their diversity a common goal – common life, common standards, common purpose: the *sequela Christi*. Religious life can be regarded as a prototype of fundamental Christian life (Acts 2.44ff). Religious life transcends confessional boundaries, and it also transcends and transforms the daily life of the brother and sister, those who do not marry for the sake of the Kingdom (cf. Matt. 19.12). Religious life and religious consecration is thus meant to be a prophetic sign pointing towards an eschatological reality, a New Heaven and a New Earth, where all are one in Christ.

Abbrevations

CIC   *Codex Iuris Canonici*, (Catholic) Code of Canon Law (Jan 25, 1983)

CR   *Catechism of the Catholic Church*

LG   *Lumen Gentium: Dogmatic Constitution on the Church*, Vatican II (Nov 21, 1964).

OPR   *Ordo Professionis Religiosae: the Rite of Religious Profession* (Sacra Congregatio pro Culto Divino, Feb. 2, 1970).

PC   *Perfectae Caritatis: Decree on the appropriate Renewal of the Religious Life*, Vatican II (Oct 28, 1965).

SC   *Sacrosantum Concilium: Constitution on the Sacred Liturgy*, Vatican II (Dec 4, 1963).

---

troparion when he assumes the liturgical vestments before celebrating the Divine Liturgy. Similar nuptial imagery is used (at least in the Russian tradition in relation to the little habit: after the ceremony, the newly tonsured candidate spends the whole night in prayer in the church. Then the monastic choir of monks or nuns arrives at midnight with lighted candles, singing the hymn: 'Behold the bridegroom comes...' All religious – monks and nuns – are seen as the Bride of Christ, one of the wise virgins who were awake and had oil in their lamps. (Source of information: Fr. Kliment Huhtamäki.)

References

Abbot, Walter M. (ed.). 1967. *The Documents of Vatican II*. London: Geoffrey Chapman.

Augé, Matias. 2000. Rite of Religious Profession in the West. In *Handbook for Liturgical Studies* IV, ed. Anscar J. Chupungco, 315-330. Collegeville: The Liturgical Press.

Berger, Teresa. 1999. *Women's Ways of Worship. Gender Analysis and Liturgical History*. Collegeville: The Liturgical Press.

Berntson, Martin. 2003. *Klostern och reformationen*. Skellefteå: Artos & Norma.

Boisvert, Laurent. 1988. *La consécration religieuse*. Paris: Cerf.

Brodd, Sven-Erik. 1972. *Evangeliskt klosterliv i Sverige*. Stockholm: Verbum.

1999 (rev. ed.).*Catechism of the Catholic Church*. London: Geoffrey Chapman.

Crouiset, Marguerite-Marie. 1972. Virginité et vie chrétienne au regard du rituel de la consécration des vierges. *La Maison-Dieu* 110:116-128.

Dahl, Soeur Eva. 1981. La vie monastique et la Réforme: deux interpellations réciproques. *Nouvelle Revue Théologique* 103:679-695.

De Candido, Luigi. 2001. Vie consacrée. In *Dictionnaire de la vie spirituelle*, eds. S. De Fiores/ T. Goffi, 1160-1170. Paris: Cerf.

Emsley, Matias. 2000. The Rite of Consecration of Virgins. In *Handbook for Liturgical Studies* IV, ed. Anscar J. Chupungco, 331-342. Collegeville: The Liturgical Press.

Eusebius. *The History of the Church*. G. A. Williamson/ A. Louth (trad./ed.), The Penguin Classics. Hammondsworth: Penguin Books, 1989.

Foley, Edward. 1989. *Rites of Religious Profession*. Chicago: Liturgy Training Publications.

Hausman, Noëlle. 1988. Pour la 'Professio super Hostiam'. *Nouvelle Revue Théologique* 110:729-742.

Laghé, Birgitta. 2004. National but Foreign: Female Religious Communities in the Church of Sweden. In *Nuns and Sisters in the Nordic Countries after the Reformation*, ed. Y. M. Werner, 255-304.

Lambin, Rosine. 2001. La voile dans le Christianisme et ses racines dans la religion romaine. *Yearbook of the European Society of Women in Theological Research* 9:189-202.

Legrand, Hervé. 1993. La réalisation de l'Église en un lieu. In *Initiation à la pratique de la théologie* t. 3, eds. B. Lauret/Fr. Refoulé, 143-345. Paris: Cerf.

Malchau, S. & Nilsen, E.-B. 2004. Tables and Figures. In *Nuns and Sisters in the Nordic Countries after the Reformation*, ed. Y. M. Werner, 419-436.

Martola, Yngvill. 2001. *Worship Renewal*. Tampere: The Research Institute of the Evangelical Lutheran Church of Finland.

Metz, René. 1972. Le nouveau rituel de consécration des vierges – Sa place dans l'histoire. *La Maison-Dieu* 110:88-115.

'Monachisme'. 1979. In *Dictionnaire de Spiritualité ascétique et mystique*, ed. M. Viller ecc. t. 10, fasc. 68-69, col. 1524-1617. Paris: Éd. Beauchesne.

Nilsen, Else-Britt. 1991. Luthers oppgjør med klostervesenet i 'De votis monasticis'. *Norsk Teologisk Tidsskrift* 92:15-28.

– 2001. *Nonner i storm og stille. Katolske ordenssøstre i Norge i det 19. og 20. århundre*. Oslo: Solum Forlag.

Nin, Manel. 2000. Monastic Profession in the East. In *Handbook for Liturgical Studies* IV, ed. Anscar J. Chupungco, 307-313. Collegeville: The Liturgical Press.

Paul VI, 'Magno gaudio'. *La Documentation catholique* 1964:690.

Puglisi, James F. 1996. *The Process of Admission to Ordained Ministry. A Comparative Study*, Vol I. Collegeville, Minn: The Liturgical Press.

Raffin, Pierre. 1970. Liturgie de l'engagement religieux: Le nouveau rituel de la profession religieuse. *La Maison-Dieu* 104:151-166.

– 1992. *Les rituels orientaux de la profession monastique*. Spiritualité orientale 4. Bégrolles-en-Mauges: Abbaye de Bellefontaine.

Ravasi, L. 1968. La professione 'super hostiam'. Vita Religiosa 4 (1968) 615-619.

Rituel de la profession monastique (RPM). 1981. Roma: Diaconie Apostolique.

Rituel de la profession religieuse (RPR).1992. Paris: Desclée-Mame.

The Rites of the Catholic Church as Revised by the Second Vatican Ecumenical Council –Volume Two (Rites II). 1991. Collegeville: The Liturgical Press.

Robinson, N. F. (1916). *Monasticism in the Orthodox Churches*. London: Cope and Fenwick.

Rogerson, Barry. 2001. A Translation of the Church of Norway's Ordination Rites. In *Studia Liturgica* 31:211-240.

Schneiders, Sandra M. 2001. *Selling All*. New York/Mahwah, N.J.: Paulist Press.

v. Severus, Emmanuel. 1984. Feiern geistlicher Gemeinschaften. In *Gottesdienst der Kirche Handbuch d. Liturgiewissenschaft* Teil 8, ed. Hans Bernhard Meyer, 157-189. Regensburg: Verlag Friedrich Pustet.

Simon, Monique. 1997. *La vie monastique, lieu oecuménique*. Paris: Cerf.

'Stati del Nord-Europa'. 1997. In *Dizionario degli Instituti di Perfezione*, ed. G. Pelliccia and G. Rocca. t. IX, col. 139-171. Roma: Edizioni Paoline.

Strieder, Leon F. 2001. *The Promise of Obedience. A Ritual History*. Collegeville: The Liturgical Press.

Sundback, Susan. 2001. Female cloisters in the Nordic Countries – monasticism returning? Manuscript.

Thorkildsen, Dag. 1997. Religious Identity and Nordic Identitiy. In *The Cultural Construction of Norden*, ed. Ö. Sörensen & B. Stråth. Oslo: Scandinavian University Press. 138-160.

Tugwell, Simon. 1983. Dominican Profession in the thirteenth Century. *Archivum Fratrum Praedicatorum* 53. 5-52.

Werner, Yvonne Maria. 1997. *Det kvinnliga klosterväsendet i Norden 1860-2000: En kvinnlig motkultur i det moderna samhället.* Manuscript.

– 2002. *Kvinnlig motkultur ock katolsk mission. Sankt Josefsystrarna i Danmark och Sverige 1856-1936.* Stockholm: Veritas.

– (ed.). 2004. *Nuns and Sisters in the Nordic Countries after the Reformation.* Uppsala: Studia Missionalia Svecana LXXXIX.

Appendix

Rites received for Perpetual Commitment to Religious Life in the Nordic Countries

Religious Family, Congregation	Community	Sex	Country	Church Family
	New Valamo and Lintula	M/F	Finland	Orthodox (Finnish Orthodox)
	Treenignhetens-kloster	M	Sweden	
Benedictines[1]	Vor Frue Kloster, Åsebakken	F	Denmark	Catholic
Benedictines of St. Lioba	Sankt Lioba Kloster, Fr.berg	F	Denmark	Catholic
Benedictines	Mariavall, Tomelilla	F	Sweden	Catholic (former protestant)
– Secular oblates	''	F		
Benedictine	Benedikts Hus, Tomelilla	M	Sweden	Catholic (formerly Protestant)
Benedictines	Mariadöttrarna, Omberg	F	Sweden	Catholic (formerly Protestant)

Benedictines	Östanbäcks kloster, Sala	M	Sweden	Protestant
Cistercians				
Common observans	Maria Hjerte Abbedi (Sostrup), Grenå	F	Denmark	Catholic
Carmelites				
Reformed – Brethren	Tågarp	M	Sweden	Catholic
Reformed – Nuns	Barmhärtiga kärlekens Karmel, Glumslöv	F	Sweden	Catholic
Reformed – Nuns	Totus Tuus, Tromsø	F	Norway	Catholic
Reformed – Nuns	Hafnarfjördur	F	Iceland	Catholic
Franciscans				
Ordo Fratrum Minorum	Province of NL Oslo	M	Norway	Catholic
Ordo Fratrum Minorum	Province of NL Lindköping	M	Sweden	Catholic
OFM-lay members	Oslo+ Lillestrøm	M/F	Norway	Catholic
Convetuals	Jönköping	M	Sweden	Catholic
Conv.-lay members		M/F	Sweden	Catholic
Helige Franciskus Systraskap	Klaradalkloster, Rävlanda	F	Sweden	Protestant
Dominicans				
1. Brethren (only formula)	Province of France Oslo	M	Norway	Catholic
Brethren (only formula)	Province of France Lund	M	Sweden	Catholic
2. Nuns	Lunden kloster, Oslo	F	Norway	Catholic
3. Sisters				
– Notre Dame de Grâce	Katarinahjemmet, Oslo	F	Norway	Catholic
– URSD (Roman Union of St Dominic)	Stockholm, Märstad	F	Sweden	Catholic
– Tourelles	Rögle	F	Sweden	Catholic

Birgittines				
Old observance	Pax Mariae, Vadstena	F	Sweden	Catholic
Hesselblad	Trondheim	F	Norway	Catholic
Hesselblad	Turku	F	Finland	Catholic
Jesuits (only formula)	Stockholm	M	Sweden	Catholic
Sisters of St Joseph, Chambéry	Copenhagen	F	Denmark	Catholic
Sisters of St Joseph, Chambéry	Oslo	F	Norway	Catholic
Sisters of St Elisabeth (Neisse)	Oslo	F	Norway	Catholic
Little Sisters of Jesus	Copenhagen	F	Denmark	Catholic
Amantes de la Croix de Hue	Oslo	F	Norway	Catholic
Maria Magdalenas Systrar	Nacka	F	Sweden	Protestant
Diaconnesses de Reuilly	Diakonisseklosteret Engen, Kolbu	F	Norway	Protestant
Den Uppståndne Frälsarens Systraskap	Överselö Klostergård, Stallarholmen	F	Sweden	Protestant
Helgandssystrarna (Holy Spirit)	Alsike Kloster, Knivsta	F	Sweden	Protestant
Ordo Salvatoris, augustinii	Augustinerorden, Stånga	M	Sweden	Prostestant
'Consecrated virgin living in the world'		F	Denmark	Catholic

1. Two alternatives: Monastic profession with and without the rite of consecration of virgins.

5. Institutionalization and Contextualization of Rites of Ordination and Commitment

Though this is perhaps more apparent in some rites than in others, two tendencies seem universal in ritual development, including the development of rites for ordination and commitment. First, they tend to be institutionalized, that is, integrated into an established ecclesiastical structure or perhaps living their own lives as micro institutions of their own. At the same time rites cannot escape being contextualized, taking forms and colours from the cultural and ecclesiastical surrounding in which they live.

Bent Hylleberg analyses the rites for baptism and ordination in the Nordic Baptist Churches. Siding with the radical Anabaptist tradition and its modern promoters, Hylleberg sees believer's baptism as an 'ordination to mission', which in principle makes confirmation and all forms of commitment and ordination unnecessary or, even worse, a form of repetition of baptism and thus a replication of the standards for baptised Christians. Unfortunately there is no clear evidence of this understanding of baptism in the baptismal rites in the Nordic Baptist Churches, nor are there any references to the interrelationship between baptism, the 'priesthood of all the baptized' and the 'priesthood of some of the baptized' in the rites for the ordination of pastors in the same churches. Hylleberg considers this a deviation from 'Christianity', brought about by the tendency of the Nordic Baptist Churches to be shaped in the image of the surrounding institutionalized 'Christendom' of the established Evangelical Lutheran Churches in the Nordic Countries.

Hasse Neldeberg Jørgensen outlines the story of the ordination practice of the free Lutheran Congregations in Denmark. The modern Danish Church Father, N.F.S. Grundtvig, who inspired the electoral congregation movement in ELCD and the free Lutheran congregations, formally outside ELCD structure, strongly emphasised the importance of (infant) baptism without arguing against the tradition of ordaining pastors. This led the free Lutheran congregations to celebrate the ordinations or installations of pastors in various free ways. During the second half of the twentieth century bishops of ELCD were permitted to officiate at such ordinations, but only as 'private persons'! Independently of the individual pastor's actual path of 'ordination' in free congregations, a number of them have been accepted without re-ordination as pastors in ELCD.

Gudrun Lydholm presents the rites for commissioning/ordination to officership in the Salvation Army in the Nordic Countries in relation to the theological development of the Salvation Army internationally. Traditionally the Salvation Army stresses the vocation to ministry of all believers/soldiers and the adoption of the available measures best suited to mission. Today the Salvation Army increasingly sees itself not only as part of the universal Church but also as a church in its own right, though other churches note the lack of the sacraments of Baptism and Eucharist as well as of Apostolic Succession in the ordained leadership of the Army. Since 1978 the term 'ordination' has been introduced but practiced in rather different ways at the ceremonies for commitment to officership in the Salvation Army. This is no less so in the Nordic countries, with their different Salvationist traditions and ecclesiastical contexts. The Salvation Army thus provides a distinctive example for the study of the significance of the processes of institutionalization and contextualization of ordination rites.

Ghita Olsen examines 10 different rites for the sending out of missionaries from Nordic mission societies and churches. The patterns of development are very diverse, as the rites are sometimes used in established or free churches and sometimes in independent mission societies with rather loose relations to a mother church, so that the mission society may tend to act as a micro church in itself. In the Churches of Sweden and Finland, which are moving in the direction of a threefold concept of the ordained ministry, the rites for the sending out of missionaries are being moved from the ordination section of the Service Books, as missionaries are now to be blessed and sent out but certainly not to be ordained. It is thus in the 'low church' traditions of the Norwegian Missionary Society, for example, that we find rites with an instrumental character. Olsen's survey leaves the impression that rites for the sending out of missionaries tend to be the poor relation among rites of ordination and commissioning in the Nordic Churches.

Baptism as Commitment to Ministry and Mission: A Consideration of the Rites for Baptism and Ordination in the Nordic Baptist Churches

Bent Hylleberg

In the theology of Baptists, where *credo-baptism*[1] has remained the pattern of baptismal practice, reflection on the relationship between the theology of baptism and the theology of ordination is to be expected. This article examines the relationship between 'the priesthood of *all* the baptized' and 'the priesthood of *some* who are ordained' in the liturgies of baptism and ordination of the Nordic Baptist Churches.

Jürgen Moltmann has pointed out, that '[t]he special stress on ordination and sacred ministry – to the point of raising it to the rank of sacrament – apparently always crops up when the church goes over to the practice of infant baptism' (Moltmann 1998, 314). Moltmann continues:

> The baptism of those who are not of age is always in danger of making the community spiritual babes too, for no special value in the sense of a call can be ascribed to infant baptism as such. Just as confirmation must supplement infant baptism [for lay people], so too must ordination [for the clergy] as the visible act of the call to a special ministry. ... In a congregation of baptized believers, baptism and confirmation coincide, and ordination approaches baptism directly, as the conferring of a special charge. It does

---

1. In what follows the term credo-baptism is used for 'believers' baptism' and paedo-baptism for 'infant baptism'.

not confer any higher dignity than baptism and merely gives specific form
to the person's special call (Moltmann 1998, 314).

Accordingly we will look for the theology of ordination among Nordic Baptists in a context dominated by a paedo-baptizing Lutheran folk church.

Furthermore theologians from the tradition of credo-baptism more and
more frequently point out that baptism has to be understood as 'ordination for
mission' (Williams 1963, 29; McClendon 1994, 390f; Yoder 1998, 53ff, and
Kreider 1993, 84ff). If this is a valid theology for baptism, what kind of
consequences does such a theology have for our theology of ordination as
Baptists? Is it possible that we as Baptists do not have to continue to speak
about 'baptism *and* ordination' in order to begin to reflect theologically about
'baptism *as* ordination'?

In the following analysis of liturgies for baptism and ordination in the
Baptist Unions of Denmark, Norway and Sweden we find our resources in two
published liturgies (Norway: Taranger 1994, and Sweden: Persson 1987) and
one unpublished guide (Denmark: Anhøj 1998).[2] Baptists in Norway and
Sweden are used to Handbooks; Baptists in Denmark do not have this tradition. But all the Nordic Baptist traditions have a common relaxed attitude to
written formulae. The liturgies are not compulsory standards that have to be
adhered to, but options that can be used either directly or as inspirational
guidelines (Taranger 1994, 4). Liturgies are a question of spirituality not only
for the ministers but primarily for the congregations (Persson 1987, 8). What
follows here is a study of the three liturgies for the act of baptism and a
comparison between these and a similar analysis of the liturgies of ordination.

Baptismal Liturgies in the Nordic Baptist Churches
Texts

Following the introduction that is common to all of them, the Nordic baptismal liturgies may be examined under three headings: presentation of the
candidate for baptism, the act of baptism itself, and the reception of the
baptized into the church fellowship.[3]

The introduction begins with the singing of a baptismal hymn. The candi-

---

2. *The Swedish Handbook*, Till Församlingens Tjänst, is intended for all Swedish-speaking
   groups of Baptists in both Sweden and Finland, i.e. five different Baptist Unions. In
   1997, three of the Swedish groups formed a new Union, 'Nybygget'. Since 2002 this
   Union has been called, the Evangelical Free Church ('Evangeliska Frikyrkan').
3. The three Nordic liturgies of baptism will be analyzed with the Swedish (SE) as the

date(s) for baptism and the one who will administer the baptism (normally the pastor) take their places in front of the baptismal pool, facing the congregation. The act of baptism is introduced by the reading of passages from the New Testament. The readings are chosen from the accounts of the baptism of Jesus (Matt. 3.13ff), of baptism in the early Church (Acts 2.36-40; 8.35-38) and from biblical teaching about baptism (Rom. 6.3-4; Gal 3.27-28; 1 Peter 3.21-22). The Great Commission (Matt. 28.18-20) is always included. These biblical texts may be read by the candidate(s) as well as the pastor.

Then follows the first part of the act of baptizing, the *presentation* of the candidate. This may be done, 1) through a 'brief personal testimony' given by the candidate. 'It is a sufficient testimony if the candidate standing in the baptismal pool answers 'Yes' when asked if he/she believes in Jesus Christ' (NO); 2) through a dialogue between the pastor and the candidate, or 3) just through the pastor's presentation of the candidate. Then the pastor (SE) asks the candidate two questions: 'Do you believe in Jesus Christ as Lord and Saviour?' and, 'Do you want to be baptized into Christ in order to live a new life with him?' To each question the candidate answers 'Yes'. After this personal confession of faith in Christ the congregation unites in the common confession of faith, either by singing a baptismal hymn (DK) or by reciting the Apostles' Creed (SE). The presentation closes with the 'baptismal prayer', a Trinitarian prayer led by the pastor, in which he gives thanks for those who today 'are baptized into Christ to a new life and to fellowship with his people' (SE).

The second part of the liturgy, the *act of baptism* itself, takes place in the baptismal pool. The pastor descends into the water followed by the candidates (one at a time), while the congregation usually sings hymns or listens to the choir. In DK and NO the pastor now asks the candidate the two questions mentioned above. After the candidates' confession of faith, but before baptizing, the pastor will say: 'NN, as commissioned by my Master – ('At the command of Jesus Christ', NO and DK) – and on your own confession of faith in Jesus Christ as Lord and Saviour, I baptize you in the name of the Father, the Son and the Holy Spirit'. The baptism takes place by lowering the baptizand completely under the water once. After each act of baptism the

---

basis, since this is the most developed rite. The analysis will be synoptic, and reference will be made to the Norwegian (NO) and the Danish (DK) liturgies if there are important deviations. Comments on this article have been received from my Swedish and Norwegian colleagues Sune Fahlgren and Billy Taranger. Their comments have been included where the practices in general deviate from the Handbooks.

congregation will sing a threefold 'Amen' (DK). Before leaving the baptismal pool the pastor turns to the congregation quoting Mark 16.16: 'Whoever believes and is baptized will be saved'. In the Norwegian liturgy the invitation is followed by a symbolic act: the congregation lights a candle for each baptismal candidate, while one candle is left unlit. As the pastor points at this light he says: 'This light symbolizes the call of God. It will be lit, when one who today hears the call, decides to follow the command of Jesus and is baptized on his/her confession of faith in Christ'. The last newly baptized person leaves the baptismal pool followed by the pastor. While they are changing dress, one or more of the church members give thanks to God for the gift of baptism, for the person(s) who have been baptized and for the growth of the church (SE), or the congregation sings a hymn of praise (DK).[4]

The third part of the liturgy of baptism, *the reception into church membership*, closes the act of baptism. This part is called the welcome (SE) or the reception for membership (DK). It is 'characterized by joy and warmth'. The newly baptized stand in front of the congregation while the pastor welcomes them and reads selected scriptural passages about church growth (Acts 2.41f), church unity (1 Cor. 12.13; Eph. 4.3-6), discipleship (Rom. 12.9-12; Col. 2.6-7) and service (1 Pet. 2.9-10). Then the newly baptized kneel and the pastor 'and assistants' (NO: 'deacons', DK: 'church members') ask for God's blessing over them, an act of intercessory prayer that closes with all joining in the Lord's Prayer (DK, NO). In all liturgies it is emphasized, that the reception is a welcome into the universal Christian Church, *in casu* the local Baptist church: 'Those who believe and are baptized become one with Christ and his people on earth' (NO). As an expression of care for the fellowship the congregation answers in the affirmative to the question: 'Will you sustain NN

---

4. The Swedish Handbook is corrected by Fahlgren 2003 when it says that the invitation – where all who will 'receive Jesus Christ as their Lord and Saviour' are invited to be baptized according to the Scriptures (here Acts 2.38 is quoted) – is placed in the section named above as the 'Introduction'. Normally the practice in Sweden has become the same as in Denmark and Norway, where this invitation to be baptized is given from the baptismal pool after the baptismal act(s). In Sweden – according to the Handbook – the act of baptism is completed when in the baptismal pool the pastor lays his hand on the head or shoulder of the newly baptized person and pronounces the priestly or apostolic benediction, but he can also choose the following words: 'NN, you are now a disciple of Jesus Christ: if you are baptized into Christ, you are also clothed with Christ'. According to Fahlgren 2003 this practice has changed, and the reception into membership now takes place, as it does in Denmark and Norway, where the pastor's prayer and his benediction, whilst he lays his hand on the one just baptized, belong to the third part of the liturgy, the 'Reception into church membership'.

with your care and with your prayer?' (DK, NO). The newly baptized are then welcomed with a handshake and are given a certificate of baptism (with a passage of Scripture) and eventually a gift (a Bible) and envelopes for church offerings (DK). The Swedish liturgy of baptism includes a word of commission to be used – after the Lord's Supper – at the close of the worship service (Rom. 6.3-4; Col. 2.6-7), underlining that those just baptized, together with the congregation, are baptized to live 'a new life' in the service of others 'overflowing with thankfulness'. The commission is the final part of a normal service of worship in all three liturgies. It may be worded: 'Go in peace, serve the Lord with joy' (NO).

Contexts

The act of baptism is part of an ordinary Sunday Communion service: 'Baptism is a central part of the preaching and confession of the church and belongs naturally to the celebration of worship in the congregation' (SE). The candidate(s) for baptism will normally arrive dressed in a white baptismal gown and, at the beginning of the service, will walk with the pastor through the sanctuary to take a seat at the front of the church. The hymns to be sung at a baptismal service are chosen according to the character of the service, but cannot be analyzed here since they are not specifically mentioned in the liturgies. The baptism itself takes place after the Scripture reading and the sermon, in order to emphasize that the gospel call to faith, baptism and discipleship comes before the act of baptism. That is why the liturgies speak about 'believers' baptism' and 'confessional baptism', that is, 'credo-baptism'. After the baptism follows the celebration of the Lord's Supper, before praise and commission close the service of worship: 'To a complete baptismal service belongs, according to early Christian tradition, the celebration of the Lord's Supper' (SE). Baptism is practiced everywhere by total immersion: 'Baptism takes place by immersion. The immersion may be done in different ways. The most common way is that the person to be baptized is lowered backwards into the water. Alternatively the one to be baptized kneels in the baptismal pool and is bent forward under the water or even sits on a stool in the baptismal pool and is lowered into the water' (SE). Immersion is a symbol of our burial and resurrection with Christ – 'in order that ... we too may live a new life' (Rom 6.4).

Theology of Baptism in the Liturgies

This survey of the three liturgies of baptism produced by the Nordic Baptist Churches allows us to draw a number of conclusions about the meaning of baptism and the ministry of the baptized. For this purpose we shall focus on the elements usually included in the liturgies and on the key players involved in the process of baptism.

Elements included

The liturgies show that baptism in water in the name of the triune God and received through confession of faith is *God's act of salvation*. This is seen in contextual remarks: 'In baptism God acts through his Holy Spirit and realizes the promises related to the baptism' (SE). It also appears in the liturgy, in the thanksgiving after the act of baptism: 'We thank you for reminding us in this way how we through baptism may surrender ourselves to you and how you deal with us' (SE). That this has to do with forgiveness of sin is apparent from the chosen Scripture reading (Acts 2.38) and from the baptismal prayer ('God, you have created us to a life in freedom, release us from the powers which bind us'), as well as from the Lord's Prayer which ends the thanksgiving after the act of baptism (SE). The element of faith is emphasized just as markedly in both text and context. In the thanksgiving after the baptism it is said: 'Thank you for NN who has now been baptized by faith in your promises', and in the contextual remarks we read: 'Baptism according to the New Testament is believers' baptism through which the baptizand receives God's grace as revealed in Christ' (SE).

Text and context also underline that 'baptism according to the New Testament is baptism to a life in obedience [to the Word of Christ] and discipleship [in Christ]' (SE). This element and the power needed for this is emphasized in the liturgies in different ways. The baptismal prayer says: 'When we baptize with water, you give your Holy Spirit', and we pray: 'Let your Holy Spirit fill the one who is baptized with life and light and hope' (SE). The Danish liturgy emphasizes even more strongly *the equipping by the Holy Spirit* with spiritual gifts for service. The prayer during the laying-on of hands says: 'Lord, we thank you for NN, whom you now through the power of the Holy Spirit have made a member of your body. Fill him/her with the power of the Holy Spirit and equip him/her for the task of discipleship that he/she may prove to be what he/she has been made.'[5] The epicletic character of the prayer is quite clear here. The work of the Holy Spirit has conveyed the preaching, communicated the call of the Gospel, created the faith and the confession,

---

5. The Nordic Baptists do not interpret the act of laying-on of hands. Baptists in Great Britain say in their liturgy of baptism that it is 'a sign of blessing and an act of commissioning, and to ask that they may be fully equipped for their vocation as servants of Jesus Christ in the Church and in the world' (Green 1991, 103).

passed on God's promises through baptism in water and now endows the baptized for further service in the light of the Kingdom to come. The eschatological perspective is seen in the prayer of thanksgiving for the baptism: 'We thank you for the gift of the Spirit. Help us to live in our baptism, to have confidence in your grace and faithfulness, and to serve one another as you, our Lord, served others. Give us strength to do this by your Holy Spirit', and it is marked even more clearly when, at the end of this prayer, the congregation recites the Lord's Prayer together (SE).

Finally, the text and context demonstrate that baptism connects the baptized to *the Christian Church*. The contextual remarks explain that 'baptism, according to the New Testament, is a conversion baptism which has its place at the beginning of the Christian life', and that it 'is baptism into Christ and into his body, the church' (SE). The baptismal prayer says: 'We thank you that we may be baptized into Christ and be united with your people in service and praise' (SE), and the congregation gives thanks explicitly for the baptized as a gift from God: 'We thank you that we may receive NN as your gift to the congregation' (SE). The baptized is incorporated into God's covenant people with one definite purpose – 'a chosen race, a royal priesthood, a holy nation, God's own people, in order that you may proclaim the mighty acts of him who called you out of darkness into his marvellous light' (1 Pet. 2.9) (SE).

From the broader context it appears that before the act of baptism there has been *a time of preparation*. By virtue of the preaching of the Gospel, the presence of the congregation, and the creative power of the Holy Spirit, the one who asks for baptism has listened to and received God's call. The desire of this person to be baptized is caused by *God's call*. It is a desire that is publicly pronounced to the leadership of the congregation. In former times the one to be baptized was often tested and made 'the good confession' to the congregation – at a church meeting before the service at which the acceptance for baptism took place. Today some instruction will normally be given before the celebration of baptism, while the reception takes place in the act of baptism itself, through the baptism in water followed by the prayer with laying-on of hands.

Key Players Involved

The one who officiates at the baptism is normally the pastor of the church – though one of the deacons or another member of the church appointed by the congregation may substitute. The one who officiates at the baptism will also pronounce the blessing with the laying-on of hands, while the baptismal prayer following the act of baptism is led by 'one or more people' from the congregation (SE). In the epicletic prayer with the laying-on of hands at the reception of the baptized (DK, NO), members of the council of elders (NO) or members of the church (DK) also participate in addition to the officiant. It is in principle the business meeting, acting as the church leadership that, according to the wish of the one to be baptized, decides who shall represent the fellowship at the intercessory prayer.

The Meaning of Baptism

The analysis of the liturgies (text) and the context in which they function shows the importance that Nordic Baptists attach to baptism. The person who asks for baptism understands in advance of the baptism that he/she is called by God. The instruction that takes place before the celebration of baptism is best understood as an examination before baptism. So the liturgies reflect both the *vocatio* and the *examinatio* aspects. Credo-baptism does not only celebrate and confirm the already existing call (expressively), but (instrumentally) in the baptism God gives his forgiveness and equips the one who is baptized with the power to serve through the prayer of the congregation. The disciple who is in this way called, forgiven, equipped, and blessed ('*benedictio*') is through baptism connected to the Church of Christ both in the form of its fellowship ('*communio*') and its service ('*diakonia*'). As part of this fellowship the baptized is incorporated into 'the priestly service of the baptized' for the world ('*sacerdotium*') and understands therefore his/her service as apostolic ('*missio*'). The specific kind of service or function (charge) that the baptized should take on, as part of the life and work of the church, is to be decided by the congregation according to the spiritual gifts of the baptized.

Liturgies for Ordination in the Nordic Baptist Churches

The liturgies for ordination are comprehensive and comments on the contexts are many (Persson 1987, 196-219; Taranger 1994, 84-104; Anhøj 1998, 42-43, 51-55). There are liturgies for ordination not only of pastors (SE, NO, DK), but also for services within the Baptist Unions including international missionary work (SE, NO), for local deacons, for leaders of the church and other co-workers (SE, DK), and for social workers serving in institutions outside the area of the local church (DK). An analysis only of the liturgies for the ordination of pastors follows here. The terminology varies a great deal, without precision.[6]

---

6. The Swedish liturgy has a special problem since it is a common liturgy based on the

Texts

The liturgies of ordination may be divided into three main parts. In the first, *the preliminaries to the act of ordination*, the leader (ordaining minister) presents the ordinand to the congregation (NO, SE). The ordaining minister then addresses the ordinand (SE and NO, in DK the congregation is also addressed), after which several biblical texts are read to emphasize God's call and election (e.g. Is. 6.1-8; Jer. 1.4-7; Matt. 4.19; Rom. 10.13ff), to point to the character of service (e.g. Matt. 9.36f; Acts 20.24,28; Eph. 4.7,11-15), and to emphasize the necessity of the equipping by the Holy Spirit for the ministry (e.g. John 20.21ff; 1 Cor. 12.4-7; 1 Tim. 4.14ff). Now follows in SE and NO – but not in DK – a section with questions to the ordinand, followed by promises.

The ordinand responds in the affirmative to a number of questions, which the leader asks 'aware of the presence of Jesus Christ' (SE): The ordinand confirms, 1) his/her *faith* 'in the triune God' (NO), and in 'Jesus Christ as Lord and Saviour (SE, NO), and 2) his/her *call* to the service for which he/she is being ordained: 'Are you sure that God has called you to serve as ...' (SE). The ordinand furthermore promises, 3) *faithfulness* – both to God by 'abiding in God's word', by fulfilling his/her service 'by the grace of God and in the power of the Holy Spirit' (SE), and by 'leading a life that is worthy of the call' (NO) – and to 'the church community that today consecrates you' (NO), and he/she promises to participate in a 'trusting cooperation' (SE). Finally the

---

varied practice in five Swedish-Finnish Baptist Unions (Persson 1987, 196f). What follows here starts from SE and NO. The liturgies will be analyzed synoptically. Where there are deviations in DK these will be mentioned. In DK the word 'ordination' is used when it has to do with a ministry valid within the national Baptist Union while 'inauguration' (*'tiltrædelse'*) is used about the act of intercessory prayer (with or without the laying-on of hands) that may be used at the dedication of a new pastor or of other co-workers in the local church (Anhøj 1998, 53). NO may use the term *'ordinasjon'* (Taranger 2003) in the same manner as in Denmark, but it is more common to speak, as in Sweden, of *'innvielse'* (NO) and *'avskiljning'* (SE). SE uses 'avskiljning' for 'dedication' with prayer and the laying-on of hands of both pastors and (different from DK) of local church leaders (presbyters) and co-workers (deacons), while 'intercessory prayer' (*'förbön'*) is used with others who are 'entrusted with special tasks'. Both SE and NO speak about 'ordination' when referring to missionaries in international service – even when they will not be working as pastors! – SE and NO are consistent in using the word 'pastor' for the term 'priest' (*'præst'*) more usually used by the Lutheran Church in Sweden and Norway, while DK says 'minister', as the Lutheran Church in Denmark also does. NO and SE as well as DK speak about 'installation' (*'indsættelse'*) when the pastor is dedicated for a new ministry. For DK, see also Hylleberg 1989, 133ff.

ordinand commits himself/herself to, 4) *professional secrecy* by keeping to your-self 'what has been entrusted to you, in the practice of your high call' (NO), and 'not revealing to anybody, what a person has confessed or told you as a spiritual adviser' (SE). In SE the leader closes with the affirmation: 'God will help you to keep what you have promised!' and he/she reminds the ordinand about the intention of the church: 'This congregation has through its call to you declared its readiness to receive you as a servant of Jesus Christ and as a steward of the Gospel and to assist you in all possible ways in this task'. Then the congregation is encouraged through Scripture readings to be faithful to-wards the ordinand (1 Thess. 5.12f; Heb. 13.17).

The second part, *the ordination prayer*, is in all three liturgies an intercessory prayer with the laying-on of hands. Before this prayer, reference is made to historic continuity: 'According to the apostolic way we will now by prayer and the laying-on of hands consecrate you to the service to which God has called you' (SE). The prayer may be a free prayer for which the liturgies give some guidance. From this it occurs as Trinitarian prayer (DK, SE), primarily with an epicletic character: 'Eternal God, let your Spirit descend upon this servant,... equip him/her with all that is needed to do your will' (NO), and 'Give NN the power of the Holy Spirit and spiritual gifts that he/she together with the church with humility and frankness may carry out the good news' (SE). The prayer also expresses the concern that the pastor's service may have Christ-like character: 'We pray that people may hear the voice of Jesus when your servant is guiding and preaching, and may see the hands of Jesus when your servant baptizes and distributes the gifts of the Lord's Supper' (SE, NO). The prayer ends with the Lord's Prayer said by the whole congregation, before the bene-diction is pronounced over the ordinand. Then follows in SE the commission: 'Go with gladness and frankness into the call that God has given you!' In Norway they close with this declaration: 'In the name of our Lord Jesus Christ, the Lord of the Church, we declare you consecrated to service as a pastor in the Baptist Union'.

The third part by which the act of ordination is closed has the character of a *welcome* to the ministry. The newly ordained may receive a Bible as a gift (SE) or a handshake (DK, NO). If they are married their spouse is asked to come forward and then they are both welcomed to their common service (DK). All three liturgies include handing over to the ordinand a certificate of ordination. In SE the act of ordination closes with a doxology (Jude vv. 24-25).

Contexts

The ordination of pastors takes place either at the synodical level ('annual Union conference', NO and SE) or in the local church, where the ordinand is to serve (DK). Both in Sweden and Norway (Taranger 2003) the ordination at the synodical level is followed by an installation in the local congregation. In DK the ordination takes place in the local church at a special celebration of worship for the whole congregation where representatives from the local church, neighbouring churches and the Baptist Union participate in the liturgy. Following the act of ordination, the newly ordained preaches the sermon and leads the congregation in the celebration of the Lord's Supper. The ordination has validity within the national Baptist Union, and may even be valid for pastoral service within the global Baptist body.

The pastoral ministry following the ordination is very comprehensive. From text and context it appears that the pastor is ordained to take on (SE) the duties of a shepherd and a teacher, including preaching the Word, administering baptism and the Lord's Supper, education and pastoral care, and 'to serve the church and your fellow human beings'. The same tasks appear within the two other liturgies. However, NO adds the ministry of intercessory prayer and the work of an evangelist. Common to the ordination of pastors and missionaries within all three traditions is that it is regarded as a once-and-for-all act, not to be repeated. Neither titles nor education are decisive for ordination; only the functions for which the ordination takes place are 'decisive and indelible' (SE). Though it is 'rarely used' (Fahlgren 2003), the SE liturgy contains as an indication of this a recommendation on 'Departure from ministry' to be used when 'gratitude is shown at the end of ministry' (SE).

Besides the ordination for pastors and missionaries there is also ordination for a number of other ministries. On the congregational level SE speaks about the 'separation' or 'setting apart' ('avskiljning') of 'local church leaders and co-workers'. DK speaks about 'dedication' ('indsættelse') for special ministries', where, for example, local church leaders, treasurers or children's and youth workers are mentioned. At the synodical level 'dedication' ('indsættelse') applies, for example, to the general secretary, theological teachers and evangelists. In SE and DK intercessory prayer is more important than the gesture of laying-on of hands that often goes with it, though this is always used at the 'commissioning' ('indvielse') of pastors.

The Theology of Ordination in the Liturgies

This survey of the three liturgies of ordination produced by the Nordic Baptist Churches allows us to draw a number of conclusions about the meaning of ordination and the ministry of the ordained. For this purpose we will focus on the elements usually included in the liturgies and the key players involved in the process of ordination.

Elements Included

The structure of the act of ordination may be divided into three parts. To the first belongs *the call* which is primarily understood as God's call communicated by the church: 'The dedication for this holy service rests upon God's call, acknowledged and confirmed by the greater fellowship' (NO). The 'inner compulsion' (NO) is thus combined with 'an outside call' from the local church or the national church communion. In addition to this, DK mentions an examination to take place at the ordination council. Before the ordination representatives of the local church, neighbouring churches and the Baptist Union get together to listen to and have a discussion with the ordinand, who accounts for his/her call, basic theological understanding and view concerning the task of the church (Anhøj 1998, 55). The council is an essential forum for discussion. It is, however, only theoretically able to prevent an ordination, since the call of the church is prior to this council (DK). In Norway the council is able to block the planned ordination, if necessary (Taranger 2003).

In the second part *the ordination itself* takes place with prayer and the laying-on of hands. Here the making of promises has a central place in two of the liturgies (SE, NO), while the epicletic prayer about the equipping and blessing by the Spirit is central to all three liturgies. The ordination is understood expressively, not instrumentally, and this is evident from the many expressions of wish in the liturgies. It may be heard in this passage (NO): 'As we believe that you (the ordinand) are acting in obedience to God's call, it may seem unnecessary to ask for further assurances about your faith and the seriousness of your intention, but in order that the congregation may better observe your wishes and intentions, we ask you to respond to the following questions, which we are asking you in Jesus' name'. The making of promises is psychologically motivated here. The same rejection of an instrumental interpretation, but in this case for theological reasons, is evident from a deliberate choice of terminology in which SE emphasises that titles are secondary while the ministries understood as functions are 'indelible' to the church. The 'indelible character' (*'character indelebilis'*) is constituted by the ministerial functions themselves, carried by the gifts of the Spirit, bestowed by the Spirit 'for the common good' (1 Cor. 12.7), for as long as the individual continues in ministry.

The third part of the act of ordination seems to be more randomly chosen with great variety in relation to the *handshake* and the presentation of a Bible 'by which the church symbolically confirms its call to the pastor to preach God's word' (SE). The functions that the ordained pastor is expected to take on are manifold. One or two of them show the influence of the national

(Lutheran) churches. The promise of secrecy may best be understood in this perspective (Persson 1987, 198). In DK this is also seen in the wording on the certificate of ordination, according to which the ordinand may 'administer church ceremonies with civil validity'.

Key Players Involved

The leader of the ordination is in principle the general secretary of the church communion involved, since he has been entrusted with an 'episcopal' service at the synodical level (Kyrø-Rasmussen 1967, 91f), but others may be chosen to take his/her place provided that the person chosen has 'been ordained to serve him/herself' (SE). No reason is given for this request. The principal of the theological seminary will normally participate and will then chair the ordination council (DK) or present the ordinand to the congregation (NO). Members of the local church, representatives of neighbouring churches and of the Baptist Union will read the scriptural passages before the intercessory prayer. All who have participated in the Scripture reading will take part in the laying-on of hands. The general secretary will normally say the ordination prayer and pronounce the benediction over the ordinand, but all participants may also pray spontaneously here (SE, NO).

The Meaning of Ordination

The analysis of the text of the liturgies and the context in which they function show the importance that the Nordic Baptists attach to ordination. Ahead of the ordination has gone a double calling. In the ordination the church will hand the ministry over to the one who has previously accepted both God's and the church's calling, and who has been equipped by the Holy Spirit with such spiritual gifts as may qualify them for ministry. The church (the ordination council) has examined the educational qualifications that the ordinand has received as well as his/her discipleship of Christ in thoughtfulness and service (life and ethos). The liturgies reflect in this way both the *vocatio* and the *examinatio* aspects. The promises given by the ordinand and the admonitions given by the ordaining minister to the congregation both express the wish that the parties may cooperate in a fruitful relationship with one another, for the blessing of many and for the furtherance of the Kingdom of God. The prayer with the laying-on of hands is understood as the congregation's intercessory prayer for God's blessing over a new co-worker ('*benedictio*') entering into an extensive task, primarily through ministry as a shepherd and a teacher. For this purpose the ordinand is commissioned ('*missio*'), and the congregation receives him/her with gratitude as a gift from the hand of God ('*receptio*'). The liturgies do not speak about any special power ('*potestas*') or about a special priesthood ('*sacerdotium*'), that would place the ordained 'above' the congregation, but he/she takes here place as a servant 'in' the church in order to work 'together with' the congregation for the benefit of the church's mission and the salvation of the world. The Nordic Baptists never speak about 'office' ('*embede*', DK, or '*Amt*', German) but always about 'ministry' ('*tjeneste*') (Persson 1987, 196).

The Relationship between Baptism and Ordination in the Nordic Baptist Liturgies

The liturgies for *ordination* contain no references to the ordinand's baptism or to anyone else's. It is, however, vital that the ordination takes place in the midst of the congregation. The very first part of the Swedish Handbook mentions the rite of 'intercessory prayer for those who are entrusted with special tasks'. This rite includes among other things the four New Testament texts that mention the gifts of the Spirit (Rom. 12; 1 Cor. 12; Eph. 4; 1 Pet. 4). The liturgy for the 'consecration' ('*avskiljning*') of pastors and missionaries continues in this vein. The ordained ministries are thus seen in the light of the manifold ministries. In NO the ordination of pastors is kept in the same context of ideas. Prayer is said that the ordinand 'together with your people... may hold true worship and faithfully administer baptism and communion'. DK gives thanks because God is calling ministers into 'a special service', just as he 'can use all of us'.

Baptist *ecclesiology* has as its point of departure the congregation gathered around the risen and present Christ. The congregation therefore exists for the incarnation of the Gospel in the world. The question of the ministry of the individual is based on the spiritual gifts and the decisions of the fellowship and is primarily a matter of arrangement: 'All things should be done decently and in order, for God is a God not of disorder, but of peace' (1 Cor.14.33). The church serves the '*shalom*' of the Kingdom of God in the world. For this purpose all the baptized are equipped and commissioned. No one stands 'above' the church but all stand 'in' and 'together with' the others in the common service. The ordained ministries do not belong to the '*esse*' of the church though they are most often counted as of its '*bene esse*'.[7] Thus it is said (SE):

---

7. This ecclesiological view has been described perfectly in §1-6 of the Ministry section in the BEM text, whilst only the rest of this Ministry section has received little support from Nordic Baptists. See DK and SE responses to BEM (Thurian, Vol. II, 246ff, and Vol. IV, 200-205 respectively).

The Christian Church has, throughout its long history accomplishing its calling, divided different tasks among its members. As church communions and local churches ordain and engage somebody for a special service it is not in order to release the other members from the service in word and deed. Instead the purpose is that the church shall function better and that its members shall be able to share in a more effective way the responsibility of the Church and of its service in the world (Persson 1987, 196).

This purpose does not always seem to be fulfilled. Ordination of 'the few' does not in general further a sense of responsibility among 'the many'. This is empirically ascertained where 'a priesthood of some believers' is created in the midst of 'the priesthood of all believers'. The special ministries do not always create room for a diversity of ministries, and the ministries often huddle together around the few ordained. In addition – and even more important – is the theological insight that the analysis reveals, that ordination most of all looks like a 'duplication' of *credo-baptism* in which the '*vocatio-benedictio-missio*' sequence is repeated for the few. This creates *de facto* a division among God's people, in which the seed of the fragmentation of God's people ('*laos*') is laid. Also the terminological confusion about ordination among Nordic Baptists reveals the theological problems related to ordination. Here we have a questionable practice seeking a good theology. At Moltmann's suggestion a different perspective should therefore be developed.

The Relationship between Baptism and Ordination in Christianity and Christendom

In order to investigate Moltmann's thesis we may look into what happened in the early Church. The original Christian rite of initiation was conversion baptism. This baptism took its inspiration from three different events in the life and ministry of Jesus: his baptism in the Jordan (the anointing for ministry), his death and resurrection (the gift of salvation), and the outpouring of the Spirit at Pentecost (distribution of charisms for ministry). The paradigm shift from Christianity to Christendom – when *Corpus Christi* changed to *Corpus Christianum* between about 300 and 500 AD – influenced the balance of these three components (McDonnell 1999, 308). Eventually paedo-baptism was understood only from the perspective of Easter, stressing the remission of sins and the gift of salvation, but eliminating the patterns of Jordan and Pentecost. Christian baptism, interpreted as empowering with the Spirit for ministry and mission, taken on by the community of the Saints, decreased. A tendency to locate the action of the Holy Spirit in post-baptismal blessings was established. Paedo-baptism reduced baptism to a *conditio sine qua non* for the coming 'real' blessings (Bradshaw 2001, 277). Therefore vows, confirmation, and ordination offer themselves irresistibly to different groups of Christians as substitutions for the blessings that originally belonged to credo-baptism interpreted as a rite of initiation from which the power of the Spirit and its charismata flow for ministry and mission. The laying-on of hands, epicletic prayer, and even 'ontological change' eventually became part of these different substitute blessings. We may name these blessings 'substitutional acts' because they followed paedo-baptism in order to fulfil what originally was intended by credo-baptism itself.

In the case of the *laity*, a post-baptismal blessing seems to surface within the first three centuries. It may be argued that, in the New Testament, there seems to be a relationship between credo-baptism in water, laying-on of hands and intercessory prayer for the gifts of the Spirit. The first explicit references, outside the New Testament, to a rite of laying-on of hands in baptism are found in Tertullian, Cyprian and Hippolytus. When paedo-baptism became dominant, the close tie was disrupted between baptism in water, laying-on of hands with prayer for the Spirit's empowering for ministry, and first communion within the church fellowship (Hannsen 1987, 193). Shortly after 400 AD paedo-baptism succeeded in the western church (Wright 2001). And in the middle of the fifth century it was stated with reference to paedo-baptism: 'In baptism we are reborn to life, after baptism we are confirmed for combat; in baptism we are washed, after baptism we are strengthened' (Bradshaw 1992, 150).

A second substitute praxis evolved within the *religious orders*. Monasticism began to formulate its thinking within a two-baptism framework, with the second baptism received later in life, making real the first baptism received in infancy, and being seen as the full flowering of the reality given in that first baptism. This framework created a distinction within the church between the 'just' (believers who live in the world, the *'parochianoi'*) and the 'perfect' (the former 'Christians', *'paroikoi'*, 'resident aliens', who now started to renounce everything, including marriage). The ascetics built a monastic wall around the actualization of infant baptism (McDonnell 1991, 313). Credo-baptism had been substituted by paedo-baptism for the majority, and vows which gave birth to the *'sancta'* dimension of the few. The charisms had been monasticized, excluding Christians who marry, who do not renounce and leave the world. In a civilization where everyone was now christianized by paedo-baptism (established by compulsion in Justin's edict of 529) holy communities entailed a new identity. Monastic profession was often described as a 'second baptism' (Kreider 2001, 45).

Thirdly, ordination of the *clergy* may also be interpreted as a substitute blessing. It is significant that there is no evidence of a liturgy of ordination before Hippolytus (about 205). In the middle of the third century Cyprian testified to the concept of ordination: 'The bishops with their clergy constituted a priesthood which could act on behalf of the rest' (Bradshaw 2001, 278). This broke down the older concept that 'the whole people of God' constituted a royal priesthood functioning before God in worship for the benefit of the world. This did not happen without protest, and this even came from the centre of Rome. In 428 Pope Celestine I protested because a newly ordained bishop in Arles had been wearing clothing that differentiated him from the laity. It was right that the clergy be distinguished from 'the common folk' as well as from non-Christian people, but let this be 'by our learning, not by our garments; by our mode of life, not by what we wear; by purity of thought, not by peculiarities of dress', which the pope called 'superfluous superstition' (Kreider 1993, 84). The pope fought without success. A century later the Fourth Council of Arles ordered 'that no one was to be ordained to the priesthood or diaconate without having demonstrated the fruits of "*conversion*" for an entire year' (Kreider 2001, 44). In Christianity conversion was a condition for credo-baptism understood as 'a change of belief, behaviour and belonging, accompanied by experience' (Kreider 1999, 109). In Christendom conversion had become a *sine qua non* for ordination, the substitute blessing that followed paedo-baptism for the clergy. Obviously the clergy were often recruited from the monasteries.

In Christianity 'church' and 'world' were visibly distinct, yet affirmed in faith to have one and the same Lord. This pair of affirmations is what the so-called 'Constantinian transformation' changed. The most pertinent fact about the new state of things in Christendom is that the two visible realities, 'church' and 'world', were fused – a 'fusion' of which Constantine was the architect, Eusebius the priest, Augustine the apologist, and the Crusaders and Inquisition the culmination' (Yoder 1998, 89). Now there was no longer anything to be called 'world'. It is not always recognized in what structural connection this change stands with the new distinction that now arose inside the church:

[T]he doctrine of the invisibility of 'the true church' sprang up in order to permit the affirmation that on some level somewhere the difference between belief and unbelief, i.e. between 'church' and 'world', still existed. But this distinction had become invisible, like faith itself. Previously Christians had known as a fact of experience that the Church existed but had to believe against appearances that Christ ruled over the world. After Constantine one knew as a fact of experience that Christ was ruling over the world but had to believe against the evidence that there existed 'a believing church'. Thus the order of redemption was subordinated to that of preservation, and the Christian hope turned inside out (Yoder 1998, 57).

'Baptism *and* ordination for Ministry' as opposed to 'Baptism *as* Ordination for Ministry'

A transformation of the Church as described above gives us different points of departure when we speak about the liturgy and theology of ordination. Basically it is possible to formulate two different perspectives on ordination – one in churches that speak about ordination from the perspective of paedo-baptism, and another one in churches that interpret credo-baptism as ordination.

The first perspective – speaking about paedo-baptism *and* ordination – is described in the *magnum opus* of James F. Puglisi in its two different forms in the Roman Catholic Church as well as in the churches of the Reformation. From my perspective it is interesting to wonder where Roman Catholicism will go with two bright new liturgies for baptism, which alter the pattern of both paedo-baptism (*Ordo Baptismi Parvulorum*, 1969) and credo-baptism (*Ordo Initiationis Christianae Adultorum*, 1972), for the first time since the tradition of Augustine's time was frozen in the liturgies developed in 1614 according to the Council of Trent (1545-63).

The second perspective, interpreting credo-baptism *as* ordination, comes from the Anabaptist movement at the time of the Reformation. An analysis of the baptismal liturgy of 'the theologian among the Anabaptists', Balthasar Hübmaier, concludes:

> According to Hübmaier, the Church had been unnecessarily stratified. The advent of the multiplicity of both monastic vows and clerical orders had devalued the role of the laity in the Church. The practice of infant baptism had removed both the requirement for a prior confession of faith and its subsequent two-pronged obligation, to utilize the powers of the keys and to preach to the unregenerate. For Hübmaier, baptism following a confession of faith in Christ was ordination enough for everyone (Johnson 1995, 84f).

Today ministry is an issue on which the radical Reformation churches and their heirs who practice credo-baptism are divided among themselves. Some of them, Baptists especially but also Pentecostals, maintain patterns of pastoral ministry that are compatible with the rest of Protestantism except that they turn down the sacramental ontology in order to upgrade the authority of the congregation as a whole in calling and governing the minister. But the clergy remained largely unchallenged. The Baptists' view developed somewhat 'unconsciously, being dictated more by considerations of expediency and necessity rather than by considerations stemming from a re-examination of the nature of the church and its vocation in the world' (Kreider 1993, 94). Today most Baptists adopt the ordained ministry of the non-conformist paedo-baptizing tradition (Fiddes 1989, N. Wright 2001, opposed to Warkentin 1982).

A significant minority will, however, make a far more radical critique, being neither Catholic nor Protestant (Walter Klaassen 2001). In this tradition (Kreider 1993, McClendon 1994, Yoder 1998, see also Fahlgren 1998) ordination is seen from the perspective of credo-baptism *as* ordination for ministry and mission: 'These communities, supported by a strong current of contemporary biblical scholarship and an undercurrent of missionary theology, would argue against the fundamental concept of the sacramentally and professionally 'set apart' ministry, whether on the grounds that priesthood is done away with in the new covenant, or because all God's people are priests and every one is a charismatic minister' (Yoder 1998, 286).

The Anabaptists were a movement of restoration. They restored the entire community to their New Testament role as 'saints in common', including the task of discernment, also known as the power of the keys, no longer leaving it to the ordained clergy. This communal ministry of discernment based on credo-baptism has to take responsibility for 'the task of recognizing vocations, acknowledging and encouraging gifts, and helping the gifted to see their role within the rule of God' (McClendon 1994, 144), that is, to mobilize all the baptized for ministry according to their gifts and charismata. They do not think along the lines of a set-apart ministry for individuals, but of *a people set apart*-ministry. This does not mean that there can no longer be itinerant 'apostles' or 'evangelists' or local 'bishops' or 'elders'; it does mean that these must be seen as being only part of the fullness of Christ. For according to this view bishops are part of the laity, and according to this view every Christian is a cleric. Christian leadership is not achieved by exalting (or by denigrating) the gifts of the few, but by discovering that the Spirit has a gift for each. Every member is a minister (McClendon 1994, 369f).

Such a view has consequences for the interpretation of both leadership and baptism. First, if *leadership* in the church is 'a gift among gifts granted in the fullness of Christ, then ordination (not provided in the New Testament) and hierarchy (opposed there) are not essentials of leadership, and may concretely resist the realization of that fullness' (McClendon 1994, 371). The role of the designated leaders was to serve the community by enabling every member in his or her ministry of 'inreach' as well as outreach, so that the church could function in a 'divinely coordinated multiple ministry' (Kreider 1993, 89) following the word of Christ: 'You have one teacher, and you are all students; you have one Father, the one in heaven; you have one instructor, the Messiah' (Matt. 23.8ff). Secondly, *baptism* creates brothers and sisters, co-workers – '*synergoi*' – in ministry and mission for the Kingdom of God:

> They had entered into this common ministry by baptism. Through the laying-on of hands, they had been commissioned to a life of ministry, entered into a new order, and experienced 'ontological' change. And they had been empowered for this new life of service by the outpouring of the Holy Spirit. For them baptism was thus ordination (Kreider 1993, 87).

Conclusion

This article began with an analysis of the rites for baptism and ordination in the Nordic Baptist Churches. We saw that, in this tradition of credo-baptism the theology of ordination has become homeless. It is nothing less than a 'duplication' (a repetition) of credo-baptism, because in it the '*vocatio-bene-dictio-missio*' sequence that applies to all in baptism is repeated in ordination for the few. It creates an atmosphere of irresponsibility on the part of the baptized, but is also reveals a derailment of New Testament ecclesiology, pneumatology and ministry. Furthermore we recognized that the theology of the ordination liturgies in the Nordic Baptist Churches is formed more in the tradition of 'Christendom' than in that of 'Christianity' though the liturgies have been produced by Christians who still practice credo-baptism. Looking for reasons for this lack of consistency we may first of all point to an unwitting lack of theological reflection about the theology of ordination. This can be partly explained by the influence of our paedo-baptizing Lutheran setting, but also by a lack of courage to stand up for the radical position known from the Anabaptist theologians at the time of the Reformation.

In the second part of the article we dealt with Moltmann's suggestion that whenever the church ceases to practice credo-baptism and introduces paedo-baptism a special stress is laid upon ordination and ministry. When the church tried to adapt to the culture of the Roman Empire, its offered privileges, and its growing pressure to make the Christian faith the ideology of the empire, without competitors, a radical transformation of the Christian faith and its liturgies took place. Different and innovative substitute blessings were introduced to mark the apostolic and holy *notae* of the people (*laos*) of God in a situation where the 'resident aliens' ('*paroikoi*') had become parishioners ('*parochianoi*'). These blessings were occasionally called a 'second baptism' following paedo-baptism which was reduced to a soteriological *conditio sine qua non* for the substitutes.

Although Nordic Baptists in their liturgies of ordination still perpetuate the theology of ministry and mission that belonged to Christendom we have to sign up for a more radical change. To perpetuate these features in a post-Christendom culture is not only an anachronism; it is detrimental to the health of a church that realizes the need for a ministry and mission of the whole people of God ('*laos*') in tomorrow's world. If the priesthood of all the baptized interpreted as ordination for ministry and mission is to increase, then the special priesthood of ordination of some believers must decrease. We need a Copernican change. '[L]ike the proverbial cuckoo in the nest, the two will not comfortably co-habit' (David F. Wright, in Bulley 2000: ix).

References

Anhøj, Olaf. 1998. *Liturgihåndbog for danske baptistmenigheder.* (www.baptist-kirken.dk).

Bradshaw, Paul et al. 1992. *The Study of Liturgy.* London: SPCK.

Bradshaw, Paul. 2001. The Effects of the Coming of Christendom on Early Christian Worship. In *The Origins of Christendom in the West,* ed. Alan Kreider. New York: T & T Clark.

Bulley, Colin. 2000. *The Priesthood of Some Believers. Developments from the General to the Special Priesthood in Christian Literature of the First Three Centuries.* Carlisle: Paternoster.

Fahlgren, Sune (ed.). 1998. *På spaning efter framtidens kyrka.* Stockholm: Libris.

– 2003. E-mail to the author of 06.03.2003.

Fiddes, Paul. 1989. *A Leading Question. The Structure and Authority of Leadership in the Local Church.* London: Baptist Publications.

Green, Bernard. 1990. *Prayers and Patters for Christian Worship.* Oxford: Baptist Union of GB.

Hanssen, Ove C. 1987. *Handspåleggelsens funksjon ved kristen initiasjon i Apostlenes Gjerninger.* Lunds University.

Hylleberg, Bent. 1989. Ordination og indvielse i Det danske Baptistsamfund. In *Under bøn og håndspålæggelse. Indvielse af missionærer, diakoner og præster,* ed. Hans Raun Iversen and V. Tranholm-Mikkelsen. Frederiksberg: Anis.

Johnson, Todd E. 1995. Initiation or Ordination? Balthasar Hubmaier's Rite of Baptism. In *Studia Liturgica* 25: 68-95.

Klaassen, Walter. 2001. *Anabaptism: Neither Catholic nor Protestant.* 3rd edition. Ontario: Pandora/Herald Press.

Kreider, Alan. 1993. Abolishing the Laity. An Anabaptist Perspective. In *Anyone for Ordination?* ed. Paul Beasley-Murray, 84-111. Kent: MARC.

– 1999. *The Change of Conversion and the Origin of Christendom.* Harrisburg, Pennsylvania: Trinity Press.

– 2001. Changing Patterns of Conversion in the West. In *The Origins of Christendom in the West*, ed. Alan Kreider. New York: T & T Clark.

Kyrø-Rasmussen, K. 1967. *Hvad skal vi med kirken?* Aalborg: Baptisternes Forlag.

McClendon, J. Wm., Jr. 1994. *Doctrine: Systematic Theology,* Volume II. Nashville: Abingdon Press.

McDonnell, K. and G. T. Montagne. 1991. *Christian Initiation and Baptism in the Holy Spirit. Evidence from the First Eight Centuries.* Collegeville, Minn: The Liturgical Press.

Moltmann, Jürgen. 1998. *The Church in the Power of the Spirit.* London: SCM.

Persson, Lars Åke (ed.). 1987. *Till församlingens tjänst. Handbok.* Stockholm: Libris.

Taranger, Billy (ed.). 1994. *I menighetens tjeneste. Håndbok.* Oslo: Norsk Litteraturselskap.

– 2003. E-mail to the author of 03.03.2003.

Thurian, Max (ed.). 1986-1988. *Churches Respond to BEM*, I-VI. Faith and Order Papers 129, 132, 135, 137, 143, 144. Geneva: World Council of Churches.

Warkentin, Marjorie. 1982. *Ordination. A Biblical-historical View.* Grand Rapids: Eerdmans.

Williams, George H. 1963. The Ancient Church, AD 30-313. In *The Layman in Christian History*, ed. Stephen C. Neill and Hans-Ruedi Weber. Philadelphia: Westminster Press.

Wright, David T. 2001. Augustine and the Transformation of Baptism. In *The Origins of Christendom in the West*, ed. Alan Kreider. New York: T & T Clark.

Wright, Nigel G. 2001. Inclusive Representation: Towards a Doctrine of Christian Ministry. In *The Baptist Quarterly* XXXIX, 4: 159ff.

Yoder, John Howard. 1998. *The Royal Priesthood. Essays Ecclesiological and Ecumenical.* Scottdale, Pennsylvania: Herald Press.

Ordinations in the Free Lutheran Congregations of the Grundtvigian Movement in Denmark

Hasse Neldeberg Jørgensen

N.F.S. Grundtvig (1783-1872) was a Danish theologian, priest, hymn writer, historian, and politician. His influence on Danish church life and the hymns sung in Denmark is enormous.[1]

The extent to which Grundtvig's ideas have influenced Danish church life is, however, not easy to identify and assess. Grundtvig's theological thinking can be very difficult to interpret and its influence, for example on the rites and the organisation of the church and its congregations, is often a matter of local interpretation and practice.

Freedom was one of the key words in all Grundtvig's work. Some may consider him a liberal or a radical, and he certainly opposed the established church, but he was not a spokesman for the fragmentation of the Evangelical Lutheran Church of Denmark (ELCD) into autonomous congregations only linked to another larger community according to their own choice. However, it was his clear perception that the church organisation and its buildings are only the visible framework within which the life of the congregation is enacted (Allchin 1997, 68). Complete freedom should exist within the church. Grundtvig had a much higher regard for the community of believers than for the church as an institution. The pastors of the church should be free in the discharge of their office. He often stressed the necessity of allowing pastors a free hand with regard to the choice of liturgy and rites. In one of his key books, *Elementary Christian Doctrine (Den kristelige Børnelærdom,* 1868), he says that pastors should only be obliged to teach and preach in accordance with the Holy Scripture *to the best of their belief* and to administer the Holy Sacraments

---

1. For an introduction in English to Grundtvig, see Allchin 1997.

to the best of their belief and in accordance with the Lord's command (Grundtvig, 9:500).Grundtvig shared Luther's view that priests should be ordained and he did not oppose the practice of laying-on of hands with prayer. However, in the centre of the liturgy, as he saw it, the Apostles' Creed has pre-eminence. For Grundtvig the Creed with its connection with baptism was 'the one needful thing', which – as the Word of God – would create faith as it mentioned it.

Although freedom was very important to Grundtvig and he talked about a 'free church', he would not suggest the establishment of congregations outside the ELCD, which since 1849 has been a folk church under state authority and in which all church legislation must be approved by Parliament. Under the influence of Grundtvig's thought, an additional law, passed in 1868, gave parishioners the right to form free congregations within the framework of the Church. These congregations are called '*valgmenigheder*', – '*valg*' meaning both to elect and to choose. These free 'electoral congregations' consist, therefore, of believers who choose to belong to a particular congregation and are allowed to choose their pastor themselves. As it is, the ELCD consists of two kinds of congregations: parish congregations and electoral congregations, of which there are currently 30.

In his old age Grundtvig summed up his views and said that free congregations *outside* the ELCD should only be seen as a very last resort (Grundtvig, 10:362). However, about fifteen free Lutheran/Grundtvigian congregations were actually established outside the ELCD during the last decades of the nineteenth century. Another eleven were established in Schleswig, south of the German-Danish border, where there was a significant Danish minority after the 1864 war, a war that Denmark lost. Nine of these congregations were dissolved soon after the area was voted back into Denmark in 1920.

The Grundtvigian Free Congregations (GFCs) are very close to the ELCD but are totally independent in their organization. They have always had the freedom to install or ordain their own pastors, using liturgical and ritual practices other than those of the ELCD. At least 42 pastors were ordained in the GFCs in the period 1874-2002. To this number must be added at least 20 others who were ordained for ministry in the GFCs in the German-occupied southern zone of Jutland from 1864 to 1920. In the same period 10 cases are recorded of pastors ordained in a GFC and later accepted as ELCD pastors without any consideration of re-ordination.

Ordination in the Grundtvigian Free Congregations

The questions to be dealt with in this article are the following: How did the GFCs approach ordination for ministry and why did they handle it as they did? How do they do it today? Do the ordinations in the free congregations represent a special Grundtvigian point of view on ordination? Is there a recognisable unity between the free congregations? If not, is every ordination a kind of *ad hoc* rite made up for one particular event, invented by the congregation, the person who ordains and the one who will be ordained? And last, but nonetheless important, how does the ELCD view these free ordinations?

Grundtvig did not oppose the ordination of pastors as such. Originally he was in favour of apostolic succession as we know it from the Church of Sweden and the Church of England. However, in the 1830s he changed his perception of ordination. It ceased to matter to him any longer if it were a bishop who ordained or not. What mattered was the laying-on of hands with prayer for the gift and enlightenment of the Holy Spirit. Only the Holy Spirit truly calls the shepherd, he said, referring to Acts 20 (Grundtvig, 9:403-04, 570-71).

The first Ordination

The first ordination of a pastor who had been called to a GFC took place in 1874. The free Danish congregation in Rødding, just south of the Danish-German, border had for a long time wanted their own pastor. They had agreed on Cornelius Appel. He was a teacher and not, as all other candidates for ministry were, a theologian educated at the University of Copenhagen. The ordination was planned to take place at the Folk High School in Askov, just north of the border. The school was part of what might be called the 'Grundtvigian family'. The founding of schools like that had been inspired by Grundtvig's thinking on education (Allchin 1997, 167). They were small residential colleges, which worked with young adults, for the most part from a peasant background.

In the planning of this ordination, it was not even mentioned that the congregation should try to arrange it in a parish church. The people behind this remarkable event in the history of the Church in Denmark knew that it really was a grey area they were entering. The ordination service took place in the school's assembly hall. A number of Grundtvigian electoral congregations and their parish priests participated. Except for a few they all followed a request to wear their official dress, a black cassock with a white ruff. Appel was ordained by the first electoral congregation pastor in Denmark, Vilhelm Birkedal from Ryslinge. The ordinand wore a cassock, which he had borrowed for the occasion.

In 1912 the ceremony was described and commented on by a Grundtvigian priest, Lavrids Nyegaard, Birkedal's son-in-law. Nyegaard states that the first free ordination was not in accordance with Grundtvig's perception of an ordination. He reports that the Apostles' Creed was said during the ordination and that the ordinand was presented with five questions, to which he had to express his assent and promise to act accordingly: these questions concerned the faith of the Church, as contained in the Apostles' Creed; the right distribution of the Sacraments as instituted by the Lord; the preaching of the Gospel with the enlightenment given by the Holy Spirit and in accordance with the confessions of the Church; the building up of God's congregation, to the best of his ability, and acting as a Christian in the spirit of love and faith (Nyegaard 1912, 160-161; Schrøder and Helweg 1874, 19). For Nyegaard it was wrong that all these promises were not followed by Grundtvig's phrase '*to the best of my belief*' (Nyegaard 1912, 161).

After the questions and promises the rest of the ordination took place in accordance with the usual rite used in the ELCD, including conferral of the office of ministry. Thereafter both pastors and lay people from the congregation of Rødding took part in the laying-on of hands.

The ordination in Askov had legal consequences for the participating pastors. Schrøder and Helweg, the headmasters of the school, published a booklet with their statement about the event. It was a reply to the diocesan Bishop of Ribe, who was anxious to know exactly what had happened. Furthermore they found it important to inform the so-called 'Meeting of friends', which was a nation-wide group of Grundtvigians that met annually in Odense. Charges were made by the Ministry of Church Affairs against the pastors. The Supreme Court finally adjudicated on the matter. The pastors were sentenced to only moderate fines, not because of their participation but because they had worn the cassock during the ordination![2]

The official dress was obviously the important sign when the meetings between pastors from the ELCD and those from the free congregations and assemblies were to be classified as official or unofficial. Without his cassock, a pastor from the ELCD was apparently considered a private person. This particular Danish cassock then became a topic of discussion for the free pastors. Most of them preferred to be dressed as 'a proper pastor'. By using the cassock they were able to demonstrate that even though they were pastors of free

---

2. The cassock is official dress and wearing it required specific permission from the government Ministry of Church Affairs. The pastors of the free congregations were allowed to use the cassock only a few years later, in 1912 (Roesen 1976, 358).

congregations they had a close relationship with the ELCD. This was a demonstration, so to speak, that the Evangelical Lutheran Church in Denmark consisted of parishes, and electoral and free congregations!

The Grundtvigians met in Askov in 1881 to formulate demands to the ELCD for more freedom according to the principles that Grundtvig had expressed. The oath of the pastor should be very short, they thought, just 'to the best of one's belief to teach in accordance with the Holy Spirit and to distribute the Sacraments as commanded by the Lord' (Lindhardt 1978, 103). Among other changes, they wanted the definite possibility of ordaining non-theologians, if they were considered qualified, and freedom for the congregations themselves to call the new pastor, instead of the pastor being appointed by the Ministry/King. The immediate success of the so-called 'Askov Address' was limited but in 1901 a new liberal government came to power in Denmark. Many of the politicians were closely related to the Grundtvigian movement and several of the Askov demands found their way into legislation. For example, in 1903 the parish councils were given the right to choose from among applicants for the post of parish priest and to recommend to the Ministry of Church Affairs who should be appointed; children were allowed to receive Holy Communion before confirmation and the local congregation could choose together with their priest which of the different forms of liturgy they wished to have. However, one of the main demands of the Askov Address, that the pastors' oath should be changed and simplified was not acted on. Candidates for ordination actually made (and still make) two promises: one to the bishop at ordination, in which they promised that their preaching would be in accordance with the Word of God as found in the Bible and witnessed to in the confessions of the church. A second promise, made in writing just before or after ordination, acknowledges that the Word of God is found equally in the Bible and in the confessions of the church. This second promise further states the new pastor's obligation of obedience to church law and to the authorities of ELCD. The expression 'equally' in the second promise clearly indicates Grundtvig's influence and his view of the importance of the Apostles' Creed, but it has left the ELCD with two oaths, given in or around the same rite, but clearly expressing different points of view about the confessions.

In 1915 a group of people, gathered around Jacob Appel, the headmaster of Askov Folk High School, tried once again to convince the politicians of the importance of a 'free people's church'. Jacob Appel was the son of the first GFC pastor in Rødding. He had for a period been the government minister for church, education and culture. Now he and his friends argued, in an 'Askov Address', for a church federation, very free and consisting of electoral congregations. In order to allow even the most liberal priests to hold office in the church, there should be no specific confession. However, their proposal was completely rejected and it was obvious that the parish system could not be done away with (Lindhardt 1978, 108).

The meetings that resulted in the Askov Addresses might in other countries be seen as assemblies of a synodical character, and certainly in a way that is what they were. It is obvious that the group of Grundtvigian delegates from all over Denmark had a purpose, an articulated demand for change within the ELCD. On the other hand the Grundtvigians themselves vehemently refused to call these events a synod. The movement had from the beginning opposed any kind of church organization where laity and priests have a framework for discussion of church matters that might result, for example, in changes in church legislation.

Again and again the interpretation of freedom for Christians and their congregations is the argument against organized synods with a juridical involvement. The Askov Addresses therefore represent a unique expression in the history of the Grundtvigian, non-organized movement, in Denmark.

More Congregations, More Ordinations

By the end of the nineteenth century many Grundtvigian groups considered forming either electoral congregations or GFCs. At Askov Folk High School, a form of College offering training for ministry in the free congregations was established (Lund 1965, 75-76). Initially it was not for Denmark but for the Danish congregations in the USA and South America that the training was planned. The Danish bishops refused to ordain non-theologians for ministry abroad. One of the students was Niels Dael who became an important figure in the GFCs and in the ordinations of their pastors.[3] Dael was ordained in 1886 by the GFC pastor Rasmus Lund on the island of Mors.[4] Rasmus Lund had himself been ordained in the ELCD. Niels Dael spent a number of years in Argentina as a pastor to the Danish emigrants. When he came back to Denmark in 1908 he became the pastor of the GFCs in Høve and Havrebjerg in Zealand.

A few years later he bought a farm called Liselund where he founded a school similar to the one in Askov. Dael called his school a 'School for the Congregation'. A number of men who later became pastors in GFCs attended

---

3. Niels Dael was portrayed in Jensen 1957.
4. Following a discussion on children's right to participate in the Holy Communion the congregation on Mors chose to change their status from an electoral congregation to a GFC. They left the official church!

his courses. Niels Dael ordained most of them, either on Liselund or in the church where their congregation met for worship. This ordination practice eventually led to his being given a nickname among the Grundtvigians, 'the bishop of the GFCs', but he certainly was never appointed bishop by any synod or assembly. Events simply took place as they did and, like many other things related to the Grundtvigians, especially in the GFC's, there is a notable lack of a solid and articulated theology behind practice and an articulated and clearly expressed point of view on matters concerning the life of the congregations and the church as such. In the 1930s Dael took an active part in the discussion on women pastors and ordained the first one. As in 1874 with the free ordination south of the Danish-German border, it was again in this area that the first female pastor exercised her ministry. Her name was Maren Sørensen from Valsbøl. For many years, without ordination, she had preached, baptised and distributed the Holy Communion. In 1940 she was ordained without an actual calling from a particular congregation or even any prospects of becoming a pastor.[5]

It is important to note, that Dael's ordinations were accepted in the ELCD. A theologian called Helge Hostrup was ordained by him in 1925 for ministry in the GFC in Frederiksborg (*Højskolebladet* 1926:1) and only two years' later he was employed as an assistant vicar in the ELCD without any form of re-ordination. Another example is that of the well known Grundtvigian pastor, Aage Møller, who was also ordained in 1925. This ordination took place without any identification of calling. The congregation in Rønshoved, where he was to be the next pastor was so very free that they did not accept any kind of organisation; no council, no list of members. When Møller was ordained, three teachers from Askov, along with the pastors, took part in the laying-on of hands. Aage Møller was later called as pastor to an electoral congregation in Mellerup without anyone ever questioning his ordination.

Niels Dael's ordination rite was very simple. He himself never commented on the theological implications in writing, but as far as it has been described in reports of the ordinations that took place, it can be summed up as follows: the ordinand stood facing the altar where Dael was presiding; Dael preached and then addressed the ordinand in a very personal way and invoked a blessing on his work as a pastor. Then the ordinand knelt and during the laying-on of hands Dael said the Apostles' Creed followed by the Lord's Prayer and closed the rite with the Aaronic blessing. The important thing for Niels Dael was to

---

5. The law permitting the access of women to ordination within the ELCD was passed in the Danish Parliament in 1947.

follow the New Testament pattern as he understood it: laying-on of hands during epicletic prayer[6]. As far as can be seen from reports in contemporary journals, representatives of the laity always participated in the laying-on of hands, just as they had at the first ordination in Askov in 1874.

Ordinations by ELCD Bishops

In 1939 the GFC of Aagaard in Jutland called a new pastor. It was a young theologian named Richard Andersen, who had been a teacher at the Folk High School in Rødding for about two years. He did not approve of the ordinations at Liselund and wished to be ordained by a bishop. He then called upon Bishop Noack, diocesan Bishop of Haderslev. He was invited to an interview with Noack and was told the actual date of the ordination. Richard Andersen wondered why the bishop had not commented on Aagaard's status as a GFC, so he asked: 'I suppose that the bishop is aware that the congregation in Aagaard is a GFC?' 'Yes, I realise that', the bishop said 'but I expect that you do not have a religion of your own?' Andersen certainly did not! (Hansen, 1987: 96). The Ministry of Church Affairs later reprimanded Bishop Noack, not for having ordained a GFC pastor but for ordaining him together with an ordinand appointed to office as a parish pastor in ELCD.

Exactly the same happened in 1953 when Bishop Ølgaard of Odense ordained the GFC pastor Helge Noe-Nyegaard in the cathedral. He was not a theologian, but holder of a MA degree (Noe-Nyegaard 2000). A very important document has survived from this ordination, a 'Certificate of ordination'[7], which the bishop gave to Helge Noe-Nyegaard. Such a document is not known from any other ordinations of GFC pastors, and the document is even more remarkable in that it says that the ordination is only valid for service as a pastor in Trængstrup GFC and does not allow the pastor to apply for or to hold office in the ELCD.

What are the theological consequences? Does is mean that the ordination did not have the universal remit that ordinations normally have? The bishop must surely have been aware of the fact that the ELCD never rejects ordinations from other Christian denominations. The only hindrance might be the applicant's lack of academic background, as ordinands at that time had to be theologians educated at the university or be in possession of a related academic

---

6. He points this out in an article in *Højskolebladet* nos 12 and 13, 1925, where he points to the sending out of Paul and Barnabas as the basic model – and the Holy Spirit as the real ordainer.
7. A copy of the document is in the author's possession.

training. In contrast to this quite another expression was used in 1916, when the GFC in Holstebro had their new assistant pastor ordained by the senior pastor. When priests and laity were laying-on hands the ordaining minister said, 'The Grundtvigian Free Congregation of Holstebro hereby gives you, Jens Nielsen Krustrup, in the name of the congregation of Jesus Christ, authority to serve as a pastor here and everywhere where Christians may need your service' (Lillelund 1985, 41). They obviously did not doubt that they were members of and even acting on behalf of the universal Church.

In 1954 the first ordination of a GFC pastor in the Free Church took place in Rødding. Once again this congregation wrote an important chapter in the history of church life in Denmark. The diocesan Bishop of Ribe performed the ordination according to the rite of the ELCD, but there was a significant difference, as the chairman of the congregation council and the ordinand's father participated in the laying-on of hands (*Højskolebladet* 1954, 534). The bishop announced that for him it was a moment of particular importance, because it had been his predecessor in the Diocese of Ribe who had taken legal action against the priests who participated in the first ordination of a Rødding GFC pastor in 1874.

The connection between the ELCD and the GFC was obvious to everyone and had been so for many years. The influence of the Grundtvigian movement was vast and to a certain extent church legislation as such was influenced by Grundtvig's thinking. The connection was significantly proved when the new ELCD hymnbook was published in 1953. It contained a great number of Grundtvig's hymns, approximately one out of three, and was practically regarded as an additional confessional document of the ELCD. Of the 791 hymns in the 2003 hymnal, a quarter are by Grundtvig.

A group of bishops discussed the formalities of ordination of GFC pastors with the Ministry of Church Affairs, and in 1955 it was agreed in writing that they were allowed to ordain, though their ordinations were to be regarded as private acts with ecclesiastical but not juridical consequence (Roesen 1976, 359). This is certainly very strange indeed: the bishop ordains because he is a bishop, not as a private person. Furthermore it had been accepted for many years that GFC pastors could hold office in an ELCD parish congregation. By law it was also accepted that non-theologians could apply for a post in the ELCD when they had been GFC pastors for seven years.

Ordained or Not?

It is quite clear from the available sources that ordinations in the GFC are indeed very different in their liturgical structure and perception. A number of pastors have been ordained by bishops and even signed the priestly oath of the ELCD. It appears that there are at least six different possibilities for ordination represented in the GFC family:

Ordination in a GFC church by another GFC pastor
Installation in a GFC church by another GFC pastor
Installation in a GFC church by an ELCD pastor
 (electoral congregation pastor or parish priest)
Ordination in a GFC church by an ELCD pastor
 (electoral congregation pastor or parish priest)
Ordination in a GFC church by an ELCD bishop
Ordination in a cathedral by an ELCD bishop

The installation is indeed very Lutheran. Luther emphasised the importance of the presentation and installation of pastors in the congregation that had actually called them. The question therefore arises as to what ordination is and whether it is necessary for the pastor's ministry and administration of the Sacraments. What difference does it make? It might be expected that any GFC pastor applying to hold office in the ELCD would be met by a requirement for re-ordination. However, there has not been one single example of such a requirement since the first ordination took place in 1874. In 1976, August Roesen, the most senior official in the Ministry of Church Affairs, described the GFCs as holding a unique position in relation to the ELCD (Roesen 1976, 355-57). They have many rights and their priests are accepted as colleagues and as rightly ordained.

The ordinations by Niels Dael have been mentioned in particular. A more recent example is from Aagaard in 1976. Gunnar Kasper Hansen, pastor in Aagaard from 1976 to 1991 recalls the day of his ordination/installation as follows: 'We had a normal Sunday service... Just before the hymn preceding the homily, Richard Andersen (who himself had been ordained by the Bishop of Haderslev, in Haderslev in 1939) gave an address in which he said that he, on behalf of the congregation, hereby installed me as the new pastor (with a handshake, as far as I recall) and then I presided for the rest of the service' (Hansen 2000). That certainly is a very 'low church' concept of ordination, which is practised in a number of GFCs. However, the really interesting aspect is that, since 1991, Hansen has been a pastor in the Danish congregation in Brussels, which is an ELCD congregation. No one ever doubted that the installation was valid as an ordination.

It might be argued that the expression 'anything goes' seems to describe the situation in ELCD. However, matters are not so simple. Apart from a few

examples of very 'low church' ordinations it is important to note that all the
ordaining ministers who participated in GFC ordinations had themselves been
ordained either by a bishop or by a pastor who had been ordained by a bishop.
As a further illustration of the close relationship between the three different
kinds of Lutheran congregations it is worth noting that 2 out of 10 GFC
pastors and 7 out of 26 electoral congregation pastors previously held office as
parish priests in ELCD before they were called to one of the 'free congregations'.[8]

Free Ordinations – Free Church?

It is obvious that the variety of ordination rites, views and approaches to
ordination in the GFCs calls for some reflection on whether there is in fact a
kind of free church movement in these congregations. Evidently they are very
autonomous in their structure and there has never been, as mentioned earlier,
any kind of Grundtvigian synod, at least not in a strict and organised form, to
decide what should be preferred and what should be rejected. However, for
many years, until an intermission in 1920[9], the Meetings of Friends (*Ven-
nemøder*) discussed items of mutual interest, and the meetings in Askov in
1881 and in 1914 (the second Askov Address was not published until 1915)
could be regarded as synods. These meetings were of course without any
juridical consequence for the congregations participating: that would have
been a major departure from Grundtvig's ideals for a free congregation in a
free church. The contour of a free church is difficult to identify. The impression is that the GFCs have always regarded themselves as free in relation to the
ELCD, which has, however, been their context and their closest family. It
might be claimed that the free congregation model represents a way of fulfilling Grundtvig's ideals for the Evangelical Lutheran Church as closely as possible without actually being part of the state church. As to the influence from
the free congregations, it could be said that they have always allowed and
certainly expected the laity to take an active part in ordinations, both as readers

---

8. See *Teologisk Stat* 2000, but also note that 8 of the congregations share 4 pastors.
9. Since 1950 there have been annual meetings of the Union of Grundtvigian Electoral
   Congregations and Free Congregations, but this Union has been careful not to articulate common demands or proposals for the future of ELCD. For some non-Grundtvi-
   gian groups in the church, the Union represents a conservative line. The overall view of
   the 40 congregations in the Union seems to be that it would be contrary to Grundtvig's
   ideas on congregational freedom if the Union were to formulate doctrines or common
   statements.

and in the laying-on of hands. This possibility did not exist officially in the ELCD until 1987.

Conclusion

It is arguable that the ordinations in the GFCs represent at least a possible version of a Lutheran ordination, in which it is made visible that a candidate becomes a pastor because they have been called to be so. As matters stand, all members of both electoral congregations and the GFCs are allowed to vote when a candidate is elected for ministry in their congregation. That fact, together with the ordination in the church where they will minister as pastor and last, but not the least, the laying-on of hands seems quite Lutheran and can obviously be regarded as a reflection of the *rite vocatus* of *Confessio Augustana* XIV. Here there is an election, a sending to and a reception by the congregation. However, it is only possible to reach the above conclusion, if it may be presumed that the matter has been articulated and presented as a theological reflection on Lutheran and Grundtvigian premises. Especially here there is a major problem, as no such overall accepted theological reflection has been documented in the sources found so far. This may be because it seems to contradict Grundtvig's perception of freedom for each congregation. On the other hand there certainly seems to be an underlying and common understanding of the relationship between pastor and congregation similar to that described by Luther (Luther 1982, 139-40). Nevertheless, research on the Grundtvigian Free Congregations must rely on their practice as the source of information, as they have neither doctrinal statements, nor synodical decisions, nor liturgical regulations.

References

Allchin, A.M. 1997. *N.F.S. Grundtvig: An introduction to his Life and Work.* Aarhus: Aarhus University Press

Grundtvig, N.F.S. 1904-09. *Udvalgte skrifter*, vols. 1-10. Ed. Holger Begtrup. Copenhagen: Gyldendalske Boghandel, Nordisk Forlag

Hansen, Gunnar Kasper (ed.). 1987. *Aagaard Frimenighed 1887-1987*. Aagaard: Aagaard Frimenighed.

Hansen, Gunnar Kasper. 2001. Personal account.

Højskolebladet 1876 –. (periodical).

Jensen, Jens Marinus. 1957. *Præsten Niels Dael, Liselund*. Aarhus: Forlaget Aros.

Lillelund, Schultz-Jakobsen and Bojsen-Møller. 1985. *Holstebro Valgmenigheds-kirke 100 år*. Holstebro.

Lund, Hans. 1965. *Askov Højskole 1865-1915*. Copenhagen:Gyldendal.

Lindhardt, P.G. 1978. Den anden Askovadresse. In *Kirkehistoriske Samlinger 1978*. Copenhagen: Selskabet for Danmarks Kirkehistorie.

Luther, Martin. (1520). Asger Chr. Højlund (ed.). 1982. *Om kirkens babyloniske fangenskab*. Copenhagen: Credo Forlag.

Noe-Nyegaard, Helge. 2000. Personal account.

Nyegaard, Laurids. 1912. *Vilhelm Birkedal. En levnedsskildring*. Vol. 3. Copenhagen: Nationale Forfatteres Forlag.

Roesen, August. 1976. *Dansk kirkeret*. Hillerød: Den Danske Præsteforening.

Schrøder, L. and Helweg, L. 1874. *Om Corn. Appels Ordination. En meddelelse til det kirkelige Vennemøde den 8.de Sept. 1874*. Odense. Document printed in 'Chr. Milo's Officin'.

Rites for Commissioning/ Ordination to Ministry in the Salvation Army in the Nordic Countries related to the Theological Development in the Salvation Army internationally

Gudrun Lydholm

The Salvation Army has its roots in the Wesleyan tradition, and particularly the transatlantic[1] revivalism, in nineteenth century England. William Booth was ordained as a minister in the Methodist New Connexion.[2] It was from there that he and his wife left for independent ministry, carrying with them Wesleyan theology and practice.

The Salvation Army considers the year 1865 to be its year of birth. In that year, William Booth joined a tent mission in East London, of which he soon became the leader. It was originally an ecumenical endeavour with people from different churches who wanted to reach the masses of East London with the gospel. It developed into a permanent mission, the East London Mission, and later when it spread into other parts of the country, it became the Christian Mission. In accordance with Methodist tradition, it was organised with a yearly conference, with William Booth as General Superintendent. In 1878 a

---

1. The reference here is to the revival within the nineteen century Holiness movement with roots both in North America and England. Figures such as Charles D. Finney and Phoebe Palmer had a profound influence on both William and Catherine Booth.
2. William Booth was the founder of The Salvation Army. His co-founder and wife was Catherine Booth. She was very much the thinker and theologian behind it all, and also a well-known public preacher and speaker.

mission statement said, 'The Christian Mission is ... a volunteer Army'. The word 'volunteer' was deleted and the word 'Salvation' inserted. Thence the military metaphor became the basic metaphor. Flags, uniforms, ranks, bands and so on, came into being within the first year, together with military discipline and rule.[3] In accordance with Methodist tradition the Christian Mission and the early Salvation Army practised infant baptism and shared the Lord's Supper as a monthly celebration.[4]

In the theology and the practice of ecclesiastical order, William and Catherine Booth shared John Wesley's conviction that it was biblical to connect Church order to the mission of the Church. Wesley wrote:

> What is the end of all ecclesiastical order? Is it not to bring souls from the power of Satan to God? And to build them up in his fear and love? Order, then, is so far valuable as it answers these ends; and if it answers them not, it is nothing worth (Baker 1981, 2:205-206).

Like John Wesley, the Booths were convinced that there was no single pattern of Church order in the New Testament. Therefore denominations were free to

---

3. The military metaphor was in keeping with the spirit of the time, and it spread in UK so that for every Mission Station in 1878 there were 20 corps in 1886, and for every evangelist in 1878 there were 25 officers in 1886. It soon crossed the borders into continental Europe, to USA, India and other places.

4. In 1883 the Salvation Army abandoned sacramental practice, for pragmatic reasons, from fear of dissension and division about the mode of administration, for example, on the matter of unfermented wine, women officers administering the sacrament and so on, and for theological reasons. Theologically, there was a strong conviction that the emerging Army was free to respond to the guidance of the Holy Spirit in the same way as the New Testament Church had been. As Salvationists understood it, in true apostolic succession, they felt themselves free to adapt the message of the gospel to meet the needs of their specific mission. There could therefore be discontinuity with the history and tradition of established churches. The Holy Spirit's guidance and biblical example came before strong ecclesiology. In addition, there came from some quarters of the nineteenth century Holiness movement a deep distrust of ritualistic practices that might lull believers into a false sense of security regarding their relationship with God. Communion with Christ, in Holiness teaching, was the outcome of an inner transformation, an entire sanctification, where the purity of Christ was mirrored in the life of the believer. In contrast, the sacraments appeared to be outward practices, indicating superficial religion without inner power. Catherine Booth in particular was the advocate of this stance and voiced it very strongly. Instead of infant baptism a dedication ceremony of the infant was introduced.

establish ordination and Church order which was in keeping with their practices.

Significant for Methodism, particularly at this time of revival in the new Wesleyan groupings, was the practice of putting new converts to work in the church. This practice was developed and stressed even further in the later Salvation Army. It was the priesthood of all believers put into practice. Connected with the belief in the priesthood of all believers is Martin Luther's notion of vocation.

As people are called to different vocations, the Salvation Army acknowledges that all believers are engaged in ministry. Whatever vocation Salvation Army soldiers are engaged in, the focus of their life is to serve God and to bear witness to his saving power. The ministry is very clear – all are called and charged to be followers of Christ and to let their life reflect this calling. Some are called to the specific ministry of preaching, teaching or administration – to spiritual leadership, to make this their vocation. In the Salvation Army this calling will most frequently be to officership. The officer is first and foremost a soldier with the same calling and charge as all other soldiers, but with a specific calling to spiritual leadership. This leadership may take different forms: for the majority it is to be leader and 'pastor' of a corps. It can be as a leader of a social institution or outreach, as a missionary, or as an administrator and 'overseer'. The officers bind themselves to 'martyria', 'missio' and 'diakonia' and to maintain Salvation Army teaching (See on the Officers' covenant below). The vocation of officership does not mean that preaching, teaching and leadership cannot be part of the ministries of soldiers, but it is emphasised that an ordination to spiritual leadership is especially integral to officership. Salvation Army officers are given authority to exercise their spiritual leadership by the call of God, confirmed by God's people.

The soldiers and officers are sent to the world and it is understood that all vocations, all ministries are 'diakonia' – service. Such service must take body and shape in ministry that seeks the lost.

Commissioning to Different Kinds of Ministry

The basic commissioning is to soldiership. It is the foundation of all other commissioning, including the ordination to officership. The soldier's enrolment is not normally repeated.

Enrolment as a soldier can be equated in its meaning with believers' baptism as it recognises the truth that all who are in Christ are baptised into one body by the Holy Spirit.[5] It is in keeping with the belief that divine grace can be received without the use of any material element.[6]

The Swearing-in of Soldiers

The conditions for being sworn in as a soldier are: witness to salvation through faith in Christ; a time of preparation, where the doctrines, principles and evangelistic witness of the Army are taught and accepted; an acceptance by the corps census board, and a signing of the soldier's covenant – articles of war.

The ceremony takes place in a public meeting such as Sunday worship and will generally be performed by the corps officer. The flag will be present.[7] There will be an affirmation of faith – perhaps a reading or reciting of the doctrines (Salvation Story, ix, and Salvation Army songbooks), a reference to the articles of war of which the last passage will be quoted: 'I witness that I freely enter into this covenant, convinced that the love of Christ requires the devotion of my life to his service for the salvation of the whole world. I am determined, by God's help, to be a true soldier of the Salvation Army'.

Then follows the question: 'Do you declare in the presence of God and this congregation that you undertake, by the help of the Holy Spirit, to live and work as a true soldier of Jesus Christ and of the Salvation Army, according to the witness and promises you make this day. If so, raise your right hand and say: I do'.

The officer will charge the soldier to keep the promises and, by God's grace, be a blessing to the world in which he/she lives. The articles of war, which have been signed, will be presented with the words: 'In the name of the Lord whom we love and serve, I accept your declarations and receive you as a soldier of the ....corps of the Salvation Army'. The ceremony concludes with a prayer of dedication, during which the soldiers kneel under the flag.

---

5. By baptism the Army understands the gracious act of God, by which, in response to repentance and faith in Jesus Christ, the person dies to the old self and rises to the new. Thus they are initiated into Christ and incorporated into his body (Rom. 6.3-6; Gal. 3.27).
6. The witness of the Salvation Army is simply that the presence of the risen Christ may be fully realised, and the divine grace freely received, without the use of any material element. The Salvationist believes most ardently in the real presence (Coutts 1975, 97)
7. In all Salvation Army ceremonies with the character of a dedication the Salvation Army flag is used. Its three colours, red, blue and yellow symbolise faith in the triune God and in God's works of grace –salvation and sanctification.

The Commissioning and Ordination of Officers

Foundational for officership and ordination to this is a call to spiritual leadership. It is a personal call, but not a private one. It is a response to the communal call of the Army. 'It is important to notice that the making of an officer has two aspects. From one aspect the initiative is from God in the calling, equipping and sending forth of this minister. From another the community has its own important role to play in the process. The Army must test the call of a candidate, discern the gifts of the Spirit in this person and receive what is a gift from the Spirit to the Church. It also authorises the officer to serve in a leadership capacity and is responsible for the welfare and ongoing training of the new leader.'[8] When a soldier claims a personal call to officership, it is taken very seriously and it will be tested in the local corps and at divisional and territorial level.[9]

The Covenant

The first part of the Commissioning to officership is the signing of the covenant. The cadets will normally spend a day in solitude, prayer and reflection. At the end of the day or the following day the Covenant Service will take place at the Training College. It will centre on the covenant, perhaps with a meditation on each of the promises. The covenant states:

> Called by God to proclaim the Gospel of our Lord and Saviour Jesus Christ as an officer of The Salvation Army, I bind myself to him in this solemn covenant, to love and serve him supremely all my days, to live to win souls and make their salvation the first purpose of my life, to care for the poor, feed the hungry, clothe the naked, love the unlovable and befriend those who have no friends, to maintain the doctrines and principles of the Salvation Army, and, by God's grace, to prove myself a worthy officer. Done

---

8. Quotation from a working paper by Major Ian Cooper in connection with the Army's response to the BEM document
9. The Army has over the years been very sensitive to the calling of individuals and has had the courage to take many 'risks' with people who lacked formal education and visible gifts for leadership or had a dubious past. During training many 'hidden' gifts have come to the surface and during their officership people have given the most amazing service and reached 'the unreachable' with the gospel. They have developed a gifted leadership that was unthinkable at the 'humble' beginning. Some 'risks' have of course not produced such good results. This practice is very much in keeping with the Army's conviction that the aim of ministry is to save souls. Mission is the overall purpose in accordance with the quotation of John Wesley noted at the beginning of this article.

in the strength of my Lord and Saviour and in the presence of the Territorial Commander,[10] Training College officers and fellow cadets.[11]

It is a very solemn occasion. The signing of the covenant takes place at the mercy seat during time of meditation and prayer where each cadet is given plenty of time for prayer and the actual signature. [12] When it is signed the cadet gives it to the TC who countersigns it.

Ordination and Dedication

This is a grand public occasion of worship with soldiers and officers attending from all over the country; there are flags, music and singing. It is performed by the TC on behalf of the General.[13]

At the beginning of the ordination service the cadets will march into the hall following their flag and with a smaller flag attached to their uniform tunic. The training principal will present the cadets and hand them over to the TC. During the ceremony the cadets make a public affirmation of faith: 'In the name of God, the Father, the Son and the Holy Spirit, and in the presence of officers, soldiers and friends of the Salvation Army here assembled, we declare that we believe....' The 11 Doctrines are then proclaimed and the TC questions the cadets:

---

10. Hereafter TC
11. This passage 'to feed the poor ....' from the ordination ceremony was inserted into the covenant in 2001. The covenant has in its essence been the same for years. The first covenant I could find in SA archives in London was from 1918. Due to the destruction of International Headquarters during Word War II a lot of historical material has been lost. I found a Danish covenant from 1923 and the wording was the same. Looking at reports from copies of the *War Cry* in the 1880s it seems that the structure of covenant and commissioning services has been in place from very early days.
12. The 'mercy seat' is the Salvation Army altar at the front of the hall. A cadet being trained for officership will normally be living in a communal setting for two years with theoretical and practical training. The most important objective of the training is the spiritual formation. Ordination takes place after these two years. Distance learning continues for the next 5 years.
13. The TC has the legal responsibility for Salvation Army personnel, activities and possessions within the area: he/she is the spiritual 'overseer'. Often the area is the same as the national borders of the country as is the case with Denmark, but when it comes to the other Nordic countries Norway/Iceland/the Faeroe Islands are an entity, and so are Sweden/Latvia, and Finland/Estonia. The General is the world leader of the Salvation Army spiritually, legally and administratively, and is the only elected person. A High Council consisting of TCs from around the world and other senior leaders elects him/her for a 5-year period.

Do you promise faithfully to maintain and proclaim these truths? (We do)

Do you regard it as your duty to bear witness to the whole world, to strive to lead mankind to its only Saviour and, for Christ's sake, to care for the poor, feed the hungry, clothe the naked, love the unlovable, and befriend those who have no friends? (We do)

Do you promise by Christian example, holy living, boundless charity, and adherence to the principles and discipline of our Movement to show yourselves faithful officers of the Salvation Army? (We do)

The following part is to each individually. Usually, at least in the Nordic countries, the cadet will kneel during this part. 'Accepting your promises and recognising that God has called, ordained and empowered you to be a minister of Christ and of his gospel, I commission you an officer of the Salvation Army.'

When all have been ordained and commissioned the TC offers the prayer of dedication. By this prayer the officer is committed to the help and guidance of the Holy Spirit, and to the intercession of the community. It has not been customary for the TC to lay his/her hands on the officer during the prayer, but this symbolic act seems to have come into use in recent years at least in the Nordic countries.[14] After this dedication, the officer will receive his/her appointment and the Officer's commission.

The wording of the ordination presented here was introduced in February 2002.[15] The previous wording was introduced in 1978 and made use of the word 'ordination', which had not previously been part of Salvation Army terminology:[16] 'In accepting these pledges which you have each made, I commission you an officer of the Salvation Army and ordain you as ministers of Christ and his gospel.' The authority given is that of spiritual leadership understood as servant leadership.[17] It is an ordination to the world: that is the focus, whatever the appointment. An officer is considered an officer for the

---

14. Below, where the practice between the Nordic countries will be compared, it is evident that the imposition of hands has been used quite frequently. It depends not so much on the difference between the countries as on the TC who is performing the ordination.

15. It was sent out as a memorandum from the General on 15th February 2002 to all TCs and other international leaders. Such a memorandum is expected to be followed by the different territories, and thus this wording has been in use since 2002.

16. This wording became controversial. See details below in the section on the contemporary international forum: development in the terminology of ordination and commissioning.

17. It means to be willing to do whatever is needed for the sake of the work and of people,

rest of their life (if they do not leave the work) and retired officers are retired from the work but not from officership.[18]

The dedication, ordination and commissioning is not repeated if it is agreed that an officer is to return to the work after having left it. He/she will be re-accepted, and this is seldom part of any public event, but a personal encounter between the TC and the officer.

The Installation of Territorial Leaders

The installation will be performed by the General or on behalf of him/her by another TC or international senior leader. It is a public event with representatives from the whole territory. The introduction to the ceremony recalls the original calling, covenant and ordination as a basis for this new responsibility, then comes the Challenge with the symbols of the Word of God (to preach the truth), the Flag (to maintain the essentials of Salvation Army teaching), the Mercy Seat (the focus on salvation and sanctification), the people (to serve them and accept responsibility for their spiritual well-being). After this the Charge to preach the word of God, to preserve and protect Army teaching, to raise up officer candidates, to provide pastoral care to officers, to maintain Army discipline, to provide full opportunity for people to utilise their gifts and fulfil their calling, to administer SA work, property, finance, social programmes. After the promises have been given the dedicatory prayer is offered. The ceremony concludes with the Induction, '... I now install you as leaders of ... '.[19]

As the installation is international, it will be the same in whatever country it is done. It will be repeated when territorial leaders are sent to a new territory.

Similarities and Differences

All three types of commissioning are public occasions: they take place within the worshipping community and signify a transition to a new status or func-

---

but each appointment will also give the officer specific authority. As the commanding officer of a corps the authority given is wide-ranging. It is not democratic but consultative leadership.

18. In all international statistics the total number of officers, both active and retired, will be given. A retired officer is often called upon to step in with vacancies, for advice, for performing funerals, weddings, dedications or swearing-in of soldiers.

19. Most frequently a married couple, both of whom hold the same rank, are installed as territorial leaders. (Traditionally a Salvation Army officer is either single or married to another officer.) The challenge, charge and dedication concern both. The legal authority is given only to the one (generally the man) who is the TC. The spiritual leadership is a shared responsibility.

tion within the community. The ceremonies are basically the same in all the Nordic countries. The basic one and the foundation for any other commissioning is the swearing-in of a soldier. It is a real transition to the status of a soldier of Christ. It is an affirmation of faith, a confession of salvation and a personal dedication to a life marked by the discipline of a soldier.[20] The difference in Salvation Army identity within the Nordic countries and between the Nordic countries and the Army internationally, which is dealt with below, is also evident when it comes to soldiership.[21]

The claim is that ordination to officership does not signify a transition to a new status, but to a new function within the Army. This can be challenged. Even though soldiership is the basis and in practice soldiers often take upon themselves the work of officers and to a certain extent the authority as well, it is on the question of authority that the above is not true: soldiers doing their work do not have authority and are met with the expectation that they are just part of an interim arrangement, before the 'real' one, the officer, takes over. The grandeur of the occasion signals an importance and significance, as if a new status were given. Theologically this has not been given serious consideration. By having the military metaphor as the basic metaphor, the concept of hierarchy follows as a matter of fact. An officer is given a rank at commissioning – the rank of Captain – and, in due course, promotion to different ranks will be given.[22] Visually the hierarchy with different levels of authority is obvious, as the officers have epaulettes on their uniforms, which signify their rank. Their epaulettes are different from the soldiers' epaulettes, which do not signify rank, just soldiership.

The function (or status) of spiritual leadership is based on authority and on

---

20. Many soldiers have been brought up in the Army, been dedicated as infants, sworn in as junior soldiers, attended Sunday school and junior soldier classes, been trained as corps cadets. Hence it is an affirmation of a personal decision in the faith they have been brought up in. Often it is an affirmation of a personal salvation experience. Other soldiers have just come to a personal faith and experienced salvation. Finland represents a significant difference, as the first category is a tiny minority.

21. All the Nordic countries have a Lutheran state or majority church. This is reflected among SA soldiers most of whom were baptised as infants. With this as a background, the swearing-in as a soldier is for some acknowledged as primarily a dedication to service, for others it is the beginning of a new life in Christ. The church rites and sacraments are a part of some Salvationists' lives. This is most frequent in Finland and Norway, less so in Sweden and rare in Denmark.

22. The rank of Major will come after 15 years. All ranks above that, Lt. Colonel, Colonel and Commissioner are due to promotions to territorial leadership or other international positions.

the officer's dedication to life-long service, availability to be sent anywhere within the country or within the world and to a simple lifestyle. The installation to territorial leadership is basically a confirmation of the ordination ceremony and a new dedication to greater leadership responsibilities.[23]

The flag is used in all three ceremonies, because they all have the element of affirmation of faith and dedication to service.

The Nordic Understanding of the Rite Compared with the International Understanding

Even though the rite is basically the same all over the world, as it is translated from the original English version, the understanding of it differs. This difference in understanding seems to be caused by the kind of identity that is given to officership and soldiership. This identity is influenced by training and education, especially the training for officership.[24] But that is only one aspect: there is also the aspect of ecclesiology.

Internationally, the discussion about whether the Army is a church has been intensified since the BEM process.[25] The claim previously had always been that the Salvation Army was not a church, but an evangelical movement. The reality, however, is that it functions as a church and is accepted as such. The corps is a worshipping community, which exists 'to save souls, grow saints and serve suffering humanity'. For the soldiers and for many who belong in a different way, it is their spiritual home, where they are incorporated into the body of Christ and feed on him. Today the church identity is widely recog-

---

23. An important aspect is the authority to ordain officers, re-accept officers and terminate an officer's service.
24. There is a variation from one country to another in the quality and focus of education programmes, though the outline is the same. This is due to teaching staff, books, materials, and the extent to which academic values and practical values are stressed. Variation is also evident in the Nordic countries.
25. A response to the BEM process was published in Needham 1987. In some countries where there is no doubt that the Army functions as a church, it can seem strange that the discussion on the Army's church identity presupposes a general image of a church as something static and ritualistic. There is a fear of losing the mission focus and innovation of a movement.

nised[26], even though many feel uncomfortable with the word 'church'. This discussion is alive in the Nordic countries in varying degrees.[27]

A further factor is the religious legislation and practice of the country. This has a profound influence on church life as well as on the identity of its members and ministers. The crucial question is, 'What is the relationship between state and church?' 'Is there a separation between the two or is there identification?' The question of identity seems to be decisive for how the ceremony is understood or what is 'projected' onto it.

The Nordic Context

In the Nordic countries there are strong links between the state and the Lutheran majority churches. As the countries' borders are not only political but also identical with national and cultural borders, there is a majority cultural identity within the borders. In this situation there is a close identification between culture and church, culture and official Lutheran Christianity.

This situation has affected the identity of soldiers and officers and also the Nordic Salvation Army's ecclesiology. Belonging to the church has been expressed through rites. In the Salvation Army in the Nordic countries the greater celebrations of life have often taken place within the official church – in infant baptism, confirmation, weddings and funerals.[28] This has meant that

---

26. The mission statement is: 'The Salvation Army, an international movement, is an evangelical part of the universal Christian Church. Its message is based on the Bible. Its ministry is motivated by love for God. Its mission is to preach the gospel of Jesus Christ and meet human needs in his name without discrimination'.

27. There has been discussion in Denmark for a number of years. The Swedish separation of state and church has intensified the discussion there. In Norway it has been on the agenda of the officers' forum. In Finland the thought of the Army being a church is foreign, but a debate has started to take place.

28. As mentioned above, the Salvation Army does not administer the sacraments. They are considered to be an outward sign of an inward grace and not necessary for salvation and sanctification. Jesus Christ is the one, true, original sacrament which the sacraments signify. The claim is that his real presence can be experienced as we feed upon Christ without material means such as water, wine and bread. However, any Salvationist is free to participate in any church's sacraments. There is a considerable gap between Salvation Army beliefs and the Lutheran sacrament of baptism and the theology that surrounds it, but tradition is stronger than theology in this respect. This is the overall picture. The great differences in practice between the countries are dealt with below. To this must be added that the Salvation Army ceremonies in some of the countries are performed in addition to church ceremonies: after baptism the dedication of the child may take place in the corps, the church wedding may be followed by a Salvation Army wedding. Funerals are of course an exception to this practice.

the 'big' events in life has been disconnected from the worshipping community to which the soldier belongs and have been an isolated event in that sense. On the other hand, it has meant an allegiance to the official religious culture.

Celebrations or rites carry a great significance because they separate the ordinary from the extraordinary. They are a concentration of life, of values and meaning. That some celebrations to a large extent have been linked to the official church and not to the corps has had an impact, especially on ecclesiology and the identity of officership. The officer's role has been minimised, when the church's rites took precedence over the unique Salvation Army ceremony, such as the enrolment of soldiers. The officer has been the one in charge of the everyday business and the ordinary worship life, the Salvation Army's own celebrations, but not the ones celebrating the perhaps more significant events in people's lives. On interviewing Salvation Army officers and soldiers in the Nordic countries, it has been evident that there is an uncertainty about the identity of officership as well as of the Army's ecclesiology.[29] The grand celebration of ordination and commissioning with its strong mission focus has been difficult to link to the reality of corps life. In times of stagnation, when the enrolment of soldiers is a less frequent occasion, the unique Salvation Army identity is not being affirmed through this celebration.

In the interviews a clear difference has been apparent between the younger and older generations. A stronger Salvationist identity (and therefore a stronger officership identity) is rather evident in the younger generation and weaker in the more mature generation. Some of this might be accounted for by the ordination ceremony (which changed after 1978 with the insertion of the word 'ordination' to signify status as a minister) or perhaps more importantly by the debate that followed. A further development is taking place.[30]

The International Context

As the majority of officers are leading a corps, it is this role which dominates the officer identity in the Nordic countries as well as in other parts of the

---

29. There is a reluctance to use 'churchy' expressions – for example, the word 'meeting' is preferred to 'worship' or 'service'.

30. A change in officers' identity has been taking place for a number of years and is still going on: the separation between state and church in Sweden, for example, is having an impact. I will go on to show how different forms of legislation, in different countries, are reflected in this identity change.

world.[31] Where there is a separation between church and state the Salvation Army officer is more frequently accepted as a minister of religion both by the public as well as by the soldiers, and the corps is looked upon as a church. All celebrations take place within the corps as the worshipping community. The officer performs infant dedications, junior soldier enrolments, the swearing-in of soldiers, weddings, local officer commissioning and funerals. Even though the Army is seldom part of the main religious culture, its own ceremonies are not disconnected from the more general ones such as weddings and funerals. All take place within the Army corps and all are performed by the corps officer. There is a greater focus and acceptance of his/her vocation of spiritual leadership. The officer's identity is therefore generally different from the Nordic understanding and perception. The status in society is different. The officer will be called upon for chaplaincy service at disasters, in prisons, hospitals, airports, in the armed forces, and in other ways.

Similarities and Differences

The actual commissioning is the same and so is the plan for training for officership. All confess to being called by God to proclaim the gospel of Jesus Christ. The covenant with the strong emphasis on '*martyria*', '*missio*' and '*diakonia*' is the same. The commissioning is seen as a ceremony giving authority for leadership with a strong mission focus. The celebration marks the fact that the officer is set aside for these tasks. The commissioning does not highlight a specific priestly role of church maintenance and pastoral care for the members of the Army. The reality of the change from a mission movement to a church is not reflected in the rite, but in the interpretation of it. Therefore the identity, role and actual tasks are 'projected' onto the understanding of this celebration. Even though a lot of the daily work is the same – the officer leads the corps, counsels the people, evangelises the district, is in charge of worship, social outreach, administration and finance and so on, there is, however, a difference in the Nordic countries compared with the international scene.

One of the great differences is that the 'priestly' role, with involvement in the rites at the crucial point in people's lives, such as birth, marriage and death, is more rare or non-existent. In countries without official majority churches,

---

31. As the Salvation Army is working in 108 countries it is impossible to give a fair picture of the international context, as it differs considerably; but the 'model' context which I am referring to as the international is the Anglo-American context. It is the dominant one when it comes to theology and administration, not only in United Kingdom, North America and the Commonwealth countries, but in international leadership as well.

officers will perform these rites not only for their own people, but often for people from the wider community. This is not generally the case in the Nordic countries.

The identity of officers, and the understanding of what the rite ordains them to be, differs between the international and the Nordic context. My thesis is that some of the explanation may be found in the fact that a number of rites are performed in the Lutheran Church and not in the corps. This is caused both by the interrelationship between church and state, by church legislation and by the self-understanding of the Army within a given country.

The Understanding of the Rite within the Nordic Countries

The Salvation Army territories in the Nordic countries differ from each other when it comes to numbers of officers and soldiers. Norway is by far the biggest, by comparison with size of population. Numerically, Sweden and Norway are about the same; so are Denmark and Finland when it comes to numbers of soldiers, but not of officers.

Denmark

The Salvation Army in Denmark was recognised as a faith community with the legal right to perform weddings on 27th January 1971.[32] This made a significant change in identity and self-understanding.

The Salvation Army here differs from the other Nordic territories in not having its own school for officership and therefore no public occasion for the ordination ceremony in the country. This has been the case for more than 30 years. Danish cadets are trained in Oslo or London.[33] In Oslo the Danish TC ordains the Danish cadets, in London they are ordained by the English TC.

The influence of the lack of available training and ordination in Denmark has apparently been significant. It has removed this grand celebration from the Danish soldiers and officers and estranged them from its rite.[34] This might be one of the explanations for the small number of soldiers who apply for training to officership. The reason cannot be found in lack of involvement or service,

---

32. On 1st January 1970, a new marriage law came into force and made it possible for faith communities to perform weddings.
33. The choice between the two is decided by the cadet's academic achievements. Today when most of the cadets have a good qualification or degree, nearly all of them go to London.
34. In 1999 a group of Danish soldiers (Valby brass band) visited Moscow and took part in the Commissioning of the Russian cadets. It made a profound impression on them

as the majority are very active soldiers and take leadership roles upon themselves at local level, but perhaps the lack of challenge, which the commissioning and ordination gives, accounts for the smaller number.

That the influence from the international training in London has been strongest can be seen in the officers' identity. There is for most a clear understanding of ordination as being for spiritual leadership as a servant of Christ with the authority equal to other ministers. The discussions concerning the Salvation Army's church identity have been going on for forty years and more. It has caused debate and difference of opinion, but the dialogue has been kept alive and has informed the situation.

Before World War II officers generally did not bring their own children to the Lutheran Church for baptism. Even though the majority of soldiers at that time brought their children to the church, a fair number did not pursue this. Until 1971 the legal aspect of weddings was dealt with at the Mayor's office and the religious part at a Salvation Army wedding. Some would have the wedding in the church and the Army wedding as an addition, but only a tiny minority. In 1971 recognition as a faith community made it possible for officers to perform weddings. Since then most Salvationists' weddings take place in the corps. When it comes to Salvationists' funerals most are performed by an officer. That has been the case for many years. These celebrations are part of corps life together with the Army's specific ceremonies.

Finland

The Salvation Army's situation in Finland seems to be at the other end of the scale from the Danish experience, with Norway and Sweden in between. When the Salvation Army started in the country, Finland was part of the Russian Empire. Even today, the registration of the Salvation Army as a foundation reflects this situation.[35] The question of a Salvation Army church identity has not been seriously debated until recently, and affiliation to the Lutheran Church is very strong.

---

to experience a dedication and ordination, which they had never seen before. This spiritual experience and the insight gained made the younger ones consider officership as an option for life.

35. As was the case with the Army's start in other countries, the Army registered in any way that was possible. Often no registration as a religious body was possible, and this was the case with Finland. The unique situation is that, even though registration was altered after independence, no kind of registration as a religious body has ever been done. There is one registration for all activities as a foundation doing Christian work and engaged in business with a humanitarian objective.

The overall understanding of the ceremony has been as a commissioning primarily to *diakonia* and mission. The concept of being ordained to spiritual leadership and to a ministerial function has not been significant and very often absent from the understanding. A majority see themselves as corps workers more than spiritual leaders. Even though all have been trained according to the same international pattern, the emphasis has been stronger on the *diakonia* part of officership than on the pastoral.[36] All have been ordained by basically the same ceremony, but the understanding is still different.

A possible explanation might be linked with the alteration of the ceremony in 1978. The average age among officers is higher in Finland than in the other Nordic countries, so only a few have been 'ordained'. The debate which followed this alteration has not been on the agenda in Finland. However, the situation is changing, and a discussion on the identity of the Salvation Army is starting to take place, reflecting the international discussion of whether it is a church or not.[37] The situation until now has been nearly 100% state church membership parallel with soldiership.[38] It means that infant baptisms, confirmations, weddings and funerals[39] take place within the state church. Often Salvation Army ceremonies have been added to these.

Ordination to officership has taken place quite frequently in Finland, but not regularly as in Sweden and Norway, due to lack of cadets. In May 2001 four new officers were ordained. As in other countries, such an event gathers large congregations, and there is a response from soldiers to the challenge to officership that the ceremony gives. Finland has twice as many officers as Denmark, with the number of soldiers about the same. A significant change is taking place amongst the younger officers, as identity is discussed and as young people of Finnish origin are coming back to Finland from abroad to work in the Army.

---

36. Some Finnish officers have been trained in UK, Sweden and more recently at the Russian school. Those trained and ordained abroad have brought another officer model with them. This is visible in the present dialogue and discussion.
37. In parliament a new law on religious freedom is being processed and in the wake of this work groups have been formed and dialogue is taking place within the Salvation Army.
38. In Finland both the Orthodox and the Lutheran churches are the country's official church. Both church affiliations are present in SA but with a vast Lutheran majority.
39. The funeral will always be performed by an Orthodox or Lutheran minister depending on the original church affiliation. In official dialogues the view has been stated that 'foundations' do not perform funerals.

Norway

The Salvation Army in Norway is registered as an organisation and not as a faith community or church. It is a similar situation to the Finnish one, but with the difference between a foundation as in Finland and an organisation as in Norway.

The celebration of ordination to officership takes place nearly every year in Oslo. This happens during the yearly congress, when there are days of public worship on a grand scale for people coming from all over the territory. Soldiers and officers experience this ordination ceremony repeatedly, and this influences the identity of the officers and the soldiers' recognition of the spiritual authority given.

There is a similarity between the situation in Finland and in Norway when it comes to a very strong affiliation to the Lutheran Church. The vast majority of Salvationists have their children baptised in the church (and have a Salvation Army child dedication afterwards); nearly all weddings will take place in the church (with a Salvation Army wedding later). The officer has no legal right to perform weddings and generally people choose the church instead of the Mayor's office for the legal part. Unlike Finland, an officer performs funerals

In spite of this similarity it is a very different Army, with a much clearer Salvation Army identity. One of the differences is that officers consider themselves spiritual leaders and ministers for their congregation, their corps, and are accepted in this way by the soldiers.

The debate on the church identity of the Salvation Army is alive and has been taking place for a long time. At the moment it is more a discussion on the extent of affiliation to the Lutheran Church than on the Army's own church identity. The reason for this is that the corps in reality functions as a church. The majority of soldiers have a Salvation Army background, have grown up in the Army and consider the Army their spiritual home. They give their time and talents to the Army. The soldiers who come new to the Army take up the same attitude and practice.

The officers consider themselves ordained to be spiritual leaders. The officers' training increasingly has this focus. This is reflected in the understanding of the ordination ceremony. There is a difference between the younger and older generation in the focus of their officer identity here as in Finland. The difference is that the number of younger officers – those ordained after 1978 – is much bigger, and that the debate on the ceremony and on ecclesiology has been present and alive.

Iceland

The situation in Iceland is the same as in Norway, when it comes to registration as an organisation. All rites, including funerals, take place within the Lutheran church.

The fact that the ordination ceremony does not take place in the country makes the situation similar to Denmark. But as a fair number of officers and soldiers attend the annual congress in Oslo and witness the ordination ceremony there, the rite is still alive for them and influences their perception of officership. All officers are trained in Norway and there is an exchange between the two countries when it comes to officers' service.

Sweden

The Salvation Army in Sweden was acknowledged as a faith community with the legal right to perform weddings on 28th March 1952.[40] Following the separation of state and church in January 2000, a new registration took place. The Salvation Army became a registered faith community on 10th March 2000.

As is the case with Norway, the ordination ceremony takes place every year during the congress. The concept of a congress is the same – public worship on a grand scale for the whole territory. And, as in Norway, participation in these forms influences officers' identity and the soldiers' recognition of the authority given to spiritual leadership.

The situation in Sweden is somewhere between Denmark and Norway when it comes to the relationship with the Lutheran Church. The number of officers and soldiers is about the same as Norway. The vast majority will bring their children to baptism in the church and have been baptised themselves, so there is a membership of the Lutheran Church as in Norway and Finland.[41] Since 1952 most Salvationists' weddings have taken place in the Army hall and

40. This was the case with a number of Free Churches based on the law on religious freedom of 26th October, 1951.
41. The separation between church and state is so new that there is no clear indication of what will happen when it comes to infant baptism as the entrance to membership. Some are leaving the church and giving their church tax to the Army. Not only Salvationists, but also people from the general public have made this decision. There were 900 the first year and 200 the next, but exactly how many of these are Salvationists is not recorded.

been performed by an officer. Funerals have been performed by officers since the 1920s.[42]

The officers consider themselves spiritual leaders and ministers for their corps and are accepted as such by the soldiers. The training has spiritual leadership as focus and aim, and therefore ordination is understood as giving authority for that.

The discussion on Salvation Army church identity has been alive for many years and has mostly followed the Danish and international pattern. The performance of weddings and funerals as part of an officer's service has clearly signalled the Army's church identity and the officer's identity as a minister of religion. A number of officers have terminated their membership of the Lutheran Church and have the Army as their only 'church'. The separation between state and church is very likely to cause a further development in this direction in the coming years.

The Ordination Ceremony

As mentioned earlier the wording at the ordination, which was introduced in 1978, is the same, translated from English into the national language. The part which follows the promises made is as follows: 'In accepting these pledges which you have each made, I commission you as an officer of the Salvation Army and ordain you as ministers of Christ and his gospel'. This part of the ceremony is never printed in the orders of service; only the promises are there.[43]

In asking Nordic leaders to examine their wording some differences came up.[44] The leaders' nationality varies, but the wording has been used in whatever country they served:

Commissioner Sven Nilsson is Swedish and has been TC in Denmark and Sweden: 'We have listened to the declaration of dedication that you have all read, and the promises you have given. I hereby ordain you as officers of the Salvation Army, separated and dedicated to service for Christ and his gospel'.

---

42. It has been possible for Salvation Army weddings and funerals to take place within Lutheran church buildings. After the separation between state and church this is still possible, but now it costs a certain amount of money.

43. Norway has this wording printed in the copy of the ceremony, which the TC has, but not in the order of service. In the other countries the TC chooses the words even though it is expected that the international text will be used.

44. I have contacted three other TCs of Norwegian origin and one Danish TC, but either I have not got an exact wording or description, or the wording has been a precise translation of the international text of 1978.

Commissioner Birgitta Nilsson is Swedish/American and has been TC in Sweden: 'Through your declaration of dedication you affirm the covenant you have sealed with God and proclaimed your intention to serve the Lord. Now I dedicate you as an officer of the Salvation Army with all that the holy office contains'.

Commissioner Ingrid Lindberg is Swedish and has been TC in the Philippines, in Denmark and Finland. Placing hand on head, she says: 'I hereby dedicate you as an officer and servant of Christ and his gospel in the name of the Father, the Son and the Holy Spirit'.

Commissioner Edward Hannevik is Norwegian and has been TC in Denmark and Norway. Placing hand on head, he says: 'In accepting these promises you have given, I commission you an officer of the Salvation Army and ordain you as a servant for Christ and his gospel. May the blessing of almighty God rest upon your service; may the wisdom and guidance of the Holy Spirit be yours in rich measure; may the wonderful presence of Jesus always be a joy to you. Amen'. Then the Aaronic blessing follows.

Colonel Carl Lydholm is Danish and presently TC in Finland. Placing hand on head, he says: 'Acknowledging that God has called you, Christ has ordained you and the Holy Spirit has empowered you to preach the gospel, I receive your promises and commission you as an officer of the Salvation Army. May the blessing of almighty God rest on your service; may you be filled with the love and grace of Jesus; may the anointment, wisdom and joy of the Holy Spirit be given you in rich measure'. Then the Aaronic blessing follows.[45]

In the Nordic countries the act of ordination seems to be developing in a more solemn direction than perhaps is the case internationally. This can be seen in the imposition of hands in the majority of the examples. This act can be seen as a blessing, a confirmation of the calling and an acceptance of the candidate into officership. In the case of Hannevik's and Lydholm's versions it is more than just a blessing – there is an epiclesis in the act and wording of the ordination. At present it is not possible to say how much impact this development and the reflection behind it will have in the years to come.

All the examples given are Christ-centred, as is the original English version. It is his gospel that is in focus. Birgitta Nilson's version is, however, different. She does not use the words 'ordination' and 'commissioning' and does not mention Christ and his gospel, but is dedicating the officer to 'holy office'

---

45. This reflects the international discussion, as explained below. This wording was one of the suggestions. The final wording referred to earlier was sent out internationally from the General's office on 15th February 2002.

('*heliga ämbetet*'). This is quite unique in a Salvation Army setting and might be an isolated personal choice of hers.

The discussion on church identity and the development of the ordination ceremony over the last twenty to thirty years, with the inclusion of the word 'ordination', might be one of the reasons for the more distinct officer identity, which can be seen in the younger generation in the Nordic countries. The same reason might account for the difference of identity between the younger and the older generation.

The Contemporary International Forum

Development in the Terminology of the Ceremony of Ordination and Commissioning

The development from an evangelical movement to a church has taken place over a long period, even though it has not been clearly expressed in words until the last ten to twenty years. About thirty years ago, there was discussion about how to explain what an officer was commissioned to. This discussion took place very much as a result of ecumenical dialogue. In these dialogues it was felt to be important that an officer should be accepted on equal terms with other ministers. One of the ways to achieve this was to use similar language to that of other churches in the commissioning ceremony. An international Salvation Army discussion took place. In 1978 it was decided to use the term 'ordain' in the ceremony and the wording became as follows: 'In accepting these pledges which you have each made, I commission you as officers of the Salvation Army and ordain you as ministers of Christ and his gospel'. The different territories were encouraged to use this wording and in translation use whatever word 'ordain' would signify in common church use.

This was welcomed by many parts of the Salvation Army and certainly in the Nordic countries, where the development towards a 'church' identity was in process. In other parts of the world it was not agreed upon, especially in UK, where there was dissatisfaction with this development. It became an internal discussion in many countries as well as in international publications. The division of opinion did not strictly follow geography; there were differences of opinion almost everywhere.

Basically there was discussion on the whole idea of being a church. It was feared that the use of the word 'ordain' might lead officers to see the priestly role as their dominant function and forget the prophetic aspect, with its focus on mission or the diaconal challenge. The reality is that the 'church' identity has been accepted and the 'priestly' role of the officer has become more visible, if not dominant. The development in the Nordic countries has also moved in this direction, in spite of all the differences in officer identity.

There has been unease ever since in some quarters with the word 'ordain'. In 2000, General John Gowans, who is British, used an alternative wording in the commissioning ceremony in London and some weeks later in Atlanta, USA: 'Accepting your promises and recognising that God has ordained you to preach the Gospel, I now commission you an officer of the Salvation Army'. I felt that something new was being introduced and wrote to him to ask why he had altered the wording – Was it an unease with the wording 'I ordain'? I suggested that his wording more clearly confirmed Salvation Army belief in God as the one acting. A correspondence took place and the suggestion to expand his version and let it be debated was accepted. It reads as follows: 'Accepting your promises and recognising that God has called you, Christ has ordained you and the Holy Spirit has empowered you to preach the Gospel, I now commission you an officer of the Salvation Army'. The rationale for this expansion was to underline God's call which is basic to officership, to highlight the fact that ordination is from Christ, in whose service the officer is meant to be, and to include the empowerment of the Holy Spirit, which is believed to be crucial for any service. It was trinitarian. The matter was sent to the International Doctrine Council and to a hearing of leaders from different parts of the world. The final decision was to keep the three verbs, but not to relate specific acts to the three Persons of the Trinity. It was argued that the correct use would be God the Father, God the Son and God the Holy Spirit and that would be too 'heavy' a wording.

International Theological Development

Theological discussion on who a Salvationist is, how the spirituality is expressed and nourished and what the Salvation Army believes has taken place internationally. Long-term commissions and *ad hoc* committees have been working and the debates on these issues have been kept alive in different ways. A Spiritual Life Commission published its report in 1998 with the aim of enriching worshipping life. This was translated in all the Nordic territories as in most other Salvation Army territories and is showing its effect in a greater focus on worship and the need to enrich it.

The International Doctrine Council wrote *Salvation Story* (1998), *Study Guide to Salvation Story* (1999) and *Servants together – the ministry of the whole people of God* (2002) to give an account of Salvationist faith and ministry today in a contemporary way. A first international theology and ethics symposium took place in Canada in 2001, with 50 theologians and ethicists from different parts of the world under the title: *Salvationist theology and ethics for the new millennium.* [46]

Worship as the Foundation for Salvationist Theology

The introduction to *Servants together* states:

> Salvation Army theology has sometimes tended toward a theology of the individual rather than of the Church. The first section of this book is careful to place the concept of ministry in the broader theological context of the calling of all God's people to a discipleship of worship, community and mission. The mission and ministry of the individual can only properly be understood in the context of the priesthood of 'all believers'. The Church is seen as a worshipping community intent on corporate as well as individual mission, with worship and community being integral to a biblical understanding of ministry.

There is a growing understanding of how much worship and celebrations influence and form theology. To a large extent, worship forms personal faith and develops understanding and commitment. An indication of this is the great influence that songs and hymns have on faith development and personal devotions. As part of the focus on the importance of worship, an intensified debate on the Salvation Army's position on the sacraments is taking place.[47]

Conclusion

The celebration of a rite for commissioning/ordination to ministry has a profound influence.

Even though this is the case, other factors are also decisive and will be 'projected' onto the understanding of the rite. This is illustrated in the Nordic

---

46. There was participation from the Nordic countries in all these commissions: the Nordic influence has thus been present, in addition to the evident influence of the international debate on the Nordic scene.

47. Generally this is a debate about the Lord's Supper and a growing wish to reintroduce this sacrament into Salvation Army worshipping life. In *Salvation Story* and *Salvation Story Study Guide*, a more theological approach was taken to explain the position. This is being developed further, so that a clearer theology will emerge in the coming years. In the unique Nordic situation the debate on the sacraments is also centred on the Lord's Supper, but it includes baptism as well.

situation. The setting of the celebration is the same everywhere; the process and the words are the same, but the understanding of what is going on and what authority is given differs from country to country. The reason for this is that there are different concepts of officer identity. This identity is to a certain degree shaped by existing legislation on religious matters, the relationship and affiliation between the majority churches and the Salvation Army and by Salvationists' understanding of the nature of the Salvation Army's identity.

References

Baker, Frank (ed.). 1981. *Letters of John Wesley 1-2*. Oxford: Oxford University Press.

Cooper, Ian. 1983. *A theology of Salvation Army officership –paper in response to BEM*. London: Heritage Centre.

Coutts, Fredrick. 1975. *No Discharge in this War*. London: Hodder and Stoughton.

Espersen, Preben. 1999. *Kirkeret*. Copenhagen: Jurist og Økonomforbundets Forlag.

Frelsens Hærs ceremonibog. 1981. Copenhagen: Frelsens Här.

Green, Roger J. 1996. *Catherine Booth*. Grand Rapids: Baker Books.

Handledning för Frälsningsarméns Högtider. 2004. Stockholm: Frälsningsarmén.

Hanson, AT and Hanson, RPC. 1987. *The Identity of the Church*. London: SCM.

International Doctrine Council (Earl Robinson, Ray Caddy, Roger J. Green, Gudrun Lydholm, Phil Needham, Christine Parkin) publications and papers: Papers from territories (Australia Eastern, Brazil, Canada, Finland, Germany, Pakistan, Philippines, Sri Lanka, Sweden, USA East, USA West) as a response to a working paper on *Towards a Salvationist Theology of Spiritual Leadership*. 1998. This paper and the responses laid the ground for *Servants together*.

Needham, Phil. 1987. *Community in mission – Salvationist Ecclesiology*. London: Salvation Army.

One faith, one church – the Salvation Army's response to Baptism, Eucharist and Ministry. 1990. London: Salvation Army.

Puglisi, James F. 1996, 1998, and 2001. *The Process of Admission to Ordained Ministry*, I-III. Collegeville, Minn.: Liturgical Press.

Response from the Salvation Army to BEM. Papers from working groups in territories around the world in reply to International HQ's first draft of the SA response to BEM. London: Heritage Centre. Papers on the BEM discussion from International Leaders' Conference (Berlin 1984). London: Heritage Centre.

Response to BEM from Denmark. 1986. Copenhagen: Frelsens Här (booklet).

Response to BEM from Sweden. 1986. Stockholm: Frälsningsarmén (booklet).

Salvation Story. 1998. London: Salvation Army.

Salvation Story Study Guide. 1999. London: Salvation Army.

Servants together – the ministry of the whole people of God – Salvationist perspectives. 2002. London: Salvation Army.

Salvation Army Ceremonies

Historical material – Covenant Cards – London: Heritage Centre.

Frelsens Härs arkiv. Copenhagen.

Frälsningsarmens museum. Helsinki.

Salvation Army Ceremonies. London

Draft for the revision of Frelsesarmeens Ceremonibog, Norway.

Memoranda from the General on wording at ordination 1978, same 1992 and 2002

Papers and articles from Salvation Army in Canada on the use of the word 'ordination' from 1970 onwards.

Correspondance with General Arnold Brown, Canada, on the introduction of the word 'ordination'. 2000.

Correspondance with General John Gowans on the new wording at commissionings. 2000-2001.

Correspondance with Nordic TCs (active and retired) on wording at ordinations. 2000-2001.

Workers for the Harvest: A Comparative Study of Rites for the Sending out of Missionaries by Nordic Mission Societies and Churches

Ghita Olsen

The commission to engage in mission concerns the whole church. In principle every church member is a missionary, and baptism is the foundation for the sending. Yet mission societies and churches have specific rites for the ssending out of missionaries. We will look at ten such rites from the Nordic context. The rites are from twelve mission societies and churches, representing both established churches and Free Churches.[1] We will examine the differences and similarities in the rites, the function of the rites and what they express about the ministry of a missionary and the role of the sending congregation.

Seen from an ecumenical perspective it is a fundamental criterion that a prayer accompanied by imposition of hands is said when an individual is given

---

1. The largest missionary organisations in Norway, Sweden, Finland and Denmark were contacted in February 2002, and these are the rites received. The rites from the Baptist Union of Norway and Danmission came from other researchers on the project, 'The Theology and Terminology of Ordination and Commitment'. A few other organisations either replied that they do not use a specific rite or they sent incomplete information. Information from Iceland came late and is not included in the study. The Union of Icelandic Mission Societies (SIK) for many years used the same rite as the Norwegian Lutheran Mission (NLM). The bishop ordains missionaries sent out by SIK. The rite in use today is based on the rite for the ordination of deacons, but is still very similar to the rite used by NLM.

a public commission by the church. We will therefore examine if and how this prayer is significant in the rites for the sending out of missionaries.

Presentation of the Mission Societies and Churches

The rites examined are from the following twelve Nordic mission societies and churches:

The Finnish Evangelical-Lutheran Mission (FELM) is an official missionary organisation of the Evangelical-Lutheran Church of Finland. It was founded in 1859. At the end of 1999, there were 274 FELM missionaries working in 23 different countries in Africa, Asia, Europe and Latin America.

Messengers is a Lutheran missionary organisation based in Finland. Its main commitment is to transmit the Gospel by radio to those parts of the world that cannot easily be reached through traditional missionary work. Currently, Messengers is involved in financing Christian radio programmes in about 30 languages in the Middle East, the Far East, Asia, Africa and Europe. In addition to financing Christian radio programmes, Messengers has missionaries involved in missionary radio and in parish work.

The Lutheran Evangelical Association of Finland (LEAF) started its foreign missionary work in 1900, in Japan.[2] Since the 1970s, it has also carried out missionary work in Kenya, Papua New Guinea, Zambia, Cameroon, and Russia. LEAF has about 60 missionaries.

The Norwegian Missionary Society (NMS) is an independent organisation within the Church of Norway that works together with churches in 13 countries on four continents and has about 150 missionaries.[3]

The Norwegian Lutheran Mission (NLM) is an independent organisation within the Church of Norway, founded in 1891 as the Norwegian Lutheran China Mission.[4] Today NLM works both in Asia and Africa.

The Baptist Union of Norway (BUN) was founded in 1879 and started

---

2. FELM, Messengers and LEAF use the rite of the Evangelical-Lutheran Church of Finland (*Kyrkohandbok* 1995, 174ff). Sources: , **cf.** Pekka Harne, FELM, 18th **att.** Pekka Harne, February, 2002; Tuula Korpiaho, Messengers, 18th **att.** Tuula Korpiaho, February, 2002 and; Seppo Suokunnas, LEAF, 11th , **att.** Seppo Suokunnas, March, 2002.
3. Received 8th February, 2002, from Turid Ølberg, NMS headquarters in Stavanger.
4. Received 18th February, 2002, from Astrid Eilertsen, NLM headquarters in Oslo.

foreign mission in 1915.[5] They work in Albania, Republic of Congo, Nepal, Thailand, Vietnam and Cameroon.

The Church of Sweden Mission (CSM), which is an official part of the Church of Sweden, has about 60 missionaries employed to work in 14 different countries.[6]

The Mission Covenant Church of Sweden (MCC- S) is a community of 840 Swedish congregations.[7] MCC started foreign missionary work in 1881 and today works in Ecuador, Nicaragua, Republic of Congo, Eastern Europe, Middle East, India, Pakistan, Japan and China.

The Swedish Evangelical Mission (SEM) was founded in 1856 as an independent mission society within the Church of Sweden and initially an Inner Mission movement.[8] However, foreign mission was taken up from the start, and as early as 1865 the first missionaries were sent to Ethiopia. Today SEM works in Eritrea, Ethiopia, India, Malawi, Sudan, Tanzania and Sweden. Since 1997 the work abroad has been integrated with the Church of Sweden Mission and Church of Sweden Aid.

Danmission was established on 1st January 2000 as a continuation of the Danish Santal Mission (founded in 1863) and the Danish Mission Society (founded in 1821).[9] Danmission works in India, Bangladesh, Nepal, Mongolia, The Philippines, Cambodia, China, Tanzania, Madagascar, Egypt and Denmark and has at present 60 missionaries and volunteers. Danmission is an independent mission society within the Evangelical-Lutheran Church in Denmark.

This is also the status of the Danish Sudan Mission (*DSM*), founded in 1911.[10] DSM works in five African countries.

The Danish Evangelical Mission (DEM) is also an independent mission so-

---

5. Received 4th February, 2002, from Bjørn Øyvind Fjeld.
6. Booklet received 6th March, 2002, from Ella Wolde Selassie, Church of Sweden; text identical with the rite in the Church of Sweden's Service Book, except for the rubrics (*Den Svenska Kyrkohandboken* II 1988, 64f). The draft of a rite drawn up by Per Harling in 1998 (parts of which have been used) was also received from Olle Kristenson, Church of Sweden Mission.
7. Received October 2003, from Rev. Per-Magnus Selinder, Secretrary for Theology and Ecumenics in the MCC of Sweden. This rite is part of a revised Service Book, which came into use in Advent 2003.
8. Received 6th March, 2002, from Ella Wolde Selassie, Church of Sweden.
9. Received from Hans Raun Iversen, February 2002.
10. Received 26th February, 2002, from Margit Ganderup-Nissen, DSM headquarters in Christiansfeld.

ciety within the Evangelical-Lutheran Church in Denmark, founded in 1948.[11] DEM works in Ethiopia, Liberia and Botswana in Africa. In 2001 DEM had 10 missionaries and a number of short-term volunteers.

Terminology and Structure of the Rites

There is some variation in the terminology used for this rite, and who celebrates it also varies. Figure 1 gives an overview of the differences:

Figure 1

ORGANISATION	TERMINOLOGY	OFFICIANT
FELM, Messengers, LEAF	blessing (*velsignelse*)	a bishop
NMS	commissioning (*vigsling*)	not specified
NLM	commissioning (*innvielse*)	the chairman
Baptist Union of Norway	commissioning (*innvielse*)	the secretary general
CSM	sending out (*sändning*)	a bishop
MCC of Sweden	Setting apart (*avskilja*)	the mission leader
SEM	ssending out	the district leader
Danmission	commissioning (*indvielse*) and ssending out	a pastor
DSM	ssending out	a pastor
DEM	commissioning (*indvielse*) and ssending out	a pastor

It is significant that during the latest 30 years the terms used in these rites have changed. For instance in Sweden there was a change from the term '*vigning*' ('ordination'), used in the 1942 Service Book, to the term 'sending' in the 1969 Service Book. In Finland there was also a change from the term '*vigning*', used in the 1963 Service Book, to the term 'blessing' in the 1984 Service Book. These changes reflect the fact that the rite is seen neither as an act of ordination

---

11. Received 27th February, 2002, from Benedikte Pedersen, DEM headquarters.

nor only as a matter of ssending out to some distant place, but fundamentally as a matter of mere sending based on baptism (Eckerdal 1985, 464).[12]

Figure 1 also reflects the fact that the relationship of the mission societies to the church varies. In Sweden and Finland there is a close connection between the Evangelical-Lutheran Church and the societies. CSM and FELM are official missionary organisations of the Church of Sweden and the Evangelical-Lutheran Church of Finland respectively, and a bishop is the officiant in their rites. The rite used by FELM, Messengers and LEAF is a rite for the blessing of missionaries authorised by the Evangelical-Lutheran Church of Finland and a part of the church's Service Book.

In Norway and Denmark the mission societies are within the church, but not under the authority of the church. It is therefore someone from the organisation, possibly the leader/a pastor, who officiates atcelebrates the ceremony.

NLM, the Baptist Union of Norway, the MCC of Sweden and SEM are Free Churches or Free Church organisations.

The main elements and structure of the various rites also vary, as seen in the table below. The requirement that they take place in an ordinary service or High Mass applies to all the rites. It is also common to all rites for a group of assistants to participate in the reading of the biblical texts and/or the deed and in the imposition of hands during the central prayer of the ceremony. There is no information on who chooses the assistants or who they are to be.

Many of the rites include a Presentation section. It is usually stated who the missionary is, by whom they are called to serve as a missionary, and where they will work as a missionary. Two of the Presentations (NLM and SEM) include the reading aloud of a deed.

---

12. A further study of changes in terminology would be valuable for the understanding of the theology behind the rites, but goes beyond the scope of this article.

Finnish rite	NMS	NLM	BUN	CSM	MCC-S	SEM	Danmission	DSM	DEM
Presentation	Presentation	Introductory prayer	Presentation	Readings	Presentation	Address[13]	Address	Intro prayer	Presentation
Readings	Introductory prayer	Address	Readings	Address	Address	Presentation	Readings	Address	Readings
Commitments	Readings	Readings	Exhortation	Presentation	Readings	Commitments	Exhortation	Readings	Commitments
Blessing	Address	Presentation	Commitments	Commitments	Commitments	Readings	Commitments	Commitments	Prayer
Prayer	Exhortation	Commitments	Prayer	Prayer	Prayer	Prayer	Prayer	Prayer	
Sending	Commitments	Prayer		Sending	Sending	Sending	Sending		
	Prayer	Sending							
	Sending								

The terminology and main elements of the rites indicate that the mission societies and churches understand the rite as a blessing ceremony for those who are sent with the commission of the organisation or church. The second table showed that three elements are found in all the rites: scriptural readings, the missionary's commitment and a prayer with the imposition of hands.[14] We will go into detail on these elements. As the ceremony takes place as part of a service, we will also examine the role of the congregation present.

---

13. The original 'sändningstal' is a technical term for a commissioning address delivered by the officiant.
14. Called 'Prayer' in the table.

A Closer Look at Three Central Elements

We will examine the three common elements of the rites to see what is said of the ministry of a missionary through the biblical readings, the exhortation and promises, and the central prayer.

The Scriptural Readings

The scriptural readings are expected to express the biblical basis, responsibility and blessing of the specific ministry. The readings in the various rites are as follows:

FELM, Messengers and LEAF
Matt. 28.18-20 – the great commission
John 15.16 – 'You have not chosen me, but I have chosen you and appointedgiven you to go and bear fruit, fruit which lasts, that whatever you ask the Father in my name he may give you.'
John 13.15, 20 – Christ as example, and whoever receives Christ's messenger receives Christ
Acts 1.8 – Christ's final charter and promise of the outpouring of the Holy Spirit
Rom. 10.12-15 – on the absolute need for a messenger to bring the Good News of salvation
It is possible to choose other readings.

NMS
Matt. 28.18-20 – the commission to world evangelism
2 Tim.1.7-8a, 9-10 – do not be ashamed of the gospel or Matt. 25.35-40 – the righteous meet the needs of others in the service of love.
2 Cor. 5.17-20 – on being a new creation in Christ, on the ministry of reconciliation and being ambassadors for Christ

NLM
Matt. 28.16-20 – the great commission
1 Cor. 12.4-6 – on the diversity of gifts and ministries
1 Cor. 12.7-11 – on the various gifts
1 Pet. 4.10-14 – on being good stewards of God's grace
2 Tim. 1.7-9 – do not be ashamed of the gospel.
1 Pet. 2.9-10 – you are a chosen generation, a royal priesthood.
2 Tim. 1.13-14 – be loyal to the faith.

BUN
Two alternative reading series are given:
Gen. 12.1-2 – God's promise to Abram.
Matt. 9.35-38 – on Jesus' preaching and healing and the words on the harvest and the workers
Acts 1.8 – Christ's final charter and promise of the outpouring of the Holy Spirit.
or Matt. 28.18-20.
Acts 13.1-3 – on the separation of Barnabas and Saul for work
2 Tim. 2.1-7 – on strength and endurance as a good soldier of Jesus Christ

CSM
The ceremony always takes place on a Sunday and the biblical readings of the actual Sunday are used. However, Matt. 28.18-20 is often included.

MCC-S
The rite prescribes three or four readings. Suggestions are:
Matt. 28.18-20 and Mark 16.15
Acts 13.2-3 – on the separation of Barnabas and Saul for work
Matt. 25.35-36, 40 – the final judgement
1 Cor. 12.4-6 – on the diversity of gifts and ministries
2 Cor. 5.17-20 – on being a new creation in Christ and the ministry of reconciliation
Ps. 86.9-11 – all nations shall come and worship before God.

SEM
The reading of Matt. 28.18-20 is required.
Other readings can be chosen by the district leader or the assistants. Suggestions are given, e.g. 1 Cor. 12.4-7 on the diversity of gifts and ministries.

Danmission
Two readings are mandatory:
Matt. 28.18-20 – the great commission
Rom. 10.13-15 – on the absolute need for a messenger
In addition to these two readings, two others may be chosen from a list of ten.

DSM
The only reading is Matt. 28.18-20.

DEM
Ps. 86.9-11 – all nations shall come and worship before God
Matt. 28:18-20 – the great commission
Rom. 12.4-8 – on being one body in Christ and the various spiritual gifts
John 10.14-16 – the good shepherd who goes also to the sheep outside the fold

Conclusion

Not surprisingly all the rites include Matthew 28.18-20, the commission to bring the Good News to the whole world.[15] This reflects the mission tradition of the Enlightenment (Bosch 2000, 341) which was dominant until the 1950s and to which all the mission organisations in this study belong. Since then the concept of *missio Dei* has become predominant in modern theology of mission (Bosch, 389). Of New Testament texts, the Gospel of John is the most representative of *missio Dei* thinking, but in these ten rites the relevant parts of the Gospel of John (such as chapter 17 or chapter 20) are rarely used. The exceptions are the Finnish rite and the second choice of readings in the Danmission rite. On choice of readings the rites seem to be rather 'outdated'. The new situation of mission might call for other biblical readings.

When we look at the readings, we find in the Free Churches, NLM, BUN and MCC of Sweden, a tendency to focus on the gifts and the personal qualities of the missionary, such as strength and endurance. The Finnish rite emphasises that the missionary must live as an example to others. The other churches and organisations show a tendency to focus on the task of the missionary. The readings speak of the absolute need for a messenger, of reaching the sheep outside the fold, of preaching the gospel and drawing people to Christ.

Exhortation and Commitments

As shown above, all the rites have a specific commitment section. Some of the rites have an exhortation just before this section or as part of it. Subsequently the missionaries are expected verbally to commit themselves to the ministry by giving one or more promises. The commitments may be sealed with a handshake of fellowship. Of the ten rites this is only the case for the Norwegian NMS rite and the Danish rites, possibly due to the common roots of ordina-

---

15. CSM uses the texts of the actual Sunday, but normally Matt. 28 is also read. The first of the possible series of readings in the rite of the Baptist Union of Norway does not include Matt. 28.

tion rites in the Church of Norway and the Evangelical-Lutheran Church of Denmark dating back to the Church Rite of 1685.[16]

The *Finnish rite* contains no exhortation before the promises. The missionaries promise to receive the mission commission, to be faithful and to live as examples to the congregation.

NMS: This section has similarities to the ordination of pastors in the authorised service book of the Church of Norway. The last exhortation of the exhortation section is identical with the last exhortation to pastors: 'To live by the word of God and by study and prayer penetrate more deeply into the holy scriptures and the truths of the Christian faith' (*Gudstjenestebok* 1996, II: 169).[17] The missionaries are exhorted to be obedient to the Lord and faithful to the Word of God and the confession of the church. In the single promise they promise to do faithfully what they have just been exhorted to do.[18]

NLM: In this rite this section has a confessional character. The first three questions begin: 'Do you believe...?' The missionaries asked if they believe that the Bible is the Word of God, that Jesus Christ is true God and true human being, and so on, taken from the Apostles' Creed and the Nicene Creed. Then they is asked if they believe that 'it is only due to [Jesus Christ] and comprehended through faith that we have forgiveness of our sins and our rights as children of God'.[19] The fourth question asks the missionaries to declare (insofar as they know thimselves!) that his faith is in agreement with the confessional basis of the Church of Norway. In the fifth question the missionaries are asked if they will live a life worthy of servants of the Lord. The central words are faithfulness, diligence, readiness. This is a repetition of the wording of the deed read aloud earlier in the ceremony (in the Presentation section).

BUN: The missionaries promise to be faithful to God and the Baptist Union in their service, to work for good collaboration in the mission field and accept the leadership of the Baptist Union of Norway.

---

16. See Iversen, Part II.6.
17. Translated from the original Norwegian text: 'Leve efter Guds ord og i studium og bøn trænge dybere ind i de hellige skrifter og den kristne tros sandheder'.
18. A missionary sent out by NMS can instead of this rite/ceremony choose a rite/ceremony called '*forbønnshandling*', ('act of intercession'). This rite is without exhortation and promise. According to a letter of 8th February, 2002, from NMS employment adviser Turid Ølberg, those who are sent for a short period tend to choose this, while those who are sent for a longer period normally choose '*vigsling*', the commissioning ceremony analysed in this article.
19. The Norwegian text says: 'at vi alene ved hans fortjeneste, grebet i troen får våre synders forladelse og barnerett hos Gud'.

CSM: The missionaries are asked if, with the help of God, they will carry out the task to which they has been called.

MCC-S: First the missionaries must confess their faith in Jesus Christ as crucified, dead and resurrected. Next they must confirm their willingness to be sent to the specific place and to serve in fellowship with the church there and with the gifts of grace they have received.

SEM has no promises. The deed read aloud earlier in the ceremony (in the Presentation section) contains an exhortatory element, when it states that a missionary is called to be faithful towards the Lord and the Church.

Danmission: The missionaries are exhorted to proclaim to people that God's Kingdom is at hand and they must repent and believe in Jesus Christ (cf. Mark 1.14); to act with love towards them and live among them as is seemly for servants of Christ. In the single promise the missionaries promise to take on this ministry according to the grace that God will grant.

DSM: The missionaries are asked if they are willing to travel, as missionaries, to the specific place mentioned.

DEM: The missionaries promise to undertake the ministry and do it according to the grace that God will grant. They are exhorted to do this task for the honour of God, for the edification of God's Church and its unity, and for the benefit and salvation of their fellow human beings.

Conclusion

The exhortation and commitments admonishes the new missionaries to personal faith and obedience to Jesus Christ and to the church or organisation that is sending them out. Most of the rites emphasise the missionaries' faithfulness (to God, the Word, the Church).

We find two types of commitment: one confessional or credal (NLM, MCC-S) where the missionaries are commissioned on the basis of a declaration of faith. In this case they first have to affirm that they stand in the right relationship to Scripture and Creed and that they have the will to be faithful. We might say that the inner calling of the individual for the task ahead is emphasised. In the other type of commitment, the main element is that missionaries promise to do what they have just been exhorted to do and/or take on the specific ministry they have been called to by the church or organisation. Here the outer calling is emphasised.

The Prayer with Imposition of Hands

One of the characteristics when an individual is given a public commission in the church is the imposition of hands accompanied by prayer (Brodd 1998, 4).

This prayer invokes the Holy Spirit, praying that he may confer charisms for the specific ministry on the person. Moreover it is an act of intercessory prayer for God's blessing on the person and on his ministry. As mentioned above, this prayer is found in some form in all the rites, but different terms are used for this action. NMS and DEM call it 'imposition of hands and prayer', while DSM uses the term 'sending with imposition of hands'. The Finnish rite calls it 'blessing for the missionary commission' and CSM 'blessing and sending'. The MCC-S and SEM call it 'intercessory prayer'. BUN calls it 'prayer of commissioning during the imposition of hands', NLM 'commissioning', and Danmission 'commissioning and sending'. We will take a closer look at the content of this section of the various rites.

FELM, Messengers and LEAF: The wording of this section is quite similar to other rites of the service book of the Evangelical-Lutheran Church of Finland, for example, the rite for deacons. The bishop says: 'With the authority that according to God's will is given to me by Christ's Church, I bless you for the service of mission, in the name of the Father, the Son and the Holy Spirit'.[20] The bishop and the assistants then place their hands on each missionary's head and the bishop prays a short prayer of blessing: 'May God, the Triune, bless and sanctify you that you may always and everywhere serve Christ's Church. Amen'.[21] After the removal of the hands, while the missionary is still kneeling, the bishop prays a prayer of thanksgiving and for blessing on missionary work in general. It ends with an eschatological affirmation: 'Lord, we look forward to that day when you will be praised in every tongue and your law will fill heaven and earth'.[22] The section ends with the Lord's Prayer.

NMS: The prayer is very similar to the ordination prayer in the ordination rites in the Service Book of the Church of Norway (*Gudstjenestebok* 1996). The text of Matt. 9.37-38 is interwoven with this prayer for workers for the harvest, a tradition that goes back to Luther.[23] Then there is a prayer that God will send his Spirit with the gifts required for the ministry to be undertaken.

---

20. Translated from the original Swedish text: 'Med den myndighet som enligt Guds vilja har getts mig av Kristi kyrka välsignar jag er till uppdraget i missionens tjänst i Faderns och Sonens och den helige Andes namn'.
21. Translated from the original Swedish text: 'Må Gud, den treninge välsigna och helga dig, så att du alltid och överallt tjänar Kristi kyrka. Amen'.
22. Translated from the original Swedish text: 'Herre, vi ser fram mot den dag då du prisas på alla tungomål och ditt lov uppfyller himmel och jord'.
23. This prayer for workers for the harvest goes back to the ordination prayer in Martin Luther's ordination rite from the Wittenberg Ordinal 1537/1539 (Puglisi 1998, 4f).

It ends with a declaration that the missionary is now rightly called and holds the authority and responsibility that belongs to 'his [or her] holy calling'.

NLM: A free prayer with imposition of hands. It ends with the Lord's Prayer. The prayer refers to the preceding confession, when it opens with the words: 'In accordance with this your confession and promise, we commission you in the name of the Triune God to the work you are called to'.

BUN: The secretary general prays either a free prayer or a set prayer that God will send the Holy Spirit with gifts of wisdom, counsel, knowledge, strength, love and devotion. This section ends with a declaration: 'In the name of our Lord Jesus Christ, Lord of the congregation, we declare that you are commissioned to the service of a missionary'.[24]

CSM: The rite itself mentions no prayer with imposition of hands, but the rubrics of the booklet used by CSM specify that at this point in the service the missionary/the whole missionary family go to the altar. They kneel and during the imposition of hands, the bishop prays: 'Go out to your ministry in the name of the Father, the Son and the Holy Spirit'. [25] To the children the bishop says: 'The God of your baptism is with you all days and until the end of time'.[26] There is no *epiclesis* and no specific gifts are prayed for. The prayer is clearly meant as a general blessing of the whole family.

MCC-S: The mission leader prays a free intercessory prayer. The rite itself does not mention imposition of hands, but in the constitution of the MCC-S the imposition of hands during this prayer is prescribed.[27] The section ends with the declaration: 'God has found you worthy of trust and has taken you into his service'. [28]

SEM: The section begins with a reference to apostolic Tradition followed by a free intercessory prayer.

Danmission: During the imposition of hands the pastor prays for blessing on the missionaries and for God's help.

DSM: The content of the prayer is for God's blessing on the missionaries, that he will keep them humble and in good health and let people encounter

---

24. The text in Norwegian is: 'I vor Herre Jesu Kristi, menighedens herre, navn erklærer vi dig for indviet til missionærtjenesten'.
25. The Swedish text says: 'Gå til din tjänst i Faderns och Sonens och den helige Andes namn'.
26. The Swedish text is: 'Ditt dops Gud är med dig alla dagar till tidens slut'.
27. Received as electronic file from Rev. Per-Magnus Selinder, Secretrary for Theology and Ecumenics in the MCC of Sweden, 28th February, 2002
28. The Swedish text says: 'Gud har funnit er vara värda förtroende och tagit er i sin tjänst'.

the Gospel through their service. Unity between the missionaries and the ones who send them out is emphasised. The prayer contains no *epiclesis*.

DEM: The prayer asks for blessing on the missionaries and their family, that God will keep them humble and in good health and send the Holy Spirit that they may draw people to God through their service.

Conclusion

When we look at this central part of the rites for the ssending out of missionaries, we must ask what the character of the rite is and what action the rite communicates. Is the rite instrumental – does God act, so that a missionary is created? Is there a transformation of the object of the rite and transference of different gifts of the Holy Spirit? Or is the rite expressive – an act of confirmation of the calling, both the individual's inner calling and the calling by the mission society or church. Or is it an intercessory prayer indicating rather vague wishes and expressions of hope (Brodd 1998, 4)?

The answer as to whether the rites are instrumental or expressive is not obvious. One rite, the one from NMS, is clearly instrumental. The order of events is: a prayer that God will send his Spirit and various gifts, followed by a declaration that the missionary now is rightly called. Something has happened. BUN includes the same elements, but as seen above, the commitments section of this rite has an expressive character.

The majority of the rites take more than anything else the form of an intercessory prayer, a prayer for *blessing* on the missionary and his task.

The Role of the Congregation

It varies a great deal how detailed the rites are about the role of the congregation present, but in all of them a group of assistants takes part in the imposition of hands, and in many also in the reading of the biblical texts. (Nevertheless the pastor may officiate without assistants at the *Danmission* rite.) In *SEM* some of the assistants take part in the free prayer during the imposition of hands. In the *Finnish* rite it is one of the assistants who does the presentation of the missionary. In the *CSM* rite, after the commitments, it is possible for short greetings, possibly biblical, to be given to the missionary by representatives of the sending organisation or congregation. In general the assistants may be the chairman and/or other members of the mission society board, members of the parish council, representatives of international mission, and so on. Often this is not specified in the rite and depends on tradition, on the person who is officiating at the rite, or on other considerations.

The *NMS* rite stands out as the rite with the most comprehensive role specified for the congregation. Its rubrics provide for the possibility that the presentation of the missionary may be done by the chairman of the parish council. The Introductory prayer is formed so that it alternates between officiant and congregation. Afterwards the congregation sings an epicletic hymn. Assistants take part in the imposition of hands, and finally the members of the congregation are exhorted to support the missionary with their love and in their prayers.

Final Conclusion

We may conclude that imposition of hands with prayer is part of all the rites analysed, as are scriptural readings and a commitment by each individual missionary. But there are visible differences between the rites of an established church or a Free Church. The Free Church rites of NML, BUN, MCC-S and SEM have a more expressive, credal and free character than the other rites and a focus on the individual sent out, while the remaining rites of the mission societies associated with established churches focus more on the sending and have a more instrumental character, with the *NMS* rite as the most distinct in this matter, because they are close to the Church of Norway.

We can also conclude that the rites for the ssending out of missionaries primarily communicate an act of intercession by which the missionaries are strengthened for their task and upheld by the acknowledgement and prayers of the congregation.

The rites are not seen as acts with parallels to that of the ordination of a pastor, as was found in an earlier study of Danish rites (Iversen 1989); they are not only a matter of ssending out a missionary to some distant place, but a matter of sending based on baptism. The reason for this development may well be the influence of the Lima document of the Faith and Order Commission, *Baptism, Eucharist and Ministry* (BEM) with its emphasis on the threefold ministry of bishop, priest and deacon. The Lima document has resulted in a strengthening of the position of the deacon in the Nordic churches. In some of the churches the deacon is now regarded as part of the ecclesiastical office.[29] In line with this development for deacons, the rites for the ssending out of missionaries seem to have changed. What we mainly find today are acts of intercession – prayer and wishes for a blessing on the missionaries and their task.

---

29. See article on the rites for deacons (Part II, 3).

References

Baptism, Eucharist and Ministry (BEM). 1982. Faith and Order Paper 111. Geneva: World Council of Churches.

Bosch, David. 2000. *Transforming Mission: Paradigm Shifts in Theology of Mission*, 15. ed. Maryknoll, New York: Orbis Books.

Brodd, Sven-Erik. 1998. Preliminära anteckningar till frågan om hur man analyserer och jämför ordinations- välsignelse- och installationsliturgier som dogmatiska texter. Consultation at Farfa 16-20.4 1998.

Den Svenska Kyrkohandboken II. 1988. Stockholm: Verbum.

Eckerdal, Lars.1985. Svenska kyrkans gudstjänst. Genom bön och handpåläggning, *Vignings – jämte installationshandlinger – liturgiske utvecklingslinier.* Bilaga 6. Statens offentliga utredningar 1985:48. Stockholm.

Kyrkohandbok för den Evangelisk-lutherska Kyrkan i Finland III. 1995. Vasa: Församlingsförbundets Forlag.

Iversen, Hans Raun. 1989. Missionær-, diakon- og sekretærindvielser i Danmark. In *Under bøn og håndspålæggelse. Indvielse af missionærer, diakoner og præster*, ed. Hans Raun Iversen and V. Tranholm- Mikkelsen, 65-117. Frederiksberg: Anis.

Puglisi, James F. 1998. *The Process of Admission to Ordained Ministry*, vol. II, The First Lutheran, Reformed, Anglican, and Wesleyan Rites: A Comparative Study. Collegeville, MIN: Liturgical Press.

Thunberg, Lars. 1989. Missionærtjenestens egenart. In *Under bøn og håndspålæggelse. Indvielse af missionærer, diakoner og præster*, ed. Hans Raun Iversen and V. Tranholm-Mikkelsen, 200-205. Frederiksberg: Anis.

6. The Role of the Congregation in Rites of Ordination

Rites of ordination and commitment cannot be studied comprehensively unless what they are able to communicate in the context of the congregation present is taken into account. Do the rites really communicate what their authors intended when they did all their careful theological, liturgical and perhaps even ecumenical work in the process of creating them? Do the rites include the congregation as a participatory subject in the liturgy – or do they leave the members of the congregation in the position of observers or spectators in their own church?

Einar Sigurbjörnsson highlights the Lutheran custom of replacing parts of the liturgy of the Latin Mass with hymns for the congregation to sing in the vernacular, as was and is done in the rites for the ordination of pastors and bishops in the Evangelical Lutheran Churches in the Nordic countries. The singing of the ordination hymns analysed may be seen as the better part of the congregational participation in the ordination rites.

Hans Raun Iversen analyses the rites for the ordination of pastors and bishops in the Evangelical-Lutheran Church of Denmark. The overall aim of the authors of these rites, in use since 1987, was to create modern rites as faithful as possible to the rites of the 1537 Danish Church Ordinance. Discussion during this process centred on theology, in particular on the concept of ordained ministry and the historical legitimacy of various concepts of ministry. The question that was not addressed at all is how far it is actually possible to communicate the same message as the Reformation rite communicated in its original context by attempting to recreate rites drawn up in 1537 and to use them in the present day.

Communicating the Theology of Ordination through Hymns in the Evangelical-Lutheran Churches of the Nordic Countries

Einar Sigurbjörnsson

Hymns have played a major part in Lutheran Worship. Luther himself wrote several hymns: some were translations or adaptations of Medieval hymns but others were original poetry. Among Luther's hymns were paraphrases of biblical Psalms and Canticles, and parts of the Catechism.[1] In order to make the ideal of worship in the vernacular easier, Luther and his collaborators also had some of the traditional parts of the liturgy paraphrased as hymns. This is most evident in the German Mass of 1526 where the *Credo* and the *Sanctus* were written as hymns (WA 38: 423-431; LW 53:1-90). In the *Formula Missae* of 1523 he had already suggested that in addition to the Latin parts of the Mass, German hymns should be sung.[2] The hymn writing tradition gradually grew and developed and included not only liturgical material but catechetical and private devotional material. This was also inspired by Luther's view that people learn poems better than prose and, therefore, poets should paraphrase biblical material into verses and hymns.[3] Biblical poems, both paraphrases of biblical

1. For Luther's hymns see WA 35; Jenny 1985; LW 53:189-309. In this article, I quote the American translation of Luther's liturgical writings in LW 53.
2. LW 53, 36; Cf. Article 24 of the Augsburg Confession, On the Mass: *'Servantur et usitatae caerimoniae fere omnes, praeterquam quod latinis cantionibus admiscentur alicubi germanicae, quae additae sunt ad docendum populum'* (BSLK, 91).
3. Cf. 'Preface to the Burial Hymns – To the Christian Reader'. LW 53: 330: 'But if anyone should have the gift and desire to put these verses into good rimes, that would help to have them read more gladly and remembered more easily. *For rime and verse make good sayings and proverbs which serve better than ordinary prose*' (Italics mine).

books and meditations, were widely used by people and in most Lutheran churches hymns gradually replaced the traditional parts of the liturgy. In this article hymns used in the liturgies of ordination in the Lutheran Folk churches of the Nordic countries will be described.

Luther's Ordination Rite

In his Ordination Rite of 1535 Luther recommends two hymns (LW 53:122-126). The first hymn, to be sung by the choir (*'Chorgesang'*), is *'Veni, sancte Spiritus'* followed by a versicle from Ps. 51: 'Create in me a clean heart, O God, and renew a right spirit within me' – and the collect for Pentecost: *'Deus qui corda fidelium'*. It is not altogether clear whether Luther is referring to the antiphon *'Veni, sancte Spiritus, reple tuorum corda fidelium'* or the sequence for Pentecost *'Veni, sancte Spiritus, et emitte cælitus'*.[4] It is improbable, however, that Luther is referring to his own hymn *'Veni, sancte Spiritus gebessert'* which he wrote for Pentecost 1524, since he says that the hymn as well as the following responsive prayer and the collect for Pentecost are to be sung in Latin by the choir and he does not use the German name of the hymn, *'Komm, heiliger Geist, Herr Gott'*.[5] After the laying-on of hands, Luther's hymn *'Nun bitten wir den heiligen Geist'* is sung by the congregation.[6]

This choice of hymns, together with the other parts of the ordination liturgy, reflects Luther's understanding of ministry as a ministry of the Word. The Word of God is the means by which the Holy Spirit creates faith and, therefore, ministers must be endowed with the Holy Spirit in order to fulfil their mission. It is through the hymns that the congregation is called to pray that the Holy Spirit bestow his gifts upon the ordinands and that the congregation may through the ministry of the Word be led to faith. Ordination implies a 'sending' (*'missio'*), by the Lord and, therefore, the rite provides a Pentecostal context (Puglisi 1998, 10).

---

4. Cf. LW 53: 124 and Puglisi 1998, 7, where he explains that the traditional hymn according to Medieval Pontificals was *Veni, creator Spiritus*. Luther also translated this hymn into German, *Komm, Gott, Schöpfer, heiliger Geist* – Come, God, Creator, Holy Ghost, LW 53, 260-262, Cf. LBW 1978, no. 473.

5. The first verse of the hymn is a versification of the antiphon *'Veni, sancte Spiritus reple tuorum corda fidelium'* but the other two are prayers for the gift of the Holy Spirit for faith and steadfastness. See LW 53, 265-267 and LBW 1978 no. 163.

6. 'Now let us pray to the Holy Ghost', LW 53, 263-264; LBW 1978 no. 317

The Nordic Rites

All sixteenth century Nordic ordination rites recommend the same hymns as Luther did in his ordination rite. *'Veni, sancte Spiritus'* – most probably the antiphon, and in churches of the Danish tradition, followed by the collect for Pentecost – is to be sung in Latin, and, after the ordination and before Holy Communion, Luther's hymn *'Nun bitten wir den heiligen Geist'* is sung in the vernacular. The Danish tradition was valid for Denmark, Norway and Iceland and was established by the Church Order of 1537 and the Danish-Norwegian Rite of 1685 (Lausten 1989; DNKR 1685; Lindhardt 1978; Puglisi 1998, 30-39).[7] The Swedish tradition was valid in Sweden and Finland and established by the Church Order of 1571 and the Church Law of 1686 (Hellerström 1940, 227-233; Puglisi 1998, 53-63.). It is interesting to note that in spite of the fact that in Denmark apostolic succession was not retained and the Danes seemed to be more critical of episcopacy than the Swedes, the rite for the ordination of bishops in Denmark was more elaborate than that of the ordination of priests and even more elaborate than the Swedish rite for the ordination of bishops (Puglisi 1998, 15-23, 29, 34-39, 58-62). This is apparent from the fact that when a bishop was ordained two Psalms, Ps. 8 and Ps. 134, were to be sung in Latin besides the two traditional hymns, and the Church Order states that by these Psalms ministers are reminded of their call and mission (Latin text in Lausten 1989, 141-142). This custom is retained in the 1685 Rite (DNKR 1685, 122). The choice of Ps. 134 is obvious, and the Church order explains that this Psalm is to be sung for the preachers, to remind them of the fact that they are to stand with elevated hands in praise of the Lord and proclaim the true blessing offered by Jesus Christ, the true seed of Abraham, and oppose all temptations of the Devil (Latin text in Lausten 1989, 142). To modern readers the choice of Ps. 8 is not so obvious. But the choice of this Psalm is quite in line with Lutheran christological understanding of the Bible in general and the Psalter in particular. According to this understanding, Ps. 8 referred to Christ and the election of humankind to salvation in Christ. Luther writes, for example, on Ps. 8 in his exposition of 1537:

> This psalm is one of the beautiful psalms and glorious prophecy about Christ, where David describes Christ's person and kingdom and teaches who Christ is, what kind of kingdom He has and how it is formed; where this King rules, namely, in all lands and yet in heaven; and the means by

---

7. Cf. Iversen (Part II.6) and Einar Sigurbjörnsson and Kristján Ingólfsson (Part II.2).

which this kingdom is founded and regulated, namely, only through the Word and faith, without sword and armor.[8]

The psalms were sung in Latin, thus not communicating much to the congregation except the part of it that understood Latin, which was the clergy present and the school boys who were singing. The ordaining minister is, however, to expound on one or two verses and thereby the theology of ministry was communicated to the congregation.[9] Thus the congregation is called to active participation, not only in the prayers expressed in the epicletic hymns but also when they were reminded, through the exposition, of the mission and call of the ordained ministry.

The first Swedish ordination rites were published in the Church Order of 1571 (Puglisi 1998, 53-63; Hellerström 1940, 227-231). The hymns sung are the same as proposed by Luther, the antiphon '*Veni, sancte Spiritus*'and Luther's hymn '*Nun bitten wir den heiligen Geist*'. In addition to these two, at the ordination of bishops a responsory, '*Sint lumbi vestri praecincti*'('Let your loins be girded') from Luke 12.35-36, was to be sung in Latin.

The Modern Period

Denmark

In the nineteenth century, the Danish ordination rites were revised and this affected the choice of hymns. The '*Veni, sancte Spiritus*' with versicle and collect was continued in Latin chant but it was recommended that the antiphon and prayers be sung in Danish. In the rite for the ordination of bishops, Ps. 8 disappeared and its hymnic paraphrase was not retained. Ps. 134 was retained in its hymnic paraphrase but it was also allowed that the Psalm itself be sung in Danish (Lindhardt 1978, 20-46).

The present ordination rite was authorized in 1987.[10] It is based on the nineteenth century ritual revisions. Besides the antiphon '*Veni, sancte Spiritus*', which is either sung in Latin or Danish, there are three hymns recommen-

---

8. LW 12, 98. Verse 2 was said to refer to the preaching of the Gospel, LW, 111.
9. These two Psalms were paraphrased into hymns and found in Danish and Icelandic hymnals in the sixteenth and seventeenth centuries (Lausten 1989, 240-241; Páll Eggert Ólason 1924, 146, 198).
10. Cf. Iversen (Part II.6).

ded.[11] The first one is no. 291 *'Du, som går ud fra den levende Gud'* ('You who proceed from the living God') or another hymn to the Holy Spirit (RB 1992, 134). This hymn is among the hymns for Pentecost in the Danish Hymnal and by proposing this hymn the ordination rite emphasizes the Pentecost context of ordination. The hymn is Grundtvig's translation, or rather adaptation of the English hymn, 'O, Spirit of the Living God' by James Montgomery, written for a missionary congress in 1836 at which missionaries were sent out (Malling I: 297-300). The original hymn has six stanzas with four lines each. Grundtvig's adaptation also has six stanzas, but each stanza has six lines. Besides being longer, Grundtvig's text is also much richer in metaphor than the original.[12] The first stanza is a prayer to the Holy Spirit to be near us in a dark world which is opposed to God's Son. The second stanza is an intercession for those whom the Spirit sends, that he may give them tongues of fire and yet mild speech, thus alluding to the sending of the Holy Spirit at Pentecost in tongues of fire which gave the apostles courage to speak for all. The third and fourth stanzas pray that the sending of witnesses may bear fruit in good deeds and praise to God. The fifth stanza prays that the whole world may believe and the sixth stanza expresses confidence that the Holy Spirit will fulfil God's plan for salvation so that no one will perish except the 'generation of damnation' (*'fortabelsens æt'*). This shows Grundtvig's denial of universal salvation and his faithfulness to confessional Lutheranism which states that the Spirit creates faith where and when God wills.[13]

The rite retains the traditional *'Veni, sancte Spiritus'* and the collect for Pentecost, which may either be sung in Danish or Latin. As an alternative, after the initial invocation by the bishop, the congregation may sing the second and third verses of *'Du, som går ud fra den levende Gud'*. It is interesting to note that the translation of *'Emitte spiritum tuum, Domine, et creabuntur. Et renovabis faciem terrae'* is very 'clericalist':

---

11. A new hymnbook was authorized in Denmark in 2002 and put into effect at Pentecost 2003, DDS 2002, and I quote the hymns according to the numbers there, though the Service Book quotes the former 1953 Hymnal.
12. Grundtvig's adaptation was translated into Icelandic (see below). It is also translated into Norwegian and four verses are in the present Norwegian Hymnal, at no. 218 among the hymns for Pentecost.
13. Cf. Augsburg Confession article 5: *'Nam per verbum et sacramenta tamquam per instrumenta donatur spiritus sanctus, qui fidem efficit, ubi et quando visum est Deo . . .'* (BSLK 58).

(Bishop): Lord, send your Holy Spirit to create ministers for you – (Congregation): and renew your congregation day by day.[14]

After the presentation of candidates, no. 485 or 486 or another appropriate hymn is sung, and in the hymnal both 485 and 486 are marked as ordination hymns. The former hymn, no. 485, is by Thomas Kingo (1634-1703), *'O Jesus, præst i evighed'* ('Oh, Jesus, priest in eternity'). Kingo wrote it as a Gospel hymn for the first Sunday after Easter.[15] The hymn is a meditation by the congregation on the magnificence of the preaching ministry based on the Gospel of the day, John 20.19-31, on Christ's sending of the Apostles by breathing on them and giving them authority to bind and loose sin. Jesus is the eternal high priest who reconciled the world to God. The ministers of the Church are sent to bring the ministry of reconciliation, and, as Christ was anointed by the Holy Spirit by the Father, he strengthens his ministers by the same Spirit to preach God's word. Directly referring to John 20.22, it says that Jesus still breathes on his ministers so that they are endowed with power to bind and loose sin.[16] The hymn emphasizes that this noble task is not laid upon the shoulders of angels but of weak and frail humans. The final verse is a prayer by the ordinand that he/she may honour the ministry.

The other hymn, no. 486, is Grundtvig's ordination hymn *'I dag på apostolisk vis'* ('Today in apostolic manner') (Malling II: 336-337). 'Apostolic manner' is a direct reference to a phrase in the ordination rite.[17] The first stanza is interesting and refers to the congregation as the acting subject: 'Today in apostolic manner we lay our hands on new instruments for the glory of Jesus and to the light and consolation of the Lord's little ones'. This implies that it is the Church which acts in ordination through the ordaining ministers. There are interesting metaphors in the second and third stanzas: the church transcends the present congregation which is here today but will vanish tomorrow, whereas it is Jesus who is eternal and for each age creates witnesses around the earth. The meaning implied seems to be that the congregation present is a temporal manifestation of the eternal church which has the perpetual duty of appointing ministers through the hands of the officiating ministers. In the

---

14. *'(Biskoppen): Herre, udsend din Helligånd, så du skaber dig tjenere – (Menigheden): og fornyer din menighed dag for dag'* (RB 1992, 135).
15. Malling IV: 164; the text was revised in the nineteenth century.
16. The same metaphor was also used in the old wording of endowment in the 1685 rite. Cf. Iversen (Part II.6) and Einar Sigurbjörnsson & Kristján Ingólfsson (Part II.2).
17. See Iversen, Part II.6.

fourth stanza the congregation asks the Lord to accept the ministers from their hands and equip them with God's Spirit of truth and as witnesses of faith, hope and love. This metaphor is a direct reference to the Church Order of 1537 which interprets the laying-on of hands as an offering of the ordinand to God.[18] Stanzas 5 to 9 are prayers that God equip them for their ministry and in the eighth stanza God is asked that he himself may be their preacher.

The final hymn proposed is Luther's 'Nun bitten wir den heiligen Geist', no 246.

In the rite for the ordination of bishops, Ps. 134 may be sung as the introit. Another hymn proposed is Luther's 'Erhalt uns, Herr, bei deinem Wort'.[19] Otherwise the hymns proposed are the same as in the rite for the ordination of priests, except that between the four lessons Decius' hymn 'Allein Gott in der Höh sei Her' – 'Aleneste Gud i Himmerig' – is sung.[20]

Norway

Norway came under the Swedish crown in 1814 and gradually began developing its own liturgical tradition which as far as ordination was concerned was based on the Danish tradition. The first Norwegian Service Book was authorized in 1889, the second in 1920 and the present one in 1992 (Fæhn 1994, esp. 407-414).

The present rite proposes two hymns for ordination (GNK 1992, 162-173, 201-213). The first is 'Veni, creator Spiritus' – or another hymn of epicletic character – which may be sung between the lessons. This choice of hymn is very interesting from an ecumenical point of view since this hymn was part of the ordination rite in the Middle Ages and still is in the Roman Catholic Church but not in Lutheran rites. The second hymn, sung after the ordination proper, is Luther's 'Nun bitten wir den heiligen Geist'. Both hymns, 'Veni, creator Spritus' and the first stanza of Luther's hymn may also be sung at the ordination of catechists, deacons and bishops (GNK 1992, 175-182, 187-194, 206-209). As in Denmark the invocation to God, in the antiphon 'Veni, sancte Spiritus', to send his Holy Spirit is that new ministers may be created (GNK 1992, 164, 176, 187). It is interesting to note that at the ordination of bishops there is no hymn proposed after the ordination, and the rubric only says that this is to be a hymn of prayer (GNK 1992, 213). At the ordination of bishops

---

18. Lausten 1989, 143 (Latin text). This view of ordination is expressed by Philip Melanchthon in his *Loci communes* of 1543, 140-141.
19. 'Behold os, Herre, ved dit ord', DDS 2002 no. 337, ('Lord, keep us Steadfast in thy Word'), LW 53, 304-305; LBW 1978 no. 230.
20. DDS 2002, no. 435; 'All Glory be to God on high.', LBW 1978 no.166.

the antiphon and invocation are omitted, which implies that the Church of Norway regards episcopal ordination more as an installation than an ordination.

In the 1984 Norwegian Hymnal there are 12 hymns under the heading, Ordination to ministry (or service) within the Church, nos. 676-687. Among them is Grundtvig's 'Today in apostolic manner' (no. 678). Some hymns refer to the diaconate: no. 683, for example, is a translation from Swedish,[21] and some, such as no. 679, refer to missionaries.

There are several hymns that refer to the ordination of priests. Two of them are old hymns which in Norway were converted into ordination hymns. The former, no. 676: *'Vor prest som oss skal lære'* ('Our priest who shall teach us') is originally a German hymn, *'Aus meines Hertzens Grunde'*, which was translated into Danish by Jakob Madsen (Matzøn) in 1603 as *'Jeg vil din Pris udsjunge'* ('I will sing your praise') (DDS 2002, no. 737). In Norway it was made into an ordination hymn by B.M. Landstad (1802-1880) (Malling II: 4 80-483). The second, no. 677, is by Thomas Kingo, *'Guds menighet! Luk opp din munn'* ('God's congregation, open your mouth for praise!'). The hymn was originally written as an exposition of 1 Thess 5.12-23, the Epistle for the 26th Sunday after Trinity, with the opening: *'O kiere Siæl, luck op din Mund'* ('Oh, my soul, open your mouth to praise'), but in Norway it was adapted for ordination and 'soul' replaced by 'congregation'.[22] The third hymn, no. 681, is by Gustav Jensen: *'Ei for å tjenes Herren kom'* ('Our Lord did not come to be served'): it emphasizes that ministry is service with reference to Mark 10.45. Some hymns use the Gospel metaphor of harvest and workers which Luther also used in his ordination prayer, for example, nos. 680 *'Knel, du Kristi vitneskare'* ('Kneel, you crowd of Christ's witnesses') by B.M. Landstad and 684: *'Høstens Herre, når du sender'* ('Lord of the harvest, when you send') by Bjørn Braun (1913-1980). One hymn, no. 687, uses the metaphor of temple and builders: *'På Herrens tempel bygges fra pinsefestens dag'* ('The Lord's temple is ever being built, from the Feast of Pentecost') and seems to be a hymn for the ordination of missionaries. Another hymn, no. 682, is a prayer by the ordinand: *'Min Herre har kalt meg og glad vil jeg gå'* ('My Lord has called me and in joy I will go') by Sigvald Skavlan (1839-1912). Still another hymn, no. 680, is an

---

21. *'Din kjærleik, Jesus evig er'*, by T.E.F. Lönegren: *'Din kärlek, Jesus, gräns ej vet'*, in the Swedish hymnbook, DDS 1986 no. 91.

22. In the new Danish Hymnal, DDS 2002, some verses of this hymn are no. 378 under the heading 'Communion of Saints': *'Hvor kan jeg noksom skønne på'* ('Where can I sufficiently express God's love?')

exhortation by the congregation to the ordinands that they may be courageous in ministry and a prayer to Christ that he may send them his Holy Spirit: *'Knel du Kristi vitneskare'* ("Kneel, oh crowd of Christ's witnesses') by M.B. Landstad.

There are three hymns written in the latter half of the twentieth century, nos. 684, 685 and 686. Hymn no 684, *'Høstens Herre, når du sender'* ('Lord of the harvest, when you send') by Bjørn Braun seems to be meant for the sending or consecration of missionaries. At the beginning the hymn mentions the fact that there are many different vocations within the church. Some go to the end of the world, others keep watch in prayer (*'bønnevakt'*), and yet, every vocation is from the Lord for which we give thanks. In the last stanza the prayer is for strength also for those who have worked so hard: 'Say to all that were called: "It was I who called you"'.

Hymn no. 685 is a hymn for the ordination of priests: *'Med kall fra Gud og Kirken blir nye prester sendt'* ('With call from God and the Church new priests are sent') by Olav Hillestad (1923-1974). The first stanza describes the ministry of priests as that of preaching the Word and administering the sacraments. Priests speak on God's behalf and act in the place of Christ in proclaiming the message of reconciliation and peace. The second and third stanzas are a prayer for the priests in their difficult and yet happy work of admonishing (*'refse'*) people for their sins and keeping them from falling. The hymn also thanks the Lord for new witnesses and reminds God of his promise to give the Holy Spirit to his ministers.

The third hymn, no. 686, *'Herre, du kalte disipler blant folk uten rikdom og rang'* ('Lord, you called disciples among people of no wealth or position') is by Liv Nordhaug (1926-). This is an interesting hymn which builds upon these contrasts: the greatness of God and of God's calling and the frailty of human beings. This illustrates that God gives strength to the weak, so that the work of the Church is a miracle: empty and poor hands are filled with miracles from God; the weak God sends are strong when they tread the way of calling and promises.

Iceland

The first Icelandic Hymnal with a section entitled, 'Ordination Hymns' was published in 1871 and there are three ordination hymns, nos. 525-527.[23] One

---

23. SB 1871. One of them, no. 527, is an adaptation of the Swedish hymn by J. Svedberg *'O, gode herde du Som gav ditt liv för fåren'*, in the Swedish Hymnal of 1937, DSP 1937 no. 222 but not in the present hymnbook. It is not in SB 1972.

of them is an old hymnic adaptation of Psalm 134 but changed here into a hymn for ordination; the others were new hymns by Icelandic hymn-writers. A common characteristic of these hymns is that they are christological and use the image of a priest shepherding his flock at the chief shepherd's command. In the 1886 hymnal Ps. 134 disappeared in favour of a translation of Grundtvig's *"Du som går ud fra den levende Gud"* ("Andinn Guðs lifanda' af himnanna hæð") by Stefán Thorarensen (1831-1892) (SB 1886 no. 594). The other two were revised. In the 1945 hymnbook, two of these were retained (SB 1945 nos. 610 and 611) but both disappeared from the hymnbook in 1972.

In the present hymnal which was authorized in 1972 there are two hymns for ordination (SB 1972 nos. 266 and 267). Both are to be sung according to the rite of ordination in the 1981 Service Book of the Icelandic Church.[24] Besides these a hymnic adaptation of Ps. 117 by a seventeenth century poet, Jón Þorsteinsson, who was killed by Algerian pirates who plundered his parish in 1627, is sung before the antiphon '*Veni, sancte Spiritus*' and the collect for Pentecost.[25]

At the beginning of the ordination service a new hymn written by Bishop Sigurbjörn Einarsson is sung, *'Kristur, sem reistir þitt ríki á jörð'* ('Christ, who established your Kingdom on earth': SB 1972 no. 267). The hymn is a prayer to Christ that he will give his Spirit to all those he sends and will lead his flock and kindle the fire of love in their hearts. The final stanza is prayer to the Holy Trinity where each person is addressed, that the Father may be with us in all we do, that the Spirit may be awake in us and that Christ may let his cross conquer in the lands of darkness, his love warm up frozen soil, and that he may come to take all power on earth.

After the ordination a hymn by the seventeenth century poet Hallgrímur Pétursson (1614-1674) is sung. This hymn is from the tenth of his 50 Passion hymns,[26] where the poet meditates on the high priest Caiaphas who, empow-

---

24. HB 1981, 183-190, 194-206, see further Einar Sigurbjörnsson and Kristján Ingólfsson, Part II.2.
25. *'Lofið Guð, ó, lýðir, göfgið hann'* ('Praise God, O peoples'), SB 1972, no. 24. This hymn had been part of the ordination rite before the publication of HB 1981. See Einar Sigurbjörnsson and Kristján Ingólfsson, Part II.2.
26. Hallgrímur Pétursson's Hymns of the Passion – *Passíusálmar* – have been published regularly since their first publication in 1666 and are very widely read, and *inter alia* one hymn is read daily on the national radio during Lent. They have been translated into several languages, Danish (1995), Norwegian (1979), English (1966 and 2001) German (1974), Hungarian (1974), Italian (1995) and Dutch (1996) and published by Hallgrimskirkja, Reykjavík.

ered by the spirit of his office, had prophesied the death of Christ (cf. John 11.50 and 18.14) but during the trial of Jesus had obeyed the spirit of darkness. This leads the poet to the prayer that God will never take his Spirit from him and to the admonition to priests that they proclaim the word of truth and rely on God's help. Priests must bear in mind that they are to meet their judge at the hour of judgement and then they will be asked about the disciples their carelessness had led into perdition. Five of this Passion hymn's 17 stanzas are here made into an ordination hymn containing a prayer for the Holy Spirit and an admonition to the preachers.

At the ordination of bishops, the same hymns are recommended but after the ordination, instead of Hallgrimur Pétursson's hymn, the *Te Deum*, in a translation of Luther's version, may be sung (SB 1972, no. 39; LW 53:171-175).

For the ordination of deacons, the Service Book recommends two hymns. The first is Luther's '*Nun bitten wir den heiligen Geist*', no. 335 in the Hymnal, and the second one is no. 288, '*Guðs kirkja er byggð á bjargi*' which is a translation by Friðrik Friðriksson (1868-1961) of the hymn by Samuel John Stone (1839-1900), 'The Church's one foundation is Jesus Christ her Lord' (LBW 1978 no. 369). In 1996, Bishop Sigurbjörn Einarsson translated a Swedish hymn by Arne H. Lindgren '*Öppna mig för din kärlek*' (see the following section): '*Gef mér þinn kærleik, Kristur*' which may be used at the ordination of deacons.

Sweden

The present Swedish Service Book of 1987 does not recommend any hymn for ordination services except the antiphon '*Veni, sancte Spiritus*', which is hymn no. 361 in the Swedish Hymnal (DSPB 1986). The same was the case with the older Handbook of 1942 (DSKHB 1987, 333-359, 381-396). In the older Hymnal of 1937 there were three hymns on the ministry of priests (nos. 222-224) and one to be sung at the ordination of bishops (no. 226). Only one of these is in the new 1986 Hymnal: '*Av dig förordnat, store Gud*', which was no. 224 in DSPB 1937, is no. 419 in DSPB 1986 with a new beginning. '*Du själv förordnat, store Gud*'. The new Swedish Hymnal has two parts, the first part containing hymns no. 1-325 is an ecumenical part, common for most churches in Sweden, and the second part is specific for each church. In the case of the Church of Sweden, this latter part contains hymns no. 326-700.[27] Accordingly, there are two sections in the hymnal with the heading 'Witness

---

27. See the preface to DSPB 1986 by Swedish Archbishop Bertil Werkström.

– service – mission', the first containing nos. 86-102 and the second nos. 412-420. In the former group there are several hymns intended for the diaconate, nos. 91-96, and in the latter part two hymns relate to the ordination of priests and bishops, nos. 419 and 420.[28]

In the Church of Sweden, ordinations always take place at an ordinary Sunday Mass, which means that the season of the year is decisive for the selection of hymns. As a processional hymn at the beginning of the ordination of priests and bishops, hymn no.1, the *Te Deum* in the hymnic version of Ignaz Franz (1719-1790) translated by Olov Hartmann (1906-1982) is usually sung, and nos. 419 and 420 are normally used. No 419 is a hymn originally by Jesper Svedberg (1643-1735) but rewritten in 1986 by Olle Nivenius (1914-2000) mostly in order to revise the language. However, there is one theological change in the first stanza: the original emphasized that the ordained ministry is instituted by God and explained the greatness of its service. The new version says that it is God who has ordered us to call witnesses for him; it prays for those who now are to be ordained in 'apostolic manner'. The hymn prays for the ordinands and all ministers of the Word that they may be faithful servants and lead us to the true priest, our Lord.

Hymn no. 420 is a new hymn by Olov Hartmann, *'Herren, vår Gud, har rest sin tron högt bland serafer och änglar'* ('Our Lord has his throne on high among seraphim and angels'). This hymn is very rich in biblical imagery. The first stanza uses the calling of Isaiah in Isaiah chapter 6. The Lord calls from on high to us who are here below on this needy earth, asking, 'Whom shall I send?' and we must answer, 'Here am I, send me'. The next stanza refers to John 21: the disciple knows the countenance of the Lord who asks, 'Do you love me? Feed my lambs.', and the congregation answers on behalf of the ordinands, 'Lord, you know my love'. The third stanza refers to the commissioning of Christ in John 20.19ff. The disciples are behind closed doors and suddenly the Lord is there with his commission and the answer is Thomas' confession, 'My Lord and my God'. The final stanza is a prayer to Christ, using first a military imagery that he may help those on whom his mantle falls, that they may use his word in holy warfare without looking back, and then praying that he give faithfulness to his Church until his will is done and God's kingdom come. This hymn emphasizes the greatness of the ordained ministry,

---

28. Since neither the Hymnal nor Handbook mentions any hymns, I wrote to the liturgical secretary of the Swedish Church Dr. Nils-Henrik Nilsson and thanked him for the following information that he gave me about the hymns that are normally used at ordinations.

linking it with the prophetic vocation of Israel and the apostolic commissioning, and views ministry as a service to the Lord and by the Lord in a hostile world.

In the first part of the Hymnal there are several hymns related to the diaconate. One of them is no 91, *'Din kärlek, Jesus, gräns ej vet'* ('Your love, Jesus, is without boundaries'). This hymn has been translated into Norwegian (NOS 1986, no. 683) and Danish (DDS 2002, no. 365). The hymn refers both to the Song of the Suffering Servant (Isaiah 42.1ff) and to Jesus' words that those who wish to be great must be the servant of all (Matt. 20.25-28). Another is no. 96 and is very often used at the ordination of deacons: *'Öppna mig för din kärlek'* ('Open me for your love') by Arne H. Lindgren (1922-).[29] This hymn is a prayer by the ordinand that God will open her/him to the love of the Lord for which the world has great need and which it can receive only if it flows through God's servant.[30]

Finland

In the Swedish-Finnish hymnal which was authorized in 1986 and published in 1987 (SPELKF 1987) there are five hymns in the section, *Ministers of the Lord* (nos. 245-249).[31] One of them (no. 248) is Olov Hartmanns above mentioned hymn, *'Herren, vår Gud, har rest sin tron högt bland serafer och änglar'*. Another, no. 246, *'Herre, du som trofast vårdar all din återlösta hjord'* ('Lord, who in faithfulness watch your redeemed flock') by Bengt Olof Lille (1807-1875) is to be sung at the election of priests where the electors pray for grace that the vote may fall on the right candidate.[32] Still another, no. 249, is a prayer by ministers that they may be faithful ministers of the Word and act in unity: it is a new hymn by Seppo Suokunnas (1945-): *'Herre, du har anförtrott oss en uppgift i din kyrka'* ('Lord, who have entrusted us with a mission in your Church'). The other two, nos. 245 and 247, are hymns intended for the occasion of ordination. No. 245: *'Inför dig vår herde här i sin kallelse skal träda'* ('Before you, our priest now enters his calling') by Bengt Olof Lille, is a prayer to the Lord that he may strengthen and bless the

---

29. I myself attended the ordination of a deacon in Lund Cathedral on 24th August, 2003, where this hymn was sung.
30. This hymn was translated into Icelandic by Sigurbjörn Einarsson in 1996, Cf. above.
31. I am indebted to Professor Emeritus Karl-Johann Hansson for giving me information on the Finnish hymns.
32. In the DSPB, 1937, there was a similar hymn for the election of priests. It was omitted in DSPB 1986 – perhaps it would be dangerous to have the Holy Spirit interfere with the democratic process!!

Shepherd with his Spirit in the priest's task of preaching and consoling, and that the priest may watch over the Lord's flock in faithfulness. It also prays that 'we' – the congregation – may rightly listen to the preacher so that he may lead us to God. No 247: *'Du, Jesus Kristus, i din skörd arbetare vill sända'* ('You, Jesus Christ, want to send workers to your harvest') by Max von Bonsdorff (1882-1967) is also a prayer to Christ that he may endow those who are standing around the altar with his strength, that they may be faithful servants, filled with Christ's light. In the final verse the Lord is asked to ordain them himself. This hymn is thoroughly christological in content. Christ is addressed in the prayer that he may give strength and faith and feed them with his Word.

Conclusion

The theology communicated in the hymns used at ordination in the Nordic folk churches is very faithful to the foundational liturgies of the sixteenth century. The antiphon *'Veni, sancte Spiritus'* and Luther's hymn *'Nun bitten wir den heiligen Geist'* have been parts of the liturgy, especially in Denmark. According to Lutheran theology, the minister is a minister of the gospel and the sacraments, which are the means of grace through which God creates faith. Therefore, ministers must be equipped with the Holy Spirit to be the acting subjects in conveying the message of reconciliation and hope. The majority of Nordic hymns sung at ordination services are epicletic in character either direct prayers to the Holy Spirit, like Luther's hymn, or prayers to God that he may give the gifts of the Holy Spirit to the ordinands. In several hymns Christ is addressed but most christological hymns are pneumatological and trinitarian as well. The hymns do emphasize the solemn occasion of ordination, the magnificent vocation of ministers and the necessity of formation by the Holy Spirit in all their lives.

According to the Lutheran Confessions, ministry is instituted by God. Most of the ordination hymns interpret this doctrine, including the modern ones. Grundtvig's hymn *'I dag på apostolisk vis'* and Olov Hartmann's hymn *'Herren, vår Gud, har rest sin tron'* are perhaps the strongest in this respect. Eschatology is also prominent in some hymns, for example, Hartmann's hymn, and in the Icelandic hymn.

Hymns are parts of the liturgy celebrated by the congregation itself. It is through the hymns that the congregation is an active participant in the liturgy. In the hymns, the congregation prays for the ministers and for themselves that God may give the necessary gifts to the ministers and faith to the congregation itself.

References

BSLK. *Die Bekenntnisschriften der evangelisch-lutherischen Kirche.* 1967. Göttingen: Vandenhoeck & Ruprecht.

DDS 1953. *Den danske salmebog.* 1953. Copenhagen: Det kgl. Vajsenhus' Forlag.

DDS 2002. *Den danske salmebog.* 2003. Copenhagen: Det kgl. Vajsenhus' Forlag.

DNKR 1685. *Danmarks and Norgis Kirkeritual 1685-1985,* 1985. Skarrild: Udvalget for Konvent for Kirke og Theologi.

DSKHB 1942. Den svenska kyrkohandboken. 1942. Stockholm: Svenska kyrkans diakonistyrelses bokförlag.

DSKHB 1987. *Den svenska kyrkohandboken.* 1987. Del. II. Stockholm: Verbum.

DSPB 1937. *Den svenska psalmboken.* 1937. Stockholm: Svenska kyrkans diakonistyrelses bokförlag.

DSPB 1986. *Den svenska psalmboken.* 1986. Stockholm: Verbum.

Fæhn, Helge. 1994. *Gudstjenestelivet i Den norske kirke.* Oslo: Universitetsforlaget.

GNK 1992. *Gudstjenestebok for den norske kirke. II: Kirkelige handlinger.* 1992. Oslo: Verbum.

HB 1981. *Handbók íslensku kirkjunnar. 1981.* Reykjavík: Kirkjuráð hinnar íslensku þjóðkirkju.

Hellerström, A.O.T. 1940. *Liturgik.* Stockholm: Svenska kyrkans diakonistyrelses bokförlag.

HSB 1910. *Helgisiðabók íslenzku þjóðkirkjunnar.* 1910, Reykjavík: Ísafoldarprentsmiðja.

HSB 1934. *Helgisiðabók íslenzku þjóðkirkjunna.* 1934, Reykjavík: Ísafoldarprentsmiðja.

Jenny, M. 1985. *Luthers geistliche Lieder und Kirchengesänge.* Vollständige Neuedition in Ergänzung zu Band 35 der Weimarer Ausgabe. Köln, Wien: Böhlau Verlag.

Lausten, M. S. 1989. *Kirkeordinansen 1537/39.* Copenhagen: Akademisk forlag.

LBW 1978. *Lutheran Book of Worship.* 1978. Minneapolis: Augsburg Publishing House.

Lindhardt, P.G. 1978. Historisk om bispe- og præstevielsesritualerne. In *De biskoppelige handlinger. Præste- og bispevielse, provsteindsættelse og kirkeindvielse.* Betænkning afgivet af Kirkeministeriets liturgiske kommission, 7-83. København.

LW 12. Jaroslav Pelikan (ed.). Selected Psalms. *Luther's Works. Vol. 12.* Philadelphia: Fortress Press.

LW 53. Ulrich S. Loupold (ed.). Liturgy and Hymns. *Luther's Works. Vol. 53.* Philadelphia: Fortress Press.

Malling, Anders. 1962 ff. *Dansk salmehistorie.* Copenhagen: J.H.Schultz Forlag.

NOS 1984. *Norsk salmebok* 1984. Oslo: Verbum.

Páll Eggert Ólason.1924. *Upptök sálma og sálmalaga í lútherskum sið á Íslandi.* Reykjavík: Fylgir Árbók Háskóla Íslands.

Puglisi, James F. 1998. *The Process of Admission to Ordained Ministry. A Comparative Study. Vol. II. The First Lutheran, Reformed, Anglican and Wesleyan Rites.* Collegeville, Minn.: The Liturgical Press.

RB 1992. *Ritualbog.* 1992. Copenhagen: Det Kgl. Vajsenhus' Forlag.

SB 1871. *Sálmabók til að brúka við guðspjónustugjörð í kirkjum og heimahúsum.* 1871. Reykjavík: Prentsmiðja Íslands.

SB 1886. *Sálmabók til kirkju- og heimasöngs.* 1886. Reykjavík: Sigfús Eymundsson.

SB 1945. *Sálmabók til kirkju- og heimasöngs.* 1945. Reykjavík: Forlag Prestsekknasjóðsins.

SB 1972. *Sálmabók íslensku kirkjunnar.* 1972. Reykjavík: Kirkjuráð.

SH 1942. *Den svenska kyrkohandboken.* 1942. Stockholm: Svenska kyrkans diakonistyrelses bokförlag.

SH 1987. *Den svenska kyrkohandboken.* 1987. Del. II. Stockholm: Verbum.

SPELKF 1987. *Svensk Psalmbok för den evangelisk-lutherska kyrkan i Finland.* Antagen av kyrkomötet i februari 1986. Vasa Boktrykeri AB Fram.

WA 35. Lieder. D. Martin Luthers Kritische Gesamtausgabe. Bd 35. Weimar 1883ff.

WA 38. Ordinationsformulär. *D. Martin Luthers Kritische Gesamtausgabe. Bd. 38.* Weimar 1883ff.

Rites for the Ordination of Pastors and Bishops in the Evangelical-Lutheran Church of Denmark: A Communicative Perspective

Hans Raun Iversen

There are two authorised ordination rites in the Evangelical-Lutheran Church of Denmark (ELCD): one for the ordination of pastors and one for the ordination of bishops.[1] This is in itself a striking fact, which can to some extent be understood through the process of analysing the content of the rites.[2] A fuller understanding does, however, require knowledge of the historical background of the ordination rites as well as their ecclesiastical setting in the Evangelical-Lutheran Church of Denmark.

This article first analyses the rites as they are printed and used as liturgical texts, according to the ELCD Service Book in current use. Both rites were

---

1. According to the Danish National Constitution of 1849 § 4 this church is 'the Danish Folk Church and as such supported by the state'. For further information on the religious scene in Denmark, see Iversen, Part I above. The Danish word used for ordination rites is '*vielse*', though the common word in everyday parlance is '*ordination*'. The word '*vielse*' is also used for marriage, whilst '*indvielse*' is used for the consecration of a new church or churchyard. The first rite after the Reformation used the word '*ordination*' – the word '*vielse*' was authorised only in the 1685 rite and has continued in use in subsequent rites.
2. See Iversen 1989 for a discussion of the fact that no other ordination rites have been authorised in ELCD, though such rites have been used especially for deaconesses, deacons and missionaries for almost 150 years. One Liturgical Commission – the one that created the 1963 *Prøveritualbogen* (the 'Proposed Service Book', which was never authorised) – had the idea that a rite for the ordination of deacons and deaconesses should be included in the Service Book. For the most recent development, see Malmgart (Part II.3 above).

authorised on 6th March 1987 and slightly revised for the 1992 Service Book. For the analysis of the textual content, the method agreed at the Farfa Consultation in April 1998 has been followed.³ More light is then shed on the results of this first analysis by relating the current liturgies to the three previous pairs of ELCD rites (1537, 1685 and 1898), as ordination liturgies are strongly historically determined in ELCD.⁴ Thirdly, the results of the first two analyses are related to the wider context of their theological and legal setting in the Danish Folk Church.

The specific question raised here is, 'What is being communicated to the congregation (and at a bishop's ordination, to the public, via television) during ordinations in ELCD? In order to introduce this perspective, two basic questions about the intention and communicative ability of rites are identified at the outset.

Understanding and Communicating Ordination Rites

It is a fair assumption to make that rites must be self-explanatory; the churches should be held responsible for the theology being communicated in their liturgies, for these liturgies, as texts and as ritual performances, are a vehicle for the communication of theology.⁵ This is a reasonable requirement even for churches such as the Lutheran Churches which do not subscribe to the *lex orandi lex credendi* principle. As ritual texts are meant for performance and not for reading, it is necessary to take into account not only what the texts say but also what they communicate by the way in which they are performed. The leading composite question for analysis is thus: Who is saying and doing what to whom within the rite, on behalf of whom, in which way and in which context? What are the results? With whom is the overall performance com-

---

3. 'Theology and Terminology of Ordination: a Research Project on the Authorisation of Rites and Procedures in the Nordic Churches', 1998, Consultation at Farfa 16-20 April, 1998 (unpublished material). See Part I above.
4. The best historical analysis of these rites is found in Eckerdal 1989. For the wider Lutheran context, see Puglisi 1998 (3-70), which includes an analysis of the Danish rite drawn up at the Reformation (30-39). For more detailed information on these developments, including proposals put forward at various times for new rites that were never authorised, see Lindhardt 1977.
5. In the so called Snedsted pastors' trial the local as well as the regional court pronounced that 'the rites of the Folk Church must be seen as interpretations of its confessional basis', and 'the rites must be taken as valid, though not exclusive representatives of Evangelical-Lutheran positions' (Judgement in Thisted Byret 27.6.1996 and Judgement in Vestre Landsret 19.1.1999).

municating? However, the question of communication is particularly complicated. An examination of the ELCD rites faces a double challenge to understanding for the following reasons.

In the first place it is obvious that the Liturgical Commission which finished its work in 1978, and to a lesser extent the bishops who revised the Commission's recommendations before the authorisation of the rites in 1987, did so very much as historians, who wanted to reconstruct and preserve the rites developed at the time of the Danish Reformation. That leaves us with the question of how far they succeeded in applying the intention of the Reformation rites to the situation of the Danish Church today, in order to ensure that the rites they were authorising did not simply repeat, with slight adjustments, what the reformers had said, without really communicating the Reformation theology in today's context. Or even worse: Are these rites, which are taken from a particular context, where the church was opposing sixteenth century Roman Catholic concepts of ordained ministry, communicating something entirely different from their original message in today's totally new situation, where pastors are seen as civil servants who specialise in religious affairs and regarded as appointed to be religious caretakers and employees of the secular welfare state?

Secondly there is also a general question that must be asked about the ability of traditional rites to communicate to a congregation wider than a restricted number of trained theologians. In the theoretical debate on rites as means of communication, there are currently two major schools of research:

One school, whose representatives include Roy A. Rappaport, trusts rites to be able to pass on their own message, independent of the prejudice and for-understanding – or lack of relevant horizon – of the participants. The rites simply seem to work – as is definitely very often the case within ELCD on occasions such as baptisms, weddings and funerals. 'Although usage may not be faithful to it (the rite), that which is represented in liturgy is not fiction, and the performance does more than *remind* individuals of an undying order: it *establishes* that order' (Rappaport 1979, 197).

A second school argues that participants in rites understand and receive according to their own intentions, attitudes and concepts. Thus more participatory 'performative rites' may work even better than 'liturgical rites', where the primary concern is to have the rite correctly enacted (Humphrey and Laidlaw 1994, 8-14). This is in fact the whole point of using rites in an often theologically ignorant folk church context: participants do receive and understand a lot, but they do so in their own ways, quite independently of the intention of the pastors and theologians who create the rites. On the other hand the rites are necessary, for without them folk church members cannot express the meaning and mark the transitions that they each in their own way experience in the rites. This is particularly so when those who are present are themselves direct participants in the rite, as is the case with weddings and funerals, where the performance of the participants interacts directly with the fixed traditional rite, which the pastor represents (Rubow 2000, 45). A liturgical rite cannot communicate, if people attending it do not, as individuals, have the experience of being given an active part in the rite. The pastor's prayers are not directed to the same end as the lay people's prayers, if the experiences and situation of the lay people are not reflected in them. Thus the ordination rites are in a very difficult position, when placed in a folk church congregation.[6]

Present Danish Evangelical-Lutheran Ordination Rites as Text and Performance

The rites for the ordination of pastors and bishops are very similar. *The pastor's ordination* is part of a special evening service and can take place on any day of the week. It normally takes place in the cathedral of the diocese where the pastor has been called to serve in a particular parish, though it may also take place in another church, such as the new pastor's parish church. As there will normally be more than one candidate to be ordained at the same service, and many of them have been called to temporary posts only, the ordination will most often take place in the cathedral as the central and 'neutral' place. *The bishop's ordination* is part of a normal Sunday Service (without Eucharist!) in the cathedral of the diocese in which the new bishop has been elected to serve. All the pastors and church elders from the diocese attend and more than one hundred officials from all branches of society – first of whom is the Queen. As part of its 'public service', the national television network always transmits a bishop's ordination.

---

6. Obviously empirical research would be needed to establish evidence of what the 1987 ordination rites communicate to a contemporary folk church congregation, to lay people gathering in the church to watch the ordination ceremony. No systematic, empirical research has been done so far. One observer reporting from the ordination of a bishop in Ribe in 1980 concluded: 'In fact I have the feeling that nobody knows why a bishop has to be ordained: he is probably first and foremost an administrator – a civil servant. If a few people think that this appointment is such an important thing, it could be done by shaking hands, signing and having a dinner for those in favour of that' (Ruge 1980, 63). If nothing else is conveyed here, at least the for-understanding of the reporter, as probably shared by most ELCD-members, seems very well expressed!

The Structure of the Two Rites

The structure of the two rites is deliberately the same.[7] Parts at 10-16 and the parts printed in capitals at 1 and 6 below are added to the normal service and are specific to the ordination service:

1. Prelude WITH ENTRY PROCESSION
2. Layman's[8] entrance prayer
3. Entrance hymn from The Danish Hymnal (DDS).[9]
4. The greetings between officiating minister (always a pastor) and congregation
5. The entrance collect ('*kollekt*') by the officiating minister
6. Entrance scripture reading (1 COR. 3.3-8 OR EPH 4.1-13, ON THE HUMBLE AND GOD-GIVEN SERVICE OF MINISTERS IN THE CHURCH)
7. The Apostles' Creed (compulsory in normal Sunday Services in ELCD, only adopted as a compulsory part of the ordination service in 1987)
8. Hymn (DDS 248 or another Holy Spirit hymn for a pastor's and DDS 296 for a bishop's ordination)
9. Brief sermon by a pastor at a pastor's ordination only.
10. Presentation (announcement of the candidate for ordination)
11. Prayer from the pulpit for the ministry of those who are to become pastors/bishops.
12. Hymn (special for the occasion of ordination: DDS 294 (by Grundtvig) or 293 (by Kingo) for a pastor's and 248 (by Luther in Grundvig's version) for a bishop's ordination)
13. Sung ordination prayer: *Veni, sancte Spiritus* in Danish (sung antiphonally by bishop and congregation) or Latin (by bishop and choir)
14. Sermon from the altar by the bishop to the candidate(s)
15. Four readings from the Bible
    a. Matt. 28.16-20 or John 20.21-23 (the sending of the disciples/the mission of ministers)
    b. John 15.1-5 or John 15.12-16 or Matt. 10.24-27 (on Christ, his Church and its servants)

---

7. The full text of the 1987 pastor's ordination in the Danish original version, arranged synoptically together with the previous rites of 1537, 1685 and 1898, is available on www.teol.ku.dk/ast/ansatte/Hans%20Raun%20Iversen-ordination.htm.
8. A custom found only in ELCD, where a lay person, in practice normally the 'clerk' ('*kordegn*'), says a prayer on behalf of all the laity.
9. The numbers noted in the following refer to the 1953 edition of the Danish Hymnal.

c. 2 Cor. 5.14-21 or Eph 4.7-13 or 1 Cor. 4.1-5 or 2 Cor. 3.4-8 – or Phil. 2.5-11 for a bishop's ordination (on serving in Christ)

d. 2 Tim. 4.1-5 or Titus 1.5-9 or 1 Pet. 5.2-4 or Phil. 2.5-11 – or Acts 20.28-32 for a bishop's ordination (on leadership in the congregation)

16. The ordination
    a. The bishop's exhortation about the ministry of a pastor/bishop
    b. Promise by the candidate(s) –their affirmative response to the exhortation
    c. The handshake between the candidate(s) and the bishop and those assisting him (at a bishop's ordination only between the candidate and the two bishops assisting; at a pastor's ordination normally including all those who had participated in the entry procession (at 1 above) and those who would be taking part in the laying-on of hands (16e below)
    d. For a bishop's ordination only: presentation with an episcopal cloak and a cross
    e. Ordination prayer concluding with the Lord's Prayer during the laying-on of hands

17. Hymn (DDS 246)

18. The service continues with the Eucharist, after a pastor's ordination, or with a sermon by the new bishop, after a bishop's ordination, at which there is no Eucharist.

A. Trinitarian Perspectives

Classical Trinitarian formulae are used in all the three editions of the collect used in the service (at 5) and in the *Veni, sancte Spiritus* (at 13) – asking the Triune God to equip his Church with pastors and bishops. The collect (at 5) belongs to the Danish church tradition and the ordination prayer at 13 to the classical ordination tradition. If taken fully into account the rite is given a strong Trinitarian and epicletic introduction by the Grundtvig hymns (at 8 and 12) together with the *Veni, sancte Spiritus* – as context for the weaker *epiclesis* in the prayer during the laying-on of hands (at 16e).

B. Continuing the Work of Christ

The pastor is to be a 'faithful pious preacher' of the Gospel of Christ (at 5). So is the bishop (at 5), who is 'furthermore' to carry out supervision in the congregations (at 10). Otherwise it is left to the biblical texts and the hymns to say that the pastor or bishop who is being ordained is to carry on the work of Christ, following in his footsteps, and to specify how he is to do this. Bishop

Henrik Christiansen, who was influential in the final arrangement of the order of the present four series of texts for the readings claims that the content and foundation (*'mandatum Dei'*) of the ordained ministry (*'ministerium ecclesiasticum'*) is fully expressed in the biblical readings, regardless of which texts are chosen for a particular ordination service (Christiansen 2003: 9).

C. The Gifts of the Holy Spirit

The *Veni, sancte Spiritus* (at 13) asks for the gift and enlightenment of the Holy Spirit. In the prayer during the laying-on of hands (at16e) God is asked to strengthen the candidate(s) with the Holy Spirit for their ministry as workers for the harvest, preachers and stewards of the Gospel. There is, however, no mention of personal gifts of the Holy Spirit to be received by the person being ordained. The majority of the hymns (most of them written or translated by Grundtvig) invoke the Holy Spirit to strengthen and unify the Church.

D. Baptism and Ordination

In the rites for the ordination of pastors and bishops, there is no mention of baptism as the foundation, nor is the congregation mentioned or the pastors' and bishops' call to work with congregations. Baptism is mentioned only in the reading of Matt. 28.16-20, which is included as a text about the task of pastors and bishops – not as a text on the common calling of all the baptised. Bishop Christiansen argues that Matt. 28 here is 'a full expression of how ordination is building on the covenant of baptism – as a ministry in, for and with the baptised and baptising people of God. In the context of ordination Matt. 28 stands significantly for baptism as the foundation and for the sending out – and thus for the content of the ministry to which ordination sends and equips' (Christiansen 2002, 6). However, it is rather questionable to what extent this interpretation is heard by anyone except the bishops who agreed that this was the meaning of Matt. 28 in this context.[10]

---

10. Bishop Christiansen defines ordination in ELCD as 'a divine service, in which the congregation and the representatives of the ordained ministry (*'ministerium ecclesiasticum'*) – in ELCD the bishop – on behalf of the Church publicly confirm the pastor's election, which has been undertaken by the representatives of a congregation and, according to the present Folk Church order, recognised by the Ministry of Church Affairs. At the same time, it is made clear that the Bishop in question has tested and accepted the said person for ordained ministry in the Folk Church' (Christiansen 2003, 4).

E. Relationship to the Congregation

Both texts for the entrance reading (at 6) mention the unity and disunity of the Church and the role of leaders in relation to that. Both ordination prayers (at 13 and 16e) emphasise that ministers exist for the benefit and growth of congregations. The four biblical readings (at 15) also deal indirectly with the relationship between pastor/bishop and congregation/church. However, in neither of the two rites does the congregation appear as the body that elects, approves or receives the new pastor or bishop, not to speak of their participation in the ordination. It is furthermore questionable whether topics mentioned in the biblical readings and formal prayers are heard and understood at all, if they are not experienced in the direct wording and performance of the rite

F. Concepts of the Church

The rites hardly make any distinction between the Church universal, the Lutheran Church and the local congregation. They seem to indicate that there is only one church – identical with the acting church, the Evangelical-Lutheran (Folk) Church of Denmark. In the presentation prayer from the pulpit the traditional mention of the congregation to which the new pastor has been called has been taken away to give a more open and ecumenical perspective on ordination (according to Christiansen 2002, 8).

G. Call and Confirmation

The rites emphatically state that a call has already taken place and they confirm it (see 10 and 16). This is clearly the case, even though the performance of these impressive rites and *expressis verbis* the first part of the ordination prayer (at 16e) indicate that the candidate is being created pastor/bishop during the rite! A significant difference between a pastor's and a bishop's ordination is that the candidate for pastor's ordination enters the church in his (newly bought) pastor's robe, the cassock, whereas the bishop enters in his (old) pastor's cassock.[11] The bishop is later dressed in the bishop's cassock and cross as part of the rite (at 16d).[12] At a pastor's ordination the common practice is for the pastor who is to be ordained to wear an alb over his black pastor's cassock.

---

11. What cannot be seen by the congregation at a distance is that the new bishop's 'pastor's cassock' is in fact quite new, as the bishops wear velvet at the front of their cassocks!
12. Bishop Christiansen refers to Grundtvig's strong emphasis on true ministry as a gift of the Holy Spirit – and Gospel, Creed, Bible etc. as belonging to the congregation, which should therefore not be given to the pastor in particular. The pastor should only be given what he is given by the Holy Spirit, as only the Holy Spirit can install pastors

Quite a number of pastors testify to feeling that they fully become pastors only when they enter the church again, having taken off the alb during the hymn after the ordination (at 17), even though the alb is taken off outside the church and not as part of the rite.

H. The Significance of the laying-on of Hands with Prayer

The ceremony with the promise and handshake (at 16 b and c) may appear impressive. Even more impressive and thus – as it seems – the central point of the rite is the ordination prayer during the laying-on of hands by the bishop and the group of assistants (at 16 e). This can amount to a great number at a pastor's ordination, but only five at a bishop's ordination. The centrality of this is underlined by the repetition of 'Amen' after the concluding Lord's Prayer. The popular saying goes that the young theologian is made a pastor by having his backbone removed by the bishop and his assistants during their laying-on of hands. Something like this is indeed what this performance looks like, when watched from the congregation, though the theological content is about conferral of ministry and *epiclesis*.

I. The Effect of Ordination

There is no specific statement in the rite of any precise effect, such as sending, receiving or being authorised. However, the newly ordained leave the church together with and in the very same dress (without the alb) as their fellow pastors/bishops – indicating that the newly ordained person is now like his/her fellow ministers. This is particularly clear at a bishop's ordination, where the new bishop is vested in the episcopal cloak and receives the cross as the last part of the ordination rite (see 16d, cf. note 12).

J. The Apostolic Dimension

The rites strongly emphasise that ordination is following apostolic traditions and patterns (at 10, 13, 15, 16a and e). Since 1987 the Apostles' Creed has been included as a compulsory part (at 7) of the ordination rite, as is also the case for all Sunday services in ELCD, a development that followed Grundtvig's

---

in the Lord's flock (Christiansen 2002, 7). On the other hand Bishop Christiansen finds it very important that the bishops are given their special cloak and cross during their ordination to signify the responsibility of oversight which they have over and above the responsibility of a pastor (Christiansen 2002, 8). Therefore Bishop Christiansen took care to have this vesting of the bishops mentioned in the new 1987 rite. Since 1923 the Danish bishops have had a bishop's cross, but most of them have considered this cross to be a 'private' matter, even though is pertains to their office.

discovery of the Apostles' Creed as a 'word from the mouth of the Lord' (see below under L, The Promises). Bishop Christiansen finds that the apostolic dimension of ordination has its strongest emphasis in the many long hymns sung during ordination (Christiansen 2003, 14-15).

K. Subjects and Participants

Strictly speaking only seven people are needed for a pastor's ordination: the bishop; a pastor as officiating minister of the ordinary parts of the service and the presentation (10 and 11); four assistant pastors (for 15 and 16c and e), and the candidate(s). If the bishop so decides, all the pastors present, and even some representatives from the congregations involved, may participate at 1 and at 16c and 16e at a pastor's ordination. Normally all pastors participate in this way, but lay people – for example, representatives of the parish boards which have elected the new pastor(s) – participate on a regular basis in only a few of the dioceses.[13]

At a bishop's ordination several people are needed for the procession: the Bishop of Copenhagen; the dean of the cathedral as officiating minister of the ordinary parts of the service and for the presentation (at 10 and 11); all the area deans of the diocese; all the other bishops of the National Church; one bishop from each of the Nordic Lutheran Churches, and the bishop-elect. The readings (at 15) are normally done by four Nordic bishops, whereas only the two Danish bishops from neighbouring dioceses and the most senior and the most junior pastor of the diocese participate at 16c, d and e. To prevent the risk of the new Danish bishop being involved in (episcopal) *successio apostolica*, which ELCD does not believe in but nevertheless seems to be afraid of (Lindhardt 1977,46) no foreign bishop will ever lay hands on a bishop of ELCD (See note 20). The three Danish bishops are the only ones who participate in the part of the rite that takes place in front of the altar. In 1987 it was proposed that lay people should participate in the laying-on of hands at the bishop's ordination, as was the case in the 1537 Church Ordinance (*De biskoppelige handlinger* 1978, 69, 80). However, this Danish tradition, which might have complicated

---

13. In the Diocese of Roskilde lay people's participation in the procession and the laying-on of hands has been normal practice since 1978. Bishop Christiansen considers that this goes against the Lutheran Confession according to which ordained ministry ('*Predigtamt*', '*ministerium ecclesiasticum*') is instituted by God (*Confessio Augustana* – hereafter CA –5). The *rite vocatus* required according to CA 14 must not be confused with the delegation of the ministry from the lay people as their participation in the laying-on of hands may indicate (Christiansen 2002, 5).

the ecumenical situation even further, was not accepted by the bishops, when they completed the work on the present 1987 rite.

In both rites the congregation of lay people is present and participates in the ordinary parts of the service and in the singing of the many good and long hymns as has always been the case in ELCD services (cf. Iversen 2002). In the parts of the service that are specific to the ordination, the congregation is given the chance to join in the first 'Amen' after the ordination prayer together with the bishop ('All say "Amen" to this', at16e). In practice, only those who are standing very close to the bishop – mainly the pastors – will manage to join in this Amen. There is no other involvement on the part of the congregation in the central parts of the ordination rite.

L. The Promises

The content of the candidate's promise (at 16 a, b) is formulated following the traditional nineteenth century confessional Lutheran patterns. The bishop 'by virtue of [my] office' receives the promise. According to what is promised here at the ordination, the pastor's preaching is to be in accordance with the Word of God, as it is found in the Bible and to which the confessional documents of the Church 'witness'.[14] In the promise or oath ('præsteløftet'), which the pastor-to-be has to sign before ordination, the Word of God is said to be found equally in the Bible *and* in the confessional documents of the Church. Under the influence of N. F. S. Grundtvig (1783-1872), this un-Lutheran formula, which from the time of orthodoxy (seventeenth century) replaced the oath to the King found in the 1537 Church Ordinance, was never revised. For Grundtvig it was important that the Apostles' Creed, as the universal baptismal creed of the Church, was formulated by Jesus himself and as such 'a word of God' even more than most of the Bible. This point of view has had a strong influence on Danish rites, where the Apostles' Creed, including the renunci-ation of Satan, is always used in all forms of liturgy. Later on the problems with liberal theology also hindered attempts to reformulate the hyper-confessional wording in the pastor's oath. This orthodox pastor's oath, however, never affected the promises made by the pastor in the ordination rite (in the 1898 rite the Word of God is said to be found only in 'the prophetic and apostolic writings': the confessional documents are not mentioned.) Thus the pastor even today gives two different and contrasting promises in the same process,

14. The Apostles', Nicene and Athanasian Creeds, with the *Confessio Augustana* and Luth-er's *Small Catechism* form, equally, the confessional basis of the Danish Church since the Danish Law of 1683.

an ecumenical-Lutheran one during the rite and another one, which may be understood in a narrow confessional way, before the ordination takes place (Harbsmeier 1989, 208f; Lindhardt 1977, 26, 42-47).

M. The Corporate Dimension

As processions are very rare in the Danish Folk Church,[15] it makes a very strong impression on the congregation to see the procession with all the pastors in black and the bishop at the head, or at a bishop's ordination all the bishops and deans with the Bishop of Copenhagen leading them. The ordination in front of the altar with pastors (and bishops) crowding around it (perhaps with a few lay representatives, if it is a pastor's ordination) also leaves members of the congregation with the impression that they are passively observing a rite in which the fellowship of pastors or bishops is creating a new member of their special order – to which admission is gained by going through this distinct rite of incorporation into the body of ordained colleagues.

N. Entry into Spiritual Leadership

It is hard to see where the rite admits the candidate to any form of spiritual leadership – except as a preacher and guardian of the right Gospel in the Lutheran sense of that, as it is expressed in the pastor's promise and the prayers (at 11 and 16a-c and e). At a bishop's ordination the new bishop's sermon immediately after the ordination can be seen as a test or demonstration of his ability to lead the church by preaching the Gospel. The newly ordained pastor is – wisely? – not tested in the same way.

O. Differences between Rites for the Ordination of Pastors and Bishops

There are only small differences between the two rites even though each rite makes a quite different impression on the congregation.

The rite and the biblical texts are the same – except that there is the option at a bishop's ordination of reading Phil. 2.5-11 and Acts 20.28-32 (on Paul talking to the bishops in Ephesus). There is a difference, however, in that the one verse of the free Danish version of the ancient Trinitarian *Hymnus Angelicus*, later know as *Gloria in Excelsis Deo* ('*Aleneste Gud i Himmerig*', DDS 360) is sung by the congregation between the different readings at a bishop's ordination.

The hymns are almost the same at the ordination of pastors and bishops:

---

15. Apart from ordination the only other occasion when there would normally be a procession is the consecration (*'indvielse'*) of a new church.

DDS 296, Luther's hymn on the Word is used at a bishop's ordination, instead of DDS 294 or 293 used at pastors' ordinations, as the candidate to become bishop is already ordained pastor (at 8 and 12).

In the exhortation on the bishop's ministry it is emphasised that the bishop is still to be a servant of the Word but now 'furthermore' a supervisor of pastors and congregations. In the ordination prayer (at 16e) the Holy Spirit is asked to 'form and enable' the bishop as well as the pastor for the new ministry. In 1898 the bishop was only to be 'enabled'! Eckerdal's interpretation is that there are now two types of ordained ministries in the Danish church (Eckerdal 1989, 58). According to the Liturgical Commission the correct understanding is, that 'form and enable' are equivalent symbolic expressions, and as the bishop is no more than the pastor the same expressions have to be used for both of them (*De biskoppelige handlinger* 1987, 67, 81).

Nowhere in the rite is it explicitly claimed that pastor or bishop receive authority in the church. The only trace of this is in the peculiar wording that appears in the ordination prayer (15 e). Of pastors it is said, 'we now according to your Word entrust them with the holy preacher's and pastor's office'; for a bishop there is a prayer for the person 'who is now being entrusted with a bishop's ministry in NN diocese'. This is what is left of the strong (feudal) words about delegation of office found in the 1685 rites and, in a rather weaker version, in the 1898 rites. It is peculiar that both these forms, which were totally omitted by the Liturgical Commission, appear now in passing so to speak.[16]

It is also to be noted that the bishop is said to have a 'ministry' ('*tjeneste*') whereas the pastor has an 'office' ('*embede*', '*Amt*'), which the bishop of course already has!

---

16. Bishop Christiansen has a very definite explanation, though, without prior explanation, it is hard to hear and understand this new wording in the ordination prayer in the way he does. According to Christiansen the little word 'now' in the short new sentence 1) expresses the '*institutum est*' of CA 5 (the newly ordained person is 'now' being entrusted with what God himself has instituted); 2) indicates that now is the legal moment when the bishops and pastors pass on the order of ordained ministry to their new colleague, and 3) indicates that this is the moment when the Holy Spirit is being asked to equip the new pastor/bishop. In other words this little 'now' makes the whole rite instrumental in the classical way, as this is the exact moment when ordained status is being transferred – dogmatically, legally and by the Holy Spirit himself (Christiansen 2003, 8). This is obviously debatable, but even if the argument is accepted ELCD still needs to find other ways of including the lay congregation in the rite (cf. Puglisi, 2001, 230).

The subjects of each rite, the participants and the whole setting of the services appear, however, quite different. This may be due to the vesting of the bishop, to which there is nothing similar for pastors, except the removal of the alb outside the church (normally in the vestry) after the ordination, and the new bishop's exercise of his authority by preaching immediately after his ordination. Moreover, for a bishop's ordination, there is the whole setting with the procession and a hundred high-ranking officials, including the Queen, at the front of the church.

Conclusion

Apart from the biblical readings, the Apostles' Creed and the long theologically dense hymns, the Danish Evangelical-Lutheran rites for the ordination of pastors and bishops have preserved expressions of Trinitarian ordination theology in the prayers (at 5, 13 and 16e). In their performance the two rites are, however, basically forms for the masters (the ordained bishops and pastors) to introduce and authorise the disciples (the candidate(s) for ministry) to be like themselves. This is done according to what is emphatically called 'apostolic tradition', while the congregation looks on and does practically nothing during the ordination as such. Only at a later stage at a Sunday morning service in the local congregation – at the installation – the pastor is introduced and recommended to the congregation by the area dean on behalf of the bishop – and thus received by the congregation. (There is no such installation for the bishop, as he is ordained in the cathedral of the diocese where he is to serve.)

In particular, the handshake after the promise made by the pastor/bishop to be ordained clearly communicates the message that ordination is enrolment into the club of pastors/bishops. Interestingly this is the part of the rites that has caused most of the problems at the ordination of women, when conservative male pastors, who have participated in the rite as supporters of conservative ordinands, have refused to shake hands with the female pastors ordained during the same service. As the state and/or God, who has entrusted the pastor with his/her office, is not visibly present and participating and as it would be too much like 'episcopalism' if the ordaining bishop were the only one shaking hands with the candidates, the whole group of ordained ministers present receives the new minister by shaking hands with him/her. This is of course a nice gesture – especially when everybody shakes hands with everybody else – but it is hard to see that is has a proper place at the centre of the ordination rite. It seems that this habit, which has been interpreted as a sort of 'democratisation' of the handshake with the bishop only, is unique to ELCD tradition. What is intended as a democratisation within the clergy group in fact looks like an introduction into the clergy club.

The Current Rites against the Background of Previous Danish Ordination Rites

In the 1537 Church Ordinance ordination is called a 'custom', that is, a ceremony only ('*Inthet andet end én skick vdi Kircken*'). A great deal of emphasis is placed on the process of praying for, electing, testing and calling the new pastor. The act of ordination itself is what Eckerdal calls 'an act of prayer by the church' (Eckerdal 1989, 20). The text repeats that everything must be said in a loud voice, so that the people can hear what is going on, and that the bishop and the congregation must be close enough to one another for the congregation to see what is going on. The rite is found in two closely related forms, one for pastors and one for bishops, of which the rite for the ordination of a bishop is the oldest known from an Evangelical-Lutheran church. Generally speaking the 1537 rite is close to that of 1987 – as the latter is deliberately constructed as its modern parallel. Unlike Luther's rite both of the 1537 rites include a promise (a vow to the king to be sworn by the candidate(s) before the ordination in the church); the handshake is included in the bishop's ordination only but was officially introduced in 1685 for pastors also. According to the text on the ordination of a bishop, elders (lay people) (may) participate in the laying-on of hands. There is no mention of this at the pastor's ordination, and it is not found in the 1685 rite.

The 1685 Rite transformed the ordination rite into what Eckerdal calls 'an act of feudal delegation (endowment)' (Eckerdal 1989, 21). Partly influenced by the recovery of feudalism during the time of absolute monarchy (from 1660) and partly due to Anglican influence the act of delegation (or conferral of office) by the bishop to his vassal, the candidate, was developed and made the central part of the rite. The oath to the ordaining bishop with the subsequent handshake has taken the place of election by, sending to and reception into the congregation, as found in the 1537 rite. The congregation is no longer supposed to do anything but pray at a distance – not as a part of the rite of ordination. Even the 'Amen' after the ordination prayer is only to be said by the clergy – and the second 'Amen' by the bishop alone.

The 1898 ordination rite represents a compromise between the two former rites. The act of delegation is still strong but the ordination prayer during the laying-on of hands has returned, with significantly epicletic wording. A revealing part of the bishop's ordination – also typical of its time – is the fact that the bishops celebrate the Eucharist with one another – while the congregation watches but is not invited to participate.

In the latter part of the twentieth century the act of delegation was severely attacked, not least by the official Liturgy Commission[17], which was itself vigorously attacked, particularly by Professor Regin Prenter and the high church movement of the 1960s and 1970s (Prenter 1980; Glenthøj 1992). Against that background the bishops – as they took over and completed the 1987 rite – were mainly concerned about the Liturgical Commission's recommendations that ELCD should return to the good old pattern of 1537. At the same time they secured a form of endowment or 'entrustment' with *'potestas'*, mentioning it in the introduction to the ordination prayer (16e), thereby also placating the protesting high church pastors.[18] Consequently the bishops did not take much time to consider the theological content of the rite or the role of the congregation in the act of ordination. Nor did they consider the ecumenical texts on the ordained ministry such as the BEM document. Against this – briefly described – historical liturgical background the ELCD ordination rite ceased to be a feudal giving and receiving of authority between bishop and candidate and became a collegial incorporation of a new member into the fellowship (the *ordo*) of the clergy.

Apart from the significant rewording of the introduction to the ordination prayer the bishops did not change much of the recommendations made by the 1978 liturgical commission before they had the new rite authorised in 1987. The number of collects to choose from was cut down from seven to three (at 5), and the number of Epistle texts from four to two (at 6). The order of the texts for the four readings was changed, so that none of the four basic topics mentioned in brackets (at 15) could be omitted. Only one text, Matt. 7.7-11, which seems to have been suggested because Luther used it for his baptismal rite (!), has been omitted. The bishops did not accept the Commission's recommendation that a bishop's ordination should end with the Eucharist. They knew that it would be impractical (and unpleasant for the many high ranking guests) to have the big congregation included in a Eucharist with all the state and church officials. In the exhortation for the new bishop the commission suggested, that the new bishop should 'take care of himself and his entrusted work', but the bishops returned to the old wording and the 1987 rite says that the new bishop shall 'take care of himself and for the congregation, with which he has been entrusted'. The bishops also returned to the traditional wording of the epicletic prayer for the gift of the Holy Spirit for the new bishop, in the prayer during the laying-on of hands. Again here the Liturgical Commission was so eager to emphasise that nothing new was really being

---

17. This criticism is the most dominant idea in *De biskoppelige handlinger* 1978.
18. Cf. Bishop Christiansen's interpretation, referred to at note 16.

added to the pastor's ordination when the pastor was ordained bishop, that it omitted the classical *epiclesis* in its recommendation for the prayer during the laying-on of hands at the bishop's ordination.

Eckerdal emphasises that the new rite is a congregational rite (Eckerdal 1989, 57). Ostensibly a place has been given to lay people and the clerical act of delegation has been removed. However, in practice the members of the congregation are only present as a context in which the ordination takes place. They are there as they are at the traditional Danish Sunday Service: it takes a lot of good will to see the congregation as the subject of what is going on, as the singing of the many long hymns is almost the only part in which the congregation is actively involved in the rite (and even that part is sometimes taken over by professional choirs).

The Ecclesiastical Setting of the Present Rites

The Folk Church in Denmark (ELCD) is very much a state church. The so-called folk church dimension is, however, evident at the congregational level. This is the case in as far as the congregation boards elect the pastors and bishops – practically without interference from church or state authorities. When the congregations have elected them the pastors and bishops are, however, formally government civil servants employed by the state Ministry for Church Affairs.

Paragraph 37 of the law that governs congregation boards reads: 'When exercising his duties of office, including the care of souls, the pastor is independent of the congregation board'. This paragraph – inserted as a compromise to silence the pastors when legislation was first introduced to create permanent congregation boards in all parishes in 1912 – is still a cornerstone in the self-understanding of the majority of pastors in the Folk Church of Denmark, even though, to a very large extent, it is in practice meaningless, as pastors have to co-operate with the congregation boards in almost every part of their work, according to other parts of the church legislation and practice.

It is significant to note that the Liturgical Commission began its 1978 recommendations on the rites for the ordination of pastors and bishops with a long historical analysis of the development of the Danish rites. There is no mention whatsoever of a biblical perspective on ordination. The report begins with a historical description (by Professor P. G. Lindhardt) written in a historically and ecumenically ignorant vein:

There is no need to take account of the Catholic rites for the ordination of bishops and pastors, which we know from the late medieval Pontificals of Lund and Roskilde. In all respects the ceremonies they contain, which reflect the Roman understanding of sacramental rites (with the ordination of bishops as the superior rite) are so different from the Evangelical ordinations that there is no conceivable reason to compare them.[19]

A great deal of historical work, of varied worth, was covered in what follows in Lindhardt's introductory article but the result is a foregone conclusion. It is to be found in the brief comments on the recommendation for a new rite. As the first rites from the time of the Reformation were not known in authorised texts, the Commission 'found it most proper as a point of departure to take the ordination rites for pastors and bishops, as found in 'The Right Ordinance' of 1537/1539'. Further it emphasised that both of these rites are 'congregational'. Therefore the new rites have to be formed in such a manner 'that it is clear that the pastor or bishop to be ordained has already received his/her calling by the election of the congregation and the appointment by state authority' (p. 48).[20]

The present rites for the ordination of pastors and bishops together with the lack of other official ordination rites in the Folk Church of Denmark, reflects – and reinforces – the precarious balance of power between state, clergy and congregation. At the same time they show a rigid – theologically rather unreflected – use of the confessional doctrines in CA §§ 5 and 14. The congregation board members, whose involvement in the ordination service is rather

---

19. Cf. e.g. Smith 2002, who argues convincingly that there was continuity between the medieval and the early Reformation Church on matters of ordination and public ministry.

20. This position was decisive in the Danish debate on the Porvoo Common Statement, and the refusal of the Danish Evangelical-Lutheran bishops to join its proposed Lutheran-Anglican fellowship in the 1990s. Episcopal succession was removed from the Danish Church at the time of the Reformation, when new Danish bishops were ordained by Pastor Johannes Bugenhagen, Luther's delegate to Copenhagen. As in the Liturgical Commission the most influential point of view in the Danish Church among theologians, is still that ordination is primarily a public celebration of the calling of a pastor or bishop, which has already taken place (cf. note 10). It is therefore not necessary that it is a bishop – still less a bishop with apostolic succession – who ordains a new pastor or for that matter a new bishop. The major point – on the part of the theologians – in the Danish attack against the Porvoo Statement was the statement's teaching on the threefold ministry, and thus the superiority of the bishop's ministry. Apart from lack of understanding of the statement itself, the main attitude taken by the lay people in the congregation boards, who also tended to be negative to the statement, seems to have been resistance to the actual power of bishops (and pastors). When the theologians said that the bishops were going to be more powerful, if the church signed the Porvoo Statement, the lay people had no option, as they feel that bishops (and pastors) are already too powerful in the church (cf. Lodberg 2002).

passive, have already played their decisive part, as they are sovereign in electing pastors and bishops by voting – and thus they have secured the *'rite vocatus'* of CA 14. This reflects a well-known division of labour in the folk church: lay people pay the bill and make the most powerful decisions. The rest – including the rite – is left to the clergy. The old formula 'pay, pray and obey' has been changed to 'pay, elect the pastors/bishops according to your democratic choice, and let them be ordained by their fellow pastors/bishops to do the rest of the job together with their fellow pastors/bishops'.

Ole Bertelsen, when Bishop of Copenhagen, began his sermon at the ordination of Bishop Herluf Eriksen on 25th May 1979 as follows:

> Let me be frank and begin by asking in the midst of this congregational gathering. Is it not too grandiose and stately to make a person take up his work in such a gathering? What sort of sense is there in this? And how suitable is it? Of course, we do not need to pay attention to how far this is in accordance with the time we happen to live in, but we cannot avoid wondering if this is in accordance with the main purpose of the Christian Congregation: the Gospel of Christ, crucified and risen! In my opinion we should not be too serious in this respect. The word seriousness is not found in the New Testament – This book is full of words like joy, peace, power, life, hope, love.... We are having a feast today. We are admitting a bishop to continue his service in the dynamic message of joy... (Bertelsen 1980, 12).

Three out of six of Bishop Bertelsen's published sermons at bishops' ordinations begin by defending the rite (Bertelsen 1980). The Bishop is not trying to explain the meaning of the actual rite, but pointing out that after all, in the light of the Gospel, the performance of the rite is not very important. He is, however, revealing that he himself is not at all at ease having to lead such a grandiose ceremony, which is not easily connected to the Gospel which the Church is here to proclaim. However, the bishop also has to obey and follow the rites as the state is paying him to do.

Conclusion

The Danish Evangelical-Lutheran rites for the ordination of pastors and bishops have much valuable theological content. However, the hard questions this analysis raises are these:

How can ELCD practice *lex orandi lex credendi* in any sense if only the bishops who made the compromises leading to the present ordination rites, have the right understanding of what is going on during the ordination service? Probably it cannot.

Are the1987 rites for the ordination of pastors and bishops an example of a tradition (of 1537) being surrendered and betrayed instead of being transmitted (cf. Puglisi 2001, 280)? Did the Liturgical Commission and the bishops succeed in re-introducing the 1537 rite (the actual performance of which we know very little about), or did they create a splendid new and very different rite by putting something similar to the 1537 rite into the totally different context of the late twentieth century? The latter would seem to be the case.

How can we expect the congregation to understand and appreciate the ritual enactment of a rite with which the ordaining bishop himself is not at all at ease? We probably cannot.

The Liturgical Commissions and the bishops at no time analysed the differences between the Reformation situation – in which a new rite had to legitimise a new Lutheran Church after the break from the old Roman Catholic Church – and today's situation in Denmark, where the state church tradition is so strong that whatever is said is heard within that framework. A congregational rite cannot be created today simply by devising a rite that is anti-Catholic. It would have to be an anti-State-Church rite – and not a rite that seems to fit hand-in-glove into the modern state church practice, where the pastors act as a group of civil servants.

It is legitimate, though not necessarily theologically sufficient, to wish to articulate today what the Reformers articulated in their day, but if what is to be communicated is also to be understood, this can hardly be done by repeating now a rite that is almost 500 years old.

References

Bertelsen, Ole. 1980. Gud i Vold. *Prædikener og taler ved bispevielser 1975-1980*. Århus: Aros

Christiansen, Henrik. 2002. Personal letter of 17th April 2002 to Hans Raun Iversen on the procedure and the theology behind the 1987 ordination rites in ELCD.

– 2003. Indvielse af præster og biskopper. *Kritisk Forum for Praktisk Teologi*, 93: 2-17.

Danmarks og Norgis Kirkerite (1685). Genudgivet af Udvalget for Konvent for Kirke og Theologi, 1985.

De biskoppelige handlinger. Præste- og bispevielse, provsteindsættelse og kirkeind-

vielse. 1978. Betænkning afgivet af Kirkeministeriets liturgiske Kommission. Betænkning nr. 848. København.

Eckerdal, Lars, 1989. Indvielse til tjeneste i det kirkelige embede and Den danske folkekirkes indvielsesliturgiske tradition i et luthersk liturgisk fællesskab. In *Under bøn og håndspålæggelse. Indvielse af missionærer, diakoner og præster*, ed. Hans Raun Iversen, 13-64. København: Anis.

Glenthøj, Jørgen. 1992. Forandringer i det hidtil gældende, danske ordinationsrite af 1898 i forhold til nyt autoriseret rite for præstevielse af 6. marts 1987. *Præsteforeningens Blad* 50: 1017-1020

Harbsmeier, Eberhard. 1989. De danske folkekirkelige prædiken – økumenisk betragtet. In *På enhedens vej. Bidrag til den økumeniske bevægelses historie i Danmark i det 20. århundrede*, ed. Peder Nørgaard-Højen, 208-217. Århus: Anis.

Humphrey, Caroline and Laidlaw, James. 1994. *The Archetypal Actions of Rite*. Oxford: Clarendon Press.

Iversen, Hans Raun. 1989. Missionær-, diakon- og sekretærindvielser i Danmark. In *Under bøn og håndspålæggelse. Indvielse af missionærer, diakoner og præster*, ed. Hans Raun Iversen, 65-117. København: Anis.

– 2002. Overvejelser omkring en spørgeskemaundersøgelse af salmesang i Norden, *Hymnologiske Meddelelser* 1: 76-82.

Kirkeordinansen 1537/39. 1989. Tekstudgave med indledning og noter ved Martin Schwartz Lausten. København: Akademisk Forlag.

Lindhardt, P.G. 1977. De danske ordinationsriteer. *Kirkehistoriske Samlinger* 1977: 7-50.

Lodberg, Peter 2002. The Danish 'No' to Porvoo. In *Apostolicity and Unity: Essays on the Porvoo Common Statement*, ed. Ola Tjørhom. Geneva: WCC Publications.

Prenter, Regin. 1980. *Kaldet af Gud eller mennesker?* Bemærkninger til De biskoppelige Handlinger Præste- og bispeindvielse, provsteindsættelse og kirkeindvielse. Betænkning afgivetaf Kirkeministeriets liturgiske Kommission. Skarrild: Kirkelig Samling om Bibel og Bekendelse.

Puglisi, James F. 1996, 1998, 2001. *The Process of Admission to Ordained Ministry*, Vol I-III. Collegeville, Minn.: Liturgical Press.

Rappaport, R. 1979. *Ecology, Meaning and Religion*. Berkeley: North Atlantic Books.

Rubow, Cecilie. 2000. *Hverdagens teologi*. København: Anis.

Ruge. Mette. 1980. Bispevielse. Ribe 11/5 1980, in *Kritisk Forum for Praktisk Teologi* 2.

Smith, Ralph F. 2000. *Luther, Ministry and Ordination Rites in the Early Reformation Church*. New York: Peter Lang.

PART III

Ecumenical and Liturgical
Perspectives on Ordination

1. Ecumenical Perspectives

All churches tend to have ordained ministers, according to a certain order, varying from church to church. The ministerial orders of our churches have therefore become a key issue on the ecumenical agenda. To contribute to this agenda this book is focusing on the theology and terminology of rites for ordination. The following three contributions attempt to place the studies found in this book in the context of current ecumenical studies and dialogues on the unity of the Christian Church with special reference to mutual recognition of the ordained ministers of the churches.

Ola Tjørhom discusses research in and dialogues about ordained ministry within the broader field of ecumenical research and dialogues. He recommends that in the pluralistic scene of church life in the Nordic countries the churches should make up their minds and use the term ordination only when introducing bishops, pastors and deacons to ministry by the way of sacramental liturgy. He further argues for the importance of research into the interrelationship between theology and terminology in the churches' ordination rites.

James F. Puglisi, SA, gives an account of the present state of ecumenical dialogues on ministry and ordination. He emphasises the convergence in ecumenical theology, placing the ordained minister in and over against the congregation, as the theology of ordained ministry is grounded in Christology and placed in ecclesiological relationship with the priesthood of all the baptised.

Grant White highlights the Orthodox understanding of liturgy and ordination as the background to his discussion of the Orthodox position in the ecumenical dialogues on ordained ministry. He points out that the Orthodox Church finds itself closer to the Roman Catholic and the Anglican Churches than to Protestant Churches in term of the understanding of the necessity of ordination, performed by a bishop, as a *mysterion* closely connected to the Eucharist. He also outlines important ongoing issues, which the Orthodox Churches still have to come to terms with – internally as well as ecumenically.

Ecumenical Research on Ministry and Ordination: Some Remarks and Observations

Ola Tjørhom

Initially, I would like to emphasise that I see this research project as an important initiative for several reasons. First, with some notable exceptions, research on ordination and ordination rites must be characterized as an 'endangered species' in most of contemporary Nordic theology. Secondly, while being crucial to the ecumenical venture and the accomplishment of the goal of visible unity, only a limited amount of ecumenical reflection is available on these topics. And thirdly, the fact that the present initiative is conducted within a truly ecumenical framework with researchers from several church traditions serves as a reminder of a basic, but still often neglected concern: ecumenical research is best conducted ecumenically! Thus, this project fills a marked gap in current Nordic theology as well as in our ecumenical efforts.

Ecumenical Research: between Mere Comparison and Pure Activism

Basically, there are two ditches that must be avoided in the field of ecumenical research. The first one is to reduce this concern to the level of a purely formal comparison; the second is to confuse research on church unity with impatient 'activism'. The main problem with the first of these approaches is that if you try hard enough, almost anything may seem to have a certain similarity. This is illustrated in the story about the man who came across a potato that looked exactly like a bear that had curled itself up and, thus, looked exactly like a potato ...! The point here is that a mere comparison has little to offer when it is conducted in isolation. Consequently, ecumenical research must be related to specific challenges in the present ecumenical situation. At the same time, the activist approach implies that we depart from the field of proper research and its task to reveal rather than to implement. Moreover, ecumenical activism tends to confuse the goal of unity with the steps towards unity – an attitude that ecumenical research should be most concerned to avoid.

Trying to identify an intermediate approach between the two extremes of mere comparison and pure activism, the following concerns are in my view of crucial significance:[1]

1. Ecumenical research is marked by a fundamental obligation to the goal of visible unity in the sense that it is directed towards offering an appropriate description of this goal as well as identifying possible steps and stages that may lead to its realisation. However, the concrete implementation of the goal in question is, of course, the responsibility of the churches.
2. Ecumenical research aims to clarify both the measure of diversity that is compatible with unity and the limits of diversity. Here a correction of a most static perception of ecclesial diversity as something that allows the churches to 'remain as they are' within the framework of a 'reconciled denominationalism' or an *Ökumene in Gegensätzen* is a vital concern.[2]
3. In the wake of this, ecumenical research should be committed to developing and assessing different concepts of unity. However, there is a clear need in this connection to move beyond the intense debates of the 1970s and 1980s on the so-called 'models of unity' – partly since most of these models were confessionally conditioned and partly because there is a growing awareness that unity cannot be accomplished through more or less abstract 'models'.
4. Ecumenical research is particularly relevant in the perspective of the ecumenical dialogues – bilateral as well as multilateral ones. However, in a situation where many of these dialogues increasingly resemble an

---

1. I have tried to develop several of the following concerns in more detail – though within a general ecumenical framework and especially with regard to the need for an appropriate unity concept – in O. Tjørhom, 'The Goal of Visible Unity – Reaffirming our Commitment', *The Ecumenical Review*, 54, no. 1-2 (April 2002), 162 ff.
2. A rather striking recent expression of the consequences of such an approach can be found in a statement by the Evangelical Church in Germany on church fellowship, in which the goal of unity is repeatedly identified with '*geordnetes Miteinander bekenntnisverschiedener Kirchen*' ('an ordered togetherness of churches that maintain different confessions'). See *Kirchengemeinschaft nach evangelischem Verständnis: Texte der EKD*, No. 69, 2001.

endless piling up of abstract consensus that is not being converted into living fellowship and where questions are being reopened over and over again, our research in this area must include an effort to identify and explore new ways forward.

5. Much evidence suggests that we are approaching the borders of 'consensus ecumenism' or 'doctrinal ecumenism', and that there is a need for research that does not limit itself to more or less abstract doctrines, but also includes the practices of the churches. Here I think of liturgies and spirituality as well as the churches' mission and service in the world. The simple fact is that unity is intended to lead us into a common life and, thus, requires far more than an abstract 'agreement'.

Especially within current Protestant ecumenism, there is a growing emphasis on what is labelled 'ecumenical methodology'. On the one hand, there are many fundamental and methodological questions that must be clarified in this connection – emerging as a vital task for our ecumenical research. And there are several examples that such deliberations can be most helpful. On the other hand, the proclivity to identify this concern with an assumedly sophisticated, but highly abstract acrobatics where we are supposed to agree on certain foundational 'ideas' while keeping our densely parochial faiths and our even more parochial practices unchanged and unchallenged, is in my view ecumenically counterproductive. A clear example of this attitude can be found in the – rather Hegelian – insistence that we should reach agreement on an abstract *'Grund'* ('foundation'), while continuing to present this *'Grund'* in radically differing or even directly contrary *'Gestalten'* ('shapes'). However, such an 'idealistic' approach will only contribute to a perpetuation of static denominational diversity and not bring us one single inch closer to the realisation of the goal of visible church fellowship.

Research on the Church and Church Ministries: Some Basic Presuppositions

Generally, research on the Church and its ministries must be anchored in Holy Scripture. However, in this field there is a special need to see things in an historical perspective – or in the perspective of church tradition, if you like. The New Testament reflects an initial phase in the Church's development. When it grew and its life changed, new structures had to be developed that go significantly beyond the structural patterns of the first Church. This was particularly the case in regard to church ministries. First, the passing away of the apostles made it necessary to initiate different forms of leadership and authority. Secondly, the existence of several churches or 'congregations' in the same city required extended episcopal oversight. And thirdly, the 'universalization' of the Church within the Constantinian empire points towards new forms of episcopal collegiality as well as a universal ministry of unity under the auspices of the Bishop of Rome. When seen in the perspective of ecumenical research, the point is neither to reject this development as a deviation from an authentic biblical pattern nor to canonize it as a result of the work of the Holy Spirit. The point is rather to realise that research on church ministries requires a historical approach that transcends pure biblicism as well as an isolated doctrinal or dogmatic assessment.[3]

The question of structures for the ministries of the Church must be raised within the context just indicated. Obviously, I cannot go into the intense debates on this question in detail. Allow me, however, the following brief remarks in favour of the so-called threefold structure of the early Church:

1. Although this structure cannot be found in its full form in the New Testament, we can discern there a development that points towards such a structure – already having the service of priests and deacons, and reflecting the need for *'episkopoi'* as the Church grew.

2. Since the Church according to its nature is primarily local and universal, it can be argued that we need ministries that correspond to both these dimensions. Here priests together with deacons attend to the local congregation. Bishops serve as a link between the local and universal level by representing the local Church universally and the universal Church locally. And the universal nature of the Church may also seem to require a kind of ministerial manifestation – be it personal or collegial, and without necessarily identifying it with the Bishop of Rome.

3. The Lutheran insistence on the basic oneness of the Church's ministry should primarily be understood as a theological concern in the sense

---

3. For a broader account of the ecclesiological framework of church ministries and the nature and purpose of these ministries, see *i.a.* O. Tjørhom, *Kirken – troens mor: Et økumenisk bidrag til en luthersk ekklesiologi* (The Church – Mother of Faith: An Ecumenical Contribution to a Lutheran Ecclesiology), Oslo: Verbum Forlag, 1999. Cf. also O. Tjørhom, *Visible Church – Visible Unity: towards an Ecumenical Ecclesiology*, Collegeville, Minn: Unitas Books, the Liturgical Press, 2003. Furthermore, a vital contribution from a Swedish free church perspective should be noted here: *Kyrka, Ämbete, Ledarskap: Självförståelse och visioner* (Church, Ministry and Leadership: Self-understanding and Visions), Örebro 1995.

that it shows that all ministries must somehow be anchored in the service of Word and sacrament that constitutes the Church. However, this does not exclude a certain measure of structural differentiation.

In relation to the theological framework of research on church ministries, the following factors play a vital role:[4] First, the ministry of God's people as a whole – within which the ordained ministries are placed, while having a special responsibility for providing appropriate spiritual leadership – is essential at this point. Here the interconnectedness as well as the difference between the so-called common priesthood – or better; the priesthood of all baptized believers – and the publicly ordained ministries must be clarified. All these ministries are crucial within the Church as the body of Christ. But if they are falsely confused or muddled together, it will have negative repercussions for all of them.[5] Secondly, apostolicity and the concern for apostolic continuity also belong to the theological framework of research on church ministries. While not being a repetition of the unique service of the apostles in their capacity as eyewitnesses to Christ's work, this service is continued in the space of the Church through its ordained ministries together with the faithful as a whole. And throughout church history, the bishop has been perceived as a special sign of apostolic continuity. Thirdly, just as the Church is not an end in itself, but the priest of creation and the first-fruits of reunited humankind, church ministries must be seen in the perspective of the Church's mission and service in and for the world. In this connection, the need to provide a link between '*leitourgia*', '*diakonia*' and '*missio*' is of particular significance. Subsequent to this, the concept of '*sacramentum mundi*' is of relevance to the ministry as well. All this

---

4. Cf. on this also C. Braaten, *The Apostolic Imperative: Nature and Aim of the Church's Mission and Ministry*, Minneapolis: Fortress 1985. For an ecumenical approach to apostolicity, cf. O. Tjørhom, 'Apostolicity and Apostolic Succession in the Porvoo Common Statement – Necessary or a Mere 'Optional Extra' in the Church's Life?', in O. Tjørhom (ed), *Apostolicity and Unity: Essays on the Porvoo Common Statement*, Grand Rapids: Eerdmans, 2002.

5. The problems that are connected with the relationship between the ministry of the faithful and the ordained ministries of the Church tend to pop up in a radicalised and even almost acute form in churches where predominantly secular democratic ideals have been incorporated. This is clearly the case in most Nordic Lutheran folk churches. Politically speaking, such ideals are absolutely vital, but they become more ambiguous when they are seen in an ecclesiological perspective. Surely, the Church is no '*societas inaequalis*'. Yet, it is a community where all are equals in dignity, but still unequal in regard to tasks and responsibilities. This lesson can be drawn from St. Paul's powerful exhortation on the Church as the body of Christ in 1 Cor. 12.

indicates that research on church ministries must be ecclesiologically embedded – simply because these ministries are instrumental to the Church as 'Christ's sacrament to us' (de Lubac). More concretely, the present framework shows that the ordained ministries stand both in and over against God's people as a whole.

Ordination: The Theological Problems at Stake

Let me here start with some brief remarks on the discussion of ordination in recent dialogue statements that deal with church ministries. Some texts – primarily on the Protestant side – are simply content to list ministry and ordination as topics that require further clarification, without seeing them as divisive.[6] Other texts only contain short references to ordination, while presuming that the churches involved basically agree on this topic.[7] However, the three following texts are particularly relevant at this point: Faith and Order's Lima statement (*Baptism, Eucharist and Ministry*, 1982) has a full section on ordination. Additionally, two documents from the second phase of Roman Catholic-Lutheran dialogue are important here. This is primarily the case with regard to *The Ministry in the Church* (1981/82), which even includes several ordination liturgies, without discussing these liturgies in detail. But *Facing Unity: Models, Forms and Phases of Catholic-Lutheran Church Fellowship* (1985) should also be taken into account in this connection, especially Hervé Legrand's appendix that deals with the fundamental structures of the rites of episcopal ordination in the early Church.

As to which questions emerge as the main problems in the ecumenical dialogue on ordination, as far as I can see, the following topics play a most important role at this point:

1. The question of *the formal and ecclesial validity of ordination* is particularly crucial – one might even say fateful – in the dialogue between the Roman Catholic Church and the churches of the Reformation. This mainly depends on the insistence in *Unitatis Redintegratio* § 22 that the ministry of 'the separated Western churches' is marked by a so-called '*defectus ordinis*'. Though this defect should probably be understood more in terms of a lack of fullness than as a total absence of

---

6. Cf. especially the 1973 *Leuenberg Agreement*, but partly also the 1984 Methodist-Lutheran statement *The Church: Community of Grace*.
7. This is the case with the 1992 *Porvoo Common Statement* as well as several other documents from the Anglican-Lutheran dialogue.

anything that is essential to the Church, it cannot be denied that it emerges as one of the most divisive topics in the present dialogue process. However, the Vatican II *Decree on Ecumenism* also includes an explicit acknowledgement that the Holy Spirit makes use of the churches of the Reformation as instruments of salvation (cf. §3). And one may argue that it is difficult to see how churches that fulfil this key function can be substantially deficient. Accordingly, a pneumatological approach may be the best way to proceed in this field.[8]

2. Subsequent to the question of validity, *the sacramental nature of ordination* must be clarified. This topic points towards and includes problems that relate to the Christological implication of ordination and the *character* of the ordinand. Here, however, the dialogue texts reflect a notable convergence. While Roman Catholics distinguish between the chief sacraments of baptism and the Eucharist and other sacramental acts, already the Lutheran Reformers were prepared to describe ordination as a sacrament – as demonstrated by Melanchthon in art. XIII of the *Apology of the Augsburg Confession*.[9] Moreover, it is explicitly confirmed in art. VII of the same *Apology* that the ordinand can be seen as acting '*in persona Christi*'. And while art. V of *Confessio Augustana* makes it clear that the '*Predigamt*' is instituted by God, art. XIV insists that only those who are '*rite vocatus*' – i.e. properly called in the sense of being ordained – shall officiate in Word and sacrament on behalf of the whole Church. As for the question of the '*character indelebilis*', there is a growing consensus that what is at stake here is the lifelong duration of ordination and not an ontological quality. Since ordination is both Christologically and pneumatologically anchored, this act should also be perceived as *transmitting a particular charism* – or more precisely the charism of spiritual leadership.[10] This means that

8. This problem is discussed further in O. Tjørhom, 'The Catholic-Lutheran Dialogue – Status and Challenges', in P. Nørgaard-Højen (ed.), *Catholic-Lutheran Relations Three Decades after Vatican II*, Rome 1997.
9. If ordination is understood as a sacrament, the laying-on of hands should be seen as its concrete 'element'.
10. Let me here just briefly mention that I see no need to go into earlier debates on the interrelation between structures and charismata – respectively Christology and pneumatology – in this connection. I am simply saying that most theologians today seem to realize that we are here dealing with perspectives that are not mutually excluding, but rather complementary – and that they should, therefore, not be pitted against each other.

ordination confers both the God-given authority to exercise such leadership and the spiritual equipment for exercising it. Seen in this perspective, it becomes evident that an *epiklesis* is essential to all rites of ordination. This factor has often been rejected on the Protestant side as an expression of some kind of automatism.[11] It should, however, be conceived as a sign of the participation of the Holy Spirit in the act of ordination.

3. While being primarily vertically anchored as a manifestation of God's setting apart and equipping of the ordinand, ordination also includes a more 'horizontal' dimension. The key concern here is partly that the ordinand is included in the fellowship of all those who have been ordained to a special ministry in the Church across time as well as space, and partly a commissioning and endorsement of priests, bishops and deacons by the faithful. The main intention at this point is that the ordained persons are charged with the responsibility to prevent things which belong to all of us from being annexed by individuals or small groups. Thus, the ordained ministries are supposed to protect the true communality of Christian life. The practice of so-called lay presidency increasingly emerges as a vital ecumenical problem. Yet, the partly sub-theological nature of this problem is confirmed by the fact that there is a wide variety of practices in this area within several of the confessional families and churches. While Lutheran and other Reformation Churches previously kept up a certain degree of lay presidency on the basis of 'the principle of need' in order to cope with the lack of priests, such measures today seem to depend more on the likes and dislikes of people in the congregations than on real 'need'. However, in spite of the many different evaluations of this practice, there can be no doubt that it effectively and substantially undermines ordination.[12]

Finally, I would like to mention – if briefly – that when the goal of visible structural unity is at stake, a largely abstract 'mutual recognition' of ordination

---

11. Interestingly – or rather embarrassingly, in the early 1980s, the Bishops of the Church of Norway in their response to the Lima document explicitly welcomed Faith and Order's emphasis on the invocation of the Spirit, while at the same time effectively removing most remnants of an *epiklesis* in the new liturgies of the church.

12. On an appropriate theology of lay people, the contributions of Yves Congar are still most valid. See especially *Jalons pour une théologie du laïcat*, Paris: Cerf, 1964 and *Sacerdoce et laïcat*, Paris: Cerf, 1962.

and ministries cannot be regarded as sufficient. In fact, one often gets the feeling that such a 'recognition' is used primarily as an artificial grip to avoid the theological problems we face in this area – allowing the churches to 're-main as they are'. However, when our aim is a dynamic growth towards visible unity, far more is needed. With regard to ordination, this will include forms of regular mutual participation in these acts and an ensuing full interchangeabil-ity of all ordained ministries. Seen against this background, it also becomes clear how important ordination is in an ecumenical perspective. In general terms, the topics just listed should be kept on the agenda of the current research initiative, which hopefully will be able to contribute to a clarification of several of them.

The Theology and Terminology of Ordination: an Important Dialectic

One of the most important aspects of the present research project is its em-phasis on the dialectic between the theology and terminology of ordination. As far as I know, such an approach is quite rare in the field of ecumenical research. Basically, we must be open to the possibility that a common theology is hidden behind the vast variety of terms and concepts that are being used in relation to ordination. An example of this can be found in the claim that even if the Church of Norway does not apply the term 'ordination' to its episcopal con-secrations any more, the revised ordinal includes most of the constitutive elements of such an act. Simultaneously, however, there are cases where the opposite is true, i.e. where common terminology conceals marked variations in practice as well as theology. This seems to be the case in view of the vast differences between a sacramental and a non-sacramental perception on this point – despite the fact that both positions tend to apply the concept of 'ordination'.

Seen against this background, the following more general conclusions can be drawn when it comes to dialectics between the theology and terminology of ordination: First, real convergence cannot be deduced on a purely conceptual level, but requires that a parallel convergence on the basic structure of ordi-nation can be identified in the churches' liturgies and ordinals. Secondly, in this connection the concrete practices of the churches must be seen as just as important as their doctrines – because an abstract approximation that remains invisible on a practical level is of clearly limited value in an ecumenical per-spective. And thirdly, in order to be able to uncover a sustainable convergence in this field, we must distinguish between proper ordinations – only being applicable to those who share personally in specific public church ministries, that is priests, bishops and deacons – and the many acts of prayer, dedication and installation that may be used in connection with a vast variety of tasks and services in the Church's life. This implies that the threefold ministry provides a significant basis in defining the ordination-concept. Generally, there seems to be a growing need to defend and preserve the word 'ordination' today. This is confirmed by the fact that the word has almost totally vanished from the current ordinals of the Church of Norway.[13] Not the least in this area, our traditional theological vocabulary has been put under massive pressure through the adoption of management-type leadership rhetoric within *inter alia* many neo-charismatic groups with their somewhat tedious efforts constantly to re-invent the wheel.

In terms of the present research project, this implies that the identification of a certain convergence behind terminological differences definitely deserves to be properly investigated. It may even represent a most constructive ecu-menical opportunity. However, in order to contribute to the realisation of visible unity, such a convergence must be authenticated, affirmed and visual-ized by the churches' liturgical practices as well as their theological reflection.[14] At this point, the approach to apostolicity and apostolic succession in the *Porvoo Common Statement* may offer a feasible model: on the one hand, Por-voo maintains that the *'res'* of apostolicity can be kept up even in times when several of its *'signa'* have been lost. On the other hand, the churches that have lost these signs are admonished not to 'remain as they are', but rather to regain as many of the apostolic signs as possible and to have them reintegrated into their lives.[15] In my view, this applies to ordination theologies and liturgies as well. Also at this point, we should not settle for a minimalist common de-nominator, but rather aim at fullness – because ecumenism is meant to make us richer and not poorer.

Observations on the Material of the Research Project

I now turn to some more specific, if brief and preliminary comments on the material in this research process. The sources at hand are extremely rich,

---

13. As far as I have gathered, the revised ordinals and liturgies of installation in the Church of Norway only once speak of the priest as 'ordinand', while the term 'ordination' is never used explicitly in these liturgies.
14. Generally, this is based on the vital insight from so-called liturgical theology that liturgy is theology and the parallel insistence that there is a vital interaction between liturgical practice and theological reflection.
15. See on this §§50 ff. of the *Porvoo Common Statement* – and particularly §52.

comprehensive and – one might add – almost a little overwhelming. In order to avoid anticipating the systematic and analytical assessment of the different parts of the material, I shall at this point limit myself to the following more general observations:

1. The comprehensiveness and richness of the research material must be seen as a positive asset that also reflects the richness of the act of ordination and its crucial ecclesiological significance. Yet, there are huge variations here both content-wise and methodologically. Accordingly, there is a need to develop a common pattern or matrix for the study of ordination liturgies – in view of the comparative task as well as the theological and ecumenical assessment. Further, a clear distinction between proper ordination liturgies and other acts of prayer, initiation and installation is needed. And as already suggested, the three-fold ministry of the early Church may serve as an appropriate foundation and criterion at this point.

2. The collected material exposes huge variations not only *between* the churches, but also *within* some of the church families involved. This particularly appears to be the case in Nordic Lutheranism – theologically as well as liturgically. I doubt that this depends primarily on cultural factors and contextualization, as the cultural differences in question are in fact limited. The variations mentioned should probably be perceived more as results of diverging ecclesiologies. Here the discrepancy between a Western Nordic line, which today seems to be particularly strong in Denmark and Norway, and an Eastern Nordic tradition manifested in Sweden and Finland, plays a crucial role.[16] At present, the main watershed on this point appears to be the degree of openness to ecumenical impetus. Generally, however, the existing *internal* diversity does not seem to be used as an ecumenical opportunity.

3. The special character of liturgies calls for close attention when they are treated as research objects. On the one hand, I fully agree that liturgy is theology and doctrine. On the other hand, liturgy is clearly more than abstract doctrine – it is implemented, enacted and lived theology. Ordination liturgies should, thus, also be understood as a 'performance' or as an enacting of different aspects of the drama of salvation.

---

16. Even if this may be somewhat too simplistic, one may argue that while Sweden and increasingly also Finland adhere to a 'Catholic' interpretation of the Reformation, Denmark and Norway are more traditionally Protestant. Cf. Jyrki Knuutila's article (Part II.2).

And in this 'performance', what we *say* is only a part of the matter – what we *do* is clearly important, too. Moreover, in liturgy we are concerned to manifest visually the words we speak. All this implies that our liturgies are 'performances' more in the sense of the early medieval mystery plays than in the sense of the idea dramas of Ibsen and Strindberg. These concerns must be reflected in our research.

Methodologically, the research project includes three differing, but also interconnected approaches: A descriptive and documentary task – presenting a vast scope of ordination liturgies: a comparative task – conducting a comprehensive comparison of the liturgies in question; and a systematic-analytical task – identifying common features as well as variations between the liturgies. In my view there is ample reason to hope that new ground can be broken on alle these points. If so, the present project will render vital services to the continued ecumenical dialogue on church ministries and ordination

Allow me finally to return to the goal of our ecumenical endeavours in the field of ministry and ordination. As already indicated, an ever more frequent tendency to settle for an abstract mutual recognition of ministries and ordination acts can be observed in this area. Such attitudes are also reflected in some of the contributions to this research project. Against this background, I would like to repeat that the concept of 'mutual recognition' today increasingly appears to emerge as an expression of static diversity – allowing the churches to 'remain as they are'. It should, thus, rather be understood as a step towards unity or as an effort that is directed towards a common ministry. Such a ministry should not be perceived as a uniform entity. However, it requires a joint theological foundation, a common structural framework and a shared general direction. Moreover, 'mutual recognition' in relation to ordinations must be concretised through liturgies that converge in content and structure, through regular common participation of bishops in these acts and some kind of licensing of those who exercise their ministry in other churches, as practised within the Porvoo communion. Personally, I am convinced that this is the only feasible way to proceed when we are aiming for the traditional goal of the ecumenical movement – namely visible unity, in order that the world shall see and believe.

Key Issues in the Ecumenical Dialogues on Ordination

James F. Puglisi, SA

This article will attempt to survey the bilateral and multilateral inter-confessional dialogues with a view to discovering if there is any convergence in the way the churches speak about ordination, its meaning, its constitutive elements, its theology or theologies. Let me begin by looking at some of the points of convergence to try to determine what the key issues are. In order to obtain some perspective on what has now turned out to be a very extensive number of statements on ministry, it is also necessary to take note of the divergence which likewise occurs in these dialogues. So let us begin.

Catalogue of Texts

I have compiled a listing of the dialogues that treat the question of ministry. This list is not meant to be exhaustive but indicative of the work that has been done in the dialogues on the question of ministry (see the appendix). It will be impossible to treat each and every one of these statements. However, I will attempt to designate some of the key issues that have arisen in these discussions and offer one or two examples from the texts themselves. A first approach to the question at hand leads us to the constatation of three major themes that are treated in almost all of the dialogues on ministry: 1) the identification of where the ordained ministry is situated in relation to the ministerial nature of the whole people of God and the role of the ordained ministry in the Church, 2) the question of the relation between apostolic continuity of the Church and apostolic succession and 3) the structuring, meaning and exercise of the ordained ministry. Obviously there are other issues that are raised that will be indicated as we progress but I think that these three themes have shown themselves to be key issues for the churches in dialogue and are of importance for the current project.

The Context in which the Ordained Ministry is Placed

A clear context begins to emerge from these bilateral discussions, namely that none of these dialogues will treat the question of the ordained ministry in isolation. Inevitably the dialogues treat of the question of ministry in the framework of its relation to the ministry of Christ and secondly in the context of the Church. Great care is taken in establishing the *Christological basis* of the ordained ministry from the beginning. Ministry is described in relation to Christ and Christ's ministry; he is the point of reference. At the heart of Christ's ministry is the fundamental witness that he gives to the Father. What characterizes this ministry is the idea of service or *diakonia*. A first conclusion that we can make here is that a principal concern of the churches is to see the category of service as being the primary one for articulating ministry in general and secondly that all Christian ministry has its referent in the ministry of Jesus himself. Much care is taken to connect every form of ministry to that of Christ and in this context the Church's ministry is presented. Since all who are baptized are baptized into the Body of Christ and in the threefold dimension of his mission, namely they share in the prophetic, priestly and royal dimensions of his mission. The Orthodox-Catholic dialogue on ministry affirms that 'in the New Testament Christ is referred to as apostle, prophet, pastor, servant, deacon, doctor, priest, *episcopus*' (Orthodox-Catholic International Dialogue [=O-RC] 1988:§2).[1] He is sent by the Father and hence is attributed the title of 'true apostle'. In its turn the Church is likewise sent to carry out the mission that Christ entrusts to her. The ministry of the Church is made possible by the action of the Holy Spirit. Thus we see the pneumatological dimension of the ministry introduced. This dimension thereby brings into perspective the Trinitarian nature of ministry including that of Christ.

We may see this clearly stated in an example from the Reformed/Catholic Dialogue, *The Presence of Christ in Church and World* ([=R-RC] 1977):

> The sending of Christ and the equipment of the Church in his service are also works of the Holy Spirit. The mission of the Holy Spirit belongs to the constitution of the Church and her ministry, not merely to their effective functioning. Too often, imbalances in theology of the ministry are the

---

1. For the sake of clarity it is necessary to cite the paragraph numeration so that the passages may be found in other translated versions of the text. A shorthand abbreviation has been chosen for many of the dialogues which will be given in square parentheses [] the first time the reference appears and then only the abbreviation will be used in succeeding references.

result and sign of an insufficiently Trinitarian theology. It is by the power of the Spirit that the Lord sustains his people in their apostolic vocation (R-RC 1977:§94)

It is interesting to see the Reformed/Catholic dialogue present the Trinitarian aspect of ministry which will normally be a key issue for the Orthodox in their discussions with other churches. We should not under-estimate the importance of the Trinitarian dimension since it locates the principle dimension of salvation in the merciful activity of the Father who through the life, ministry, death and resurrection of the only Begotten Son, reconciles all peoples to himself and to each other in the communion of the Holy Spirit (WCC [=Accra] 1975:§M5; *cfr.* Lutheran World Federation & Secretariat for Promoting Christian Unity [=L-RC] 1972:§48; Roman Catholic/Presbyterian-Reformed Consultation [=RC-P/usa] 1972:§2).

The second context that may always be seen present in the dialogues is the *ecclesiological* one. This context is of major importance since it considers the role that the Church plays in the actualization of Christ's ministry through the power of the Holy Spirit. We need to verify through a serious analysis of the ordination texts of the churches if and how this dimension is expressed. If the churches can recognize the actualization of the ministry of Christ in other churches this would be an important step toward the mutual reception of ministry. Linked to this notion is another key concept, namely that of apostolicity. The Church is apostolic in the sense that it witnesses to what the community in the Spirit has received from the apostles. This witness also contains the mission of the Church to be an agent of the reconciliation of God offered through Christ to the whole world. An issue that is repeated several times in the dialogues is that of the fact that all the baptized share in this ministry of the Church, and the mission of the Church is to bring to all peoples the Good News of salvation. In reality this means that the Church is apostolic in two senses. First it is apostolic because of its foundation or source, namely that it is founded on the witness that was given to Christ by the apostles. Secondly the Church is apostolic in terms of the mission it has received to be ambassadors of reconciliation to the whole world (*Groupe des Dombes* [Dombes-M] 1973:§4; Lutheran World Federation & Secretariat for Promoting Christian Unity [=L-RC-ministry] 1981:§16f).

The corporate sense of the exercise of the ministry by all the baptized is clearly affirmed in all the texts. This is rooted in the concept that has come to be called the 'priesthood of all believers' or 'baptismal priesthood' into which we are initiated through the saving waters of Baptism. The scriptural foundation for this concept is to be found in 1 Pet 2.9 which appears in almost all of the dialogue texts (Lutheran-Roman Catholic Dialogue in the United States [=L-RC/usa] 1970:§10; L-RC 1972:§48; Dombes-M 1973:§31).[2]

What is not always clear is the relationship of the 'priesthood of all believers' to the priesthood of Christ. Some have expressed it as a relationship of sharing in Christ's Priesthood (L-RC/usa 1970:§10) or as an 'extension of Christ's ministry, including his priestly office' (R-RC 1977:§96). On the whole the dialogues are cautious about making a close identification of these terms for the reason that the New Testament does not link the notion of priesthood as applied to the community to the unique priesthood of Jesus Christ (Tillard 1973). One would suppose that the modes of linking the two are of capital importance. They must be linked not in terms of identity but in terms of participation, something that not all churches are ready to do. It must be remembered that the biblical understanding of priesthood as applied both in the Old Testament and in the New Testament to the people is to be under-stood in a collective or corporative sense.

In the past the use of the 'priestly' category to describe the ministry of the Church has been overly restricted and reduced the ministry to its cultic sense leaving in the shadows the prophetic and royal dimensions. We need to ask ourselves if by this restriction we may sufficiently express the fullness of Christian ministry as it is lived in the daily living of the baptized. It is in the context of the ministerial aspect of the whole Church that the dialogues will then begin to speak of the special or ordained ministry. An important point to bear in mind as we study the ordination texts is to see how this balance between the ministerial aspect of the whole Church and the special ministry of some is articulated. It is only against this backdrop that we can also grasp the originality of the ordained ministry within the Church. Biblically this may be illustrated by studying the Pauline texts on the distribution of diverse gifts by the same Spirit (Brockhaus 1975).

Other Dimension in Ordained Ministry

Methodologically the dialogues have tended to express what the churches hold in common for establishing a solid basis as the point of departure rather than stating contentious positions. In this way constitutive elements of the ministry that are commonly held begin to become obvious. This is not to say that the

---

2. See also the authoritative work done by a Lutheran scholar that corrects the exegetical reading of the biblical texts used by Martin Luther for the position of the universal priesthood of all believers (Elliott 1966).

dialogues have avoided points of contention but rather they desired to start from a common ground to be able then to deal with the differences.

We have seen that what is universally held by the churches as a starting point is the Christological context of the ministry that is pneumatologically grounded hence set within a Trinitarian framework (L-RC-ministry 1981:§19-22). Next all ministry is seen as being located in an ecclesiological context. Finally the dialogues understand the diversity of ministry as being a gift that God makes to the Church in order that she may fulfil her mission to the world.

From this perspective then the dialogues can speak of a special ministry (L-RC/usa 1970:§9; R-RC 1977:§§96f), office of ministry (L-RC 1972:§§50, 56, 59), ministerial office L-RC 1972:§56, 61; Anglican-Roman Catholic International Commission [=ARCIC] 1973:§6), ordained ministry (Anglican-Lutheran Conversations [=A-L] 1972:§76; ARCIC 1973:§§2, 7; Methodist-Roman Catholic [=M-RC] 1976:§80), pastoral ministry (Dombes-M 1973:§20; WCC Baptism, Eucharist, Ministry [=BEM] 1982:§§1-6) and so on. We can add that a key concept for talking about ordained ministry is to situate it in the context of the whole people of God (L-RC/usa 1970:§9; L-RC 1972:§50; ARCIC 1973:§2; M-RC 1976: §80; R-RC 1977:§96; Dombes-M 1973:§20). Two important factors can be seen here: first, that the ordained ministry is conceived of as one of the many ministries that God gives to the Church that are called forth by the Spirit; secondly, this kind of ministry is distinct from the many ministries in the Church. The dialogues can even make a statement such as is to be found in the Reformed/Catholic discussions (R-RC 1977:§96): 'The calling to the priesthood of all those who share in the body of Christ by baptism does not mean that there are no particular functions which are proper to the special ministry within the body of Christ' (cf. Dombes-M 1973:§20). The ordained ministry has even been considered as an integral dimension of the structuring of the Church (Dombes-M 1973:§11; L-RC 1972:§56; ARCIC 1973:§6; Faith and Order 1975:§M13).[3] The special or ordained ministry is usually seen at the service of the baptismal priesthood (ARCIC 1973:§§7, 13; L-RC/usa 1970:§12; M-RC 1976:§98).

Distinctive Characteristics

The ordained ministry is seen as existing as a reminder that Christ is the very source of its faith, hope and unity. The *Groupe des Dombes* expresses this very

---

3. See the conclusions following a theological analysis of the rites of ordination in the churches (Puglisi 2001, 264-277).

succinctly: 'The mark of the pastoral ministry is to ensure and signify the Church's dependence on Christ, a source of its mission and foundation of its unity' (Dombes-M 1973:§20). This way of understanding the distinctiveness of the pastoral ministry helps to see the representative nature of the ordained ministry. Some of the dialogues have come to speak of the twofold representative-ness that may be ascribed to the ordained ministry inasmuch as it represents the community before Christ and Christ to the community (M-RC 1976:§79; L-RC 1972§50; L-RC-ministry 1981:§14; L-RC/usa 1970:§13). This aspect is what I have described elsewhere as the 'vis-à-vis' or 'over-againstness' dimension of the ministry. Precisely because the ordained is a member of the baptized faithful but through the process of ordination, the ordained person receives a charism, gift of the Spirit for the sake of serving the whole, this person stands 'face to face' in relationship with their brothers and sisters to confirm them in their faith and challenge them in their service to the world.

A concern of the dialogues is to see the special ministry not only as serving the Gospel under which it stands but also as a gift from God to the community that lives by the Gospel (ARCIC 1973:§13). To say this another way, there is an attempt to explain the distinction in function and service of the special ministry in relationship to the ministry of all the baptized. Once again this is an issue which the churches need to attend to in the revision of their ordination texts. How clearly is this relationship made both in text as well as in ritual action?

The Meaning of Ordination

The churches attempt to clarify the meaning of 'ordination' since this word has various nuances, depending on the language that it is used in. The Lima document (BEM) notes that there is not clear meaning derived from the New Testament itself. However, this document tries to illustrate the meaning of ordination in this way at §40 (Faith and Order 1982):

> Properly speaking, then, ordination denotes an action by God and the community by which the ordained are strengthened by the Spirit for their task and are upheld by the acknowledgment and prayers of the congregation.

I think that the BEM document has had as much influence on the bilateral discussions as have the Dombes discussions. In both of these we can find the basic meaning identified by four characteristics whereby ordination is seen as:

an invocation to God to grant the gifts of the Holy Spirit for the needs of the ministry;

a sacramental sign of the answering of this prayer by our Lord who confers the necessary charisms;

a welcome extended by the whole Church to the new servants and their reception into a college of ministers;

the commitment of the minister to the ministry with which the minister is entrusted (Dombes-M 1973:§35; Faith and Order 1982:§§41-41).

What also seems to be emphasized in the notion of call or vocation is that no one has a right to this particular task based on personal choice or capacity (L-RC/usa 1970:§18; M-RC 1976:§78). The human process of electing and appointing is not seen as sufficient for admission to the special ministry within the Church. The liturgical action is an expression and confirmation of the calling and sending of the Lord. Hence a key issue here is the process of admitting someone to this ministry. There seems to be a good amount of consensus that it is the Spirit's work and prayer in the form of the *epiklesis* and the ritual gesture of the laying-on of hands that is the liturgical expression that mediates the Spirit's bestowal of this particular form of ministry in the Church (O-RC 1977:§98; M-RC 1977:§78; L-RC 1972:§59; A-L 1972:§78; Dombes-M 1973:§34, Faith and Order 1982:§§41-50). While this is the case, at least in theory, the practice of the churches needs to be examined in the light of this affirmation. What is actually the role of the diverse groups of actors in the process of admission to ordained ministry? Is there a verification of the fact that indeed and not just ritually, the faithful participate in the choice of ministers in the churches? Many of our churches have a very high theology about the role of the faithful in the life of the church but is this theology actually realized in fact?

On the whole when the dialogues mention the special or ordained ministry they refer to the ministries of bishop, pastor/priest and deacon. This fact then becomes an issue when we look at what the churches actually do in terms of whom they are ordaining. This is one of the reasons why it was important to look at the meaning of the terms that we are using in the practice of the churches. Is there a theological justification for the ordaining of every one from church sacristan or organist to bishop? Obviously the dialogue statements do not provide a complete answer to this question but from their contexts it becomes fairly clear that when they are speaking of ordained ministries they are referring to the ministries of bishop, presbyter and deacon.

Open Questions

Some questions still have not found consensus in the various dialogues. By way of conclusion I would like to list these. First the question of the function of the exercise of *episkopé* is a crucial one. Oversight in the Church can be exercised according to several models. The churches are fairly well agreed that some form of pastoral oversight needs to be exercised within the Church (M-RC 1976:§88; Faith and Order 1975:§26; R-RC 1977:§102; The Porvoo Common Statement [=Porvoo] 1993: §A5). The issue of under what form shall this *episkopé* be exercised remains a question to be discussed further and it reaches to the discussion of the Petrine ministry as well. Much will depend upon the structuring of the individual churches. The question of the threefold ministry of bishop, presbyter and deacon remains an open question. BEM makes several suggestions and various dialogues have considered the issues that exist between congregationally ordered churches and episcopally ordered ones (Faith and Order 1982:§§25-26 and 28-31; Lutheran-Roman Catholic Commission on Unity [=L-RC-church] 1993:§204; *Groupe des Dombes* [=Dombes-E] 1978:§1). The important issue remains the way in which the episcopal, presbyteral and diaconal functions will be carried out. What appears clearly in the dialogue texts is that whatever the final form will be there must be a collegial exercise of the office involved (Dombes-E 1978:§§40-43; L-RC/usa 1970:§15).

Next the question of apostolic succession and continuity of the Church needs to be clarified in terms of the relationship that exists between the two. Just as the ministry of the whole Church is the englobing reality for the special or ordained ministry, so too is the context of the apostolicity of the whole Church for the succession. The rites of ordination will need to deal with this issue in some way. The issue of the authority of the ordained ministry and the question of status within the Church are likewise issues to be looked at.

Lastly the large question that looms over many of the discussions is that of the papal ministry and the role that it has to play in the whole question of the ministerial structure of the Church. With these questions on the ecumenical agenda we will certainly have enough to keep us talking to one another for a while.

References

Anglican-Lutheran Conversations [=A-L] 1972. Pullach Report. In Meyer and Vischer, 1984, 14-34.

Anglican-Lutheran Conversations [=A-L-Niagra] 1987. The Niagara Report on «*episkopé*». In Gros, Meyer and Rusch, 2000, 12-37.

Anglican-Roman Catholic International Commission [=ARCIC] 1973. Ministry and Ordination. In Meyer and Vischer, 1984, 78-84.

Anglican-Roman Catholic International Commission [=ARCIC-clarifications] 1991. Clarifications of Certain Aspects of the Agreed Statements on Eucharist and Ministry of the First ARCIC. *Information Service* 87:237-242.

Brockhaus, U. 1975. *Charisma und Amt. Die paulinische Charismenlehre auf dem Hintergrund der frühchristlichen Gemeindefunktionen.* Wuppertal: Theologischer Verlag Rolf Brockhaus.

Burgess, J.A. and J. Gros, eds. 1989. *Building Unity. Ecumenical Dialogues with Roman Catholic Participation in the United States.* NY/Mahwah, NJ: Paulist Press (Ecumenical Documents IV).

Burgess, J.A. and J. Gros, eds. 1995. *Growing Consensus. Church Dialogues in the United States 1962-1991.* NY/Mahwah, NJ: Paulist Press. (Ecumenical Documents V).

CDF/PCPCU 1991. Vatican Response to ARCIC I Final Report. *Origins* 21, 441-4473

Chambésy 1978. Reflections by Orthodox and Roman Catholic Theologians on Ministries. *OiC* 14: 289-295.

Church of Sweden-Roman Catholic Diocese of Stockholm (=L-RC/swe) 1989. The Office of Bishop: *Report of the Official Working Group for Dialogue between the Church of Sweden and the Roman Catholic Diocese of Stockholm.* Geneva: Lutheran World Federation. (LWF Studies, 1993-94/2).

Consultation on Church Union (=COCU) 1977. In Quest of a Church of Christ Uniting. *Mid-Stram* 16: 49-92.

Elliot, J.H. 1966. *The Elect and the Holy. An Exegetical Examination of 1 Pet 2.4-10.* Leiden: E.J. Brill (Supplements to *Novum Testamentun,* 12)

Faith and Order. 1975. *One Baptism, One Eucharist and a Mutually Recognized Ministry. Three Agreed Statements* [=Accra]. Faith and Order Paper 73. Geneva: World Council of Churches.

Faith and Order.1982. *Baptism, Eucharist and Ministry.* Faith and Order Paper 111 (BEM). Geneva: World Council of Churches.

Gros, J., H. Meyer and W. G. Rusch, eds. 2000. *Growth in Agreement II. Reports and Agreed Statements of Ecumenical Conversations on a World Level, 1982-1998.* Faith and Order Paper 187. Grand Rapids: Eerdmans; Geneva: WCC Publications.

Groupe des Dombes [=Dombes-M] 1973. *Towards a Reconciliation of Ministries: Points of Agreement between Roman Catholics and Protestants.* In McAdoo 1975, 89-107.

Groupe des Dombes [=Dombes-E] 1978. The Episcopal Ministry. *OiC* 14: 267-288.

Lutheran-Roman Catholic Commission on Unity [=L-RC-church] 1993. *Church and Justification*. In Gros, Meyer and Rusch 2000, 485-565.

Lutheran-Roman Catholic Dialogue in the United States [=L-RC/usa] 1970. *Eucharist and Ministry*. In Burgess and Gros 1989, 102-124.

Lutheran World Federation & Secretariat for Promoting Christian Unity [=L-RC] 1972. *The Gospel and the Church. The Malta Report*. In Meyer and Vischer 1984, 179-184.

Lutheran World Federation & Secretariat for Promoting Christian Unity [=L-RC-ministry] 1981. *The Ministry in the Church*. In Meyer and Vischer 1984, 248-275.

Lutheran World Federation & Secretariat for Promoting Christian Unity [=L-RC-unity] 1984. *Facing Unity*. In Gros, Meyer and Rusch 2000, 443-484.

McAdoo, H.R. 1975. *Modern Ecumenical Documents on the Ministry*. London: SPCK.

Memorandum 1973. *Reform und Anerkennung kirchlicher Ämter: ein Memorandum der Arbeitsgemeinschaft ökumenischer Universitätsinstitute*. München: Kaiser: 11-25.

Methodist-Roman Catholic [=M-RC] 1976. *Dublin Report*. In Meyer and Vischer 1984, 340-366.

Meyer, H. and L. Vischer, eds. 1984. *Growth in Agreement. Reports and Agreed Statements of Ecumenical Conversations on a World Level*. Faith and Order Paper 108. Ramsey, NJ: Paulist Press; Geneva: WCC Publications.

Norwegian Catholic-Lutheran Discussion Group 1991. The Ministry of the Church. In *Statements by the Catholic-Lutheran discussion group in Norway 1982-1991*. Oslo: Church of Norway. Church Information Service.

Orthodox-Catholic International Dialogue [=O-RC] 1988. *The Sacrament of Order in the Sacramental Structure of the Church*. In Gros, Meyer and Rusch 2000, 672-679.

The Porvoo Common Statement [=Porvoo] 1993. *Together in Mission and Ministry*. The Porvoo Common Statement with Essays on Church and Ministry in Northern Europe. London: Church House Publishing.

Puglisi, James F. 1996, 1998, 2001. *The Process of Admission to Ordained Ministry. A Comparative Study*, vols. I-III. Collegeville: Liturgical Press.

Roman Catholic/Presbyterian-Reformed Consultation [=RC-P/usa] 1972. Ministry in the Church. A Statement by the Theology Section of the Roman Catholic/Presbyterian-Reformed Consultation, Richmond, Virginia October 20, 1971. *JES* 9, 589-612.

Tillard, J.-M.-R. 1973. What Priesthood has the Ministry? *OiC* 9: 242-247.

World Alliance of Reformed Churches & Secretariat for Promoting Christian Unity [=R-RC] 1977. *The Presence of Christ in Church and World.* In Meyer and Vischer 1984, 456-463.

Appendix

List of Dialogues
Exclusively on Ordained Ministry

1. *Eucharist and Ministry.* (L-RC/usa-1970). Burgess and Gros 1989, 102-124

2. *Ministry and Ordination* (ARCIC-1973). Meyer and Vischer 1984, 78-84

3. *Elucidation.* (ARCIC-1979). Meyer and Vischer 1984, 84-87

4. *Ministry in the Church.* (RC-P/usa-1971). Roman Catholic/Presbyterian-Reformed Consultation [=RC-P/usa] 1972, 589-612.

5. *Memorandum* – 1973 (6 German ecumenical institutes). Memorandum 1973, 11-25.

6. *One Baptism, One Eucharist and a Mutually Recognized Ministry* (Accra) – 1974. Faith and Order 1975.

7. *Baptism Eucharist Ministry.* (BEM) –1982. Faith and Order 1982.

8. *Towards a Reconcilaition of Ministries.* (Dombes-M) -1973. McAdoo 1975, 89-107.

9. *The episcopal ministry* – 1976, (Dombes-E). Dombes-E 1976, 267-288.

10. *Reflections on ministries* – 1977 (O-RC/ch). Chambésy 1978, 289-295.

11. *The ministry in the Church* – 1981, (L-RC-ministry). Meyer and Vischer 1984, 248-275.

12. *The sacrament of order in the sacramental structure of the Church* – 1988 (O-RC). Gros, Meyer and Rusch 2000, 672-679.

13. *The Niagra Report on «episcope»* – 1987. Gros, Meyer and Rusch 2000, 12-37

14. *The Porvoo Common Statement* – 1993. Porvoo 1993, 30f

15. *The Ministry of the Church* 1986 (L-RC/nor). Norwegian Catholic-Lutheran Discussion Group 1991.

16. *The Office of Bishop* – 1989 (L-RC/swe). Church of Sweden-Roman Catholic Diocese of Stockholm (=L-RC/swe)1989.

17. *Episcopacy* – 1987 (L-M/usa). Burgess and Gros 1995, 118-128.

18. *Joint Statement on Ministry* – 988. Burgess and Gros 1995, 495f.

Ministry in Another Context

1. *Dublin Report* – 1976 (M-RC). Meyer and Vischer 1984,356-362.

2. *Ministry* - 1976 Ch. VII (Consultation on Church Union). COCU 1977: 82-92.
3. *The presence of Christ in Church and World* – 1977 (R-RC). Meyer and Vischer 1984, 456-463.
4. *The Gospel and the Church* – 1972 (L-RC). Meyer and Vischer 1984, 179-184.
5. *Pullach Report* – 1972 (A-L). Meyer and Vischer 1984, 23-26.
6. *Facing Unity* – 1984 (L-RC-unity), §§86-149. Gros, Meyer and Rusch 2000, 443-484.
7. *Catholic response to ARCIC* I – 1991. CDF/PCPCU 1991, 441-447.
8. *Clarifications of certain aspects of the agreed statements on Eucharist and Ministry of the First ARCIC* – 1994 (ARCIC- Clarifications). ARCIC-clarifications 1991, 237-242.

Orthodox Understanding of Liturgy and Ordained Ministry with Special Reference to the Ecumenical Dialogues

Grant White

Liturgy and Theology: an Orthodox Perspective

In the past fifty years there has been something of a revival of Orthodox theology. The credit for much of this must go to many of the theologians of the Russian emigration following the Bolshevik Revolution and their successors.[1] The Institut Saint Serge in Paris and St. Vladimir's Orthodox Theological Seminary in Crestwood, New York, became major centres of this emigré theology which has significantly influenced Orthodox practice in Western countries.

Although there is a tradition of dogmatic theology in Orthodoxy, modelled after Catholic and Protestant scholastic theology, in the past forty years Orthodox theologians have argued that the classic western division of theology into the categories of systematic, moral, ascetical, liturgical, actually does more harm than good. It tears apart the living reality of *theologia*, which cannot be defined simply as systematic theology. *Theologia* embraces the entire experience of life incorporated into Christ's body, lived in the power of the Spirit, to the glory of the Father. This experience will necessarily be eschatological and ascetic, as the Church waits and watches in hope for the return of the Bridegroom. At the same time, *theologia* necessarily embraces the world, for Orthodox emphasize the Incarnation and Resurrection as God's confirmation of the goodness of the world God has created and loves so fiercely.

---

1. For a bibliography of the works of these theologians to 1971, see Zernov 1973.

The import of all this is to emphasize that for Orthodox there cannot simply be a 'theology of liturgy' existing in its own subsection of dogmatic or practical theology. Although it has become something of a cliché to say so, the truth is that we Orthodox believe that all theology is liturgical, because it is all directed to the glorification of God who has redeemed the world through Christ, in the Holy Spirit. To put the issue in terms of ordination and its theology, many Orthodox theologians today would suggest that to focus solely on a 'moment' of ordination which can be named with precise terminology which in turn can be translated from one language to another is to miss the larger point, namely, that ordination is part of what the Church does because of what it is and whose it is. Alexander Schmemann suggests that the transformation of liturgy into an object of theological inquiry represents a profound change (and a change for the worse) from an earlier, patristic view of liturgy, Church, and world in which the categories of sacred and profane had been overcome in the eschatological reality of the Church. Schmemann argues that Christian liturgy is not 'sacred' in the sense of an action intended to make something holy which is not, but that it is (now Schmemann is speaking of the Eucharist) 'sacramental, i.e., a series of transformations ultimately leading the Church, the *ecclesia*, into the fullness of the Kingdom, the only real "condition" of the transformation of the elements' (Schmemann 1990, 20). Perhaps it would be fruitful to think of ordination liturgies as well as a series of transformations – both of the Church and of the individuals being ordained.

The Shape of Ordination Liturgies in Orthodoxy

When we speak about 'ordination' in Orthodox Churches today, we have to begin with the fact that there is not one set of ordination rites used by all Orthodox around the world. There are several families of Orthodox ordination liturgies. Each liturgical family is unique, although of course there have been mutual influences and borrowings between and among them over time. In his study of ancient Christian ordination rites, Paul Bradshaw divides the Eastern Christian rites into eight families: Armenian, Byzantine, Coptic, East Syrian, Georgian, Jacobite, Maronite and Melkite. Of these, the most geographically widespread is the Byzantine, a true 'world liturgical tradition' alongside the Latin (Catholic) Rite. We must also keep in mind that of the above traditions, the Maronite and Melkite are used exclusively by Eastern Rite Catholics, and to the best of my knowledge the Byzantine, Coptic, East Syrian, and Jacobite are in use among both Orthodox and Eastern Rite Catholics.

Paul Bradshaw has argued that 'amid all the diversity of the various ordination rites of East and West can be discerned a number of elements that are found in many or all of the traditions and that seem to point to a basic pattern of practice followed in the early centuries of the Church's history with regard to the appointment of bishops, presbyters, and deacons' (Bradshaw 1990, 20). He suggests that this 'basic pattern' includes the following:

Context: Sunday Celebration of the Eucharist
Approbation by the people
Proclamation/bidding
The Prayer of the People
The Sign of the Cross
The Imposition of the Hand
The Ordination Prayer(s)
Concluding Ceremonies
   The Kiss
   Bestowal of Symbols of Office
   Declaration of Ordination

Today the actual location of the ordination liturgy within the celebration of the Eucharist varies from tradition to tradition. In addition, the East Syrian tradition allows for the ordination of presbyters and deacons outside of the Liturgy of the Eucharist, and in the Byzantine tradition deacons are ordained in the context of the Liturgy of the Presanctified, because they are able to minister at it as well as at the Sunday and feastday celebration of the Eucharist (Bradshaw 1990, 21).

The diversity of ordination prayers in the Orthodox Churches bears witness to a diversity of theological, linguistic, and even biblical traditions within Orthodoxy. There are enough differences among the Eastern Christian liturgical families that any kind of generalization about their ordination prayers is difficult. If I were to single out two emphases which I think run through all traditions, it would be the emphasis on the work of the Holy Spirit in the selection and ordination of the candidates, and the emphasis on the apostolicity of the ministries of bishop, presbyter, and deacon.

For the sake of comparison with other Nordic ordination rites, I will turn now to a few areas of common ecumenical interest. In particular, I will address the status of Orthodox ordination rites as sacraments, the role of the people in the ordination liturgies, and the technical terminological question of *cheirotonia* versus *cheirothesia*. Again I must emphasize that the diversity of Orthodox liturgies and liturgical practice today means that here I have to speak in general about Orthodox ordination liturgies, rather than with reference to any one Orthodox liturgical tradition. However, because in general the Orthodox Churches have retained the elements outlined by Bradshaw above, I will refer to that general outline.

As was the case in western Christianity until the time of Peter Lombard, the precise number of sacraments in Orthodoxy today remains a somewhat open question. Not all Orthodox count the same liturgical actions as belonging to the category of *mysteria*. For example, in the Syrian Orthodox and Church of the East traditions, the number of *raze* (a Syriac word corresponding to the Greek *mysteria)* has varied. It is worth emphasizing that this view of the number of the sacraments is basically a continuation of patristic viewpoints on the subject. Of course, one can find in patristic literature a variety of enumerations of the *mysteria*. But as with so many topics in patristic writings, those enumerations appear only occasionally, in response to a variety of questions or situations. These occasions for numbering the *mysteria* are not directly parallel to the complex of theological and philosophical issues which drove medieval western theologians to fix the number of the sacraments in the Latin Church.

Since at least the seventeenth century, Orthodox theologians of the Byzantine tradition have come to speak of seven *mysteria* of the Church, of which ordination is one. It must be noted, however, that this way of speaking about what the Church does liturgically is somewhat foreign to Orthodox theology. Yes, it has its uses in that it allows Orthodox to talk with those churches which deem it a matter of importance to delimit the number of the sacraments (both Roman Catholic and Protestant), but the danger, of course, is that by fixing the number of the sacraments we artificially remove them from the wider context of the good world created by God, a world which by virtue of its having been created by God and redeemed by Christ, is itself sacramental. I understand that speaking this way about sacraments risks disintegrating into a kind of fuzzy pantheism or nature-worship. This danger probably is one reason why Orthodox Christians insist so strongly on linking the created world with what God has done and is doing in Christ.

The role of the people in Orthodox ordination liturgies today is difficult to discuss phenomenologically, because of the diversity of Orthodox liturgical families and even of current ways of enacting the ordination liturgies. At the very least, we can note that the various Orthodox Churches have retained the approbation of the people, a practice attested already in the church order literature of the third and fourth centuries. However, one might be excused for asking precisely what the people's acclamation, 'He is worthy' has to do with the role of church members in choosing and/or ratifying their bishops, presbyters, and deacons. This is not to suggest that there is no role, but that that role bears some extended reflection. Besides the *axios,* the participation of the people depends on the context of the ordination liturgy. Thus when ordinations happen in the Divine Liturgy, then in theory there will be a congregation present and actively participating in the appropriate responses, hymns, and the Nicaeo-Constantinopolitan Creed. We need, however, to recover everywhere the Sunday celebration of the Divine Liturgy as the context for ordinations. We have departed from our tradition when we ordain bishops, presbyters, and deacons outside of that Sunday celebration.

It is something of a commonplace today that Orthodox view 'real' ordination as that act designated by the Greek term *'cheirotonia'*, and refer to mere 'appointment' or 'designation' to an office as *'cheirothesia'*. This distinction came to the fore at the beginning of the 1950s, when the debate about the ordination of female deacons began to emerge in Greece. Since then, the issue has been taken up by those arguing for and against the ordination of women to the diaconate and presbyterate in the Roman Catholic Church. However, Cyrille Vogel demonstrated in 1974 that before the eighth century the two terms were actually used interchangeably (Vogel, 7-21, 207-238). Both had to do with the liturgical action of laying hands on persons and things, not only in the context of ordination but also in Baptism and the Eucharist. The question is what theological value one attaches to the post-eighth century development, in which the terms came to be differentiated.

Orthodox Liturgical Texts in Modern Languages

Orthodox Christians sometimes claim that one of the virtues of Orthodox worship is that it is in the language of the people. We can point to the herculean labours of St. Innocent of Alaska or St. Nicholas Kassatkin in Japan as examples of Orthodox who have given their lives in large part to the translation of Orthodox liturgical texts and other writings. We also note, correctly, that Sts Cyril and Methodius translated the Byzantine liturgical texts into the South Slavic language of the day, inventing an alphabet for that language in the process. All these statements are true, but they reflect only part of the reality. Less often discussed is the fact that many parishes in Europe (and in North America, although less frequently) continue to celebrate the Divine Liturgy in Church Slavonic or Byzantine Greek, while others use the languages of the national groups from which the founders of the parish originally came. Thus Orthodoxy has come to be identified in some parishes with the use of a particular language (whether Slavonic or Greek or Romanian or other). We can see here of course the dynamics of national and/or ethnic identity, in which the retention of the mother tongue is intended to help *diaspora* communities maintain their social cohesion. Use of the mother tongue in worship obviously helps recent immigrants and older immigrants unable to use the common language(s) of the society in which they live. But its exclusive use raises an often insuperable barrier between the Church and those who are interested in joining it. Thus the issue of which languages to use in liturgical celebrations concerns the mission of the Church as well as the Church's liturgical practice.

In the case of the Byzantine tradition, most of the translation of the Divine Liturgy and of other texts has taken place in missionary contexts such as Japan, Central Asia, China, and Alaska. Translation at least of the Divine Liturgy into modern western European languages has also taken place. As early as 1865 the Holy Synod of the Russian Orthodox Church called for the translation of liturgical texts into Finnish, a move which can be understood in the context of the mid-nineteenth century rise of nationalism and movements for the use of national vernaculars rather than the language of the imperial rulers.

We must distinguish here between mission and *diaspora*. Today one often hears the Orthodox Churches of North America and Western Europe referred to as 'diaspora churches'. I question this view, and the linguistic assumptions accompanying it. I wonder if the category of *diaspora* has any theological meaning when one is talking about the one, holy, catholic and apostolic Church. In other words, can the Church ever be in *diaspora* when its fundamental quality is catholicity? Or, to put the question in other terms, if eschatological waiting in hope for the consummation of God's will for all the cosmos is the *sine qua non* of the Church's life, then either *diaspora* is a universal situation, or none of us live in *diaspora*, or both are the case.

To say all this is not to question the fact that there exist in the Nordic countries, Western Europe and North America Orthodox communities made up of people who are refugees, exiles torn from their homelands and forced to live in cultures often radically different from their own or that respect for basic human rights, not to mention veneration of the image of God in all human beings, means that people must be allowed to use their native tongue. What I am questioning is the false identification of Orthodoxy with any single language or, if you will, the notion that, in order to embrace Orthodoxy, it is necessary also to embrace a particular ethnic or linguistic identity.

Ordination: Orthodox Perspectives

If we take seriously the above critiques of the classical western separation of theology from liturgy and ethics, our discussion of the theology of ordination must begin from the liturgical texts themselves rather than from more abstract statements. At the same time, Orthodox participation in bilateral and multilateral ecumenical conversations since the inception of the Ecumenical Movement necessitates our also taking seriously what Orthodox have said about ordination in such contexts. The question of texts is too large to address here, except again to note the tradition of ordaining within the Sunday celebration of the Eucharist. Once again, a comprehensive treatment of each of these topics lies beyond the scope of this article. However, I hope at least to identify some major themes.

Let us turn first to what Orthodox Christians have said in ecumenical discussion about ordination and ministry. I take these statements to be particularly important because they represent Orthodox attempts to formulate their views in comparison and contrast to and with other churches. In some sense they are the most recent ecclesial discussions of ordination and ministry, even if they do not have the authority which a statement of a Great and Holy Council would possess. I must also emphasize here that Orthodox see the necessity and importance of participation in ecumenical conversation. There is no question here of withdrawal from ecumenical engagement, in spite of the difficulties Orthodox have had in the World Council of Churches in recent years.

The sources I shall briefly discuss come from bilateral and multilateral conversations. Not surprisingly, the Orthodox-Roman Catholic bilateral dialogue has discussed ordination in the most depth. The 1986 statement of the U.S. Orthodox-Roman Catholic Theological Consultation on Apostolicity affirms the sacramentality of apostolicity. After having located the experience of apostolicity in 'the mystery of Christian initiation', the statement notes that 'as an essential element in the life of the whole Church and of every Christian, apostolicity therefore is by no means unique to or limited to the realm of hierarchical ministry' (U.S. O-RC 1996, par. 9, 127). At the same time, however, the Consultation goes on to discuss apostolicity and the ordained ministry:

In our consultation attention was drawn to at least two corollaries which may follow from this understanding of apostolic faith: (a) The apostolicity of ministry is generally seen as derived from the continuity of the community as a whole in apostolic life and faith: the succession of ministers in office is normally agreed to be subordinate to that ecclesial apostolicity. (b) Apostolicity seems to consist more in fidelity to the apostles' proclamation and mission than in any one form of handing on community office. These observations alert us once again to the danger of reducing apostolicity simply to forms and institutional structures. Yet we also must resist any temptation to locate apostolicity in what is merely individual or in what falls outside the mediated nature of the divine economy – as happened and still happens, for example, in the gnostic claim to immediate experience. Apostolicity is experienced not in atemporal isolation but rather in the Church's social nature as a community of faith and in its historical continuity and permanence – even in concrete forms and patterns once given the Church's life by its relation to the civilization of the Greco-Roman world (U.S. O-RC 1996, par. 10, 127-128).

For our purposes I underscore the statement's emphasis on what it calls the 'historical continuity and permanence' of the Church as a necessary *locus* of experiencing apostolicity today. Thus apostolicity must be rooted in 'the mediated nature of the divine economy'. To put it in western theological terminology, there is a sacramentality to apostolicity, including the apostolicity of the ordained ministry. Orthodox would say that apostolicity is necessarily related to the *mysteria* celebrated by the Church, which in turn are rooted in the *mysterion* of the saving will and action of God in Christ, through the Holy Spirit. What for other Christian traditions (even after the influence of the Liturgical Movement) might seem to be a liturgical conservatism or even simple adherence to hidebound forms is seen in its authentic light as an expression of that very insistence on the necessity of our experiencing apostolicity within the historical, concrete parameters of 'the mediated nature of the divine economy'.

The Joint International Theological Comission met in 1988 at New Valamo, Finland, and produced the text with the unwieldy title: 'The Sacrament of Order in the Sacramental Structure of the Church with Particular Reference to the Importance of Apostolic Succession for the Sanctification and Unity of the People of God'. The text speaks of the ordination of bishops 'under its sacramental aspect':

> Episcopal ordination, which according to the canons is conferred by at least two or three bishops, expresses the communion of the churches with that of the person selected: It makes him a member of the communion of bishops. In ordination the bishops exercise their function as witnesses to the communion in the apostolic faith and sacramental life not only with respect to him whom they ordain, but also with respect to the church of which he will be bishop. What is fundamental for the incorporation of the newly elected person in the episcopal communion is that it is accomplished by the glorified Lord in the power of the Holy Spirit at the moment of the imposition of hands (JI O-RC (1988), par. 27, 136).

The Commission goes on to say, 'Episcopal ordination confers on the one who receives it by the gift of the Spirit, the fullness of the priesthood . . . [the bishops] lay hands and invoke the Holy Spirit on the one who will be ordained as the only ones qualified to confer on him the episcopal ministry. They do it, however, within the setting of the prayer of the community' ((JI O-RC (1988), par. 28, 136). The 1989 *Joint Reaction* of the U.S. Orthodox-Roman Catholic Consultation does not comment on these two paragraphs, although it contains several critiques of the New Valamo statement.

A year earlier the Joint Committee of Orthodox and Catholic Bishops (United States) had issued a short declaration on ordination which outlined three 'general points of agreement': (1) the three sacred orders of diaconate, presbyterate and episcopate have a sacramental nature; (2) these orders are exclusively conferred by bishops with unquestionable apostolic succession; and (3) ordination implies a setting apart' (JO O-C (1988), 150). In addition, for both Catholics and Orthodox, ordination is permanent, hence, 'the sacred ordination never becomes invalid' (JO O-C (1988), 151). Each church accounts for this permanence of ordination in different theological terms, although the text explicitly discusses only the Roman Catholic theology of sacramental character.

To summarize these statements, Orthodox in dialogue with Roman Catholics have produced statements which stress the consonance and even commonality of the two traditions' views on ministry and ordination. Yet Orthodox note differences between themselves and Catholics. A good example is the common affirmation at New Valamo of the invocation of the Holy Spirit at the moment of the laying-on of hands coupled with the distinction the 1988 American Consultation makes between Orthodox and Catholic terminology with regard to the permanence of ordination. The future of this dialogue is unclear in view of the near-collapse of the relationship between the two churches following the fall of Communism in 1989.

Orthodox-Lutheran Bilateral Conversations

In his extensive study of Orthodox-Lutheran dialogue from 1959 to 1994, Risto Saarinen discusses the topic of ordained ministry as a dialogue subject (Saarinen 1997, 116-127, 133-137, 257-265). Saarinen suggests that perhaps the most significant acheivement of this dialogue in its many forms was reached by the 1986 Sofia consultation between the then-*Bund der Evangelischen Kirchen in der DDR* and the Bulgarian Orthodox Church. He says,

A common theology of ordination is outlined in which both churches affirm 1) external and internal vocation, 2) episcopal ordination, 3) the consent of the congregation, 4) prayer, invocation of the Holy Spirit and laying-on of hands in ordination liturgy. Differences are listed in 1) the closer understanding of the sacramentality of ordination, 2) the hierarchical gradation of ministry, 3) the content of apostolic succession and 4) the ordination of women (Saarinen 1997, 261).

At the same time, Saarinen detects a significant difficulty in this bilateral dialogue with the entire question of ecclesiology. Of the Orthodox side he notes: 'Throughout the dialogue documentation one can perceive a certain *lack of interest* towards developing concrete ecclesiology. Although the global dialogue was to discuss ecclesiology as its first topic . . . the extensive preparatory material does not offer much in terms of concrete models' (Saarinen 1997, 263-264). This lack of concrete views of the church also hindered the Lutheran side in more than dialogue. Saarinen suggests further that the lack of constructive ecclesiological proposals was due to the predominance in the dialogues of a Russian Orthodox 'school theology' which 'stressed the external observance of canonical rules, especially that of the apostolic succession of bishops' (Saarinen 1997, 263). In the light of the Orthodox-Roman Catholic statements above stressing the necessity of concrete, historical manifestations of apostolicity, Saarinen's characterization here of the Orthodox position on apostolic succession needs to be rethought.

Orthodox Responses to BEM

If Orthodox (at least until recently) have stressed the consonances and commonalities between Orthodox and Roman Catholic theologies and practices of ordination, the situation is slightly different with the Orthodox responses to the 1982 Faith and Order convergence text *Baptism, Eucharist, and Ministry*. The responses of the churches to BEM were collected from 1986 to 1988 in the six volumes of *Churches Respond to BEM*. Later studies analysed the responses in the hope of further Faith and Order work toward a common expression of the apostolic faith today (Faith and Order 1990). In general, the most critical Orthodox responses to BEM related to its Ministry section. In particular, more than one Orthodox response criticized the document for not explicitly stating that ordination was a sacrament, that in some places the document seemed to imply that ministry was simply representative, and that the document did not stress the importance of the concrete office of bishop, as opposed to the more general notion of *episkopé* or oversight. It is not surprising that the Orthodox responses in the multilateral context of Faith and

Order would be heavily critical. I think that the responses reflect in part the well-known Orthodox fears that the World Council of Churches has marginalized Orthodox theological concerns.

Conclusion and Open Issues

From what I have said above about the shape of Orthodox Christian ordination rites, it becomes clear that there is a gap between the clarity and relative simplicity of the early rites and the rites as they are today. This distance between early and present ordination rites presents something of a problem for anyone wanting, on the basis of the liturgical traditions themselves, to describe the theology of ordination in Orthodox tradition. For if one proceeds from the rites themselves, one must ask the difficult question: which phase in the history of the rites is authoritative? There is no consensus on this question among Orthodox theologians. For the representatives of the so-called 'neo-patristic' school, the Fathers' teaching embodies the norm of Orthodox theology. However, one must be careful not to read Lossky, Florovsky and others as reading the patristic tradition as narrowly as Protestant theologians. That is, that although Protestant theology tends to conclude the patristic period with Augustine, Orthodox theology does not. Of course, many Orthodox theologians would disagree with the very notion that the periodization of history has theological value. And so, some Orthodox theologians have spoken of the patristic period extending to the present. This statement is theological, not historical. That is, the authority of the Fathers (i.e., of Tradition) extends to theologians up to the present time. Historicism is (in theory) excluded as an option.

And yet, other Orthodox theologians today offer one or another version of what my teacher Robert Taft used to refer to as the 'pick-a-century game'. Or perhaps, I might add, the 'pick-a-nation' game. Whether it be pre-1917 Russian Orthodox practice, eighth century Constantinopolitan rubrics, or some other rosy past, there is also in Orthodox theological circles today the desire to go back somehow. In these times of post-Communist searching for a viable identity, Orthodox around the world (not only in those countries whose peoples suffered under Communist tyranny) often evince the desire to return to eras and positions of authority gone forever. There is also here a sense of reaction against, or at the very least response to, a world whose technology expands more quickly than we have the capacity to respond, a world in which ancient hatreds, fuelled in part by religious allegiances, have proved stubbornly, perversely resistant to the death others wish for them. I suggest that this theological road leads to the proverbial dead-end. In the past twenty years,

Orthodox theology of this vein has been particularly susceptible to the influence of nationalism, an ideology denying the very catholicity of the Church. In spite of the firm embrace of neo-patristic theology by Orthodox theologians in western countries, the fact of continuing jurisdictionalism in those countries suggests that neo-patristic theology is not a compelling alternative to the ideology of national and ethnic identity.[2] These are pessimistic reflections, to be sure. But we had first to outline the theological landscape today before proceeding to describe an Orthodox theology of ordination.

We must now turn to the question regarding what method to use in accounting for Orthodox theology of ordination, especially in the context of these collected articles and the ecumenical conversation they represent. In my view, the most helpful way is to discuss Orthodox views with an eye to Protestant and Catholic theologies of ordination. The advantage of this approach is that it at least tries to engage other theological traditions as it attempts to account for its own. The disadvantage is that there is the potential for polemic and misrepresentation of other views. I shall do my best to avoid the latter, but I leave it to the reader to decide if I have been successful.

Obviously, one could write several volumes on this subject. Let me simply suggest three points of comparison in the hope that others will continue the conversation.

The Bishop, Ministry and Sacramentality

In Orthodox practice, God ordains by the hand of the bishop. There can be no ordination without the bishop. Unlike many if not all Protestant traditions (I count here the Anglican tradition as separate), episcopal polity is not an arbitrary decision of the Church, subject to change, but is the will of God for the Church. We return to the argument about history to which I alluded above. Orthodox believe that the bishop is of the *esse* of the Church. There is an argument here about the role of the bishop involving more than simply 'good order' or 'authority'. The bishop is a sign and a guarantee of the apostolicity and catholicity of the Church, and thus is the one by whose hand God ordains. Readers will note here the similarity to Catholic teaching, although the issue of the ecclesiological function of the Pope makes the comparison inexact. As is well known, the large disagreements about ministry which sur-

---

2. An exception is Finland, which so far has successfully resisted the jurisdictionalism found in neighbouring Sweden, for example. We should also note that the existence of SCOBA in North America, and of such organizations as Orthodox Christian Laity, point to the possibility of change.

faced in the churches' responses to the 1982 Faith and Order text *Baptism, Eucharist and Ministry* (BEM) in no small measure had to do with objections to the text's suggestion that the threefold ministry of bishop, deacon, and presbyter was somehow normative. I would also suggest that the objection to a normative threefold ministry correlates with objection to what some responses called the 'sacramentalizing' tone of BEM. Does substituting *episkopé* for *episkopos* solve the problem? Probably not for Orthodox, although it is premature to shut the door on the question.

Eucharist and the Functions of Ordained Minstry

The early liturgical texts and references to ordination more often than not say that ordination takes place on Sunday, in the context of the celebration of the Eucharist. As to the former, this practice has died out in much of the Orthodox world. As for the latter, it continues to serve as the context for the ordination of presbyters and bishops, and in some churches for deacons as well. Although some of the reformed Protestant ordination rites suggest that ordination take place in the context of the Eucharist (and of course this is normative in Catholic practice), as far as I am aware the Eucharist is not a mandatory or normative context. I stress this point because for Orthodox and Catholics alike, the function of ordained ministries has to do fundamentally with liturgical roles at the celebration of the Eucharist. I want to be clear here: I am not saying that other Christian traditions do not also link ordained ministry with liturgical roles, or that other Christian traditions do not view presidency at the Eucharist as a function of ordained ministry. However, the question is about the necessary relationship between Eucharist and ordained ministry – and here I think Orthodox, Roman Catholics and Anglicans are much closer to each other than they are to Protestants.

The conversation becomes more difficult, it seems to me, when our partners in the context of ecumenical discussion of ordained ministry assume that Orthodox automatically view the exercise (and even existence!) of ordained ministry as somehow a defense of heavy-handed authority, oppression, and injustice through hierarchy. Of course, in the past and even now some Orthodox bishops, priests, and deacons have been heavy-handed, oppressive, and unjust. But Orthodox see such realities not as signs that the system itself is flawed, but rather as evidence that fallible human beings exercise these ministries.

Related to these matters of system and power is the question of ordination as a 'right'. Although no Christian tradition possessing an ordained ministry asserts (to the best of my knowledge) that every member of the church has the right to be ordained if he or she wishes, still it is the case that rights-based language is largely foreign to Orthodox theological tradition. Some will view this fact as evidence of the shortcomings of Orthodox ethics! Perhaps a more balanced view will suggest that the question of who can or cannot be ordained cannot be discussed adequately using terminology and assumptions deriving from eighteenth century political philosophy, but that the Tradition itself must be more thoroughly understood and embraced in order to talk adequately and fruitfully about this question. Still, Orthodox would do well to ask ourselves how then the Tradition mandates our acting for justice. Obviously, the Scriptures and the Fathers (look at Chrysostom, for example) give us a solid foundation for such action – but the hard work of engaging the Tradition on this point remains to be done.

Ministry and the Iconic

There is a long tradition in Christianity, beginning with Ignatius of Antioch, of viewing bishops, deacons and presbyters as icons of God and the Apostles. In Orthodox tradition, ordination involves the bestowal of that iconic character. Obviously, we can spot here a circle in which one's view of God will shape how one sees the clergy, which in turn moulds how we see God, and so on. If one assumes that hierarchy represents oppression and injustice, then of course one will immediately dismiss an iconic view of ordained ministry as a means of perpetuating oppression and injustice. Or perhaps if one professes a 'low' theological anthropology, one might question the very possibility at all of human beings serving as icons of God.

However, an iconic understanding of ordained ministry can also proclaim a foundational reliance on the grace of God, as well as a theological anthropology that takes sin seriously but still maintains that *synergeia* is possible and necessary. I think that this Orthodox perspective is related to, but differs somewhat from the discussion in Roman Catholic tradition around the function of the priest *in persona Christi* in the Eucharist – it is a different discussion, but related. However, I think Orthodox theology can develop in drawing the theological implications of an iconic view of ordained ministry, for the whole Church. That is, one can argue that the iconic character of ordained ministry is a gift of God, but one which is grounded in the fundamental possession of the image of God that all human beings have. If ordination bestows an iconic character on ordained ministry, how does baptism grant all Christians the gracious gift, through the Spirit, also of possessing an iconic character? And further, how does this iconic character – of both the ordained and all the baptized – bestow on us the gift and responsibility to discern more fully and actively the image of God in our neighbour?

References

Borelli, John, and Erickson, John H. (eds). 1996. *The Quest for Unity: Orthodox and Catholics in Dialogue.* Crestwood, New York and Washington, D.C.: St. Vladimir's Seminary Press and United States Catholic Conference.

Bradshaw, Paul. 1990. *Ordination Rites of the Ancient Churches of East and West.* New York: Pueblo.

Faith and Order. 1990. *Baptism, Eucharist & Ministry. Report on the Process and Responses.* 1990. Faith and Order Paper 149. Geneva: World Council of Churches.

Joint Committee of Orthodox and Catholic Bishops. (1988) (JO O-C). 1996. *Ordination (1 October 1988).* In Borelli and Erickson 1996.

Joint International Orthodox-Roman Catholic Theological Commission (1988) (JI O-RC). *The Sacrament of Order in the Sacramental Structure of the Church, with Particular Reference to the Importance of Apostolic Succession for the Sanctification and Unity of the People of God.* In Borelli and Erickson 1996.

Saarinen, Risto. 1997. Faith and Holiness: *Lutheran-Orthodox Dialogue 1959-1994. Kirche und Konfession* 40. Göttingen: Vandenhoeck & Ruprecht.

Schmemann, Alexander.1990.Theology and Liturgical Tradition, In *Liturgy and Tradition: Theological Reflections of Alexander Schmemann,* ed. Thomas Fisch. Crestwood, New York: St. Vladimir's Seminary Press.

U.S. Orthodox-Roman Catholic Theological Consultation (U.S. O-RC). 1996. Apostolicity as God's Gift in the Life of the Church. In Borelli and Erickson 1996.

Vogel, Cyrille. 1972. Chirotonie et chirothésie. Importance et relativité du geste de l'imposition des mains dans la collation des ordres. *Irénikon* 45: 7-21, 207-238.

Zernov, Nicolas (ed.). 1973. Russian Emigré Authors: A Biographical Index and Bibliography of Their Works on Theology, Religious Philosophy, Church History and Orthodox Culture 1921-1971. Boston: Hall & Co. Russian title: Русские писатели эмиграции: библиографические сведения и библиография их книг по богословию, религиозной философии, церковной истории и православной культуре.

2. Liturgical Perspectives

Ordination is a liturgical process. Thus the theology of ordination depends fundamentally on the concept of liturgy in the ordaining church. Historically and ecumenically the relationship between theology and liturgy varies from radical Protestant Churches, where liturgy is primarily a channel for the communication of theology, to Orthodox Churches, where theology basically is liturgy, as there are no other, or at least no better places to gain theological insight than the liturgy. In between these two positions we find the Roman Catholic Church, which makes a distinction between theology and liturgy, but most certainly also has a distinct theology of liturgy.

Paul De Clerck introduces the Roman Catholic understanding of liturgy in the context of the Second Vatican Council's teaching on liturgy. Liturgy for the Catholic Church is actions of God, mediated by human beings, that is Christian congregations and their liturgical leaders. Thus liturgy is a basic source for the understanding of the work of God as well as the identity of the Church as the Church is being recreated by God through the liturgy – in Baptism and the Eucharist and at Ordination as well.

Päivi Jussila outlines a modern Lutheran understanding of liturgy as an interrelation of love, knowledge and prayer. Not unlike the Orthodox Church she perceives liturgy as a process of transformation. Liturgy is the language of the Christian community, through which it participates in the fellowship of the Trinitarian God. In the power of the love of God, the love to God, created in the liturgy, leads the community to knowledge about the will of God – alongside transforming its members as individuals – through Baptism, Eucharist and Ordination.

Ninna Edgardh Beckmann discusses the relevance of gender in ordination rites. She sees the lack of gender reflections in this field so far as a result of the necessity for female theologians to use the rites as entrance to the authority of a pastor, as this possibility has been opened only little by little in the Nordic Churches during the last 50 years. However, the current interest in feminist rituals is likely to affect study of the forms, theology and language of ordination rites in order to transform the present rites in a more gender conscious way.

A Catholic Understanding of Liturgy

Paul De Clerck

It could be said that liturgy is like Janus, the Roman god of beginnings, as it too is a double-headed entity. On the one hand it is human action, which requires a gathering of men and women. Thus, it is visible, recognizable and situated in time and space. On the other hand, the nature of liturgical action is spiritual. It is not simply a question of a sport, an art or another cultural activity as it contains texts presented as the Word of God and other texts, called prayers, which are addressed to God.

Liturgy therefore shares in the *ambivalent* nature of the Church. It has two charges:

> The Church is essentially both human and divine, visible but endowed with invisible realities, zealous in action and dedicated to contemplation, present in the world, but as a pilgrim, so constituted that in her the human is directed toward and subordinated to the divine, the visible to the invisible, action to contemplation, and this present world to that city yet to come, the object of our quest.[1]

After developing this characteristic of the liturgy, I will show the relationship between liturgy and theology; I will highlight the goal of liturgy as a passage for the assembly to enter into the mystery of Christ, and I will address the relationship between liturgy and culture.[2]

---

1. Second Vatican Council's Constitution on the Sacred Liturgy, *Sacrosantum concilium*, 2.
2. A recent overview of Catholic liturgy can be found in the handbook of the Pontifical Liturgical Institute of Rome: A. J. Chupungco (ed.), *Handbook for Liturgical Studies*, 5 vols. Collegeville: The Liturgical Press, 1997-2000. More specifically on the theology of the liturgy, see P. De Clerck (ed.), *La liturgie, lieu théologique*. Paris, Beauchesne, series

A Divine Action Realized by the Mediation of a Human Action

As soon as one speaks of liturgy or sacramental realities, the term 'mediation' is essential. It signals, in effect, the ambivalent nature of the realities addressed above. It allows for the movement and the relationship between ecclesial action and the work of God to be achieved.

Let us take baptism as an example. It is clear for everyone that this sacrament is an action of the Church, celebrated on such-and-such a day, at such-and-such a time, with certain people and according to a prescribed rite. Yet, it includes prayers addressed to God, which force us to consider that this action of the Church is not limited to terrestrial (worldly) activity. This is even clearer in the light of the profession of faith, which is not an affirmation of the qualities of a group, as a national anthem or the platform of a political party would be. It names God, a God who is Trinity. What is more, it initiates a relationship between this triune God, those baptized on this day and the other members of the assembly, because the rite asks *them all*: '*Do you believe* in God the Father..., in Jesus Christ..., in the Holy Spirit...?'

This analysis of the liturgical action thus underscores its ambivalent nature. Baptism cannot be defined simply as a celebration of the birth of a child or of the conversion of an adult, or even as the way in which a group reinforces itself. The existence of prayers, in its unfolding, serves to break the human circle, to allow the 'breaking-in' of another partner. In addition, these prayers ask this invisible Partner to accomplish the most decisive actions of baptism: to make one pass from death to life, to infuse the Holy Spirit, to aggregate to the community. A divine action is accomplished through the mediation of a phenomenal activity.

This example draws our attention to the nature of the minister of the liturgy and makes the connection with ordinations. In liturgy, it is essential never to confuse the liturgical actor and the author of grace! The prayers in which we ask God to act and the texts which in general accompany the action should keep us from making this error. In a broader sense, the analysis we have made of baptism underscores the fact that the principal actor of the liturgy is Christ and his Spirit:

Sciences théologiques et religieuses 9, 1999 and De Clerck 'Une théologie de la liturgie. "Pour la gloire de Dieu et le salut du monde"', in *La Maison-Dieu* 221, 2000/1, 7-30 (English trans: 'Theology of the Liturgy: "For the glory of God and the salvation of the world."', in *Studia Liturgica* 30, 2000/1, p. 14-31.

The liturgy, then, is rightly seen as an exercise of the priestly office of Jesus Christ. It involves the presentation of man's sanctification under the guise of signs perceptible by the senses and its accomplishment in ways appropriate to each of these signs. In it full public worship is performed by the Mystical Body of Jesus Christ, that is, by the Head and his members. From this it follows that every liturgical celebration, because it is an action of Christ the Priest and of His Body, which is the Church, is a sacred action surpassing all others. No other action of the Church can equal its efficacy by the same title and to the same degree.[3]

This passage expresses very well that the principal actor is God, even if the action is realized by the Body of Christ which is the Church.

In the vocabulary used by many writers in this book, the Catholic notion of liturgy understands this action as 'instrumental' much more than as 'expressive'.

Liturgy, Faith and Theology: Their Interrelationship

We can affirm that liturgy is a theological discipline, even if it is not clear for everyone, including some in the Catholic world. For the most part in academic programmes liturgy does not receive the same status as would exegesis or Christology. Is it possible to deepen the relationship between theology and liturgy?

Let us return to the example of baptism. It includes, as we have said, a profession of faith. Moreover, baptism is its birthplace: it is in the baptismal liturgy that the different 'symbols of faith' were hammered-out, since it is these symbols that the catechumens proclaim on being thrice plunged into the saving waters. According to the model of the New Testament, the profession of faith had a Trinitarian structure. It has also known augmentation over the centuries, as a result of doctrinal developments; this is how the Symbol of Nicaea became that of Nicaea-Constantinople and integrated some pneumatological elements defined by the council of Constantinople (381). This demonstrates that the liturgy depends on theology, more precisely on Christian doctrine that the Church receives from Scripture and reflects on over the course of centuries. Thus, it is theology that influences the liturgy.

Yet, the Catholic idea of liturgy also maintains that liturgy is a vehicle which brings to life the fundamentals of faith. This idea recalls in this sense the adage

---

3. Constitution on the Sacred Liturgy, 7.

lex orandi, lex credendi, in which the word order indicates that the influence goes from the liturgy tòward faith.[4]

In the general sense, the adage underlines that the liturgy makes the baptized enter more deeply into the Christian mystery. It highlights that the liturgy cannot be completely defined as a collection of rites which guarantee the identity of a human group. Its celebration has no other aim than to recreate the paschal mystery. Thus, after the proclamation of the Gospel, Catholic liturgy puts this acclamation on the lips of the assembly: 'Praise to You, Lord, Jesus Christ'; it indicates clearly who is the author of the Word that has just been heard and who it is that just spoke to those he loves. In the same broad sense of the adage, we can say that the fact that an ordination rite exists, announces an essential fact of the Church with respect to her ministers. If ordinations are celebrated in the context of a liturgy, it must not be simply a question of conferring ecclesiastical powers, without which the celebration would be useless, or simply a question of following protocol. The adage suggests that, if the Church celebrates an *ordination liturgy*, it must do so by virtue of the faith of which, in one way or another, God is the author. The *lex orandi*, in this case the manner by which the Church ordains, makes us understand the *lex credendi*, the theological interpretation of ordination.

The adage originally had a more precise meaning. In the thought of its author, Prosper of Aquitaine, disciple of Saint Augustine and secretary of Leo the Great, the *lex orandi* makes it possible to know the *lex credendi*. The phrase from which the adage is derived expresses the idea thus: *ut legem credendi lex statuat supplicandi*, in order that the commission of praying (allusion to 1 Tim 2.1-2 where prayers for all human beings are asked) determines the law of belief, i.e. the true faith (in the context, faith in the grace of God, in opposition to the semi-Pelagians.) Thus, it was originally an heuristic principle; study of the liturgy allows one to know the true faith. This reinforces the idea of the liturgy as the action *par excellence* of the Church. But this heuristic principle can only be considered valid today if the liturgical inquiry is done fully, that is, if it is based on the history of liturgy and comparative liturgy. For it is not any liturgical fact, taken haphazardly, to which can be ascribed such an important

---

4. On the various understandings of this maxim, see P. De Clerck, '"*Lex orandi, lex credendi*": Sens originel et avatars historiques d'un adage équivoque', in *Questions Liturgiques* 59, 1978, 193-212. (English trans. by Th. Winger: '"*Lex orandi, lex credendi*": The original Sense and historical Avatars of an equivocal Adage', in *Studia Liturgica* 24, 1994/2, 178-200), and De Clerck '"*Lex orandi, lex credendi*": Un principe heuristique', in *La Maison-Dieu* 222, 2000/2, 61-78.

epistemological value. In Prosper's argument, the *lex orandi* signified first of all the biblical foundation (here 1 Tim 2.1-2), then the ecclesiastical reception, i.e. the fact that the churches throughout the world put into practice this law in the prayers of intercession and, at a third level, the content itself of the prayer which asks God for the grace of conversion.

An example of this would be the presence of an *epiclesis* in the eucharistic prayers. We know that the Roman Canon, the only eucharistic prayer of the early Roman rite, does not have a very pneumatological *epiclesis*, unlike all of the Eucharistic prayers of the other liturgical families. Comparative liturgy teaches us thus therefore about the *lex orandi*, and it enriches the *lex credendi*, here the theology of the Eucharist, showing that it integrates the role of the Holy Spirit.

The Aim of the Liturgy: to Become the Body of Christ

The liturgy is a celebration in which the subject is the People of God, who are gathered, not simply the minister. The theoretical proof is that all the liturgical prayers are composed in the plural 'we'; only a few, those which have a devotional character, are written in the singular 'I'. The fact that the majority of the prayers are expressed by the minister, in the name of the assembly, often gives the opposite impression, as if the priest were associating the assembly with his own action. The invitational character of the liturgy allows us to understand nevertheless that even if it is the minister who proclaims the prayer, it is the whole assembly which prays. The prayers are preceded, in the Roman liturgy at least, by an invitation, said by the minister in the plural: 'Let us pray'. These words invite all of the participants to enter into the prayer, silently, while the minister 'collects' (a Gallican term, used today by the Roman liturgy to describe the opening prayer of the Mass) the prayer of the assembly and expresses it out loud.[5]

The participation of the assembly is therefore an essential element of all liturgical activity. The principle is evident, even though clergy and laity alike may still thwart it with current secular habits. The Conciliar Constitution on the Sacred Liturgy understands it in this way:

> Mother Church earnestly desires that all the faithful should be led to that full, conscious, and active participation in liturgical celebrations which is

---

5. See P. De Clerck, 'Le caractère ecclésial des oraisons', in *La Maison-Dieu* 196, 1993/4, 71-86.

demanded by the very nature of the liturgy, and to which the Christian people, 'a chosen race, a royal priesthood, a holy nation, a redeemed people' (1 Pet 2.9, 4-5) have a right and obligation by reason of their baptism.

> In the restoration and promotion of the sacred liturgy the full and active participation by all the people is the aim to be considered before all else, for it is the primary and indispensable source from which the faithful are to derive the true Christian spirit. Therefore, in all their apostolic activity, pastors of souls should energetically set about achieving it through the requisite pedagogy (Constitution on the Sacred Liturgy 14, §1 and 2).

This quotation expresses well that participation is not a 'fad' but that it corresponds to the nature itself of the liturgy, work of the Body of Christ which is commissioned by virtue of its baptism. It also designates the liturgy as the primary and indispensable source of Christian life, contrary to the personal devotions which for so long were the nourishment of the Christian people.

If the liturgy has for its subject the People of God and concretely the assembly gathered for the celebration, it has as its aim the transformation of this assembly into the Body of Christ, in the Spirit. As grapes in a vat are pressed into wine, catechumens become Christians by the process of initiation. The goal of liturgy is to ensure that the people who have gathered will be converted by hearing the Word of God and becoming more fully the Body of Christ.

Augustine and the Ecclesial Concept of the Eucharist

This goal was clearly that which Saint Augustine ascribed to the Eucharist, and especially to communion. Several of his sermons to neophytes comment on the act of communion in this way:

> Brothers, these mysteries carry the name 'sacraments', because the appearance does not correspond to their profound reality. What do we see? A material object. But the spirit discerns a spiritual grace. Do you want to understand this body of Christ and his members? Listen to the Apostle saying to the faithful: 'You are the body of Christ and his members.'
> (1 Cor. 12. 27)

> If you are the body and members of Christ, then it is your sacrament that is placed on the table of the Lord; it is your sacrament that you receive. To that which you are, you respond 'Amen', and by responding to it you assent

to it. For you hear the words, 'the Body of Christ' and you respond 'Amen'. Be then a member of the Body of Christ that your 'Amen' may be true [PL 38, 1247; CCC 1396]. [6]

A prayer after communion expresses it very clearly:

Lord our God,
allow us to find in this communion
our strength and our joy,
so that we may become
what we have received, the Body of Christ.[7]

Mystagogia

The most properly liturgical way of arriving at this evangelical and ecclesiastical goal is expressed by the term *'mystagogia'*, a Greek word which means 'entrance into the mystery'. *Mystagogia* entails, first of all, a manner of celebrating liturgical actions with respect, subtlety and exactness so that one can see right away that this celebration is a matter of something other than just a meeting or a show. Here we touch upon what is called the 'art of celebrating', because it is not only a question of knowledge [*savoir*], a *logos*, but also of know-how [*savoir-faire*], an *ergon* (in Greek: work). This art is perceived in the gathering when the assembly *knows how* to listen to the Word of God, *knows how* to approach the altar, *knows how* to sing together. It is a particularly important requirement for some of the actors, that is, the lectors, the cantors, the ministers of hospitality, and above all the priest who is charged with the sacramental representation of Christ.

Mystagogia also designates the liturgical period which occurs between Easter and Pentecost and concludes the process of Christian Initiation. According to the *RCIA* [Rite of Christian Initiation of Adults (1972)], at the Easter Vigil the catechumens are baptized, confirmed and invited to participate for the first time fully in the Eucharist. Yet, this celebration opens the 'Period of *Mystagogia*' so that they might receive all that has been given them. This liturgical time has a symbolic nature; it shows that while Christian initiation is finished, the Christian life is never finished; it manifests the interplay between the

---

6. Saint Augustine, *Sermon* 272 to the neophytes: PL 38, 1247; CCC 1396.
7. *Missel romain*, Post Communion prayer, 27th Sunday in Ordinary Time (translation from the French missal).

precise moment when the sacraments are celebrated and the lifetime during which they must be put into action. In this sense, the period of *mystagogia* highlights an important dimension of the liturgy — the constant return to and the continual deepening of what God gives to us once and for all.

Mens Concordet Voci

This liturgical dynamic, too, is well expressed by a maxim taken from the Rule of Saint Benedict (ca. 540). He begins his work by describing how to pray the Divine Office and the Psalms. It is only at the end of these instructions that he expresses in what spirit *Opus Dei* [the Work of God] should be done: *ut mens nostra concordet voci nostrae*, so that our spirit would be in harmony with what our voices say. Our voice, in this instance, is truly the recitation of the psalms, but its goal is the transformation of our '*mens*', translated 'spirit', 'soul', even 'interiority'. The maxim illustrates a fundamental law of liturgy; it begins by an act, corporal in nature, in this case the recitation of the psalms; and by this recitation, by the effort of our voice, our innermost being will be, little by little, touched and transformed.[8]

The maxim highlights two characteristics of the liturgy. First, it does not have primarily an expressive nature according to the categories that we spoke of earlier. The liturgical assembly is not a forum for free expression: it is a place of listening to the Word of God, and of praise-filled response, in the dynamic movement of the Spirit. Secondly, the liturgy has a corporal much more than an intellectual nature: it begins with 'a doing' and with 'an action', with gestures and songs, with the eating and drinking of the Body and Blood of Christ, so that these actions move us, transform us and nourish us. One does not come to the liturgy to express one's own ideas: the liturgy itself captures us and turns our thoughts and feelings towards God.

Liturgy and Culture: Towards Inculturation

Existing fundamentally in the order of action, the liturgy is incarnate. It relies on social contexts (the dockers of Corinth or the bourgeois of Oslo), on cultural contexts (that of late Antiquity for the Fathers of the Church, that of Luther, that of the computer age and globalization) and even on anthropo-

---

8. On the liturgical importance of this maxim see P. De Clerck, 'Une perception du corps et des sens', Ch. 2 of *L'Intelligence de la liturgie*, Paris: Editions du Cerf, 1995, 2005[2], 35-63.

logical conventions (such as physical touch, colour and so on). Liturgical history bears witness to this cultural penetration of the liturgy (or rather of liturgies), because since the fourth century liturgical families have developed, in the East (Syrian, Coptic), and in the West (Roman, Gallican, Hispanic...), characterized by the cultures in which these liturgies blossomed. In this sense, an 'orthodox liturgy' does not exist but a Byzantine liturgy, used as much today by Orthodox as by Eastern Catholics.

The Liturgical Movement, born in the nineteenth and developed in the twentieth century, allowed Christians to rediscover the essential framework of liturgy. It also made them aware of the historical circumstances of the liturgical expressions they had inherited. This discovery is more recent in Catholicism, which has been celebrating liturgy in the vernacular for only thirty years.

This awareness prompts the reflection we call 'inculturation'. Beginning with the cultural roots of the past, we hope for a liturgical adaptation to modern mentalities. This is true, particularly in the West, for the ideals of democracy and equality between the sexes, and more importantly for the expression of the Christian mystery itself. Many of the Post Communion Prayers, for example, jump directly from the request for a fruitful reception of the Body and Blood of Christ to the hope of participation in the heavenly banquet, thus short-circuiting the realities of the world and of history. What was taken for granted in the cultures of Antiquity and the Middle Ages is no longer acceptable today.

Inculturation is a major challenge. It is enough to think about the cultures of the Far East to be convinced of it; or to note that the liturgical year developed in the northern hemisphere, but that in the southern hemisphere, they celebrate Easter in autumn, at a time when nature is beginning to die! We find ourselves here before the reality of the Christian tradition which has a threefold process. First, it includes the reception of the Christian message, transmitted necessarily within a particular culture; it requires assimilation of the data which in turn modifies it to a certain degree; finally, it requires the retransmission to future generations of the data, with the obligatory adaptation of this new reception. Thus, we note, the liturgical realities are a place of major reflection regarding the interaction of Scripture and Tradition.

Conclusion

What is the significance of the fact that ordinations are celebrated in the context of liturgy?

We will try, by way of conclusion, to concretize this presentation of the Catholic understanding of liturgy in terms of the theme of this book, conse-

PAUL DE CLERCK

crated as it is to ordination. Ordinations are carried out currently in all of our traditions, by a liturgical act. This observation needs first to be nuanced or made more precise. In reality, when one begins a celebration of ordination, everyone already knows who is going to be ordained. This fact suggests that we distinguish between three moments in what we usually call ordination: the choice of those to be called, the prayer accompanied by the imposition of hands, and the Eucharist in which this celebration takes place.

The celebration itself often begins with the presentation of the ordinands, but their selection has been done beforehand. Procedures for choosing them are varied: we know that in Antiquity, bishops were chosen by the Christians faithful of the diocese; today many wish for more democratic ways than those that have been inherited from previous generations. Yet whatever may be the means of choosing, it is not equivalent to ordination itself. Thus, once one agrees on the ordinands, one proceeds to the liturgy of ordination; the heart of which is the epicletic prayer accompanied by the laying-on of hands, when the Church invokes the Spirit to give the ordinands the gifts that will be necessary for the ministry they are going to exercise. It is here that the liturgy manifests its significance. It highlights that, if the Church is able to choose people for ministry, God alone can make them into ministers. Otherwise, an administrative appointment would suffice. The ordination prayers usually contain characteristic formulations of this theological awareness. Take for example this ancient Gallican prayer for the ordination of a bishop which asks 'that your blessing (that of God) be on him, even if it is by the imposition of our hands'. One would hope that these liturgical facts, notably the epicletic character of ordination, would develop their potential and would blossom in a pneumatology of ministry.

Finally, in the majority of Christian liturgies, ordination is 'crowned' by the eucharistic celebration. Here again, the liturgical acts carry the meaning. It is not only a question of framing or of heightening the importance of the ceremony. The relationship between ordination and the Eucharist expresses something of the very nature of the ministry received: it is in the Eucharist, at the deepest level, that the Church is constructed, the Church whose ministers are charged with preserving communion. It is thus by proclaiming the Word and giving the invitation to receive the Body and Blood of Christ that they principally will realize the ministry that they have just received.

We conclude then that the liturgy expresses the Church, its identity and nature; it offers a concrete manifestation of the design of God who gathers his People. During each ordination, it shows in itself the existence of a ministry responsible for communion, instituted to show the gratuitousness of salvation, the divine origin of every action of the Church, especially of the Word of Christ and of the Sacraments of the Spirit.

Love, Knowledge and Prayer: Reflections on the Integrity of Liturgy with Special Reference to Rites of Ordination

Päivi Jussila

Way of Life

The first Christian communities were held together by the apostles' teaching, fellowship, the breaking of bread and prayers (Acts 2.42-47). The Christian way of life continues to be based on the same corporate practices; it is related to the basic needs of nourishment, companionship, remembrance and consolation. It has its *'ordo'*, its basic shape, which is shared by Christians worldwide.

Christian worship reflects this basic pattern of life. It consists of the ordinary stuff life is made of: gathering, reading, eating and sending (Lathrop 1993, 10-11). This ecumenical pattern is evident in ordination liturgies (Nairobi Statement 1996, 24-25). In other words, the basic shape of liturgy (*'ordo'*) is one of the contexts, which help us to understand the nature and function of ordination. Beginning with the *Apostolic Tradition* of the third century, the ordination rites have had a consistent structure made up of core elements, such as calling, reading, breaking of the bread, the imposition of hands, praying and sending.

The liturgies by which the Church confers various ministries have certain elements in common: calling, blessing, sending. This signifies that these ministries together serve the same Lord in the one Church. But there are also differences: Scripture readings and liturgical wording differ according to the type of ministry and responsibility (Lutheran Understanding 1983, para. 45, 15).

Traditionally, Christians have been identified as those who belong to the Way (Acts 9.2). Indeed, there is something dynamic about the Christian pattern of life, including liturgy. Ordination rites may be understood as rites of passage in which Christians mark the changing conditions of their lives. Like all other changes and transitions in the life of a Christian, they reflect the basic transition which takes place in baptism: 'Once you were not a people, but now you are God's people' (1 Pet 2.10) (Chicago Statement 1998, 14).

These rites are processes of transformation shaping not only the life of the ordinand, but also the life of the Church and all its baptized members. In other words, ordination is not an isolated moment or act in the life of the Church and the baptized. Like baptism, it carries and transforms us daily throughout our lives.

> What then is the significance of such a baptism with water? Answer: It signifies that the old creature in us with all sins and evil desires is to be drowned and die through daily contrition and repentance, and on the other hand that daily a new person is to come forth and rise up to live before God in righteousness and purity forever (Luther, Small Catechism, 360).

> Therefore let all Christians regard their baptism as the daily garment that they are to wear all the time. Every day they should be found in faith and with its fruits, suppressing the old creature and growing up in the new (Luther, Large Catechism, 466).

Ordination rites do not take place in isolation. Though liturgical texts and rubrics related to these rites are informative of the nature and purpose of the rite, the content and purpose of ordination rites should not be reduced to liturgical texts. In the end, these rites are acts of God and the Church; they are the witness of the Church to the world. What actually happens and its consequences are crucial questions for the Christian way of life.

The Trinity

Liturgy can be defined as a way of life that gives a profound unity to love, knowledge and prayer. Even if the manifestations of liturgy are rich and varied, they have something in common: they ultimately flow from the love of the triune God. From the beginning, the belief in the three-personed God has marked Christianity. It has constituted a vital part of the Christian way of life, especially in liturgy and prayer. The being of God is a relational being: God is the triune God, i.e. God is communion. In liturgy, Christians are called to participate in communion with the triune God. This relationship shapes all other relationships: to oneself, to another and to nature. The expressions 'one in being' and 'in three persons' refer to the most perfect unity in love. They describe God as love, as someone who gives himself completely to us: 'The Father gives us all creation, Christ all his works, the Holy Spirit all his gifts' (Luther, Large Catechism, 440).

A God who is one and three at the same time is a mystery beyond our comprehension. We need water, bread and wine to be in communion with God and in order to know God. Baptism and Eucharist are expressions of God's saving presence in the Church. They are also expressions of the corpo-reality and materiality of faith. They do not only belong to the 'sacred sphere' but are celebrated in the midst of the suffering world. They grant us God's grace, which is visible, edible, drinkable and audible. Just as God in Christ became human, so sacramental celebration relates closely to people's concrete situations.

Even though Lutherans do not consider ordination as a sacrament in the proper sense of the word, ordination can be understood in sacramental terms. Like Baptism and Eucharist, ordination is not an individual, isolated act. As a physical and visible act, the laying-on of hands embraces the whole of creation. It is not a remote or separate act: rather, it is a sacramental deed, open and intimate by nature, and taking place in solidarity with all.

> Ordination is not an act of separation from the other members of the Church ... Rather, it is a calling, blessing and sending for a God-given ministry in the midst of and for the people of God (Lutheran Understanding 1983, para. 52, p. 16).

Communion

Only through sharing and the exchange with others do we become truly ourselves. To live a Christian life is to be pulled out of one's isolation and to be united with Christ and the rest of humanity. All liturgical actions are communal by nature. Ordination liturgies should express clearly that ordained leadership is for the assembly. People are appointed and prayed for that they might serve in assembly roles. According to this understanding '"office" is nothing other than a place to stand and a task to do in the assembly' (Lathrop 1993, 185). Yet, in Protestant churches there are often serious disagreements over who may or may not be ordained, with little reference to the communities among whom these ordained ones will function. Protestant liturgies have often understood Christian leadership as a solitary task. And yet, as Gordon Lathrop argues, 'Christian leaders – bishops, preachers, pastors, ministers – gain their importance among us primarily because of their roles in the assembly' (Lathrop 1993, 185).

Traditionally and ideally, ordination liturgy takes place in the context of the Eucharist. In ancient eucharistic usage *koinonia* describes the oneness of Christians in the body of Christ through the one bread and cup.

> The cup of blessing that we bless, is it not a sharing in the blood of Christ? The bread that we break, is it not a sharing in the body of Christ? Because there is one bread, we who are many are one body, for we all partake of the one bread (1 Cor 10.16-17).

When the ordination rite is a part of eucharistic celebration, it becomes clear that ordination is an act of the whole Christian community in the presence of that community. Therefore, the laying-on of hands, for example, is not an isolated act performed by the ordained clergy but, rather, an act of the whole Church (Lathrop 1993, 197). The process of ordination is deeply embedded in the life of a local church. Nevertheless, the Church which ordains is not simply the local church. Every act of ordination is an expression of the apostolicity and catholicity of the one Church. 'The ordained ministry is also a sign of the unity of the Church beyond the specific Christian community since persons are ordained by the Church at large ....' (Lutheran Understanding 1983, 10, para 24; Lathrop 1993, 197-198).

The Eucharist is the sacrament of love, the bond of love. In Holy Communion we taste the very life of God, who is love. The breaking of the bread makes the Church what it is. In his sermon on *The Blessed Sacrament of the Holy and True Body of Christ* (1519), Luther explains the loving communion which takes place in the celebration of Holy Communion:

> Christ with all the saints, by his love, takes upon himself our form (Phil 2.7), fights with us against sin, death, and all evil. This enkindles in us such love that we take on his form, rely upon his righteousness, life and blessedness. And through the interchange of his blessings and our misfortunes, we become one loaf, one bread, one body, one drink, and have all things in common (Luther, *The Blessed Sacrament*, 58).

The Eucharist embraces all of life. It is an offering on behalf of the whole world.

> The eucharistic celebration demands reconciliation and sharing among all those regarded as brothers and sisters in the one family of God and is a

constant challenge in the search for appropriate relationships in social, economic and political life (BEM, 14).

Solidarity in the eucharistic communion of the body of Christ and responsible care of Christians for one another and the world find specific expression in the liturgies: in the mutual forgiveness of sins; the sign of peace; intercession for all; the eating and drinking together; the taking of the elements to the sick and those in prison or the celebration of the Eucharist with them. All these manifestations of love in the Eucharist are directly related to Christ's own testimony as a servant, in whose servanthood Christians themselves participate (BEM, 14).

Participatory Knowledge

The communion of the three Persons of the Trinity is founded on love. Therefore, imagining the Trinity does not confine itself to the activities of the mind. It requires a synthesizing of knowledge, love and prayer. 'Whoever does not love does not know God, for God is love' (1 John 4.8). We cannot know God if we do not love God. Knowledge and love go together. God's ultimate being as love presupposes the integration of knowledge and liturgy. According to patristic understanding, there is an inner connection between the act of prayer and theological reflection. In modern terms, in order to be relevant, theology has to take seriously the basic questions related to life, death and holiness that are at the heart of our being. It should deal not only with the possibility of encounter with the living God, but also with the ways and means of achieving it. The emphasis is on the living knowledge of God in prayer and acts of love. In other words, theology is not considered as an end in itself, but as a way which is meaningful for those who have encountered the triune God: '... for we cannot keep from speaking about what we have seen and heard' (Acts 4.20).

Knowing the triune God is inseparable from participating in a particular community and its liturgical practices. Liturgy presupposes the active participation of the whole assembly. What does this mean in the context of ordination liturgies? Ordination liturgy is a corporate act, which according to an ancient tradition, should take place on Sunday or a feast day within the main assembly of the church. The act of ordination is also in principle associated with a congregational service including the Lord's Supper, and the congregation is explicitly a partner in the act of ordination through hymns, prayers and acclamations (RC/L JC 1982, 42).

When ordination, i.e. the election of the candidate and prayer for bestowal of gifts, takes place in the Sunday assembly, in the midst of the people, the dialogue between leaders and assembly draws 'new leaders into the perpetual dialogue of ritual leadership' (Lathrop 1993, 197). The Early Church made an organic connection between theological reflection and liturgical experience. Liturgy was not considered an object of theological inquiry but, rather, as the living source and the ultimate criterion of all Christian thought. Therefore Irenaeus, for example, was able to say that, 'Our view is in accordance with the Eucharist, and the Eucharist confirms that which is our view' (Irenaeus IV, 18, 5).

This kind of participatory knowledge of God available in worship differs from purely rational knowledge; it is knowledge gained through action and acquired by entering into a relationship (Wood 2001). This kind of knowledge is not about looking at things, but about dwelling in them. It is not about handling things, but about becoming immersed in them. In this context we can speak about *primary liturgical theology*, which is 'the communal meaning of the liturgy exercised by the gathering itself' and *secondary liturgical theology*, which is 'written and spoken discourse that attempts to find words for the experience of the liturgy and to illuminate its structures' (Lathrop 1993, 5-6).

Participatory knowledge is understanding through love. It is mediated through practices such as the reading of the Bible, liturgical actions, sacraments, prayer, forgiveness, hospitality, witness, solidarity with the poor and service to those in need. The kind of theology we promote is closely related to the nature of the questions we raise. For example, asking what happens to the elements in the Eucharist is different from asking what happens to the Church in the Eucharist. Asking who performs the laying-on of hands is different from asking what happens to the Church during this gesture.

Eucharistic liturgy is about participatory knowledge of the triune God. It is not individualistic in character, but grows with the experience of communion. In the Eucharist the Church ceases to be an institution or a doctrine and becomes life and salvation. In the Eucharist, love, knowledge and prayer belong together. In classical terms, the content of faith, *fides quae creditur* (the faith which is believed) and the act of faith, *fides qua creditur* (the faith by which we believe) belong together, and '... the eucharistic reality embraces doctrine and life, confession and liturgical form, piety and practice' (L/RC JC 1980, 2).

In the context of academic theology, knowledge of God is normally limited to 'knowledge about'. This kind of theology is interested in systems of consistent categories and concepts. The object or content of knowledge is cut into the smallest possible, indivisible pieces after which it is put together again. Liturgy, instead, does not seek theoretical or partial knowledge of God. It seeks

God not as a piece of knowledge, but as a being. It aims at a unifying experience of communion. Knowledge without love leaves a human being in the state of terrifying loneliness and boredom.

> All things are wearisome; more than one can express; the eye is not satisfied with seeing, or the ear filled with hearing. What has been is what will be, and what has been done is what will be done; there is nothing new under the sun (Eccles. 1.8-9).

In the context of liturgy we acknowledge that our words can say something about God and yet, at the same time, suggest the ineffable. The more we get to know God the more we understand how little we know. Therefore, it is not surprising that the language of liturgy is filled with praise and doxology:

> O the depth of the riches and wisdom and knowledge of God! How unsearchable are his judgments and how inscrutable his ways! (...) For from him and through him and to him are all things. To him be the glory forever. Amen (Rom 11.33, 36).

References

Chicago Statement on Worship and Culture: Baptism and Rites of Life Passage. 1998. In *Baptism, Rites of Passage, and Culture*, ed. S. Anita Stauffer, 13-24. Geneva: The Lutheran World Federation, Department for Theology and Studies.

Faith and Order. 1982. *Baptism, Eucharist and Ministry*. Faith and Order Paper 111 (BEM). Geneva: World Council of Churches.

Irenaeus, Adversus Haereses IV,18,5, ed. J.-P. Migne, *Patrologia Graeca 7*, Paris.

Lathrop, Gordon W. 1993. *Holy Things. A Liturgical Theology.* Minneapolis: Fortress Press.

Luther, Martin. (1519). 1960. The Blessed Sacrament of the Holy and True Body of Christ. In *Luther's Works*, 35: 45-73.

Luther, Martin. (1529). 2000. The Large Catechism. In *The Book of Concord. The Confessions of the Evangelical Lutheran Church*, ed. Robert Kolb and Timothy J. Wengert, 377-480. Minneapolis: Fortress Press.

Luther, Martin. (1529). 2000. The Small Catechism. In *The Book of Concord. The Confessions of the Evangelical Lutheran Church*, ed. Robert Kolb and Timothy J. Wengert, 345-375. Minneapolis: Fortress Press.

Lutheran/Roman Catholic Joint Commission (L/RC JC). 1980. *The Eucharist*. Geneva: The Lutheran World Federation.

The Lutheran Understanding of Ministry. 1983. Geneva: LWF Studies.

Nairobi Statement on Worship and Culture: Contemporary Challenges and Opportunities. In *Christian Worship: Unity in Cultural Diversity*, ed. S. Anita Stauffer. Geneva: Lutheran World Federation.

Roman Catholic/Lutheran Joint Commission (RC/L JC). 1982. *The Ministry in the Church*. Geneva: The Lutheran World Federation.

Wood, Susan K. 2001. Participatory Knowledge of God in the Liturgy. In *Knowing the Triune God. The Work of the Spirit in the Practices of the Church*, ed. James J. Buckley and David S. Yeago, 95-118. Grand Rapids, Michigan/Cambridge: William B. Eerdmans Publishing Company.

The Relevance of Gender in Rites of Ordination

Ninna Edgardh Beckman

The starting point for this article is a lacuna, as studies on rites of ordination from a gender perspective seem to be largely non-existent. Nor was the issue covered in the original plan for the project on *Rites of Ordination in the Churches of the Nordic Countries*. At a certain point I was invited to comment on the texts from a gender perspective. I then observed that although absent in the overall planning, gender was touched upon in several studies. To get a deeper understanding of the issues raised I searched the libraries for books and articles, and was surprised to find –nothing! I may have missed some works, but later queries have confirmed my observation. The lacuna is twofold. Gender seems not to have been on the agenda in discussions on ordination rites, nor have ordination rites been on the agenda for feminist theologians.

This is the more surprising considering the amount of studies produced on the two broader issues which intersect in the study of ordination rites. There are shelves full of books on rites and liturgical language, also from a gender perspective. There is also a steadily growing pile of books on different aspects of gender and ordination, women as deacons, women as priests and so on. But on the combination of the two I have found nothing.

At a late stage in the project it was not possible to include an additional study dealing with how gender is expressed in specific ordination rites in the Nordic countries, though this might have been of great interest. What I will do instead, in this paper, is ponder the two broader fields outlined above – the debates on gender and ordination, and the expanding field of feminist liturgical studies – for indications of the relevance and theological potential of combining the two areas. I will mainly use examples from my own context, which is Swedish and Lutheran, although I will sometimes expand the discussion to other traditions.

A Relevant Absence

My main argument is that the lacuna with regard to gender and ordination rites does not indicate that the subject as such is irrelevant. A more probable explanation – against the background given by the two above mentioned areas of research – is that discussions on ordination rites have so far taken place in rooms far away from the ones where feminist scholars have treated issues of gender and power in relation to the Christian tradition. The lack of literature does in this way more probably reflect the relevance of the subject than the opposite. For most of Christian history, women have, by reason only of their sex, been excluded from ordained Christian ministry. This does not, however, mean that gender has been absent, but rather the contrary. Gender as an issue has been the more present, as women have been absent. With the liturgical scholar Teresa Berger we may conclude that 'the very absence of women in these texts, rites, and legislative practices is an integral and constitutive part of the existence of these practices' (Berger 1999, 24). This indicates the need to use gender as an analytical tool in the study of ordination rites.

In some churches the practice of excluding women from ordination has been challenged and tradition changed during the second half of the last century. But, and this is my conclusion, even Protestant women, who often have the opportunity to be ordained, have still not yet reached such a strong position as clergy that they feel free to question and criticise the rite that marks their very entry into this ministry. From the perspective of the first women in priesthood it would even have been foolish – however well motivated – to question their recently won platform of theological influence and authority. It may, however, be that the time has come for a change in this respect.

Separation and Hierarchy

I want to start with a comparison between gender and ordination, because the two phenomena have surprising similarities, which might not be obvious at first glance. Gender is the word used in English to indicate an ascribed identity, which separates some people, called women, from others, called men, and also culturally orders them into a value laden hierarchy where males and masculinity are ascribed higher value than females and femininity (Cf. Braidotti 2002).

This gendered hierarchy is in most societies seen as constitutive for human beings. A new-born baby is seldom welcomed only as 'baby', but as a boy or a girl. Gender can in this way be seen as constitutive for the formation of human identity, both at a personal and at a societal level. Although feminist theorists disagree on many things these are general statements which most would agree on.

It would, however, be more difficult to find a consensus on how the gendered subject is constructed, how gender intersects with other structures of oppression, how the relation between biological sex and gender works, and which strategies are most helpful to realize feminist visions. One of the most central and recurring internal feminist debates has concerned whether to stress women's similarity to men, as human beings (liberal feminism), or to stress the value of what women have culturally come to represent (cultural feminism). I will come back to the relevance of this debate in relation to ordination, but let us first look at the similarity between ordination and gender.

Ordination and Gender

Ordination to Christian ministry is a theological construct. As such it is always inculturated into, and performed within, a specific context, where gender is also at work. Already we note an intersection here between the two objects of our interest. Ordination as a rite is a theologically understood ceremony whereby some people, the ordinands, are separated from others, the lay people, and ordered into a value laden hierarchy, where the ordained undertake certain obligations, and are given certain authorities and privileges, which are not given to lay people. How much of authority and privilege is attached to being ordained varies between theological traditions, but also between cultural contexts. These contexts might also be reflected in the ordination rite, along with the theological understanding.

Moreover, setting someone apart in ordination has in most churches been understood as not only related to human power structures, but also to the hope for divine power. This divine authorisation is in turn closely related to church identity at a constitutive level. Ordination is in this way an ecclesiological issue.

We may conclude from this that there are similarities between present and dominant understandings of gender and ordination

in that they have to do with constructions of identity,
in that they work both at an individual and a corporate level,
in that they set some people apart from others,
in that this setting apart leads into somehow value laden hierarchies.

Legitimating Hierarchies

From the argument given above it seems obvious that the exclusion of women from ordination, practised in much of Christian history, has been influenced by, and has also reinforced, a gender hierarchy which values women less than men. With critical pregnancy the Swedish feminist theologian Maria Södling has summarised the argument for excluding women as 'the art of letting God legitimate discrimination' (Södling 1995, 265).

If this goes for ordination as such, it is also true that the specific shape of the rite, for example the use of an exclusively masculine language for God, or a typology of ministry based on exclusively male roles of leadership, may reinforce culturally constructed gender hierarchies. These are obvious aspects to look for in a critical gender analysis.

What is maybe less obvious is that the similarities between the two phenomena also open a possibility for ordination working the other way, namely as destabilising such a gender hierarchy. As an ordination rite is in a sense a setting apart into another context, or into a new status or function in the community, such a rite may also, at least hypothetically, mark a new equality. This is interesting as it opens up a possibility for the Church to work against the prevailing culture also with regard to gender, as it does in many other issues where human dignity and justice are questioned.

We may make a comparison with the baptismal rite, where the Pauline words of no one any longer being Greek or Jew, slave or free, female or male, but all being one in Christ, may be interpreted as a ritual repudiation of gender hierarchies. Ordination might in a similar way be interpreted as an explicit stripping of gendered identity into a more androgynous priestly identity. A rite of profession for entrance into a religious order may also potentially be used as a way of leaving the gendered hierarchies behind.

In reality gendered hierarchies tend, however, to persist, the androgynous priest being still socially defined as a male authority, and the female order being still dependent on the male structure for the most central rite, the celebration of the Eucharist. An analysis of a rite of ordination from a gender perspective would, however, clarify these aspects.

The Need for Critical Studies

The above sketched intersections between gender and ordination indicate that a critical analysis of the working of gender in a certain rite cannot be separated from the broader discussion on ordained ministry. The analysis of gender has also to be combined with observations of the workings of other separating categories.

Feminist theorists have in recent years tried to leave the conflicting positions between cultural and liberal feminism behind, in search of more creative ways forward, which give room for deeper insights into the way that gender intersects with, for example, class, sexuality and ethnicity in the creation of identity. In church debate this development is mirrored in an increasing debate about other forms of identity construction, such as homosexuality or disability, also leading to exclusion from ordination (Stuart 2003; Eiesland and Saliers 1998). Why is it that certain categories are excluded from the ordained ministry? What does this say about our image of God and Christ? How does it affect the community? Questions like these might be approached through an analysis of the ordination rites, as well as through a more theoretical analysis.

Including a critical gender perspective in our studies of liturgy also implies an awareness of how our research perspectives work to conceal or disclose aspects of the objects studied. A research perspective which focuses on liturgical tradition as in transition will, for example, more easily reflect changes with regard to gender, than a more static perspective. If a broad spectrum of church traditions is included – as they have been in this project – this makes it more obvious that different traditions concerning gender and ordination are possible and also ritually practised. If there is a breadth in the offices studied, such as religious orders, deacons, priests and bishops, but maybe also other ministries, this also helps to make the variations in how gender is related to ordination visible. Are the offices theologically understood as united, but threefold, as presently in the Church of Sweden? How is this reflected in the ordination rites? Are deacons ordained separately from the priests or in a common liturgy? Are male and female ordinands treated in the same way, or are there gender-related ritual differences? Which offices are regarded as not in need of ordination, and are these held mainly by women or by men?

The list of interesting questions for critical research could be greatly expanded, but some examples of what kind of questions would be relevant from a gender perspective will have to suffice. Feminist studies have always been in need of a double strategy, combining critique with constructive thinking and experimentation, and it is in approaching the more constructive side of the task that a comparison between the introduction of the ordination of women and the creation of alternative feminist liturgies might be of interest.

Women and Ordination

Let us start by looking at how the ordination of women has come about in the Nordic folk churches and primarily in a Swedish context. These reforms and the debates surrounding them are documented in an extensive literature (For Norway see Stendal 2003, for Denmark see Pedersen 1998, for Sweden see e.g. Rodhe and Rodhe 1958, Stendahl 1985, Ralfnert 1988 and Sandahl 1993).

The arguments for the ordination of women to priesthood in the Nordic context have mainly followed the above mentioned liberal/humanist line, theologically based on women and men being similar and of equal worth, created in the image of God and baptised in Christ (Rodhe and Rodhe 1958). The arguments have also been highly influenced by secular debates on women's rights (Ralfnert 1988). The exclusion of women from ordination has been seen as both reflecting and risking reinforcement of a culturally constructed gender hierarchy which discriminates against women. This in turn has to do with the line of argument against the ordination of women being strongly based on ideas of gender complementarity and the subordination of women (Södling 1995, Almer 1997).

Sometimes, however, supposed gender differences have also been used as arguments for the inclusion of women. Women have then been expected to complement the male clergy with supposed specific gender-related qualities (Rodhe and Rodhe 1958:112f). In many circumstances it has, however, been crucial, and a question of professional survival, for women clergy to stress their similarity with the male clergy.

The first generations of women who served as priests in the Church of Sweden experienced many forms of enduring exclusion, in spite of the decision taken in 1958. Examples are summarised in SOU 1981:20, an official enquiry into the situation of the first women priests. Most common according to this enquiry were demands made for them to step aside on different occasions out of regard for the conscience of priests and other personnel who did not accept the ordination of women. It was for example not uncommon for women priests to be restricted to serving in a special district of the parish and not in the main church. In a study undertaken in1993 women priests still reported that they were expected to step aside voluntarily at times when their presence could be expected to disturb someone. Surprisingly they seldom mentioned this as examples of being discriminated against. The male researcher concluded that this probably implied that the discriminating gender order was taken for granted: 'Perhaps it may be said that they are quite thick-skinned, or that they have had to develop a thick skin. Another way of putting it is to say that a certain amount of discrimination is part of everyday life, in such a way that you don't react to it: it is part of the natural order' (Hansson 1993: 106).

During the first decades in which women were ordained, there were obvious examples of discrimination also directly connected to the ordination ceremony. In preparing this article I was for example confronted with the licence given to a woman ordained in 1970. The printed pronoun 'he' in the document had been corrected to 'she' by hand, although by this time it was more than ten years since the first women had been ordained.

Another example of the reluctance to fully accept women as priests is shown in the practice, quite common for many years, of ordaining women and men at different times of the day, at the request of male ordinands who did not accept the new system. This was even given a name of its own, and was called *'särvigning'* ('separate ordination'). It also happened that women were ordained in another diocese and by another bishop because the bishop of the diocese where they were going to serve did not accept women as priests. This also received a name of its own and was called *'distansvigning'* ('distance ordination'). A discussion in the preparatory work when the legislation was adopted came to be applied in church practice as a 'conscience clause'. During the first two decades this clause was used to legitimate special treatment of women, in order to safeguard the right of male priests not to be forced to act against their conscience (SOU 1981, 20; Stendahl 1985, 111-117).

The conflicts surrounding the acceptance of women as priests in the Church of Sweden have continued. A quarter of the male clergy in 1998 still resented the ordination of women (Bäckström and De Marinis 1998).

In spite of the difficulties in resolving the conflicts, women have now served for 45 years as priests in the Church of Sweden. For a few years the Church of Sweden has also had two women bishops, themselves ordaining both priests and deacons. To a high degree these women have taken on ministry as it has been formed by male priests for centuries, although the rapid changes in society have implied more and quicker changes in church tradition during recent decades. However, I think it is fair to say that the continuous need to argue for the right to exist has held female priests back with regard to possible needs for theological changes, for example in the theology of ordination (cf. Stendahl 1985, 181 and Eriksson 1999, 329f).

Feminist Rituals

Women priests, upholding tradition in the same way as men, is one side of the present reality in the Church of Sweden. There is, however, also another current, more in line with cultural or radical feminism, where the stress lies on valuing the specific gifts and experiences of women. Feminist theologians have witnessed to the development of a feminist liturgical movement (Procter-Smith 1990; Berger 1999), starting in the late seventies, mainly in the USA, but later spreading throughout Europe and now also clearly visible in other parts of the world (Berger 2001). The movement has also been documented in Sweden (Beckman 2001).

This feminist liturgical movement is characterised by certain specific traits, the main one perhaps being its institutional independence and capacity for self-authorisation, but without ever letting go of the claim to belong to the Church. It is a movement of women creating a liturgical space of their own, built on their own experienced needs. It is anti-hierarchical, encouraging forms of shared leadership, often expressed by gathering in a circle. Liturgy is explicitly seen as involving the whole body, not only the intellect. This is expressed for example through the inclusion of symbolic actions and dance. Nevertheless changes in language, in order to make it more inclusive for women, are also typical.

New theological understandings are tried, but without claims to be universal truths. Plurality is seen as a positive value. God is named also in the feminine, and there is a stress on the close relation between God and her people. Rather than seeing the human being as a sinner, the stress is laid on humans as responsible collaborators with God. Self-sacrificing ideals are repudiated and women are encouraged to respect their own needs and integrity.

Few examples are, however, documented of alternative forms of baptism, burial or weddings in the feminist liturgical movement. This might be a result of institutional independence. New rituals are created following women's life cycle or the seasons of the year. No specific ordination is needed to perform the rituals, although in those churches where women are ordained as priests, as in the Church of Sweden, these may serve as leaders of the rituals. Most often this is done in close collaboration with lay women.

The feminist liturgical movement is a reaction, where exclusion of women is turned into something creative and positive. The rigidity and rectitude of dominant church traditions are replaced with a life-centred and inclusive horizontality, closely related to women's traditional spheres (Northup 1997).

Feminist Liturgy and the Institutional Church

The Swedish variant of the feminist liturgical movement shares many traits with other feminist liturgies, but has a closer institutional belonging. This is shown for example by the fact that female priests have played a crucial role in the movement. The liturgies have often taken place in church buildings and the Eucharist has often been celebrated (Beckman 2001).

The high acceptance of gender equality in Swedish society may in part explain these traits, as this has paved the way for a heightened sensitivity towards gender issues also in the former state church. But it might also be the case that the Swedish example, being so recently studied, indicates a change in which the liberal claims for women's right to be ordained, begin to combine with the cultural feminist claims that women's experiences finally will have to have more influence on theology than has hitherto been the case.

Such an opening up between feminists working for the full acceptance of women as clergy and feminists experimenting with alternative rituals could bring about interesting constructive theological discussions also about ordination and, consequently, about rites of ordination. The transformative force of strategies of equality could thus be joined to the transformative force of strategies of difference.

Constructive Theology

In a future constructive theological reflection one obvious source would be Christian history. As shown by a Roman Catholic theologian like Teresa Berger, or an Orthodox theologian like Kyriaki Karidoyanes Fitzgerald, women have been more prominent in the formation of Christian tradition than has been recognised by both feminist and more conservative theologians alike (FitzGerald 1998; Berger 1999).

Nevertheless a constructive feminist approach is also dependent on contemporary critique and alternative interpretations of Christian faith. The international movements working towards the ordination of women in all church traditions are interesting in this perspective, one example being the network Women's Ordination Worldwide (WOW), which has the purpose of supporting women in developing relevant forms of Christian ministry according to their traditions, personal calling and prevalent cultures, but also of encouraging women to explore new ways of ministry (http://www.wow2005.org).

Other movements work explicitly for ordination within the Roman Catholic Church, where we find organisations like Brothers and Sisters in Christ (BASIC, http://www.iol.ie/~duacon/basic.htm) and special websites, promoting dialogue around the issue, against the explicit instructions of the church authorities (http://www.womenpriests.org/index.asp). In these movements we also find a conscious ecclesiological reflection, which is important because, as clearly shown in this book, the relationship is so close between ecclesiology and the understanding of Christian ministry and ordination.

But the feminist liturgical movement might also constitute a valuable source in the reconsideration of Christian ministry and its formative rites. The institutional independence of the feminist liturgical movement has made the movement the *locus* of a more radical critique of church tradition than has been possible within the official structures of the churches. The movement has also been very open to spiritual needs in contemporary society.

When these traits are to be used as a theological source, it is, however, important also to scrutinise the perceptions of gender underpinning the liturgies. As a reaction against being marginalised in different ways, feminist liturgy has tended to be highly dependent on the specific experiences of the women involved. Sometimes this also involves an explicit reliance on ideas of specific 'women's ways of being and doing' (Beckman 2001).

Transferred to another context, this cultural feminist reliance on ideas of women's special gifts and needs may easily be used to legitimate prevailing ideas of gender complementarity, including the subordination of women. It may also be excluding in relation to women with other experiences, which is especially important as there is always a tendency for the more privileged groups to be the ones who are active and have the time and resources to engage in a liturgical group.

Instead of interpreting what is going on in the feminist liturgical movement as a specific feminine contribution, I therefore suggest that it be interpreted as a lay-based feminist movement of spiritual and liturgical renewal, which offers several contributions to the institutional churches. One contribution is the radical feminist critique, and the attentiveness to the reproduction of gendered hierarchies. Another contribution is the theological reinterpretation of tradition, based on the experiences and needs of some, but not all, women in contemporary society. These experiences are important in the ongoing reinterpretation and reconstruction of Christian tradition, not because they are specifically feminine, but because they are the experiences of the body of Christ. As such they may be an important resource, but only one, in the ongoing reconstruction of Christian tradition.

References

Almer, Johanna. 1997. Mannens lovsång till Mannen. *Svensk Kyrkotidning* 10:113-120.

Beckman, Ninna Edgardh. 2001. *Feminism och liturgi. En ecklesiologisk studie.* Stockholm: Verbum.

Berger, Teresa. 1999. *Women's Ways of Worship: Gender Analysis and Liturgical History.* Collegeville, Minn: The Liturgical Press.

– ed. 2001. *Dissident Daughters: Feminist Liturgies in Global Context.* Louisville, Kentucky: Westminster John Knox Press.

Braidotti, Rosi. 2002. The Uses and Abuses of the Sex/Gender Distinction in European Feminist Practices. In *Thinking differently: A Reader in European Women's Studies.* ed. Gabriele Griffin and Rosi Braidotti. London: Zed books.

Bäckström, Anders och DeMarinis, Valerie. 1988. *Präst- och pastorsundersökningen 1988.* Stencil: Uppsala Universitet.

Eiesland, Nancy and Saliers, Don E. (eds). 1998. *Human Disability and the Service of God: Reassessing Religious Practice.* Nashville: Abingdon Press.

Eriksson, Anne-Louise. 1999. Från mäns dominans till kvinnors dans. In *Modern svensk teologi. Strömningar och perspektivskiften under 1900-talet,* 325-348. Stockholm: Verbum.

FitzGerald, Kyriaki. Karidoyanes. 1998. *Women Deacons in the Orthodox Church: Called to Holiness and Ministry.* Brookline, Mass: Holy Cross Orthodox Press.

Hansson, Per. 1993. *Jämställdhet i Svenska kyrkan. Tre empiriska studier.* Religion och Samhälle 83. Tro & Tanke 1993:2. Uppsala: Svenska kyrkans forskningsråd.

Kvinnlig präst idag. Tio kvinnliga präster berättar. 1967. Stockholm: Natur och Kultur.

Northup, Leslie A. 1997. *Ritualizing Women: Patterns of Spirituality.* Cleveland, Ohio: Pilgrim Press.

Pedersen, Else Marie Wiberg. 1998. *Se min kjole. Historien om de förste kvindelige präster.* Copenhagen: Samleren.

Procter-Smith, Marjorie. 1990. *In Her Own Rite: Constructing Feminist Liturgical Tradition.* Nashville: Abingdon Press.

Ralfnert, Bernt. 1988. *Kvinnoprästdebatten i Sverige i perspektivet kyrka-stat.* Dissertation. Lund: University of Lund.

Rodhe, Birgit och Sten Rodhe. 1958. *Män och kvinnor i prästämbetet.* Stockholm: Svenska kyrkans Diakonistyrelses bokförlag.

Sandahl, Dag. 1993. *Kyrklig splittring. studier kring debatten om kvinnliga präster i Svenska kyrkan samt bibliografi 1905 – juli 1990.* Stockholm: Verbum.

Statens offentliga utredningar (SOU) 1981:20. *Omprövning av samvetsklausulen. Män och kvinnor som präster i svenska kyrkan. Betänkande av kvinnoprästutredningen.* Stockholm: Liber förlag.

Stendahl, Brita. 1985. *Traditionens makt. Kvinnan och prästämbetet i Svenska kyrkan.* Stockholm: Petra bokförlag.

Stendal, Synnøve Hinnaland. 2003. *'-under forvandlingens lov'. En analyse av stortingsdebatten om kvinnelige prester i 1930-årene.* Bibliotheca theologiae practicae 70. Dissertation. Lund: Arcus.

Stuart, Elizabeth. 2003. *Gay and lesbian theologies: Repetitions with critical difference.* Aldershot: Ashgate.

Södling, Maria. 1995. 'Låt man bli man och kvinna kvinna'. Om kvinnoprästmotståndet i Svenska kyrkan. In *Feministisk bruksanvisning. Essäer.* Eds Claudia Lindén & Ulrika Milles, 245-275. Stockholm: Norstedts förlag.

PART IV

Conclusion

Theological and Liturgical Considerations behind this Research on Rites for Ordination and Commitment

Hans Raun Iversen

This book provides rich material and a wide variety of approaches to the theology and terminology of rites of ordination and commitment in the churches in the Nordic countries, despite the limitations identified in the introduction. It therefore also offers the editor a great many issues for final consideration and conclusion. In an attempt to limit and organise the scope, I have taken as the point of departure for these concluding observations six basic questions that relate to the research that has been undertaken:

1. How is ordination related to God – seen as a work of God?
2. What is the relationship between baptism and ordination – as a reflection of the relationship between congregation and minister?
3. How is the relationship between congregation and minister expressed in lay participation in rites of ordination?
4. How is the relationship between various ministers in the church expressed in the various rites of ordination and installation to a range of ministries in the church?
5. How does the process of admission to ordained ministry reflect the understanding of oversight (*episkopé*)?
6. What are the diversities and convergences in the ordination rites and the understanding of liturgy in the Nordic Churches?

The Trinitarian Foundation of Ordination

Most ordination rites repeatedly mention, address, invoke, praise and pray to God the Father, God the Son and God the Holy Spirit. On the surface at least, they seem to operate with a balanced Trinitarian theology. The role of the Trinity in ordination and liturgy is, however, not primarily one of correct dogmatic teaching. A dynamic understanding of God working in a Trinitarian way is essential, if ordination is to be a theological and not only a legal or communicative act in the churches. Referring to J. D. Zizioulas, James F. Puglisi emphasizes that

> Christ... is only present in the world in and through the presence and action of the Holy Spirit. In the New Testament this affirmation is so essential, that the incarnation itself of Christ is inconceivable without the work of the Spirit (Luke 1.35). We can christologically conceive of ministry only in the context of pneumatology and this finally leads to the involvement of the whole Trinity. The ministry of the Church cannot be reduced to anything less than the action and involvement of God in history since the beginning (Puglisi 1996, 202f).

As we know from the story of the first Pentecost, after the death, resurrection and ascension of Christ, the Kingdom of God, God's own *eschaton*, is made present among us in the power of the Holy Spirit. The Holy Spirit, however, always calls the receivers of the Spirit together as a new People of God, gathering it as a baptismal and eucharistic communion – and thus proclaiming in word and deed, and in the form of its presence, the coming of the Kingdom of God. It is within – and only within – this communion that ordination for ministry in the service of God as known from Jesus Christ can take place and ordained ministers are to work.

For an ordained minister to be participating in the work of Christ – and not limiting him/herself to being a steward of practical matters within the church – it is essential that the fellowship expressed during the laying-on of hands at ordination is focused in the epicletic prayer to the Holy Spirit to equip the minister-to-be. Whoever voices the epicletic prayer, theologically speaking the core of ordination should be, but is not always, the prayer by the whole congregation for the gifts of the Holy Spirit for the specific ministry, which is now being handed over to the one being ordained. As a fully theological act, ordination cannot be celebrated without the congregation believing and expressing the belief that admission to the ordained ministry is basically the work of the Holy Spirit.[1] Only in this way can the Church see itself – and live – as

---

1. Volf puts the point in this way: '...the church needs the vivifying presence of the Spirit of God, and without this presence, even a church with a decentralised participative

a Trinitarian reality, a community with its ministers, and a community that is the body of Christ. Upheld by the work of the Holy Trinity, the Church is a communion which must reflect the communitarian being of that same Trinity. This is essential whenever the Church is proclaiming the Gospel or being rebuilt in celebration of baptism, Eucharist – or ordination (cf. Puglisi 2001, 245, 285-8). If we accept that there is participatory knowledge in liturgy, ordination is not about looking at things, but about dwelling in them, not about handling the Trinity, but about being immersed in it.[2]

Church and Minister: Baptism and Ordination

It is only too easy to make the priesthood of ordained believers overshadow the priesthood of all baptized believers. Among others the Lutheran Reformers reacted to this tendency emphasizing that over against God and human beings (*'coram Deo et coram hominibus'*), ordained ministers have no special status at all. They only have special functions within the congregation among sisters and brothers (*'in ecclesia pro fratibus'*, Puglisi 1998, 163-167).

Baptism implies commitment to service and mission. Salvation received by baptism and faith is always to be shared with others. The Gospel of the Kingdom of God can never be narrowed down to a private concern for the individual baptized Christian. Understanding what Christianity is all about, every baptized Christian must be a pastor to fellow Christians as well as a deacon to those in need and a missionary to non-Christian neighbours. That baptized Christians must be servants to everyone does not, however, mean that everyone should always do everything to everyone else at the same time. The gifts are differentiated and so the functions must be in any congregation. It is not everybody who is gifted to be a cross-cultural missionary! Nor is everybody gifted and educated to be called to perform pastoral care, public preaching or ministry of oversight. To make sure, that such important functions as these are carried out, the Church calls, ordains and installs specific ministers to take leadership in these functions. Ordination for a specific function is primarily to be understood as a congregational prayer for the person to be equipped for the specific ministry and by no means as 'a second baptism' placing the ordained person at a different level compared to other baptized Christians.

How is the interrelationship between baptism and ordination being handl-

---

structure and culture will become sterile, and perhaps more sterile even than a hierarchical church...Only the person who lives from the spirit of communion (2 Cor. 13.13) can participate authentically in the life of the ecclesial Community' (Volf 1998, 257).
2. Cf. Jussila (Part III.2).

ed in ordination rites – and for that matter in baptismal rites in the Nordic churches? The answer, in brief, is that the relationship between the theology of baptism and the theology of ordination is only rarely mirrored in the rites examined. It is most striking that, although the Nordic Baptist Churches practise believers' baptism, the relationship between baptism and ordination is not reflected in their ordination rite, nor is it in their baptismal rites, according to Bent Hylleberg's study (Part II.5). Historically, in Hylleberg's view, confirmation and ordination, and also monastic professions, have often been practiced as a sort of 'second baptism'. This is hardly the case in Nordic rites for perpetual commitment to religious life as analysed by Else-Britt Nilsen (Part II.4). On the contrary it seems that, of all Nordic rites, these rites, when examined, are seen to be most clearly building on baptism as the basis of perpetual Christian commitment. Another rather isolated example of an explicit relationship to baptism is found in the different ordination rites in the Church of Norway, where – after having introduced the 'new worker' to be ordained –the rite continues: 'In baptism we were incorporated into the people of God, and we were all 'ordained' ('*vigslet*') to be ministers (or 'servants', '*tjenere*') for God'. After referring to the teaching on the priesthood of all believers in 1 Peter, the rite continues almost literally quoting *Confessio Augustana (CA)* V: 'God has also instituted a specific ministry to proclaim the gospel and administer the sacraments, so that we can share in saving faith and be preserved in this faith'[3] In other churches – such as the free Grundtvigian congregations in Denmark, which emphasize baptism as 'the one thing needful', ordination nevertheless seems to be conducted without any reference at all to baptism.[4]

It is highly questionable whether the relationship between congregation and minister can ever be clarified theologically without a clear expression of the relationship between baptism and ordination. This is needed not least in the wording of the ordination rites. In these rites, where the theological identity and responsibility of the participating clergy is most often clearly expressed, lay people are left as observers or even as consumers if the rites do not emphasize the common ministry of all baptized in the midst of whom – and for the building up of whom – ministers are being ordained. Equally important – or even more important – is the question of how lay people take responsibility in the process of admission to ordained ministry.

---

3. Cf. Fjeld on the Lutheran Churches in Norway, in his first article, and on the United Methodist Church in Norway, in his second article (Part II.4).
4. Cf. Jørgensen (Part II.5).

Church and Minister: The Role of Lay People in the Ordination Rite

The relationship between ordained ministers, their local congregations and the wider Church is crucial in all ordination rites. The relationship may be articulated in different ways in various parts of the rites.

As an ordained minister is always a servant within the community of believers he or she must also be elected and called by the laity of the relevant congregation, or at least with their consent. The *Traditio Apostolica* from the beginning of the third century clearly states that the bishop to be ordained shall be one who has been chosen 'by all the people' (Puglisi 1996, 18f.). The theological reason for this dependency of the ordained ministers on the community of laity tends, however, to be neglected or rather transformed into a certain degree of legal influence by lay leaders in congregations, during the process of admission to ordained ministry. This has often been the consequence of the Lutheran viewpoint that what matters is that the one to be ordained is called in an orderly manner (*rite vocatus*, as stated in *CA* XIV). Such a call to ministry can easily be extended, just as the minister can be examined by proper authorities before the ordination, in such a way that there seems to be no reason why the laity's participation in the election should be expressed in the ordination liturgy, since the election is over. The fact that 'so and so' has been called is thus only announced in legal terms at the beginning of the ordination rite, and there is no place left for the laity present at the ordination to consent by confirming that the candidate (as the called or elect person is now usually termed) is 'worthy' (Greek '*axios*', Latin '*dignus*') as is still the case at ordinations in the Orthodox Church.[5]

Another explicit way of including the laity in ordination is by their participation in the processions and the laying-on of hands during the decisive epicletic prayer, which has been introduced as a possibility in the Evangelical-Lutheran Church of Denmark, though some bishops do not accept the participation of laity in the process of ordaining a person to a ministry which has, as CA V says, been instituted by God.[6] Church leaders claim that the laity present at ordination of course 'participate in the liturgy', as lay people can

---

5. See Metropolitan Johannes (Part II.1) and White (Part III.1). Volf emphasizes that 'ordination is to be understood as *a public reception of charisma given by God and focused on the local church as a whole.* . . . Ordination is essentially a divine-human act' (Volf 1998, 249).
6. Cf. Iversen (Part II.6).

join in singing the hymns and spiritually, though most often silently, in the saying of the creed and the prayers, and at least they watch and listen to the liturgy as it is being performed by the bishop and his assisting pastors. The reality of this participation depends on the practical scenario in the church, where the laity will often be placed far away from the clergy at the altar – and where the creed and the prayers are often said in a manner so that the laity – without a written order of service to hand – have no chance of joining in what is supposed to be their own creed and prayers!

The communion between laity and clergy has its basic expression in the Eucharist, which has therefore also been a part of all ancient ordination liturgies. It is, however, not always so any longer, for example in the Lutheran Churches in Norway and the Evangelical-Lutheran Church of Denmark.[7] It is hard to see how the true relational (i.e. theological and congregational) character of ordained ministry can be expressed without the context of the Eucharist as the decisive common meal for common strength from God (Puglisi 2001, 251, 262).

Eventually the interdependence between the ordained ministers and the congregation of laity may be expressed in the last part of the ordination rite when is moves from 'electio' and 'benedictio/ordinatio' to 'missio/receptio'. In a number of Nordic ordination rites the 'missio/receptio' part is, however, missing, probably often due to the fact that the ordination takes place in the cathedral, where the congregation of the pastor-to-be may be absent. The 'missio/receptio' part is thus only and often very weakly expressed in the short rite at the installation of the pastor by the area dean the following Sunday in the local church. Thus it is not clarified in the ordination rite that the calling and ordination is being done so that the newly ordained minister may be sent to and received for work in a particular congregation. The result of this – or rather the background of this – is a *clericalization* of the ordained ministry as a special profession, where ordained ministry is to be exercised to – but not having its identity within – the congregation (Puglisi 2001, 242).

The practice of ordaining pastors, for example, in diocesan cathedrals and not in the local churches of the congregations where they are to serve, is among other things often used to express the idea that ordained ministry is for the whole church – and that ordination is for life-long service, independent of the congregation, which the pastor is actually serving during his or her time as an ordained minister at work. Also representatives of other neighbouring churches may participate in the ordination, for example at a bishop's ordination, in

---

7. Cf. Fjeld and Iversen (Parts II.4 and II.6).

order to express the idea that ordained ministry is for the service of the whole church and that it is important and valid for service also in other churches. Such participation is of course only meaningful when the participants come from churches with some agreed mutual recognition of ordained ministries.

Unfortunately, the material collected in this book does not deal with the various practices of reception with or without re-ordination of ordained ministers who go from one church to another and are invited to resume ordained ministry in another church, as often happens in the Nordic countries. It seems an obvious issue for exploration – in order to challenge the churches about their – as it seems – theologically poorly thought-out practice on this point.[8]

Relationship between Ministries

Relationships between different sorts of ordained ministries are expressed in the way the rites for their ordinations converge or differ. This is the case in different respects.

In most churches only the bishop (or his equivalent) can officiate at the liturgy of ordination. This seems to indicate that for theological reasons the bishop has the supreme ministry among ordained ministers, as is also clearly demonstrated in the oldest available ordination rite, *Traditio Apostolica*, ascribed to Hippolytus of Rome.[9] Even so some churches argue that the bishop's role when officiating at the liturgy of ordination to other ministries is only following practical and functional church order, not expressing any theologically founded priority among ordained ministries.

The question of which ordained ministers participate in the various rites for ordination of candidates to different sorts of ordained ministries also seems significant. As a general rule, for example, pastors will participate actively or even officiate at the ordination of deacons, whereas deacons, as a general rule, will have no active role, except perhaps as a personal assistant to the bishop, during the ordination of pastors, where pastors are always actively involved.

---

8. Volf comments as follows: 'Certainly a previous ordination in a local church will be of significance for a different local church into which the ordained person is transferred, and it will be the more so the more intimate is the communion between the local churches involved' (Volf 1998: 251).
9. Cf. the interpretation in Puglisi 1996, 27-85 concluding that in *Traditio Apostolica* the real meaning of Christian *fraternitas* is clear: Christians are 'members of the same dignity, yes, but differentiated according to the various functions in the Body. However, despite these functional and ministerial differences, all share, in solidarity, the overall responsibility for the life of the community' (85).

This seems to indicate that deacons do not belong to a full and equal order of the ordained ministry of the Church.

There are often significant differences in the order and not least the wording and the symbols used in the different liturgies. Certain acts such us praying during the laying-on of hands may be omitted in rites that admit the candidate to a 'minor' or less recognized ministry in the Church. The different sorts of vestments worn during the ordination rites often seem to indicate not only the different function but also the different positions of the various ministries.

The unity or disunity among ordained ministers is furthermore indicated in the normal practice of re-ordaining deacons, who take over the work of a pastor, or pastors, who take over the duties of a bishop. In Lutheran Churches which emphasize that there is only one ordained ministry ('*ministerium ecclesiasticum*' as the Latin rubric to art. V in CA names it) one might expect that missionaries, who have been sent out from a certain church to preach and sometimes even to administer the sacraments in a 'mission field', could take over the work of a pastor in the home church in question without a new ordination. 'Re-ordination' has, however, normally been practiced, when a missionary 'pastor' returns and takes up a pastor's duties in his home church. In recent years the problem has often been eliminated when a missionary with pastor's duties has received his ordination from the local church in the 'mission field', which will then be recognized by the church at home. It is, however, noteworthy that Ghita Olsen finds that emphasis on 'the threefold ministry' tends to degrade the rites for the sending out of missionaries from the Nordic Churches. There is an obvious need to rethink the relationship between ordained ministry and mission work proper.[10]

A basic requirement for all ministries with all kinds of 'ordination' in the Christian Church is that they are apostolic, carrying on the message and practice which the first apostles learned from Jesus of Nazareth. As there is only one Jesus whose apostolic tradition can be carried on, all ministers have to work corporately, sharing one and the same apostolic ministry, even though they have different shares in that one ministry. Eventually this also means that no minister in any church can renounce his or her basic communion with all sorts of ministers in all Christian Churches, without denying that these ministers belong to the apostolic tradition of the one Christian Church.

10. The question is dealt with in the context of ELCD in Iversen 1989, 65-117. A new study of rites for the sending out of missionaries is provided in Olsen (Part II.5).

Episkopé and Ordination

It is no accident that the issue in *The Porvoo Common Statement* that has been the trickiest for the studies in this book is the question of episcopacy or *episkopé* in its relation to lay people, orders and the act of ordination. As we have seen in the case studies in Part II above most churches in the Nordic countries try to express the connection between *episkopé* and ordination in one way or another. Therefore the question of the relationship between episcopacy and ordination must be dealt with explicitly. What is the significance of the role of the bishop in the ordination rite? And what are the criteria for a bishop to be a proper bishop, in as far as such a position is found to be needed in the Church?

The lessons from the ecumenical dialogues leave us with no doubt that there can be no ecclesial communion without eucharistic communion – and that, according to the standpoint of the Roman Catholic Church, for example, there can be no eucharistic communion without recognition of the 'sacrament of orders' – that is, bishops seen as successors of the apostles according to divine institution.[11] Thus the questions of the role and kind of bishops, who officiate at ordination in our churches, remain core questions when dealing with the ecumenical relations between churches. At the same time –and no less important – leadership as expressed by ordination is a crucial question within each of our churches. It is an important instrument and a signal of how the churches care for and express authorized ministry and true Christian teaching within their own traditions.

There is no such thing as a simple historical succession from the apostles of Jesus to the bishops (and pope) of our churches today. It may, however, be argued, as the Roman Catholic Church does, that sound theological reflection leads to the acceptance of the episcopal ministry as an order which has developed in the Church under the guidance of the Holy Spirit – in the same way as Protestants believe that the biblical Canon came about by the work of the Holy Spirit. Francis A. Sullivan divides his argument for the Roman Catholic view into three parts:

1. The post-New Testament development (in terms of ministerial orders)

---

11. Cf. Sullivan 2001. Cf. also the contributions by Puglisi and Tjørhom (Part III.1). Puglisi (1996) discusses at length the development of episcopacy, as reflected in early ordination liturgies, during the struggle of the early Church for survival at times of persecution and heresy.

is consistent with the development that took place during the New Testament period.

2. The episcopate provided the instrument that the post-New Testament Church needed to maintain its unity and orthodoxy in the face of the dangers of schism and heresy threatening it.[12]

3. The Christian faithful recognized the bishops as the successors to the apostles in teaching authority. The reception of the bishop's teaching as normative for faith is analogous to the reception of certain writings as normative for faith. The Holy Spirit guided the Church in determining both norms, for error about the norms would have led to untold errors in faith (Sullivan 2001, 255).

Mainstream Protestants generally have no objection to the idea that the work of the Spirit may be expressed in a process of institutionalization. There may be a tension but never a pure contradiction between charisma and institution. On the contrary it is possible to speak of institutionalization as a manifestation of the Holy Spirit, 'Ordnung als Manifestation des Geistes' (Schweitzer1959).[13] So far it is quite possible for Protestants to follow Sullivan's argument. Furthermore it seems that the Reformation Churches pointing to 'sola scriptura' as the only guard for sound faith have most often been ruled by kings and princes who have pointed to themselves as 'Guardians of the Christian Faith' and have taken the authority to appoint bishops and pastors for the churches in their areas. As we have today no kings to 'guard the faith' in our churches, the questions of authorized ministry and true Christian teaching have to be dealt with. We may attempt to solve them by the help of (democratic) synods and/or (professional) teaching committees. Such arrangements do, however, not take account of the fact that lay people meet – and put their trust in – pastors and bishops as authoritative teachers of the gospel. How is this – undemocratic – fact to be dealt with?

One way of dealing with the need for teaching authority in the Church is to have authorized bishops with teaching authority and pastoral oversight over the congregations in their dioceses, and to let these bishops authorize new pastors and bishops by ordaining them and taking on the oversight of their

---

12. It might be added that Irenaeus and others who argued for – and won the case about – the fixing of the biblical Canon in the last part of the second century did so by pointing to the apostolic tradition, as it had been guided by a historical line of bishops.

13. A general discussion on the interrelationship between charisma and institution in Protestant Churches is found in Dombois 1969.

future ministry. This is, however, not enough to guard the Christian faith within a church. Bishops cannot work alone, nor can they appoint and authorize pastors without the active consent of the congregations. Therefore the connection between *episkopé*, congregation and ordination may be helpful, when carefully expressed and practiced.

The electoral process of officeholders can be described correctly only as this complex interaction of mutual giving and accepting (or also rejecting) between officeholders and the congregation (Volf 1998, 256). In fact there is a need for a mutual ministry of oversight between three partners in the church: the bishop must supervise the congregations and their ordained ministers; the ordained minister must take the daily responsibility of supervising the theological practice of the congregation; and the lay people, who participate in the calling of all ordained ministers, also have a duty to supervise the teaching and preaching of their ministers in congregation and church. It is this complex interdependence which should be expressed in rites of ordination.

Convergence and Diversity in the Structure of Ordination Rites and the Understanding of Liturgy in the Nordic Churches

James F. Puglisi concludes his study of contemporary ordination rites in Roman Catholic, Lutheran, Reformed, Anglican and Methodist Churches as follows:

> Ordination is a complex process that links ministry, concrete Church, confession of faith, and communion of the faithful. This concrete process is at once communal, liturgical, and juridical, and in all its aspects, sacramental. Christian ordination cannot be reduced to a simple rite of installation or of entrance into a charge, but it is an ecclesiastical process (*traditio-receptio*) in which a Christian receives a charism for the building up of the Church, which puts him in a new relationship – personal and lasting – with his brethren (Puglisi 2001, 264).

As we have seen in the case studies of ordination rites from the various churches in the Nordic countries, not all these ordination rites can be described as 'sacramental' and distinctly different from rites of installation. Also the reception of a particular 'charism', not to speak of a '*character indelebilis*', during ordination is not found in all rites, especially not in the cases where the decisive emphasis it put on the democratic calling of the pastors. On the other hand all the Nordic ordination rites have more or less the same basic structure and content, as follows:

- Introduction of the candidate within a congregational gathering
- Prayers
- Hymn-singing
- Confession of faith
- Readings of relevant biblical texts
- Address

and/or
- Promises and admonition, calling attention to the content of the ministry in question
- handing over of the ministry

and/or
- Prayer for the reception of the Holy Spirit during laying-on of hands

It is also generally clear that the ordination rites are needed for communal and liturgical as well as for juridical reasons. Although there may be some 'anarchic' or charismatic practices in Pentecostal-type Churches[14] normally all our churches carefully follow a practice where ordination is needed before ministers may perform their central ministerial duties. There seems to be a trend for the practice of ordination to converge towards a mainstream way of doing things, more or less independent of the official theological teaching and understanding of ministry in the churches examined.

Ordination in the Churches of the Nordic countries is clearly something different from a graduation ceremony, for example. Nobody doubts that students have graduated with all the rights and duties of a graduate, whether or not they participated in the graduation ceremony at their college or university. As a general rule, however, no one is a full minister in a Nordic Church without having gone through the proper rite for ordination to the ministry in question. Ordination is a practical and a more or less strict legal requirement for an ordained minister, someone having an 'office' ('*embede*', '*embete*', '*vigningstjänst*'). However, the question is how the rites are actually performed and interpreted theologically.

Are our ordination rites *expressive*, that is, only or at least primarily proclaiming publicly (by blessing in the midst of the congregation and petitionary

---

14. Cf. also the acceptance of 'privately ordained' ministers in the Evangelical-Lutheran Church in Denmark as described in Jørgensen (Part II.5).

prayer) what has already been effected during an already completed process of admission to ordained ministry? Or are they rather *instrumental*, i.e. performative acts by means of which the candidate for ordination is actually being ordained and thereby created – by God and the Church – as the minister he or she is going to be?

Generally speaking, the rites analyzed in Part II above are not easily identified as simply expressive or instrumental.[15] Many of them are both, for others it is very unclear how they might be described. As we have pointed out above it is also quite often unclear who has called and who is actually ordaining the candidate to the ordained ministry in question (the local congregation, the National Church, the bishop, the fellow ministers or someone else).

The tradition of introducing ministers by means of a rite, as part of the normal liturgical activity of the churches, does, however, seem to be as strong as ever before. Probably this is due to a common experience of the importance of proper ministers, who – because they are necessary for the life of the church – have to be properly ordained, though no church can be run without an active ministry of lay people, as if its life is only the business of professional ministers. To this, it seems, is added a growing sense of the importance of liturgy – and the experience (at the very least implicit) of liturgy and rites as means by which something happens as something is done to those participating in a rite. During the process of secularization that culminated in the 1970s, many Nordic Churches had difficulties in their liturgical life. Today many have come to realize that even though liturgy may be bad no liturgy at all is worse and even deadly for the churches. Thus churches are eager to introduce ministers by way of liturgical ceremonies. It might even be said that whenever a church joins the tradition of introducing its ministers by *epicletic* prayer during the laying-on of hands, the church ordains, whether it so intends or not!

References

Dombois, H.1969. *Das Recht der Gnade. Ökumenische Kirchenrecht*. Wittenberg: Luther Verlag.

Iversen, Hans Raun. 1989. Missionær-, diakon- og sekretærindvielser i Danmark. In *Under bøn og håndspålæggelse. Indvielse af missionærer, diakoner og præster*, ed. Hans Raun Iversen and V. Tranholm-Mikkelsen, 65-117. Frederiksberg: Anis.

---

15. See e.g. Fjeld on non-Lutheran Churches in Norway, Brodd on the Swedish Mission Covenant Church (Part II.4) and Olsen on missionaries (Part II.5).

Puglisi, James F. 1996, 1998, and 2001. *The Process of Admission to Ordained Ministry I-III.* Collegeville, Minn.: Liturgical Press.

Schweitzer, E. 1959. *Gemeinde und Gemeindeordnung im Neuen Testament.* Zürich: Zwingli Verlag.

Sullivan, Francis A. 2001. *Apostles to Bishops: The Development of the Episcopacy in the Early Church.* New York: Newman Press.

Volf, Miroslav. 1998. *After our Likeness: The Church as the Image of the Trinity.* Grand Rapids, MI & Cambridge UK: Eerdmans.

Common Statement:
The Meaning of Ordination

This statement is based on the research project on Rites of Ordination and Commitment in the Churches of the Nordic Countries: Theology and Terminology

In 1997 the Nordic Ecumenical Council decided to initiate a study process on *Rites of Ordination and Commitment in the Churches of the Nordic Countries: Theology and Terminology.*[1] From 1998-2003 ecumenical study groups met to examine ordination in the Nordic Churches. In addition to these, a research project, funded by NOS-H, was carried out under the joint leadership of the signatories of this statement.[2] This group was convened and coordinated by Hans Raun Iversen, Faculty of Theology, University of Copenhagen. The general results of the research project appear in the present volume.

Now that we have completed our collaborative research and listened to representatives of the Nordic Churches, we wish to share with the churches some insights gained along the way, including:

---

1. In 1997, the following were members and observers of the Nordic Ecumenical Council: The Anglican Archdeaconry of Scandinavia, the Evangelical-Lutheran Church of Denmark, the Danish Baptist Union, the Ecumenical Council of Finland, the Evangelical-Lutheran Church of Finland, the Council of Free Christians in Finland, the Swedish Free Church Council in Finland, the Nordic Salvation Army, the Greek Orthodox Metropolitanate of Sweden and Scandinavia, the Evangelical-Lutheran Church of Iceland, the Methodist Church of Scandinavia and the Baltic, the Nordic Bishops' Conference, the Free Church Council of Norway, the Christian Council of Norway, the Church of Norway, the Orthodox Church of Finland, Sigtuna Foundation, the Swedish Baptist Union, the Swedish Mission Covenant Church, the Free Church Council of Sweden, the Christian Council of Sweden, the Danish Ecumenical Council.
2. NOS-H is a common Nordic research fund set up by the Nordic National Research Councils for Humanities and Theology.

1. Some theological remarks on our research findings;
2. Some observations for the churches to consider whenever they work with their ordination rites or have the opportunity to start a study process on the theology of ordained ministry.

Whilst we shall deal specifically with ordination rites, much of what we say also applies to what are sometimes referred to as 'rites of commitment'.

I. Theological Remarks on the Research Findings of a Study of Ordination Rites in the Churches of the Nordic Countries

A: *Theological and Ecclesiological Context*

1. In all the churches in the Nordic countries it is understood that the ministry of the Church is rooted in the ministry of Christ. As is found in ecumenical dialogues, so also in the Nordic churches, there is an increasing awareness that ministry is pneumatologically grounded. This means that there is a growing understanding that the ministry of the Church is carried out through participation in the *koinonia* of the Trinity, which is actively involved in the world. This awareness provides a concrete starting point for the understanding of ordained ministry.

2. The whole Church is apostolic. All the Nordic churches also have an ordained ministry which participates in and cares for the apostolicity of the Church as its special task. Ordained ministry is situated within the Church and is at the service of the whole Church. It would be helpful if in the churches the relationship between the apostolicity of the whole Church and the apostolicity of the ordained ministry were to be more clearly understood and expressed.

3. In most of the Nordic churches there is a diversity of ministries, ordained and non-ordained. However, some of the churches have a weak theological understanding of how all ministries in the Church are a gift from God. This includes natural gifts or talents, gifts or charisms from the Holy Spirit that individual Christians put at the service of the Church, and gifts or charisms for ordained ministry that are bestowed during ordination. This whole spectrum of gifts is to be engaged for the purpose of the Church's common mission in the world and needs to be seen as a whole, so that the specific gifts of ordained ministries in the Church are not isolated as the only gifts that the life of the Church relies on.

B. Theology of Ordination to Ordained Ministry

4. Admission to ordained ministry in the Nordic churches is a process consisting of elements that are arranged in a different order in the various churches: education, formation, affirmation of equipment and gifts, calling and ordination. Some churches see the whole process as guided by the Holy Spirit. Other churches seem to be unaware that it obfuscates the understanding of ordained ministry and ordination if only one or the other of the elements of the process is emphasised or if other parts are treated as only practical matters. The churches need to make the theological significance of all parts of the whole process of admission to ordained ministry clear for everyone involved.

5. Ordination is a liturgical act focused on prayer. This is the understanding in all the Nordic churches. There is also an increasing tendency to have the invocation of the Holy Spirit during the laying-on of hands within the Eucharist as a central part of the rite. This development points to epicletic prayer as the key for understanding what ordination is all about.

6. The Nordic churches seem to be converging in the understanding that ordination is an act of the Triune God, in which ordained ministers are equipped and strengthened by the gifts of the Holy Spirit and supported by the acknowledgement and prayers of the congregation. In this convergence the Nordic churches are in line with the results of the ecumenical dialogues on ordination.

7. The basic calling of the church to mission among those outside the churches is implicitly present in the rites of ordination in the Nordic churches. More emphasis might be put on the challenge to ordained ministers to equip the whole people of God for their involvement in mission and, whenever needed, to send missionaries out for special tasks in the mission of the Church.

C. The Ecumenical Context of Ordination to Ordained Ministry

8. Influence from ecumenical dialogues and experiences from ecumenical relationships are apparent in the recently revised rites of ordination in the Nordic churches. This indicates that inspiration from ecumenical work and the formal, as well as informal, reception of the results of ecumenical dialogues have been and may continue to be utilised in the concrete processes in which churches come closer to one another in theological understanding and ecclesial practices.

9. It is important to recognise that *martyria, leitourgia* and *diakonia* as

expressions of the *koinonia* of the Church take form in a variety of ministries in churches of various denominations in the Nordic countries. This underlines that there is and will continue to be a diversity of patterns of ministries, even as the churches come closer in terms of their theology and practice of ordination.

10. The ecumenical dialogues make it clear that mutual recognition of doctrines and sacraments on the one hand, and ordained ministry and ordination, on the other, are dependent on one another. It is therefore important that the churches keep on working with the practice of ordination, where the understanding of ordained ministry is expressed and re-enforced in the churches.

11. Nordic churches without mutual recognition of ordained ministries do not normally deny the spiritual value of the service of ordained ministers of the other. In general there is, however, a need for the churches to find more and better ways of expressing their positive view of the service of ordained ministers in other churches.

D. *Theology, Terminology and Ritual Practice*

12. Parallel to ordination rites for ordained ministries, the Nordic churches have rites for lifelong commitment to service as well as rites for the installation of ordained ministers and for the sending out or installation of church workers for life as well as for a determined period of time. The churches need to consider what all these rites have and should have in common and where they should also differ.

13. The ordination rites in the Nordic churches do not always reflect clearly the churches' theology of ordained ministry. A general tendency seems to be that the actual practice of ordination expresses a deeper, i.e., more sacramental understanding of ordination than that which is expressed in the current theology of the churches. The churches need to consider what they might learn from this discrepancy.

14. A discrepancy is also often found between the ritual texts and what the actual performance of the rites communicates to the congregation and to those non-church members who might observe them. It is therefore important that the churches attempt to examine the impression and understanding that the congregation and outsiders observing the rites may be left with.

II. Proposals on Ordination Rites for the Consideration of the Churches

A: The Theological and Ecclesiological Context

1. In what way and to what extent do the rites make it understood that the Triune God, through the Holy Spirit, is at work in the whole process of admission to ordained ministry (education, formation, affirmation of vocations, gifts and equipping) as well as in the act of ordination itself?

2. How clearly does an epicletic prayer during the laying-on of hands express that ordination, carried out by the Church, is an act of God, who equips the ordinand by the power of the Holy Spirit?

3. Are the different ordination rites celebrated within the eucharistic liturgy? If not, why not and with what result? If yes, how is the relationship between the Eucharist and ordination reflected in the rite?

B. Theology for the Ordination to Ordained Ministry

4. How is the ministry of *episkopé* articulated in ordination rites? By whom is it exercised? Does this reflect the general theological stance and practice of the Church concerning oversight in the Church?

5. What is the role of lay people and how is it carried out and made theologically visible in the various parts of the process of admission to ordained ministry and especially in the ordination rites?

6. How do the ordination rites express the fact that ordained ministers are to call and equip the whole people of God for mission, the basic task of the Church?

C. The Ecumenical Context of Ordination to Ordained Ministry

7. How are the unity, holiness, catholicity and apostolicity of the Church of Jesus Christ expressed in rites of ordination and commitment?

8. How is the ecumenical openness or inclusiveness of the ordaining church expressed in the rite and reflected in the group of those who participate actively in it (e.g. by the reading of texts and in the laying-on of hands)?

9. To what degree do the rites reflect the results of ecumenical studies and dialogues in terms of theology and terminology?

10. How is the practice of the re-ordination of ministers dealt with? In cases of re-ordination, how is it made clear that re-ordination is not

invalidating the service of ordained ministers in the church from which the re-ordained minister comes?

D. Theology, Terminology and Ritual Practice

11. How far do the churches distinguish between a) ordination, b) commitment for lifelong service other than ordained ministry, c) installation of ordained ministers in a new congregation/function and d) installations or sending out of short-term church workers (including ordained ministers)?

12. When churches use the term 'ordination' (or the equivalent in the vernacular), does it refer only to ordained ministers (e.g. priests/pastors, bishops and deacons and their equivalents) or also to other co-workers in the church? What criteria are used when deciding on this terminology?

13. How far is the terminology used in the rites coherent and reflecting the actual theology of the church using them?

14. What do the rites communicate to the members of the congregation participating in ordination services and to people outside the churches watching them? What and how do the churches teach about the purpose of ordination and commitment?

Gunnel Borgegaard
Nordic Ecumenical Council, Sweden

Sven-Erik Brodd
University of Uppsala, Sweden

Risto Cantell
Department for International Relations,
Evangelical-Lutheran Church of Finland, Finland

Hans Raun Iversen
University of Copenhagen, Denmark

Else-Britt Nielsen, OP
University of Oslo, Norway

Ghita Olsen
University of Copenhagen, Denmark

James F. Puglisi, SA
Centro Pro Unione, Italy

Einar Sigurbjörnsson
University of Iceland, Iceland

Ecumenical Institute of St Bernardino
Venice, Italy

27th October 2003

Indices

Abbreviations

Abbreviations for literature, used by specific authors, are found in the references for each article.

BEM   *Baptism, Eucharist, Ministry* (The Lima Document, 1982).
BUN   The Baptist Union of Norway
CA   *Confession Augustana*
CoN   The Church of Norway
CSM   The Church of Sweden Mission
DEM   The Danish Evangelical Mission
DK   Denmark
DSM   The Danish Sudan Mission
ELCC   The Evangelical-Lutheran Church Community
ELCD   The Evangelical-Lutheran Church of Denmark
FEAN   The Free Evangelical Assemblies of Norway
FELM   The Finnish Evangelical-Lutheran Mission
FIN   Finland
GFC   Grundtvigian Free Congregation
IS   Iceland
LEAF   The Lutheran Evangelical Association of Finland
LFCN   The Evangelical-Lutheran Free Church of Norway
MCC-S   Mission Covenant Church of Sweden
MCCN   The Mission Covenant Church of Norway
NLM   The Norwegian Lutheran Mission
NMS   The Norwegian Missionary Society
NO   Norway
PMoN   The Pentecostal Movement of Norway
SAN   The Salvation Army in Norway
SDAN   The Seventh-day Adventist Church in Norway
SE   Sweden
SEM   The Swedish Evangelical Mission
UMCN   The United Methodist Church in Norway

Names

The Icelandic names are placed according to Icelandic custom (the first name before the family name).

Topics

Some words, e.g. bishop, congregation, context, Christ, liturgy, ministry, ordination, pastor, priest, rite and theology, which appear at almost every second page are not included here. The reader is referred to the Contents. See also Glossary of Nordic Terms.

Biblical References

Glossary of Nordic Terms

The main reference for the table is the current terminology of the majority Evangelical-Lutheran Churches in the five Nordic Countries. Terminology from other churches are mentioned in the comments.

Denmark: DK, Norway: N, Sweden: S, Iceland: IS, Finland (Finnish-speaking): FIN-f, Finland (Swedish-speaking): FIN-s.

English Term	Nordic Term	Country
Terms of the Ordained Ministry		
Bishop		
	biskop	DK, N, S, FIN-s
	biskup	IS
	piispa	FIN-f
Deacon		
	diakon	DK, N, S, FIN-s
	diakoni	FIN-f
	djákní	IS
Deaconess		
	diakonisse	DK, N
	diakonissa	S, FIN-s
	diakonissa	FIN-F
Dean		
(rural dean)	provst	DK

	prost	N
	prófastur	IS
	kontraktsprost	S
	rovasti	Fin-f
(cathedral dean)	domprovst	DK
	domprost	N
	dómprófastur	IS
	domprost	S, Fin-s
	tuomiorovasti	Fin-f
Ministry		
	embede	DK
	embete/tjeneste	N
	embætti / þjónusta	IS
	ämbete / vigningstjänst	S, FIN-s
	virka	FIN-f
Pastor		
	pastor	DK, N, S, FIN-s
	hirðir, forstöðumadur	IS
	pastori	FIN-f
Priest		
	præst	DK
	prest	N
	prestur	IS
	präst	S, FIN-s
	pappi	FIN-f
The Act of Ordination		
Commitment	(see promises)	
Consecration	(see ordination)	
Declaration		

	erklæring	DK, N
	vígsluheit	IS
	försäkran	S,
	prästeden, ämbetseden	FIN-s
	pappisvala (bishop.) piispan vala	FIN-f
Epiklesis (Invocation of the Holy Spirit)		
	påkaldelse af helligånden	DK
	påkallelse av den hellige ånd	N
	ákall til heilags anda, ákall um heilagan anda	IS
	Åkallan av den heliga Anden	S, FIN-s
	pyhän hengen avuksi huutaminen, pyhän hengen rukoileminen	FIN-f
Examination/Exhortation		
	formaning	DK, N
	hvatning	IS
	uppmaning	S, FIN-s
	kehotus	FIN-f
Handshake		
	håndslag	DK, N
	handtak	IS
	handslag	S, FIN-s
	kättely, kätteleminen	FIN-f
Imposition of Hands		
	håndspålæggelse	DK
	håndspåleggelse	N

	handayfirlagning	IS
	handpåläggning	S, FIN-s
	kätten päällepaneminen	FIN-f
Installation		
	indsættelse	DK
	innsettelse	N
	innsetning	IS
	mottagande installation	S
	installation	FIN-s
	papin asettaminen vakinaiseen virkaan	FIN-f
Intimation	(see presentation)	
Ordain		
	ordinere, indvie	DK
	vigsle	N
	vígja	IS
	viga	S, FIN-s
	vihkiä	FIN
Ordination		
	ordination, (præste-)vielse	DK
	vigsling, ordinasjon	N
	vígsla	IS
	vigning	S
	(präst-)vigning	FIN-s
	(papiksi) vihkiminen	FIN-f
Ordination/Consecration		
	vielse	DK
	vigsling	N
	vígsla	IS

	vigning	S, FIN-s
	vihkiminen, (bishop: piispan vihkiminen virkaan)	FIN-f
Presentation		
	intimation	DK
	fremstilling	N
	vígslulýsing	IS
	kungörelsen, kallelsen till ämbetet	S, FIN-s
	kutsu virkaan	FIN-f
Promises		
	løfter	DK, N
	heit	IS
	löften	S
	löften	FIN-s
	lupaukset	FIN-f
Scriptural Reading		
	skriftlæsning	DK
	skriftlesning	N
	ritningarlestur	IS
	textläsning	S,
	bibelläsning	FIN-s
	raamatunluku	Fin-f
Sermon (by the Ordinator)		
	ordinationstale	DK
	ordinasjonstale	N
	vígsluræða	IS
	vigningstal	S, FIN-s
	puhe	FIN-f

Sermon (in the regular Service)		
	prædiken	DK
	preken	N
	prédikun	IS
	predikan	S, FIN-s
	saarna	FIN-f

Comments on Terminology

Bishop
The term bishop is used for the ministry of episcopate (leadership) and the function of episkopé (pastoral supervision) in the Orthodox ritual, in all the Roman Catholic Rituals for Ordination as well as in the rituals in the Lutheran Folk Churches (Lutheran free churches differ).

Deacon
Neither the term deacon nor the existence of different rituals for admittance represents a guarantee of the adherence to the threefold ordained ministry as in the Orthodox and Roman Catholic churches and the Church of Sweden. The Icelandic Church considers deacons to be part of ordained ministry, Church of Finland does not and Church of Norway is in the process of clarification of this matter.

Pastor
The function of a minister of word and sacrament (ministerium ecclesiasticum) is not only named priest, but also pastor (pastor). In the Norwegian Free Churches current terms are also pastoral leader (forstander), shepherd (hyrde), officer (offiser), and elder (eldste). The word pastor is not used in official liturgies in Sweden.

Priest
(presbyter/sacerdos). At the Reformation, the Lutheran churches in the Nordic countries all maintained continuity with the Medieval church as far as terminology was concerned both with regard to liturgies and ministries. The Church Order of 1537 for Denmark, Norway and Iceland, used minister (þénari) for priest (prestur) and superintendentes for bishops, but at the same time the words priest (the Latin original uses presbyter) and bishop (episcopus) also

appeared and continued to be the terminology of the people in all countries and soon also in official legal and liturgical texts. This has not changed today. Actually various Nordic terms are used for the same ministry.

Epiklesis

In the Finnish and Swedish rituals the word "epiklesis" is not used, but the act is a part of the imposition of hands and is also marked through the singing of Veni Sancte Spiritus by the chorus.

Ordination

The term "ordination" is absent in the present rituals of the Church of Sweden and Church of Norway. However, in Norway there are references to the concept of ordination in the terms "ordinand" and "speech of ordination". In the Danish church, the titel of the ritual says "vielse", even though the common word in daily language is ordination. The Roman Catholic rituals in the Nordci countries have the same ambiguity: The heading of the chapter on ordination in the Norwegian Catholic prayerbook has the heading "Ordinasjonen" and in the preamble it talks about "ordinasjonens sakrament", but when it comes to describing the act, the chapter uses "vielse" and the verb "vie". The term ordination does not appear in the Swedish and Danish translations of the catholic rituals nor in the Finnish.

Ordination/Consecration

Used both for ordination of priests and for consecration of bishops. The vernacular concept for Ordination vielse / vigsling / vígsla / vigning / vihkiminen is derived from the verb viga (to ordain in Danish, Norwegian, Icelandic, and Swedish) and vihkiä (to ordain in Finnish). Since medieval times, the meaning of this vernacular verb has been seen and understood in Scandinavian theological languages to mean bless or consecrate and sanctify. An additional source of confusion is the use of the term vigsling/vigning both for marriages and consecration of a church building. At present the Church of Norway uses the same term vigsling for priests, cathechists, deacons, cantors, bishops and some other specialised ministries. Church of Sweden uses vigning for bishops, priests and deacons, and the term invigning for church buildings. In the Church of Denmark the word vielse is used for weddings, wheras indvielse is used for consecration of a new church or churchyard.

Contributors

Ninna Edgardh Beckman gained her doctorate in ecclesiology at the University of Uppsala in 2001 for a thesis entitled *Feminism och liturgi. En ecklesiologisk studie* (publ. Stockholm: Verbum) She is currently Associate Professor at the Uppsala Research Institute for Diaconal and Social Studies. A contributor in 2004 to *Religious Change in Northern Europe – the Swedish Case*, she is currently responsible for the coordination of the gender dimension in the project on Welfare and Religion in a European Perspective, a comparative study of the role of the churches as agents of welfare within the social economy.

Gunnel Borgegaard was Director of the Nordic Ecumenical Council, Uppsala, Sweden untilo March 2004 and now holds the post of Ecumenical Secretary in the Nordic Ecumenical Institute, Sigtuna, Sweden. She has participated in many ecumenical projects on ministry and ordination, including the process which led up to the Porvoo Common Statement and is convenor of the Anglo-Nordic Diaconal Research Project.

Sven-Erik Brodd is a Priest of the Church of Sweden and Professor of Ecclesiology and Dean of the Faculty of Theology, at the University of Uppsala. He has been a member of various ecumenical dialogues and international bodies, and lectures frequently in a wide range of countries. He is co-Director of the Anglo-Nordic Diaconal Research Project and author of numerous books and articles on ecclesiology, sacramental theology, mariology and ecumenical theology.

Risto Cantell is Executive Director of the Church Department of International Relations in the Evangelical-Lutheran Church of Finland. He holds the degrees of Master of Theology (Helsinki 1970) and Doctor of Theology (Helsinki 1980).

Paul De Clerck is Professor of Liturgy and Sacramental Theology at the Institut Catholique de Paris. He holds the Licence in theology (Louvain, 1967) and a doctorate in theology with specialisation in liturgy (Paris 1970). A member and former President of *Societas liturgica*, he is the author of many works, including: *L'Intelligence de la liturgie.* (Paris: Editions du Cerf, 1995) and is editor of *La liturgie, lieu théologique* (Paris: Editions Beauchesne, 1999).

Bjørn Øyvind Fjeld is Principal of the Ansgar Teologiske Høgskole, Kristiansand, Norway. He was awarded the degrees of Master of Theology (Norwegian Lutheran School of Theology, Oslo, 1971) and Doctor of Ministry (Trinity Evangelical Divinity School, Deerfield Illinois, 1993).

Jákup Reinert Hansen has been Minister at Sandø in the Faeroe Islands since 1982. He holds the degrees of M.Th. (Aarhus 1982) and was awarded a Ph.D. from the University of Aarhus in 2004 for a thesis entitled *Mellem Kor og Skib, Jakob Dahls færøske postiller.*

Bent Hylleberg is Dean of Studies at the Scandinavian Academy of Leadership and Theology (SALT-dk). He has studied at the Baptist Theological Seminary, Tølløse (1966-69), the University of Aarhus (M. Th. 1977) and Andover Newton Theological School, Boston (1980-81). His publications include *The History of the Danish Baptist Union* (1989) and several articles. Since 1985, he has been a member of the Baptist World Alliance's Commission on Baptist Heritage and Identity.

Helena Inghammar is a Priest in the Church of Sweden. She holds the M. Div. degree (Lund 1995) and is currently working on a doctoral thesis (Gothenburg, 2000-).

Kristjan Valur Ingolfsson is Associate Professor of Liturgy at the University of Iceland and was awarded the M.Th. degree in 1974.

Hans Raun Iversen has been Associate Professor of Practical Theology at the University of Copenhagen since 1982. He holds the M.Th. (Aarhus 1976) and has numerous publications on subjects in the field of practical theology, church history and missiology.

Hasse Neldeberg Jørgensen was Pastor of the Grundtvigian Free Congregation of Aagaard (1991-97), of the Electoral Congregation of Odense (1997-2003), and is currently Pastor of the ELCD Parish of Askov and Dean of Malt (2003-).

Päivi Jussila was until 2004 Study Secretary for Worship and Congregational Life, at the Lutheran World Federation, Geneva, Switzerland and is now a pastor in the Finnish Church. She gained her doctorate in Theology in Cambridge (1995) and her most recent publication is *See How They Love One Another: Rebuilding Community at the Base* (ed. Päivi Jussila, LWF Studies, Geneva, 2002).

Jyrki Knuutila, Lectures in practical theology at the University of Helsinki, where he was awarded the degree of Doctor of Theology in 1990 and appointed Docent in practical theology in 1991. His main research topics are ecclesiastical law, homiletics, liturgics, medieval fragments, early Finnish literature (15th – 16th century).

Karen Langgaard is Associate Professor of Greenlandic Literature and Syntax in the Department of Greenlandic Language, Literature and Media, Ilisimatusarfik (University of Greenland), Nuuk, Greenland. Her publications include 'Grønlandske salmer', in *Dejlig er jorden. Psalmens roll i nutida nordiskt kultur- och samhällsliv* (eds K-J. Hansson, F. Bohlin and J. Straarup, Åbo, 2001) and several other articles on Greenlandic hymns.

Gudrun Lydholm has been an officer in the Salvation Army since 1968. She currently holds the rank of Colonel and is responsible for territorial leadership in Finland/Estonia. She holds the M.Th. (Copenhagen 1989), was a member of the Study Committee of the Ecumenical Council in Denmark (1990-1995) and the Salvation Army International Doctrine Council since 1992. She is co–author of several books on Salvationist theology and beliefs.

Liselotte Malmgart holds the M.Th. (Aarhus 1996) and was awarded a Ph.D. from the University of Copenhagen in 2002 for a thesis entitled: *Udviklingslinier i nyere dansk diakoni.* Her publications include *Vilkår for liv og vækst. Menighedsrådsloven 1903-2003* (Aarhus 2003).

Metropolitan Johannes of Nicaea, Exarch of Bithynia and Archbishop Emeritus of the Orthodox Chuch of Finland was awarded the M. Th. (New York 1953) and doctor of theology degrees (Åbu/Turku 1966 and Thessaloniki 1971). His writings include, *The Kingdom of God in the Thought of William*

Temple, *The Relation of Unity and Uniformity in the Church according to the Spirit of Ecumenical Synods* and *The Tradition of Silence*.

Else-Britt Nilsen, OP, entered the Dominican Community at St. Katarinahjemmet (Oslo) in 1971 and from 2003 has been Superior General of her Congregation (Notre Dame de Grâce, Chatillon, France). She holds an M.A. in Sociology (Oslo 1971), Lic. Theol. (Université Catholique de l'Ouest, Angers, 1982) and Dr. Theol. (Oslo 1990). She was Research Fellow (Faculty of Theology, Oslo 1982-2001) and is Research Officer (Norwegian Ministry of Culture 2001-). A member of various national boards and committees on Ecumenism, she has been Vice-President of the Christian Council of Norway since 2002. Her publications include numerous books and articles, including writings on the following topics: the history of religious sisters in Norway and Scandinavia, ecumenism, Norwegian and Scandinavian Catholic church history, theology, rites and the role of ordained ministers.

Ghita Olsen is a Pastor in the Evangelical-Lutheran Church of Denmark. She holds M.Th. (Copenhagen 2001) and was awarded the university gold medal in 2000 for a dissertation entitled *Den teologiske debat om diakonatet i de nordiske folkekirker* (published Copenhagen 2000).

James F. Puglisi, SA, is Director of the *Centro Pro Unione* in Rome and Professor of Ecclesiology, Sacraments and Ecumenism at the Pontifical University of St. Thomas (*Angelicum*), Pontifical Athenaeum Antonianum, Pontifical Athenaeum S. Anselmo (Rome) and the S. Bernadino Institute of Ecumenical Studies (Venice). He holds a BA in sociology (Catholic University of America 1969), a doctorate in religious anthropolgy and history (Sorbonne, 1991) and a doctorate in systematic theology (*Institut Catholique de Paris*, 1991). He is a member of the Franciscan Friars of the Atonement and was elected Minister General in 2004. Among his writings are four volumes on the theology of ordination: *The Process of Admission to Ordained Ministry I-IV*, (Collegeville: Liturgical Press, 1996-2004).

Einar Sigurbjörnsson has been Professor of Theology at the University of Iceland since 1978. He holds the M. Th. (Iceland 1969) and Dr. Theol. (Lund 1974). His writings include: *Ministry within the People of God*, 1974.

Ola Tjørhom, has held the posts of Professor of Dogmatics and Ecumenical Theology at the School of Mission and Theology, Stavanger, Director of the Nordic Ecumenical Institute, Uppsala, and Research Professor at the Institute for Ecumenical Research, Strasbourg. He holds the degrees of Cand. theol. (Oslo, 1977) and Dr. theol. (Oslo, 1992). Among his numerous publications are: *Kirken – troens mor: Et økumenisk bidrag til en luthersk ekklesiologi* [*The Church – Mother of Faith: Ecumenical Contribution to a Lutheran Ecclesiology*] (Oslo: Verbum Forlag, 1999); (ed.) Unity and Apostolicity: Essays on the Porvoo Common Statement (Grand Rapids: Eerdmans, 2002); *Visible Church – Visible Unity: Ecumenical Ecclesiology in the Perspective of The Great Tradition of the Church* (Collegeville: Liturgical Press, 2004).

Grant White is Principal of the Institute of Orthodoxy Christian Studies, Cambridge, UK, and a member of the Orthodox Church. He was until 2004 Professor of Church History and Deputy Director of the Department of Orthodox Theology, University of Joensuu, Finland. He holds a B.A. in the Study of Religion (Harvard 1985), studied Syriac, church history and theology at Oxford University (1987-88), and was awarded a Ph.D. in theology by the University of Notre Dame in 1993.